COMMUNICATION
@ Work

COMMUNICATION @ Work

Ethical, Effective, and Expressive Communication in the Workplace

MARYLIN S. KELLY

McLennan Community College

PEARSON

Boston   New York   San Francisco
Mexico City   Montreal   Toronto   London   Madrid   Munich   Paris
Hong Kong   Singapore   Tokyo   Cape Town   Sydney

Editor-in-Chief: Karon Bowers
Series Editor: Brian Wheel
Series Editorial Assistant: Heather Hawkins
Production Editor: Paula Carroll
Editorial-Production Service: Argosy
Composition Buyer: Linda Cox
Manufacturing Buyer: JoAnne Sweeney
Electronic Composition: Argosy
Interior Design: Anne Flanagan
Cover Administrator: Kristina Mose-Libon

For related titles and support materials, visit our online catalog at www.ablongman.com.

Between the time website information is gathered and then published, it is not unusual for some sites to have closed. Also, the transcription of URLs can result in typographical errors. The publisher would appreciate notification where these errors occur so that they may be corrected in subsequent editions.

Library of Congress Cataloging-in-Publication Data

Kelly, Marylin S.
  Communication @ work : ethical, effective and expressive communication in the workplace / Marylin S. Kelly.
      p. cm.
  Includes bibliographical references and index.
  ISBN 0-205-34223-X
  1. Communication. 2. Communication in organizations. 3. Business communication. I. Title: Communication at work. II. Title.

  P91.K357 2006
  302.2—dc22

                                    2005054604

Printed in the United States of America

10 9 8 7 6 5 4 3 2 1   RRD-VA 09 08 07 06 05

Contents

PART ONE
Building Foundations   3

1
Communication Elements, Principles, and Ethics   4

2
Perception and Self-Concept   34

PART TWO

Building Personal Power 57

3

From Apprehension to Confidence 58

4

Powerful Listening 82

5

Nonverbal Communication 112

6

Topic Research 138

PART THREE
Building Experience   163

7

Quick Start to Informative Speaking   164

8

Models, Applications, and Processes of Informative Communication   200

9

Visual and Other Sensible Support   228

PART FOUR
Building Connections   313

14
Consequential Conversations in Interpersonal Communication 374

15
Conflict at Work 404

16
Interviews and Appraisals 438

Special Topics

Preface

Communication @ Work: Ethical, Effective, and Expressive Communication in the Workplace is designed as a primary text for business and professional communication courses. With a reliable, effective, and even exciting body of material, it is intended to be a text that students and instructors will look forward to using.

Students' communication outcomes should be effective, expressive, and—foremost—ethical. Certainly not robotic, communicators' skills must be humanized and expressed with empathy or enthusiasm and tolerance or conviction. *Communication @ Work* aims to distinguish itself from other business and professional communication texts in several ways.

TO INSTRUCTORS

The material pertinent to a business and professional speaking text is both compelling and overwhelming. Rapidly evolving organizations place incredible demands on communication instructors to prepare students for jobs. Also, the reality is that instructors often teach several courses, and any course that schedules student presentations challenges classroom management. Therefore, an instructor needs a text to provide the traditional content of the course along with contemporary practices for discussion and reference. *Communication @ Work* includes material in a flexible format that allows the instructor to (1) rely on the text to teach particular skills and concepts, (2) use the text as a springboard or reference, (3) provide back-up for students who may miss a lecture and must be prepared for an exam or speaking assignment, and (4) lead the readers into other speech communication applications.

This text aims to provide security for the instructor in the quality of its content. We are teaching in a time in which many of the traditional rhetorical principles have surfaced in attractive new clothes, and we want to ask, "So, what's new?" But we are also teaching in a time of new paradigms with terminology that employers will expect our graduates to not only recognize, but also use. This text helps the instructor meet that teaching responsibility.

Instructors will appreciate these features:

- *Reality @ Work,* a special feature specifically designed to introduce theory and practice in realistic, new, and ever-changing workplaces.

- *Contemporary Voices,* which add the voices of three popular and prolific communicators who echo the truths of communication scholarship: Peter Senge, speaking on learning organizations; Daniel Goleman, on emotional intelligence; and Stephen Covey, on principled leadership with effective habits. The selection of these contemporary and popular authors recognizes that effective learning takes place when there is a balance of familiarity and novelty. Since the bulk of the text content introduces readers to many of the communication field's researchers and writers, these "contemporary voices" build a bridge to business and other professions, blending old and new seamlessly. Instructors may center discussions on these authors' books or may delegate their excerpts as optional reading.

- Compelling interpersonal and small group activities integrated into textual material

- Chapter-end activities focusing on *technology, teamwork, ethics, writing, and speaking*

- Extensive coverage of presenting in both formal and informal settings. ("Quick Start" chapters on informative and persuasive speaking get students on their feet and speaking; in-depth chapters follow to support instructors who wish to lead their students into more intensive coverage of informative and persuasive techniques.)

- Flexible structure to allow instructors to customize the sequence of core material. (For instance, the small group/team and presentational speaking sections are stand-alone sections. Chapters do not depend on prior chapters, with the exception of "advanced" informative and persuasive speaking chapters and the more detailed chapters on teams and leadership. Those who spend less course time in presentational speaking may choose the "Quick Start" chapters for informative and persuasive speaking and the small group chapter as an overview of group process.)

- Familiar material supported with lively, updated examples

- Theory clearly explained in practical ways

- User-friendly material that is current and based on sound research in the communication and social science fields

- Practical skills and applications, engaging readers to imaginatively communicate in their future jobs

- A pedagogical approach respecting varied learning styles

- Predictability balanced with a lively pace for developing flexibility and breadth in skills

TO STUDENTS

Ultimately, this text is written to assist and support students. You as students have your own set of requirements and requests when it comes to a speech book.

- You want credible, dependable information to prepare you for work environs and communication in them.

- You want a readable, useful, informative, and engaging text—one that will help with assignments and won't put you to sleep! You don't want "cute," but you do want "interesting."

- When you truly *use* a text (as opposed to *read* a text), you *search* for specific information and depend on the text to *guide* you through unfamiliar territory. You want adequate content without being overwhelmed.

- To make this experience work, you must be able to see yourself as a classroom speaker and later as a communicator in the workplace.

- Careful consideration is given to how you learn, and the text utilizes methods leading to understanding and retention.

ORGANIZING PRINCIPLES

The writing of this text was guided by how students best develop into successful, principled communicators, whether in the classroom or the workplace. Each chapter builds awareness, knowledge, and skills incrementally. The developmental metaphor for the major divisions of the text centers on "building."

Building Foundations (Part I)

First, of course, are the foundations for communication concepts and skills. The first chapter, "Communication Elements, Principles, and Ethics," lays the groundwork in communication theory and the ethical use of communication. In this chapter students meet three popular authors who espouse sound communication theory in business and professional arenas. The roles of perception and self-concept are covered in Chapter 2, as students also consider how we perceive and are perceived by others and by organizations.

Building Personal Power (Part II)

The personal effectiveness section, with self-concept as a linchpin, prepares students to understand and build personal effectiveness by managing communication apprehension (Chapter 3), through listening (Chapter 4), through discovering the power of nonverbal communication (Chapter 5), and through adequate research (Chapter 6). The organizing principle of this section centers on communicators building from the inside out by managing their communication apprehension and by practicing active verbal and nonverbal listening. As sequenced, this section satisfies the need to teach attending skills from a personal power perspective early in the course and to alleviate some apprehension about speech presentations before progressing too far into speech preparation. Secured in the knowledge that comes from focused research, students anticipate building communication experiences. The activities in these chapters quickly involve students with content and prompt interaction with other class members.

Building Experience (Part III)

The third section, "Building Experience" teaches presentational speaking skills. Human resources, health careers, and other business and professional areas are expecting their applicants and requiring their employees to develop presentational speaking skills. In response to instructors' and students' complaints that many texts devote too few pages to this preparation, we devote a significant portion to presentational speaking. Chapter 7, "Quick Start for Informative Speaking," takes a *developmental approach as students prepare their first speeches.* (Some instructors will choose to use Chapter 7 early in the semester.) To avoid students overloading with textbook reading assignments before engaging in speech preparation, they are guided step by step to prepare and deliver informative presentations—read a little, apply it to their topic, read a little more, organize ideas, and so forth. The student needs to learn enough to speak, but the richer learning will follow because he or she has had a related, ingrained experience for reference.

Instructors may choose to add Chapter 8 for in-depth reading with their academically stronger classes. Chapter 8 gives more choices, examples, workplace applications, and analyses of informative processes. The visual and other media content of Chapter 9 is placed between the two informative chapters and the two persuasive chapters. The placement is in response to the lecture/discussion sequence used by most instructors surveyed. Chapters 10 and 11 on persuasive speaking echo the informative chapters, with a "quick start" followed by a more advanced chapter on persuasive design.

Building Connections (Part IV)

The fourth and final section looks at "Building Connections" as it amalgamates material on interpersonal and small group communication. The chapters discuss teams (Chapter 12), leadership (Chapter 13), interpersonal conversation (Chapter 14), conflict (Chapter 15), and interviews. Instructors can confidently use their own discretion in placing this section—or individual chapters—on their syllabi. The material may come early in the course in a contextual sequence of interpersonal, small group, and finally presentational speaking or be pared and distributed as time allows.

THE COMPLETE PACKAGE FOR STUDENT AND INSTRUCTOR

Ultimately, learning is a positive outcome of instructor–student communication supported by meaningful interaction between student and textbook author. Toward those ends, an ancillary package supports the use of this text:

> Instructor's Manual
> Test Bank
> Computerized Test Bank
> PowerPoint Presentation Package (available as a download)
> Companion Website (www.ablongman.com/kelly1e)

ACKNOWLEDGMENTS

I wish to thank my professional colleagues who collaborated in the more than five years of development and production of *Communication @ Work*: Carol Allen, Northern Illinois University; Nicholas F. Burnett, CSU, Sacramento; Carolyn Clark, Salt Lake City College; Terry M. Cunconan, Central Missouri State University; Michael Eaves, Valdosta University; Lisa Gebhardt, Southwestern Texas State University; Amiso M. George, University of Texas at San Antonio; Tina Harris, University of Georgia; James Hayes, Colorado State University; Thomas J. Healy, Salem State College; Carol Heinemann, DeVry University; David Hudson, Golden West College; Lawrence W. Hugenberg, Youngstown State University; Timothy E. Hunt, Lewis and Clark State College; Derrick LeMarr Coreen, Kansas State University; Deloris McGee-Wanduri, University of Houston; Shellie Michael, Volunteer State Community College; Mary L. Mohan, SUNY Geneseo; Darrell Mullins, Salisbury State University; Pamela S. Perkins, San Diego City College; M. Erin Porter, University of Texas at Austin; Walter Stevenson, Golden Gate University; Julie A. Rennecker, Case Western Reserve University; Belinda Thomson, Brescia University; Rob Walsh, Mitchell Community College. I am deeply grateful for the insights and creative talents of Michael Greer, Developmental Editor, who nurtured the development of the manuscript from conception to completion. Michael understands teamwork and collaboration as a productive art and is a colleague and friend. Karon Bowers, Editor-in-Chief, lent her wisdom and understanding of teaching speech communication in shaping this work. Brian Wheel, Series Editor, studied the project, understood its innovations and direction, and finalized the production task. I especially thank Jennifer Trebby and Heather Hawkins, assistants to the editors, who amazingly juggled a plethora of tasks without dropping a single one.

There is nothing like one's own workplace colleagues and friends! I thrived on the ideas and cherished the encouragement of McLennan Community College students, instructors, administrators, and support staff.

Most important, I could not have completed this work without the support of my wonderful family—my husband, Robert; my children, Walter, Jill, Karen, and Jeff; and my Dad. They protected my time, served as sounding boards, and encouraged me at every juncture. As executives, managers, and professionals in their organizations, they were touchstones of reality for business communication.

COMMUNICATION
@ Work

Building Foundations

I.

Communication Elements, Principles, and Ethics
2 **Perception and Self-Concept**

art I establishes the foundations for communication concepts and skills. Chapter 1 lays the groundwork in communication theory and outlines the ethical and unethical uses of communication in the workplace. This chapter also introduces three popular authors who describe sound communication theory in business and professional arenas. The fundamental roles of perception and self-concept are developed in Chapter 2, which introduces audience analysis by taking an audience's perspective during speech preparation.

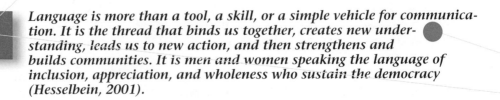

Language is more than a tool, a skill, or a simple vehicle for communication. It is the thread that binds us together, creates new understanding, leads us to new action, and then strengthens and builds communities. It is men and women speaking the language of inclusion, appreciation, and wholeness who sustain the democracy (Hesselbein, 2001).

Communication Elements, Principles, and Ethics

1

Elements of Communication

Human Communication in System Models

Communication and Meaning

Principles of Speech Communication

Diversity and Workplace Communication

Working with Emotional Intelligence

Communication Competence

Ethics and Communication

"Don't work harder; work smarter." Most of us would if we knew how, but we suspect we will have to work harder *and* smarter, and we can only hope that will be adequate. With limited time and energy, larger questions loom. How will we as individuals and organizations survive and thrive during astonishing changes? How can we unleash the creativity, talent, and energy we possess in the midst of pressure? Are there ways to enrich personal, family, and professional relationships? Communication is more than a set of skills. It is the expression of who we are, what our values are, and how we use knowledge. It is our connection with others. It is the heartbeat of any organization. Persons "in community" *communicate*.

It has been recognized for some time that a high quantity of communication does not guarantee high quality. Managers spend between 50% and 80% of their total time communicating to customers or employees or suppliers, yet Peter Drucker claims that at least 60% of all management problems result from faulty communications, especially from poor listening skills (Jim Moran

Institute for Global Entrepreneurship, 2004). Even though managers spend most of their time communicating with others (Mintzberg, 1973), employees actually receive superiors' messages only half the time (Burns, 1954). Peter Drucker (1973) recognized the following in his examination of business practices:

> Communication has proven as elusive as the Unicorn. The noise level has gone up so fast that no one can really listen any more to all that babble about communications. But there is clearly less and less communicating. The communication gap within institutions and between groups in society has been widening steadily—to the point where it threatens to become an unbridgeable gulf of total misunderstanding.

The noise and speed within business have grown exponentially since the 1970s, and still we are hard pressed to define "better communication," especially when it is so naively prescribed for business woes.

When an area critical to us changes so rapidly, we search out the voices of the times. Business, for instance, listens to the "father of modern business," Peter Drucker, as well as Rosa Beth Kanter, Jonathan Katzenbach, and Jon Anderson; this text cites them for their assessments and advice. The communication field values the scholarship of the doctors M. Scott Poole, Linda Putnam, Edward Hall, Ernest Bormann, Paul Eckman, James McCroskey, B. Aubrey Fisher, and many others; you will see these scholars' names frequently as we explore theories and principles of communication.

Concerning cited sources, a very practical problem surfaced as groups of students discussed how a textbook could better serve them and interest them. Here are two comments that showed consensus:

• "We are overwhelmed with experts' names and theories, but we don't really have a sense of who they are, and we usually forget their names."
• "We need to get to know the authors and books that business executives read. We're not sure if and how they play into the communication scene."

A response to these comments evolved into a unique feature for this text. It spans disciplines to include the voices of Peter Senge, Stephen Covey, and Daniel Goleman, all extremely familiar to the business community and its scholars. These influential authors and speakers value effective, expressive, and ethical communication, and they reinforce the idea that communication should be based on principles, self-discipline, and appreciation of others—foundations of this text. Their words and ideas are showcased in Contemporary Voices boxes running throughout the text. As you read, you will come to identify Senge with "learning organizations" and open systems thinking as set forth in *The Fifth Discipline*. He proposed a new paradigm for organizations and suggested they recognize not just what happens *within* the organization, but also how the organization interacts with its environment, including other organizations. Covey advocated a balanced life, ethical business, and "principled leadership." Covey's *Seven Habits of Highly Effective People* boldly showed that putting "first things first" and being proactive rather than reactive actually worked in highly successful businesses—and he preached ethics when they were considered naive along the fast track. Goleman popularized the idea of "emotional intelligence" and convinced organizations that emotion is part of our "wiring" and that the brain can learn more emotionally intelligent ways to communicate and interact with self and others. It is hoped that, by the end of the text, you can include Senge, Covey, and Goleman among the people you "know" and can talk about their ideas in your future business conversations.

This first chapter introduces the major elements of communication, discusses several principles of speech communication, introduces emotional intelligence as a construct for competency, overviews key communication competencies for organizations, and examines ethical applications of speech communication.

OBJECTIVES

After studying the content of this chapter, you should be able to

- Conceptualize people as communication systems
- Discuss speech communication in terms of meaning and understanding
- Explain key principles of speech communication
- Define major elements of speech communication
- Connect emotional intelligence with communication competence in the workplace
- Make ethical choices in communicating with others

• ELEMENTS OF COMMUNICATION

Alex's baby was due at any time, and his wife, Joy, didn't feel like going to Alex's best friend's wedding rehearsal dinner. However, she made sure Alex had his cell phone with him, just in case. Before dinner, Alex discretely chose the "silent and vibrate" phone setting and dropped it into the top of his boot, so he could feel it if Joy called. The father of the bride raised a toast to the couple, but Alex drew the guests' attention when he knocked over his champagne, tugged at his boot, and shouted, "Help me get my boot off! We're having a baby!"

It's at times like these that we are struck by the constraints of communication. Alex's message made sense to him, but left the other guests baffled. There was a communication disconnect. Having lived in the human communication "lab" all our lives, we take communication for granted. In order for you to become a communication systems analyst, begin by dissecting the process and taking a close-up look at each element. If an essential element malfunctions, communication stumbles. Communication is incomplete when a nurse can't understand a patient who speaks Czech, a salesperson uses a PowerPoint demonstration for a visually impaired client, or a chemist uses scientific terminology when speaking at a coach's association. Let's examine the elements of communication between people. Refer to Reality @ Work 1.1 as you read about communication elements.

ELEMENTS IN PRACTICE

John is worried about finishing some work to present at a board meeting tomorrow morning, and Tracy is pestering him to do something else

Reality
@ WORK
1.1

Presentations and discussions blend seamlessly in this interaction. How do participants anticipate these roles?

(psychological noise). John's cubicle is small, and Tracy's perfume is overpowering (physical noise). In the midst of Tracy's explanation, the phone rings (physical noise). John is already hungry and tired (physiological noise).

Tracy asks, "John, will you finish this expense report for me? My flight leaves in an hour for a really important meeting this afternoon." She sounds tense and rushed. At the same time, Tracy hands John the incomplete report and picks up her briefcase and airline tickets.

John *decodes* Tracy's verbal and nonverbal message. He translates the words into a picture in his mind that he will be completing a report after Tracy leaves. He hears urgency in her words and tone of voice. He sees physical evidence that she is on her way to the airport.

Tracy's intent is to send John the *message* that she is competent, important, and busy, but it is possible John will translate the words and actions to mean that Tracy is disorganized and demanding.

John is in his office (place context) at 6:00 in the evening (time context) when Tracy delivers her message. He presumes she chose him by default because almost everyone else had left (prior events). John knows that when Tracy returns from the convention, she is favored to become the company president (anticipated event following the communication). John and Tracy make assumptions about the appropriateness of the message (national and corporate cultures).

Source or Sender

An originator of a message is the *source* of the message. The intention is for someone to understand it. Because a source also transmits a message, the source may be called a *sender*. For instance, an engineer who presents a project to the board of directors, a physician's assistant who explains a lab report to a patient, and a lost child who bursts into tears in a store are all message senders.

Receiver

The recipient of the message is the *receiver*. The idea is not original to the receiver, as it is to the source. In baseball terms, the source or sender is the pitcher, and the receiver is the catcher. Receivers include a member of the board listening to the engineer's project explanation, a family member hearing the words and tone of voice and seeing the facial expression of the physician's assistant giving the lab report, and a clerk in the store seeing the tears and hearing the sobs of the lost child.

Encoding

Sources *encode* messages when they put ideas into codes that receivers can understand. Codes may be verbal or nonverbal and may or may not be chosen intentionally. A communication *symbol* is anything that prompts meaning. When the message is *intentionally* encoded, we call the symbol a *sign*. Messages often combine several types of codes. In Reality @ Work 1.1, Tracy used several *codes*. She chose language—English, in this case—to make a request and justify the request. She used the phrase "really important" for emphasis, and her vocal tone and rate reinforced the urgency. Other nonverbal communication—picking up the briefcase and tickets—sent the message that she was on the move and in a hurry.

- *Verbal codes:* All languages are verbal codes. Words may be spoken, written, or coded by other linguistic means, such as American Sign Language (ASL).
- *Nonverbal codes:* All other codes are nonverbal codes. These include vocal sounds, gestures, eye communication, facial expressions, appearance, and timing.

Decoding

For *decoding,* a receiver takes a physically delivered code and interprets it—that is, connects the sensory data to the receiver's existing knowledge. From a multitude of signs and symbols, the receiver must select the ones that are most relevant to the communication.

Message

The *message* is primarily the idea that the source intends to send and the receiver purposefully receives. Sometimes, however, a receiver misinterprets a message or decodes one the source did not intend to send. An interviewee may intend to send the message that he is competent and confident, yet his words and fidgety behavior send the message that he is incompetent and nervous.

Channel

The *channel* is the physical means by which the message is conveyed. In face-to-face communication, three powerful channels are available: sight, sound, and touch. When used for an audience of several hundred, a public address system is also part of the channel. The choice of channel itself sends and shapes the message. For instance, a face-to-face meeting with the CEO carries a different impact than an e-mail message would. Communication goals determine which channel works best.

TABLE 1.1 • Criteria for Channel Selection

Who is receiving the message? Are you communicating with an individual, a group, or an audience? What is your relationship with the receiver? Is privacy or confidentiality needed?

How much information are you sending? Is it too much to retain at one hearing? Will the receiver need a hard copy?

How carefully do you need to word the message? Is the message a sensitive or official matter? Will the receiver need to refer to it for directions, data, guidelines, or legalities?

Do you need to communicate an attitude or the nature of the relationship?

How soon does the message need to be received? How critical is the timing of the message?

What kind of feedback do you need? Do you need to see and/or hear the other person to assess reaction? Do you need immediate feedback?

Work communication offers a menu of channels: face-to-face, phone, e-mail, instant messaging, memoranda, letters, faxes, and teleconferences. E-mail is fast, does not require the communicators to find a time to get together, gives time for wording, and makes it easy to keep a "saved" or hard copy. The telephone adds voice and immediacy, but removes time for careful wording, for making copies, and for flexibility in scheduling. Public speaking limits feedback but efficiently delivers the message to many people at one time. Face-to-face communication opens visual as well as verbal channels but is sometimes difficult to schedule or may overwhelm some people, causing them to become defensive or self-conscious.

Teleconferencing opens a visual channel so that communicators can see one another. Interestingly, participants in teleconferences experience heightened awareness of both the access and the limitations regarding whom they can see and when ("I wish the camera had been pointing at him when he heard me give those statistics"), and when they are being seen ("Could they see how disgusted I was?"). Camera technicians control a large part of the communication channel. As always, "message sent" does not guarantee "message received."

Finally, written communication is the most formal channel, the most legally binding, and the most likely to survive in its original form. Anything that is written can potentially become evidence in a court of law. Refer to Table 1.1 to guide channel choices.

ACTIVITY 1.1

CHOOSING CHANNELS

Tracy and John talked at John's desk in Reality @ Work 1.1.

1. *Which communication channels were open for them?*
2. *Who chose the channels?*
3. *Which advantages did the chosen channels have?*

9:00 A.M.	Phone conference with clients in Atlanta, Georgia, and Sacramento, California.
11:00 A.M.	Technical team meeting in my cubicle.
12:00 noon	Brown bag lunch at desk to hear CEO's monthly state of the organization address, streamed to my cubicle; prepare questions for live feedback.
1:00 P.M.	Check "high importance" flagged e-mail.
2:00 P.M.	Teleconference with Zurich branch. (Note to self: I'd rather be skiing in Zurich.)
4:00 P.M.	Update statistics and time line in Gantt chart; import into PowerPoint for presentation in the morning.
5:00 P.M.	West Coast colleagues request advice from our risk communication team. (3:00 P.M. their time.)

FIGURE 1.1 • Daily Schedule of a Marketing Manager

Technology shadows traditional channels of communication. Let's check your schedule for today in Figure 1.1.

Due to the cost of time and money involved in travel, virtual conferences are replacing many face-to-face meetings. Even explorers on Antarctica are "connected" through the single satellite that orbits between poles. Virtual environments facilitate problem solving, design, and training. Patients live or die in virtual surgery, buildings are constructed and examined three dimensionally and structurally, and marketing divisions "visit" other countries and test their products demographically. The single thing that transforms people who share a goal into a team or into an organization is their ability to communicate, and virtuality unites distanced people for real-time dialogue. Of course, a channel is essential for real or virtual communication. Two additional elements that are truly inescapable are context and noise.

Context

All communication occurs within a *context*. Context includes time, place, culture, people present, events occurring immediately prior to the communication, and events expected to occur following the communication. Public speakers learn to analyze the contexts for their presentations in order to be most effective. Channel choices depend upon context, as is obvious in the example provided in Reality @ Work 1.2.

FLIGHT OF THE NERD

"Please fasten your seat belts and return your pocket protectors and laptops to their full, upright, and locked position. The Nerd Bird is ready for takeoff" (Imperato, 2000). Systems analysts, marketers, engineers, project managers, and executives (even Michael Dell) are at work in the air between Austin, Texas, and Silicon Valley in California. Intel, IBM, Dell, Motorola, Schlumberger, and

Reality
@ WORK
1.2

Texas Instruments are companies that live at both ends of the "digital pipeline" between the two states. Flight attendants say it's hard to serve a meal around all the laptops. One sales manager complained, "I can't talk about confidential stuff on-board this tube. All my competitors are here, too!"

1. *How does changing a work context change communication behaviors?*
2. *Is flight time considered work hours?*
3. *How are these employees supervised, and how do they supervise others?*

Noise or Interference

Noise, by definition, is anything that interferes with the communication process. *Physical interference* is commotion from the immediate environment, such as loud noises in the hallway, warm room temperature, an uncomfortable chair, or, for the "flight of the nerd," the din of the airplane. *Physiological interference* is experienced inside the person physiologically, such as having a headache or feeling tired. *Psychological interference* happens in a person's mind and can be the loudest noise of all. For instance, your concern about a calculus exam is so "noisy" that you can't hear the English professor. Planning a date this weekend, anticipating a job interview, and experiencing emotional trauma are examples of psychological noise. Of course, if your stomach is rumbling (physical noise) because you are hungry (physiological noise), and the person next to you can hear it, you may suffer embarrassment (psychological noise).

The next two elements are actually special kinds of messages that "bookend" the main message. Feedback gives a response to a message, and feedforward prepares the listener for the message.

Feedback

Feedback is the response to the source's message. Effective feedback reduces misunderstandings, because the source gets insight into how the receiver has interpreted the message. Ideally, in speech classes, students receive feedback from professors and classmates about their communication skills. Direct feedback includes comments about the effectiveness of a presentation. Indirect feedback, such as questions from classmates, reflects a better understanding of how much the audience understood.

Suppose you criticize an employee's work, and the employee becomes so discouraged that work productivity diminishes, and then you criticize further. Each message (behavior as well as words) is both cause and effect, and devoid of any kind of feedback, an employee's confidence likely diminishes.

Feedforward

Feedforward is another special kind of message. It prepares listeners for the main message, such as when a manager begins a conversation, "With fewer employees, each of us must take on increased responsibility." Feedforward in public speaking prepares the audience for the content and emotional tone of the message. For example, employees anticipate a positive report when a CEO starts out with: "Time to celebrate here at Infomaze!" Equipped with basic terminology, let us next discuss how the elements relate to one another.

• HUMAN COMMUNICATION IN SYSTEM MODELS

Model airplanes won't take us to London, but they will help us study how airplanes take flight. Models illustrate processes and show relationships and connections. Thus, a model of communication would be helpful. Keep in mind, however, that interrupting a *living* system's process alters what it really is. For instance, a biology student can observe the muscle, vessels, and valves of a pickled frog heart, but the frog's heart isn't doing what it was designed to do—pump frog blood. Human communication is also a living process, and when we freeze it in a lifeless model, we distort it. Therefore, models are helpful but imperfect. Imagine designing a circuit board, blueprint, schematic diagram, or other model to represent human communication. This section notes the evolution of communication models.

Systems are characterized as "open" or "closed." Linear models in their most uncomplicated forms flow in one direction and end with the reception of the message, and therefore can be compared to a *closed system model*. A closed system by definition does not affect or have effects outside its unique parameters and does not interact with other systems.[1] An *open system model* shows interaction constantly bringing about change in an infinite number of other systems and within itself. The dynamics of an open system seem more suited as a representation of human communication. In actuality, any model will be an overly simplified representation of the complexities of human beings communicating.

Earlier, traditional models of communication offered a linear view, with models showing the transmission and the reception of messages along a straight, one-dimensional path. The advantage of linear models is their easy-to-remember simplicity. See Figure 1.2 is a representative linear model with feedback.

In face-to-face communication, however, messages are sent and received simultaneously, rather than taking turns back and forth like a shortwave radio. When communicators interact, they affect and are affected by one another, and the message inevitably is altered in the process. A transactional model, as in Figure 1.3, adds interaction and continual feedback to earlier models, but falls short of illustrating human communication with adequate complexity for our analysis.

Human communication is better understood as a life system, rather than as a two-dimensional model. An open systems approach advances the idea that all the components of a model are interrelated and that a change in one component prompts changes in other parts of the system. *Output*—end results—feeds back into the system as *input* to potentially affect future behaviors (Tubbs, 2001, p. 21).

---

[1] Because two people communicating are arguably two systems interacting, each person being a system, then a true linear model can only represent intrapersonal communication—that is, communication within oneself.

FIGURE 1.2 • Linear Communication Model with Feedback

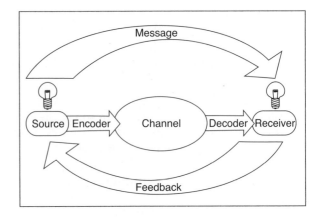

FIGURE 1.3 • A Simplified Transactional Communication Model

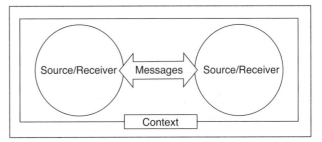

CONTEMPORARY VOICES 1.1: SYSTEMS THINKING

We turn to one of our three featured contemporary voices, Peter Senge, to introduce systems thinking:

> A cloud masses, the sky darkens, leaves twist upward, and we know that It will rain. We also know that after the storm, the runoff will feed into groundwater miles away, and the sky will grow clear by tomorrow. All these events are distant in time and space, and yet they are all connected within the same pattern. Each has an influence on the rest, an influence that is usually hidden from view. You can only understand the system of a rainstorm by contemplating the whole, not any individual part of the pattern. (Senge, 1994, p. 6)

Senge laments how limited our models of organizations and the workplace are:

> We are woven into the systems' fabric and are too close to see overall patterns of behavior and change. Instead, we tend to focus on snapshots of isolated parts of the system, and wonder why our deepest problems never seem to get solved. (Senge, 1994, pp. 6–7)

Systems thinking is a conceptual framework that helps us see existing patterns more clearly:

> In effect, the art of systems thinking lies in seeing through complexity to the underlying structures generating change. Systems thinking does not mean ignoring complexity. Rather, it means organizing complexity into a coherent story that illuminates the causes of problems and how they can be remedied in enduring ways. (Senge, 1994, p. 128)

A featured strand throughout this textbook is the writings of three gurus of contemporary thought in organizations today. Here you meet Dr. Peter Senge, a leader in researching and teaching leaders in businesses and organizations. A self-described "incurable systems thinker," Dr. Peter Senge takes organizational learning to the next level. *Harvard Business Review* named *The Fifth Discipline* one of the seminal management books of the past 75 years, and the *Journal of Business Strategy* (September/October 1999) named Senge one of the people who had had the greatest influence on business strategy overall. Senge is a senior lecturer at and director of the Center for Organizational Learning at the Sloan School of Management, Massachusetts Institute of Technology (MIT), and chairperson of the Society for Organizational Learning, which is a global collaboration of corporations, researchers, and consultants (Society for Organizational Learning, n.d.). He is credentialed academically with a B.S. in engineering, an M.S. in social systems modeling, and a Ph.D. in management from MIT. The Society for Organizational Learning includes as member organizations Intel, Harley Davidson, Ford, Royal Dutch/Shell, Procter & Gamble, and AT&T, to give a small sample. Senge is also a founding partner of Innovation Associates, located in Massachusetts and Canada.

Open systems theory is a powerful organizational philosophy that influenced thought in engineering, biology, sociology, and economics some time before becoming a framework for studying organizations. In order for us to understand and improve a process, we must *conceptualize* the process. No wonder Peter Senge insisted that businesses and industries turn to systems as their "mental model," rather than to the assembly line view under which they had functioned for decades. Daniel Katz and Robert Kahn (1966) apparently were the first to refer to organizations as open systems, similar to living organisms in that they continually change in response to practical needs (Geus, 1997). An open systems organization exchanges resources and ideas among its employees (as in a closed system) *and* with outside sources. Although a systems model gives us paradigms for clearer concepts, we still limit the accuracy of the model as soon as we make it two dimensional.

Feedback is an important part of systems thinking (King, Young, & Behnke, 2000, p. 365). A building's air conditioning thermostat, for example, has a feedback system. It gathers information about the temperature in the building and, on the basis of that feedback, "decides" to deliver more warm or cool air (Littlejohn, 1992, pp. 365–392). This example helps us generalize a helpful definition, whether feedback is a function of engineering design or an analysis of genetic adaptation: Feedback is the process that provides knowledge to inform strategic adjustment for improvement. Systems thinking emphasizes that every "influence" is both *cause* and *effect* (Senge, 1994, p. 75).

• COMMUNICATION AND MEANING

In a large lecture hall, the professor proclaims to his class, "To work with language, learn the rules. For instance, in the Russian language, a double negative remains a negative, and in Spanish, the more negatives used, the more negative is the message. However, in English, a double negative forms a positive, like driving forward and reversing, finishing where you started. However, there is *no*—I repeat, NO—language where a double positive forms a negative." A dis-embodied voice zinged from the back of the hall, "Yeah, right."

Rules guide our use of verbal and nonverbal codes, but words and other symbols cannot carry messages. The clever student caught literal and cultural uses of "yeah" and "right" and predicted that his listeners would, in good humor, enjoy the paradoxical and equivocal nature of language. Let's explore some basic concepts of meaning.

Meanings Are Events

Meanings cannot exist independently; they must be attached to experiences of some sort. In communication studies, we call these experiences *events*. Meanings, then, are events occurring in contexts and attached to symbols. Therefore, we internalize these symbolized meanings to label our experiences. Even objects, in this regard, are events. For instance, although oysters are objects, one's initial experience with oysters is an event, and the event creates a meaning for "oysters." If you and a friend first see oysters at a fresh fish market in Gulf Shores, Alabama, and the next evening you enjoy oysters on the half shell in New Orleans on a beautiful evening with jazz playing in the square, you attach these events to the label "oyster." Meanings for events are unique to each person.

Meanings Carry an Emotional Dimension

Carried away with the delight of oysters, you order them again the next day, but your friend can't even look at an oyster, much less eat one. He recalls the smelly fish market and monotonous music. An emotional set becomes a part of the total meaning of our words and symbols. Even common, little words affect us, and our word choices influence our behavioral choices. "Can't never could do anything," a familiar saying, reminds us that saying the word *can't* predisposes us to not try. The previously mentioned professor may now tell himself, "Never say never."

Meanings Are in People, Not in Words

Words do not guarantee that receivers magically will know the sender's intended meanings. Words trigger meanings, and each person's experiences have created different personal meanings. Meanings thus live inside people, rather than mechanically attaching to words.

Meanings, Symbols, and Referents Work Together

The triangle of meaning in Figure 1.4, shows the relationships among (1) symbols (primarily words in our examples), (2) referents (objects, events, ideas, etc.), and (3) thoughts. Each point of the triangle connects in a specific way with each of the other two points. Look at the chair you are in—a *referent*. You *refer* to this thing with the word *chair*. The word is not the actual object, nor is it the *thought* about the object. Neither is your thought the same thing as what you are sitting in or the word referring to it. If you are French, you say *chaise*, a different symbol for the same chair. Write the word *chair* on the chalkboard. Try sitting on that. Many communication breakdowns occur because people forget that a word is not the same as what it refers to. (For example, Joe had a mean-

FIGURE 1.4 ● The Triangle of Meaning

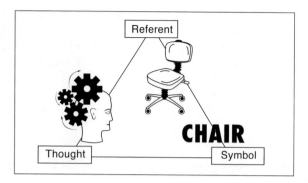

spirited, unfair boss in his last job. Now you are his new boss. Just the word *boss* prompts defensiveness in Joe. Joe has confused the *word* with the *referent.* Now the word *boss* includes you, but he is still reacting to his old meaning rather than what he knows about you.)

We employ language in order to share meanings with one another. We never have perfect understanding, but by processing feedback and experiences, we approximate an understanding. The closer we can come to sharing a meaning, the better the quality of our communication. Another way to look at the process of sharing meaning is to think of it as narrowing context until senders and receivers see an event very similarly. The narrower context moves the communicators from abstract language use to specific, concrete use.

Meanings Depend on Contexts

All communication occurs within a context. Context includes who is present, what the physical setting is, and what the relationship is. Context relies heavily on culture, time, and message sequence.

The Context of Culture

Messages depend largely on the cultural context of the moment and the communicators' individual background cultures. There are many kinds of culture. Have you ever known people who assumed that everyone did things the way their high schools or communities did, until they attended college and saw differently? Schools and communities thus exist as cultures. Even gender is treated as culture. Certainly, nations and countries show cultural differences. Likewise, organizations develop unique cultures. One organization views itself as a large, nurturing, productive family. Another organization resists the warm, fuzzy image and focuses on the bottom line. It's practically impossible to have impact in an organization until you become familiar with an organization's culture.

HOTEL BUSINESS IN OTHER LANDS

Mary Anne Russell (personal communication, May 2000), in discussing the hotel industry in various countries, described a time when she centralized marketing and reservations by computer for an international hotel chain. In Switzerland, she suggested that the hoteliers needed to "address the various

Four businesswomen confer with audience at a business seminar. How does this setting (context) influence senders' encoding choices? What ethical dimensions rest on the quality of the messages sent?

segments of the market." The Swiss wanted to know what she meant. She explained that they should attract customers by appealing to their particular needs. The Swiss said, "We wouldn't steal customers from other businesses! That would not be ethical." Surprising her again, when she consulted in Japan, such resistance did not exist, although theirs, too, is a rich and traditional cultural background.

Messages are meaningful at a specific point in time. The time of day, season of the year, and the length of time between visits affect the communication. The phrases "good timing" and "bad timing" indicate that sequencing shapes meanings. Therefore, people ask such things as "Is this a good time to talk about a problem in our department?"

The *environment* is the physical surroundings, including the building or location, furniture, acoustical qualities, temperature, overflowing in-boxes, and books on the shelf. The communication of environment includes *audience*—the ones who can hear and observe the conversation. Some topics are inappropriate to discuss publicly, and word choices change depending on who is listening.

ACTIVITY 1.2

STEEL OR UPHOLSTERY?

In small groups, discuss the differences between having a conversation (1) in a doctor's examining room as you sit (scantily clad) on an examining table and look at stainless steel instruments in a glass cabinet and (2) in the doctor's office as, fully dressed, you sit in an upholstered chair visiting with the doctor, who is seated behind a mahogany desk and surrounded by degrees and certificates.

Meanings Are Denotative and Connotative

Denotative meanings are the meanings commonly shared by those who use a language—in other words, the dictionary definitions. *Connotative* meanings are the personal, subjective, and emotional meanings that individuals attach to words.

• PRINCIPLES OF SPEECH COMMUNICATION

Principles are rules or laws that are inherent to the nature of something. Understanding principles of speech communication better equips us to make appropriate decisions.

Communication Is Inevitable

You cannot *not* communicate. Communication is inevitable, and the reasoning is straightforward:

- People constantly behave.
- All behavior potentially communicates.
- Therefore, people are constantly communicating.

A human being is like a radio station, sending out a signal whether or not anyone is tuned in. As long as a person is alive, those signals are going out.

SOUNDS OF SILENCE

1. George quietly listens to the department head as she presents a new benefits package. The department head interprets George's silence to mean he is satisfied with the package.
   Has George agreed to the benefits package?
2. A patient is comatose and hooked up to monitors.
   Is the patient communicating?

ACTIVITY 1.3

Communication Is Dynamic

Speech communication affects everyone in the interaction, just as in a football game, after the ball is snapped, the teams react to what other players do and to what the ball does. In addition to all the coaching and game plans, a good player has to be aware of the moment.

Likewise, speech communication is dynamic and will not behave statically. Even silence affects others, analogous to a linebacker standing in place after the ball is snapped, at which moment the quarterback notices an open receiver.

Speech Is an Interactive Process

Staying with the football analogy, the players at the line read keys from the opposing team and at the same time remember the formation that has been called prior to the snap. Thus, one person's action affects the other person's action—in this case, physically. In speech the impact is emotional and intellectual. Break apart the word *interactive: Inter* means between, and *active* means behavior. The word *process* here means continuous, with neither fixed beginning nor ending.

Speech Communication Is Irreversible

We all have felt words slip out and immediately wished we could take them back, but speech is not a reversible process. In a court of law, a judge sometimes instructs the jury to disregard the last statements of the witness and has the words stricken from the record. But can jurors really forget? In order to forget, they would have to remember, and they would have to keep remembering what they were supposed to forget to avoid discussing it. These instructions "take an issue off the table" in jury-room discussions, but an impact has been made nevertheless. Likewise, when we criticize, compliment, argue, and give opinions, our statements affect other people, and the meanings live on indefinitely in those listeners. Receivers use their brains to interpret messages, and their brains are forever physiologically changed. The words live on.

Speech Is Unrepeatable

Have you ever tried to describe some hilarious event, but, discouraged by the listener's apparent lack of appreciation, end up commenting, "You just had to have been there"? Remember, a spoken message is itself a unique event, and contexts subtly, but continually, change. That is why we may not catch on to a math concept until we hear it for the third time. Even as our words potentially live forever, they are at that same moment dying.

Spoken Messages Have Content and Relational Dimensions

A relational dimension of communication *always* exists, and it is especially apparent in face-to-face communication. Attitudes are communicated primarily through nonverbal means (tone of voice, handshake, facial expression, etc.). Relational messages include a person's emotional state and a person's attitude about the other person. A project director can say, "I got your written report" and send a message by her tone of voice of either "I love your report" or "I could care less."

More Communication Is Not Necessarily Better Communication

At work, clearer and more frequent communication usually clears the air and builds consensus, but sometimes communication clarifies and intensifies the conflict. Unfortunately, the more some people work together, the more they know that they don't want to work together.

●━●━● DIVERSITY AND WORKPLACE COMMUNICATION

Various perspectives affect meaning, context, and, in fact, all the principles and elements of communication. We heartily acknowledge the complexity and diversity within organizational climates. Organizations often "leverage diversity" to cultivate diverse talents, but they must, at the same time, recognize the melding of gender, ethnicity, and generational cultures.

• • • • TIPS   • • • • Organizational Communication and Communication in Organizations • • • •

The phrases "organizational communication" and "communication in organizations" are used interchangeably in many sources. The best way to determine

Although we can assume scientific data is the content of this discussion, what interpretations can you make about the relational dimensions present in the interaction?

the meaning is to pay attention to the context. When you recognize a source as making a distinction, it will be along these lines.

Organizational communication includes the following:

- Messages that organizations present about themselves publicly, including messages to customers, clients, or the general public
- Communication between organizations, such as between the federal government and pharmaceutical companies
- The formal flow of communication within the organizational culture, according to organizational charts, regardless of who holds the position

Communication in organizations depends largely on the nature of the business and encompasses the following:

- The formal and informal flow of communications within the organization, both by organizational chart and by the persons who hold the positions
- Interpersonal communications among employees
- Team and small group communications
- Communications between employees and clients (which has some qualities of both types—organizational communication and communication in organizations)
- Tasks in which communication is the core business, such as an exchange of intellectual capital

• • •

Gender

Some general information clarifies the picture of gender in workplace comparisons:

- Men have greater access to social or interpersonal power than women, and they differ in their ability to influence others (Carli, 1999).
- Women delivering discipline are perceived as less effective and less fair than men (Atwater, 2001; Atwater, Carey & Waldman, 2001).

- Men and women are similar in leadership style and overall effectiveness (Eagly & Johnson, 1990; O'Leary & Ickovics, 1991).
- Although equally effective in all aspects of supervision, women display more transformational leadership behavior than men (Atwater, 2001).

Communication style is inherent to a person's self-concept and is difficult to change. Women attempting (somewhat outside their comfort zones) to use a male communication style may feel they are being rude or even mean. Men feel less powerful and more vulnerable when they become less assertive. Most likely because of cultural expectations, men and women using their gender opposite's style are judged less favorably by others.

A mixture of styles emerges from gender acculturation. Peter Drucker makes an important point about our changing work context: "Knowledge work knows no gender; men and women do the same jobs" (Drucker, Spring 2000). Male or female, people have more choices than ever in how they work.

• • • • TIPS   • • • • Gender Communication • • • •

Gender communication research has brought attention to differences in styles. The research overall concludes that there are more differences among women and among men than between men and women. Some researchers find it more useful to identify subjects by communication gender style. That is, a particular woman may have a more dominating style—a male style, and a particular man may focus more on building rapport, a female style. Generally speaking, organizations benefit from a blend of styles, and leaders should learn a variety of skills, contingent on the situation. Nevertheless, several behaviors in American culture correlate to the gender of the communicator.*

- Men tend to interrupt women more than they interrupt men, or than women interrupt either men or women.
- Men have a tendency to "solve" or "fix" problems as soon as they hear about them.
- Women seek intimacy and rapport through their verbal conversations. At work they ask for others' opinions and look for consensus. Men may interpret this as uncertainty and indecisiveness.
- Men maintain their status through conversational banter and opposition. This inhibits some men and many women from communicating.
- Women tend to downplay their authority, trying not to "lord it over" others. This usually works with women, but it makes them vulnerable to a man challenging their authority.
- Men want to maintain status and perceive asking questions as going "one down" in the "one-upmanship" conversational game. They may judge negatively those who ask questions.
- Women use more indirect communication than men and may not be heard as clearly.
- At meetings, men are more likely to speak out, and women are more likely to speak privately.

---

* Read, for instance, works by Deborah Tannen, such as *That's Not What I Meant*.

• • •

Age

Remarkably, four generations work with one another in American corporations today. With increased life expectancy and threats to retirement funds, more employees stay in the workplace additional years, yet "reporting relationships no longer correlate to age or experience . . . no precedent exists" (McCann, 2002). Even blue collar workers show generational differences, due in part to the shift from employment in manufacturing to employment in service (Gibson & Papa, 2000). "Nearly 70 percent of participants in a recent Web poll said they're experiencing a 'generational rift'" (McCann, 2002). This is a broadly held perception, and yet, in spite of these changes, Rosabeth Kantor says that "people in their 60s and beyond have embraced e-culture both enthusiastically and effectively. What our youth do bring to e-culture are energy, passion, and rejuvenation. . . . There's something to be learned in both directions" (Hodgetts, 1995).

In one study, supervisors see problem-solving and communication skills as stronger in engineers over age 45. Human resources personnel rate older and younger engineers about the same in technical knowledge and teamwork. In adaptability and ability to keep up with new developments, the younger engineers rate higher than the older engineers (IEEE-USA, 2000).

Ethnicity

Workplaces now assume diversity by cultures among employees. One project in global automotives involved a team functioning from more than a dozen time zones, six languages, and four continents. Diversity by ethnicity in the workplace is a given. A member of one global team asked online, "Does anyone here speak English?"

An executive in a Saudi organization complained, "We have twenty-seven different nationalities working together in our organization. Most come from countries where people were brought up not to say bad things about the people they work with. So it's hard to get honest performance feedback." Yet, another executive at a Netherlands' bank observed, "Some people here give feedback to score in a macho game of one-upmanship; they pay no attention to the impact on the person receiving it, they're far too blunt" (Goleman, 1998, p. 149).

Other demographic profiles evolve to shape the American scene. More management and professional positions are being filled by minority employees and, as is legal, without regard for race. Such blending of American cultures obscures contexts and challenges communications.

• WORKING WITH EMOTIONAL INTELLIGENCE

Being "smart" is not enough. In communication, quantity does not necessarily breed quality, and diversity introduces more complexity into organizational communication. The new yardstick is not just how smart we are, or how much training and expertise we have, but also how well we handle ourselves and each other. Increasingly, employers use this new yardstick in choosing who is hired and who is not, who is let go and who is retained, who is passed over and who is promoted.

Daniel Goleman contends that emotional intelligence (EI, or sometimes, with a reference to IQ, called EQ) has more to do with an individual's success over a lifetime than does IQ. He addresses key communication competencies, and his emphasis on communication, teamwork, and leadership speaks to our mission in business and professional speaking.

CONTEMPORARY VOICES 1.2: A DIFFERENT WAY OF BEING SMART

Salovey and Mayer coined the term *emotional intelligence* in 1990 and described it as "a form of social intelligence that involves the ability to monitor one's own and others' feelings and emotions, to discriminate among them, and to use this information to guide one's thinking and action."

In the early 1990s, Daniel Goleman became aware of their work, which eventually led to his book *Emotional Intelligence.* Goleman is the second contemporary voice in this textbook's learning strand. Goleman explains the physiology of emotions through neuroscience research, and he supports his construct with conclusions from more than 500 corporations. Certainly a "different way of being smart," emotional intelligence is nonetheless a long way from fluffy emotionalism. Goleman says we experience an "emotional hijacking"—that is, emotion overcomes the logical pilot on a productive path—when the physiology of emotion bypasses the logical processing part of the brain. "We cannot manage feelings of which we are unaware" (Lambert, 1998).

EI competencies are similar to the old-fashioned idea of "maturity" and can be categorized by competency sets: (1) self-awareness, self-confidence, and self-control; (2) commitment and integrity; and (3) the ability to communicate and influence, to initiate and accept change. Goleman agrees that communication is very high on, maybe on the top of, the list of desirable traits sought in employment.

Use of the new yardstick begins by assuming that employees have the intellectual ability and technical know-how to accomplish their job tasks. It measures the next level of personal qualities, such as initiative, empathy, and adaptability. Empathy develops first in self-awareness, and then in awareness of others' emotions. At that level, a person begins developing competencies in teamwork, leadership, and persuasion.

Emotional intelligence may seem oxymoronic, because our society has long associated intelligence purely with intellect, analysis, and rationality, but Goleman deals with the feeling side of life—joy, hurt, anger, sadness, jealousy—and asserts that human beings can also handle these states intelligently. Truly, intellect and rationality do little good unless the emotional response is informed, managed, and used effectively.

ENROLLING THE BRAIN

The most encouraging conclusion is that emotional control can be taught. In other words, even for individuals who are shy or who seem to have a genetically shortened fuse, education of the emotions is effective. The limbic brain—the emotional brain—is quite primitive compared with the neocortex—the thinking brain. "The thinking brain comprehends something after a single hearing or reading. The limbic brain, on the other hand, is a much slower learner—particularly when the challenge is to relearn deeply ingrained habits" (Goleman, Boyatzis, & McKee, 2002, p. 103). Recent research is heartening in this regard and informs the writing of this text:

- Although the emotional brain needs more practice (Zull, 2002), training can produce changes in the brain centers, creating new neural tissue as well as new neural connections and pathways throughout adulthood (Bennett-Goleman, 2001, cited in Goleman, Boyatzis, & McKee, 2002).

- Competencies can develop, with new habits replacing old ones, even in adulthood, and changes at the limbic system level show enduring effect (Boyatzis, 1994; Boyatzis, 1999; Boyatzis, Leonard, Rhee, & Wheeler, 1998; Edelman, 1987).

Dr. Goleman was educated and has taught at Harvard, where he also earned his doctorate. He covered behavioral and brain sciences as science editor for the *New York Times,* so it must have been especially satisfying when *Emotional Intelligence, Why It Matters More Than IQ* made the *Times'* Best Seller list. Another major work, *Working with Emotional Intelligence* (1998), includes two additional years of research and internal studies of nearly 200 large companies and their most successful employees. *Primal Leadership* (2001) presents conclusions for ongoing research, especially focusing on the competencies that have been shown to be teachable skills that are useful at the forefront of leadership.

Perhaps this is the time to explore the effects of emotionally unintelligent people, as seen in the next activity.

THE OBLIVIOUS BOSS QUIZ

How oblivious would you rate a boss making the statements in this activity? In small groups, rate each boss's statement:

ACTIVITY 1.4

- 0–2 Out to lunch (synapse misfire)
- 3–4 MIA (physically present, but mentally "missing in action")
- 5–6 Down for the count (ineffective; time to leave the ring)
- 7–8 One of Neptune's moons (clueless and circling another world)
- 9–10 Comatose (minimal signs of life)

_____ 1. "Don't waste my time with complaints."

_____ 2. "Say what? I don't want to hear it. Go on. No kidding. Get down. You're not serious."

_____ 3. "Send your ideas to my assistant to be screened before you use my time. She can explain them to me."

_____ 4. "Impress the clients with a highly technical solution, but don't confuse them."

_____ 5. "We have six laptops to check out somehow."

_____ 6. "Your future isn't what it once was."

_____ 7. The project manager says, "This project lacks leadership."

_____ 8. "Hey, boy, gotta minute?"

_____ 9. "You are valuable to the organization, but your work is not important."

_____10. "Donna is in Seattle today, so you will have to present the plan to the client. Donna's the only one who understands the design, so just put together something."

_____11. "Alphabetize the list in numerical order."

_____12. "Make these incompatible software packages work together."

_____13. "Good morning, ladies and gentlemen. The bylaw subcommittee finished their work in the last hour and e-mailed you a 200-page packet with 63 changes. Are you ready to vote on each change?"

_____ 14. "Your height doesn't qualify you for a larger cubicle. Perhaps you can raise your chair some."

_____ 15. "I don't want to hear about lack of resources. Just get it done."

Assuming you have learned and will learn from the mistakes of these clueless bosses, let's categorize and become acquainted with the concept of communication competence and explore several of the major communication competencies.

COMMUNICATION COMPETENCE

Grounded in communication and business research, this textbook searches for a reasonable way to categorize the competencies that repeatedly surface. There is no doubt that qualities and competencies forwarded in the discipline of communication make up the majority of the Goleman construct of emotional intelligence. Therefore, it relies on Goleman to further validate the competencies' choices and structure them for our study.[2]

Communication, by way of definition, occurs when individuals engage in a transaction in order to reach a shared understanding of an event. Communicators negotiate meaning through the sending and receiving of messages.

Communication competence refers to a person's ability to apply communication skills appropriately, and *communication efficacy* is the amount of personal confidence in valid communication skills. People who have an aptitude for learning and who value themselves as well as others are more likely to become competent communicators. Competent communicators get jobs done, solve problems, persuade others, negotiate, soothe, question, and explain. These are the people you want to work with.

Three decades of research in organizations sends a consistent message: Employees are more likely to lose their jobs due to poor people skills than to poor technical skills. In a national survey of what employers are looking for in entry-level workers, specific technical skills were less important than the potential employee's underlying ability to learn on the job. After that, employers listed the following skills and qualities as desirable (Goleman, 1998):

- Listening and oral communication
- Adaptability and creative responses to setbacks and obstacles
- Personal management, confidence, motivation to work toward goals, a sense of wanting to develop one's career and take pride in accomplishments
- Group and interpersonal effectiveness, cooperativeness and teamwork, skills at negotiating disagreements

In response to a 1990 study from Fortune 500 companies, the Creative Education Foundation listed critical workplace skills (Ryan, 1999). More than half of the competencies related to communication in organizations. Oral

---

[2] As the Consortium for Research in Emotional Intelligence continues its work; Goleman adjusts his EI construct to reflect the consortium's findings.

communications, interpersonal abilities, and teamwork abilities are the top skills interviewers seek in applicants[3] (Carnevale et al., 1989).

The National Communication Association (1997) analyzed responses from questionnaires sent to personnel interviewers at 500 businesses. Over 90% of the respondents said communication skills are essential for success, but regrettably, only 60% found applicants to be prepared with those skills at interviews. Furthermore, approximately 90% agreed that an employee's ability to communicate is one of the determining factors when giving promotions. College degrees and pertinent job skills are essential to get graduates in the corporate door, but the minimum is inadequate for success. When employees lose jobs, the most recorded reason of record is "poor communication skills."

This textbook's focus in business and professional speaking communication is communication within organizations. In other words, this course is about *your* individual communication as a part of your job. Several competencies—descriptiveness, empathy, openness, and expressiveness—appear repeatedly and are introduced in the following sections.

Descriptiveness, Clarity, and Accuracy

Message integrity relies on accurate descriptions. Messages, like buildings, should have structural integrity. They should be accurate and complete and should not oversimplify, enhance, or distort data. They should present facts, tone, and attitudes accurately. Descriptive language focuses on problems and solutions, rather than who gets blamed and who takes credit. Communicators' research informs others' decisions, so the findings should be reported descriptively.

DESCRIPTIVE CHOICES

Select which message in each pair contains the more accurate description.

●
ACTIVITY
1.5

1. a. "It can't be helped."
   b. "I don't know how to change the outcome of this event."
2. a. "They don't know what they are talking about."
   b. "I have some recent information that the technical group hasn't heard yet."
3. a. "I will be back in my Robson Street office no later than 2:00 this afternoon."
   b. "I will be back in the office later today."
4. a. "Write a thorough report on the project."
   b. "Submit a report on the project listing the client's specifications and the completed tasks to date."
5. a. "Great progress today. Let's schedule the same time tomorrow to continue our discussion."
   b. "Great discussion. See you tomorrow."
6. a. "A complex problem requires a robust solution."

---

[3] By 1996, employers said the three most highly sought-after skills in new hires were oral communications, interpersonal abilities, and teamwork abilities.

"Make a matrix listing the client's requests and the team's proposed responses."

Answers

1. (b) The first message begins with "it" and is in the passive voice. "I" takes responsibility and describes the speaker's relationship to the problem.
2. (b) "They" tends to separate a group from the "we" or "I" who is speaking. The inclusion of the phrase "recent information" adds to the completeness of the message. The "I" statement shifts from blaming to being a contributor.
3. (a) An address and a time frame are given. A vague "later" may be intentionally ambiguous, if the speaker is trying to avoid seeing someone.
4. (b) "Thorough" can mean interminably long or a paragraph about the project's current status.
5. (a) A supportive comment is made and the plans are specific.
6. (b) The first statement is highly abstract. The second statement helps focus future action.

Empathy

Empathy means feeling with another individual, as conveyed in the concept of "walking in another person's shoes." Empathic leaders are attuned to a wide range of emotional signals in individuals and groups. "Empathetic people are superb at recognizing and meeting the needs of clients, customers, or subordinates" (Goleman, Boyatzis, & McKee, 2002, p. 50). Empathy thus isn't a mushy, emotional mentality: "That would be a nightmare—it would make action impossible" (Goleman, Boyatzis, & McKee, 2002, p. 50).

Empathy detects how others feel in the moment, and uses compassionate listening and supportive responses. Even employees' bad moods send disruptive messages to clients. For instance, in cardiac care units where the nurses generally were in a "depressed" mood, the death rate among patients was four times higher than on comparable units (Schneider & Bowen, 1995). Saying and doing what's appropriate includes calming fears, assuaging anger, joining in good spirits, and sharing values and priorities. The unwittingly off-key, unempathic employee sets off negative reactions (Goleman, Boyatzis, & McKee, 2002, pp. 30–31).

Openness

Relationships require *openness,* but deception is just the opposite—*closed.* In a closed climate, suspicions and rumors grow. Conversely, effective communicators disclose (1) appropriately, (2) incrementally, and (3) reciprocally in order to develop trust between the communicators. Author Susan Scott, in *Fierce Conversations* (2001), challenges people to live in the "here and now" and engage in real communication, instead of lazily skirting openness, authenticity, and when necessary, confrontation.

"I'd say you're unlocking the value of a person when you communicate openly with them," Mark Loehr, a managing director at Salomon Smith

Barney, observed . . . "When you communicate openly, you open the possibility of getting the best out of people—their energy, creativity. If you don't, then they just feel like cogs in a machine, trapped and unhappy." (Goleman, 1998, p. 175)

Expressiveness

Expressiveness makes attitudes and emotions known to others. Faces and voices of expressive individuals communicate compassion, excitement, amusement, reluctance, apprehension, and so forth. Exaggerated expressiveness can come across as unstable, unbusinesslike, or manipulative, but without expressiveness, communication becomes flat, ambiguous, and possibly deceptive. Expressive words enrich messages, and a friendly handshake reinforces "I'm so happy to see you." A concerned look, on the other hand, may confuse the other person, until words explain: "I think I just locked my keys in the car."

Why do people enjoy shopping in some stores and dread others? The expressiveness of people in the store, especially the employees, sets the tone. It thus makes sense that in a study of 32 stores of a U.S. retail chain, the stores with the most positive salespeople showed the best sales results (George, 1995, as cited in Goleman, 2002, p. 16).

Cheerfulness and warmth are the most contagious moods in working groups, with irritability less contagious, and depression hardly contagious at all. The brain's open-loop circuitry interprets smiles and laughter so quickly that we immediately and involuntarily laugh and smile in response (Barsade, 1998; Barsade & Gibson, 1998).

• ETHICS AND COMMUNICATION

The most powerful tool any of us has is ethical communication. Although if we have been exploited and swindled by unethical communicators, we have difficulty remembering how resilient and strong ethical communication is, at least in the long run. Communication "swindling" is deceptive and hurtful, because "swindlers" meet their own needs at the expense of others. Unethical communication distorts or withholds information, twists advice, and misrepresents plans.

Ethical Communicators Interact Responsibly

Ethics, by definition, are the principles of conduct that govern a person or group. Former Supreme Court Justice Potter Stewart said that ethical people know "the difference between what you have a right to do and what is the right thing to do" (Young, 1992). To be ethical is to be honest and straightforward, avoiding deceitful, unscrupulous, or unfair methods and goals (Gregory, 1993, p. 13). Bowen H. McCoy, managing director of Morgan Stanley & Company, investment bankers, states the following:

> Ethics involves the art of integration and compromise, not blind obedience and conformity. Ethics calls for tolerance of ambiguity; yet, it is an action-oriented, interpersonal process. [It] signifies a heightened ability to seek truth that stems from core beliefs and to decide consciously on one's action

in a business context. Ethics deals with free choice among alternatives. (McCoy, 1983, cited in Andrews & Baird, 2000)

Ethics and sound economic development go hand-in-hand, and now organizations say that ethical business is better business, especially after the business scandals in the early 2000s. When an organization articulates its values, it influences the values of its employees and shapes the way outsiders perceive it. To be ethical is to play fairly.

Global issues complicate ethical considerations. Ethical businesses rely on ethical communicators, but when a corporation conducts business with 40 to 50 countries, whose ethical standards should it follow?

Reality @ WORK 1.4

COMMUNICATING ORGANIZATIONS' VALUES WITH ETHICAL ACTIONS

Levi Strauss & Co., long famous for its jeans, has more than 34,000 employees and $5.2 billion in sales. The company had a track record of ethical and humane practices, such as retaining workers during the depressed 1930s, integrating in the 1960s, and heralding AIDs as a corporate cause in the 1980s. It was even drafting a program to develop a formalized code of ethics when *NBC Nightly News* aired a report that accused a Levi contractor in Saipan of imposing virtual slavery conditions on local workers. Levi audited its largest clothing contractor on the island to determine whether the contractor conducted "their business consistent with a set of ethical values not inconsistent with those of Levi Strauss & Co." The audit resulted in a canceled contract and a $9 million settlement against the contractor. By 1992, Levi teams began investigating practices in the 50 countries where they did business, proactively upgrading, suspending, or terminating contracts accordingly. In China in 1993, Levi surrendered most of its $50-million-a-year operation.

Yet another NBC report uncovered horrible conditions in the Bangladesh operations. Underage 12-year-old children were working in the factories, but the children's work kept their families from starving. Some of the children were sole supporters with few choices: work in the factories, beg on the streets, or become prostitutes. Levi's solution was to pay the children's wages while they attended school until they reached legal working age.

Levi's code of ethics and performance guidelines for overseas suppliers, *Business Partner Terms of Engagement,* led the way, and Wal-Mart, Nike, Reebok, and Sears adopted similar codes (Rappaport, 2000).

Ethical Communicators Recognize Power and Responsibility in Their Communications

Some people insist, "I'm just going to say what I think," when what they *really* want to do is cut someone down. Ethical communicators carry responsibility for *what* they say, *how* they say it, and their choices of when, where, and to whom they speak, as well as for their nonverbal communication. Ethical communicators

- Handle information responsibly and accurately and send messages that are accurate, unbiased, and complete.
- Use words responsibly and avoid derogatory or discriminatory language.
- Send honest messages through accurate impressions and avoid manipulation through exaggeration or distortion.

- Pay attention to responses and feedback.

In KPMG's 2000 Organizational Survey, its concern about "a culture of lying" in businesses was more insightful than readers at the time knew, since ethical breaches of conduct by Enron and other major corporations were yet to make headline news. Employees justify their deceptions, saying they fear a loss of public trust in the company if they tell about the violations they observe.

Employees must have a "safe and confidential way of reporting misconduct without fear." Ethical companies with honest work environments "will thoroughly communicate their standards to employees and provide training that helps workers achieve their stated performance goals" (Mallory, 2000, pp. 6–8b).

Senge, Covey, and Goleman's ideas converge in their discussions on ethical practices. Due largely to Stephen Covey's work, ethical approaches in the workplace are increasingly explicit, not hidden. His signature book, *Seven Habits of Highly Effective People* (1989), motivated people to openly discuss the matter of principles at work. Covey reminds us that principles are self-evident and are fundamental to and inherent in the good of people everywhere. "Principles are guidelines for human conduct that are proven to have enduring permanent value" (Covey, 1990, p. 35).

CONTEMPORARY VOICES 1.3: PRIMARY GREATNESS

And now let's meet our third contemporary voice, Dr. Stephen Covey, who is as responsible as anyone today for bringing the need for ethical behaviors to organizations' attention. In *Principle-Centered Leadership* (1992), Covey says character that demands ethical behavior, not sparkling personality, is the substance of "primary greatness."

"We may have the 'right' rhetoric, style, and even intention, but without trust we won't achieve primary greatness or lasting success" (Covey, 1992 pp. 57–58). Covey says three character traits in particular are essential to primary greatness:

- *Integrity,* "the value we place on ourselves." "If we can't make and keep commitments to ourselves as well as to others, our commitments become meaningless" (p. 61).
- *Maturity,* "the balance between courage and consideration" (Covey citing Hrand Saxenian, Harvard Business School, p. 61). "While courage may focus on getting bottom-line results, consideration deals more with the long-term welfare of other stake holders" (p. 61).
- *Abundance mentality,* which believes that "there is plenty out there for everyone." It is the opposite of the "scarcity mentality," in which life is viewed as a limited pie—if one person gets a large piece, there is less for the rest to share (p. 62).

Trustworthy persons communicate ethically and are above reproach, build trust through reliability and authenticity, and admit their own mistakes. They confront unethical actions in others and communicate tough, principled stands.

SUMMARY

This chapter defines the major elements of communication, discusses several principles of speech communication, introduces key communication competencies, and examines the ethical application of speech communication. Key communication competencies for business practices are descriptiveness, empathy, and expressiveness.

Human communication can be represented with several elements: the source of the message, with a functional encoder; the receiver of the message, with a decoder; a substantial message, which involves a channel, context, and noise (interference); and feedback and feedforward. Although linear and transactional models help us identify communication elements, open systems models accommodate the complexity of human communication.

Although rules guide our verbal and nonverbal usage, words and other symbols cannot carry messages. Symbols trigger meanings from our previous experiences, or *events*. Words trigger meanings, and each person's meanings are different. Therefore, meanings are in people, not words. All communication occurs within a context, which relies heavily on culture, time, and the sequence of messages. Denotative meanings are the common ones most of us speaking a language share, whereas connotative meanings are the personal, subjective, and emotional meanings that individuals attach to words.

Principles of speech communication explain communication dynamics: Communication is inevitable, dynamically affects everyone in the interaction, and is irreversible. Spoken messages have content and relational dimensions. Furthermore, more communication is not necessarily better communication.

Ethical practices are what we do to act on ethical principles. Ethical communicators interact responsibly, but unethical communicators distort or withhold information, twist advice, and misrepresent plans. •

ACTIVITIES

1. **Presenting to Others:** To understand a variety of workplaces, interview people in careers that interest you. Make notes on what you learn, so you can present your findings to a class in less than five minutes.

   - Tell whom you interviewed and in what field.
   - Describe typical activities or tasks in the interviewee's job.
   - What is it about this field of study that interests you?
   - List three topics from this study of speech communication that relate to this field of study.

2. **Technical Support:** The Society of Competitive Intelligence Professionals (SCIP) is a nonprofit group with over 6,000 members representing some 44 countries. The Alexandria, Virginia–based entity provides books about human intelligence and a website (www.scip.org) providing a database of 350 experts and a list of conferences all over the world. SCIP deplores the word *spying,* pointing to its code of ethics posted on its website (www.scip.org/ci/ethics.asp). Describe SCIP's code of ethics in light of ideas from the Contemporary Voices features in this chapter.

3. **Journaling the Experience:** America's Career Infonet at www.acinet.org lists competencies for various careers as compiled by the U.S. Department of Labor. Journal your plan for meeting the requirements of your field.

4. **Presenting to Others:** What are we guaranteed by the First Amendment, which deals with "freedom of speech"? What are practical guidelines for exercising that freedom? Locate an article discussing freedom of speech as applied in a court of law. What was the reasoning behind the decision? Do you agree or disagree with the decision? Why? Present your conclusions to your small group in a three-minute speech.

5. **Ethically Speaking:** Ethical practices are what we do to act on ethical principles. Read Covey's suggestions for exercising maturity and integrity. How would you change the list? Give a three-minute presentation about a workplace situation that illustrates one of Covey's practices (Covey, 1992, p. 77).

   • Never make a promise we will not keep.

   • Make meaningful promises, resolutions, and commitments to do better and to be better—and share these with a loved one.

   • Use self-knowledge and be very selective about the promises we make.

   • Consider promises as a measure of our integrity and faith in ourselves.

   • Remember that our personal integrity or self-mastery is the basis for our success with others.

6. **Team Work:** Goleman (1998, pp. 39–40) presents results of a large survey by H. Fountain that was made public in "Of White Lies and Yellow Pads," the *New York Times,* July 6, 1997. As a team, find related articles of similar substance and report your findings to class.

   The Ethics Officers Association commissioned a survey of 1,300 workers across all levels in American companies and discovered that about half admitted to being a part of unethical business practices.

   • Lied to or deceived a customer: 9%

   • Falsified numbers in reports or documents: 6%

   • Lied to superiors on serious matters or withheld critical information: 5%

   • Taken credit for someone else's work or idea: 4%

   • Engaged in copyright or software infringement: 3%

   • Forged someone's name on a document: 2%

   • Reported false information when filing government forms, such as tax returns: 1%

FOR FURTHER READING

Covey, S. R. (1990). *The seven habits of highly effective people: Powerful lessons in personal change* (1st Fireside ed.). New York: Simon & Schuster. Explore articles by and about Stephen Covey and others at www.franklincovey.com/foryou/articles/index.html.

Goleman, D. (1998). *Working with emotional intelligence.* New York: Bantam Books. The official website for staying current in emotional intelligence research is www.eiconsortium.org.

Senge, P. (1994). *The fifth Discipline.* New York: Doubleday/Currency. The official website for Senge's Learning Organizations is www.solonline.org.

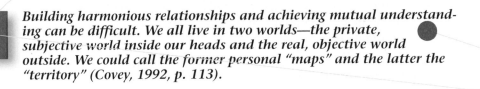

Building harmonious relationships and achieving mutual understanding can be difficult. We all live in two worlds—the private, subjective world inside our heads and the real, objective world outside. We could call the former personal "maps" and the latter the "territory" (Covey, 1992, p. 113).

Perception and Self-Concept

The Stages of Perception

How We Perceive Others

How We Perceive Ourselves (Self-Concept)

How We Perceive Organizations and Events in Organizations

We communicate with one another according to the way we see one another. This is the only reality available with which to interact. "At the root of most communication problems are perception or credibility problems," writes Stephen Covey in *Principle-Centered Leadership* (1992, p. 109). Disarmingly simple, the study of *perception* opens insights to powerful skills. We function in our world as we see it, and everyone sees it somewhat differently. Kathleen Kelley Reardon, in *The Secret Handshake: Mastering the Politics of the Business Inner Circle* (2001), describes how the perception of power works in a business setting:

> When I visited a friend at a West Coast firm, I entered the building to find that the many banks of elevators didn't seem to have indicators of the floors to which they'd take you. Nor was there a display board of office locations to which I might refer. I wandered about the lobby with several other people, including a lost mail courier. After a while, we noticed that some people waiting for elevators seemed to be staring at the floor. We looked down to find, embedded in the granite floor, the numbers indicating which floors each elevator stopped at. . . .
>
> The building seemed to say: "We are understated here because we don't need to be otherwise. . . . We are very important. If you were truly rich or important, we would have met you in the lobby. . . ." It was a very uncomfortable place, the kind that makes you want to spill something. (pp. 151–152)

This chapter explores the perceptual process and three outcomes of perception: how we see others, how we see ourselves, and how we see organizations and their events.

OBJECTIVES

After studying the content of this chapter, you should be able to

- Explain the three stages of the perceptual process
- Recognize several perspectives that shape interpretations/evaluations of self, others, and events in the workplace
- Value accuracy and avoid inaccurate and distorted perceptions
- Communicate more accurately and less defensively
- Understand that communication in organizations relies on people's perceptions

Because our individual perceptions are our individual realities of events, people, and the world in general, it serves us well to consider how those perceptions develop.

THE STAGES OF PERCEPTION

By definition, *perception* is the interpretation and evaluation of a collection of information directly available to the perceiver. Direct information (available only through our five senses) is called *sense data*. To make sense of it, we *organize*, or group, the sense data. When we "make sense of it," we are *interpreting*. Furthermore, we factor our values into our interpretations by *evaluating* the collected, organized sense data. Finally, we respond and interact with others according to our interpretations.

"We should probably neither think of perception as the start nor the finish of the process, but rather as the entire act" (Russell, 2000, p. 1). The three stages of perception are sensing, organizing, and interpreting/evaluating. The example in Reality @ Work 2.1 will get us started.

Reality @ WORK 2.1

ANTICIPATING MEANING

Julie arrives at work, frowning and slamming the door behind her. She mumbles "Hello" to Bob in the cubicle across from hers. Bob greets her, "Hey, Jules, how's it going?" She drops a stack of papers on her desk. Bob does a quick memory search, trying to figure out why she is frowning, slamming, and dropping. Maybe she's mad at him. Last week he *did* get a choice assignment that she wanted. Wait a minute! Didn't she say she had a dinner date last night? Perhaps that didn't go well. Hmmm. Could those papers have something to do with her mood? Bob considers possible interpretations of Julie's behavior. Should he say something, or will he end with a foot in his mouth? He needs to learn more from Julie before coming to a conclusion.

Stage 1: Sensing

Sensing requires the selection of data available through the five senses. Because more data are available to us than we can process, we select some information over others. We can process it quickly, but there is only so much we can do in a fixed amount of time. Not only time limits us; we physically can't see or hear all the sense data available. The eyes can take in 10,000 times more information than the brain can assimilate, and we see only one seventieth of the light spectrum. We don't recognize sounds under 20 or over 20,000 cycles per second (Andrews & Baird, 2000, p. 230).

Several selection factors affect which things we pay attention to:

- *Intensity:* We pay attention to the things that are the brightest, loudest, smelliest, most energetic, and so forth.
- *Contrast, or change:* We notice what is different.
- *Repetition:* We notice things because we've heard or seen them many times before.
- *Psychological comfort:* We select information that reinforces our beliefs and ideas.
- *Motivation:* We note certain people, events, or items because they interest us or are important to us.
- *Experience:* We learn from our experiences what to expect, and those expectations shape our perception.

ACTIVITY 2.1

SELECTION FACTORS

Which selection factors are at work in the following?

1. A nurse notices a patient has not eaten.
2. An accountant cannot understand why a popular employee's books show $1,000 in the red at the end of each month, with no logical explanation.
3. A project manager pushes her team to work extra hours, thinking that the division manager wants project completion at all costs. When three of the five team members complain, and the division manager chastises the project manager, she feels betrayed.
4. A pilot's attention turns to a dial tipping into a red zone, and he listens for warning beeps.
5. Persons engaged in the dating scene notice quickly whether someone is wearing a wedding or engagement ring.

Stage 2: Organizing

The *organizing* stage connects collected sense data to meaningful interpretations. By organizing, we impose a pattern onto our observations to help us make sense out of something. "We do not perceive things to be random, unrelated occurrences. Rather, we tend to organize our perceptions into coherent patterns" (Hayes & Baird, 2000, p. 232). For instance, a "predicting pattern" might conclude "At the hospital, women in white shoes who are standing together are nurses."

SARAH'S STORY

Sarah said her parents still treated her like a child. She lived at home and worked 20 hours a week to defray expenses while she attended a local college. "You'll always be our little girl," Dad said. Mom asked, "Will you ever grow up?"

On campus, she was pleased to find she was being included in newly forming friendship groups. Isn't that part of the college experience? Because she lived at home, she needed to not hesitate when people included her in an evening out. She limited herself to only two nights a week to hang out or party. Sarah was a bit jealous of her new college friends, living in apartments, cooking for themselves, and having friends over at all hours. She had noticed, however, that when they had exams, their apartments got pretty messy. She was glad Mom had charge of that. She heard a couple of friends from out of state say they had to schedule maintenance for their cars. Thank goodness Dad took care of that for her. One thing she *could* do was shop, and it can't hurt to look—until the credit card bill comes in. She hadn't told her parents she had a credit card. After all, the Banc of the Planets had congratulated her on being in college and had provided a card. The Banc of the Planets was not sounding so friendly now.

Academically, she knew she was a capable student. (After all, her high school math teacher had praised her for diligence and coached her for math competitions.) She was a kind person and capable worker, so she continued volunteer work she had taken on in high school, plus a new one on campus. But, unlike high school, her grades were low Cs, except a B in math. She would have to put in some long hours to prepare for the second round of exams.

Meeting the problem head on, she told the community organizations why she couldn't volunteer this semester. She increased her work hours, meanwhile, to chip away at the credit card penalties. (She wasn't ready to tell her parents about the card yet.) Studying at home was hard, because her mother frequently asked her to run errands or do chores. That was a real dilemma, since Sarah wanted Mom to *see* that she was working hard. Her Dad said, "Just show me the grades, and I'll pay your next semester tuition." She wondered whether she had actually been studying hard or whether she had just stayed busy.

With another year to live at home before transferring to a university, Sarah decided she needed to talk to her parents about a more adult relationship. She

We know that some nurses are men, and we know that white shoes do not always go with the job, but *generally* the pattern holds true. We use these patterns—generalizations—to interpret what we observe and to predict others' behaviors.

In order for our generalizations to be useful, we *stabilize* these generalizations, a process that began the moment we began trying to make sense out of this world on which we were born. Stabilizing helps us predict repeated events, and it is something we must *learn* to do.

Astronaut Jim Lovell, played by Tom Hanks, in *Apollo 13,* enjoys the irony of perception of size over distance, as he holds his thumb up to block out the very moon on which he hopes to walk. The internal rule about size and distance helps us make sense of common events, and we use organizing principles so automatically that it takes effort to step back and look at them. A more complex application is provided in the case study, Sarah's Story.

In addition to categorizing and stabilizing, people tend to use other organizing principles, such as these:

was tired of feeling she couldn't please her mother and worried she would disappoint her father. She knew that she wanted their perception of her to change. But how? She remembered how she and her math professor had had a comfortable conversation that had begun by discussing a problem she missed on an exam. Having the exam copy in hand seemed to help. Perhaps something logical and tangible would pave the way again. She prepared a chart of a typical week, showing the class meeting times and the number of hours required to prepare for each class. She also included work hours, social time, community service time, and time to do family chores. Guessing that her Dad would question her objectivity, she checked her schedule with a campus advisor, who said, if anything, she needed to decrease her work hours or drop a class. She needed to work to pay her debt, and she was afraid to tell her parents if she dropped a class.

Sarah then showed the schedule to her parents. She was pleased with the tone she set—logical and calm: "You warned me that college was hard, and I thought I had listened. What I hadn't realized is how much there is to juggle. I passed this first round of exams, but I want my grades to be higher. So I would like to see what you think of a schedule I've made. I've already checked it with a campus advisor. I value your advice and need us to be a team." Her father shifted into his "business voice," obviously liking the structure Sarah proposed. Her parents were skeptical but negotiated reasonable expectations with her. Her mother admitted she resented the cost of college and opportunities she never had, and she "punished" her daughter with more chores whenever she saw her sit down. Sarah pointed out that she had already cut back on volunteer work. She had overcommitted, mostly to escape from home and studying, she admitted. They discussed the costs of repeating a course versus the minimum wage she was earning from her job. The discussion was an adult discussion—a big step in her desired direction.

What can Sarah do to change the way her parents treat her?

What evidence do you find in this case study of stabilized perceptions? Explain.

Unlocking a stabilized perception depends on having a different set of sense data or different organizational pattern. What will Sarah need to do? What will her parents need to do?

- *Proximity* assumes that closeness counts. The cliché is, "Birds of a feather flock together." For instance, if John goes to lunch with a group known to be highly critical of management, then others may assume John is likewise critical of management.

- *Good form* describes our need for closure. Here the adage is, "If it looks like a duck, walks like a duck, and quacks like a duck, it must be a duck." For instance, we assume all supermarkets function the same way and would be surprised if there were no check-out lines.

- *Common end,* also called *common fate,* comes from experiencing similar outcomes. For instance, you know five friends who went to medical school, and now they all live in large homes and drive BMWs. Lynn recently received acceptance for medical school, and you assume that in ten years she, too, will live in a beautiful home and drive an expensive car.

Stage 3: Interpreting/Evaluating

Our minds "make sense" out of events around us, such as a boss implementing a suggestion we made, a friend driving up in a new car, and a colleague ignoring a friendly greeting. *Interpreting* attaches meaning to selected and organized sense data. Assumptions, generalizations, and conclusions are all interpretations. We generalize how professors behave in class. We assume that Lynn will complete medical school and that John is critical of management. "Jumping to conclusions" implies that the interpreter did not have all the facts (adequate sense data) or organized the facts inaccurately. In a way, we never have *all* the facts, and of course, some interpretations are higher in quality and accuracy than others, but beware of jumping to conclusions.

Evaluating is a kind of interpreting that we constantly do. The word *evaluating* implies the application of meaning according to our individual value system. The most obvious evaluative interpretations are heard in statements that judge another person, the person's behavior, or the person's possessions. Compliments and criticisms make obvious the values of the speaker. Evaluations surface in almost every—if not every—communication.

When we make interpretations, we use what is happening at the time to know what is real, rather than a figment of the imagination. For instance, we need to know that the red light we are looking at is in the present and not one stored in memory from the past. An amazing 90% or more of an interpretation depends on past knowledge stored in the brain (Gregory, 1998, p. 3).

Perceptions determine how we view organizations and events at work. One person's problem is another person's opportunity. The perceptual shift from *problem* to *opportunity* mobilizes employees to find answers.

 HOW WE PERCEIVE OTHERS

Perceptions determine how we see others and how others see us. As we noted in the section on stages of perception, we form impressions of each other from limited information. For instance, after an interview, we decide whether this is a person with whom we want to work. As another example, speakers collect information about their audiences to understand the needs and interests of their listeners. The following discussion surveys perspectives that shape our perceptions, filters that limit those perceptions, and common perceptual distortions.

Perspectives Shape Perceptions

Your perspective of an event depends largely on who you are, your experiences, and your background. Several obvious frames of reference affect people's perceptions.

The Gender Perspective

Gender affects the ways we are seen and the ways we see others. "That's a man's point of view. What do the women think about this?" is a comment indicating that people think gender is a major factor in a person's needs and decisions.

What evidence do you see of gender equanimity in this photograph from the Center for Disease Control?

Even in communication styles, stereotypes in Western culture emphasize the perceived differences: "A woman wouldn't be able to tell that many people they won't have jobs next month." "We need a man to face the press corps—someone who won't freeze when they drill him with questions." You may not be surprised to learn that the stereotype does not hold up in research. There are actually more differences *among* men and among women than *between* men and women (Weaver, Fitch-Hauser, Villaume, & Thomas, 1993; Wood & Lenze, 1989). Some authors see communication between genders as similar to cross-cultural communication (Tannen, 1990).

We err in thinking the differences indicate that men and women see things totally differently and communicate with totally different styles. That being said, men and women have many communication similarities and several notable differences (Aries, 1989; Aries, 1996; Kramarae, 1988; Tannen, 1990). For instance, men are more likely to perceive conversation as a way to compete, attain power, and solve problems. Women, however, are more likely to perceive conversation as a means to affiliate with others, find things in common, and build cooperative climates. Men, on the one hand, are more likely to "see" a competitive world in which they win or lose "points" with each conversation. As a result, they are more likely to have the ability to remember detailed facts from a dialogue. Women, on the other hand, are more likely to see a world in which cooperation and affiliation are the foundations of effectiveness, which leads them to read nonverbal cues more skillfully.

The changing roles of women in the workplace confound men and women's perceptions. Currently, women hold approximately one third of all managerial positions, and the number of female-owned U.S. firms has more than doubled (Trentham, 1998). The future portends a different profile. The *2002 American Workplace Report* from the Employment Policy Foundation says, "In the next three decades, women will overtake men in management and professional positions." By 2030, women are projected to hold 54% of the management and professional jobs (Employment Policy Foundation, 2005).

What confusion has this shift caused? Men and women are perceived and judged according to cultural role expectations, or stereotypes. "Working women were once kept beneath a glass ceiling because they were considered too 'nice.'

Need and competences cut across the barriers of age, race, and gender. In this photograph, an OSHA team, made up of staffers from throughout the United States, discusses air sampling procedures at the World Trade Center site. Since September 11, OSHA has taken more than 3,500 air and bulk samples for asbestos, silica, lead and other heavy metals, carbon monoxide, and numerous organic and inorganic compounds, as well as noise.

Now they're being held back because they aren't nice enough," according to an article in *Psychology Today* (A. Wilson, 2000). Another study says that seemingly competitive women are judged job competent but less sociable, and thus less hirable, than those thought of as less competitive. In contrast, job-competent, but socially incompetent, men are described as hirable (A. Wilson, 2000).

The Generational Perspective

We likewise perceive people and events according to their and our ages. Currently, the workplace spans five generations. The baby boomers (born soon after World War II) are now in their fifties, and they bring attention to late career and retirement issues. Generation X has hit its stride in the workplace, having produced almost instantaneous millionaires. It isn't unusual for Gen-Xers to choose second careers in their forties. Gen-Yers have already stood on the shaky ground of a downward-sliding economy and a nation at war.

The Career Role Perspective

We make assumptions about others according to their roles. Whereas product developers use sophisticated equipment to "build the better mouse trap," marketers ponder whether enough people will actually buy a new, improved, and more expensive mouse trap. In communicating, we may identify one of our roles outside of work as relevant to a comment. For example, "As a parent of toddlers, I am concerned about the safety of the mouse trap" or "As a member of the NRA, I say, shoot the little rodents!" More often, we take on relevant professional roles, stated or implied: "We're not set up to deal with that fee structure in accounting." "From a nursing perspective, that large a case load in chemotherapy will drastically reduce off-site support to patients."

ACTIVITY 2.2

PERSPECTIVES BY PROFESSIONS

Write a paragraph summarizing why people in different professions have different perspectives of the same facility. For instance, describe a hospital from an architect's perspective, a doctor's perspective, and a hospital administrator's perspective.

The Cultural Perspective

Diverse cultures teach different values and customs. It is so easy to think that our way is the only way, but the business world crams cultures together, making it abundantly clear that conducting negotiations across cultures creates more problems than communication within the same culture. Conflicting cultural perspectives seem as if one person is doing a waltz and the other a tango (Bazerman, 2000). For instance, cultures vary in their assumptions about a "fixed pie," that is, a limited amount of resources, and cultures differ in their perceptions of risk.

Having thought about gender, generational, role, and cultural perspectives, let's turn to ways of thinking and knowing that affect all of our perceptions.

Several Factors Filter Perceptions

Remembering basic tenets and accounting for common tendencies increases perceptual accuracy (Hayes & Baird, 2000, p. 233):

- *Familiarity:* The more familiar we are with a person, the more likely we will make accurate interpretations. One exception, surprising to most of us, is that we are no more likely to figure out when a relative or close friend intentionally lies to us than when a stranger does.
- *Intent:* Listeners anticipate speakers' intentions as they interpret their comments.
- *Context:* For an example of the effect of context, what is appropriate with close friends is different from what is appropriate in a business meeting.
- *Labels:* Prior information and labels affect how we perceive someone. For instance, if we learn someone is an executive, we may decide that person is condescending to nonprofessionals.
- *Projection:* We tend to see our own characteristics in others. We project positive characteristics onto people who we like and negative ones onto those we do not like. "She seems so much happier now that she is using my exercise plan."

Because these filters shape, and often distort, our perceptions of others, we must learn how ordinarily useful tendencies go awry to distort perceptions and how to correct or avoid these distortions.

Common Perceptual Distortions

Perhaps it would be easier if our fallacious viewpoints appeared as total mirages or obvious tricks of the senses, but instead they appear as a semblance of truth twisted into a somewhat different creature. It is difficult to excise the fallacy while retaining the truth.

Stereotypes

Stereotypes generalize ideas about a category of people as a result of the organizing stage in the perceptual process. That makes sense, because putting people into categories simplifies our perceptions and helps us predict how people will act. "Perceivers regularly construct and use categorical representations to simplify and streamline the person perception process" (Macrae, 2000, para. 1). These categories are harmful when we stabilize our perceptions only according to a category ("typical engineer," "computer nerd," "flaky artist") and do not see people as individuals. Stereotypes become reinforced as we collect additional examples to support them (Hamilton, 1979). "Because their security comes from within instead of from without, [principle-centered people] have no need to categorize and stereotype everything and everybody in life to give them a sense of certainty and predictability. They see old faces freshly, old scenes as if for the first time" (Covey, 1992, p. 37).

Familiarity corrects stereotyping. The better we know someone, the more we see the person as an individual. The following comments illustrate this concept: "As a high school teacher, she is very strict, but she's a softy with her own kids," or "He's not your usual computer nerd. He's hysterically funny." Avoid *labeling*, in order to see the person before the label.

Attribution Theory

"To what do you attribute that?" With *attribution,* we assign cause. "He failed on that project *because* he got caught up dealing with details and forgot the larger picture." "She is a natural for sales *because* she is a 'people lover.'" "He is very shy, *so* don't expect him to support your ideas at the meeting." "His career has been going downhill *ever since* he began wasting so much time on the golf course." These preceding examples could be accurate attributions or erroneous attributions (misperceptions).

One type of error, *overattribution,* attributes too many events to a single cause. For instance, two companies merge, causing anxiety among employees about their job security and new job requirements. Management may be prone to blame any employee problem on the recent merger, although some of the problems would have been there with or without the merger. With *self-serving bias,* an error resulting from psychological discomfort, perceivers put a positive spin on themselves in their interpretations. "You are criticizing me because you are jealous of my talent." The *fundamental attribution error* assigns cause to "just the way things are." "That's a supervisor for you—caring more about

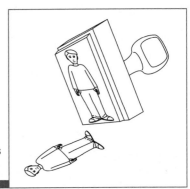

The term stereotype is an old printing term for a way to reproduce images. Do we carry stereotypes to stamp onto others?

scheduling than us." "Don't worry. Jeri always throws little fits when deadlines get close. That's just the way she is."

The most important correctives to attribution errors undo the distortion:

- Recognize that knowledge of a situation is always incomplete.
- Don't make assumptions about someone else's intent.
- Realize the tendency to protect the self-concept.
- Avoid assigning cause too broadly.
- Monitor one's personal internal labels, because even unspoken ones affect one's perception of others.

ATTRIBUTIONS

In small groups, discuss the most common interpretations for each problem, and discuss how attribution shapes those perceptions.

ACTIVITY 2.3

1. *All* the TV channels are showing "ant races."
2. SuLynn's calculus professor reviews her semester's grades: C, D, F, F, and A.
3. A professor is surprised by Avery's most recent grade—a D after four previous As.
4. A paramedic at the scene of an accident sees that a baby is not crying and has a blue coloration and shortness of breath.
5. An accountant cannot understand why a very popular employee's financial record shows $1,000 in the red at the end of each month for the past year.
6. An ordinarily quiet employee explodes, "Hell, no, I won't work Saturday! I didn't take this job to neglect my family."

Primacy and Recency

Primacy effect means that what happens first or early in the encounter has the largest impact on the interpretation. With primacy effect, the more common of the two, we get "first impressions" that strongly affect later perceptions. That is why the first five minutes of an interview count so heavily (Gladwell, 2000). The tendency to quickly form impressions comes from a natural survival instinct to respond to danger—fight or flight.

Someone who relies on the most recent information to be the most accurate information on which to base interpretations is subject to the "recency effect." People generally are not as prone to recency effect as to primacy effect, but we see forms of recency effect when someone asks, "What have you done for me lately?" or comments, "Did you hear the last thing she said at her interview? That statement 'gave away' her *real* attitude."

For example, the first time you meet your boss, he is griping about something at work. However, he cheerfully greets coworkers the next morning. A "primacy person" interprets this as follows: "The boss is a negative person, but he pretends to be positive with his cheerful greetings." A "recency person" interprets the same events as follows: "The boss used to be a complainer, but he has obviously changed into a cheerful person."

To perceive people more accurately, treat your first (or last) impression as a hypothesis, or "best guess," as to what that person is like. Continue evaluating additional information to improve the accuracy of your overall impression of that person (familiarity). A person who tends to rely on recency effects should add to his or her flexibility in seeing people as constantly changing and only one component in the history of the relationship.

PRIMACY AND RECENCY

1. Dr. Jones reports from her 1967 research on acid rain, and Dr. Smith reports his 2002 research on the same topic.

   Given that the research is equally reliable, which research would you use to help you analyze current air quality? How did you make your decision?

2. You are a physical therapist, and your patient has increased her endurance and strength steadily. Today, your patient showed decreased strength in her pretreatment evaluation.

   In planning her treatment, will you pay more attention to today's level of strength, her earlier level, or both? Why?

─────── ●

Prophecies

CONTEMPORARY VOICES 2.1: EFFECTS OF PROPHECIES

Chronic troublemakers and slackers—labeled LPs, or "low performers"—were more burden than asset to the U.S. Navy. What did the Navy do about the "undermotivated problem sailors"? The Navy first dealt with their supervisors, who were taught to perceive the problem sailors in terms of potential. The supervisors learned to expect the best out of these low performers and to communicate that expectation, disregarding the problematic histories.

The supervisors let the LPs know they believed in their ability to change, and that positive expectation proved powerful: The LPs began to do better on every front, receiving fewer punishments, showing better overall performance, even improving their personal appearance. It was the Pygmalion effect in action: Expecting the best from people can be a self-fulfilling prophecy. (Goleman, 1998, pp. 149–150)

From *Working with Emotional Intelligence* by Daniel Goleman, copyright © 1998 by Daniel Goleman. Used by permission of Bantam Books, a division of Random House, Inc.

The true story related in Contemporary Voices 2.1 demonstrates the power of expectations—expectations based on interpretations of previous events. This self-perpetuating phenomenon (one of many dynamics explained by theories of perception and self-concept) traps us in the cliché that "What you expect is what you get." Fortunately, this time the power of perception was used ethically and helpfully, due to the context and the intent of the Navy supervisors. *Self-fulfilling prophecies* are predictions a person makes about himself or herself to which that person behaviorally responds, reinforcing the prediction. In this way, a person labels himself or herself. Another way these prophecies occur is when a person is labeled by someone else and believes that label. An individual's self-concept, developed from early childhood, remains largely unexamined. Therefore, many prophecies come from labels given to us by others, such as by parents and caregivers. The sources vary, but the label has an effect only if the person *believes* the label. To correct potential problems with prophecies, be careful of the power of labeling and be wary of the vulnerability of being labeled.

In the sections on perceptual distortions, notice that the general advice is to familiarize yourself with additional information about the person or situation, examine your reasoning, and avoid the use of labels to guide conclusions.

CORRECTING PERCEPTUAL INACCURACIES

ACTIVITY 2.5

1. Adjusting Stereotypes
   a. In teams of two, list three groups that are a part of your identity, such as your gender, major, athletic group, high school, college, arts group, age group, or race. Have your partner do the same.
   b. Take turns presenting identity groups and telling what you think the stereotype is of the group, how you resemble the stereotype, and how you are *not* like the stereotype.
   c. Discuss how your perception of the other individual now differs from the stereotypes.
2. Flexing with Attributions
   a. Collect your own attribution statements for three days. These are statements such as "My history professor used a sinister tone of voice in announcing the exam because she thinks all students are lazy and doesn't like us," "George sounded rude, but you have to know that that is just the way George is," and "I made a C on the essay because he has me pegged as a C student."
   b. Analyze your statements to determine whether they are likely to be in error because of the fundamental attribution error, overattribution, or self-serving bias.
   c. Discuss two of your statements with a classmate. Can you or your classmate think of other reasons for the other person's behavior?
   d. What can you do to determine more accurately if your conclusions are correct?
3. Living Now with Primacy
   a. Tell your partner about a time someone jumped to an incorrect negative conclusion about you. Listen as your partner tells a similar story. Discuss how you felt about those bad "first impressions" from others. Were you able to change those impressions? How?
   b. Tell about a time you jumped to a conclusion about someone too quickly and perhaps felt embarrassed. How did you discover you had made an inaccurate conclusion?
4. Standing on History: Recency
   a. Share with your classmate a time you were disappointed in someone or felt betrayed. (Focus your discussion on your perception of the person after the disappointment rather than on the details of a betrayal.) Did you respond that the person had changed or was never the person you had thought he or she was?

b. Tell about a longtime friendship, relationship with a relative, or friendship at work in which you were disappointed but realized that 99% of the time this person had been very reliable. How did you handle the situation?

5. Helpful Prophecies

a. Tell about a label you believed and became. The label could be from a parent, teacher, coach, or someone at work. Was it a helpful or harmful label?

b. Tell about three labels you regularly put on other specific individuals. Discuss how your response begins to shape the other person. Are the labels you give—the prophecies you make—helpful or harmful?

HOW WE PERCEIVE OURSELVES (SELF-CONCEPT)

Perception not only determines how we see others, but also shapes how we perceive *ourselves*. The communicator, whether sender or receiver, brings personal communication skills, personal background and experience, and a sense of self into the communication. For instance, if you perceive yourself as an expert on the topic, you enter the conversation with confidence. If you see yourself as a cooperator, you communicate differently than if you see yourself as competing for a promotion. If you feel yourself to be the victim of office politics, you communicate differently than if you see yourself as having a position of power. As we have seen with *communication style*, self-concept is largely the way "individuals perceive themselves interacting with others" (Kirtley & Weaver, 1999).

Sources of the Self-Concept

Just as we collect sense data that lead to our interpretations of what other people are like, so we interpret the sense data relating to ourselves to determine what *we* are like. Covey (1991) says, "Lasting solutions to problems, lasting happiness and success, come from the inside out" (p. 62). "Outside in" results in miserable people, stuck in the roles of victims.

"Perception of self" is the same thing as "self-concept." Each person has a collection of thoughts about who he or she is. The human psyche protects itself from too much information coming in too quickly about the "self." Ego-defense mechanisms seek to protect us, although they can delude and eventually create a dysfunctional self-concept (Boyatski, 2001, p. 6).

Robert Sternberg (1995), in *In Search of the Human Mind,* offers a more specific and culturally relevant definition of self-concept: "our sense of *independence* (our autonomy and individuality) and *interdependence* (our sense of belonging and collectivity). Some cultures place more value on the group, whereas other cultures place more value on the individual. These and other influences of culture and personality blend to bring about interpretations of self (Sternberg, 1995, p. 454). Parallel to cultural influences are other things that shape self-concept: (1) Significant persons in our lives teach us what we are like, (2) we compare ourselves with others to see how we measure up, and (3) we observe our own responses, impulses, and thoughts.

SOURCES OF THE SELF-CONCEPT

ACTIVITY
2.6

"We are who we are told we are."

"We are the many decisions, both large and small, that we make."

1. *Discuss the truth that you find in each of these statements. Which quotation do you prefer? Why?*

2. *Do you make decisions about who to believe when they tell you things about yourself?*

3. *Do toddlers make informed decisions about who they are?*

4. *How early in life do children have concepts of themselves?*

Self-Efficacy

Generally, employees who perceive themselves as capable in key areas of their jobs seem to perform better on the job than those of similar ability who lack confidence in their abilities. Even among high-IQ individuals, the ones who showed more self-confidence in childhood and teen years became more successful in their careers (Holahan & Sears, 1995). The perception of one's capacity to perform is *self-efficacy* (Hackett & Betz, 1981; Schoen & Winocur, 1988).

A study of 112 entry-level accountants (Saks, 1995, cited in Goleman, 1998) demonstrated a correlation between those who came into the organization with high self-efficacy and those who had high job performance ratings from their supervisors 10 months later.

The flip side was found in workers who lack self-confidence. Common traits are a fear of seeming inept, giving up on their own opinions and ideas when challenged, chronic indecisiveness, shying away from risk, and failing to voice valuable ideas (p. 71).

Employees with high self-efficacy are more likely to embrace new challenges, stay focused on required tasks, and interact well with others. People like doing often what they perceive they do well. By repeating the tasks, they improve their abilities in those areas (List & Renzulli, 1991). One study focusing on communication (Douglas, O'Flaherty, & Snow, 2000) noted that young adults perceived themselves as having more frequent communication difficulties than those close to them thought they had.

Healthy Self-Concept

How can people feel better about themselves? Because one's perception of one's self is woven strand by strand over a lifetime, it's difficult to know how to change it. The truly healthy self-concept is both flexible and resistant to change—a delicate balance. We don't directly build self-concept. We build "self," and in the process we perceive that self. We benefit directly as we feed back that good image into ourselves, indirectly as others reflect it to us, and organizationally as our workplace becomes a healthier work environment, another part of our identity.

CONTEMPORARY VOICES 2.2: BLAMING OTHERS

Covey (1992) conceives self-concept, self-efficacy, and organizational effectiveness as interdependent. People with unhealthy self-concepts are prone to blame other people for whatever goes wrong. That blame says, in effect, that the blamer is "out of control" of his or her circumstances: The victims of the blame potentially gain power. Self-awareness and personal responsibility empower oneself. "Between what happens to you and your response is a degree of freedom. And the more you exercise that freedom, the larger it will become. As you work in your circle of influence and exercise that freedom, gradually you will stop being a 'hot reactor' . . . and start being a cool, responsible chooser—no matter what your genetic makeup, no matter how you were raised, no matter what your childhood experiences were or what the environment is" (p. 42).

HOW WE PERCEIVE ORGANIZATIONS AND EVENTS IN ORGANIZATIONS

We interact with others according to our perceptions of them, and we do the same thing with organizations. For example, because trust is built on perception, we "trust" Red Lobster to serve fresh fish, and we "trust" Visa to charge us accurately.

Analogies Shape Perceptions of Organizations

The perception is the reality, or at least as close as we are going to get to what is actually happening (Gregory, 1998). Never is that truer than in organizational behavior. Employees have a relatively fixed view of their organizations and their roles in them. References to perception and related analogies pepper business-related articles and books. For instance, L. K. Lewis (2000) examines the problems of implementing change in organizations and says, "Problems are not objective but *perceived*. Defining whether an implementer was 'truly' accurate will always be problematic and dependent on the time *frame* and point of reference of the respondent or judge. *Framing* these questions in terms of *perceptions* is therefore a more useful and realistic approach" (p. 47, italics added for emphasis). Because common, overlapping metaphors guide organizational perceptions, let's look at the three most frequently used in business literature.

Frames

We use the word *frame* several ways: "I've been framed." "What is your frame of mind?" "Let's reframe the question." Frames also provide metaphors for several related concepts currently discussed in the communication literature.

- The communication *context* is referred to as a frame. The physical setting, time, and cultural dimensions of the communication event compose a communication frame.

- The communicator's *frame of reference* includes the communicator's background, knowledge, and experiences. For decoding, a communicator uses imagined pictures in order to make communicators' symbols meaningful. Each time a communicator encodes a message, that message relies on recalled knowledge and experiences.

- Most specific to the study of perception in communication, a frame is an *organizing principle* leading to congruous interpretations. To *reframe* is to interpret a situation and all that is packaged with it differently than before. Because frames may explain the communicator's intention or may attribute causes, framing and reframing are persuasive communication skills.

Paradigms

Paradigm is another broad term. The Greek word root is *paradigma,* which means a pattern or map for understanding and explaining certain aspects of reality. Paradigms usually appear in the form of a metaphor, analogy, or mental model that serves as a frame of reference. Joel Barker (1992), in *Paradigms: The Business of Discovering the Future,* says paradigms are patterns of rules and assumptions that "define our boundaries and tell us how to behave in order to be successful." Paradigms "give us new ways of viewing the world and solving problems" (Barker, 1992, cited in Newstrom and Davis, 1997, p. 32). Because we are comfortable with old paradigms, we don't shift easily to new ones. Outsiders to an organization seem to be better at introducing new paradigms to the organization.

A new, complex paradigm awakens creative possibilities. *Encyclopaedia Britannica* at one time looked to be the clear winner in the information marketplace, and students cited *Britannica* in their research papers as a first line of defense. Meanwhile, *Funk & Wagnall's Encyclopedia* struggled to maintain a share of the market, when an up-and-coming company named Microsoft bought the failing encyclopedia and shifted it to a different paradigm—personal computers as a path to all sorts of information—and called it Encarta.

What is your metaphor—or paradigm—for going to college? You may see college as either a job or an adventure, and every course as either a new country or a prison sentence. Others "pay the price" of attending college in order to get good jobs. Your view of college shapes your day-to-day activities and priorities. A *paradigm shift* requires taking a different perspective to see a situation in a new way, affecting attitudes along the way.

Many people view organizations through a mechanical paradigm.

> The organization is like a machine; if something is broken, it needs to be fixed. If you can find the problem, get the right part, stick it in, and turn it on, it will work. But organizations are not mechanical; they are organic. To see organizations through the agricultural paradigm is to see them as living, growing things made up of living, growing people. Living things are not immediately "fixed" by replacing nonworking parts; they are nurtured over time to produce desired results. (Covey, 1992, p. 212)

Mental Models

Mental models determine how we perceive events and how we talk about events. They marry frames with paradigms, as revealed in several excerpts from Senge (see Contemporary Voices 2.3).

CONTEMPORARY VOICES 2.3: MENTAL MODELS

New insights fail to get put into practice because they conflict with deeply held internal images of how the world works, images that limit us to familiar ways of thinking and acting. That is why the discipline of managing mental models— surfacing, testing, and improving our internal pictures of how the world works— promises to be a major breakthrough for building learning organizations. (Senge, 1990, p. 174, citing Kuhn, 1970)

Mental models can be simple generalizations such as "people are untrustworthy," or they can be complex theories, such as my assumptions about why members of my family interact as they do. But what is most important to grasp is that mental models are *active*—they shape how we act (p. 175) . . . .

As Albert Einstein once wrote, "Our theories determine what we measure." For years, physicists ran experiments that contradicted classical physics, yet no one "saw" the data that these experiments eventually provided, leading to the revolutionary theories—quantum mechanics and relativity—of twentieth-century physics. (p. 175, citing Kuhn, 1970)

Senge (1990) prescribes a dynamic mental model that constantly and collectively learns and reinvents itself. Anticipating Anderson's (1992, 1998) warning of a common resistance to new paradigms, Senge (1990) also includes paradigms in his discussion of mental models, giving a clear example of resistance to change:

Computers are integral to cars these days. Whether a Mercedes Benz or a Chevrolet, a SUV or luxury sedan, multiple functions depend on tiny semiconductors and microprocessors. Why did it take so long for the manufacturers to include these remarkable devices in their designs? One obstacle to earlier use was that designers accepted the *mental model* of a bulky computer, far too large to be mounted inside an automobile (p. 18).

1. *Describe two of your mental models.*
2. *A physician first concludes from symptoms the possibility of a disorder, then tests for it. Why are some diseases difficult to diagnose? Apply Einstein's comment to another field, such as accounting, computer programming, or engineering.*

Picture yourself as a computer programmer. With a fixed mental model of "self as computer programmer," you go to college, learn three or four programming languages, and get a job upon graduation. Predictably, you expect to be the sole occupant of a cubicle, enter code by yourself, and activate a few brilliant solutions. Now shift to a model of you as "employed in a technical field" and "involved in creating products." With the new mental model, if a new skill were needed—maybe one that did not even exist when you were in college—you would be open to learning and adapting to a changing workplace. Furthermore, working on a team or presenting a product to a client would fit your mental model and be less likely to throw you off balance.

Mental models also help us to perceive a company's identity, such as when IBM and Apple employees picture themselves serving the masses through IBM's "service" and Apple's "computing power for the masses" concepts. Unfortunately, the wrong mental models can block us from seeing how organizations and their employees can function. Can a cola company own a restaurant? Or a tobacco company produce cheese? If the mental model had been confined to a cola beverage, the Coca-Cola Company would never have included Olive

Garden restaurants. Nor would Phillip Morris have merged with Kraft. Stakeholders and the general public have mental models of organizations too, generally shaped by slogans and images.

Perceiving Positively in Learning Organizations

The remedy for disabled learning organizations relies on individuals and the organization as a whole using different ways of thinking. Senge (1994, pp. 5–13) brought up the problems, so we turn to him for solutions, as he teaches us areas—in his word, disciplines—absolutely critical for learning organizations.

CONTEMPORARY VOICES 2.4: FIVE PERSONAL DISCIPLINES

The first discipline, *personal mastery,* forms a compact between personal and organizational learning. The members of an organization must keep learning in order for the organization to continue learning. Personal mastery continually clarifies critical issues and puts us on a path to "see current reality more clearly" (Senge 1994, p. 8).

Second, *mental models* are "deeply ingrained assumptions, generalizations, or even pictures or images that influence how we understand the world and how we take action" (Senge 1994, p. 8).

Third, *building shared visions* requires a communication of a shared perception of the organization in such a way that the whole organization is moving toward the shared vision as one.

Fourth, *team learning* starts with genuine dialogue, a fluid exchange of ideas and knowledge among the team members. Teams are the fundamental learning unit in the organization.

Finally and fifth, *systems thinking* forms a framework for conceptualizing interrelationships among individuals and the organizations they are in, between parts of an organization and the whole organization, among organizations, and between organizations and the world. Learning organizations, by definition, engage in systems thinking. Noting the overwhelming complexities in today's world, Senge calls systems thinking the fifth discipline and views it as the cornerstone for organizations' perceptions of their world. The perceptual shift is from seeing people as capable only of reacting, rather than seeing them as participants in the shaping of their realities and their futures (Senge 1994, 69).

To truly understand business and professional communication is to grasp the underlying dynamics of perception. Compare the concepts of the five disciplines with the content of this text. *Personal mastery* requires that we perceive things more clearly and with less bias. Personal mastery likewise relies on understanding one's self-concept. *Mental models* surfaced as analogies that help us see things in new ways to initiate creative solutions. Also, in the section on analogous thinking, we saw that *shared visions* motivate organizations that otherwise would be satisfied with the status quo. As the basic functioning unit in learning organizations, *teams* are so crucial that two chapters of this text are devoted to them. Finally, *systems thinking* moves us to get the big picture and to recognize the inherent interdependencies. This text views the characteristics of systems thinking as a factor in communication principles (Chapter 1). Systems thinking is apparent at all communication levels—intrapersonal, interpersonal, small groups and teams, and public speaking—and in all perceptions—self, others, and organizations.

SUMMARY

U nderstanding the perceptual process opens the door to understanding human communication. This chapter looked at three outcomes of perception: how we see others, how we see ourselves, and how we view the organization and events at work. The three stages of perception are sensing, organizing, and interpreting/evaluating. Sensing requires the selection of data available through the five senses. Organizing seeks out an organizing principle in order to link the collected sense data to meaningful interpretations. Interpreting attaches meaning to the selected and organized sense data. Assumptions, generalizations, and conclusions are all interpretations. Evaluations are picked up in almost every—if not every—communication.

Several perspectives—actually, frames of reference—affect many people's perceptions. These perspectives include gender, age, career, and culture. One common perceptual distortion is stereotyping, which generalizes ideas about a category of people. Attribution theory presents overattribution, self-serving bias, and the fundamental attribution error as other distortions. Finally, distortions occur from depending on first or last impressions (primacy or recency) and on self-fulfilling prophecies.

The communicator brings a perception of self—self-concept—into the communication. Self-efficacy is one's perception of one's abilities, especially in a work or learning setting.

Analogies give us ways to think about organizations, events in those organizations, and our roles in them. Frames are contexts, frames of reference, or organizing principles. A paradigm is an analogy that serves as a frame of reference. Paradigm shifts allow us to see organizations from a different perspective in order to see more of the potential of the organization. Mental models help us "see" a particular company's identity through the company's shared vision.

Perception and communication are fundamental to everything else studied in business and professional communication. Personal mastery requires that we perceive with less bias and relies on understanding one's self-concept. Mental models and shared visions give momentum to organizations that otherwise would be satisfied with the status quo. Teams are the basic unit of organizations. Systems thinking sees the "whole" as dynamic interacting parts feeding into and gleaning from other entities. Communication is involved in and contributes to the perceptions of self, others, and organizations. •

ACTIVITIES

1. **Team Work:** Conduct a team experiment. Bring several people into a room and give them 2 minutes to observe all that they can within the room. Take them to another room where they have 10 minutes to list what they observed. Probably they will stop writing before the 10 minutes are up. Then ask questions such as (1) How many males and how many females were in the group? (2) What color shirt was the person who brought you into the room wearing? (3) Was there a clock in the room? (4) How many windows were in the room?

    As a team, write a report of your findings and conclusions.

2. **Presenting to Others:** Find a news story and an editorial on the same topic. Report to the class key differences you found between reporting the news story and editorializing about it.

3. **Team Work:** Terry Anderson (1998) discusses frames of references in *Transforming Leadership:* "Individuals who lack control over their frames of reference become more self-centered and tend to have shallow relationships with others" (p. 112). Anderson contrasts people who behave assertively with those who behave aggressively or passively. Assertive people are more in control of self and do not tread on others' territory or passively accept others placing blame on them. He says that aggressive people are "usually not in control of their thoughts, feelings, and behaviors. They either cannot or will not take charge of their frames of references. Therefore, they have trouble controlling their actions, and others suffer as a result" (p. 112). Passively behaving people, on the other hand, "overcontrol their frames of reference to the point of self-suppression. They place others before themselves even if they (or others) have to suffer for doing so" (p. 113).

   In small groups, discuss Anderson's comments and determine which three meanings for *frame* Anderson uses.

4. **Journaling the Experience:** Health careers function in a different paradigm from the old one in which doctors were seen as gods who would decide on a patient's fate. Now doctors consult with patients, giving them treatment options, and patients participate in their treatments. What is the current mental model for those graduating from medical school? Write your thoughts and conclusions in your journal.

5. **Ethically Speaking:** Watch the movie *The Big Chill* and compare the generational differences in perceptions and ethics that you see.

6. **Technical Support:** In *Fast Company* (www.fastcompany.com/online/25/one.html), Polly LaBarre notes that the "old style of leadership—a model that reflects the days when hierarchy and command-and-control reigned"—is familiar, but asks whether it is appropriate for Net-based leaders today. Twelve leaders answered her in this article.

   a. What use of analogies do you find?

   b. What evidence do you find of high self-efficacy with these leaders?

   c. Connect their answers with two other concepts in this chapter.

FOR FURTHER READING

Reardon, K. K. (2000). *The secret handshake: Mastering the politics of the business inner circle.* New York: Doubleday/Currency. As one critic says, "Great book. Nasty subject." Reardon argues that office politics are here to stay, so either arm yourself or be robbed.

Check out Mind Illusions at www.aboutlearning.com for some fun with perception.

Read more about mental models at www.solonline.org.

Six Seconds is a 501(c)3 public benefit corporation that was incorporated in California on September 30, 1997. The organization was founded to support the global emotional intelligence movement and promote a more caring, positive environment in schools and organizations. It can be found at http://6seconds.org.

Building Personal Power

With self-concept as a linchpin, Part II prepares students to understand and build personal effectiveness by managing communication apprehension, by listening, and by discovering the power of nonverbal communication. The organizing principle of Part II centers on communicators building from inside out by managing their communication apprehension and by practicing active verbal and nonverbal listening.

At the core of our existence as human beings lies a powerful drive to be with other people. There is much evidence that in the absence of human contact people fall apart physically and mentally; they experience more sickness, stress and suicide than well-connected individuals. For all too many people, however, shyness is the primary barrier to that basic need. (Carducci, 2000, p. 1)

From Apprehension to Confidence

3

Communication Apprehension and Confidence

Managing Communication Apprehension

Strategies to Build Confident Speaking

Support Others in Overcoming Communication Apprehension

Unfortunately, some individuals' perceptions place them in scary worlds, and their responses are based on fears and phobias. The fear of communicating is *communication apprehension* (CA), familiar as "stage fright" and shyness. Public speaking is America's number one fear (Whitworth & Cochran, 1996), and even public figures such as outgoing David Letterman report shyness. Forty-eight percent of Americans are shy, an increase of about 10% over the last 15 years (Carducci, 2000).

Some people become apprehensive simply reading about communication apprehension, and almost everyone has avoided speaking publicly at some time.

"Since most people prefer death over public speaking, at a funeral almost anyone would rather be in the coffin than delivering the eulogy," quips comedian Jerry Seinfeld. Public speaking frightens most people some of the time and some people most of the time. Unfortunately for shy people, businesses want employees who make their expertise available by communicating effectively and enthusiastically. A shock for newcomers in the corporate world is that even for technical experts, the job demands communication skills. Those who consistently avoid making presentations and shy away from group tasks create a ceiling to their career advances and lean on colleagues to speak for them.

CONTEMPORARY VOICES 3.1: STAGE FRIGHT

It's every public speaker's worst nightmare. My friend, a psychologist, had flown from the East Coast to Hawaii to address a convention of police chiefs. Delayed planes and missed connections made him lose a night's sleep, leaving him both exhausted and jet-lagged, and his speech was first thing the next morning. My friend had been apprehensive about the talk to begin with, since he was taking a controversial stand. Now exhaustion was rapidly converting that apprehension to outright panic.

My friend began by telling a joke—but stopped just before the punch line. He had forgotten it. He froze, his mind a blank. Not only couldn't he remember the punch line, he couldn't remember his speech. His notes suddenly made no sense, and his attention fixed on the sea of faces, riveted on him. He had to apologize, excuse himself, and leave the podium.

Only after several hours' rest was he able to compose himself and give his lecture—including the complete joke—to great applause. Telling me later about his initial bout of panic, he said, "All I could think of was all those faces staring at me—but I couldn't for the life of me remember what I was supposed to say." (Goleman, 1998, p. 73).

From *Working with Emotional Intelligence* by Daniel Goleman, Copyright © 1998 by Daniel Goleman. Used by permission of Bantam Books, a division of Random House, Inc.

ACTIVITY 3.1

WHAT WOULD YOU HAVE DONE?

You have just read a story told by Daniel Goleman in *Emotional Intelligence* (1998, p. 73). Which of the following statements represent your reaction to the story? Mark "True" for the statements that parallel your thinking and "False" for the statements that do not represent your thinking.

1. *I don't have to worry about this happening to me, because I would never accept the invitation to speak.*
2. *The speaker should have prepared better and made speaker notes.*
3. *I don't like controversy, so I wouldn't speak to an audience that I knew would disagree with me.*
4. *I need to remember that this can happen, even to professionals. When I anticipate different events occurring, I can prepare for many contingencies.*
5. *This man should get a clue! He was apprehensive even before he missed flight connections and sleep. He should have canceled the speech as soon as he felt apprehensive.*
6. *One thing to learn from this story is to book an earlier flight.*
7. *I know exactly the feeling the speaker had, and I will never put myself in that position. I simply am not interested in jobs that require public speaking.*
8. *What was going on here? Usually an audience will not reassemble another time for a speech. Either the speaker had a very important message or was a very important person.*

9. *I would take the first flight home—or at least to another island! I couldn't bear to face that audience again.*

10. *Sometimes I get emotionally or physically overwhelmed and cannot do a job as well as usual. A speech is a type of job, so it's "business as usual." Sometimes a person has to do what a person has to do.*

Answering "True" to numbers 1, 3, 5, 7, and 9 indicates that you do not picture yourself as a speaker, especially in difficult situations. You may have defense mechanisms in place to avoid public speaking.

Answering "True" to Numbers 2, 4, 6, 8, and 10 indicates that you can imagine yourself as a public speaker and are imagining ways to avoid ineffective or embarrassing speaking situations.

This practical and personal chapter moves quickly from theory to application, nurturing realistic confidence. Because *your* experience is unique, you will want to understand what happens to *you*. In spite of the discomfort some people feel while reading, or even thinking, about communication apprehension, many have untapped potential to manage CA and boost personal effectiveness. Even if shyness isn't a problem for you, you need to understand the experiences of others. After all, you will probably manage employees with CA, work with shy peers, and interact with shy clients. Therefore, this chapter discusses sources and consequences of communication apprehension and the best practices for managing apprehension and building communication confidence in self and in others.

OBJECTIVES

After studying the content of this chapter, you should be able to

- List the consequences of shyness in U.S. culture
- Explain several sources of communication apprehension
- Analyze implications of current research
- Describe types of communication apprehension
- Manage apprehension and build communication confidence
- Interact with others in the workplace more sensitively

● COMMUNICATION APPREHENSION AND CONFIDENCE

Communication apprehension is a fear of communicating. It is the opposite of feeling competent and confident, which makes a person feel fluid, appropriately relaxed or energized, and responsive to present situations. James McCroskey defines it as "an individual's level of fear or anxiety associated with either real or anticipated communication with another person or persons" (McCroskey, 1989, cited in Hutchinson & Neuliep, 1993, p. 16). Some experience CA when talking one-on-one, and others relate it to giving a speech.[1]

MISLEADING ASSUMPTIONS

Assumption 1: Because we have talked most of our lives, we can talk comfortably to anyone and in any situation.

Assumption 2: A person with convictions can speak up for those convictions.

Assumption 3: All you have to do to change is to "toughen up."

Discuss the three assumptions in small groups.

1. *Are the assumptions true or false?*
2. *What assumptions do you make about communication apprehension?*
3. *What impact does communication apprehension have in the workplace?*

As with other transactions in open systems, the level of confidence comes partially from one's self and partially from one's input and feedback from others. The communicator's confidence or apprehension in turn feeds into the system. This explains, for example, how confident communicators comfortably present ideas and become known for having good ideas, whereas apprehensive communicators are not seen as contributors.

The Costs of Communication Apprehension

Personal attributes held high in our social esteem are leadership, assertiveness, dominance, independence, and risk-taking. Hence, a stigma surrounds shyness. (Carducci & Zimbardo, 1995)

Some shyness comes across as endearing or flirtatious, and shy people are seen as excellent listeners and good friends who go about their work quietly. Indeed, some people really are "the strong, silent type," but silence should be a choice, not a manifestation of fear. Overall, the costs of shyness pile up quickly. Remember, though, that shyness differs according to the setting. Some people are most apprehensive when in small groups, whereas CA may hit others only when giving a public speech. On a personal level, shy people are more insecure about dating and relationships, more likely to have fewer friends, more likely to be lonely and less satisfied with their jobs, less likely to get promotions and raises, less likely to be in leadership roles, and more limited in workplace opportunities (DeVito, 2000).

---

[1] Research on the fear of communication includes the all-too-familiar experiences of "stage fright" and "shyness." CA is also researched under the topics of *anxiety* and *reticence. Apprehension* has a milder connotation than *anxiety,* but both terms indicate an internal fear response. *Reticence* grows out of a person's beliefs and perceptions, and the term generally means a quiet, reserved behavioral response, as in being reticent to join in conversation or speak to a class. "When people avoid communication because they believe they will lose more by talking than by remaining silent, we refer to it as reticence" (Phillips, 1984, p. 52, in Daly and McCroskey, 51–56). Communication *avoidance* is a defining characteristic of CA.

"Without a circle of close friends or relatives, people are more likely to worry. Lacking the opportunity to share feelings and fears with others, isolated people allow them to fester or escalate" (Carducci & Zimbardo, 1995). "High shys" feel socially inadequate and are usually incompetent in expressing emotions. They typically avoid people or situations in which they could feel shy in any way, which only makes matters worse for them. Tragically, shy persons are more likely than those who are not shy to abuse alcohol and drugs as social lubricants. Shy individuals exaggerate what could go wrong (a self-prophesized cycle) and procrastinate, and procrastination is a symptom of loneliness.

Organizations expect competent, outgoing communicators who can speak to review boards, to clients, and to the public. Even if you do *not* experience shyness, you should learn about shyness in order to help the shy people with whom you work (a percentage that is probably higher than 40%). When people aren't paralyzed by fear, they are more open and supportive of others, but the change starts with the self.

Your Communication Apprehension Profile

Think of your own experience with communication apprehension. This section offers a widely used diagnostic self-test for situational communication apprehension. Following the self-test is a discussion of two broad types of communication apprehension: situational and trait. Whereas situational apprehension is based on the contexts for communication, trait apprehension is a pervasive, continual part of a person's personality. That is, situational CA is specific to a recurring type of situation (McCroskey, 1984), and it is normal for a person to be scared (high CA) in *some* situations.

SELF-TEST: SITUATIONAL COMMUNICATION APPREHENSION

COMMUNICATION APPREHENSION IN GENERALIZED CONTEXTS

ACTIVITY 3.3

This instrument is composed of fifty statements concerning your feelings about communicating with other people, divided into five categories. Please indicate the degree to which each statement applies to you by marking whether you (1) strongly agree, (2) agree, (3) are undecided, (4) disagree, or (5) strongly disagree with each statement. There are no right or wrong answers, and many statements are similar to other statements. Work quickly; record your first impression.

Context-Based Communication Apprehension

General
1. When communicating, I am generally calm and relaxed. 2
2. Generally, communication causes me to be anxious and apprehensive. 4
3. I find the prospect of speaking mildly pleasant. 3
4. When communicating, my posture feels strained and unnatural. 4
5. In general, communication makes me uncomfortable. 4
6. For the most part, I like to communicate with other people. 3
7. I dislike using my body and voice expressively. 3
8. I feel that I am more fluent when talking to people than most other people are. 4

34

9. When communicating, I generally am tense and nervous. 4
10. I feel relaxed and comfortable while speaking. 3

Group Discussions

11. I am afraid to express myself in a group.
12. I dislike participating in group discussions.
13. Generally, I am comfortable while participating in group discussions.
14. I am tense and nervous while participating in group discussions.
15. I have no fear about expressing myself in a group.
16. Engaging in a group discussion with new people is very pleasant.
17. Generally, I am uncomfortable while participating in a group discussion.
18. I like to get involved in group discussions.
19. Engaging in a group discussion with new people makes me tense and nervous.
20. I am calm and relaxed while participating in group discussions.

Meetings

21. I look forward to expressing my opinions at meetings.
22. I am self-conscious when I am called upon to express an opinion at a meeting.
23. Generally, I am nervous when I have to participate in a meeting.
24. Communicating in meetings generally makes me feel good.
25. Usually I am calm and relaxed while participating in meetings.
26. I am self-conscious when I am called upon to answer a question at a meeting.
27. I am very calm and relaxed when I am called upon to express an opinion at a meeting.
28. I am afraid to express myself at meetings.
29. Communicating in meetings generally makes me feel uncomfortable.
30. I am very relaxed when answering questions at a meeting.

Interpersonal Conversations

31. While participating in a conversation with a new acquaintance, I feel very nervous.
32. I have no fear of speaking up in conversations.
33. Talking with one other person very often makes me nervous.
34. Ordinarily, I am very tense and nervous in conversations.
35. Conversing with people who hold positions of authority causes me to be fearful and tense.
36. Generally, I am very relaxed while talking with one other person.
37. Ordinarily, I am very calm and relaxed in conversations.
38. While conversing with a new acquaintance, I feel very relaxed.
39. I am relaxed while conversing with people who hold positions of authority.
40. I am afraid to speak up in conversations.

Public Speeches

41. I have no fear of giving a speech.
42. I look forward to giving a speech.
43. Certain parts of my body feel very tense and rigid while giving a speech.
44. I feel relaxed while giving a speech.
45. Giving a speech makes me anxious.
46. My thoughts become confused and jumbled when I am giving a speech.
47. I face the prospect of giving a speech with confidence.
48. While giving a speech, I get so nervous I forget facts I really know.
49. Giving a speech really scares me.
50. While giving a speech, I know I can control my feelings of tension and stress.

Scoring

General   =   30 − (total of items 2, 4, 5, 7, 9) + (total of items 1, 3, 6, 8, 10)

Group   =   30 − (total of items 11, 12, 14, 17, 19) + (total of items 13, 15, 16, 18, 20)

Meetings   =   30 − (total of items 22, 23, 26, 28, 29) + (total of items 21, 24, 25, 27, 30)

Interpersonal =   30 − (total of items 31, 33, 34, 35, 40) + (total of items 32, 36, 37, 38, 39)

Public   =   30 − (total of items 43, 45, 46, 48, 49) + (total of items 41, 42, 44, 47, 50)

Compare the score on each of the other four scales with your general score and identify situations that cause you to be more apprehensive. A score above 30 indicates some communication apprehension, and scores above 35 indicate a comparatively high level of communication apprehension. Remember that this is your perception of apprehension and your experience communicating. The self-test does not compare you to other people, nor does it reflect what others notice about you.

From Virginia P. Richmond & James C. McCroskey, *Communication Apprehension, Avoidance and Effectiveness*, 5th ed. Published by Allyn and Bacon, Boston. MA. Copyright © 1998 by Pearson Education. Reprinted by permission of the publisher.

Three *situations* in which many persons experience CA are (1) speaking to strangers, (2) communicating with bosses, and (3) giving speeches that are graded in class. *Trait apprehension,* on the other hand, is an internal experience that exists regardless of the situation: It is "an enduring tendency to react to many situations with anxiety and fear" (Reiss, 1997). When people with high trait apprehension face what they perceive as threatening situations, including public speaking, they are likely to increase their situational anxiety (Reiss, 1997; Mladenka, Sawyer, & Behnke, 1998).

An additional response is *anxiety sensitivity,* wherein individuals are overly concerned about how they physically feel, or about the physical consequences of becoming anxious. Anxiety sensitivity triggers a cognitive process in which individuals overestimate their levels of anxiety. This experience differs from trait anxiety in that it does not rely on past experiences (Reiss, 1997). Anxiety sensitivity increases situational anxiety (Taylor, 1995), explaining a way that anxiety feeds on itself and elicits an extreme emotional/physical response.

With this background in the contexts and costs of communication apprehension, we are in a position to improve our experiences and outcomes. We benefit by learning how our bodies respond in the perceived fight for survival in a communication world.

The Physiology of Communication Apprehension

When the mind is calm, working memory functions at its best. But when there is an emergency, the brain shifts into a self-protective mode, stealing resources from working memory and shunting them to other brain sites in *hyperalert*— a mental stance for survival.

CONTEMPORARY VOICES 3.2: THE ANCIENT BRAIN

Public speaking requires a harmony in mental, emotional, and physical skills. According to Goleman (1998), the emotional brain learns differently from the thinking brain. Studies in neuroscience show that the survival-focused ancient brain not only houses the center for emotion but also the skills needed for managing ourselves effectively and for social adeptness (p. 6). When stress kicks in, the individual is flooded with stress hormones, mainly cortisol, which may stay for hours. Cortisol enforces survival instincts (fight or flight) by robbing energy from a person's working memory and intellect. This in part explains why communication apprehension leaves us feeling helpless and unable to remember what we planned to say (p. 76).

The ancient brain, geared to survival, reacts physiologically to a seemingly threatening situation by dumping natural chemicals into the bloodstream. Situations remind the brain of what it has learned from similar situations, and if those experiences have been negative, the brain perceives a threat. For many of us, the moment of terror was standing on stage saying our "lines" to parents and teachers. If we thought "They laughed at me, and it wasn't supposed to be funny," we felt humiliated. If we thought, "I made them laugh and I love to make people laugh," we were pleased. A child carries a generalized notion of "speaking equals possible punishment" into adulthood (McCroskey, Andersen, Richmond, & Wheeless, 1981; Mladenka et al., 1998), whereas positive expectations and encouragement build communication confidence.

Feedback strongly influences what people want to avoid or to attempt, but more resilient persons accumulate a variety of possible responses. One response is particularly characteristic of these hardier souls: They start to psychologically and physically calm their distress *during* encounters. They recognize early signs of distress, reframe the situation, and use productive coping mechanisms.

Carducci and Zimbardo (1995) reviewed research literature in an attempt to answer the question, "Are people born shy?" Inheritable biological characteristics partially explain the development of communication apprehension

(McCroskey, 1997). Recent research involving second-graders has shown there is a gene linked with shyness (Arbelle, Benjamin, Golin, Kremer, Belmaker, & Ebstein, 2003), but the number of people with it is inadequate to explain the number of shy adults. Although we know that overprotected children are more likely to grow up shy than those who are allowed to have a variety of interactive experiences, the number of overprotected children with shy genetic tendencies *still* does not add up to the large number of shy adults. Why are so many adults shy? The obvious answer is that much of our shyness is learned along the way. Adult-onset shyness may be due to life-changing events such as divorce or being fired from a job (Carducci & Zimbardo, 1995).

Communication Apprehension at Work and School

Novelty, conspicuousness, past experiences, and *being evaluated* contribute to apprehension and shyness in the workplace. Many people become apprehensive during employment interviews.

A GREENHORN'S INTERVIEW

ACTIVITY
3.4

John Greene is scheduled to interview for an accounting position at an accounting firm. The director of personnel, Lena Astor, plans to interview four qualified applicants for the position, and in keeping with company policy, she asks the same questions of each interviewee. Greene recently graduated from college, and this is his first interview. The interview is more formal than a casual conversation, and Greene isn't sure what to expect. He certainly looks sharp in his new "interview" clothes. He knows Ms. Astor has the authority to recommend an applicant. Greene is the center of the conversation, and he feels conspicuous. Gratefully, he recalls the practice interviews he did, building skills to answer questions and looking the part of a competent professional. Unfortunately, Ms. Astor looks a little like his fifth grade teacher—the one who made him read poetry to the football team. Maybe he can concentrate on her sounding more like his professor, who assured him he would do a "great job."

Discuss the following areas in light of John Greene's situation.

1. *Novelty: What is new to John in this experience?*
2. *Good past experience: What positive history does John call on in this situation?*
3. *Bad past experience: Did negative past experiences influence John's perception?*
4. *Conspicuousness: What added to John feeling in the spotlight?*
5. *Evaluation: Was John under evaluation?*

Table 3.1 presents the most common factors that people say scare them about another type of communication, public speaking (Bippus & Daly, 1999). These factors can be organized by those that precede the speech and those that occur as a result of the speech. Narrowing and defining your experiences enables you to compile a diagnostic list for yourself. Notice whether you can minimize any of the factors.

Self-conscious distortions, as seen in the left column of Table 3.1, feed on speakers' perceptions. These factors are often exaggerated by the speaker,

TABLE 3.1 • Common Fears Regarding Public Speaking

Self-Conscious Distortions	Communication Deficiencies
Fear of not meeting audience expectations	Perceived skills deficiency
Believing that one is dissimilar and subordinate to the audience	Lack of experience
Increased self-focusing	Poor preparation
Audience scrutiny	Fear of evaluation
A contagion effect in which adjacent speakers' anxiety increases an individual speaker's own anxiety	An uninterested or unresponsive audience

thereby increasing anxiety. Furthermore, notice the last item, which, in effect, says that stage fright is contagious. When people vent their frustrations and display their emotions about speaking, their anxiety spreads to intensify others' fears.

This chapter heightens one's awareness of dealing with self-conscious distortions, and this text should help you to overcome communication deficiencies caused by reasons in the right column of Table 3.1. Move through the items on the table. First, and ironically, many students think they are supposed to know skills they've never been taught nor experienced, even before their careers begin. Unprepared speakers have good reason to fear, and these speakers also quite likely fear being graded. The problem with the audience may be due to skill deficiencies, speaker perceptions, or recalcitrant, apathetic audiences. These same distortions and deficiencies affect employees more strongly than students, because communication evaluations are a major part of day-to-day work. Among other stress avoidance strategies at work, CA coping behaviors include missing meetings and making dogmatic statements to "lay down the law." Managers with positive attitudes and forthright communication can hardly imagine that an employee is intimidated at all, much less by them, but no matter how friendly a CEO, the amount of power residing in the position intimidates most employees.

MANAGING COMMUNICATION APPREHENSION

To deal with CA, we must work *through* it, not around it. This chapter has discussed theories, types, and manifestations of communication apprehension; now it moves to practical techniques for managing it. You can train the brain's emotional centers to work in tandem with its executive centers in order to manage your impulses and painful emotions. Reading about CA is not enough for overcoming its negative patterns. You must retrain your thoughts and behaviors, substituting helpful new habits for your destructive old ones.

Appropriate emotional control reflects reality. It does not deny or distort reality. Also, an emotional experience is *in response to* an event, not *because of* an event. With knee-jerk emotional reactions, we find it hard to conclude that events don't "make" us feel certain ways, but habitual thought patterns ingrain emotional responses, although "thinking behavior," through repetition, can change.

For instance, Gene's boss calls on him during a meeting to give an impromptu report about one of his projects. Gene feels an initial wash of emotion that lasts under two seconds. By that time, he is interpreting why he blushed and felt suddenly nauseous. If he interprets those physical signals as fear, he begins to experience fear. If he interprets those signs as surprise, he decides that those symptoms were because he was caught off balance, but now that he thinks about it, he is flattered with his boss's confidence in him.

1. What effect could the first interpretation have on Gene?
2. What outcome could the second interpretation have?

Our goal is to *manage* communication apprehension, not eliminate it. Apprehension can function productively, such as giving one a sense of excitement to energize one's presentations and alertness when interacting with a CEO.

The remainder of this chapter offers techniques that are especially helpful in regard to public speaking, speaking in groups, and interpersonal communication. The techniques may at first seem awkward, but these are the techniques that, if practiced, have the best chance of managing CA.

Correct Breathing to Support Speech and Control Anxiety

Breathing is a good thing, and don't let anyone talk you out of it, even during a speech. Anxious speakers complain of tightness in their chests and difficulty regulating breathing, and they often end up panting or shallowly breathing, which only increases anxiety.

Speaking borrows body parts. We don't have an organ dedicated solely to producing sound and speech. Even vocal chords close to keep food from falling into our lungs when we talk while eating. Breath is the energy of speech, and if forced to make a choice, choose breathing over speaking. It is no wonder that we have difficulty when we are nervous and speaking. It may seem strange to become more conscious of how we breathe, but like many habits, we must understand it in order to control it.

Carducci and Zimbardo (1995) suggest, "To tame your racing heart and churning stomach, learn how to relax. Use simple breathing exercises that involve inhaling and exhaling deeply and slowly." The goal is to get the most air with the least effort. The lower parts of the lungs have a larger capacity than the upper third used for shallow breathing. Relaxation techniques typically include conscious breathing. Athletes, especially swimmers, may keep a supply of air and intentionally gulp in the top third, but speakers need to fill the lungs with supportive air.

1. Stand up. Place your fingertips over the diaphragm and your thumbs at the base of the ribs.
2. Inhale through the nose, noting that the diaphragm flattens and increases in diameter, sort of like flattening an upside-down orange. It pushes out.

3. Exhale slowly and evenly. Push the last bit of air out of your lungs by allowing the diaphragm to curl up and into the rib cage, while keeping your chest high and shoulders back. (This allows the diaphragm to relax and return to its original shape.)

4. Practice moving the diaphragm while maintaining good posture, noting what happens with your breath. You do not have to "suck" in air. You simply flatten the diaphragm, and the air comes in effortlessly. (This is due to a change of air pressure of the thoracic, or chest, cavity as compared with the air pressure on the outside. Nature abhors a vacuum. Fortunately, you do not have to know all the physics in order for it to work.) When you run out of air while speaking, pause and flatten the diaphragm, allowing air to refill you. The listeners will have a "thinking break," while you replenish your air supply in under one second.

Accumulate Successful Experiences

Apprehension in part comes from a fear of being out of control. Collecting positive experiences in reasonably controlled, safe settings builds confidence. Use the speech class for all it's worth—join class discussions, work in teams, and give presentations. Especially take advantage of giving speeches in class to overcome stage fright. Reinforce skills beyond the classroom by serving in community organizations, churches, and professional associations. The service you provide often elicits warm responses from these organizations.

Students' anxiety is highest immediately before giving a speech. The second most anxious time is when the speaking assignment is first announced. Accept these peaks of apprehension as normal and short-lived. Research and planning periods actually lower apprehension and are, therefore, a productive management technique. Several other techniques are helpful beyond the initial stages of commitment and initiation of preparation. Begin by writing about the facts and feelings of apprehensive experiences, and enlist a friend's support in overcoming those obstacles.

Replace Irrational Thoughts

Debilitating and irrational thoughts crowd out helpful ones. Put communication into perspective. You are speaking, not performing brain surgery. The "what if's" can be paralyzing. "What if they laugh at me?" "What if I lose my train of thought?" "What if I start drooling and babbling nonsense?" Instead, ask yourself, "What is the worst thing that could happen?" (OK, drooling and babbling nonsensically would be bad.) Otherwise, see if you could live with that consequence. When a female student took three deep breaths before a speech, a couple of buttons popped off her shirt; she turned her back to the class and held her shirt together. She turned back around, grinned, and said, "Now that I have your attention . . . ." The class enjoyed her humor and composure—and yes, they laughed *with* her.

Instead of "Anything worth doing is worth doing well," perfectionists think, "Anything worth doing is worth doing perfectly." Perfection is an unrealistic expectation in public speaking. Don't aim for perfection; aim to do a very good job. Analyze your audience and prepare material for them, but do not

A self-conscious speaker may distort these listeners into an impossibly knowledgeable and critical audience. Focus instead on perceiving attentive and competent listeners.

Listener-centered presenters connect with their audiences. Notice the openness and responsiveness that these presenters show when speaking and listening.

expect to do it all perfectly. "Procrastinating perfectionists" find the task so daunting that they wait until too late to prepare. They excuse themselves by thinking they could have done wonderfully, if only they had not procrastinated. They do not risk trying, for fear of facing their imperfection. "Tedious perfectionists" hone each step of preparation in great detail, but run out of time. These perfectionists gather enough material to write a book and write detailed outlines, but never practice delivering the speech.

Use the Imagination Positively (Cognitive Restructuring and Reframing)

Reconstruct experiences imaginatively. Irrationally, some communication students label themselves as poor public speakers before anyone has taught them how to present to audiences. Furthermore, they avoid preparing and practicing, because they don't like thinking about failing.

Skillful cognitive restructuring reduces these negative appraisals of self. To reduce destructive self-judgments, become aware of negative thoughts and counter each with a positive statement. *Task coping statements* highlight behaviors to ensure better performances (O'Hair, Frederich, & Shaver, 2002, p. 144). Examples are, "If I talk loudly enough for students in the back to hear, my voice will sound confident" and "I will have my notes on a card that can rest on a table or speaker's stand."

Put your "picture" into a different "frame." Remember how John Greene (see Activity 3.4) reframed his interviewer as a person who gave him confidence, and he removed the picture of her as an insensitive teacher. Old frames trap you with false assumptions. A self-centered frame taunts: "Everyone will see me making a fool of myself." An outwardly focused frame enjoys: "I can't wait to see your faces as you hear the interesting ideas I've prepared for you." Presenting a well-prepared speech is an act of generosity—a gift—to the listeners.

Desensitize to Stressors

Ironically, we make our own stress and are our own worst stressors. Systematic desensitization is "based on the theory that a person cannot be relaxed and anxious at the same time." *Systematic desensitization* replaces stressful thoughts with pleasant, relaxing images. When a person becomes sensitive to an anxiety-causing situation, he or she can desensitize the intensity of the negative reaction. It is helpful to have someone trained in systematic desensitization to talk you through this technique the first couple of times. Systematic desensitization is one of the most successful techniques for managing conditioned anxiety. Over time, the link between anxiety and communication weakens.

1. Make a list, from lowest to highest, of events in the situation about which you feel anxious. For instance, a new employee preparing to present to a client team may list the following: becoming thoroughly familiar with the product, deciding how to sequence the presentation, practicing, presenting to clients, and especially the anxiety-ridden moments just prior to presenting.

2. Resting in a comfortable position, inhale slowly and deeply, and exhale slowly and completely. Relax, focusing only on breathing.

3. Tighten each fist, and hold the contraction for several seconds. Release the fist, relaxing the muscles. Think about how the fist feels in the relaxed state.

4. Continue moving through the muscles of the arms, trunk, hips, legs, and feet, first tightly contracting the muscle group and then relaxing the muscles.

5. Allow your body to sink heavily against the floor or chair supporting you. Experience gravity and "heavy muscles."

6. In the relaxed state, call to mind a very peaceful, pleasant scene. Imagine yourself in the scene, feeling very relaxed.

7. Stay relaxed and call to mind the item on your list that caused the least anxiety. In the example employee's list, that would be researching the product. "I feel relaxed and happy. I am at my desk. I will open the documents on the product and enjoy reviewing them."

8. Move through the list items, one by one, associating relaxation with each item.

9. If you notice your muscles tightening or anxious thoughts intruding upon your relaxed state, return to your pleasant scene and repeat the contract-and-relax sequence through the various muscle groups. As you increase in

experience, you will be able to imagine the scene immediately and go right to the muscle group where you felt some tightening.

• STRATEGIES TO BUILD CONFIDENT SPEAKING

Butterflies (and occasionally buzzards) light on speakers from time to time. The more you practice speaking, the fewer the buzzards, if you have an effective practice strategy. Imagine the audience. Imagine them following the thoughts and material. Imagine their favorable responses.

Prepare to Speak Extemporaneously

The basic speech delivery styles are as follows: (1) memorized, (2) manuscript, (3) impromptu, and (4) extemporaneous. A speaker doesn't usually memorize a speech. The exception would be when a speaker plans to give the same message to numerous audiences. Memorizing a speech takes time, advanced skills, and nerves of steel.

Most of us don't even have time to *manuscript* a speech, that is, to write out a speech word for word and then read it. Although there is little danger of a speaker forgetting a manuscripted speech, reading a speech creates a distance between speaker and audience. The speaker loses eye contact and sticks to the script, no matter what the response of the audience is. The most common manuscript speeches are key policy speeches given by government officials or officials responsible for making and reporting policy, when casual misstatements could have dire political consequences.

Impromptu speeches are frequently requested, but not fully expected. Usually, topics for these are familiar and occasions are fairly predictable. The skills you develop in preparing and presenting scheduled speeches carry over to skills for impromptu speaking.

Extemporaneous speaking is the type most commonly used in the workplace. Unlike impromptu speaking, extemporaneous speeches are carefully researched and prepared in advance. The speaker uses speaking notes to move through the speech. The style is communicative and conversational. Learning to speak extemporaneously gives you an edge in the workplace, because it is efficient and effective. Resist writing out and reading every word of a speech, but don't wing it either. Beginners often forget to allow adequate time to practice. Some experts suggest you spend half your preparation time practicing your speech. Media coaches tell clients not to memorize their remarks, and instead advise, "Write out your talking points, then build anecdotes around them" (Applegate, 1999).

Design Notes That Work

Use words to trigger ideas. Include statistics or brief quotes that you have difficulty remembering. Beware of too many small note cards, subject to a "misdeal." Try bright ink or a highlighter on key words. Mark in your notes where you should be midway and near the end of your speech. Make your conclusion prompt obvious so that you won't forget to make your concluding statements.

Practice in Conversation

Informally discuss your topic with friends to get experience in wording your ideas and information. Pay attention to your friends' reactions and questions and what holds their interest. Notice how you sequence the ideas and which facts, explanations, and examples are most effective.

Practice on Your Feet

Stand up! Speak out! Hold your notes, or place them where you can see them, and practice your speech from start to finish. Pretend that the audience is in front of you, or gather a practice audience. Imagine who will be in the audience, what they look like, and where they will sit. Imagine where the key people will sit. Practice out loud and on your feet once a day over a four-day period. If you are pushed for time, wait at least an hour between each of the four practice sessions.

Each time, pretend that this is your only opportunity, and that you must communicate with the audience now or never. If you don't like the way you say something, correct it aloud, as if to them. For instance, if you leave something out, say to your practice audience, "Before we move on, let me explain this." In other words, prepare for the unexpected as well as the expected with adaptive strategies.

Use Physical Energy

Prepare yourself for the physical experience of presenting. Walk to different spots in the room as you practice, adding gestures and facial responses. Some media coaches suggest practicing in front of a mirror or video camera to see whether you are overly gesturing, bobbing your head, or keeping your hands in your pockets (Brown, 1999). If you have an adrenalin overload the day of the speech, briskly walk for a couple of minutes before going into class. Retain some of the energy, however, because it will add enthusiasm and credibility to your speech. Clinging to the lectern in a white-knuckle flight position increases tension.

Gather Feedback with Eye Contact

As you speak, observe persons in the audience so you can assess interest, gather feedback, and include them in the communication. Let your eyes linger for a second or two to establish a genuine connection before making a transition to connect with another person. Regularly greet classmates with a smile and a second of eye contact along with your "Hello." When they respond, briefly look at them and smile. Don't prolong eye contact, just establish a connection and move on.

Practice with Equipment

Get familiar with the physical surroundings of your speech location. If you are using visuals, practice with them. Check that everyone will be able to see. Dress according to the usual temperature of the room, and consider how you will look and how comfortably you can move about the room. Conferences and other professional settings often provide microphones and media equipment, so check that you know how to turn them on; adjust focus, light, or sound; and otherwise use them effectively. If possible, practice with projection equipment ahead of time.

• SUPPORT OTHERS IN OVERCOMING COMMUNICATION APPREHENSION

When we are strong inwardly, we have the energy to focus on others. Even confident, on-top-of-the-world people should realize that others working with them may suffer from confidence glitches. Wonderfully, those who help others ultimately help themselves.

If you are assertive and confident, you may not understand what is going on in Josh's mind. On the other hand, if you are shy and reticent, teaching Josh may be uncomfortable and tedious. Similarly, if you are shy, Mallory may intimidate you, and if you are very assertive, the two of you may have a head-on collision. Three communication consultants analyzed the situation with Mallory and Josh and offered these suggestions.

Expert Advice for Instructing Josh

Public Settings

Some people are intimidated in public settings, and "public" sometimes means just one additional person present. If this describes Josh, then work with him one-on-one. Anyone else's presence would interfere with him processing the

Practicing when you are shy

Do you know someone in hiding?

instructions. In fact, even *you* are a distraction. Tell him that this is important "information," and he will be given "the next couple of days" to let it "soak in." Josh will be relieved that he can study this evening alone. Most people are more secure in learning "information" than in learning "skills." "Skills" suggests mastering new capabilities.

Written Instructions

Give Josh a set of written instructions. Sequence what you say with what is written. Because he can read the written instructions later, he can concentrate on what you say. Tell him that these are his copies and he can write any notes he needs.

Notes and Questions

Suggest Josh take notes as needed. Repeat necessary instructions, giving him time to write. Do not expect questions—ask them for him. For instance, "I've gone a little fast. Would you like to see that function again?" or "What would you like me to repeat? Perhaps the menu for accounting?" Do *not* say, "Stop me anytime." Instead say, "Would you like a print screen for this?"

Over-the-Shoulder Learning

Josh will prefer "looking over your shoulder" or sitting next to you. He wants to observe you, and he does not want you to observe him. He worries he will make mistakes or look foolish. He certainly does not want to be conspicuous. He wants a grip on the skill *before* he has a grip on the mouse.

Intervals and Practice

Allow Josh to practice with the software at intervals. Set up the computer so that he is working offline and "can't mess up anything." Read Josh's nonverbal communication and reinforce your interpretation with verbal communication to determine whether Josh prefers (1) watching you go through the steps one more time, (2) being at the computer while you verbally lead him through the steps, or (3) being left unobserved with the written instructions.

Stressed-Reduced Timing

Summarize previous steps, allow practice time, or take a brief break whenever you notice Josh getting tense. Always give Josh some time to practice what he has learned without you being there. This reinforces the skill and gives him a breather. While he is alone, he may write down questions to ask when you return. He will be more likely to ask questions in the future.

Comforting Words

Use words and phrases such as "play," "fool around," and the reassuring "don't worry." "I need to take care of some other business right now. I hope you don't mind having some time to play around with this software. Don't worry. You're offline and can't mess up. Any problems are my fault, not yours. If you get tired of thinking about this, use the time to do the paperwork in personnel, and I'll meet you back after lunch. By the way, Bill, whom you met in purchasing, is a good resource. Feel free to work with him on the software." Now Josh has a second person to help him, hopefully someone with whom he feels comfortable. He also has an alternative assignment, in case he is overwhelmed.

Encouraging Words

Give many encouraging words. "I cannot believe you are already doing this." "Well, you're a quick study!" "You have wonderful analytical skills. You follow the reasoning in this application." Even when things go wrong, use them for positive instruction. "Oh, good. A problem. Now I'll feel useful!" "OK, great example of something that easily happens. A program's strength is often its weakness. That's the case here. Let's work through fixing this problem." "Good for you. You spotted a problem."

Security in the Wings

Mentoring is an assignment over time. Wean Josh slowly, assuring him that he understand the basics and that you are always available. "After all," you tell him, "I've given you a lot of information in just a few days. If you need an answer or a review, I'm here." Hopefully, Josh will be comfortable in making requests and asking you questions by this point. Because of his reticence, Josh probably will wean himself as soon as he feels confident.

Interdependence

Beware of Josh becoming dependent on you. Ideally, as Josh becomes adept at each new skill, he will grow independent in doing his work and interdependent with you and others as new challenges arise. Establish connections by suggesting to Josh, "Get the P.O. forms from Dave," and "Find out how Barbara solicits vendors." Do not lead him to every destination and become a twosome every day at lunch. Include others, and be unavailable at times.

Consultants' Advice for Instructing Mallory

Public Setting

Mallory is ready and confident! She prefers learning from you to learning at home and alone. People energize her, and she doesn't mind being put on the spot.

Notes

Encourage Mallory to take notes that she can refer to later. Her tendency will be to run to you or another employee if she forgets something. Remind her to first look at her notes.

Questions

You will not have a problem getting Mallory to interact. In fact, she may leap ahead and ask questions that will get your instructions out of order. In that case, you can comment, "Great question. I think we will get to that in a few minutes.

If I don't, remind me." If she really bombards you with questions, laugh (kindly, not with an evil inflection!), saying, "This is going to be fun. I love your eagerness. Let me take things one step at a time." If Mallory comments on a particular screen, you may offer to "print it to add to her other written instructions."

Over-the-Shoulder Learning

Mallory will look over your shoulder or sit beside you only a short time before she wants to try out her new skills, and sometimes ones she doesn't have. She would prefer that you look over *her* shoulder most of the time. Her hands are itching to get to the keyboard. Preview your teaching method to assure her that she will quickly have her turn at the keyboard. "Here's the way we will do this. I will show you where to enter data and how to submit the form. Watch me and be sure to make notes about special cases. After that, it will be *your* turn to try it. Once *you* develop correct habits with that section, *we* will move on to another section." Notice the uses of "you" and "I" here. The focus is on Mallory's acquired skills, and the idea of "correct habits" is introduced. Finally, "we" suggests a partnership instead of turn taking.

Interval Practice

Mallory may almost knock you out of your chair to try out the application. Establish a pattern of (1) explanation, (2) practice, and (3) approval. That is, after you explain a procedure, she practices it. When you are confident of her ability in that skill, you move to the next.

Timing for Effective Learning

Summarize steps to anchor concepts. Allow practice time for Mallory to reinforce skills. Take a brief break as needed.

Supportive Words

Mallory probably realizes her ebullient spirit. Her can-do attitude and aggressive learning style may take her far, and you don't want to squelch her. Laugh with her frequently, and let her know you enjoy her enthusiasm. Do not let her confidence mislead you into thinking she does not need compliments and positive comments. "Great job!" "You really are catching on fast!"

Action Words

Mallory will respond well to words that imply dynamic activity. She likes "solving," "creating," "determining," and "eliminating." "Challenges" and "consequences" do not intimidate her. Whereas learning something at the moment panics Josh, Mallory is hungry for the moment.

Interdependence

To her detriment, Mallory may be so eager to be seen as competent that she does not rely on you and others when she needs to. Explain reversible and irreversible consequences and be clear about costly errors. Act neither superior to nor "in awe" of her. Depend on her as appropriate.

Josh and Mallory will benefit from employers or coworkers who under-stand their apprehension as well as their eagerness. Feeling superior because someone else is shaking and shy is usually a reaction of someone who con-stantly worries about being judged. People value the people who bring out their value. There is an unconscionable loss of human resources due to com-munication apprehension. Many communication students recognize CA in others and, in the process of helping others, discover that their own fears dimin-ish. Hopefully, you are now more aware of the causes and manifestations of CA and will be a leader to those who have unwittingly capped their contributions.

SUMMARY

This chapter explores causes and effects of communication apprehension (CA), often called stage fright or shyness. Communication apprehension has consequences for one's self and for others in interpersonal relation-ships, small groups, and public speaking. Shyness is costly in terms of time, emotional energy, social support, job satisfaction, and human resources. Trait anxiety, or trait shyness, is internal to the individual and exists regardless of the situation. Situational anxiety is specific to a situation and may occur in one-on-one conversations, small group interactions, or public speaking. Fewer peo-ple are "born shy" than report shyness as adults; thus, CA is largely learned along the way to adulthood.

Techniques for managing CA include respiration control; experience in controlled environments such as a speech class; awareness of when anxiety peaks; becoming accountable for personal prescriptions to counteract CA habits; reframing and cognitive restructuring; counteracting irrational think-ing and perfectionism; and desensitizing. Habitual responses are changed by learning new habits through experience and repeated practice.

Speakers infrequently manuscript or memorize speeches. It is more effi-cient to prepare for extemporaneous speaking. The extemporaneous speech is carefully researched and prepared in advance; it is not impromptu. Several tech-niques help the extemporaneous speaker use energy productively, including designing notes that work, practicing in conversations, and practicing with equipment. •

ACTIVITIES

1. **Journaling the Experience:** In a journal, write descriptions of three times you wanted to speak but lacked confidence to do so. Tell how you would like to behave in similar situations in the future, and write your "prescriptions" in your journal. For instance, decide to participate in class, present a report, or ask for library assistance. Choose behaviors and settings that challenge you slightly but have little risk of negative consequences. Discuss your decisions with a supportive friend, and ask the friend to sign the "prescription contract" in your journal. Journal your behaviors, feelings, and outcomes as you practice your new behaviors. Follow up by discussing your progress and setbacks with your friend.

2. **Technical Support:** Search online in recent communication, psychology, and business communication journals to locate research articles by James McCroskey and Phillip Zimbardo on communication apprehension and shyness. Summarize five conclusions of their research.

3. **Presenting to Others:** List five things that you want the class to know about you. Write two or three words per item as speaking notes. While everyone is seated in a circle (or double circle), tell the class about your items.

4. **Team Work:** Work through the breathing activity in pairs, taking turns reading the instructions while the other person performs the behavior to a point of relaxation. Discuss one setting that you need to reframe or imagine differently.

5. **Ethically Speaking:** Often we intend to help people who are worried about something, and yet we say things that discourage them. What helpful things can you say to coworkers to encourage them to open up when they want to?

FOR FURTHER READING

You will find excellent links on communication apprehension at www.roch.edu/dept/spchcom/ca_links.htm.

An enjoyable site with a free discussion of techniques to overcome stress is www.learnwell.org/stress.htm.

Outstanding researchers and writers on communication apprehension and shyness include Carducci, McCroskey, and Zimbardo, as in the following:

Carducci, B. (2000, January). Shyness: The new solution. *Psychology Today, 33,* 38–78.

Carducci, B. J., & Zimbardo, P. G. (1995, November/December). Are you shy? *Psychology Today, 28,* 34–82.

McCroskey, J. C. (1997). *Why we communicate the ways we do: A communibiological perspective.* A Carroll C. Arnold Distinguished Lecture presented at the annual convention of the National Communication Association, Chicago, IL, November 20, 1997, and published in McCroskey, J. C., & Beatty, M. J. (1984). Communication apprehension and accumulated communication state anxiety experiences: A research note. *Communication Monographs, 51,* 79–84.

Everyone, when they are young, has a little bit of genius; that is, they really do listen . . . then they grow a little older and many of them get tired and listen less and less. But some, very few, continue to listen. (Gertrude Stein, quoted in Adler, (1983)

Powerful Listening

4

The Values of Listening

A Model of Listening

Barriers to Accurate Reception

Listening Skills and Strategies

Responding to Help Others

Feedback in an Open System

Very likely in your upcoming professional job, you will write a technical report, read a software application manual, and present a project proposal. Sounds like work, and important work at that. But what about *listening* to five project proposals, *listening* to a staff discussion, and *listening* to a complaining employee—all before lunch? Speakers feel important when giving their opinions and contributing information, but listeners quietly accumulate power by understanding others and taking in information.

This chapter looks at how and why we listen and examines what organizations expect in listening competence. After defining the functions of listening, it identifies barriers to effective listening and presents specific listening and responding skills.

OBJECTIVES

After studying the content of this chapter, you should be able to

- Use a variety of listening styles
- Define the functions of listening
- Increase personal listening abilities

- Evaluate the ethics of listening strategies
- Select effective responses
- Use participative feedback

 ● **THE VALUES OF LISTENING**

Listening is a valuable, acquired set of skills, far from the passive behavior many people assume. Some people have more innate ability for listening, but listening efficiency does not exactly correlate with intelligence or other communication skills, and, fortunately, listening skills can be learned. Although you need patience, you can immediately benefit from these skills in classes, at work, at home, and in the community.

Benefits of Listening

Skilled listeners know what particular individuals or groups mean by certain words. As Burley (1982) states, "Active listening is most valuable when used to develop the mutual understanding that is necessary to solve important problems. It involves knowledge of the words being used, the various meanings that words may have for other people, and the feelings and behaviors that are generated by the use of words."

Values to Individuals and Organizations

We know that organizations rely on good listeners, because organizations learn from their members and from other organizations, obviously adding value with increased accuracy. Conversely, listening deficiencies cost corporations millions of dollars every year. For instance, delivering the wrong product takes time to deal with a disgruntled customer, triples the shipping costs, requires time to inventory, and leads to deteriorating customer trust. The irritated customer, meanwhile, returns the product and purchases it elsewhere.

●
ACTIVITY 4.1

COMPLEX CONTEXTS AT WORK

In a September planning meeting, the staff at TechTiles, Inc., discuss Link-a-Lot, a new product that recently was approved with some modifications. Tomas, the design manager, says, "I know all of you have heavy schedules, so we will push to get designs to production the first week in November." Joy, the production manager, then realizes that November is the earliest they can *begin* production, and she figures a minimum of 10 days are needed to set up production, if materials are ordered immediately. (At this time, a secretary hands a recent printout of sales to Noeli, the marketing manager.) Ed, knowing November and December are the busiest time of the year for packing and shipping, estimates, "Let's see. It takes a week to package the first 5,000 Link-a-Lots. The earliest we have an opening for packaging is December 23." With some relief, he sighs, "At least we will finish the biggest part before the holidays!"

Noeli has been reviewing the printout and whispers to Kaput from accounting, "This product could put annual profits at an all-time high for TechTiles, instead of us giving up our bonuses." They catch Ed's last comment and nod agreement. (Noeli decides to begin marketing the new product immediately, to make profits from last-minute holiday shopping. The meeting begins to wrap up, when someone asks "Noeli, do you want to share those numbers with everyone before we leave?" Noeli reports the completed sales for the year through August 31.

1. *Summarize what happened at the meeting. What was the listening context?*
2. *Do participants always take turns speaking and otherwise carefully listen at meetings?*
3. *Identify communication noise at this meeting.*
4. *Where could listening errors occur?*
5. *What could be done to prevent the staff leaving the meeting with misunderstandings?*

The example was compiled from personal interviews performed in 2000.

Listen carefully, because rewards are rich, but risks are costly. Rewards include increased knowledge, understanding, insights, and trust. Not listening leaves people vulnerable due to the increased risks of ignorance, confusion, naiveté, and distrust.

Listening Time

One indication of the value of listening is the amount of time we spend listening. In a classic study, Paul Rankin (1928) reported that adults communicate about 70% of their waking time. Of the four basic communication functions—reading, writing, speaking, and listening—the largest portion of time is spent in listening. In fact, we read and write roughly a fourth of the time we communicate, and the other three fourths we spend speaking and listening. In a survey of industrial managers, Burley (1982) affirmed that employees spent more time listening than any other communication activity and yet discovered that employees received no direct training in listening skills, as summarized in Table 4.1.

Workplace Expectations

Eighty percent of a research population of senior executives said they wanted employees to be good listeners, yet these same executives ranked listening as the skill most lacking by their employees. Executives value listening, as seen in the 60% to 90% of their working days spent listening (Kotter, 1982; Sachs, Rutherford, & Marchant, 1999). "In view of the vast discrepancy between the

TABLE 4.1 • Listening Time and Training

	Time Spent (%)	Training Received (%)
Reading	10	60
Writing	15	30
Talking	30	10
Listening	45	0

amount of time spent listening and the training received, it is not surprising that leaders in industry, business, and education today seek to improve their ability to communicate, especially in the art of 'active listening'" (Bryant, 1987). Good listeners bring ideas, solve problems, and take the corporate pulse. Trial lawyer Gerry Spence urges others to really listen to prospective jurors and witnesses, and jury selection specialist Jo-Ellen Demetrius advises listeners to hear beyond words alone. Other professionals repeatedly stress the importance of listening skills.

Reality
@ WORK
4.1

WHICH JOBS NEED GOOD LISTENERS?

- In "Listen First, Talk Later," authors Prince and File declare, "The distinction between top *[financial] advisers* and the rest is that the top advisers really, really listen" (Prince & File, 1999). The authors analyzed why some trust officers were so much more effective than their coworkers, as measured by new business brought in over the previous 12 months. In interviews, the clients of the highly successful advisors unequivocally agreed that their advisors really listened to them. The advisors were patient as the clients spoke, and they acknowledged what the clients had said.

- *Information systems managers* report a reversal from hiring the "leave-me-alone-with-my-computer" types, largely because they try to recruit people with strong interpersonal skills.

- One *recruiter* in San Francisco noted improved interpersonal skills among *technical teams:* "Today, the programmer must work with the user. You no longer put a 'techie' in a corner office, have them program all day, send in a sandwich occasionally, and never let them get near the user" (Blake, 1998).

- An *applications manager* at an insurance company complained, "Since many of our *systems* people listen with only half an ear, they don't ask questions that get to the root of the problem. They confuse a person's literal meaning with the real meaning. There becomes a dispute over what was actually agreed upon. That results in end users getting systems that they never asked for and can't use!" (Blake, 1998).

- Michael Rich, a Harvard-educated *physician* at Children's Hospital in Boston, argues, "Medicine is not a religion; it's a service industry. Yet as doctors, we often block ourselves from getting information that we most need to serve our patients. We need to listen to patients within their framework. They're the experts; they live with their illness every day. We can learn from them" (Rekha, 2000, p. 304). In a recent British study of more than 800 patients, the patients reported they wanted good "communication, including listening to and exploring their concerns (88% to 99% of those interviewed)" (Murray, 2001, p. 1).

- *Suppliers* listen for the demand of the marketplace. Steve McCallion of Ziba Design (with clients such as FedEx and Intel) and Andrew Grant at Ford (as European and *consumer-marketing-insights manager*) agree that you must go to your customers and listen to them. "Customers have higher expectations and more choices than ever. Which means that you have to listen more closely than ever" (Rekha, 2000, p. 1).

- "For every minute a *salesperson* spends listening, he or she will save four minutes overcoming objections," says Bill Acheson (Murray, 2001), University of Pittsburgh, consultant to Merrill Lynch, Prudential Securities, and SunAmerica.

- At the annual convention of the Independent Insurance Agents of America, one *agent* and *consultant* said the task "boils down to knowing your customer and listening to your employees" (Ruquet, 2000).

Listeners' Roles

Contexts and relationships define major listening roles we assume in everyday life. We play, learn, help, lead, participate, and communicate through our listening. With a variety of listening skills, you should be able to listen in all the roles appropriately.

TYPES OF LISTENING

ACTIVITY
4.2

____ 1. Do you sometimes enjoy listening to the sounds around you, much as you would enjoy seeing a beautiful scene or tasting ice cream?

____ 2. Do you listen to an organization's stories to learn the history and values of the organization?

____ 3. Do you enjoy listening to learn new information?

____ 4. Do you prefer learning concepts from another person explaining them rather than reading about them?

____ 5. Do you listen to a friend simply because the friend needs someone to listen?

____ 6. Do you listen to understand a person's problem before trying to help the person?

____ 7. Do you listen to people who work with you in order to get their ideas?

____ 8. Do you listen to authority figures out of respect for what they know?

____ 9. Do you listen for the "big picture"?

____10. Do you listen to understand an organization's political climate?

____11. Do you listen, verbally and nonverbally, to the audience while you are speaking?

____12. Do you listen to feedback following a speech you give?

Scoring

11–12: Highly versatile listener

9–10: Versatile listener

7–8: Missing out on some opportunities

5–6: Come back from lunch

After reading this section on listening roles, return to this activity to label the questions with "C" for *listening connoisseur,* "Lr" for *listening learner,* "F" for *listening facilitator,* "Ld" for *listening leader,* "St" for *listening stakeholder,* and "Sp" for *listening speakers.*

Listening Connoisseurs

Listening connoisseurs seek quality and value. Listening connoisseurs savor the moment in engaged communication. Aesthetically pleasing listening experiences, such as listening to music or poetry, recharge their spirits and engage their minds.

Listening Learners

Listening learners use skills that help them understand and remember what they hear. Listening to learn requires more energy than listening for entertainment and occurs in classrooms, on playing fields, from educational television programming, and with information exchanges at work.

Listening Facilitators

Facilitators help when they listen, and they listen before they help. When we listen to others reason through problems, we help them move from problem holders to problem solvers. Doctors, for instance, should first listen to the patient before deciding on a diagnosis and treatment. Information technologists should first listen to the needs of the client before addressing those needs through programming.

Listening Leaders

Leadership fluidly moves across organizations, with various employees taking leadership roles depending on the situation. If people stop listening to you, you know for certain it is time to stop and listen to others. As Kevin Cashman writes (2000, p. 9), "Effective leaders recognize they can accomplish great things only by being in relationship with others, practicing authentic listening and acknowledging the contributions of others." In fact, listening is one of the secrets to gaining power in an organization.

Listening Stakeholders

Those who have a vested interest in the success of an organization—its stakeholders—listen for ways to integrate systems, simplify systems, and make systems more effective. In business, people communicate with those who help them accomplish a task, and these people may be team members, bosses, personnel in other departments, or customers. The emotional payoffs from these interactions focus on rewards inherent to the job (DiSanza & Legge, 2000, pp. 55–56).

Listening Speakers

Listener-centered presenters connect with the audience. Sensing the communication event, they paraphrase, summarize, and elaborate as necessary. Listening speakers stay tuned to audiences' reactions to learn whether the audience hears, understands, agrees, or is even interested in what is being said.

A Transforming Activity

Listening transforms persons and organizations. It causes physiological changes, affects behavioral decisions, opens paths of persuasion, lays the groundwork for negotiation, and sets the tone for fundamental changes in organizations. The brain's physiology structurally and chemically changes when we listen, and we make decisions based on what we learn through listening. Being heard and being understood almost always precede voluntary and cooperative transformations in others.

NEGOTIATING CHANGE

Public-policy negotiator Susan Podziba, who teaches negotiation at Harvard and MIT, has brokered agreements between conservationists and fishermen, calmed the rhetoric of pro-life and pro-choice activists after an abortion-clinic shooting, mediated divorces, and worked with a struggling city to rewrite a charter. She says, "Listening is as important in negotiating as stating what you want. Negotiating any long-term relationship requires trust. Building trust doesn't exclude pursuing your interests. It means being forthright and listening carefully to the other side" (Hoult, 2000).

Speakers expect to change their listeners, but, curiously, listeners transform the speakers when they cause speakers to change their minds while talking in the presence of others. Speakers are likely to become increasingly objective as they hear their own ideas.

Transformational listeners prefer dialogues over monologues. In face-to-face dialogues, people are more likely to learn, to remember, and to share ownership in an idea. Interestingly, people who overhear a conversation about a topic actually remember more than those who listen to a lecture on the same topic. Two persons talking with no one listening is not a dialogue; they are simply having monologues in tandem.

Good listening is the first step for fundamental transformation within an organization: "You first have to build a listening organization—a company whose people have their ears to the ground" (Balu, 2000, p. 304). Joseph Beatty (1999, p. 281) claims good listening is a fundamental avenue for understanding one's own character as well as that of the other person and making its transformation possible.

• A MODEL OF LISTENING

Although they are a bit tedious to unravel, it's in the intricacies of listening that we discover the roots of effectiveness and ethical communication. Figure 4.1 shows a spiraling, ever-widening, tornado-like shape—a type of helix. The listening functions superimposed upon the helix are *receiving, interpreting, critical*

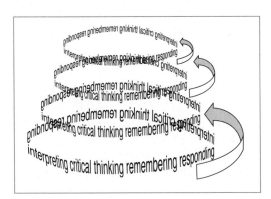

FIGURE 4.1 • A Model of Listening: The Listening Helix

TABLE 4.2 • Stages or Elements of Listening According to Various Theories

Brownell (1986)	Barker (1971, p. 7)	Steil, Barker, and Watson (1983, p. 11)	*Communication @ Work* (Kelly, 2005)
Hearing	Hearing	Sensing	Receiving
Understanding	Attending	Interpreting	Interpreting
Remembering	Understanding	Evaluating	Evaluating
Interpreting	Remembering	Responding	Remembering
Evaluating			Responding
Responding to messages			

thinking, remembering, and *responding* (essentially in no particular order). In reality, the functions' sequences vary to account for an individual listening experience. The helical model widens at the top to indicate that our understanding of events grows as we listen.

Physically hearing is only one part of a predominantly mental activity, in which we listen to *hear* something, *make sense* of it, and *remember* it. An article in *Human Communication Research* (Bostrom, 1996) says that the word *listening* is used broadly and includes attending and thinking skills (p. 304). Rest assured that we have good theoretical footing, as Table 4.2 shows in a comparison of various theories' labeled categories.

Referring back to the listening model in Figure 4.1, consider the intertwining functions. A communicator receives a message, understands basically what the speaker is saying, values it enough to put it into memory, and continues to listen, thereby receiving the message even more meaningfully, and so forth along the helix. That is, topic involvement and increasingly complex thinking skills build over time. Let's discuss each of the model's functions: receiving, interpreting, evaluating, remembering, and responding.

Receiving

Receiving is most often thought of as hearing, that is, using the mechanisms of the ears and the requisite neurological circuitry. For communication studies, however, the receiving function of listening goes beyond hearing to include *any* sensory receptors. To pay attention, we must first take in the sensory stimuli, focusing on the message sender and preparing to physically receive the message. Receiving is a rudimentary, but amazing, part of the listening process and lays the groundwork for understanding.

• • • • TIPS   • • • • Hearing-Impaired Listeners • • • •

Although reception problems occur with hearing loss, some hearing-impaired people otherwise *listen* very well. Face-to-face communication is especially effective when listeners receive messages on more than one sensory channel.

• • •

Interpreting

Understanding requires *interpreting*—making sense out of sounds, primarily words, and knowing what they mean. Communication is accurate only to the extent that receivers interpret correctly what the senders meant. At each level of interpretation, a listener decides whether to continue listening, until at higher levels on the helix, listeners use sophisticated interpretation skills, including listening in depth, discerning, predicting expectations, interpreting emotions and attitudes, and—ultimately—discriminating and analyzing.

Reality @ WORK 4.3

LEVELS OF INTERPRETING

Interpreting goes from level 1, with a basic interpretation of the message, up to level 4, in which an employee uses discriminating and analytical interpreting skills (personal group interview generating a typical scenario, 1992).

Level 1 Interpretation

Bob wants me to shut the door and discuss something. I decide to listen. Bob asks about my family and tells about his. I continue to listen.

Level 2 Interpretation

Bob wants to talk privately. He will bring up his topic after a few conversational exchanges. I'm supportive and curious, and decide to listen. Bob tells me he is concerned about losing his job. I continue to listen.

Level 3 Interpretation

Bob is worried, feels vulnerable, and is concerned about others learning of his predicament. I feel honored that he trusts me enough to discuss it with me. I will listen as long as he needs to talk. Bob tells me he has seen a re-organization chart and doesn't see his job title on it. He is worried about maintaining his health insurance.

Level 4 Interpretation

Bob does not have evidence that he will lose his job. He may even be up for another position and promotion, so far as the chart is concerned. I wonder why he brought up health insurance in particular. I will continue to listen to discriminate between what Bob knows and what he is guessing. I will listen for messages that explain his focus on health insurance.

Message from Bob: "We need to talk. Shut the door, please."

Discriminating Listening

Just as "discriminating" consumers choose the better product, discriminating listeners discriminate between information and propaganda, between research and personal experience, between official business and small talk, and between information that keeps them abreast and information on which they must take action. Discriminating skills, then, are used at every level of listening.[1]

---

[1] Some readers become confused about the use of the word *discriminate*. Discriminating *between* two or more items means noting how they are different from one another. This is different from discriminating *against* a group, which means telling how people are different in order to denigrate them, or put them down. Discriminating listeners discriminate *among* or *between*, rather than against.

Analytical Listening

In the analytical function, listeners mentally examine:

- Meanings of messages, such as speakers' intentions, conceptual content, possible applications, relational implications, and emotional/attitudinal meanings
- The emerging structure of messages, including themes and connections
- Relevant causes

Evaluating

To the critical thinking of "interpreting," we add another dimension, "evaluating." *Evaluative* listening—both detached and empathic—helps listeners think about the source, quality, validity, and worth of messages. (The word itself—e-*valu*-ative—implies that a value system is applied.) Early in the dialogue or speech, listeners evaluate how important a particular listening experience is before deciding to continue listening. Later, at higher levels of the listening model, listeners use more sophisticated thinking tools to determine the validity and worth of the message, the quality of the information, and the credibility of the source.

Evaluative listening is important when listening to persuasive speakers. Measure the value of the topic, the soundness of the reasoning, and the quality of the support for the argument (Wolff & Marsnik, 1992, p. 93).

We take on roles—identities—in the listening process. A person's listening identity changes in response to his or her evaluative listening. A listener may choose to take on an objective, detached identity or a subjective, empathic role. Objective, detached listeners distance themselves from issues to collect facts without personal bias. Detachment requires distancing oneself from "whatever threatens to distort the understanding of what is there" (Beatty, 1999, p. 4). Subjective, empathic listeners identify with the speaker, try to see the situation from that person's point of view, and seek to understand how it makes the person feel. They do not necessarily agree with the speaker.

Remembering

We need the ability to store information in order to use the other listening functions. Learning and remembering are interrelated activities that involve "large areas of the brain rather than . . . small networks of brain cells" (Wolff & Marsnik, 1992, p. 34). The fast, constant pace of listening uses short-term memory to store data for only a few seconds, just long enough for listeners to decide whether to keep listening. As listeners process the message further, they rely on long-term memory. Short-term memory has a limited storage capacity and is easily disrupted. In fact, most people need a memory strategy to retain more than seven items after hearing one repetition (Miller, 1956; Morris, 2000). Long-term memory, on the other hand, stores data for hours, weeks, or even until the final exam.

Responding

Face-to-face communication typically supplies verbal and nonverbal feedback to the communicators. Until the listener responds, the speaker is not assured

Two kinds of noise, psychological and environmental, influence these communicators.

that communication has taken place, and so responding upholds part of a listener's responsibility. Responding implies attention, even at the lowest levels of the model. Further up the model, feedback usually becomes more interactive, more frequent, and more complex, ranging from asking questions for clarity or expressing agreement to making analytical statements or asking more involved questions. Of course, sometimes a speaker blocks feedback ("I'll talk, you just listen"), in which case listeners internalize the dialogue in order to move to the higher critical thinking skills.

BARRIERS TO ACCURATE RECEPTION

It's not enough to know what listening is; we also need to know what gets in the way of listening, so we can clear the way to accurate reception of messages. Physiological, contextual, and psychological issues possibly contort our listening outcomes.

Physiological Barriers

Physical limitations block complete reception, whether due to hearing loss or the mind racing ahead to stay occupied.

Hearing Disabilities

Hunger and sleepiness physically interfere, to say nothing of headaches, allergies, and sport injuries. Hearing loss is probably the most obvious physical barrier. Emphasizing how common hearing loss is, the Occupational Safety and Health Administration (OSHA) says frequent exposure to higher than 85 decibels (db, a measurement of sound intensity) results in permanent hearing loss. The Better Hearing Institute (1987) lists chain saws, subway trains, jackhammers, and screaming children at a damaging level. More alarming, noises exceeding 110 decibels produce hearing loss if endured for one-half hour or less. Sources of such noise include speakers in cacophonous night clubs (110 db), inboard motor boats (110 db), jet planes (120 db), gasoline-powered lawn mowers (130 db), rock concerts (140 db), and rocket launches (180 db). (If you use this list to get out of mowing the lawn, don't follow up by asking for tickets to a rock concert!)

Rapid Thought

Do you find yourself taking "mental vacations" while a professor demonstrates a tedious calculus problem, a friend stretches out a story, or a meeting drones on and on? We actually think faster than people talk, and so we tend to go off on mental tangents. People talk at about 120 to 180 words per minute, and our brains process at approximately 400 to 800 words per minute. This lapse is called the speech-thought-time differential (STTD). Years ago, researchers found that if they cut and spliced taped material to shorten it by two and a half times, listeners comprehended it better (Goldstein, 1940; Garvey, 1949; Miller & Licklider, 1950). The result makes sense when you consider that many college students read at about 300 words per minute. The extra time due to STTD tempts us to go on mental tangents.

Contextual Barriers

All communication occurs in a context, and all contexts have communication noise—that is, something that interferes with communication. Three contexts in particular—location, culture, and gender—shape the listening experience.

Location

Interference in the environment weakens listening capabilities (Hagedorn, 2001). Physical noise is specific to the immediate environment, or location, of the communication. Interviewers, for instance, like to control an interview setting so that the interviewee will not be distracted.

Location helps frame the communication. For instance, chewing out a coach from the stadium seat is very different from walking into the locker room in front of the team to state your complaints. (Not that you would do either!) Also, critical comments have added impact when the location is such that someone is humiliated or embarrassed because of *where* you chose to criticize.

Culture

Cultural presumptions shade meanings, especially in regard to how directly a message is stated, the appropriateness of interactions (who may speak to whom, when, where, and about what), and whether groups (collectivism) or individuals are more highly valued.

Cultural vocabulary mismatches cause communication errors: In one type (let us label it type A), communicators use different languages that have some similar words; in the other (type B), a person does not understand technical, professional, or some other type of jargon used by the other communicator, as in these examples.

- An informational technology project designer tells a client that she will "attach a firewall to the back office functions." Her client responds, "I thought you were designing computer software for off-site sales. You need to talk to the Manager of Physical Resources about the fire code for our building."
- A marketing representative for a U.S. luggage firm launches the company's new line of luggage, NOVA, at an annual international trade market. After

an enthusiastic reception at the national trade market, the representative is surprised at the resistance, even derision, among Spanish-speaking buyers. A sympathetic soul, seeing his confusion, explains that "No va" means "no go" in Spanish, hardly a good statement for travelers.

Gender

Men and women listen differently. Women are more likely to use listening to build relationships, and men are more likely to listen to get information. Deborah Tannen (1986) says women and men listen so differently that it is as if they were speaking different languages. If the communicators are either two men or two women, they are more likely to anticipate how the other will interpret the message. When men communicate with women, the women are more likely to position themselves as the listeners and the men are more likely to be lecturers and to take on the roles of expert and authority. Women do more nodding and "uh-huh's" to indicate they are listening than do men. Men are more likely to interrupt for dominance, but women are more likely to interrupt to "join" the speaker. Women use listening to further their primary goals of building rapport and establishing closer relationships. Men especially value listening to gain information to solve problems.

GENDER STYLES

George, LaShonda, Lewis, and Marianna chat during a conference lunch break. They had all previously worked together in purchasing; however, under a new CEO, Lewis and Marianna moved to marketing. The next day George and LaShonda rehash the conversation.

ACTIVITY 4.3

George: Lewis said they are really busy in marketing. Remember how he used to complain about being bored over here?

LaShonda: Yeah, but he surely doesn't like his job in marketing.

George: He's bound to. He's making more money than he did in purchasing.

LaShonda: From the sound of his voice, he's unhappy with his new boss. He seems worried about his job.

George: He didn't say that. When I asked him how things were going, he said his workload was about the same, although Marianna was putting in more hours than he is. George travels two days a week, but sometimes, Marianna is out three days.

LaShonda: Of *course* Marianna's doing everything she can to please the boss. She's kissing up for a promotion.

George: Lewis said it was a dead-end job.

LaShonda: Not for Marianna. She thinks some changes are about to be made. Of course, she didn't want to move at first. She almost quit, you know.

George: I think you're jumping to conclusions.

LaShonda: Don't get snappy with me. I know what I heard.

1. *What kind of messages did LaShonda report?*
2. *What kinds of messages did Lewis report?*
3. *Who was right? Who was wrong?*

Psychological Barriers

Probably the most difficult barriers to overcome are the ones inside our heads—
the psychological ones, where we trip all over ourselves listening!

Difficult Relationship

Senders' and receivers' perceptions of each other color their messages. For
example, a difficult relationship may create an impenetrable barrier to genuine communication. Similarly, some work connections are tainted by history
at or outside work.

Preoccupation

Anxiety, boredom, and higher priorities motivate us to mentally stray from
a speaker's message. Perhaps our own plans, dreams, and concerns interest
us far more than the Senate Republicans' economic position, the United
Way campaign, or historic dates. A different kind of preoccupation develops when we multitask, such as searching for a document while talking on
the phone.

Intimidation

Shyness causes many people to be inattentive, especially when the person feels
conspicuous. Being in the presence of a boss or being "star struck" warps reception. At times, an experience or difficult content overwhelms a listener, and an
adrenaline rush adds a physiological hindrance to a psychological one. Even
those not easily overwhelmed occasionally miss a person's name in an introduction, because of a moment of self-consciousness.

Egocentrism

Egocentric individuals think, "It's all about me." They regret wasting time on
other people's ideas. Their own ideas are all that commands their attention.
Their attitude can be labeled, "I'm OK; too bad about you." They process every
topic by how it affects them.

Prejudices and Biases

Prejudices serve as filters to sort messages according to likes and dislikes. The
"friend or foe" filter is an example of an influential filter. For instance, if we
identify a coworker as competing for our job, we may suspect his or her messages are manipulative.

Faulty Assumptions

Assumptions are conclusions we have drawn, often prematurely. Although
some assumptions are necessary, we must keep in mind we have made a logical leap into the unknown.

Defensiveness

Defensive statements defend self-esteem or turf. We ward off wounding messages, but, in doing so, we miss many beneficial ones. Defensive listeners hear just enough to know what they want to attack. We most often tune out (1) people we don't like, (2) people who are likely to criticize us, (3) long-winded conversationalists with little substance, and (4) overbearing people.

Irresponsibility

Another roadblock takes place when we place the responsibility on others to hold our attention, teach us what we need to know, and tell us what to think. When we do not take responsibility for listening in a dialogue, by default we turn it into the other person's monologue.

• LISTENING SKILLS AND STRATEGIES

Having discussed different listening goals and studied listening obstacles, we are ready to employ solutions, including techniques to improve listening skills. Fortunately, and unbelievably to some, listening is a teachable, learnable skill. Improvement is possible, and it can be done in classes or in a current job situation. Although *hearing* can be mindless, *listening* must be *mind-full*—mentally alert and focused. When two persons connect in shared understanding, it is close to magic, as if for a moment two persons were of one mind.

Use Academic Settings to Build Listening Strength

Like training for athletic competition, listening training takes commitment, dedication, and endurance. Ironically, some of the most effective behaviors are common sense, and yet they require the most effort. Use the following practices to become an "Olympic listener."

- Let the other person talk.
- Ignore distractions.
- Seek the speaker's picture.
- Take time to listen.
- Empathize with the speaker.
- Note what you learn.

Get Active

Be physically prepared to actively listen—rested, nourished, and alert. For that "ears flapping forward" feeling, pretend that there will be a pop quiz at the end of class. Don't let words flow through your ears and out through pens without registering the message in memory. Instead of waiting to become interested, listen immediately and expect interesting ideas. That is, *quit other tasks, quickly attend,* and quietly listen.

Be Accurate

Since the average person listens with only a 25% listening efficiency, do not expect a perfect, "photographic" record of everything you hear. Examine mental pictures to improve listening accuracy.

• • • • TIPS   • • • • Picture-Puzzle Listening • • • •

1. Picture in your mind what the speaker describes.

2. Examine your picture for what the speaker actually said versus which parts you "filled in." For instance, if someone said, "Linda was late for the dinner party, and the next thing we knew, she was on her way to the hospital," are you *assuming* that the scene took place at night, at a restaurant, and Linda got sick?

3. Stay attentive to gather additional information—more pieces of your picture puzzle.

4. Reflect your understanding back to the speaker: "So you think it was something Linda ate that made her sick?"

5. Ask questions to add puzzle pieces to the picture. The sequence of events (where each puzzle piece belongs) is important. Don't take the speaker off track. You heard the speaker say that the trip to the hospital was *after* Linda arrived for dinner. Relevant questions include, "What did Linda eat? Had the food been on the table long by the time she arrived?" On the other hand, if you failed to pay attention when the speaker told you that Linda was nine months pregnant, your irrelevant questions reveal your poor listening.

6. Allow silence, so that the speaker can recall what he or she wants to say. Sometimes silence allows the speaker to express deeper concerns.

• • •

Stay in for the "Burn"

A strength training program incrementally adds number of repetitions and amount of weight lifted. Similarly, listening training increases the length of time and the difficulty of the material. A reasonable goal is to listen intensely for five minutes four times during an hour and commit to memory two things each time. Jot notes. For the in-between times, use your usual listening and note-taking style. As you conquer this level, increase the time and difficulty of material. This is not as easy as you may first think, so meet realistic goals before moving to the next level.

One of the biggest challenges is to listen to difficult material. If chemistry is your most difficult college course, adopt a productive attitude for listening. If, as a professional, listening to technologically sophisticated concepts throws you, start there. New, difficult material is not understood all at once. Pick up what you can and let your mind play with the other ideas you are hearing. When you study later, the words and ideas will be more familiar. Start by learning definitions and listening for tips on doing your work.

Use Notes to Remember

Stay focused by taking notes and use them to help you recall what you heard, reviewing them within 24 hours to improve retention. Review difficult, conceptual material several times to "layer in" understanding. Build vocabu-lary generally and specifically for the subject. Read background material or assignments. Work with the ideas ahead of time. Structure with outlines or maps. Listen for previews, overviews, and summaries. Discover what is impor-tant by listening for key words and noting nonverbal emphasis as given by the speaker.

Listen with Learning Styles

All people do not learn in the same way. Some learn best by listening to sounds, others by seeing material, and still others through movement and touch.

• • • • Language Hints at Learning Styles • • • •

Audio

Listeners receive words from speakers. Students who are competent with lan-guage and who prefer hearing descriptions and instructions are *audio learners.* After hearing instructions about serving a tennis ball, they "hear" it in their minds as they follow the steps. These learners are more likely to say things such as "I hear you," "His words pierced through me," "I like the sound of your idea," and "That's music to my ears." In recalling how to work a problem, in their heads, they hear the professor explaining it in class. Signpost language, transitions, previews, and summaries are especially important to audio listeners.

Visual

Most people are *visual learners.* They "listen with their eyes." Nonverbal com-munication is largely their domain. Visual learners benefit from diagrams, charts, illustrations, and demonstrations. Visual learners want the tennis teacher to show them what to do—just talking about it doesn't help. When they try to remember class information, they try to "see" the answer in the textbook or on a visual. Phrases that indicate visual learners are, "I see what you mean," "Let's look for an answer," "I can see an end in sight," and "What a bright idea!" Mapped notes, sketches, and mental imagery assist visual listeners.

Kinesthetic/Tactile

"Learning by doing" describes *kinesthetic/tactile learners.* They prefer hands-on activities and tactile learning activities. They learn best if they can do some-thing. They "let their fingers do the walking." As tennis players, they "don't know how until they do it." They want to get their hands on the racket and try hitting a few balls, so the instructions will make sense. The kinesthetic/tactile learner would say, "I can reach the end of the book by tomorrow," "Let's get the feel of this procedure," and "Time to roll up our sleeves and work; let's get a move on it." Kinesthetic/tactile learners need to move and use touch to learn. Having a textbook open along with notes helps. They should buy notebooks and pens that feel right to them. Hard candy or gum can even help them "eat up" and "digest" the material they learn.

• • •

Attitudes Shape Listening Experiences

Skilled listeners develop mind-sets that include openness, empathy, objectiv-ity, and adeptness at picking up all levels of the message. Listening is a bal-ancing act, contingent upon the speaker, the topic, and the listener's personal

Analyze this photograph of a guided tour. Who is communicating openness nonverbally? Who is being attentive and who is not? What are various signs of involvement you see? How do the situations affect the interactions?

involvement. For instance, in deciding whether to listen nonjudgmentally or critically, giving the speaker a fair hearing is appropriate more often than not; even so, some individuals have abused the listener's ears repeatedly, and disconnecting may be the listener's tool for survival. Other times a speaker filters out destructive comments, but continues to listen for what the speaker plans to do or to find flaws in the speaker's arguments.

Open

Openness is a willingness to listen to another individual for understanding, since it neither attacks, judges, nor defends. Openness has much in common with nonjudgmental listening and empathy. Two key aspects of openness are intellectual hospitality and willingness to listen to what the other person has to say. A person with "intellectual hospitality," in the words of John Dewey (1944), shows an "active disposition to welcome points of view hitherto alien" (p. 175). Open listeners recognize the difference between words and what the words represent and can separate their own ideas from the other person's ideas.

A second dimension of openness is "the willingness to listen to the other without communicating judgments or prejudices one has that could discourage the other from expressing his meaning or conveying his experience. This is not acceptance of the other's values or behavior but only the communicated assurance that one will make a fair attempt to understand the other without interfering judgments, blame, or the expression of prejudices that might inhibit the other's account" (Beatty, 1999, p. 9).

Empathic

Empathy begins with listening, as we seek to match another person's experience with our own past experiences in order to understand his or her reaction to a situation more fully. "We need to hear at a deeper level than just the words and context. Do we hear the fears, concerns, and beliefs? When we listen at this level, we start to receive new information and understanding; and people feel acknowledged and empowered by us to solve the situation on their own" (Cashman, 2000, p. 9).

Empathic listening is evident when the responder paraphrases the speaker's emotions, and it is also evident when the responses show a lack of defensiveness and self-serving behaviors.

PROJECT MANAGERS' EMPATHIC LISTENING

Empathic listening is the highest form of listening. We seek to understand. We genuinely try to appreciate the speaker's frame of reference. Even if we don't agree with their analysis and conclusions, we withhold our judgment, we value their contribution, and we respect their work. We abandon defensiveness and if necessary, admit that we may have missed something in our own analysis.

Empathic listening is occurring when we hear phrases such as "I think you're onto something with this revised application architecture" or "I misunderstood the influence of the data model on the poor application performance we've been experiencing." As project managers, we're expected to lead and coach others. Through the example of our listening behavior, we can reduce miscommunication and build confidence, morale and channel the creativity of the team toward effective problem solving. When we listen empathetically and attentively, everyone will be happier. (Schulz, 2001, pp. 2–3)

Objective

It's hard to be involved and, at the same time, remain *objective,* but often a listener's objectivity is exactly what the speaker wants. In a book or movie, do you imagine and feel a character's troubles as if you were that character (as the empathic listener would) or can you be the objective observer, getting the fuller story from "off-stage"? Objective listeners never become characters. They observe characters and their interactions.

> Objectivity means listening for the facts and also weighing in the human emotional and relational elements, on imaginary balanced scales. Interpersonal communication brings data to the observer in the form of the nonverbal communication of the speaker. This direct contact allows you to observe all the nuances of a person's body, language, tone of voice, and expressions. It gives you the maximum opportunity to be a good listener. Additionally, it gives the other person all the same benefits. (Rohlander, 2000, p. 22)

Adept at Discerning Message Levels

Messages are made up of layers of content messages and relational messages. There are also emotional, political, or intellectual messages and messages about messages (metamessages). "Let's go someplace private to talk about this" probably indicates substantial and important content. It also means that not everyone is included in this message, and the listener is somehow privileged. In the workplace, you often find a practical agenda and, right beneath the surface, a political agenda.

Listen Ethically

Effective and ethical listening is both a skill and a philosophy for making communication decisions, as the next three subsections show.

Sound judgments require objective listening.

Defense and Offense

Communication is not like a game with one side on defense and the other on offense. In some instances, listeners simultaneously defend against attacks and gather weapons. Other times, communicators feel safe, without need to defend or offend. Good managers learn to maintain some caution as they listen, but avoid paranoia about every message.

In a courtroom, communicators *expect* defensive and offensive listening. They listen for errors and vulnerabilities in opposing arguments and use them to their advantage. Similarly, businesses with competing products listen differently than businesses that cooperate toward a common goal.

"Listening to attack" inside the company stirs resentment and hostile competition. Observe, for instance, the defensive and offensive listening styles of employees competing for a promotion. Even salespeople on commission working the same area assume a defensive stance unless they understand mutual benefits.

Confidentiality and Alignments

Behind closed doors and over cups of coffee, secrets are told, as individuals align with one another. "Who says what to whom" defines who is aligned with whom. Unfortunately, people frequently "prove" their closeness with others by telling their secrets. If the first party discovers a third party has been told the secret, two possible reactions follow: Either the first party feels betrayed or welcomes the third party into the alignment. Meanwhile, the second party has overstepped boundaries by sharing the confidence. (Of course, sometimes that first person *expects* the confidence to be shared and implies as much.) The *grapevine* is the informal communication network that exists in every organization. It has rabid listeners and rapid deployment. News dispersed as confidences spreads rapidly as persons reinforce their alignments with one another.

Exploitation

Malicious self-serving *exploiters* use confidences to their advantage. They position themselves to minimize vulnerability, while launching their own attacks. They try to undermine others' successes and to promote their own causes.

These win–lose thinkers assert, "You have to step on a lot of people to climb the corporate ladder." Ethical listeners know that ethical listening helps both parties win.

• RESPONDING TO HELP OTHERS

When a person tells you a problem, what do you do? With the other person expecting a response, you have choices to make. An effective choice makes the difference between helping to solve a problem and blocking understanding. First, of course, you will carefully listen to the problem. Listeners who jump to conclusions about the problem assume superiority, fail to get necessary information, and waste communication time. A question to think about while listening is, "Who *owns* the problem?" Sometimes the problem belongs only to the speaker. Other times the situation presents problems for both the speaker and the listener.

Considering the person's problem and responding to it are two separate behaviors. Thought should precede response, but not every thought has to be expressed. Some of these thoughts skillfully translate into responses; others should remain unspoken. When listening to help, (1) hear the content, (2) examine the motives and intentions, (3) learn the facts and feelings, and (4) provide a helpful and appropriate response.

Advising

The responses most habitually given to a problem holder are advising and judging. Sometimes they work, but often they are disastrous. Here's why: To advise is to attempt to direct the behavior of another individual.

Imagine you are to pick up Jake and Veronica to go to a meeting. You have a new car, your pride and joy. (As long as we are imagining, what car would you like? A sporty yellow BMW?) You pick up your first rider, Jake, who sits in the front seat. The two of you, chatting, breeze along a busy street to get Veronica. You are almost to her street (which *you* know is blocked by construction on this end) when passenger Jake grabs the steering wheel and yanks it to turn onto Veronica's street. After all, he didn't want you to miss your turn. Probably, that's the last time Jake rides in *your* front seat. It is not his car, he wasn't driving, he endangered both of you, and you had already made a decision based on information you didn't think was necessary to share.

Jake's behavior is analogous to giving advice. The advisor takes over another person's problem and decides the direction in which to take it. On the other hand, if Jake had seen a toddler step off the curb and his action saved the child's life, you would have felt gratitude instead of being angry. Advice is best

- When the other person wants the advice
- When the listener is in a role that requires qualified advice or guidance
- When time is short and the problem is critical
- When the advisee is not capable of self-advising

Our motivations are usually good, but people prefer their own solutions. They usually don't want our advice; they just want us to listen.

Judging

Judging, or evaluative, responses often go hand-in-hand with advising responses. They, too, assume a position of superiority: "I'll be the judge of what is best to do, and I'll tell you what to do." Whether positive or negative, the gavel is raised, ready to sentence the victim. Judging responses include praise, compliments, constructive criticism, negative evaluations, and derogatory comments. Judging comments range from "That sounds good" and "Let's rethink that" to "Where did you get a stupid idea like that?" Even a head nod or frown can be a judgmental response.

On the other hand, the role of a coach requires constructive criticism and advice. If you pay a golf professional for lessons, you expect some correction and suggestions. Judging responses are helpful

- When the other person expects or seeks evaluation
- When you have the expertise to make evaluations
- When the other person is not capable of making informed evaluations

Others often ask whether we think they did the right thing, but beneath it all, they may resent the power of our coveted approval. (Observe adults who are hypersensitive to their parents' comments.)

● ● ● ● **Common Costs of Advising and Judging** ● ● ● ●

- Others develop dependency on our judgments and advice.
- Others fail to learn to solve their own problems.
- Others fail to develop skills in evaluating their own work and behaviors.
- Others blame us if the advice is wrong and resent us if the advice proves correct.
- Others do not build confidence in their own abilities.
- Others avoid us.

● ● ●

Advising and evaluating responses require skillfulness.

- Be sure others really want advice. When they say, "What would you do?" respond with "I don't know; what do you think is best?" or "You know more about this situation than I do." Often their questions are simply "turn taking" in conversations.
- Be sure you are the best one to give the advice or make the evaluation. One lost job does not mean you are the expert on what everyone should do when losing a job.
- Offer the response tentatively—"I'm not sure whether this will work."
- Reinforce the relationship, no matter the outcome—"Let me know what you decide. I'll be pulling for you."

Linking

Linking responses help the person with a problem gain perspective on the problem through sound analytical thinking. Alert to various patterns in the problem owner's narrative, the listener responds by dissecting a problem, offering alternative points of view, uncovering deeper meanings, or suggesting causes. A person usually reveals a problem layer by layer rather than telling it sequenced and intact. (Two exceptions: when the person has told the story repeatedly to others or with internal dialogue and when a speaker wants the listener's extended attention and uses the problem to detain the listener.)

Linking responses come only after extended listening. They are very helpful when communicators are truly thinking together, but these responses are harmful:

- When the listener takes control and assumes superiority
- When inaccurate causation is assigned
- When the listener analyzes inaccurately and sends the speaker on a senseless tangent

Skillful linking responses

- Present suggestions, not declarations, of the parts or causes of the problem
- Allow corrections of inaccurate or incomplete analyses
- Leave the speaker in control of the direction of the conversation
- Leave the speaker in control of solving the analyzed problem

Questioning

Skillful questions seek information about the problem. They are motivated by the need for understanding, not by self-serving curiosity or a desire to gossip. Genuine questions seek answers nonjudgmentally: "When did this happen?" "How often does this happen?" "Who else was there?" "What information is available to you?" Other questions add dimensions to the conversation: "How does this make you feel?" "What are your options?" As a responder, don't control the conversation or let questioning take on the form of interrogation. By the way, saying, "I was only asking because I care" does not soften the emotional effect of "grilling the suspect."

Skillful questioning takes advantage of the listening model studied earlier. As you receive, interpret, and evaluate, identify missing or confusing information, ask questions to seek clarity, and repeat the process of receiving, interpreting, and evaluating the answers.

Reflecting

With reflective responses, listeners reflect (mirror) speakers' messages back. The concept is simple: Which would you rather do—get ready in the morning with or without a mirror? The listener becomes the speaker's "mirror," providing the problem owner with a clearer look at the problem. *Reflecting* is also called *paraphrasing* or *echoing,* because listeners put into their own words what speakers seem to communicate. At first, communicators worry this response style isn't helpful. Just the opposite is true. Reflecting lets speakers know they are heard and understood as listeners focus on them and their messages. A number of risks listed for other responses dissolve in the face of these nonjudgmental, nondirective responses.

Carl Rogers (1961/1995, pp. 243–245; 1980/1995, pp. 7–8), the father of active listening responses as advocated in his client-centered approach, recognized problem ownership, valued listening as a therapeutic approach, and concluded that the speaker, who knew more about the problem than he could, inherently possessed the resources to solve the problem. Thomas Gordon popularized "Active Listening" first for parents and later for leaders and in the workplace. Dr. Gordon added the question, "Who's got the problem?" When the other person has the problem, he suggests using a combination of questioning, paraphrasing content, and reflecting an understanding of emotions and inner thoughts. He emphasizes that Active Listening requires time, patience, and withholding judgment. As a responder in the workplace and in other relationships, evaluate whether you are in a position to use reflective responses.

- Do you have adequate time to listen?
- Can you withhold judgment or advice in this situation and in your role?
- Is the problem sufficiently complex to require the investment in Active Listening?

Dimensions to consider for reflecting to speakers include the message content, emotion or attitude, and relationship.

Reflecting the Message Content

Probably the safest response is to objectively reflect content: "So you took the job at Raytheon"—the speaker now knows that you heard the basic message. Sometimes the reflection is more involved: "You took the higher paying job at Raytheon, even though the type of work is less challenging than what you do now." At the most complex end of the reflective continuum are the linking responses discussed earlier, such as, "The higher pay offsets the lack of challenge in your opinion, and you see the opportunity to develop some of your own ideas with the extra time." To avoid having the problem holder assume you agree, add messages such as, "This is what is happening with you. What you think about the situation is more important than what I think about it."

Reflecting the Message of Emotion

All messages have an emotional dimension that drives the conversation, the experience of the problem, and the decision outcomes. Reflective listeners let speakers "see" their emotional faces. Responders select words that identify the types and intensities of emotions, and because people often act out their feelings without verbalizing them, responders may supply words. Problem holders should recognize from the tone of the response that they are encouraged to correct any reflected messages. For instance, if a listener responds, "Sounds like you are furious about the change in management," the speaker can correct, "Well, maybe not furious, but I am irritated because my opinion was ignored." "I understand" is an *inadequate* response. When listeners do not want to commit to feeling as the speaker feels, they should say something like, "I am not in your situation and don't know how I would feel, but I can see how you would be anxious."

Nonverbal communication reflects a speaker's message as the listener mirrors to some degree the speaker's facial expression and posture. Lean forward, watch the speaker's face, and anticipate via facial expressions the upcoming message. This "anticipatory set" communicates receptivity. Reflecting emotions is a skill used with empathy.

Attitudes may blend with emotions, but sometimes a predominant "positive attitude" frames a current, upset emotion: "You've been leery about the new CEO for some time," or "This isn't like you to be so disheartened."

Reflecting the Implied Relationship

Metamessages communicate about the relationship in which the primary message occurs. Discussions align communicators with one another and define their relationship. For example, Brad likes discussing problems that he's confronting in developing a spreadsheet with Peggy, because they value one another's expertise. As Peggy listens, she responds with a message about the relationship, "We always enjoy tossing these ideas around. I hope it helps you as much as it helps me."

• • • • RESPOND • • • •   • • • • TIPS

- **R**eflect the content.
- **E**cho emotions and attitudes.
- **S**how interest nonverbally and relationally.
- **P**rovide precise and accurate reflections.
- **O**ffer objectivity.
- **N**ever change from the speaker's topic.
- **D**ecide which questions to ask.

• • •

• FEEDBACK IN AN OPEN SYSTEM

A classroom environment simulates working in open systems (where feedback is available from inside and outside the organization). Here you can gain experience in giving and responding to feedback.

At Work

Organizations are systems that rely on feedback in order to adapt to what is *really* going on with people in the organization.

CONTEMPORARY VOICES 4.1: MUSHROOM MANAGEMENT

Until our information system accounts for people as well as things, we will operate our organizations in the dark. Of course, some people don't mind the dark, especially those who are into "mushroom management," the primary ethic being "Keep people in the dark, pile lots of manure on them, and when they are fully ripe, cut off their heads and can them."

Covey prefers a plea for openness and honesty: "From the cowardice that is afraid of new truth, from the laziness that is content with half-truth, from the arrogance that thinks it has all truth, O God of Truth deliver us" (Covey, 1992, p. 225).

Confirmation and Disconfirmation

To *confirm* someone is to recognize the person's presence and to cause that person to feel worthy. Confirmation hears and values a speaker's message. *Disconfirmation* is just the opposite, where the speaker's message is not acknowledged and valued. Confirmation is shown with eye contact, nodding, and verbal responses. Disconfirmation comes as put-downs, cold shoulders, or wandering eyes. People actually prefer rejection over disconfirmation. Naturally, it is easier to listen to messages confirming us and our actions than to listen to messages that cause us to doubt our worth and value.

Criticism

Feedback at work often comes in the form of positive or negative criticism. Listening to criticism is an extremely difficult task. A natural response is defensiveness; after all, a little defensiveness is a good thing. You don't want to take in all criticism as absolute truth. Too much defensiveness, however, precludes learning from other people's views and expertise. Skillful responses to criticism exemplify the power of listening, as you "train" your critics and are able to get helpful criticism when you need it. There are four basic skills to this:

1. Listen to the criticism.
2. Reflect, or paraphrase, the most important parts of the message, content, emotion, attitude, and/or relationship.
3. Seek clarification.
4. State your plan.

In the preceding steps, notice how the listener directs the conversation and confirms the critic through attentive listening and paraphrasing, before controlling the remainder of the communication by seeking clarification and presenting an action plan. The listener shifts from potential victim to assertive, secure leader.

ACTIVITY 4.4

TAKING CRITICISM

EXAMPLE OF OLD SCRIPT

Supervisor:	The store window display you designed looks too sparse.
Marion:	What do you mean by *that*? You're just not used to edgy displays.
Supervisor:	Why do you get so defensive when I say something? If we don't sell clothes, you don't have a job.
Marion:	Fine. Now you're threatening me with my job.
Supervisor:	I'm just saying we have a job to do. So fix the display.

EXAMPLE OF NEW SCRIPT

Supervisor: The store window display you designed looks too sparse.

Marion: You are disappointed in the display, because, as you say, it is sparse. Do you object to how few clothes are in the display or the wire models I've used?

Supervisor: The models catch attention against the silver background, but we need to attract mall shoppers with more of our new lines of clothing.

Marion: O.K. The models stay, and I'll add other combinations of outfits behind them against the silver, like shadows, but in different colors. What do you think?

Supervisor: Good thinking! Let's see how it works.

1. *What are pivotal points in each script?*
2. *Who took control in each script?*
3. *Who listened, and what did they "hear"?*

With Audiences

As a less experienced speaker, you may be anxious about the kind of feedback you'll get; later, however, you will be anxious to get the feedback that will help you adjust to an audience's needs. "Listening to audiences" requires a speaker to interpret nonverbal communication while delivering a speech. Thus, a monologue becomes a dialogue as audience and speaker interact. Connect with individuals with eye contact, a responsive laugh, or a question during the speech to get their reactions. The longer the speech and the smaller the audience, the more verbal interaction may be effective.

Applause or follow-up discussions are immediate, positive feedback. Seldom will people stay around to insult your speech, and some will compliment your presentation. Expect communication professors and coaches to give you objective feedback. They are trained to generalize the reactions of various audiences, to diagnose the strengths and weaknesses of speakers, and to use feedback for the improvement of speakers. Keep your balance as you listen, though, and know that the coach cannot know every audience member's possible reaction. Realize that your communication experiences are important and that you benefit from objective feedback.

SUMMARY

Learning organizations require good listeners. Executives rank listening as the skill most lacking by their employees. Listening means making sense of what we hear and then remembering it. Listening can be modeled with a helix, in a continuum of receiving, interpreting, evaluating, and responding.

Physiological, contextual, and psychological blocks interfere with accurate listening. Listening must be *mind-full* to direct mental alertness toward the speaker and the message. Effective listening is active, requires physical readiness, and is precise. Listening training increases the length of time and the difficulty of the material.

Skilled listeners usually give feedback to speakers that indicates attitudes of openness, empathy, and adeptness at picking up all levels of the message. Listener responses include advising, judging, linking, questioning, and reflecting. Advising and judging are habitual and risky response choices. Questions allow the speaker to fill in gaps for understanding. Reflective responses paraphrase content, emotion, attitude, or a relational message of the other person.

Responses in the form of feedback may confirm or disconfirm the speaker. When feedback comes in the form of criticism, the recipient is challenged to be nondefensive. Feedback is valued at work and in public communication. •

ACTIVITIES

1. **Journaling the Experience:** Listen for at least five examples from the following list and write in your journal how you discriminated between or among the different types of messages. Label the various kinds of messages according to content, emotion, attitude, and relational focus.

   a. A message the professor said to the class and a message the professor said to you

   b. Emphasis of facts that will be on the exam and facts used to keep you interested in the lesson

   c. Instructions you are to follow immediately, instructions you are to follow after class, and instructions you are to use in your career

   d. A humorous remark and a serious remark

   e. A hypothetical example and a real example

   f. Disgust and teasing

   g. An important name to remember and a name used in citing a source

   h. Sarcasm and cynicism

   i. Separate items on a list spoken, but not written, in class

   j. When the professor leaves one point and moves to the next point

   k. When to take notes and when to stop writing and listen carefully

2. **Presenting to Others and Team Work:** In small groups, distribute six index cards and a pair of scissors to each member. Each member makes one cut (through one of multiple cards) and hands them to the person on his or her right. Privately, each person arranges his or her cards and makes visual or verbal notes about their arrangement. Each speaker uses his or her notes and describes the arrangement, as group members attempt to sketch it from the description.

3. **Ethically Listening:** Which prejudices other than gender, race, and ethnicity are filters that block you from listening to individuals? In a small group, discuss one prejudice per participant that distorts listening and how to remedy the distortion. How do the prejudices disconfirm the other communicator?

   a. Size

   b. Foul language

   c. Lack of education

   d. Bad grammar

   e. Regional dialect

    f. Getting physically too close

    g. Aggressive personality

    h. Rudeness

    i. Laziness

    j. Bad breath, body odor, or strong perfume

    k. Inappropriate or peculiar clothing or appearance

    l. Loud voice

    m. "Attention sluts"

4. **Ethically Speaking:** Identify prejudices, biases, and faulty assumptions you recognize in the following statements. Discuss your answers in a small group.

    a. "I've taken geology. Whatever this rock hound says won't be new to me."

    b. "Of course you get criticized at work. I never see you stay late."

    c. "Why should I listen to a biology instructor correct my grammar?"

    d. "I know the solution for this project and don't want to hear why we can't do it."

    e. "She's not too bright. She stutters."

    f. "I'm not going to have some techno-nerd coach me in baseball."

    g. "I worried when I hired him that he'd be a complainer. He's the middle child, you know."

    h. "With his poor grammar, he obviously can't contribute worthwhile ideas to the project."

    i. "He's too young to be any help to me."

    j. "No woman's going to tell me what to do."

5. **Technical Support:** Access the History Channel's speech archives to hear audio of historic speeches. Select a speech and listen for main points in the speech. Listen again, this time for emotive language, appeals to the audience, and deliberate pauses. List the main points and record other observations in a one-page paper. The archives are located at www.historychannel.com/cgi-bin/frameit.cgi?p=http%3A//www.historychannel.com/gspeech/speeches/archive.html.

FOR FURTHER READING

Buckman, R. (1997). *What you really need to know about cancer: A guide to patients and their families.* Baltimore: The Johns Hopkins University Press.

Burley-Allen, M. (1995). *Listening: The forgotten skill* (2nd ed.). New York: John Wiley & Sons.

An excellent site for problem solving involving ethical considerations is http://onlineethics.org. In particular, study the listening component of communication in the case study at http://onlineethics.org/reseth/appe/vol3/hazmat.html.

Test your fraud detection expertise at www.cfenet.com/membership/prepdemo/ to understand how biases affect listening and other observations.

Although we continually send and receive nonverbal messages, most of us are not fully aware of the ways that we communicate nonverbally. Still, if you watch carefully, you will see that most leading professionals (e.g., doctors, lawyers, politicians, corporate chief executive officers, and contract negotiators) are excellent nonverbal communicators. Some people call it charisma. Others call it style. Whatever it is, they have it! (Department of Defense, 2000)

Nonverbal Communication

5

An Overview of Nonverbal Communication

Cultural Influences on Nonverbal Communication

Nonverbal Communication for Presentations

Nonverbal Communication at the Conference Table

From the first moments of an interview to the intensity of boardroom negotiations, nonverbal communication does most of the talking. "Seven seconds is all that people need to start making up their minds about you," warns Roger Ailes, chairman and CEO of Fox News and coauthor of *You Are the Message* (Dahle, 1998). You may not speak in those first seven seconds, but you definitely make impressions by your nonverbal communication. For instance, in getting jobs, 75% of those who make a favorable impression in their first five minutes of an interview get hired, as compared with only 10% otherwise (Blakeman et al., 1971, p. 57). Organizations as diverse as the Marriott Hotel Corporation (Sundaram & Webster, 2000, p. 378) and the Environmental Protection Agency (McCaslin, 2000, p. A6) train employees in nonverbal communication skills. Nonverbal miscommunications are costly, so skills become critical. Further complicating matters, nonverbal symbols and signals vary by culture, and many negotiations and sales cross cultural lines.

This chapter examines the principles and major types of nonverbal communication, specific cultural issues with respect to nonverbal communication, and workplace applications of nonverbal communication.

OBJECTIVES

After studying the content of this chapter, you should be able to

- Define nonverbal communication and its characteristics
- Discuss major areas of study regarding nonverbal communications
- Follow guidelines for interpreting nonverbal signals
- Use nonverbal communication competently in the workplace
- Recognize, respect, and respond to cultural differences

 AN OVERVIEW OF NONVERBAL COMMUNICATION

Nonverbal communication is the study of all forms of communication other than that provided by language alone. Anything other than words alone that symbolizes and signals meaning is a part of this area of study. To say nonverbal communication is "communicating without words" is somewhat misleading, because even vocal inflection and tone of voice add dimensions of meaning to words.

The sayings "Actions speak louder than words" and "What you are speaks so loudly that I can't hear what you are saying" attest to the importance of nonverbal messages. In fact, when nonverbal messages contradict spoken ones, usually the nonverbally coded messages are the ones believed.

Characteristics of Nonverbal Communication

People often misinterpret behaviors and make assumptions about the cultural and personal values they portray, thereby ignoring fundamental characteristics of nonverbal communication.

Nonverbal Communication Is Inevitable and Constant

A basic communication axiom is, "You cannot *not* communicate." You can stop talking, but you cannot stop behaving. People breathe, smile, frown, sit, walk, stand, fidget, gesture, and blink. All behavior signals some sort of meaning, intentionally or unintentionally. Most of the signals are nonverbal, analogous to a radio station broadcasting night and day whether anyone is tuned in or not.

Nonverbal Communication Is Learned Behavior

As children, we learn how to communicate nonverbally much as we learn to use language (Palmer & Simmons, 1995, cited in Sundaram & Webster, 2000). Once learned, we incorporate it, both consciously and unconsciously, into our everyday communication behaviors (Burgoon, 1991). Most people believe that the nonverbal message is the truth and is due to the "nature" of the sender.

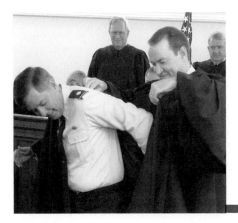

What is the setting in this scene? What are the official roles of these men, according to their nonverbal signals? Check your interpretations against the information that accompanies the photograph, as follows. Col. James Van Orsdol (right) helps Lt. Col. Lindsey Graham don a judge's robe in a courtroom, after Graham was sworn in as a new judge for the Air Force Court of Criminal Appeals. Graham, an Air Force reservist, is a U.S. senator from South Carolina in civilian life. Van Orsdol is a former chief judge for the court.

Nonverbal Communication Is Powerful

How much of the message in face-to-face communication is sent with words (verbally) and how much is sent through other channels? Unquestioningly, nonverbal messages overwhelm most verbal messages. You can't expect an audience to believe a speaker saying, "I'm really happy to be here" if the speaker's voice and face show boredom. Researchers say that nonverbal signals carry 2 to 13 times the information of verbal cues (Archer & Akert, 1977; Argyle, Alkema, & Gilmour, 1971, cited in Swenson & Casmir, 1998).

Ironically, the most often quoted percentages showing the importance of nonverbal communication distort the research done by Mehrabian and Ferris (1967) and Mehrabian and Wiener (1967). Leading textbooks stated, for example, "Mehrabian indicates that 93 percent of meaning in a conversation is conveyed nonverbally—38 percent through the use of voice and 55 percent through the face" (Dodd, 1995, p. 153 in Lapakko, 1997) and "Words, [Mehrabian] says, contribute 7 percent, vocal elements 38 percent, and facial expressions 55 percent (Ehninger, Gronbeck, McKerrow, & Monroe, 1986, p. 277 in Lapakko, 1997). Many people concluded from such statements that the total message is only 7% verbal, with the remaining 93% nonverbal. Actually, the formula was derived from two small, limited-sample studies (Mehrabian & Ferris, 1967; Mehrabian & Wiener, 1967), and neither study involved all three channels (verbal, vocal, and facial). Mehrabian himself says:

> My findings are often misquoted. Please remember that all my findings on inconsistent or redundant communications dealt with communications of feelings and attitudes. This is the realm within which they are applicable. Clearly, it is absurd to imply or suggest that the verbal portion of all communication constitutes only 7% of the message. Suppose I want to tell you that the eraser you are looking for is in the second right-hand drawer of my desk in my third floor office. How could anyone contend that the verbal part of this message is only 7% of the message? (Mehrabian, quoted in Lapakko, 1997, p. 65)

Nonverbal Communication Is Ambiguous

If somebody winks at you, is the person teasing, flirting, or blinking away dust? Could this be sexual harassment or a signal that you are included in the deal? Any single nonverbal behavior can have multiple meanings, and a single meaning can be encoded with various nonverbal behaviors. Communication researcher Judee Burgoon (Burgoon & Le, 1999, pp. 105–124) thinks that within a culture we have limited and usually ambiguous meanings for each nonverbal cue, similar to language. A researched compilation of nonverbal behaviors from the perspective of limited meanings is available through the Discovery Channel or Discovery Magazine website, or at www.discover.com/web_pick/index.html.

Nonverbal Communication Is a Part of the Whole Communication

Nonverbal communication is multichanneled, and receivers interpret a meaningful and simultaneous composite of nonverbal cues, including eye movement, gestures, vocal inflection, and body posturing. "No nonverbal cue is an 'island.' It is continually surrounded by a host of nonverbal behaviors which together may delimit and clarify meaning" (Burgoon & Le, 1999, p. 107). For instance, when doctors pay attention to words *and* to body language, patients feel more involved in their own treatments and doctors notice subtle symptoms that enable them to catch other problems (Prose, 2000). Nonverbal communication and verbal communication interact in several ways to complete a message.

- Nonverbal communication *substitutes* for verbal communication, as in the "A-OK" signal, a wave good-bye, or a kick under the table.
- Other times, nonverbal communication *emphasizes* the message, for example, with increased vocal volume or a clenched fist.
- Nonverbal communication *reveals the attitude of the speaker,* perhaps through a frown when talking about an upcoming meeting.
- *Incongruous messages* are those in which the nonverbal and verbal messages contradict one another. For instance, you say, "I am so excited to be here," but you are frowning and sound bored.
- Nonverbal communication also *complements,* or completes, verbal messages, as in smiling and signaling a person to sit down while saying, "I am interested in your project."

Categories for the Study of Nonverbal Communication

Nonverbal communication spans the spectrum from gestures to aromas and from a sense of time to a sense of space. We can simplify this expansive study with a few categories.

Kinesics

Kinesics, popularly called "body language," is the study of physical communication, whether by movement or physical appearance. Among kinesics' areas, the study of body orientation and gestures holds particular importance to us. *Body orientation* refers to what degree interactants face one another. We create psychological distance by turning away from the other person, either by angling the entire body, by turning the shoulders, or by averting the eyes (a compensation phenomenon). The forward body lean and open body posture are considered warm, courteous, and nondominant. Just the opposite—a backward body lean and closed posture—conveys dominance, unfriendliness, and emotional distance (e.g., Burgoon, Birk, & Pfau, 1990; Mehrabian & Williams, 1969, cited in Sundaram & Webster, 2000, p. 381). Knowing this, we can "read" whether someone is ready to move on or avoid us, and we can better understand the signals others may pick up from us. Imagine how confusing it is to a client when a consultant says, "Tell me more" and, at the same time, leans back and crosses his or her arms.

Gestures are the hand and arm movements that create, amplify, or emphasize a message. Gestures become essential when they substitute for words. Actually, emphasis gestures seem to help the speaker more than the listener. Certain gestures (such as snapping the fingers in the air) help speakers retrieve words from memory (Bond, 1999).

Eckman (1992) offers several useful categories for the study of body movements:

- *Emblems* can be readily translated into words. Common emblems in the United States are the "A-OK" sign, "sshhh" for quiet, and saluting a superior. Emblems are specific to a time and culture and are deliberate (Ekman, 1992, p. 102). Where we have to be careful is in automatically using an emblem common to our own culture that might be insulting in another culture.

- *Illustrators* do just as the name implies: They illustrate, point out characteristics, and usually accompany language. For instance, we point to give directions, indicate size, or outline a shape in the air. Illustrators increase with involvement and excitement about a topic and decrease with low interest or not knowing anything to say. If someone is giving a presentation for the first time or is weighing each word carefully, he or she will probably use fewer illustrators (Ekman, 1992, pp. 106–107).

- *Affect displays* exhibit emotions. *Affect* (with an "a") refers to an emotional state, as in "affective state." Your face is your emotional showcase.

- *Regulators* are the things we do to control the flow of conversation. Regulators include head nods, gestures, and leaning forward to show interest and to keep others talking, as well as looking away, interrupting, and holding up a hand to stop other speakers.

- *Adaptors* are small pieces—remnants—of a larger behavior, often dealing with a physical discomfort. Adaptors include the things we do in part in public that we would do to full satisfaction if no one were looking. For instance, an itchy nose gets only a brief bit of pressure if someone is watching. Other adaptors are an up and down movement of a finger to the side of one's face rather than the larger behavior of nodding "yes" and a back-and-forth stroke to the chin instead of shaking the head "no." Adaptors give meaning to phrases such as "itching to leave" and "fidgety and impatient."

Haptics: Touch Communication

"Stay in touch." "Reach out and touch someone." "I'm deeply touched." The communication of touch (*haptics*) is the strongest and most primitive of all communication. Research shows that touch facilitates compliance and favorable social behavior from strangers in the U.S. (Remland & Jones, 1994). For instance, a light touch on the upper arm caused people to be more likely to sign a petition (Smith, Gier, & Willis, 1982) and, in another study, to sample (and more likely buy) a new food product in a supermarket (Hornik, 1987; Hornik & Ellis, 1988). The tendency to comply held true even for people who generally disliked intrusive behavior (Buller, 1987).

As we become skillful with language, words substitute for touch in sending many messages. At these times, a compliment replaces a hug; a word of encouragement replaces a held hand, or criticism replaces physical restraint. As touch and words combine, the message becomes strong and believable.

Touch, however, can also send damaging messages, which devalue another person. In the workplace, when is it appropriate to touch and when is it not? The amount and type of touch varies appropriately, according to culture (Hall, 1966; Shuter, 1977), situation, relationships and roles of the interactants, gender, and age. An important distinction comes from *why* one person touches another. Touching another person to tend to that person's needs is quite different from touch to fulfill one's own needs. Incidental touch as a part of focusing on a task gives an additional criterion to consider. In health care facilities, patients are touched by lab technicians, nurses, and doctors. Clearly, these should be task-related touches to take care of patients' needs, while caretakers explain about what is happening or divert a patient's thoughts during a procedure. Accompanying messages should never be sarcastic, sexual, or in any way inappropriate.

Touch can communicate either respect or disdain in the workplace. Professor Stanley Jones (1994) surveyed hundreds of workers over a 10-year span to reveal the touches that most often threaten or offend. Of the 10 categories, the three most serious ones are as follows:

- *The coercive sexual proposition* implies that job-related rewards or punishments are tied to the proposition.
- *The "humorous" sexual advance* occurs with touch to an intimate body part, presented as a joke and sometimes accompanied by a verbal proposition.
- *The physically aggressive touch,* considered by employees as an extreme violation, includes pokes, punches, or pushes and may be reinforced with verbal messages.

Other relevant categories that offend employees include overly friendly touches that are confusing, touches that subtly pressure a person to fulfill a task need, demeaning touches (pats on the head or caretaking touches), and touches that interfere with or interrupt tasks (Del Valle, 1998).

Considering how often touch is inappropriate or misinterpreted, the formalized, socially accepted handshake takes on increased importance. The handshake gives us a nonthreatening way to approach an individual with a cultural symbol of friendliness, and a firm handshake makes the best impression overall (Chaplin, Phillips, Brown, Clanton, & Stein, 2000). Research subjects with firm handshakes were found to be "more extraverted and open to experience and less neurotic and shy" and were rated somewhat higher on characteristics that included conscientiousness, agreeableness, emotional stability, openness, emotional expression, and "outgoingness" (Chaplin et al., 2000, p. 114). Although other assertive behaviors backfire for women, earning them negative first impressions (Butler & Geis, 1990; Eagly, Makhijani, & Klonsky, 1992), women who used firm handshakes were seen more positively than those who offered a typical feminine handshake (Chaplin et al., 2000).

• • • •**Handshakes** • • • •   • • • • **TIPS**

Because business negotiations in America usually begin and end with a handshake, here are some hints for getting it right.

- With a firm grip, focus on conveying confidence, sincerity, and power. Too tight a grasp may hurt the other person, signal a power play, or intimidate the other person.
- A loose grip or shaking only the fingertips comes across as uncommitted, weak, and perhaps insulting.
- Use caution with surgeons' and pianists' hands and with people who have arthritis or otherwise painful hands.
- One or two limited up-and-down movements emphasize purposeful communication, so do not yank or force the other person's movement. (You are not playing the slot machines.)
- Smile and otherwise support the handshake with a warm tone of voice.
- Shaking hands after a business negotiation signals closure, seals agreement, and promotes a sustained positive relationship. Failing to offer your hand may insult the other party and may signal a "disconnect" to the relationship.
- Reinforce the handshake with a congruous message of positive words in a warm tone of voice.

                                                                                                        • • •

Facial Communication

The most important zone to read for emotions is the face. Swenson and Casmir (1998) say, "Specifically, humans look to the faces of others to help them interpret feelings and to tailor interpersonal interactions more effectively." And we look from a considerable distance, when it is important. We can pick up a smile from the length of a football field, some 300 feet. Amazingly, the face's 44 muscles can contort into 5,000 expressions, so several expressions may occur within a single second (Blum, 1998).

Emotions are crucial to forming relationships (Ekman & Friesen, 1975). We feel better about our relationships and are less likely to be depressed if we are able to identify the emotions of others (Carton, Kessler, & Pape, 1999), and people can best judge whether they are getting along with each other if they can *see* each other (Grahe & Frank, 1999). Specifically, humans look to the faces of others to help them interpret feelings and to tailor interpersonal interactions more effectively (Goode, Schrof, & Burke, 1991; Swenson & Casmir, 1998).

• • • • TIPS   • • • • Deception Detection • • • •

Many people are intrigued by the idea of telling when someone is lying, but most people aren't very good at detecting deception. Although tone of voice and body stance give us better cues about deception than do faces, a phony smile and lots of blinking betray some liars (Ekman, 1992). Skillful liars, however, use their smiles to further deceive.

• • •

If you are the boss, your employees study your face for mood and meaning (especially when verbal communication is limited). The face is the center of most communication about how likable and how credible we are, and it sets the tone for competence. We also know how to look confused in order to get a further explanation, and we signal disgust if the topic repulses us.

Circling the globe, the signal of friendliness and approval is a smile. Our social smiles say, "Excuse me" and "I'm harmless and friendly." Most of us know our social smiles, but only about 3% of us know our joyful smiles, which are recognizable by heightened eyebrows and upturned lips (Kare, 1998). A relaxed facial expression and direct eye contact communicate several types of power, including leadership, expertise, and credibility (Aguinis, Simonsen, & Pierce, 1998). You may have noticed, too, that mouths draw back in fear and push forward with anger. And, of course, a lowered brow and somber mouth indicate dominance and status (Henley, 1977; Henley & LaFrance, 1984; Leffler, Gillespie, & Conaty, 1982, all cited in Aguinis et al., 1998).

Oculesics: Eye Communication

Perhaps the most significant category for sending and receiving nonverbal messages is *oculesics,* the study of eye behavior communication (Richmond & McCroskey, 1995). For one thing, we generally like people more if they use eye contact. Normally, people look at each other while talking and periodically break a gaze that seldom lasts more than six seconds (Kare, 1998). We communicate dominance with eye contact, particularly with the whites of the eyes. Lower power status individuals look more when listening than when speaking. Higher power status individuals look more when speaking than when listening.

> Eye contact is a major source of nonverbal communication, signaling social information about intimacy and dominance. In any hierarchical system (e.g., a hierarchy of class or power), people with less power tend to engage in less eye contact with their communication partners than do those with more power (Exline, 1972). People in competitive situations often increase eye contact (Exline, 1972), even glaring at one another. Indeed, because dilation of the pupils indicates emotional arousal, business people in some cultures wear dark glasses during negotiations in order to hide their pupils. (Sternberg, 1995, p. 520)

Reality @ WORK 5.1

EMPLOYEES READ SUPERIORS' HABITUAL SIGNALS

Kathleen Kelley Reardon attended a meeting at the invitation of the CEO of a fast-growing entrepreneurial venture. He had expressed concern about communication in his organization. In *The Secret Handshake: Mastering the Politics of the Business Inner Circle,* Reardon reports her observations:

> While observing I noticed how he let a direct report know that her work had not met his standards. He visually canvassed the room, pausing to look momentarily at each person. Each one except her, that is. This continued for the entire meeting. When she did speak up, he abruptly moved on to another topic as if she hadn't said anything at all. I later learned that since he often did this kind of thing to people with whom he was displeased, it was a message she had learned to read. Rather than say, "Your profits are down and you need to get your division back on track," he simply looked past the offending person, making her, in his eyes, "nonexistent." Others at the table got the message—"I'm not pleased with her so don't you talk to her either." And they didn't. (Reardon, 2001, pp. 86–87)

Paralanguage: Vocal Characteristics

A tone of voice can make all the difference. Most of us during our careers face distraught people.

Reality @ WORK 5.2

A VOICE TO QUIET THE STORM

Bill Gates's eyes bulged behind askew, oversized glasses. Words spew from his flushed face. "He's in a small, crowded conference room at the Microsoft campus with 20 young Microsofties gathered around an oblong table. . . . Most look at their chairman with outright fear, if they look at him at all." Miserable programmers stumble and stutter, unable to calm Gates's stormy mood. Then "a small, soft-spoken Chinese-American woman, who seems to be the only person in the room who is unfazed by his tantrum," looks at him squarely. She interrupts him in quiet tones. Her words temporarily calm him. She interrupts a second time, and "he listens in silence, thoughtfully gazing down at the table." The storm lifts, "Okay—this looks good. Go ahead," and he ends the meeting (Moody 1996).

> What the woman said was not much different from what the others had been saying. But her unflappability may well have allowed her to say it better, to think clearly rather than being swamped by anxiety. Her manner was certainly part of her message sending the signal that the tirade did not intimidate her, that she could take it without becoming unhinged, that there was no real reason to be so agitated. (Goleman, 1998, pp. 82–83)

The way you say the message carries much of its meaning. *Paralanguage* is the study of vocal characteristics in communication. Paralanguage combines rate of speech, volume, inflection, emphasis, articulation, tone of voice, hesitancies, dialect, and vocalized pauses (e.g., "uh," "you know," "hmmm"). It is from a person's voice that we interpret warmth and patience, confidence and self-esteem, competence and intelligence, and health and energy. Although brief pauses usually enhance perceptions of credibility and trustworthiness

The enthusiasm shared between these communicators echoes from their voices, gestures, body postures, and facial expressions, thus creating a synchronous message.

(Scherer, 1982), overall fluent speech that is free of long pauses, hesitations, and repetitions communicates higher credibility than nonfluent speech (Erickson, Lind, Johnson, & O'Barr, 1978).

The Communication of Personal Distance and Use of Space

Anthropologist Edward Hall introduced the term *proxemics* (Hall, 1966), referring to people's use of the space around them. We consider the space immediately around us as an extension of self. Let's begin with how Hall measured and labeled the use of cultural distances (proxemics), and then consider more specifically how people claim space and the things that occupy that space (territoriality).

Proxemics presents four measured distances embedded in U.S. cultural interactions.

- *Intimate distance* is the distance starting with touch and extending to 18 inches. Intimate distance—a spatial extension of "self"—is close enough to sense details (individual hairs, color of eyes, body temperature, odor) about the other person. The person's face fills the field of vision.

- *Personal distance* immediately follows intimate distance, extending from 18 inches to 4 feet. The boundary allows us to keep others at arm's length. The near phase of personal distance is from 18 inches to approximately 30 inches. This is the distance for private discussions with close friends. In friendship settings, three or four people form a comfortable group, because the addition of people expands the space beyond 30 inches. The nature of the communication or task further influences how close employees get to each other after their initial greetings. "Closing in" on someone too closely for routine business makes the other person feel trapped. By the way, police intentionally use this discomfort when they "intrude well inside the personal zone when questioning suspects" (Suplee, 1999, p. 3).

- *Social distance,* measuring from 4 to 12 feet, is descriptive of most employee interactions. (Think of social distance as "business distance" or the "consultative zone," instead of thinking of social as a party.) At 8 feet, a midpoint of social distance, we acknowledge the presence of the other person. If you notice the distance between the doors and desks in an office environment, probably the greater the distance, the higher the person's likely power in the organization. Quite often, the distance from the door to the desk is 8 to 12 feet.

- *Public distance* begins at about 12 feet and extends to 25 feet. Beyond that, communication requires adaptation, such as a microphone, and details of facial expression are lost. Public officials and celebrities generally speak at 25 to 30 feet.

Territoriality looks at how people claim and use space. Hall argues that people, like animals, have rings around themselves and react as others enter those outlined spaces. People use several kinds of markers to delimit their territory. *Boundary markers,* such as fences and office walls, enclose territory. Modern cubicles have movable walls, and an employee's physical space literally and symbolically can change to make room for new employees or new equipment.[1] *Central markers* say what belongs to you, as when corporations put their logos on hats and t-shirts. An employee's pictures in an office indicate that the space belongs to that employee.

SPACE MARKERS

ACTIVITY 5.1

Study a work environment to see how people create or claim space for themselves.

1. *Do they mark their study areas by scattering personal belongings?*
2. *If two people working on independent projects are seated at the same table, how are they seated in relation to one another?*
3. *Is anyone able to claim an area and leave it temporarily, without anyone taking the space?*

Office layout reflects the workplace culture. Informational technology alters workplaces, and as the roles of the employees change, so does the arrangement of the space. The tangle of computer wires is becoming invisible in new office space design. Designers also use universal cabling systems, demountable partitions, raised flooring, and modular furniture to create an environment responsive to changes at work (Davis, 1996). Wireless technology dominates many environments.

THE HIERARCHY OF TERRITORY

ACTIVITY 5.2

Observe territoriality in action in the workplace. Study the size and arrangement of office space in two work environments. Which uses of territory signal authority at each place of work?

---

[1]   The initial idea of cubicles was that because workers have different space configuration requirements, the movable walls would accommodate those needs. Cubicles came to be a cost-cutting feature, however, designed to fit as much as possible into as small a space as possible for as little cost as possible.

What does the layout of this office cubicle communicate?

Appearance

The first things many people learn about you are based on what they see, so you do not want to invalidate your well-earned credibility by looking incredibly incompetent. "Clothing often serves as the criterion used by people to form a first impression" (Lehman & Lehman, 1989). Looking the part does not guarantee success, but the wrong impression can certainly get in the way, and grooming is an important part of a person's appearance (Mack & Rainey, 1990). Consider the consequences of appearance during an interview:

> At least as early as the mid 1970s, research (e.g., Dipboye, Fromkin, & Wiback, 1975; Dipboye, Arvey & Terpstra, 1977) established a relationship between judgments of attractiveness and favorable interviewer ratings. Research by Cash and associates (e.g., Cash et al., 1977; Cash & Kilcullen, 1985) also affirmed the positive correlation between ratings of attractiveness and favorable ratings of applicant personality traits. . . . Gilmore et al. (1986) also found that attractive candidates were likely to be judged as having a more appropriate personality for the job, would be expected to perform better, and would be more likely to be hired. And incidentally, once hired, physical attractiveness may also have modest influence on promotion consideration. (Morrow, McElroy, Stamper, & Wilson, 1990) (Ilkka, 1995)

Chronemics: The Communication of Time

Chronemics is the study of the communication of time. We hear references to this field in common phrases such as "Time marches on," "Time flies when you're having fun," "She wouldn't even give me the time of day," "Just a second," and "These are trying times." In the United States, we view time as a precious resource to be spent wisely and not wasted. Therefore, if we spend time on something, we are emphasizing its importance. We communicate values about relationships, jobs, hobbies, interests, and ideas by the time we spend on them. If you are late for a meeting, the others present get the message that it's not an important activity to you. Time communicates—how we use it, how prompt we are, and even how much time we tolerate silence.

CONTEMPORARY VOICES 5.1: THE RESOURCE OF TIME

Senge wonders whether complaining about not having enough time, incessant movement, and "busyness" are due to our notion that a manager's job is to "keep things moving" (Senge, 1994, pp. 302–303). He says that learning takes time, and it takes time to think through new approaches to organizations. "The management of time and attention is an area where top management has a significant influence, not by edict but by example" (Senge, 1994, p. 304).

Time communication is specific to a culture, so far as what is considered late and what is considered early or on time. How much time should you schedule for an appointment? What is the appropriate amount of time for small talk before getting down to business?

USING TIME IN OTHER CULTURES

ACTIVITY 5.3

Study the material on doing business in Mexico on the Executive Planet website under "Appointment Alert!" at http://executiveplanet.com/business-culture-in/132435536243.html and doing business in Hong Kong at http://executiveplanet.com/business-culture-in/132433772647.html

Research four other countries, one in Europe, one in Asia, one in Africa, and one in South America.

1. *Write a one-page paper contrasting the use of time in Mexico with the use of time in Hong Kong.*

2. *Use your research to support or deny the following statement: Being disrespectfully late varies by culture.*

The messages of movement, time, tone of voice, and use of space are strong, but the meanings are relatively ambiguous. We can look up the meanings of some gestures, customs in making and keeping appointments, and what is seen as intrusion in various cultures, but most of the nonverbal communication we observe daily must be interpreted quickly in the complexities of the context. Building skills in interpretation is time well spent. It is second nature for some people, yet all of us benefit from considering several guidelines.

Guidelines for Interpreting Nonverbal Communication

Because nonverbal communication is inevitable, ambiguous, and powerful, some guidelines to assist us in interpreting it are in order.

*   *Observe nonverbal communication mindfully.* Pay attention to your behavior and the behavior of others. Study research conclusions to determine whether your interpretations are what most people infer from a behavior.

*   *Treat interpretations as hypotheses.* You may be quite good at interpreting, but that does not change the fact that interpretations are inferences and assumptions.

- *Suspend judgment.* Actively seek additional information to substantiate your interpretation. Rather than jumping to conclusions, ask questions, engage in further discussion, and consider contexts and cultures.

Civil inattention is an example of the ambiguity of nonverbal communication. Civil inattention is when people politely look the other way or pretend not to notice an embarrassing event. Just because your professor did not wake you during class does not mean she didn't notice. In your career, the behavior that is seemingly overlooked could have costly consequences. One diligent (and overworked) government official was passed over for a high-level national appointment, primarily because he frequently yawned at meetings.

The matter of civil inattention can be tricky, because if you confront a person's sarcastic tone of voice, angry expression, or shifting glance, the individual may explain it away, but even the nonverbal insult that is not confronted has consequences.

 ## CULTURAL INFLUENCES ON NONVERBAL COMMUNICATION

The United States Army is heavily vested in communicating across cultures. When preparing a team for an operation in another country, Lieutenant Colonel James K. Bruton (USAR), a Special Forces officer, challenges them as follows:

> Your host-nation counterpart invites you to his home for dinner. Would you know upon arrival whether you should bow, shake hands, bring a gift, take off your shoes, greet his wife, ignore his wife, or what? During dinner what subjects would you discuss? What should you avoid talking about? How long should you stay? How would you tell when it is time to leave? (Bruton, 1994, p. 28)

Some of the greatest workplace challenges arise from responding to diverse cultures. Organizations assemble employees from opposite sides of the globe, and even when everyone speaks English, not everyone uses the same nonverbal language. Furthermore, organizations conduct business internationally, and language is only part of the communication challenge. Although you may think it unlikely that you will work in all the countries we use as examples, you won't necessarily need to go abroad to use these insights. People from around the globe will come to you, in person or via technology.

Culture is made up of the human-created part of the world (Segall, Dasen, Berry, & Poortinga, 1990) and is a "relatively organized system of shared meanings" (Smith & Bond, 1994). The culture we grow up in becomes a filter for how we interpret others, which in turn affects how we behave toward others: "Our values often reflect the beliefs of our cultural background. From childhood we develop a value system that represents a combination of cultural influences, personal discoveries, and family scripts. These become the 'glasses' though which we look at the world. We evaluate, assign priorities, judge, and behave based on how we see life through these glasses" (Covey, 1992, p. 20).

Contact and Noncontact Cultures

Researchers continue to use and explore the work and hypotheses of Edward Hall (Hall, 1966; Hall & Veccia, 1990). In one area of study, he contrasted "noncontact cultures" with "contact cultures," labeling *contact cultures* as those with closer-distanced interactions, more frequent touch, and more direct body orientation (turning toward one another). Examples of contact cultures are Arabs, Latin Americans, and southern Europeans; examples of noncontact cultures are Asians, North Americans, and northern Europeans.

High- and Low-Context Cultures

High-context cultures rely heavily on nonverbal signs in the environment, and they assign meaning to such things as offices, assigned or chosen seats at conference tables, deference to others, responsive facial expressions, and formality—all of which should be observed in person and in context. Businesspeople in high-context cultures feel as if they are working in the dark unless several channels of communication are open, so a memo or phone conversation feels grossly inadequate to them. Even video conferencing controls how much information comes from other communicators, and high-context people may be frustrated with the "lack of information."

Low-context cultures, on the other hand, do not assume familiarity and state everything explicitly. They have not interacted long enough or frequently enough to recognize subtleties of facial expressions or meanings in the environment. A written contract, for instance, is important to low-context cultures, and interpersonal agreements are not finalized until they are in writing.

In Japan, a high-context culture, distance conferencing encountered strong resistance. Isao "Kami" Kamitani, senior vice president and general manager in the Denver office of Sumitomo Corporation of America, explains: "In the Japanese sense, just paying a courtesy call is an important part of protocol. My generation was educated to visit a customer and talk face to face on almost any issue" ("Westminster Firm," 1997). Travel expenses became burdensome, however. "Face-to-face meetings are preferable, and traditionally, face-to-face communication has been believed to be very important for business. But with time and cost constraints they aren't always practical," agrees Nobuharu Ono, vice president in the Nippon Telegraph and Telephone Corporation ("Westminster Firm," 1997).

Displaying Emotions

Facial expressions that communicate emotions are largely shared across cultures, but questions remain about the universality of emotional facial expressions and the accuracy of their interpretations by others. Research in New Guinea, Brazil, Chile, Argentina, Japan, and the United States shows people to be highly accurate in recognizing the meaning of facial expressions, yielding some interesting conclusions.

- Apparently some emotions are "universal": enjoyment, sadness, anger, disgust, surprise, and fear (Ekman, Sorenson, & Friesen, 1969).
- Joy and surprise are consistently recognized, but interest and shame are the least often identified (Izard, 1979).
- Sadness is more identifiable in collectivist cultures (Matsumoto, 1989). In a comparison of Japanese and Americans regarding emotion recognition,

Americans were better at identifying anger, disgust, fear, and sadness. Both nationalities recognized happiness and surprise. Matsumoto concluded that the Japanese have difficulty identifying negative emotions because expressing such emotions is socially less desirable in Japan than in the United States (Smith & Bond, 1994, p. 61).

- Friesen (1972, cited in Smith & Bond, 1994), in an unpublished but often discussed study, compared Japanese and American students' reactions as they watched a short film about body mutilation and again as they watched an emotionally neutral film. At first Japanese and American students alike showed disgust while they watched the film, but when a "scientist" in a white coat (an apparent authority figure) was present, the Japanese displayed a slightly *smiling* expression.

Emotions translate similarly across cultures, but social appropriateness varies. The ways, timing, and interactions of emotional expression vary greatly from culture to culture. What is appropriate in one country may appear uncouth in another.

Time and Culture

How late is "late" for a meeting? How early is "early" for dinner? North Americans have about a 10-minute tolerance, but in some South American countries it is excusable if you show up 4 hours late. Some cultures tolerate uncertainty better than others. *Uncertainty avoidance cultures* characteristically require more structure and plan accordingly (Levine & Bartlett, 1984). In a comparison of time management in seven countries, a strong correlation became apparent among three test variables: how accurate public clocks were, how fast people walked down the street, and how quickly a post office clerk completed the sale of a small-denomination postage stamp. You may not be surprised to hear that the United States and Japan had speedier delivery, a faster walk, and more accurate public clocks. As a globally astute communicator, you should match the pace of the ones whom you want to feel comfortable around you.

Kinesics and Culture

In a Japanese organization, if a person sits quietly, the others assume that the person is thinking, and they will not interrupt. If the person stands and moves about, others will interact more freely. Exactly the opposite is the norm in the United States. When someone is sitting quietly, then Americans interject their comments and questions (Senge, 1994, p. 302).

In an example similar to that provided in Contemporary Voices 5.3, an American, not taught to understand the Japanese negotiation style, was guilty of "cultural chauvinism" (the belief that one's own cultural way is the only way). The Japanese manager smiled and studied the multimillion-dollar business proposal. "Give me five minutes," he said. His American counterpart smiled back and waited. A few seconds later, the American's mouth twitched, and he fidgeted some more. A whopping 18 seconds later, the American interrupted the silence, bringing a startled look to the Japanese businessman, who assumed he was entitled to have more time to think to himself and wondered skeptically about the rudely impatient American (Iwata, 1995).

Spatial Communication and Culture

When working in another country, visitors risk making a negative impression unless they adapt their use of spatial distances. As a specific example, in one program (Smith & Bond, 1994, p. 102), some Englishmen were trained to stand closer to Arabs, make more eye contact, touch more, and smile more. When trainees were compared with an untrained group, Arabs liked the trainees more.

Other research looks at where people live and how they use space and touch. If you are moving south (toward the equator), plan to get closer, literally, with close acquaintances. The closer two friends' country was to the equator, the closer they were likely to sit. Also, those who sat close together rated their friendships as closer and were more likely to touch one another (Watson & Graves, 1966; Watson, 1970; both cited in Smith & Bond, 1994, p. 101).

OFFENSIVE INTERPRETATIONS

Reality @ WORK 5.3

Kevin and Amar meet to discuss an electrical transmission grid that Sullivan Utilities Corporations plans for a rural project in Saudi Arabia. Kevin showers and puts on a fresh shirt, then meets Amar in the lobby, where they discuss a place for lunch. When Kevin is about 8 feet from Amar, he says, "Hello, you must be Amar." At about 4 feet away, Kevin extends a hand. Amar steps a mere foot away from Kevin and closes the handshake to embrace Kevin's arm. With a broad smile, Amar loudly greets Kevin, staring the entire time into Kevin's eyes. Kevin, self-conscious to be so close, turns his head, lest he offend Amar with his "stale-coffee" breath. He cannot ignore the aromas of Amar's breath and body and is embarrassed that Amar is talking so loudly. Meanwhile, Amar is insulted that Kevin "denies him his breath" and wonders why Kevin "so coldly" backs away from him.

Numerous websites and travel guides discuss customs and communication to help prepare people for business in another country. Following are some introductory suggestions for business etiquette across cultures:

- Address elders, senior staff, and family first when entering a room.

- Err on the side of being too formal, rather than too informal. Develop relationships slowly.

- Pronounce names correctly as a sign of respect and an act of courtesy. Many international clients and employees prefer to be addressed by their last or formal name.

- Learn the cultural use of time and the practice of punctuality. Northern Europeans, Americans, and Japanese are the most punctual, whereas southern Europeans, Hispanics, Middle Easterners, and Filipinos are more relaxed about time. Exceptions include Saudis and Iranians, who are punctual in business dealings.

- Notice the distance persons stand from one another. The usual 4 to 8 feet used by North Americans to discuss business is too distant for some Hispanic and Middle Eastern cultures, and to back away is considered an insult.

- Recognize the importance of "saving face" in many Eastern and Middle Eastern cultures.
- Extend offers of food, drink, gifts, or privileges repeatedly; politeness requires two refusals in some cultures.
- If several people are riding in a car together, remember that the back seat is the place of honor to the Japanese.
- Notice whether others are crossing their legs, nodding approval, praising others publicly, and performing other particular behaviors in the culture.
- Saudis, Hispanics, Greeks, and Germans shake hands repeatedly. In France, it is inappropriate to shake hands with a superior. Some cultures use a gentle handshake; others use a firm or enthusiastic handshake.
- Note proper dress and greetings.
- Observe and follow the lead of others in the use of eye contact. The length of mutual gaze between British businesspeople in London (to indicate sincerity and involvement in the conversation) seems stiff and awkward to Americans. A Hispanic youth is taught to look down in the presence of someone in authority, and many Americans expect truth tellers to look them in the eyes.

 ## NONVERBAL COMMUNICATION FOR PRESENTATIONS

Your vocal and physical presence carries a large portion of your message to an audience. You want them to positively anticipate and focus on what you have to say. Let's explore the nonverbal dimensions of your presentations.

Vocal Delivery

A Harley-Davidson motorcycle and a BMW have distinctive sounds that are patented because of the high quality they signal. Have you ever walked into an office and paid attention to the employees' sounds? You can tell a great deal about the quality of the communication climate by the sounds of their voices. As a speaker, too, you project a quality of sound. Indeed, "listeners are able to accurately judge emotions from speech at rates far greater than expected by chance" (Bachorowski, 1999). Since "speech is an acoustically rich signal that provides considerable personal information about talkers" (Bachorowski, 1999), you should sound trustworthy, confident, well informed, involved in your topic, and caring of others. Here are several suggestions:

- Speak loudly enough for others to hear. Otherwise, you are asking your listeners to work harder, or you are indicating that you do not care about them. Become aware of how lively the sound is in the room. A slight feedback of your own voice helps you know that you are reaching your listeners.
- Articulate clearly. Speakers seldom speak at too fast a rate to be understood. Americans usually speak between 120 and 130 words per minute.

Articulating clearly, Martin Luther King's "I Have a Dream" speech began at a rate of 92 words per minute and ended at 145 (Lucas, 1995, p. 272). Usually, the problem is that inexperienced speakers slur over words, omitting sounds and chopping off ends of words. Practice completing the sounds in each word, articulating as if your audience had to read your lips. After all, more people than you may think read lips to supplement their hearing. Don't be stingy and sloppy in enunciating.

- Consider what your dialect and pronunciation communicate to the audience. Former President John F. Kennedy's voice was immediately recognizable, in part for his New England accent and Bostonian pronunciation. Lyndon Johnson had his Texas accent, and Jimmy Carter his southern drawl. Some regionalisms are colorful and interesting, but many are read as uneducated or uncouth.

- Use the quality of your voice to your advantage. Find the lively, rich, excited, formal, and comfortable tones in your voice. Play down whining, whispery, and nasal tones.

- Use an interesting and helpful mix of inflection and volume to emphasize ideas and hold audience interest.

When you speak English for listeners for whom English is not their first language, remember to slow down and be patient.

Guidelines

- Pronounce words correctly and enunciate clearly. Use adequate, but not exaggerated, volume.
- Summarize key points.
- Gestures are helpful only when they mean the same thing in the listener's culture.
- Use well-constructed, short sentences.
- Use visuals whenever possible, such as graphs and charts (Millet, 2004).

Avoid

- Either/or questions
- Idioms or colloquialisms, slang, jargon
- Negative questions and contractions

Physical Delivery

We are a population who grew up with televisions, and, more than ever, what we see shapes the messages we get. Walking to the front of the room or into a conference room introduces you to an audience. (Imagine hearing that a speaker "stomped," "strolled," or "ambled" into the room or to the podium!) Even your posture conveys your attitude. Movement during a speech can have a positive effect on the audience. Following are some guidelines for moving during a speech:

- Enter and exit with confidence. When it is your turn to speak, walk confidently, but not stiffly, to the speaker's stand, showing an eagerness to share your ideas. After your speech, maintain a posture of confidence as you leave the podium.

- Remember your entire audience. Turn toward different areas of the audience. Use eye contact, varying at whom you look.

- Survey your "stage backdrop" ahead of time. *Whatever* is behind you becomes the background scenery for the audience. One speaker at a Christmas banquet was clueless to what every audience member saw with amusement—his balding head was visually encircled with a holiday wreath. Another speaker, assigned to a classroom in which science was usually taught, spoke reverently about our forefathers as he stood between a dangling skeleton and a diagram of the reproductive system.

- In a conference room, you may need to move someone else's poster or erase a dry board. If there are distractions visible through a window, you may choose to stand in a different part of the room.

- Some speakers seem small and unimportant behind a huge, technically equipped podium. Consider using a remote microphone so you can move out front or using a platform in order to be more visible.

- Give the audience visual "shifts." In order to separate main points, consider moving to the left, right, or even in front of the speaker's stand. The visual shifts will help the audience recall the ideas as separate points later.

- Videotape yourself. You will quickly correct ineffective nonverbals such as pacing, distracting mannerisms, and shifting weight from one foot to the other. One student watched his video and was surprised to see himself support his elbows on the podium as he climbed up and down the stand's center support.

Comedians get easy laughs from awkward gestures, but great speakers take advantage of well-timed gestures. Beginning speakers sometimes complain of not knowing what to do with their hands. If you concentrate on communicating with your listeners and use experience to gain confidence, then natural, normal gestures will follow. Tightly clenched fists or hanging onto the podium for dear life betray a lack of confidence. Hands shoved into pockets limit spontaneity. Arms folded across the chest indicate defensiveness. So what are we to do with these appendages dangling from our shoulders? And is it all right to "talk with our hands"? Following are some hints on effective gesturing:

- Make gestures purposeful and helpful. Do not overdo gesturing. Avoid pointing at someone while making a negative point. Do not keep your hand in front of your mouth.

- Be physically ready to move when inspiration hits. Have your hands in a position where they can move without dropping notes, pulling loose change out of your pocket, or knocking over a speaker's stand.

- Gesture above the waist, so you keep attention toward your face.

- Let ideas drive gestures. When the mind works, the body naturally moves. Usually the gesture occurs with or slightly before key words in a speech.

- Gestures should be larger for large audiences. The exception is if the speech is televised, since television tends to exaggerate movement.

Eye Contact

The term "eye *contact*" is a little odd, but the metaphor is appropriate. The speaker must get "in touch" with the audience in order to communicate with them. Public speakers connect with individuals in the audience through eye contact to accommodate closing the distance between speaker and listener. Speakers in the United States who resist establishing eye contact create negative impressions for themselves. They are sometimes seen as insincere or dishonest and are almost always perceived as tentative or ill at ease (Burgoon, Coker, & Coker, 1987). After all, some of our interpretations come from the old West, and cowboys did not trust "shifty-eyed characters."

Eye contact with listeners may feel awkward the first couple of times you speak, but listeners like being included, and eye contact is the main way to include them. Use classroom speaking experiences to build confidence with eye communication.

- Prior to your presentation, designate two or three encouragers, so that you can depend on their visual support.
- Heighten interest by quietly pausing after you get to the front of the room. Look for attentive faces, letting these listeners know that you have "contacted" them.
- As you begin speaking, look at your encouragers, varying your glance. Broaden to include more listeners into your communication circle.
- Experience the effectiveness of eye contact and pause as you deliver your speech.
- Look at your audience, not your notes, as you conclude your speech. (You may look at your notes, collect your thoughts, look at your audience, and say your closing words.)
- Let your eyes speak the language of sincerity, credibility, and enthusiasm. Avoid aggressive, glaring, sneaky, or mean looks.

Responsiveness to Audience Feedback

Immediacy indicates a sense of presence—I am fully aware of where I am, and I am mindful (mind full) of you at this moment. In an employees' presentation workshop, a bright speaker stared at the back wall and delivered a perfectly worded but stiffly delivered speech. He didn't even seem to notice his audience's reactions. When they laughed at several points and looked confused at another, the speaker neither slowed down nor changed his facial expression. After the speech, the class suggested he look at them next time and "try smiling once in a while."

For the next workshop, with a concerted effort he plastered a social smile on his face and repeatedly moved his head from left to right (and quickly back to left). His classmates were holding their breaths, trying not to laugh aloud.

Once again the speaker rigidly stuck to his game plan of delivery. He lacked immediacy.

You have to look at the audience members in order to get much of their feedback—smiles, frowns, yawns, and raised eyebrows. Eye contact sends a message that you are communicating with them individually. Even laughs and moans are vocal feedback that you can use to your advantage.

NONVERBAL COMMUNICATION AT THE CONFERENCE TABLE

Our ever-present nonverbal communication speaks for us in all business encounters. We should thus pay attention to our nonverbal messages and those of others around the conference tables of negotiations and meetings.

The U.S. Department of Defense (2000) instructs, "Being aware of both nonverbal and verbal messages will give you an important edge. Skills in interpreting nonverbal communications will help you glean useful information from others involved in the negotiation. An awareness of nonverbal communication may also prevent you from harming your own negotiation position by inadvertently sending nonverbal signals that disclose confidential information or weaknesses in your position." The Defense Department gives the example that, in negotiations, an inappropriate amount of space—either too little or too much—can negatively affect a meeting.

Conference tables are typically 4 feet across, providing enough space for the individual participants and their papers, laptops, briefcases, and drinks. Chairs with arms confine an area to give elbow room. Principal negotiators should choose a central position, indicating authority and team unity. A central position also allows key participants to communicate more privately with the leader. Notice that the president of the United States sits at the center of the conference table during Cabinet meetings. Notice, also, who sits immediately next to him and across from him.

An article from *Successful Meetings* (Stettner, 1997, p. 128) emphasizes the tactical edge that reading body language can give for negotiating:

- Make baseline observations during the greeting (and usually friendly) part of the meeting. A sudden change in mannerisms later could signal problems or deception.
- Notice such added subtle signals as covering the mouth, leaning away from you, or breathing shallowly and tensely.
- The article further compares extreme or exaggerated gestures to a poker player who throws chips across the table or slams down the cards, often signaling to astute observers they have a weak hand.
- Don't fall for tricks to get you to break eye contact, such as sliding papers across the table for you to see.
- Notice warm, large, and open gestures to signal trust.

Talking at meetings is only one way to communicate in a group. The nonverbal channels carry messages as well:

Professionals should differentiate contact from noncontact cultures in order to interact at appropriate distances from one another. Which cultural distances do you think these communicators are respecting?

- Enter the room with a smile. Others will determine whether you are happy to be there and happy to be with them. Pull up to the table, ready for a productive experience.

- Look attentive, and be attentive. Lean forward. Nod in agreement occasionally. Angle your shoulders toward the speaker. Establish eye contact with the person speaking. Note the speaker's facial expressions, especially right before he or she says something.

- Take notes. Taking notes physically engages you in the meeting. Have a system for notes. For instance, bring a file folder that has a title on it. Include the memo or e-mail about the meeting and paper for taking notes. This communicates your competence as you listen, extract important ideas, and write.

- Be aware of your distracting habits, such as twisting your hair, drumming the table with your fingers, chewing the end of your pen, or smacking gum. Assume an open posture, with your arms unfolded and your hands above the table. Some people have ineffective listening behaviors, such as habitual frowns and, for women especially, bobbing or tilting their heads.

CONTEMPORARY VOICES 5.2: SOCIAL SKILLS

Adults should remember their elementary playground lessons regarding social skills. Socially skilled children on the playground observe a group playing before joining the game. "They tune in to the game first and then enter seamlessly at a natural opening. It's the same with adults: Picking up the social rhythm and timing of those we work with is essential" (Goleman, 1998, p. 137). Goleman explains, "When two people start to talk with each other, they immediately begin to fall into a subtle dance of rhythmic harmony, synchronizing their movements and postures, their vocal pitch, rate of speaking, and even the length of pauses between one person's speaking and the other's response" (pp. 136–137). Remember to stop, look, and listen to the nonverbal dimensions in a group setting.

The impact of nonverbal communication is certainly nothing new. Here is how an observer described a liar some 900 years ago: "He does not answer questions, or gives evasive answers; he speaks nonsense, rubs the great toe along the ground, and shivers; he rubs the roots of his hair with his fingers" (quoted in Goleman, 1998, p. 17).

SUMMARY

Nonverbal communication makes a difference in getting jobs and keeping jobs. Nonverbal communication is the study of all types of communication other than by language alone. It is culturally learned behavior and is inevitable and constant. Other characteristics are that it is powerful, ambiguous, and integrated as a part of the whole message. Nonverbal communication and verbal communication interact as the former substitutes for language, reveals the attitude of the speaker, or contradicts the verbal message.

The study of nonverbal communication includes physical movement (kinesics), touch (haptics), facial communication, eye communication (oculesics), space and distance (proxemics, including territoriality), vocal characteristics (paralanguage), personal appearance, and time (chronemics).

Businesses heed nonverbal communication in diverse cultural contexts. Two ways to categorize cultures are contact versus noncontact and high versus low context. Emotions are read similarly across cultures, but social appropriateness varies. The use of space and distance varies considerably by culture.

Both public speaking and conference room settings require careful nonverbal communication; speakers should pay attention to physical delivery, eye contact, and voice. Negotiators do not stop at words; they notice tone of voice, subtle movements, and facial expressions. Skills in interpreting nonverbal communications glean information and send effective messages. •

ACTIVITIES

1. **Technical Support:** Find movie clips showing business settings to illustrate characteristics of nonverbal communication in the workplace.

2. **Team Work:** Map your personal space. Have another person approach you from the front, back, sides, and at 45 degrees from the front on each side. Tell the person to stop at the point *you* feel comfortable for carrying on a conversation. Measure each of the distances. Draw a graph of your personal space.

3. **Journaling the Experience**
   a. As you walk across campus, notice how far you are from others when you or the other person first averts eye contact. What factors do you notice affecting the length of appropriate eye contact?
   b. Study several offices (or cubicles) in an organization. What is the distance from the employee's office entry to the employee's chair? Are there any gatekeepers (secretaries) with offices or cubicles blocking immediate access to an office? Do you see indicators of organizational hierarchy in the offices, such as size, floor covering, and quality of the desks?

4. **Presenting to Others:** Explore the Omnibus website to learn about social and business customs in other countries: www.getcustoms.com/omnibus.html. Using what you learn as a baseline, interview a student from another country. Focus your questions on the areas of nonverbal communication, including dress, greetings, use of time, taboos, and insults. Present your new insights to the class.

5. **Technical Support:** Research a country on travel sites, such as Fodor or Lonely Planet, on the Internet. List several customs you find about the country.

6. **Ethically Speaking:** Attend a public meeting, such as a city council or a school board meeting. Notice nonverbal cues that signal agreement and disagreement. Notice cues that signal power or a lack of power. Locate two additional sources on nonverbal communication of power.

7. **Ethically Speaking:** Design an experiment to test perceptual biases, such as the one in the following study. Report your results to the class.

   A researcher dressed as a punk rocker pretended to be looking for help from people sitting at tables in a shopping mall food court. "Although only one in 15 people consented to help the punker when she sat right next to them, and 40 percent agreed to help when she sat at a medium distance," the researchers found, "80 percent of the people agreed to help her when she took the seat farthest away." (Suplee, 1999, p. 2)

   This and other studies concluded that people are more likely to interact with somebody who looks weird if that person stays well outside the personal zone. Why do you think people are more likely to interact with the punker if the punker stays outside the personal zone? How could this tendency affect people working in helping professions, such as nursing, or in sales, such as retail clothing?

8. **Team Work:** In small groups, assign two members (a dyad) to participate in a conversation as a salesperson would interact with a customer. The remaining group members serve as observers. Half the observers should count how *often* the communicators break eye contact and whether the listener or speaker breaks contact first. The other observers should time how *long* the communicators look at each other at each time during their conversation. After the observations are complete, discuss your findings. Research has shown that generally, people in groups look more while speaking and less while listening, but in dyads people look more while listening and less while speaking (Knapp & Hall, 2002). What did your group find?

9. **Technical Support:** Explore www.executiveplanet.com and www.culturalsavvy.com/marketing_in_japan.htm to find other customs common to the United States that could be misunderstood in other countries. Describe two of these conflicting cultural nonverbal behaviors.

FOR FURTHER READING

Ekman, P. (1992). *Telling lies: Clues to deceit in the marketplace, politics, and marriage.* New York: Norton.

Hall, E. T. (1990). *The hidden dimension.* New York: Doubleday/Anchor Books. (Original work published 1966).

Knapp, M., & Hall, J. A. (2001). *Nonverbal communication in human interaction* (5th ed.). Belmont, CA: Wadsworth.

Examine your preferences regarding the nonverbal aspect of time and culture at www.innovint.com/downloads/mono_poly_test.asp

Truth is an unruly subject and, once admitted, comes crowding in on us faster than we wish. (C. S. Lewis)

138

Topic Research

6

General Research Strategies

Overview of Library Sources

Interviews, Surveys, and Questionnaires

Using APA Style for References

Using Sources Ethically and Effectively in a Speech

D
ynamic professionals are usually discerning readers, seeking out new information. No wonder others compete to include them on teams and collaborate with them in business. These lifelong learners have no more time than anybody else; their advantage lies in their ability to find excellent material. Good research skills support ethical, effective, and expressive communication—support we need in order to inform and persuade others. So, briefly, here is a description of "triple E communicators."

- *Ethical* communicators (1) care about the quality of information they give to others and (2) respect the investment of time a listener has made in them.

- *Effective* communicators (1) care about the quantity of the information, (2) know enough to back claims they make, and (3) know how the information fits together reasonably.

- *Expressive* communicators (1) choose meaningful material for their listeners, (2) use interesting information for the listeners, and (3) allow the listeners to experience the speaker's connection with the material.

This very practical chapter is designed to broaden your use of sources, encourage active research in libraries and online, and provide an abbreviated source for citing references during a speech and on a reference list.

OBJECTIVES

After studying the content of this chapter, you should be able to

- Inventory sources to see what is available within a limited time
- Use library resources
- Access and assess sources on the Web
- Conduct interviews to gather information
- Conduct and analyze research with two research designs
- Create a reference list following APA guidelines
- Cite sources during a presentation

This chapter offers (1) an overview of what is available, (2) research directions, and (3) specific sites and sources to get you started. Sound research skills will serve you in many situations—project development, preparation for discussions, background information for making decisions, presentation preparation, and inoculation from misinformation. Let's step into one of those purposes—the speech preparation process—to bring *your* reality to the research process.

 GENERAL RESEARCH STRATEGIES

The glut of available material creates a paradox: On one hand, it's easy to be overwhelmed and intimidated; on the other hand, the mound of material available from a home computer creates a false sense of security.

> More than 30 million different books have been published since the invention of the printing press. Currently, approximately 400,000 titles are published each year. Millions of articles are published every year in thousands of different journals and magazines. There are now more than 200,000 journals and magazines in the area of science alone. (DeVito 1999, p. 123)

You will want to seek out credible sources and get answers to well-formed research questions.

Define Research Goals

What is your speech? If it is an assignment, is it an informative speech, a persuasive speech, or a team presentation? What is the topic or type of topic—perhaps a business or communication topic? Think about your audience's needs and motivations to determine candidates for topics. After deciding on a general topic area, narrow it to a presentation topic and check a couple of key sources to get a feel for what's available in terms of information.

Don't waste time worrying. Get moving. Pick up a newspaper, read article titles on journal or magazine covers, get online on a news site such as CNN or MSNBC, and watch news on television. Find something that interests you now, rather than lazily recycling a topic you have outgrown or that no longer holds excitement for you.

• • •

Be open to sources that contradict your thinking, and seek out the widest range of possible opinions. Until you have the larger picture, you cannot treat your topic convincingly within context. Read a few select articles from reliable and diverse sources to see which topical issues come up repeatedly. When debaters and lawyers prepare to speak, although they research the position that they will argue, they also research other perspectives.

● **EXAMPLE 6.1**

CHANGING PERSPECTIVES

Elizabeth convincingly spoke on the necessity for the FDA's high standards on food additives. It was obvious she had engaged the audience from the question-and-answer session that followed. In response to one class member's question, she laughed and explained, "I had already written my specific purpose statement and turned it in last week. I'll bet Dr. Kelly was surprised to hear me speak against my original position. I originally thought that the FDA was power happy and made unnecessary delays in getting products on the shelves. The more I read, the more I was convinced I liked the idea of them protecting us."

●

Remember the Audience

Crystal Waterford analyzed her audience. As she prepared to intrigue her listeners and stimulate their thinking, she enlisted them vicariously in her planning. This is one of the most important stages for using your analysis of the audience. To hold others' attention, think of what holds yours. Which speakers and professors hold your attention?

Most students appreciate hearing clear explanations, meaningful examples, compelling steps of reasoning, statistics that put events into perspective, and narratives that bring events closer. Quotations from literary, scientific, and historical people bring other voices to a presentation. Therefore, hold in mind what will interest and help the audience to understand. Certainly, we understand that informative speaking depends on good information, but nothing is more important than matching sound research to an audience's needs, concerns, and possible points of resistance.

Use a Survey and Post-Hole Strategy

Survey to get the lay of the land, that is, broad overviews, perspectives, and available information. *Post-hole* to dig deeply into a topic. Surveying provides the breadth a speaker needs for equilibrium and stability, and post-holing brings depth to a speaker's understanding. You're conducting an archaeological dig on your topic.

Surveying Reveals Breadth

Think about what you already know on the topic. What connects you to it? Have you talked with an expert? Perhaps you've seen a documentary or article on the subject. Survey other sources, such as these, to get you started:

- Encyclopedias
- News magazines
- Annual reviews in social sciences and education
- Survey text
- Popular and scholarly sources online
- Your college library's online catalog
- Experts to interview

Look for key ideas, and select a topic you want to explore. Narrow the topic to something you can handle in your preparation and speaking time frames. Then follow your best leads. Keep your goals in mind. If you find an interesting side trip, make a note to follow up later, but don't go there now. Following every lead can be exorbitantly time consuming, so stay on track with your topic.

Post-Holing Adds Substance

This is the fun part. *Now* you can become engrossed. Post-holing is a strategy that means going into depth on a narrower topic.[1] Post-holing helps fill out the research and clarify reasoning and logical connections. From your initial survey, follow up on the sources that look the most promising, so you know which ones to dig into first.

- Decide which one or two databanks contain the scholarly journals for your topic—for instance, PsycLit for psychology and WilsonWeb for humanities (see Table 6.2).
- Read two or three articles, and notice which sources they use.
- Scan a book's table of contents and a few pages of interest.

Organize with Files

Make notes on your topic, making sure that every source has complete documentation so that you don't have to bother looking it up later to create your reference list. Keep authors' names, titles of articles and books, the publication dates, issues or volume numbers, and page numbers. For an online source, keep the date you retrieved the article and the URL.

With a brief, preliminary outline, create a notebook with a section for each of your main points. File your material under the appropriate section, keeping documentation attached to it. As your ideas develop, you can move pieces to

---

[1] Educators have learned that students who learn by post-holing do as well on standardized tests as those who survey many topics.

other points or omit some material from the notebook. A good way to learn how flexible this process is, is to see how another student did it. Take your time examining the development of Crystal Waterford's topic in Examples 6.2 and 6.3.

● **EXAMPLE 6.2**

THE EVOLUTION OF A TOPIC: PART ONE

Getting Started

Crystal Waterford, who wanted to serve in the Peace Corps after graduation, considered speaking on something about nonverbal communication. She wasn't sure what. Her first search (at home) on the Internet was through msn.com. She used "training+nonverbal," which yielded more than 150,000 sites, including many home pages for training consultants.

The next day she took advantage of the library's computers and the guidance of an information specialist (librarian). Her search showed a number of articles, several which seemed on target. The librarian showed her how to narrow her online search with Boolean terms and other menu options according to the source page. Crystal appreciated these time-saving tools.

An especially interesting article said that "eyes carry important communication in every culture," so she started a new search with "eyes+communication+cultures" and became enthusiastic about topic possibilities. She could organize the eye communication articles into "a field of study" or "differences among cultures." She organized her notebook with two blue dividers, to get started:

1. The study of eye communication
2. Cultural differences with eye communication

As she read further, she became impressed by the negative consequences of nonverbal miscommunications. So she added the following item:

3. Importance and purposes of study

Crystal's Outline Takes Shape

Crystal then arranged her main points and added subpoints, marked by red dividers, as she selected support, making notes as ideas occurred to her:

Topic: "Eye Communication in Many Cultures"

I. Importance and Purposes of Study
   a. Global society *[Connect this to course content, if I use this subpoint.]*
   b. "Ugly Americans" *[Introduce Edward and Mildred Hall's research in intercultural nonverbal communication.]*

II. Areas of Study
   a. Oculesics *[Define and give best examples to contrast cultures.]*
   b. Pupil metrics *[Report some humorous research and give example about merchants' reading eye pupil size.]*

III. Applications of Findings
   a. Embassies and Peace Corps *[Specific training for overseas duties]*
   b. Cross-cultural businesses *[Quotes from successful people in international businesses]*

c. The Red Cross and other service organizations *[Just saw an article about interpreting nonverbal communication in health settings—the pre-med and nursing students will love this.]*

─── ●

Research is primarily about posing clear questions. Early in the process, Crystal's rough outline gave her a strategy for organizing information as she collected it. When she examined her "chunks" of information and tried to put her main points into questions, she could see some weaknesses—primarily, that the three broad points wouldn't fit into her time limit. She decided that for business and communication majors, the most interesting and useful segment fell under "intercultural communication." The professor had said the thesis and main points should be written with complete sentences, either statements or questions. She put her main points into questions and looked at them again. It took several attempts (and a bag of Cheetos, an apple, and two ginger ales) before she was satisfied. You can see that she eliminated a main point, but retained some of the supporting material elsewhere. The few missing pieces shouldn't be hard to find.

● **EXAMPLE 6.3**

THE EVOLUTION OF A TOPIC: PART TWO

Body of Speech

Central idea: Training in nonverbal communication benefits employees in a global society.

I. Why do future employees in organizations study nonverbal communication?

   a. We are now, more than ever, a global society. [Connect this to course content.]

   b. Due to uninformed and inappropriate nonverbal communication interculturally and cross-culturally, some people in other cultures have called us "ugly Americans" for more than 50 years. [Be sure to include definition and types. Show videotape of reactions to violent acts against the United States. Use quotes from *The Ugly American.* Tell about Edward and Mildred Hall, who have done research in intercultural nonverbal communication.]

   c. Communicating good will means showing respect and building trust with associates in other cultures [Need to pull explanations from CEOs of global businesses.]

~~II. What are relevant areas of research concerning eye communication?~~

~~a. Oculesics [Define and give interesting examples to contrast cultures.]~~

~~b. Pupilometrics [Report some humorous research and give example about merchants' reading eye pupil size.]~~

III. How are conclusions from nonverbal communication research applied?

   a. What training do government and military personnel receive in nonverbal communication?

      1. Government officials, members of the Peace Corps, and U.S. Embassy employees learn new languages *and* new nonverbal behaviors before going overseas. [Give examples of specific

training for overseas duties. Put the cut material on contrasting cultures here.]
2. The military educates overseas officers in the nonverbal communication for the country where they will be based.

b. How do businesses and service organizations benefit from knowledge of nonverbal communication?
1. Many businesses cross boundaries by design, market, or employment. [Lead in with history of Eastern merchants reading pupil dilation. Quotes from successful people in international businesses]
2. Service-oriented organizations care for people of another citizenry both in and out of country. [Include Red Cross statistics here from the great article I found yesterday on reading nonverbal communication in health settings. There are several pre-med and nursing students in class to appreciate this.]
3. Eyes, instead of ID cards or thumbprints, may verify our identity in the future. [I need to get some information on this.]

Notice how Crystal's topic evolved during the research process. She saw something that interested her, received some pointers from her professor, and began researching with some guidance from an information specialist. As she dug deeper—post-holed—she found she could compile two sections of her research notebook. Probable main points gave it more shape. Rewording the main points into questions added insight about her design, and she adjusted by broadening her topic to "nonverbal communication" (not just eye communication) and narrowing it to "organizations using intercultural communication."

Conduct Ethical Research

Verify information, and learn enough to present it accurately, fairly, and in context before stating it to an audience. Make this a way of thinking: Private decisions shape lifetime character.

- Check the accuracy of facts against other sources.
- When quoting a newspaper that in turn quotes someone's speech, determine the speaker's level of expertise.
- Don't remove a quote from the context in which it was made.
- Use statistics in the context of the research in which they were reported.
- In scholarly journals, pay attention to results and to such elements as how many people were in the study and how it was conducted.

OVERVIEW OF LIBRARY SOURCES

The technology of a culture influences how people think as well as how they do research, record their information, and use audiovisual aids. In a culture that is progressing at "twitch-speed" (Prensky, 1998) it is almost

Information and commitment can be gathered from interviews. Go to news websites to get audio clips of interviews as source material.

startling to remember that pictures were first put on the Internet in 1994. (Jaffe, 1995)

No matter how small or remote your college is, you, as a student, have electronic access to some of the best material in the world, thanks to your college or university's library. Sure, it's expensive for the school, but it's not costing you extra, so take advantage of research services and experts at hand. Explore at will, and ask for help as needed. For top-notch information on almost any topic, library on-site or remote searches are by far more efficient than typical at-home, general Internet searches. Through the former, you can access hard copies, rare volumes, CDs, and extensive databases not available to the general public. Over 10,000 subjects are categorized on the Librarians' Index to the Internet site (http://lii.org/).

Juggling time to research, prepare, and practice before making presentations is challenging, and the pressure's on to get credible, current material in a hurry. Following is an overview of some of the more frequently used sources and samples of particularly helpful periodicals, reference sources, and books.

Periodicals

Magazines, newspapers, and scholarly journals are publications that are issued *periodically* (daily, weekly, monthly, or quarterly). From these sources, you can collect different points of view and a variety of material written for the general public, professionals, and scholars.

ACTIVITY 6.1

YOUR LIBRARY

You are now managing high-profile projects—your speech presentations. As a new manager, introduce yourself to one of your staff and look over your facilities. Ideally, you have been to a library orientation and established a connection there, but there is no sense trying to do this all alone.

1. *Use this section for an easy reference while you tour a few sources. Sit down at a computer, and go to your college or university library's website. Locate "electronic sources," "online periodicals," or a similar heading. Use Table 6.1 to choose general indexes. Experiment with*

TABLE 6.1 • General and Interdisciplinary Databases

The Electric Library	Rich source of a wide variety of sources; updated daily; image resources
Readers Guide to Periodical Literature	Wide variety of magazine articles on general-interest topics
EBSCO	Scholarly journals; extensive collection
Lexis/Nexis	Newspapers, magazines, journals, newsletters, legal records
ProQuest Academic Search	Powerful database of professional journals and articles

different ways to perform a topical search. Print one of the articles. With a highlighter pen, mark the material you need for citing it in a reference list. (You will find a guide for references in the last section of this chapter.)

2. Use Table 6.2 to search for areas of interest in your major field of study or a favorite course. Print an article and critique it for source credibility and readability.

3. Compare the search features of any two indexes from Table 6.1 and 6.2. Critique them on ease of navigation and search features.

Indexes to Articles

Library *indexes* are lists based on a choice of authors, topics, and publication titles (journal, magazine, etc.). Indexes integrate and prioritize features to create more useful lists for you. Electronic indexes, such as FirstSearch and Expanded Academic Index, list relevant articles.

• Both indexes and databases display a *citation,* that is, a basic bibliographical reference (not a traffic ticket). A citation gives at least the title of the article, name(s) of the author(s), name of the publication, date published, and page numbers.

• Databases usually provide an *abstract,* or brief summary, so you can tell whether you want to read an article in full. Sometimes you find all you need in the abstract. If you need the entire article, check to see whether the database provides full text for this article. If not, you need to find how your library stores the article.

• *Full text* is available on an increasing number of databases. A real boon to college students and professionals, the full-text databases allow you to read seminal research, annual reviews, and critical reviews and to follow a strand of research over time. Professional journals' databases are your best sources for *scholarly journals* (also called *peer reviewed* or *juried journals*). As a feature in most searches, your search words will appear in bold every place they occur in the document. It's a good idea to locate these sources in your chosen field.

TABLE 6.2 • Disciplines' Databases

Gale Group	A number of indexes grouped by broad disciplines
ABI	Contains most of the communication journals, along with other social sciences journals
Internet Web Text Index	References and guides for the Internet
ERIC	Education, business, science, humanities, and social sciences
Wilson Web	Abstracts and some full text; contains some communication articles
PsychLit	Psychology
Social Sciences Index	Social and behavioral sciences; some communication articles
OMNIFILE	Education, business, science, humanities, and social science
MEDLINE	Abstracts from more than 4,000 biomedical journals
Legal Resource Index	Law
CINAHL	Nursing
Humanities Index	History, philosophy, literary criticism
Social Sciences Index	Political science, sociology, criminology, psychology, sociology

Most college libraries have *general-interest indexes* and *databases,* some of which are shown in Table 6.1. Other databases focus on disciplines or academic areas, such as in Table 6.2.

News Sources

When tracking current events or seeking recent news on your topic, turn to electronic news sources such as these:

- Home pages and subscriptions to newspapers, television networks, and magazines
- News Directory, www.newsdirectory.com (access to newspapers, magazines, and television stations worldwide)
- CNN, MSNBC, ABC News, CBS News, and PBS—generally available online, but also take advantage of library indexes that search multiple sources at one time:
  - Business Newsbank
  - InfoTrac Newspapers
  - NewsBank Newsfile Collections
  - Newspaper Source

Books

The *online public access catalog* directs you to specific *books*. Replacing the card catalog system of old, the online catalog lists that particular library's books, indexed by author, title, and subject. Read the menu and computer screen instructions. Catalogs usually indicate on screen whether a book is available, and most libraries let you reserve a copy in advance.

In addition to facts, data, testimony, explanations, and illustrations, books on specific topics can help in other ways for speech preparation.

- Notice the titles and organization of chapters to get ideas for organizing speeches.
- Read an individual chapter to get an overview on a topic.
- Look up specific subjects and names in an index.
- Look at the book's references or end notes to get leads on good sources.
- Some book series, such as the *National Issues Forums,* discuss basic facts and present opposing sides of contemporary issues.
- Illustrated books in art, science, and history are good for finding visuals that you can scan electronically and save on a computer disk.

Encyclopedias

Encyclopedias are especially helpful for gaining a broad perspective. Encyclopedias overview and illustrate everything from hydroelectricity to saber-toothed tigers to Sigmund Freud. Libraries often shelve bound volumes as well as provide entire encyclopedias online or on CD-RM. The *Encyclopaedia Britannica*[2] is the gold standard of encyclopedias, *Encyclopedia Americana* focuses on American issues, and *Collier's Encyclopedia* is known for its illustrations and engaging format. Libraries also make encyclopedias available with subscriptions through the Web, such as CompuServe, American Online, Pipeline, and Prodigy.

Almanacs and Government Publications

Almanacs and government publications are useful to answer very specific questions, with data often presented statistically, by date or by historical pattern. If you don't find general information with a basic search, a librarian often can tell you exactly where to look. Information in *almanacs* is usually available online. Annual publications contain mounds of data on economics, population, weather, unemployment, diversity, health and medicine, awards, sports, and world travel.

Government publications are primary sources "without the bias or interpretation often found in secondary sources" (Duncan, 2002). The Government Printing Office in Washington, D.C., annually prints more than any other publisher in the United States. Remember that all government sources are "fair use" documents. Locate government documents through

- *CIS Indexes*

---

2   The *Encyclopaedia Britannica* dates back to Scotland in 1771.

- *CIS Abstracts*
- *Monthly Catalog of U.S. Government Publications*

ACTIVITY 6.2

U.S. GOVERNMENT SOURCES FOR DOWNLOADING

Create a list of 10 amazing facts you find in three or more of these sources:

- *Congressional Record* (1873 to date): Prints everything that is said in Congress daily during session. It is available at http://222.access.gpro.gov/su_docs/adpos400.htm
- *Statistical Abstract of the United States:* Complete statistical data on populations, vital statistics, law, environment, elections, finances, employments, defense, and much more. See www.census.gov/statab/www/.
- *Vital Statistics of the United States* and *Morbidity and Mortality Weekly:* Especially helpful for demographic and health studies.
- *Biographical Directory of the American Congress* and the *Official Congressional Directory* (1809 to date): Biographical information on government employees, congressional districts, and other useful information regarding the personnel of the government's business.
- U.S. Supreme Court Opinions (http://fedbs.access.gpo.gov/court01.htm)
- White House (www.whitehouse.gov)
- Library of Congress (http://lcweb.loc.gov/)

Other Speaker Sources

After deciding what you need, target sources in which that material is likely to appear. Student speakers recommend these as among their favorites:

- The World Factbook (www.cia.gov/cia/publications/factbook/)
- *Bartlett's Familiar Quotations*
- *Famous Phrases from History*
- *The New Quotable Woman*
- *The MacMillan Book of Proverbs, Maxims, and Famous Phrases*
- *Oxford English Dictionary*
- *American Heritage Dictionary*
- Dictionary.com (http://dictionary.reference.com)—definitions in English and other languages
- *Research-It*
- *Physician's Desk Reference*
- *Harvard Guide to Women's Health*
- World Sites Atlas (www.sitesatlas.com)
- Historical Atlas of the United States (www.epa.gov/ceisweb1/ceishome/atlas/)
- PCL Map Collection (www.lib.utexas.edu/) through Perry-Castañeda Library (www.lib.utexas.edu/maps/)

A team can cooperate to video-tape interviews to use as sources and support in presentations.

• INTERVIEWS, SURVEYS, AND QUESTIONNAIRES

Enthusiasm, involvement in the topic, and expert testimony bring authority to your presentations. An excellent way to add these qualities is to interview experts and to conduct surveys or questionnaires.

Research Interviews

Usually experts in their fields eagerly assist students in presentation preparation. Expert sources can be interviewed by phone, e-mail, or in person, and some have web home pages where you can contact them.

Prepare

Contact the person you want to interview, and make an appointment for the interview. Introduce yourself, and state the purpose for the interview, "I'm Mary Smith, and I am preparing a speech on American Blenko glass for my college speech class. In an article in *Today's News,* I read that as an American art historian, you are an expert on Blenko. Do you have time for a half-hour interview this week or next?" If the interviewee agrees to the interview, make an appointment, later confirming the time, date, and location in writing, by e-mail, or by phone.

- If you plan to tape the interview, request permission ahead of time. Some people are intimidated, and others are concerned about the tape being used out of context.

- Research the expert's biographical data, if it is available in a printed source. Remember to prepare questions to fill in missing biographical information.

- Do background research *before* the interview to benefit most from the minutes you have with the interviewee. Become familiar with key terms and major concepts, and make notes on things you want to have explained. Your questions give the interviewee an idea of how familiar you are with the topic so he or she can gear answers to your level of understanding. If you haven't put effort into educating yourself, the interviewee may spend most of the time on basic information you could have easily gotten elsewhere.

- Prepare questions for the interview. (For our purposes, we will call requests for responses "questions," although some may be in the form of a statement, such as "I would like to know which ingredients are in ruby glass.") Organize your questions in a logical order by topic. Place your most important questions at the top of each topic area, since you may not be able to get to all of your questions. If the interviewee requests questions ahead of time, send a typed copy of the major questions to the interviewee. Keep extra copies with you. On your copy, leave space for writing answers and quotes.

Several kinds of questions elicit helpful answers. *Closed questions* get specific answers. Closed questions are usually answered with "yes," "no," or brief, factual answers. They do not invite elaboration. "Are any Blenko pieces in the Smithsonian?" "What is the oldest piece in the factory collection?" "Has the factory always been in West Virginia?" *Open questions* give the responder latitude for answering. They invite the responder to elaborate, explain, give opinions, and discuss the subject. "How does American blown glass compare with Svoboda blown glass in the Czech Republic?" "Blenko is famous for their formula for red. How was it developed?" "Is blown glass a dying art?" *Probes* prompt the interviewee to respond in more depth or more specifically. "You said the glass formulas have improved. What changes do you see for the future?"

Conduct the Interview

The Set-Up Be on time and dress appropriately. Ask to set up in the location of the interview. Set up equipment as permitted. If you are audiotaping (the least intrusive), have extra batteries and audiotapes. (An alternative is an audiovideotape.) For a phone interview, arrange ahead of time to have it taped. Use a headset or earpiece/microphone, if possible, so you can write notes or type on a silent keyboard during the interview. Speaker phones bother some people, because they lose a sense of personal connection. Be ready with questions and ready to take notes as you move from the introduction to the body of substantial discussion and, finally, to a conclusion.

Introduction For the introduction, state your name again and express appreciation for being granted the interview. Remind the person of the purpose of the interview and how the responses will be used. Small talk is an important form of communication to establish rapport and an interaction pattern. This would be a good time to set up your tape recorder and get into the arrangement for the interview.

Start recording the interview. Record for about five seconds before you speak. Open with the date, your name, the name and credentials of the person whom you are interviewing, and the purpose of the interview. Transition to your first question, as in the following example:

> This is Thursday, November 14, 2002, and I am Gina Barak. Today I have the privilege of talking with Dr. Jim Hail, who is on the psychology faculty at McLennan Community College. I am researching test anxiety among college

students. Dr. Hail has expertise in educational psychology and also publishes test banks for psychology textbooks. Dr. Hail, thank you for allowing me to interview you. I am preparing a speech for my business speaking class on test anxiety among college students. I read an article in *Psychology Today,* and I wasn't clear on what is a normal amount of apprehension. Can you explain how anxiety is different from normal worry when taking a test?

The Inquisitive Dialogue   Ask questions clearly, and give the interviewee time to answer. If the interviewee seems confused about the question, rephrase the question or explain the kind of information you're seeking. Some questions and requests will occur to you during the interview because of something the interviewee said, so be flexible enough to follow up on those questions.

If the interviewee gets off track, redirect a question or bridge from something the interviewee said. Sometimes a well-intended interviewee speaks at length on your first question, probably to take pressure off you. Still, if you want to move on, you can interject with something similar to the following: "I want to talk more about that later, but first would you talk about the physical symptoms of anxiety?"

Interviewees with a high need for order prefer a question-and-answer pattern. Others yield more information in a conversation. Learn to conduct interviews both ways, but let the responsiveness of the interviewee guide your choice.

Conclude the Interview   Use feedforward to indicate that the interview is wrapping up: "I have one final question" or "You've answered my questions very helpfully. Is there something you would like to add before we conclude?" Thank the interviewee and highlight the importance of what the interviewee said: "Thank you for explaining techniques to control apprehension and for sources on anxiety. You've told me so much that I'll include in my speech. Again, thank you for your time."

Using the Interview

Give credit to individuals when you use their ideas and words. Metaphorically bring the expert to your speech, as you would in conversation or when re-enacting dialogue. "According to psychology professor Dr. Jim Hail in a personal interview last week, anxiety is a more intense experience than apprehension. I wondered whether all apprehension was bad. Dr. Hail said that some apprehension can help a person think more clearly, since more oxygen is getting to the brain. Dr. Hail pilots an airplane that he built, and he says he takes advantage of that feeling of heightened alertness when he takes off and lands his plane. We can use a similar sensation when we take an exam." In a written report, cite the interview in the text as follows: (J. Hail, personal communication, March 11, 2003). Do not include personal communications in the references list.

Surveys and Questionnaires

Surveys are useful for gathering data not otherwise available, and listeners appreciate the time you have taken to get accurate information on matters that interest them. You may wish to report to an audience the attitude on campus about a foreign policy under discussion by Congress. Make a questionnaire short, direct, and clear. Surveys can be as short as one question. Pilot questions and requests before you administer the survey to a large research population.

- *How will you ask?* Word questions carefully. Are they worded nonjudgmentally and clearly? Will the responders feel free to answer honestly?

- *Whom will you ask?* Select your survey population. Make sure they are the ones with the information you need. Don't survey professors about students' attitudes—survey students.

- *What do you need to know?* Perceptions? Times a person has experienced an event? Level of education completed? Create questions that will generate data that can be analyzed meaningfully.

- *What response types do you need?* Design methods for responding, such as "mark yes, no, or not applicable." A Likert scale gives more choices, such as from "1 to 5, with 5 being best." Open-end questions request responders' written responses.

- *What information do you need about the respondents?* Professions? Days missed due to illness? Majors? Income brackets? Remember that you cannot require people to disclose information.

- *What will you do with the data?* Plan ahead of time how to process the data and how it will be used in your presentation. Often surveyors discover they needed to ask one or two more questions or ask them differently for the data to be useful.

- *How will you report your findings?* When reporting conclusions, describe the population you surveyed and the way you analyzed responses.

Some information is quickly gathered by questioning a large group publicly. You may ask your audience, for instance, "How many of you ate breakfast this morning?" or "Who played on a high school athletic team?" The requests are not threatening, so you should get honest, pertinent answers.

Qualitative Research

Quantitative research performs numerical analyses on data. Some data are not easily or meaningfully represented in numerical form, in which case, types of qualitative research are useful. *Qualitative* research seeks to identify emerging themes, which it verifies or contradicts in comparison with other sources examining similar data. Dr. Deborah Tannen's research on gender communication in *That's Not What I Meant* and *Please Understand Me* and Dr. Judith Wallerstein's initial research for *The Good Marriage* are examples of how qualitative research informs us. Tannen retained extensive observations, which she coded and analyzed, then checked against other data sources. Dr. Wallerstein interviewed 50 "happily married" couples in search of what good marriages have in common.

Another format for collecting qualitative data is the focus group, by which the researcher brings together a group of people who have specialized knowledge or experiences. The researcher leads the group with questions and requests for discussion, being careful not to influence the answers. A recorder (equipment or person) provides a transcript of the discussion for analysis. For instance, "Eight of eleven participants contributed 15 negative statements describing their bosses. By comparison, only two participants used positive statements, each two times." "During a discussion among nine managers after a workshop on Gardner's theory of multiple intelligences, all nine agreed that they felt they would look for different abilities in others rather than think in terms of 'who is smart and who isn't.' Two said they perceived themselves more positively as a result of reading the material."

• USING APA STYLE FOR REFERENCES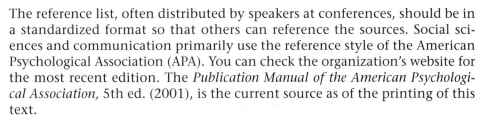

The reference list, often distributed by speakers at conferences, should be in a standardized format so that others can reference the sources. Social sciences and communication primarily use the reference style of the American Psychological Association (APA). You can check the organization's website for the most recent edition. The *Publication Manual of the American Psychological Association,* 5th ed. (2001), is the current source as of the printing of this text.

In works following APA style, the alphabetized list of references is entitled "References." The APA list of references includes only those works referred to in your paper or presentation. Remember that as a speaker, you will use the references format, which is different from the one for end notes.

- A good summary with helpful examples is on the Allyn & Bacon Public Speaking Website for students:

  http://wps.ablongman.com/ab_public_speaking_2

- Check library home pages for reference citation guides.

- Several websites updated to the *APA Publication Manual,* 5th ed., provide helpful models:

  www.docstyles.com/apacrib.htm#Examples

  www.vanguard.edu/faculty/ddegelman/index.cfm?doc_id=796

  www.lib.usm.edu/~instruct/guides/apa.html

- For specific questions on style for electronic sources, go to www.apastyle.org/styletips.html

Generally, references provide the author's last name, a comma, the author's initial(s) (followed by periods), and a date in parentheses. For books and other complete works, the title in italics follows the date. For periodicals, the article's title precedes the journal's name, followed by volume issue number and page numbers.

For APA References:

- Start a new page and center the page title like so:

References

- Start each entry at the left margin, use a hanging indent, and double space.

> Author, A. A., Author, B. B., & Author, C. C. (2000). Title of article. *Title of Periodical, xx*, xx–xxx. Retrieved month, day, year, from http//www.xxx@xxx.xxx

- Organize entries alphabetically by the surnames of the first listed author.

Comment: End with a period, except in the case of an electronic source.

Basic Components of Entries

- *Authors:* List authors in the same order as in the source, using surnames (last names) and initials. Commas separate all authors. When there are seven or more authors, list the first six and then use "et al." for remaining authors. If no author is identified, the title of the document begins the reference.

- *Publication date:* The data of publication, within parentheses, follows the listing of authors' names.

- *Titles:* If you are listing a book or a periodical article, the title comes next, with only the first word, proper nouns, and any word following a colon capitalized. Book titles are italicized; journal article titles are not. Journal article titles are not enclosed in quotation marks.

- *Facts of publication:* For journal articles, include name and volume number of journal (both italicized), and page numbers. For books, give the city of publication and the publisher.

List your sources on a separate document set up for references. Make each entry a separate paragraph with correct formatting. Sort the entries alphabetically, regardless of the type of source. (To sort in Microsoft Word, go to the Table menu and select Sort to choose a descending alphabetical sort.)

Models

Currently, APA style allows a regular indent or a hanging indent. The hanging indent is shown in these examples for common entries.

Journal Articles (magazines, newspapers, scholarly journals)

- For journal articles, capitalize the name of the publication as seen in the journal title, but only capitalize the first word, proper nouns, and the first word following a colon in the article title.

- The publication name and volume number are in italics (preferably) or underlined.

- When a volume number is given, the page numbers are not preceded by the abbreviations p. or pp.

> Blythe, T., & Gardner, H. (1990). A school for all intelligences. *Educational Leadership, 48*, 33–37.

> Caffeine linked to mental illness. (1991, July 13). *The New York Times,* pp. B13, B15. [In this entry, the author is unknown, which is quite common for newspaper articles.]

Walters, F. M. (1993, September 1). If it's broke, fix it: The significance of health care reform in America. *Vital Speeches 59,* 687–691.

Books

- Use capitalization for book titles the same way you did for journal articles titles (first word, proper nouns, and first word after a colon).
- With more than six authors, cite the first six followed by "et al."
- An editor (Ed.) is different from an edition (ed.). Use (Ed.) or (Eds.) after editors' names. For editions of a book, use (ed.) in parentheses following the title.
- Often you will run across books that compile articles or chapters written by different authors. Both the author(s) and the editor(s) are cited.

Tannen, D. (1990). *You just don't understand: Women and men in conversation.* New York: William Morrow & Company.

Campbell, L., Campbell, B., & Dickinson, D. (1996). *Teaching and learning through multiple intelligences.* Needham Heights, MA: Allyn & Bacon. [For multiple authors, use "&" as the conjunction.]

American Psychiatric Association. (1990). *Diagnostic and statistical manual of mental disorders* (3rd ed.). Washington, DC: Author. [An association, corporate, or similar entity is shown as the author.]

Shea, J. D. (1992). Religion and sexual adjustment. In J. F. Schumaker (Ed.), *Religion and mental health* (pp. 70–84). New York: Oxford University Press. [For articles and chapters in an edited book, cite the article or chapter author, then credit the edited source book.]

Conference Paper (published)

Shrout, P. E. (Chair), Hunter, J. E., Harris, R. J., Wilkinson, L., Strouss, M. E., Applebaum, M. I., et al. (1996, August). *Significance tests—Should they be banned from APA journals?* Symposium conducted at the 104th Annual Convention of the American Psychological Association, Toronto, Canada.

Chapter or Section in a Book

Stephan, W. G. (1985). Intergroup relations. In G. Lindzey, & E. Aronson (Eds.), *The handbook of social psychology* (3rd ed., Vol. 2, pp. 599–658). New York: Random House.

Journal Article from Database

Hien, D., & Honeyman, T. (2000). A closer look at the drug abuse–maternal aggression link. *Journal of Interpersonal Violence, 15,* 503–522. Retrieved May 20, 2000, from ProQuest database.

Abstract from Secondary Database

Garrity, K., & Degelman, D. (1990). Effect of server introduction on restaurant tipping. *Journal of Applied Social Psychology, 20,* 168–172. Abstract retrieved July 23, 2001, from PsycINFO database.

Government Document

U.S. Census Bureau. (2000). *Statistical abstract of the United States.* Washington, DC: U.S. Government Printing Office.

Interview

Greer, M. Medieval literature scholar. (2002, November 23). Personal interview. [Personal interviews and correspondence are not generally included in the reference list because they are not retrievable, but your professors or audiences may want to see them listed.]

USING SOURCES ETHICALLY AND EFFECTIVELY IN A SPEECH

After investing time and energy collecting sources, and after crafting a presentation, it's easy to forget your silent partners. Behind great speakers are the writers, speakers, and researchers whose work they use. Because the speaker brings these partners to the event, the speaker should introduce them.

Cite sources because it's the right thing to do. Honesty is a compelling reason to cite sources during a speech. If the authors of your sources were present, you wouldn't claim their ideas as your own, so don't do it behind their backs. For some audiences, the speaker is all the authority they need, and some speakers are adequately authoritative on their topics. Most of us, however, when we address educated, adult audiences, should supply sources for our facts, statistics, quotations, examples, and definitions.

Providing sources precludes many listeners' questions and doubts, and it increases the speaker's credibility. How and how often you mention those sources depends in part on the nature of the material and on the audience's perception of you and of the source.

- If you are respected as an expert, an audience will want to know what *you* think, rather than what a lot of other sources say. So if you are one of the leaders in the Human Genome Project, you *are* a primary source. Even so, you will probably cite other sources for statistics, quotes, and so forth.

- If you use a quotation, you can decide if *who* said it or *what* is said will have the most impact. For informative speeches presenting noncontroversial material, the audience cares more about the "what" than the "who."

- For persuasive speeches with controversial material, audiences will probably care very much about who said it, in which case, it is more effective to mention the source *before* the evidence. If the facts are more important, give the source afterward.

- If the source is not known to the audience, give the source's credentials too.

- When speaking to a professional audience in their field, and when using a highly respected and authoritative source, you increase your effectiveness by mentioning the expert *followed* by the evidence.

A problem may have occurred to you: How does a speaker cite sources and not sound like a human footnote? Citing sources during a speech is different from in-text citations in a research paper. Following are a few ideas and models for crediting sources during a speech:

- *Include key sources in the introduction:* "In my search on what we *really* know about men and women communicating, I especially appreciate the work of Dr. Judy Pearson, author of more than fifteen textbooks and hundreds of papers and journal articles."

- *Briefly establish relevant credentials for experts who the audience may not recognize:* "Doctors Richard Wallace, a professor of management, and Deborah Currier, a professor of speech communication, add international management and business communication perspectives."

- *Introduce a name with a salient point:* "Lewis Terman studied over 1,500 gifted boys and girls and kept up with them through their major life events from the beginning of his study in 1922 until his death in 1956." "According to the American Cancer Society, . . ."

- *Tie the source to the audience:* "In this morning's newspaper I saw a *Dilbert* cartoon on technical bluffing, our subject today." "Dr. John Doolittle, Dean of Veterinary Medicine on our campus, warns . . ."

- *Allow the audience to glimpse the speaker's connection with the source:* "I had the opportunity to ask Gary Green that question. I think you will be interested in what he had to say."

- *Cite the source in visual support:* A PowerPoint slide can include a quotation and the name of the person who said it.

When you are primarily using only a few sources to which you refer frequently, give the more complete information about the source early in the speech, and briefly refer to it later in order to differentiate who said what. For a single-source report, a presenter may spend time in the introduction or the first main point establishing the credibility of the source and telling the audience that this will be the basis of today's presentation.

Example 6.5 illustrates some ways student Frank Rivera credited sources in his presentation on thalidomide. Notice that he did not assume authority over his sources and chose to cite them first each time.

● EXAMPLE 6.4

CITING SOURCES WITHIN A PRESENTATION

Expert Source + Credentials + Retrieval Source + Evidence

As Dr. Robert J. Amato of the Baylor College of Medicine states in the January 4, 2002, *Current Oncology Reporter,* "This drug is the new 'in thing' in medicine. Ask any physician about the most currently significant advancements, and thalidomide will undoubtedly be one."

Retrieval Source + Evidence

According to the *Dallas Morning News* of September 11, 2001, "doctors began noticing . . . blindness, deafness, [and] malformed internal organs [among newborns]. Some babies were born with severely deformed arms and feet."

Expert Source + Evidence + Retrieval Source + Additional Evidence

Fortunately the first female head of the FDA, Dr. Frances Kelsey, did not approve thalidomide's use in the U.S.; however, the *Sydney Morning Herald* of January 19, 2002, shows that by this time the drug had already affected over 10,000 children born abroad.

Evidence + Expert Source + Retrieval Source + Evidence

Evidence: Ferraro and the doctor are the subjects of the evidence, but not the *New York Times* reporter who wrote the article

Expert source: Ferraro

Retrieval source: New York Times, June 19, 2001

Evidence: Ferraro quote

In 1998, former vice president nominee Geraldine Ferraro was diagnosed with multiple myeloma, a type of blood cancer that destroys bone tissue and kills half the people it infects. Her doctor noticed the increasing number of cancer cells and prescribed thalidomide. As Ferraro explains in the *New York Times* of June 19, 2001, "What was terrible for a healthy fetus has been wonderful at defeating the cancer cells."

The mechanics of entries in a reference list may seem tedious, and decisions about citing those sources during a speech may, on first glance, seem irrelevant, but the end results shine with professionalism. After all, the reference formats are actually time savers for professionals in a field, and citations during the speech have persuasive and information processing implications for the listeners. You are also respecting your profession and your listeners by citing sources.

SUMMARY

Ethical, effective, and expressive communication depends upon credible, current information. *Expressive communicators* (1) choose meaningful material for their listeners, (2) use interesting information for the listeners, and (3) allow the listeners to experience the speaker's connection with the material.

Analyze a potential audience and narrow a general topic to a presentation topic. Use survey techniques for an overview of a subject, and post-hole techniques to gain depth in research. Research requires posing clear questions as a guide. Ethical research additionally requires verifying the information before stating it to an audience.

Your best information comes through your college or university's library. To find books on your topic, use the library's online public access catalog. Library subscriptions to Internet databases provide access to professional journals. Large databases of scholarly, juried journals are provided digitally for students through campus libraries. ●

As accessed through the college or university website, material is filtered for the quality of sources. When using general access to the Internet, *you* must determine whether material is credible and from high-quality sources, which should be (1) respected and scholarly, (2) current and maintained, (3) polished and professional, and (4) ethical.

An interview is another and very personal way to gather information. The interview is divided into introduction, body, and conclusion. Open the interview with introductions and your purpose. Organize questions by topic and put them in a logical progression for the body of the interview. Effective questions are usually open and allow the interviewee to partially guide the direction of the interview. Conclude the interview with a brief review and words of appreciation and closure.

Citing sources precludes many listeners' questions and doubts, and increases the speaker's credibility. Give credit to sources during speeches and for written documentation, cite references according to the American Psychological Association (APA) guidelines. •

ACTIVITIES

1. **Technical Support:** Through the Allyn & Bacon Public Speaking Website (http://wps.ablongman.com/ab_public_speaking_2), find the information relevant to your next speech on "Analyize" and "Research" by using the hypertext links.

2. **Journaling the Experience:** Journal your preparation for an interview. Add a journal entry after the interview, reflecting on the experience, the value of what you learned, skills you used, and skills you would like to develop. Keep a video or audio recording of the interview.

3. **Ethically Speaking:** Conduct a general Internet search for a health topic. Evaluate five sites, indicating the ones that you would feel best about using to retrieve information to teach an audience.

4. **Presenting to Others:** Sign up to demonstrate methods for conducting a search through an electronic periodical index on your college or university library's website. Create a PowerPoint visual to assist you as you instruct the class in navigating a search on your favorite site.

5. **Team Work:** Compete in a treasure hunt for materials. Your professor will give each team a set of questions to research the answers. You will be given 10 minutes to formulate a research strategy, and the remainder of the class time to gather materials. Present the team's collection at the end of the class period.

6. **Technical Support and Presenting to Others:** Plan and present one main point for a future speech, supporting the point with:

   a. A quote and a fact gathered in your interview

   b. A research conclusion from a scholarly journal, printed from a library's electronic site

   c. A definition retrieved through a search engine to the Internet

   d. An illustration imported from an Internet source to a PowerPoint slide, such as a newsworthy slide using a White House source photograph.

FOR FURTHER READING

A number of books give an interesting taste of fascinating subjects. Here are two that will give you ideas for topics and initial resources for speaking.

Anderson, S. (1996). *The great American bathroom book* (3 volumes). Compact Classics.

Beckett, W., & Wright, P. (1999). *Sister Wendy's 1000 masterpieces.* New York: Dorling Kendersley.

Interesting and credible websites are available. For instance, try the Smithonian Natural History Museum's Science Galaxy Mosaic at http://web4.si.edu/sil/galaxy/mosaic.cfm

Building Experience

Part III concentrates on public speaking, encouraging students to design and deliver well-researched and supported informative and persuasive presentations. Experience in the classroom becomes a bridge to presenting in the workplace.

Mastery in the emotional domain is especially difficult because skills need to be acquired when people are usually least able to take in new information and learn new habits of response—when they are upset (Goleman, 1995, p. 266).

Quick Start to Informative Speaking

7

- **The Speaking Experience**
- **Topic Choice**
- **Quick Start with Research**
- **Planning the Informative Speech**
- **Speech Mapping**
- **Rehearse**

The moment you decide to avoid public speaking for the rest of your life, the CEO "invites" you to brief the board of directors on a project. No one can hide, including systems programmers, engineers, and architects, because "techies" these days routinely explain designs and products to clients. An informative presentation is an efficient form of delivering information to several people at a time. In the academic world, we call these presentations *informative speeches*. In the business world, they fall under many names: reports at meetings, public forums, walk-throughs, professional workshops, and teleconferences (Dzurinko, 1999).

The purpose of this chapter is to lead you step by step through the process of preparing and delivering an informative speech. The chapter acknowledges the difference between informing and persuading and gets you off to a quick start preparing an informative speech. The skills you learn will adapt readily to organizational settings.

OBJECTIVES

After studying the content of this chapter, you should be able to

- Define informative speaking, and recognize informative speaking in organizations
- Utilize various organizational patterns
- Understand the functions of speeches' introductions, bodies, and conclusions
- Support main points effectively
- Create an informative speech
- Strategically rehearse and effectively deliver an informative speech to a classroom audience

THE SPEAKING EXPERIENCE

In the secure environment of the classroom, we don't miss out on job promotions, and we don't lose credibility with our fellow employees. The classroom is a laboratory for building workplace skills that provides experience in designing and delivering presentations to a live audience. Outside the classroom, form follows function, and presentations conform to audience expectations.

By definition, a *public speech* presents ideas to several people gathered to listen to a speaker, and generally the speaker is the only one expected to speak. Indeed, some *presentations* (the broader term) are prototypical speeches—in other words, just what you would expect of a speech. Other presentations, however, are woven into a conversation, during which the presenter anticipates frequent interaction or interaction immediately following the presentation. Client relationships, for instance, require interaction in the development phase of a product, when the clients feel free to comment or ask questions. Another common difference is that everyone—including the speaker—may be seated during the presentation.

Though settings and expectations vary, classroom presentations provide excellent preparation for future employment. The ways the basic parts of the presentation are presented to the audience vary. This section discusses what informative speaking is and isn't, how to factor the audience into the equation, and practical criteria for informative topics. In Reality @ Work 7.1, Diane McEachern, currently with United Bank of Switzerland (financial investors and advisors) lets us see how closely training matches practice in her experiences.

Reality
@ WORK
7.1

PROFITABLE AND INFORMATIVE

Upon graduation from the University of Texas in the 1970s, Diane McEachern was sent by E.F. Hutton to its professional training school in New York. Her training included specific public speaking skills—visuals, preview and review, eye contact, voice intonation, building rapport, and more. It seemed that to her employers, becoming a professional meant becoming a speaker.

Soon after her initial training, her home community's chamber of commerce asked her to give a speech. Because most people had only hazy concepts of how the stock market operated, she chose "Wall Street" as her topic. "In giving one speech, I reached about sixty people in one hour. Furthermore, someone introduced me and established my credibility with the audience. I realized that this was so much more effective than the established practice of 'cold calling' potential clients one at a time." The informative presentation had built her credibility on financial topics.

McEachern, now with Paine Webber, saw a niche of need because more women were managing finances, so she launched a series she named "Smart Money for Women." Today, her following remains so strong that she leads monthly presentations and discussions on financial topics. Recognizing that expertise is associated with the person at the podium, McEachern advises, "Never totally relinquish the podium." If Diane invites an outside speaker, she still "commands" the podium to introduce the speaker, to answer some of the questions, and to close the meeting.

Identifying Informative Presentations

Let's compare the basic approaches of informative and persuasive speeches. They both build on a base of information and have a *thesis* or *claim* that they declare to be true. Also, they both try to persuade audiences that the facts and ideas they present are credible and important.

There are differences, however. Informative speeches instruct listeners, so they instruct and teach, but the simple dimension of including information does not make a speech an informative speech. Informative speeches explain concepts, introduce innovations, review research, teach processes, and demonstrate uses, among other purposes. Persuasive speeches, on the other hand, advocate policy, accentuate a belief or value, take a stand on a controversial issue, and lead listeners to predetermined conclusions. In summary, (1) informing is explaining a situation to the listeners, and (2) persuading is explaining a situation in light of advising what the listeners should do about it.

CONTRASTING INFORMING AND PERSUADING

ACTIVITY 7.1

An executive committee asks Lisa, a research supervisor at Alpha Pharmaceuticals, to report the progress of two work teams. The executive committee prioritizes projects and sets resources. Her teams also rely on Lisa's presentation to get additional project support.

1. *What are the committee's expectations of Lisa's presentation?*
2. *What if Lisa thinks one project is more likely to succeed than the other?*
3. *In what ways should she use informing processes? Persuading strategies?*
4. *What could offend the committee?*

A skilled informative speaker is a valuable asset to an organization. The speaker gathers information and analyzes its significance before explaining it to an audience. Good informative speakers enrich their listeners in some way.

Completing the Speaking Equation

Keeping in mind the purpose of informative presentations, let's think about your academic class as audience as well as the occasion of your upcoming speeches. You are the sender, but they are the receivers that make the communication of the message complete. All of this takes place at a particular time in a specific place. Overall, your basic challenges are to provide an audience with relevant information and to help them remember it. That starts with analyzing the audience.

Audience Demographics

Form a general picture of the people who will be listening to you—cultures, jobs, and socioeconomic levels. Consider the mix of ages, genders, academic majors, work experiences, and interests. If you know any of the audience, imagine how they will receive your presentation.

In the workplace, a mixed audience of employees from different organizations or different departments will make different—even political—interpretations of your speech.

Location and Occasion

Think about where you will be speaking. Probably you have an upcoming classroom speech, for which you're familiar with the room size, furniture, technology, and possible distractions. In business settings, you won't always be familiar with the physical arrangement. You could be teaching employees to use new equipment hands-on at a noisy factory, or you could be teaching them in a classroom away from the equipment. Such wide-ranging situations call for different informative techniques.

In the workplace, visit a location ahead of time or ask a contact person about arrangements for your presentation. Sometimes, you can request a seating or table arrangement. The more familiar you are with the setting, the less likely you will be thrown off by a technical problem.

Audience Needs and Interests

Determine the needs of your audience, what is important to them, what interests them, and what will be over their heads. Speakers motivate listeners by connecting with interests they already hold, but they must lead into unknown territory.

Audience Familiarity with Topic

An audience's familiarity with a topic governs the presenter's use of time. Consider what the audience already knows, how current they are in their information, and how versatile they are in thinking about the topic. A speaker is especially challenged when an audience has mixed levels of expertise.

 **TOPIC CHOICE**

Criteria for Informative Topics

Choose topics according to criteria that determine whether a topic fulfills an assignment without violating standards or inserting unneeded, extraneous material. Some of you as students are new to your majors, and others are soon to be in the workplace. With this range in mind, this textbook gives suggestions for appropriate topics that will prepare for the workplace, yet address a student audience.

- *Choose a topic that is appropriate for the assignment.* Whether at work or in a classroom, the topic should match the assignment, the supervisor or professor's requirements, and the time limit. Informative topics usually are about objects, processes, events, or concepts. Informative purposes may also fall under the category of definitions, descriptions, explanations, and demonstrations, if, for instance, your assignment is to demonstrate how something is made or explain industries' effects on local ecology.

- *Choose a topic that is appropriate for the community.* Meeting community standards is a criterion of ethics as well as a criterion of taste. Respect listeners' values, recognize the speech setting, and choose a topic that is appropriate for the group. You may decide that, for example, sexual harassment makes a worthwhile topic for adults seeking positions in management but wouldn't work for middle school students on career day.

- *Choose a topic from which the audience will learn something new (at least to them).* Share the satisfaction of learning something new and interesting. If the audience members do not learn something new, then you haven't instructed them. Your speech should add value to the knowledge and understanding of the listeners. "New" includes facts they didn't know, points of view they hadn't thought of, and procedures they hadn't considered.

- *Choose a topic that the audience will see as important, useful, or interesting.* If a topic is useful, important, or interesting, wouldn't the audience probably already have researched it? Perhaps, but remember that none of us has learned all that we want to know, and often what we need is guidance in what to learn. Finding an important, yet new, topic is the thrill of the hunt for a speaker.

- *Choose a topic on which you can remain objective.* Be wary of selecting topics on controversial issues or ones on which there are strong opinions. There are some exceptions, such as an informative speech that presents background information on a topic or even-handedly deals with both sides of an issue. In Activity 7.1, for example, Lisa was challenged in evaluating projects at a pharmaceutical company. In the business world, be honest with yourself about issues on which you cannot or will not give unbiased presentations.

- *Choose a topic that holds current interest and has accurate data available.* On one hand, yesterday's hot topic may seem clichéd today. On the other hand, some topics are so current that it's hard to find current, accurate information fast enough. Follow the news and sources that you check regularly about your topic, including the day you give your speech.

Table 7.1 lists some methods for finding a topic.

Speaking on Organizational Topics

Whether at work or in classes, sometimes topics are assigned, and other times you get to choose a topic. Although the planning tools of this chapter apply to various kinds of informative speeches, we will develop a speech aimed at

TABLE 7.1 • Shopping for Topics

> • *What you already know or are interested in:* Pay attention to your areas of expertise and what you like to talk about in conversation. In your other classes or community service work, what do you want to know more about?
>
> • *The current periodical section of the library:* Magazine and journal covers are designed to catch your attention, so check out covers, tables of contents, and articles that seem worthwhile and interesting. The articles will usually lead you to other sources.
>
> • *Bookstores and popular informative titles:* Likewise, bookstores display popular new books to grab your attention. Do you see a book that interests you with a topic that would work for your speech?

teaching content. As you develop your career, note the areas in which to develop expertise and present it to others.

Biographical Sketches

Focus on the life of an interesting and important person. Biographical material is readily available and varied. A number of leaders in the business world have written best-selling books or have been profiled on television or in books and magazines. You can also talk about a famous person in history, an inventor, a scientist, an outstanding sports figure, or a philanthropist.

Turning Points

Consider historically compelling pivotal events—the "Waterloo" moments in history. Major wars, natural disasters such as Hurricane Katrina, inventions, and discoveries always affect business, industry, and the marketplace. This type of topic is especially good for combining sources creatively.

The Fine Arts

Music, art, and dance topics make excellent informative speech subjects, such as a biographical sketch of a musician or artist or a particular period in the arts. Arts topics are often the subject matter for nonprofit organizations—museum tours, docent lectures, symphony lectures, and the like. Possible topics are "Henri Matisse, an Eye for Color," "Rodin, Thinking," "Mozart, From Riches to Rags," or "Jazz, the American Music." (Notice that each of these begins with a broad topic, but narrows with a second phrase to focus on a theme.)

New Technology

Read recent *Scientific American, Science,* or *Discovery* magazines to get ideas, or check electronic news sources for recent inventions and discoveries relevant to your field of study or major interest. Audiences love being among the first to learn something newsworthy. Check what's new in transportation, space exploration, global communication, synthetics, energy technology, and robotics, for instance.

Medical Research

National and international medical research costs millions—even billions—of dollars annually. Research reports are rich pipelines for material. Medical reporters for news agencies helpfully summarize findings in layman's language.

A Global Society

Economics, marketing, and business majors study global issues. What is the impact of stock trading in Japan on the stock market in New York? What are European influences on fashion? Are there collaborations among countries to find a cure for AIDS? What can you learn about countries emerging after communism dominance from visiting Prague today? (Remember that you are to stay within informative boundaries, so it's wise to choose a topic that is not controversial for your audience.)

Current Events

Have you ever researched a country in the news, perhaps one you had barely heard of before? Point out the country's location and highlight major issues to help an audience follow the news. A class learned about East Timor from a student's speech, and their interest in following news about that geographical area grew. And the ideas go on and on—giant pandas and South Pole exploration, plate tectonics reconfiguring the U.S. coasts, a frozen woolly mammoth, and treasures of the *Titanic*. You don't have to be an expert, but you *do* need to be interested.

Make a list of possible topics for your informative speech. Don't worry right now about which ideas are best. Just begin listing topic possibilities. Review your ideas to make sure you have an informative purpose in mind. (As a reminder, don't take a stand on controversial issues such as pay for student athletes, school prayer, managed health care, school vouchers, foreign intervention, and the like.) If you have chosen a topic, you are ready for a quick start to your research.

• QUICK START WITH RESEARCH

Chapter 6 explains more fully how to research a topic, but this section gives you a running start regarding collecting material.

- If you saw your topic in a magazine, newspaper, or book, start there. Did the author quote someone or cite a source in the material? Show the original source to a librarian and ask how you can find more information on that topic. You may find the original source and related articles on findarticles.com.

- Attend a library orientation session to get great ideas for efficient library research.

- Use the "electronic library" to access Infoseek or Wilson Web, and conduct a search. You can print full-text articles in the library, and you may be able to sign up at the college to access the library from your home or other location.

- Fastcompany.com and Discovery.com are interesting sources for business and science topics, respectively.
- Talk to an expert. Write out three or four good questions to ask an expert. Make an appointment for a short interview. A professor may lead you to interesting material on your topic.
- Listen to a news program that has regular science, medical, or arts reports. Use the program as one source. Pay attention to names of experts, and conduct a computer search on those names.
- Use the web pages of PBS, CNN, or MSNBC networks to find transcripts of interviews and documentaries.

PLANNING THE INFORMATIVE SPEECH

As a new "speech architect," the hardest part is getting started. Speakers don't all plan exactly alike, but most speakers follow an order similar to that shown in Quick Start 7.1. It keeps them on track and uses time well. Speech preparation centers on five basic areas:

1. Choose a general topic and write specific purpose and central idea statements.
2. Research and limit the scope of the topic, and document sources.
3. Plan the body of the speech, including the organization and support of main points.
4. Plan the introduction and conclusion of the speech.
5. Rehearse for the speech event.

Earlier you selected your topic and did preliminary research, and the rehearsal comes later, but at this stage you need to gather and organize the content of your speech. Scan Quick Start 7.1, read all referenced material, and then move step by step through it to create an informative speech.

Purpose Statement

The *purpose statement* is a planning statement—a blueprint for the speech. Study these informative purpose statements:

After hearing my speech on "Peter Drucker and the Nonprofit Organization," the audience will know relevant facts about Drucker's contributions to business practices and recognize the impact of nonprofit organizations on our society.

After hearing my speech, the audience will be able to explain Henri Matisse's inclusion in *The Wild Ones*, discuss his search for "pure color," and analyze the effect of juxtaposed colors.

At the end of my speech, the audience will be able to compare businesses in Prague today with businesses in Prague under communism.

After hearing my speech, the audience will be able to explain the path genetic research has followed toward a cure for diabetes.

● QUICK START 7.1   Plan Your Speech   ● ● ● ●

Your Decisions	Helpful Text Pages
1. Write a specific purpose statement	172–173
2. Write a central idea statement that is consistent with your specific purpose statement.	173–174
3. Tentatively select your main ideas.	
4. Examine your main ideas. Do they cover your central idea and specific purpose? Do they include ideas that are outside your speech purpose? (Adjust the main ideas or change your purpose, if needed.)	
5. Decide on an organizational pattern for the main points.)	174–176
6. Choose support for each main point.	176–180
7. Examine the support for the main points. (Have you selected support that helps the listener understand or remember that main point? Have you varied the forms of support?)	

8. Plan the introduction.
    a. Attention-getter
    b. Motivation for the audience to listen
    c. Speaker credibility
    d. Preview
	180–184

9. Plan the conclusion.
    a. Review
    b. Final memorable statement
	184–185

Notice that these purpose statements are written from an *audience's* point of view. They state the intended effect on the audience, and they specify what an audience member who hears the speech should be able to do.

You may also notice that the purpose statement practically lays out main points. There are two main points in the statement regarding the speech about Drucker. Can you find three main points in the Matisse speech statement and two points in the Prague speech statement? The diabetes speech statement does not map out the main points as clearly. It does indicate, however, a logical or chronological organization of main points by using the word *progressing*.

The specific purpose statement provides a reality check for you as you plan your speech. You may rewrite your specific purpose statement several times as you develop your speech, just as blueprints are often modified when you build a house.

Central Idea Statement

The *central idea statement* (sometimes called the *thesis* or *theme*) reflects the specific purpose statement. If you boiled down your entire speech to one statement, this is the statement it would be. State this central idea clearly to your audience early in your speech. The central idea statement should be concise and should contain an inclusive idea (an "umbrella") that unifies the speech. Write the central idea as a statement, not a question.

> **Classroom informative speech example:** "Peter Senge applies open systems theory to his popular notion of learning organizations."

> **Workplace speaking application:** "The Blue Cross/Blue Shield health benefits package for Infobility has five significant features."

Organization of Main Points

Plan two to five main points. The audience is not likely to remember more than five points in one speech. To help listeners follow you, sequence the ideas purposefully. Some beginning speakers want their accumulated knowledge to magically move into the audience's minds. Forget magical thinking! Years of experience are better for providing useful patterns of organization. This section briefly discusses four common patterns of organization.

• • • • TIPS   • • • • Speaking as Leading Audiences • • • •

Think of yourself as a tour guide for a major candy company. You catch the visitors' attention and establish your expertise by giving them background about M&M Mars. You explain the significance of this information to them and explain the order in which you will move through the plant.

Your guests follow you to the first area, where Twix candy bars are packaged. Here you explain processes and innovations affecting the candy industry. You make a transition from packaging to the area where the Twix bars are made, again pointing out key equipment and processes. And on it goes as you lead them through the plant. After the last area, you summarize tour highlights in a memorable way, thus indicating the tour has ended.

Speaking is a similar process with similar leadership. You catch the audience's attention, introduce the topic, tell why it's important, and preview the main points (areas of the plant) that you will take them through. Each featured area is presented as a related, but separate, entity. A transition is made between all areas. After the last main point, you summarize and give a final memorable statement. Keep in mind this analogy of leading from place to place as you plan your speech. Be deliberate in how you develop each point before moving to the next.

• • •

Chronological Organization

Chronos is the root word for *time,* as in *chronology;* thus, *chronological organization* organizes the main points in the order in which they occur. In a biographical sketch, the main points naturally develop from youth to old age or from early career to late career.

    I. Franklin D. Roosevelt achieves early career success, against all odds.

    II. Roosevelt's first term proved his assertive authority as president of the United States.

    III. The war years proved Roosevelt's resolve and resilience.

    IV. An illustrious career ends.

Chronological order can also be a logical order of sequenced steps, such as the steps used to reclaim and study a frozen woolly mammoth.

Topical Organization

When ideas seem to group into main points, but the main points do not require a particular order, you may choose topical organization. The following main points can be arranged in any order.

    I. Public schools are vehicles for social change.

    II. Public education is a fundamental right for all children in the United States.

    III. Federal funding complicates individual states' control of public schools.

Spatial or Geographic Organization

Spatial arrangement of points organizes according to space or geography, as in top to bottom, inside and outside, west and east, room by room, and state by state. "Federal, state, and local" is a common spatial organization. It is often one of the easiest patterns for an audience to follow when a topic is a natural fit. A speech on Yellowstone National Park can be organized geographically:

    I. Geysers and other thermal features are abundant in the southwestern area of the park.

    II. The Grand Canyon of the Yellowstone and Lake Yellowstone are the major features of southeastern Yellowstone.

    III. Mammoth Hot Springs dominates the north park for most tourists.

Causal Organization

A city planner explains small town health care systems like this:

    I. The small town hospital has given way to metropolitan health care systems. (effect)

    II. More physicians specialize as the amount of medical information increases. (cause 1)

    III. Medical tests and procedures require expensive, dedicated equipment. (cause 2)

    IV. Satellite clinics satisfy the small town residents' needs for immediate access to a personal physician. (cause 3)

Causal organization is most often seen in persuasive speaking, but you may find cause-to-effect or effect-to-cause a good fit for your informative topic as well. Students are familiar with causal reasoning from their science courses: the effects of mixing two chemicals, the causes of epidemics, the effects of force, and so forth.

An economist explains three influences on the stock market:

    I. The federal government lowers interest rates. (cause 1)

    II. The federal government lowers taxes. (cause 2)

    III. Sectors of business are growing. (cause 3)

    IV. The stock market goes up. (effect)

To explain how experts commonly predict national economic trends, the speaker could list events that historically have triggered bearish or bullish stock markets. What to present first—effect or cause—depends on the audience's knowledge. If they are more informed about the effect on the economy but do not know the causes, then one should start with the effect and then explain the causes.

Supporting Main Points

Use supporting material to substantiate your points. Predict what your listeners can understand and how they can remember what you teach. Use pertinent, helpful material and say enough, but not too much.

- All material should point back to the specific purpose you've written.
- All material should be accurate, meaningful, and reliable.
- All material should clarify the topic.

Effective speakers use a variety of supporting material. Governor Ed Schafer used several forms of support for a keynote address at the Telemedicine 2000 Conference/Exhibition in Chicago, Illinois in 1996. The governor informed attendees of an important health care option in North Dakota—telemedicine. Excerpts from his speech provide examples of supporting material, showing the effectiveness of a variety of types of support.

Explanation

Explanation is probably the first form of support you will use in your presentation. Quite often a speaker states a main point and then explains it more fully. *Expounding* means adding statements to further explain and clarify. Following is an example on the issue of confidentiality. Notice in the example that the first statement would be inadequate without the explanation of the second statement.

> Another issue . . . is confidentiality. Telemedicine consultations might involve personal medical records being shipped over computer lines to other regions of the country.

Explanation sometimes *defines* a term or concept. Shafer defines "Med Start," a term that would not be familiar to all of his audience:

> Telemedicine also provides a great tool for continuing education. In North Dakota, we are already taking advantage of telecommunication technology for this purpose. The University of North Dakota School of Medicine has a program called Med Start that links the school to hospitals throughout the state via an audio-video network. Through this network, physicians, nurses, physical therapists and any health care professionals can take a wide variety of continuing education courses taught by professors in the UND School of Medicine.

Example

An *example* illustrates or represents things, helping the listener to focus more clearly on the idea or understand it more fully. Examples may be hypothetical, such as "Imagine having telemedicine available in your community," or they may be real. Examples may be quite extensive or only a brief reference. Shafer used a brief, real example in his speech:

> In 1995, two medical facilities in North Dakota—Medcenter One and St. Alexius Medical Center—started offering telemedicine services to select communities in North Dakota.

Sometimes an example is visual. The governor mentioned a visual example he used in a different speech:

> As part of my annual State of the State address, I not only talked about telemedicine, I underwent a full telemedicine consultation and exam right there in the North Dakota House of Representative Chambers. A doctor on site consulted with a doctor off site, who was visible on screen in the Chambers and on statewide television.
>
> They examined my ear and my head—basically, the entire state got to see the inside of my head. Of course, my political opponents (and even my staff!) quipped that the light was going to shine right through my head and out my other ear!
>
> The exam was basic, but it gave people throughout North Dakota a glimpse of what telemedicine is, how it works, and what it can do.

Narrative

Narratives are stories. They share qualities with examples in that they may be real or hypothetical, brief or lengthy. Governor Shafer said, "I have countless stories to tell about how telemedicine is working in North Dakota." He told about a boy who was thrown off a horse. An emergency telemedicine consultation allowed the boy to be treated at home, thus saving thousands of dollars to the boy's family and their insurance company. He followed with narrative again:

> In another case, an 88-year-old lady named Alvina, who lives in a nursing home in Wishek, N.D., had surgery in Bismarck to close several ulcers on her feet. Through telemedicine, she was able to perform all 8 follow-up visits with a plastic surgeon. It saved her the trauma and exhaustion of traveling nearly 180 miles round trip to the specialist. Her nurses said it took Alvina three days to recover from these trips. Plus, her daughter didn't have to take time off work to drive her to Bismarck. Today Alvina is back on her feet, literally, and walking normally. Clearly, these examples show the impact telemedicine is already having in North Dakota.

Quotations or Testimony

The term *testimony* originates from courts of law. For our purposes, *quotation* and *testimony* are interchangeable. Quotations from famous people work well in introductions and conclusions, but they also provide variety and other voices in the body of the speech. Experts and their writings are quoted for definitions, statistics, explanations, and examples. Here are two pieces of testimony that Shafer used:

> The Western Governors' Association's Telemedicine Action Report of June 1995 identified six barriers to expanded inter- and intrastate use of telemedicine. The barriers identified in the Action Report are:

1. Infrastructure Planning and Development
2. Telecommunications Regulation
3. Lack of Reimbursement for Telemedicine Services
4. Licenser and Credentialing of Physicians and Other Health Care Practitioners
5. Medical Malpractice Liability
6. Confidentiality

In the preceding example, you see that Shafer cited an association and quoted the "barriers" verbatim. In the following testimony, he used an excerpt from a congressional document.

> In passing the Telecommunications Act of 1996, Congress specified that telecommunications should be used to enhance health care in America. Key language in the Act gives health care providers the right to "rates charged for similar services in urban areas in that State."

Facts

Facts seem synonymous with information; therefore, facts are in our list of supporting material. Facts are the events, dates, people, locations, and other observable information that can be verified by a reliable source. Facts are actually "examples of one" or "undeniable results." An earlier excerpt from Shafer's speech included this "example of one":

> The University of North Dakota School of Medicine has a program called Med Start that links the school to hospitals throughout the state via an audio-video network.

Statistics

A collection of related facts may be summarized and represented with *statistical* support. To correctly support an idea statistically, use accurate, meaningful data expressed in a numerical form. Statistics can give specific substance to support a statement. Do not make statistical support too hard to follow. Visuals, such as charts or PowerPoint slides, allow comparisons or retention of complex statistical support. Here is an effective use of statistical support by Governor Shafer. Notice that he rounds the number for retention.

> Approximately 200 telemedicine consultations have been completed in North Dakota to date.

In the following use of statistics, consider the sequence. The costs *follow* the sentence Shafer really wants the audience to remember.

> As telemedicine providers in North Dakota will tell you, the costs of the system and the initial cash outlays required are substantial. The basic cost for a single-site set up is $90,000. This does not include any extra scopes, which providers in our state are frequently finding to be unnecessary considering their cost ($15,000 per scope).

Comparison and Contrast

The governor used another set of statistics in order to *contrast* (show the differences) medical care in populated and unpopulated areas of the state.

> The populated regions boast 147 total medical specialists and 221 surgical specialists. The unpopulated regions, on the other hand, only have six total medical specialists and only 33 total surgical specialists.

Analogy and Metaphor

Analogies and metaphors provide figurative language to prompt a listener to use a familiar concept in order to understand an unfamiliar concept. Analogous reasoning is actually a form of comparison, much of which is implied. For instance, a student speaker used the analogy of the human eye responding to light to teach how a camera lens works. The next section of this chapter uses the cities and roads of maps as analogies for main ideas and transition statements. Be careful in using analogies that may trigger the opposite response from what you expect from your listeners.

Skillful analogies are very powerful for instruction, but weak analogies confuse listeners. Shafer did not rely on analogy in this speech, although he played on the metaphor of an empty head.

> They examined my ear and my hand—basically, the entire state got to see the inside of my head. Of course, my political opponents (and even my staff!) quipped that the light was going to shine right through my head and out my other ear!

He also led the audience to reason that this sort of physical examination was analogous to examinations for people with health issues.

> The exam was basic, but it gave people throughout North Dakota a glimpse of what telemedicine is, how it works, and what it can do.

Metaphors, abbreviated analogies, allow us to make logical leaps toward understanding a concept. Shafer, like most of us, uses metaphors, often without realizing it. Here are a few examples from his speech:

> The present *patchwork* of state laws . . . .
>
> Telemedicine also provides a great *tool* for continuing education.
>
> However, as you all know, we aren't over the *hump* yet. Nationally, and even in North Dakota who's at the *front of the pack,* we are in the very early stages of implementing telemedicine and realizing its full potential.
>
> "The *devil* is in the details" perhaps applies here.

Repetition or Rephrasing

Repeating or rephrasing a key idea can help an audience. Like underlining a statement in written material, a slight rewording gives emphasis. Governor Shafer repeated this key supporting statistic twice for emphasis:

> That's 147 specialists in populated regions, versus 6 specialists in unpopulated regions.

Use a relevant and unusual or intriguing object to focus an audience's attention on your topic.

Visuals

Any form of support may exist in visual form. Governor Shafer could have used charts or PowerPoint to present facts and statistics. The television and information ages are colliding, influencing audiences to depend on what they see. These expectations amplify the effects of visual support.

Sometimes the vision *is* the message, not just a channel for the message. Telemedicine, Shafer's topic, is a prime example. In order for telemedicine to work, the physician must *see* the patient via the medium. Otherwise, a telephone call would work. Chapter 9 details the use of visual support.

Introduction

The introduction prepares the listeners. Five things should be accomplished in the introduction:

1. The audience's attention should be focused on you and your speech. (*attention technique*)

2. The audience should know the subject of the speech. (*statement of topic*)

3. The audience should know why they are learning about this topic. (*importance of topic and motivation to listen*)

4. The audience should have confidence in you and in the quality of your material. (*speaker's credibility*)

5. The audience should have an idea of how you will sequence the material. (*preview*)

The functions of an introduction should become automatic for you. Logically, you must get the audience's attention at the beginning, and usually the preview is the last part of the introduction, but the other parts are not sequenced the same in every speech. Let's look at each part.

Audience Attention

First of all, get the audience's attention. Here are several effective techniques.

- *Ask a question.* The question can be direct or rhetorical. When a speaker uses a direct question, the speaker expects an answer from the audience. For instance, request a show of hands to the question "How many of you ate breakfast this morning?" When a speaker poses a question and does not expect the audience to answer, the speaker has asked a rhetorical question. For instance, "Have you ever been in a situation where you desperately needed medical attention, but could not afford to get it?"

- *Use a thought-provoking quotation.* A stimulating quotation or the headline of a news story evokes interest. For instance, "Pollen and diesel fumes don't mix for allergy sufferers. Inhaled diesel particles increased histamine production fivefold in allergy sufferers."

- *Use startling, surprising, or sobering statistics.* "L'Oreal sales agents selected on the basis of certain emotional competencies significantly outsold salespeople selected using the company's old selection procedure. On an annual basis, salespeople selected on the basis of emotional competence outsold other salespeople by $91,370 for a net revenue increase of $2,558,360. These higher performers also had 63% less turnover during the first year than those selected in the organization's usual way" (Spencer & Spencer, 1993; Spencer, McClelland, & Kelner, 1997).

- *Use a brief narrative.* Tell a personal story or one with which you are familiar. Perhaps tell the first part of a story and leave the audience hanging until the conclusion to get the rest of the story. "I was literally stuck inside the clothes dryer, head first. The cage I now lived in would not budge from the opening of the shiny white opening, and all I could smell was the scent of Downy."

- *Use appropriate humor.* Humor homogenizes the response of the audience quickly. Some speakers tell jokes well. Others make humorous observations or tell funny, true stories. Be sure that the humor is appropriate, leads into the topic, and does not take the audience on a listening tangent.

● EXAMPLE 7.1

Classroom Informative Speech Example

An example of an opening statement using surprising statistics is as follows: "According to a survey done by Royal Dutch/Shell, one third of the firms in the Fortune 500 in 1970 had disappeared by 1983. Shell estimated the average lifetime of the largest industrial enterprises to be less than forty years. Peter Senge, the founder and director of the Center for Organizational Learning at MIT's Sloan School of Management, blames the high mortality rate on the inability of an organization to learn."

Workplace Speaking Application

In a business setting (we'll call our fictitious company "Infobility"), you may get the audience's attention a number of ways. For instance, you could use a thought-provoking, rhetorical question: "Have you had to check in for day surgery, only to be asked frustrating questions such as 'What is your pre-certification number?' or 'Do you want us to submit your co-payment cost to your secondary coverage?'" Perhaps you would prefer a humorous statement such as, "Some people would rather do surgery on themselves than to have to submit insurance forms to cover surgery."

Statement of Topic

State your topic very clearly and early in your speech. Speakers may state the central idea at this point. Allow time to anchor the central idea with the audience.

EXAMPLE 7.2

Classroom Informative Speech Example

Continuing with our classroom introduction, we would clarify for the audience what the central idea is: "Peter Senge presents seven learning disabilities evident in organizations that contribute to their failure to thrive."

Workplace Speaking Application

At Infobility (our fictitious company) you may state, "Today we'll learn about five features of the Blue Cross/Blue Shield health benefits package that Infobility has chosen."

Importance of Topic and Motivation to Listen

Imagine the listener asking, "What's in it for me?" It makes sense to tell listeners what they can expect to gain, so they will be motivated to listen from the start. If you can't justify your choice of topic for this audience, change your topic. Some reasons for listening are that the topic helps the audience to understand current events or deals with research developments that will affect them.

EXAMPLE 7.3

Classroom Informative Speech Example

"You and I are looking toward future employment in the business community. Our understanding of common organizational learning disabilities will equip us to avoid those errors or to avoid companies entrenched in those errors."

Workplace Speaking Application

At Infobility you may continue, "Spending a few minutes today to learn about these features will save you time, money, and frustration when you are the one checking into the hospital."

Speaker's Credibility

The audience has the right to know why they should listen to *you*. You *can* build credibility without bragging. Use this part of the speech to document your major resources, to establish your interest and expertise in the subject, or to mention your conversation with an expert.

● EXAMPLE 7.4

Classroom Informative Speech Example

"I recently read *The Fifth Discipline* by Peter Senge and found his ideas informative and intriguing. A Web search on learning organizations led me to several articles, many by Senge. I followed up by interviewing Dr. Linda Dulin of McLennan Community College. She further explained the learning disability concept and critiqued Senge's contribution to the understanding of the workplace in the twenty-first century."

Another part of building credibility establishes a sense of good will and ethical treatment of the topic. The audience wants to know that you are a good person and that you care about them.

● EXAMPLE 7.5

Workplace Speaking Application

A credibility statement to the Infobility audience could be, "As the human resources director, I'm responsible for keeping informed of the benefits available to you. I anticipated your questions, so I spent two days with a representative of your insurance carrier. I'm here to answer your questions."

Preview

The preview prepares the listeners to follow the presentation. In the informational speech, the preview often lists the main points. You are setting up a road map for the audience to travel as you go through the body of the speech.

● EXAMPLE 7.6

Classroom Informative Speech Example

"First I'll briefly define what a learning organization is. Then I'll explain the learning disabilities that come from how I view myself in the organization. Finally, I'll talk about learning disabilities that come from how I view others outside the organization." You'll notice from this example that the speaker chose to use one main point to clarify the concept of a "learning organization." The seven learning disabilities could have made seven additional main points, but she grouped the disabilities under "how I view myself in the organization" and "how I view others outside the organization," for a total of three main points.

Workplace Speaking Application

"Today I'll explain the criteria the committee used in selecting a new benefits package, and then we'll look in more detail at five major features of the package." This workplace application speech would probably be at least thirty minutes long, and the main points would be as follows:

 I. The benefits committee used several criteria in selecting a benefits package.
 II. The new benefits package provides five key features.

Now let's put the parts of the introduction together for the classroom speech example:

> According to a survey done by Royal Dutch/Shell, one third of the firms in the Fortune 500 in 1970 had disappeared by 1983. Shell estimated the average lifetime of the largest industrial enterprises to be less than forty years. Peter Senge, the founder and director of the Center for Organizational Learning at MIT's Sloan School of Management, blames the high mortality rate on the inability of an organization to learn.
>
> Peter Senge presents seven learning disabilities evident in organizations that contribute to their failure to thrive, and it is these errors that I want to talk about today.
>
> Since you and I are looking toward future employment in the business community, our understanding of common organizational errors will equip us to avoid those errors or to avoid companies entrenched in those errors.
>
> I recently read *The Fifth Discipline* by Peter Senge and found his ideas informative and intriguing. A web search on learning organizations led me to numerous articles, many by Senge. I followed up by interviewing Dr. Linda Dulin of McLennan Community College. She further explained the learning disability concept and critiqued Senge's contribution to the understanding of the workplace in the twenty-first century.
>
> First I'll briefly define what a learning organization is. Then I'll explain the learning disabilities that come from how we view ourselves in the organization. Finally, I'll talk about learning disabilities that come from how we view others outside the organization.

Conclusion

The conclusion brings closure and a sense of accomplishment to the listeners. The conclusion has two requirements: Review the main points and give a final memorable statement.

Review of Main Points

Review the main points to anchor them with the audience. This will serve as a mental checklist of what was learned from the presentation. The review of the main points frequently mirrors the preview used in the introduction.

● EXAMPLE 7.7

Classroom Informative Speech Example

"So now you know what a learning organization is and seven learning disabilities that lead to organizations' disasters. We can see how our perceptions of self and of others contribute to those errors."

Workplace Speaking Application

"In conclusion, you know how the committee chose the benefits package, and you are familiar with five major features of the package."

Final Memorable Statement

The last thing you say in a speech should have impact and provide closure.

● EXAMPLE 7.8

Classroom Informative Speech Example

"As Senge says, 'Learning disabilities are tragic in children, especially when they go undetected. They are no less tragic in organizations, where they also go largely undetected.'"

Workplace Speaking Application

"As your human resources director, I want to be both human and resourceful. So please come by and ask questions anytime you want to. As you learn about your benefits package, you empower yourself to benefit from this security at Infobility."

────────────────────────────── ●

Overall, for the conclusion, aim to equal or exceed the impact and creativity of the introduction. You may quote an expert, answer a question you used in the introduction, complete a narrative you left hanging in the introduction, or refer to facts or humor used in the introduction. Other appropriate concluding remarks could be passing on the baton of expertise ("Now, you too know how to . . .") or showing a "capstone" visual or application. In substance, style, and delivery bring the speech to closure. Leave the audience with a sense of accomplishment and a timely ending.

If you plan to follow with a question-and-answer session, announce that fact after the final statement of the speech. Either you (as the presenter) or a moderator of the event should bring the question-and-answer period to closure, usually by thanking participants and showing appreciation to the group.

● SPEECH MAPPING

If your professor says an outline is required, fear not. Begin by "mapping" your speech. The map is a logical way to look at your material and later can translate into an outline. Maps show connections; outlines show subordination. A map drafts a matrix of your thinking in the planning stage.

It is little wonder that businesses use mapping techniques.[1] They are as natural as a sketch on a napkin and as tangible as an architect's blueprint. Speech maps ferret out missing and extraneous material, provide a visual presentation of ideas, and make an amalgam of ideas more manageable.

• • • • The Speech Architect's Blueprint • • • •   **• • • • TIPS**

An architect critiques a blueprint: "Do the rooms connect for a good traffic flow? Are the sizes of the rooms appropriate to their functions? Is there a good entrance? Exit?" By comparison, a speaker critiques a speech map: "Are my main points relevant and connected? Does my introduction prepare the audience? Does my conclusion bring closure?"

• • •

───────────────

[1] Gaut and Perrigo (1998) discuss how *mindmapping* combines the spontaneity of brainstorming with the structure of mapping to show connections (p. 276). *Speechmapping* is more specific and focuses on the connections among ideas and the grouping of ideas.

SUPPORTING MATERIAL IN A STUDENT'S AWARD-WINNING INFORMATIVE SPEECH

Speakers often agonize over how to use supporting material, or evidence, and where to place it in a speech. Can evidence be placed in an introduction or a conclusion? Must all evidence support main points or subpoints? To answer these questions, let's study university student Christine Meyer's informative presentation on the topic "dry water," delivered on March 25, 2002. Excerpts from this speech of definition illustrate the use of evidence—that is, supporting material—in an informative speech.* The audience on this occasion preferred varied, current, and documented (cited) sources. Even in the introduction, Christine selects facts, statistical data, and a quotation to introduce her topic and establish its importance:

1. *Move from the familiar to the unfamiliar:* According to the inventors' June 21, 2001, article in *Nature,* French physicists Pascale Aussillous and David Quere have used the water balloon model to do what nobody ever thought could be done to water—they made it dry.

2. *Establish the importance of the topic (in the introduction) with statistical data and quotation:* The World Bank webpage, accessed on March 10, 2002, and updated each weekday, asserts that "more than three million people still die each year from avoidable water-related disease" and that unless action is taken to remedy water scarcity, by the year 2025, 48 countries and 1.4 billion people will be experiencing water stress or scarcity.

In the speech, Christine maintains immediacy by using first person (I) and second person (you) and creates ethos (or good will) by describing environmentally friendly and potentially life-saving dry water.

In the body of the speech, the speaker describes dry water, discusses its uses, and explores implications of the technology. Let's note the choices and variety of support she uses in several excerpts:

3. *Definition:* Dry water is made of two key components, with water obviously being one of them. The second, though, is spores from the club moss *Lycopodium*—the pollen-like cells that *Lycopodium* moss releases in order to reproduce.

4. *Brief examples:* The Botanical Dermatology Database, last updated in October 2001, notes that *Lycopodium* has also been used for pharmaceutical purposes such as "dusting pills, suppositories, and rubber gloves" because it repels water and is safe for human use.

5. *Explication[†] and comparison:* Aussillous and Quere quickly learned that by mixing water with silane-coated *Lycopodium* spores (explains PhysicsWeb on June 24, 2001), individual drops of water become coated with the spores and take on properties similar to those of a marble or a water balloon.

6. *Explanation with facts:* When normal drops of water are placed upon a surface, they have a tendency to flatten and spread out. However, dry water droplets use the *Lycopodium* powder as a physical boundary between the water and the surface. The water is completely walled in and can neither change from its spherical shape nor escape from the powder that contains it—leaving the surface completely dry. As *Scientific American* stated on June 21, 2001, this "thin layer of powder settles between the liquid and the

surrounding air and allows the coated water to retain its spherical shape . . .
the drops can then remain on a variety of surfaces . . . without spilling."

7. *Definition, explanation (of droplet properties), and facts:* Additionally, multiple water droplets may be transported in the same container—for example, pipes or barrels—without breaking. These tiny droplets, according to the June 14, 2001, *Physical Science Update,* are "just a millimeter or so across," so when moved en masse these tiny marbles remain intact. And getting the water out of this coating is just as easy as popping a water balloon. According to the ABC News of June 28, 2001, the liquid water can be regained by puncturing the water marble—the water is released and the *Lycopodium* spores float to the top to be skimmed off—leaving behind only clean, usable water.

8. *Examples (of uses): Science News* noted on January 27, 2001, that "payoffs of [these] capabilities include improved industrial coatings, printing processes, and cooling technologies.

9. *Hypothetical example with explanation:* Additionally, *Nature* magazine of June 21, 2001, explains that dry water "might be used as a lubricant within small machines" as the *Lycopodium* coating prevents rust and minimizes the cost of lubrication and replacement parts. Its protective powder coating means that additional lubrication will not be necessary because droplets won't deteriorate or wear down as the *Lycopodium* spore coating prevents the normal process of evaporation that results from water's contact with the surrounding air.

10. *Quotation:* The Water and Sanitation Program's January 18, 2002, report on the status of the worldwide water supply explains that poorer regions do "not have adequate resources to meet water supply needs."

11. *Comparisons:* Any protection offered by the *Lycopodium* spore coating is a welcome advantage to the germ, bacteria, and parasite vulnerability of unprotected water. Additionally, the use of dry water mandates the puncturing or mass crushing of the water marbles in order to recover the usable water and the powder that contains it: a process not required by current methods of water transportation.

12. *Expert source paraphrased testimony:*[‡] *Nature* magazine notes that it is unclear how stable these water droplets are or how they will behave with age, so it's not safe to use this method of water transportation until it is proven to keep the water safe throughout the process.

The speaker avoided introducing new points in the conclusion. She did—again, skillfully and succinctly—review her main points and end with a memorable statement. Christine Myer's speech in full is available in the appendix.

---

[*] The entire speech is available on the Allyn & Bacon website supporting the text.

[†] Explication is considered a terse, clear-cut explanation.

[‡] The speaker paraphrases material from a periodical rather than quote the article directly. Ordinarily, *testimony* and *quotation* are used interchangeably, meaning the evidence comes from some kind of expert. Nor does *fact* clearly label it. The source magazine is credible, and so we recognize the source, the paraphrase form, and the reliance on a cited source.

Start the map of the speech body with the central idea in the center of a large piece of paper. Draw lines—the "roads" on the map—to each of the main points. Each main point needs support, so draw roads from each point to supporting materials for that point. If your main point has subpoints, put them in before you add supporting material. Decide where each piece of support goes, and map it accurately. If it makes sense to you, you will be able to communicate it to your listeners. If you have difficulty mapping your material, your audience will probably have difficulty following the material. As an example, Figure 7.1, maps the body of a speech given by EPA administrator Christine Todd Whitman at the 2003 National Conference on Asthma in Washington, D.C.

When you are working with a map, sketch it with pencil or on a chalkboard to allow for changes. Usually the map is of the speech body, but you can add small maps of the introduction and the conclusion, as satellites to the main map. Examine your map as you work. Are parts logically connecting?

• • • • TIPS   • • • • Transitions and Signposts • • • •

Later, when you prepare your speech, the roads translate into transitions between speech areas. *Transitions* between parts and points lead the audience along your organization paths. The sample speech in Quick Start 7.4 (see page 193) uses a transition that sets up a thesis statement that also previews main points: "Now, this may not be a scientific poll, but it is a powerful reminder that all across our nation, millions of Americans have asthma, and among the hardest ht by this disease are our children." Another transition is obvious when EPA administrator Whitman shifts points this way: "Of course, improving the air at home is only part of the solution; addressing the air quality in our schools is also vitally important."

Signposts are another part of the terrain. They are a special type of transition in which a word or phrase alerts the listeners where they are in the speech. Some common signposts are "in conclusion," "next let's look at," and "my third main point." The sample speech uses signposting with this wording: "In addition to improving indoor air quality, this administration's work . . . ."

• • •

FIGURE 7.1 • Visual Map of a Speech by Former EPA Administrator Christine Whiteman

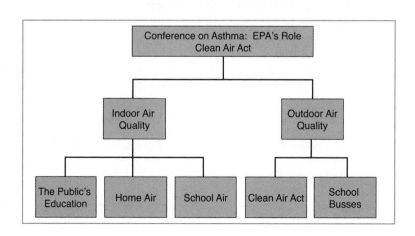

Quick Start 7.2 translates the map into an outline of the body and adds the introduction and conclusion. Speakers "talk through" their maps to see how well the structure holds together before transferring the map to an outline. Notice how the outline labels the parts of the introduction and the conclusion. Also, the body is outlined with Roman numeral "I" designating the first main point, "II" the second, and so on. A common misconception is that if you have five main points, you can slice off the first point and call it the introduction, and slice off the last point and call it the conclusion. Wrong! The main points should all be in the body. The introduction functions to interest and prepare the listeners to learn. The conclusion wraps up the presentation, but again, should not add a main point. Outlining the introduction, the body, and the conclusion as separate outlines is helpful, as in Quick Start 7.2. Notice how each part begins anew with Roman numeral "I."

● **QUICK START 7.2   Outlining the Speech** • • • •

Introduction

I. The National Asthma Education and Prevention Program leads an important event, making a difference with asthma sufferers. (Attention technique, referring to and complimenting audience)

II. Asthma is a debilitating disease. (Motivating the audience by showing the importance of the topic)

III. I have traveled to schools all around the country. (Building credibility of speaker)

IV. While we do not know all the causes of asthma, we do know that environmental triggers such as secondhand smoke, dust mites, mold, and air pollution can make asthma worse. (Preview)

Transition: Fortunately, we can address these triggers and in many cases remove them altogether.

Body

I. Pollution indoors affects those who have asthma.

   a. Education makes a difference.

      1. In a survey, three-fourths could not identify indoor environmental triggers.

      2. The National Asthma Awareness campaign and the Smoke-Free Home initiatives of EPA help parents identify environmental triggers.

      3. The president's requested $3 million increase would support our efforts at $23.9 million.

   b. Secondhand smoke affects children at home.

      1. Around 5 million children under the age of 6 are exposed to one of the most dangerous forms of indoor air pollution—secondhand smoke—at home.

      2. Of those who called EPA's Asthma Hotline last year, 43% allowed smoking in their homes.

         3. During Asthma Awareness month, EPA launched a public service announcement to encourage smoke-free homes as part of the National Smoke-Free Challenge.

   c. Air quality affects children in schools.

         1. Of the more than 50 million children in public schools, over half have health issues linked to poor indoor air quality.

         2. Over 10,000 schools utilize EPA's Tools for Schools to guide improvements, such as in ventilation systems.

II. People with respiratory illness will benefit from programs addressing the outdoor environmental air quality.

   a. The president's Clear Skies Act will require 70% reduction of nitrogen oxides, sulfur dioxide, and mercury—among the most dangerous power plant emissions.

   b. EPA expects days lost to respiratory illnesses.

         1. Currently more than 12,000 premature deaths occur due to respiratory illness.

         2. Fifteen million people lose work, school, and otherwise productive days to respiratory illnesses.

   c. The Clean School Bus USA initiative is among the programs designed to address emissions from mobile sources.

         1. New technology makes exhaust from school buses cleaner.

         2. We recommend less idling.

         3. A $5 million dollar grant assists school districts in updating their fleets.

         4. Our goal is "to ensure that by the year 2010, every public school bus on the road in all 50 states is a clean school bus, emitting less pollution and contributing to cleaner air."

Conclusion

I. From Clear Skies outdoors to our indoor air efforts, reducing the number of children who have asthma is one of the top priorities of the Environmental Protection Agency and this administration. (Review)

II. For so many Americans the struggle to breathe is a difficult hardship to overcome. By working together, we can help them surmount this disease and improve the quality of life for people with asthma all across our nation. (Final memorable statements)

REHEARSE

Practicing a speech brings an internal process to the surface. It develops the art of delivering ideas.

It's far too easy to shortchange practice time, yielding to research and development stages. This is a costly oversight. Schedule at least three rehearsals separated by several hours to "layer in" experience.

ORATING IN THE BATHTUB

The most eloquent speakers know to practice. A well-known story about Winston Churchill tells that his valet heard him orating loudly from the bathroom. Fearing that the prime minister was in dire distress, the valet burst into the bathroom, asking, "Did you call, sir?" Churchill answered, "No. I was just giving a speech to the House of Commons."

Cognitively, physically, and emotionally prepare yourself for the upcoming experience. It's time to talk, sequencing and laying out your thoughts for others to hear.

• • • • **Conversational Delivery** • • • •   • • • • **TIPS**

Deliver your speech conversationally and communicatively. Do not memorize or read your speech.

• • •

Use an extemporaneous speaking style, phrasing your ideas as you speak rather than reading from a manuscript or memorizing the speech word for word. Refer to your notes to trigger ideas. Extemporaneous speaking is different from impromptu speaking, which is spur-of-the-moment. Extemporaneous delivery relies on adequate preparation and a sense of "immediacy," or presence, with the audience.

Most students become anxious when the assignment is announced, but they relax as they get into the preparation stage. Anxiety peaks again immediately before giving the speech. This section gives quick tips to keep anxiety under control. (If you are especially apprehensive about this project or if you are usually shy about public speaking, refer to Chapter 3 for techniques to manage communication apprehension.)

As you practice, rid yourself of unrealistic beliefs, such as "I must please everyone," or "I must be perfect." No speech is perfect, nor is it perfect for every listener. The professor realizes the complexity of speaking to several listeners and will be a reasonable listener for you. Look forward to the experience. Imagine your feeling of accomplishment and success during and after the speech.

Physical behavior is easier to control than attitudes and emotional feelings. So, act capable and eager, even when you do not feel that way. As you practice aloud, repeatedly and consciously choose an attitude of confidence.

Talk Through Your Map

Take ownership of what you have learned. This is "your knowledge," and you want to also make it "their knowledge." Secure your confidence with what you have learned to this point.

To this point, you probably have been talking informally about your topic with friends, classmates, or family. Now, talk through your speech map and test how your ideas hold together. Could a person hearing your speech for the first time follow what you are saying?

Quick Start 7.3 shows speaker notes based on EPA administrator Christine Whitman's asthma address. Notice they do not follow outline form strictly. The speech itself is given in Quick Start 7.4.

● **QUICK START 7.3   Possible Speaker's Notes for Whitman's EPA Speech** ● ● ● ●

Intro
  (Lenfant), EPA co-sponsor
  Constituents
  Epidemic
  Talks in schools
  Preview—environmental triggers

I. Indoor
   a. Education
      1. Triggers
      2. Currently many uninformed parents
   b. Homes
      1. Hotline
      2. Nat'l Smoke-Free Challenge
   c. Schools
      1. 50 mil., half
      2. Indoor Air Quality Tools for Schools (10,000 schools)

II. Outdoor
   a. Clear Skies Act
      1. Nitrogen oxides, sulfur dioxide, and mercury
      2. 12,000 premature deaths, 15 mil. days missed
   b. Clean School Bus USA
      1. Exhaust, idling
      2. $5 grant—"2010 . . . every public school bus . . . 50 states . . . less pollution . . . cleaner air"

Conclusion
  Review "C.S. to indoor"
  Final statements—struggle; quality

● **QUICK START 7.4   EPA Administrator Christine Whitman's Address to the 2003
                         National Conference on Asthma** ● ● ● ●

Whitman's efficacious speech blends informative and persuasive purposes, as do most addresses by government officials. Most such presentations totally dedicated to informing are very specific to an area or are very lengthy. This speech was chosen as an informative speech sample primarily because her purpose was to update a convention body (generalized audience) on EPA's work that affects asthma sufferers. The structure of the speech is built on an organization of that information, and Whitman carefully mentions the major current programs and congressional acts. Second, she inspires the audience by her dedication to the topic and further establishes the good work of the government, president, and EPA.

Basically, Whitman organizes the speech topically, but she uses causal reasoning throughout the speech. Her support is specific and varied. She stands on her own authority in testimony. She is respectful of time and the occasion and keeps her remarks brief.

Text of Speech

Thank you Dr. (Claude) Lenfant for that introduction. I want to also thank the National Asthma Education and Prevention Program for their leadership on asthma and for making this conference possible. EPA is proud to be a co-sponsor of this important event.

It is an honor to be here this morning with the men and women who are making a real difference in the lives of millions of Americans who suffer from asthma. From physicians to health educators to school personnel, each of you is on the front lines everyday researching, managing, and fighting this disease.

For people with asthma, simple, everyday activities that most of us take for granted—climbing the stairs, walking, taking a deep breath—can be difficult daily struggles. As you well know, asthma has grown to epidemic proportions in our country and continues to increase.

During my time at EPA, I have traveled to schools all around the country, and I always ask students the same question: "Do you or does anyone in your family have asthma?" In most instances, anywhere from a third to half of the students will raise their hands. Occasionally, such as when I was in New Hampshire last week, the response is overwhelming and approaches three-fourths of the students. Now, this may not be a scientific poll, but it is a powerful reminder that all across our nation, millions of Americans have asthma, and among the hardest hit by this disease are our children.

While we do not know all the causes of asthma, we do know that environmental triggers such as secondhand smoke, dust mites, mold, and air pollution can make asthma worse.

Fortunately, we can address these triggers and in many cases remove them altogether. That is why it is so important that we not only diagnose kids with asthma and provide the proper medication, but that we also educate parents and communities about indoor asthma triggers and assist them in taking the necessary steps to make their homes and schools healthier.

Recently, EPA conducted a public survey on indoor asthma triggers, and over three-fourths of those surveyed who have asthma or have a child with asthma could not identify the top indoor environmental triggers. It is clear that we have far to go in educating Americans about these triggers, and it is imperative that we push forward with this important message. That has been a focus of our work at EPA through programs such as the *National Asthma Awareness* campaign and the *Smoke-Free Home* initiative, which helps parents identify indoor environmental triggers that make asthma worse. To support this effort, the president has requested a $3 million increase in his FY 04 budget to combat children's asthma—raising total funding to $23.9 million.

Secondhand smoke is one of the most dangerous forms of indoor air pollution—increasing the severity of asthma for one million children every year—and yet, it is one of the easiest triggers to prevent. Much has been done to decrease the effects of secondhand smoke in public places, but children who spend most of their time in homes with smokers are still being exposed at alarmingly high rates. In fact, 43% of the people who called our

Comment: Introduction and thanks

Comment: Establishing EPA's connection and credibility

Comment: Complimenting audience, mentioning the three constituencies in attendance

Comment: Establishing importance of topic

Comment: Building credibility by showing personal involvement

Comment: Focusing on topic

Comment: General preview to main points

Comment: First main point—indoor polution

Comment: Support in this paragraph is statistical, explanatory, and factual

Comment: First subpoint, secondhand smoke, soon refined to indoor pollution in homes

Comment: Support for this paragraph involves statistics, explanation of recent progress in public places, and comparison/contrast

Comment:
Introducing another EPA activity and supporting with explanation

Comment:
Second subpoint —Indoor pollution in schools. Support here is statistical

Comment:
Introducing an EPA program. This paragraph includes explanation, facts, and statistical support

Comment:
Second main point—outdoor air quality

Comment:
Support here includes explanation, facts, and statistics

Comment:
Note following support: explanation, fact and statistics, testimony; also use of "I" emphasizing ethos

Comment:
Assuring no conflict of interest and government cooperation; explaining another EPA program

Comment:
Reviewing and reiterating importance of topic and transition into conclusion

Comment:
Final statement

Asthma Hotline last year said they allowed smoking in their home, and according to the Centers for Disease Control and Prevention, around 5 million children under the age of 6 are exposed to secondhand smoke at home. During Asthma Awareness month in May, we launched a new public service announcement as part of our National Smoke-Free Challenge. It encourages parents to make their homes smoke-free.

Of course, improving the air at home is only part of the solution; addressing the air quality in our schools is also vitally important. More than 50 million children in America spend their days in our elementary and secondary schools, and studies show that over half of those schools are confronted with health issues, such as asthma and allergies, that are linked to poor indoor air quality.

In terms of environmental safety, there are a multitude of ways that schools can improve indoor air quality. EPA developed the *Indoor Air Quality Tools for Schools* program to give teachers and administrators the guidance they need to identify improvements that can be made, such as ensuring that ventilation systems are operating efficiently and outlining proper maintenance procedures. All around the country, schools are voluntarily implementing this important program. Currently, there are over 10,000 schools utilizing *Tools for Schools.*

In addition to improving indoor air quality, this administration's work to address outdoor air quality, especially the President's *Clear Skies Act,* will also have a direct impact on children suffering from asthma. *Clear Skies* will achieve mandatory reductions of 70% of three of the most dangerous pollutants emitted by power plants: nitrogen oxides, sulfur dioxide, and mercury. This will provide dramatic health benefits to the American people every year, including preventing 12,000 premature deaths and reducing by 15 million the days when sufferers of asthma and other respiratory illnesses are unable to work, go to school, or carry out their normal day to day activities because of bad air quality.

Clear Skies complements our other air initiatives, such as our work to address the emissions from mobile sources and our recently launched *Clean School Bus USA* initiative to improve the pollution performance of our public school buses. By using new technology to make the exhaust from school buses much cleaner and by eliminating unnecessary idling, we can reduce pollution from buses and improve the health of those who ride them. Last week, I announced a $5 million grant program to assist school districts in updating their fleets. Our goal is simple—"to ensure that by the year 2010, every public school bus on the road in all 50 states is a clean school bus, emitting less pollution and contributing to cleaner air."

From *Clear Skies* outdoors to our indoor air efforts, reducing the number of children who have asthma is one of the top priorities of the Environmental Protection Agency and this Administration. Of course, the federal government can only do so much, and we depend upon the work of those of you here in this room if we are to be successful in defeating this disease.

For so many Americans the struggle to breathe is a difficult hardship to overcome. By working together, we can help them surmount this disease and improve the quality of life for people with asthma all across our nation. Thank you.

Think of your speech as a gift—a present—to others. You have worked to present them something they'll appreciate, so imagine your listeners' faces as you present an interesting fact or quotation.

Even one colleague plus a presenter's imagination simulate an upcoming event.

Anchor Yourself with Notes

Use speaker notes that are meaningful to you—ones that will provide memory triggers to keep you on track. Notes are only for the speaker to see (unless your professor requests them). Make note of quotes and statistics that are tedious to memorize. Mark where you expect to be at three minutes and five minutes into your speech.

Jot down words to prompt you in the introduction and conclusion. Make the main points obvious. Commit to the opening statement to avoid making apologetic, weak opening mumblings. Beginners also need to commit to their planned conclusions. Try writing key words in red ink or bold letters. A good rule of thumb is to have no more than ten words of notes per minute of speaking, with the exception of statistics and quotes that would be hard to remember.

Practice Physically

Stand, pretend the audience is in front of you, and deliver your speech. Speak clearly and loudly. Speaking louder will slow you down, if you have the tendency to speak too fast, and adds confidence. Some coaches suggest practicing with a small audience or practicing in front of a mirror. If you have not practiced like this, you may find it awkward and laugh aloud at yourself. Practice; experienced speakers do.

CONTEMPORARY VOICES 7.1: FULLY ENGAGED

Daniel Goleman (1998, p. 109) emphasizes that people learn best when they are fully engaged in what they are doing. Observations show that the more people practice a task, the better they get, and the result is ongoing motivation to master new skills. "Great work starts with great feeling." But do not wait for the great feeling. Begin working, and let the feeling catch up to you. Pleasure and excellent work go hand-in-hand.

Practicing from start to finish is important. If you have ever memorized music to play on an instrument, you may recall that you learned the beginning better than the less rehearsed ending, but with a speech, you can practice it in its entirety every time. Make each time count in your imagination, because your imagination will store these experiences and what you have learned from them. For instance, if you forget to give an explanation, and get to a point where it is needed, you may say aloud as you practice, "But first I need to explain thus and so to you." Practice takes textbook understanding and translates it into practical and procedural knowledge.

CONTEMPORARY VOICES 7.2: PROCEDURAL KNOWLEDGE DEVELOPMENT

Goleman (1998) also explains the difference between *what you can talk about* and *what you can do.* "Knowing does not equal doing, whether in playing the piano, managing a team, or acting on essential advice at the right moment" (p. 242).

"For behavior change, on the other hand, life itself is the true arena for learning, and this takes practice over an extended period of time" (p. 244).

Reality @ WORK 7.3

CORRECTING THE TEN MOST COMMON SPEAKING ERRORS

Tina Santi Flaherty, the first woman elected a vice president at Colgate-Palmolive, GTE, and Grey Advertising, warns against common errors, for which these are the correctives.

1. Dress correctly.
2. Exude enthusiasm.
3. Rehearse repeatedly.
4. Have someone introduce you.
5. Make your speech easily followed.
6. Keep your head up (seldom looking at notes).
7. Articulate so that everyone can understand every word.
8. Choose clear vocabulary and construct sentences for the listeners.
9. Cover the room with eye contact, connecting with everyone at some time.
10. Know when to stop. Plan to spend enough time, but don't wear out your welcome.

To support a cool and collected demeanor on speech day, check Quick Start 7.5 for essentials to place in your backpack or car. Various behaviors that prepare you for speech day are noted in Quick Start 7.6.

● QUICK START 7.5   Check List for the Night Before the Speech • • • •

- Written assignments typed and ready to turn in, your name on every page
- Your speaking notes
- Charts, transparencies, computer disk or CD, or other supporting material (Pack it now.)
- Equipment, such as a projector or easel, if needed and not in the room
- Videotape, for taping your speech if equipment is available
- Appropriate clothes (businesslike and comfortable)

● QUICK START 7.6   *Mind and Body Ready for Today* • • • •

- Get some sleep, so that speaking will not feel like an out-of-body experience.
- The day of your speech, eat a healthy meal. (You want your energy to still be there when it is time to speak. This is not the day to skip breakfast and load up on caffeine.)
- Find your "zone." Remind yourself of how important and interesting your topic is. If you still feel anxious, take a short, brisk walk.
- Step by step, recall class procedures for speech days.
- Remember to breathe to energize, to relax, and to think. Fill your lungs slowly, deeply, and deliberately.

SUMMARY

Informative speaking teaches, explains, defines, and in other ways instructs an audience. Knowing the demographics, interests, and levels of expertise of audiences helps speakers communicate well with their receivers. Whether in a classroom, business, or community, inherent criteria guide the choice of topics for informative presentations. Browsing for informative topics exposes us to biographies, periods in the arts, historical turning points, inventions, medical research, and current events, to list a few. With an interesting topic selected, a student can then delve into available resources to select material for a speech.

Planning an informative speech should be a creative and orderly process of writing a purpose statement and central idea statement; selecting, organizing, and supporting main points; and creating an introduction and a conclusion. Speech mapping shows the relationships among ideas and material in a speech, and outlines help speakers sequence their material.

Physical practice of delivering the speech is essential for the best, most confident presentation. Take care of details and pack essential notes and equipment ahead of time in order to focus on the immediate occasion at the time of the speech. ●

ACTIVITIES

1. **Technical Support**
   a. Collect favorite websites for research and place them on your computer "favorites" list.
   b. Find two speeches with an Internet search. Are the ones you found informative or persuasive? Justify your answer.
2. **Team Work and Technical Support:** Graham T. T. Molitor, vice president and legal counsel to the World Future Society and president of Public Policy Forecasting, spoke in Washington, D.C., on July 30, 1999, on "The Next 1000 Years," to the World Future Society's conference on the Frontiers of the 21st Century. As a team of two or three, identify his type of organization and label at least four forms of supporting material on a photocopy of the speech, as found in the periodical *Vital Speeches*.

      I. Leisure Time Era (by 2015)

     II. Life Sciences Era (2100)

    III. Mega-materials Era (2200–2300)

    IV. New Atomic Age (2100–2500)

     V. New Space Age (2500–3000)

3. **Ethically Speaking:** Examine the arrangement of the main points in a speech by Jean Carnahan (1999, pp. 529–531), First Lady of Missouri, as she spoke at the Trailblazer's Awards Ceremony. In her speech, "Born to Make Barrels, Women Who Put Their Stamp on History," she used as examples two women who lived in the 19th century, had large personal responsibilities, were very sensitive to injustice, changed the thinking of the nation on the dominant issues of their day—slavery and suffrage, and yet never knew one another. Carnahan made creative choices in juxtaposing these women's lives in a speech. In small groups, discuss the values the speaker exposes in herself and in Stowe and Baumfree by her choices. List ethical considerations in organizing this informative speech.

      I. Harriet Beecher Stowe was the author of *Uncle Tom's Cabin* and the woman whose writings did more to arouse the conscience of the nation against slavery than anyone of her day.

     II. Isabella Baumfree later went by the name Sojourner Truth.

    III. Isabella Baumfree, a remarkable slave woman, was one of the early advocates of suffrage and civil rights.

4. **Journaling the Experience:** Keep a journal during the preparation period for the speech in Activity 5. Write about the planning process you use, helpful discoveries you make, and feelings you have as you prepare an informative speech.

5. **Presenting to Others:** Prepare and deliver a five- to seven-minute speech that meets the criteria for an informative speech. Use the suggestions for a topic from this chapter. Submit a speech map and outline to your professor before delivering the speech.

6. **Team Work:** Jan Deur (1999), vice president and acting treasurer of GTE, spoke to the Texas Business Network on "Trends in Telecommunication." In pairs, label the following excerpts (pp. 728–731) according to their forms of support.

   a. Some of you may remember the days when homes had one black rotary dial telephone, hard-wired into the wall. Your local and long distance service was [sic] all provided by one company—probably Ma Bell.

     Contrast that with today—just take a look at your business card. I daresay that most of you will have at least two phone numbers listed: a business phone and a fax number. You might also have listed a cellular phone number; a pager number; and an e-mail or Internet address. Your card is a lot more cluttered with numbers than it was 10–15 years ago!

   b. Let me give you a sneak preview of some of the gee-whiz technology—much of it Internet related—that may be headed your way in the next few years.

     Qualcomm is adding "microbrowsers" to its cell phones so they can read online data.

     Consider the possibility of receiving a message from your car that it's time for a tune-up . . . or sending an e-mail to your microwave oven to have your dinner hot when you get home.

Frigidaire is experimenting with a refrigerator equipped with a bar-code scanner. When you run out of ketchup, you just scan the label and the refrigerator orders a new bottle for you.

c. In fact, Bill Gates said he believes non-PC devices will dominate entry to the Internet within 10 years.

d. From a network of four universities in 1969, the Internet expanded across the country to 10,000 users by 1980. Today, an estimated 100 million users worldwide are linked by the Internet . . . and 300 million are predicted by 2002. The Internet is the fastest growing technology in history. And yet, when you consider that there are nearly 6 billion people in the world, the number of Internet users (less than 2%) is almost trivial. The growth prospects for the Internet are clearly enormous.

e. In comparing the data transport capabilities of copper and coaxial cable, Sender Cohen, a data communications analyst at Lehman Brothers, said, "Think of the copper telephone wire as a very thin but very intelligent pipe, and the cable wire as very fat but very dumb."

FOR FURTHER READING

To get additional guidance and support for composing a presentation, go to Allyn & Bacon's Speech Lab at www.myspeechlab.com/, http://wps.ablongman.com/ ab_public_speaking_2, or http://www.abacon.com/commstudies/.

For topic overviews, you will benefit from the National Issues Forums series through Kendall/Hunt Publishing.

Brody, M. (1998). *Speaking your way to the top*. Boston: Allyn and Bacon.

With a humorous touch, you may enjoy:

Kushner, M. (1995). *Successful Presentations for Dummies*. Boston: IDG Books Worldwide.

Empathy is crucial for wielding influence; it is difficult to have a positive impact on others without first sensing how they feel and understanding their position. . . . The first step in influence is building rapport. Persuasion is lubricated by identifying a bond or commonality; taking time to establish one is not a detour but an essential step (Goleman, 1998).

Models, Applications, and Processes of Informative Communication

8

A Model Speech

Comparing Written and Oral Communication

Types of Informative Communication at Work

Facilitating Informative Communication with Technology

Analyzing the Situation: ASSETS

Speaking to Professionals and Other Mature Audiences

Designing Presentations for Various Learning Styles

What are your goals for informative speaking? Looking beyond the classroom, you know you must succeed in your workplace communication. You already anticipate presenting to large audiences, talking to clients and managers, and instructing coworkers. You may also expect to conduct development training on site, report a project's progress, or instruct clients on the use of new equipment. Therefore, this is a very practical chapter to prepare for your future.

Chapter 7 in its entirety was dedicated to assisting you in researching, constructing, and presenting an effective informative speech, but informative speaking involves much more than one chapter can cover. This chapter further explores how to assist audiences of one or one hundred to take in information, to understand concepts, and to remember—in other words, to learn.

A model speech early in the chapter provides perspectives on organization and supporting materials—interestingly, a professional speechwriter explains the elements of her formula for an effective presentation. The chapter then overviews common informative communication in the workplace. Any of these types may serve as a classroom assignment, and, in a longer-range picture, the abbreviated suggestions clarify how to go about informative assignments in the workplace. Technology provides communication venues and supports informative efforts, so it makes sense for us to discuss several of these technologies.

Informing best takes place when communicators predict how their listeners learn, what interests them, and what motivates them. Whereas we can predict classroom audiences easily from our own extensive experience in classes, the dynamics of various audiences require additional research. The final portion of the chapter merges situation analysis, characteristics of adult learners, and interdisciplinary, informative perspectives.

> Overall, this is not an academic exercise. It is deeply rooted in making a very serious point: Our future is critically dependent on what we learn, and, unless this subject is given much greater attention, it is extremely unlikely that we will be involved in anything remotely like progress, however you define it." (Bruce Lloyd, quoted in Wagner & Minerd, 1999, p. 53)

If, as Lloyd says, our future depends on learning, it is imperative that we use the best learning tools available. The sheer volume of information is overwhelming, and businesses will depend on those who can compile and interpret the data meaningfully. "While most organizations are active users of information technology . . . they are not actively using their information assets. . . . In underutilizing information, we are literally throwing away what is perhaps our most important asset for enhancing our competitiveness now and in the next millennium" (Unruh, 1996).

OBJECTIVES

After studying the content of this chapter, you should be able to

- Identify organizational patterns and supporting materials in successful informative speeches
- Recognize purposes of specific business and professional communication tasks
- Choose among venues and formats for presentations
- Apply informative strategies tailored to a presentation situation
- Analyze career-oriented audiences to see how to best instruct them

---

• • • • TIPS   • • • • **Common Terms with Special Meanings** • • • •

- *Informative presentations:* Assisted discoveries by means of purposeful, instructional action. Informative presentations will involve participants in learning as they access and consume information. (They will not always involve a speaker on stage presenting to an audience in chairs.)
- *Learning:* Significant progress toward mastery of facts, skills, or concepts. In other words, something must change in the receiver in regard to what he or she knows or understands.

● *Audience, listener, and participant:* Anyone who receives by various channels and interacts with information you provide.

● ● ●

● A MODEL SPEECH

Jane Tully (1997), president of Tully Communications, begins her speech to the New York Women in Communications by describing her job as a speechwriter. She does this largely through figurative comparisons, including similes, metaphors, and analogies, to establish a strand around which she organizes three main points. Walk through Tully's speech (see Example 8.1) to become acquainted with her techniques and applications.

● EXAMPLE 8.1

A PROFESSIONAL SPEECHWRITER'S PRESENTATION WITH RHETORICAL COMMENTS

Thank you all for coming this evening. I'd like to begin by saying that this is the first time I've stepped out from behind the computer screen I write on to talk about the speechwriting process. Preparing this presentation for you has taught me a great deal about the work I do for my clients, and I'm delighted to share some of what I've learned with you.

A number of years ago Mary Clifford, the wife of the noted Washington lawyer Clark Clifford, gave a dinner party. Mrs. Clifford was a popular hostess, and for this occasion she planned a particularly elegant menu in honor of a special guest—Mary Garden. Ms. Garden was an aging opera singer and had been quite a glamorous diva earlier in the century. The meal was to be a feast of culinary delights, starting with freshly shucked Cape Breton oysters, flown in especially for the occasion.

When the oysters were served, Ms. Garden politely declined them. That wasn't too alarming. Many people don't like fresh oysters. But when the second course was served, she declined that, too. Mrs. Clifford became alarmed when the main course was served and her guest would have none of it. As it turned out, all Ms. Garden wanted for dinner was what she always had—a bowl of chocolate ice cream and a cup of black coffee!

There was scrambling in the kitchen, and they had to send someone on a quick trip to the store because they were out of ice cream. Mrs. Clifford managed to accommodate her guest and save the occasion, but just barely.

I tell you this story because it holds an important lesson, not only for people who entertain, but for those of us who write and deliver speeches.

You see, I have a theory that giving a speech is a lot like giving a party. You, the audience, are the invited guests. As the speaker, I am the host—at least for the moment. The speech I am delivering to you is like a meal. I want it to be nourishing food for thought—full of substance, with interesting ideas for you to chew on. I want to present it in a way that's appealing, so you'll be eager to take in my ideas. And like a good meal, I want my speech to be appropriate for this particular occasion.

If you think of a speech that way, then where does the speechwriter fit in? Actually, I like to think of myself as a kind of verbal caterer. You call on professionals like me when you don't have the time or expertise to do the job your-

Comment: Tully establishes rapport, and shows confidence in her knowledge. She lets the audience focus on her before setting up the speech focus.

Comment: She launches straight into a narrative.

Comment: Her details relate to the five senses.

Comment: She subtly teases listeners' reactions to "declining fresh oysters."

Comment: "Always" tells the audience that no one had thought to ask the guest her dietary preferences.

Comment: Listeners can identify with panic in the kitchen to accommodate a guest.

Comment: Transition to topic

Comment: Tully introduces a comparison—speech is like a party.

Comment: Tully casts herself as host and listeners as guests in figurative language that is developing into a full analogy. Later, she recasts herself as caterer.

Comment:
Tully defines her job, building credibility, but almost gives a sales pitch.

Comment:
Good save! She tells the audience that her purpose is to teach them a "recipe" for their personal speechwriting.

Comment:
She signposts ("first") and repeats first main point.

Comment:
She introduces the word "research," used more in speech composition than in planning parties.

Comment:
She introduces the topic of audience analysis.

Comment:
The subpoint is size, and supporting material explains factors affected by it.

Comment:
"Also" signposts the next subpoint: age range.

Comment:
The third subpoint is gender. She defines it and gives an example.

self, or when you have a special occasion and you want that extra something that will really make your speech stand out.

Like caterers, we speechwriters can help you in a number of ways. Maybe all you need is a little consultation on the menu, so you call on us to help you focus your message and figure out what direction to take it. Or maybe you need a few hors d'oeuvres, so you bring us in to draft some talking points or find just the right quote or story that will bring your speech to life. Sometimes you need the whole thing catered, so we serve up your speech on a silver platter—a full draft, formatted for the podium and ready for delivery. So in my role as caterer, I'd like to take this opportunity to share my basic recipe for a successful presentation. Follow this easy three-step recipe and you can't go wrong:

Know who's coming to the party,

Use only the best ingredients, and

Focus on the main course.

Comment:
Three-point preview marks the end of the introduction.

First, know who's coming.

If Mrs. Clifford had done some advance research on her guest list, she might have learned about the peculiar dietary quirks of her special guest and been prepared to graciously accommodate her. Not that she would have changed her whole menu—only adapted her plans to take Ms. Garden's eccentricity into account. Likewise, speakers and their writers need to be alert to their audience's special needs and interests. Knowing who's going to be out there helps the writer shape the message so that listeners won't simply reject the speaker's ideas one by one as they are served up.

What do we need to know about audiences? Size, for one thing. This is important because smaller audiences pay closer attention. When a group is small, the speaker can easily maintain eye contact and hold people's attention. The larger the audience, the easier it is for listeners to feel anonymous and to drift off, so a speaker has to offer more entertainment value. With large convention-sized audiences of hundreds, or even thousands of people, this is essential: bring in audiovisual support whenever you can; add stories and humor. Keep it moving, and keep it short, or you'll lose them.

To the extent that it's possible, speechwriters also want to know the age range of the audience. Will it be a group of seniors, or young professionals, or students—or a mixed group? This affects the kinds of stories, humor, and other support material we will choose to make the speaker's points. Because so much of humor comes out of life experience, the jokes Grandma enjoys may fall completely flat with your teenage son. If your audience includes a wide range of ages, you need to find humor that has a very broad appeal.

This is also true for any examples from history. A number of years ago, a friend of mine was once asked to speak to a church youth group on the subject of war and whether or not it is ever justified. He started by telling about how he had felt, as a senior in college at the height of the Vietnam War, when his draft notice arrived in the mail. A young man in the group interrupted him to say, "Oh, yeah, Vietnam. We read about that in history last week."

My friend was barely 30 at the time, and he said he had never felt so old in all his life! But it was an important lesson for him as a speaker: never assume that your audience shares your experience or knowledge of history, and be sure to give your illustrations the historical context they need—especially if you are speaking to a younger audience.

Speechwriters also want to know what the gender mix of an audience will be. Will there be more men than women, or vice versa? Again, this information affects the kinds of illustrations we choose. One of my clients, a product sales manager at Citibank, recently gave a speech to pump up a group of brokers who were being asked to meet some new revenue goals. We used a story featuring the retired Notre Dame coach Lou Holtz. The story ends with a great one-liner about a quarterback who runs 85 yards to score a winning goal. The speaker delivered it beautifully, and he got a big laugh—the vast majority of his listeners were men. It was perfect for that group, but if the audience had been more mixed, I probably would have used something different.

For the speech I'm delivering to you, I actually had to think twice about my food image. At first I thought the comparison might be a little too domestic for an audience of professional women. But after giving it some thought, I decided that since so many of the world's great chefs are men, and since we all have to eat, this image can work for both male and female audiences. My point is that it was important for me to go through the process of thinking about the gender of this audience and how that could affect the way you receive my ideas.

Speechwriters also try to find out what feelings or prejudices people bring to the subject of a speech. I've done a great deal of writing for executives at the National Geographic Society who travel around the country promoting geography education and working to bring geography back to the classroom. It's very important for them, and for me as their speechwriter, to know that many people feel about geography the way they do about math. They remember their sixth grade teachers making them memorize the 50 states or the capitals of the world. They think of geography as boring and irrelevant. Before you can persuade such people that they have to know geography to help protect the environment, succeed in the global economy, and make sense of foreign affairs, you have to acknowledge how they feel about their sixth grade lessons! Sometimes all it takes is a little humor to let your audience know that you understand where they're coming from. As soon as they get that message, they can relax and really listen to your ideas.

So . . . know who's coming to the party.

Second, use only the best ingredients. When I give a dinner party, I like to experiment with recipes that have an exotic twist—like a special ingredient I can't get down the street—maybe something I'll only find at Balducci's or the green market. The shopping is fun and interesting, and the new ingredient gives a special flavor to the whole meal.

The same is true with researching a speech. It's fun because I'm always learning something new. I have learned that it's worth going out of my way to find a little known fact or two that can help make the speech memorable. A National Geographic Society executive was once asked to accept an award on behalf of the Society from the Leukemia Society of America. In researching his remarks, I learned about a small periwinkle that grows in the tropical rainforest. This little flower is the source of the medication that saves the lives of 95 percent of the children who contract childhood leukemia. With that fact, the speaker was able to relate National Geographic's interest in saving the environment to the life-saving work of the Leukemia Society. The extra effort it took to find that little tidbit of information was really worth it.

Once you have the information you need for a speech, spice it up! A speechwriting guide called *American Speaker* points out that "Good quotes in a speech, like good seasoning in a stew, are meant to add zest without detracting from the essential nature of the dish and its basic ingredients." That's true not only of quotes, but of anecdotes and humor as well. These elements must add something to the speech, not detract from it. I think most audiences are impatient with speakers who start out with a belly laugh, then take off in an entirely different direction.

Comment:
As an example, Tully refers to this speech and shares her thought process in choosing a food analogy for this audience.

Comment:
The fourth sub-point, "feelings and prejudices," relies on an extended example for support.

Comment:
Reinforces her credibility.

Comment:
Explanation and comparison as support.

Comment:
Tully repeats the first main point before moving to second point.

Comment:
The party again introduces a main point.

Comment:
Subpoint: a fun and interesting process.

Comment:
She uses an engaging personal example.

Comment:
Emotional appeal in example personalizes the speaker.

Comment:
Second subpoint: spice it up!

Comment:
Some advice again follows, just as a recipe would have ingredients followed by directions.

Comment:
Tully varies her supporting material with a quotation that includes metaphoric language.

Not only is this annoying, but what a waste of a good story! The whole reason for telling stories in your speech is to help people pay closer attention and remember your ideas. So make sure your illustrations relate to your message, and make the connection clear for the audience.

Most stories can be used to make any number of points. When you find a good one, feel free to use it whenever and wherever it will do the job, and don't worry too much if it's been around awhile. I disagree with those who say you can't use the same story twice. Like a great piece of music that we enjoy hearing again and again, a good story can be told more than once, as long as it's freshly interpreted. Even if they've heard it before, audiences appreciate the creative connection you make between the story and your message. Let me give you an example. There's the one about the little girl who was studying first aid in her fifth grade class. One day when she went home there was a car accident right in front of her house. The next day she ran to school to tell her teacher all about it.

"Here was a man with his arm bleeding, but I knew what to do!" she said. "Oh, good," her teacher said. "Did you use first aid?"

"Oh, yes," she said. "I put my head between my legs so I wouldn't faint!"

Now that story has all kinds of possibilities. I once used it in a commencement address for a group of teachers who had finished an extension course, to make a point about how well prepared they were to return to the classroom. But it would work just as well in a corporate setting. Use it to support your education or training message, to talk about applying academic learning in the real world. It's also a story about communications, so you could use it to illustrate an idea about management communications and how we personalize the information we're given. Or use it to talk about crisis response. How well prepared is your organization to deal with crisis? Or think about using it in a speech about health care. It could illustrate a message about how our changing health care system is responding—or not responding—to real needs. A little creative analogizing can take a story like this a long way.

Your audience will enjoy the story, but more than that, they'll enjoy the way you use it to reinforce your message.

So . . . know who's coming to the party, use only the best ingredients, and third, focus on the main course.

Every great meal has a great main course, a piece de resistance. And every successful speech has a main focus, a central idea that listeners can take home. This is the concept that pulls the whole speech together and helps your audience remember your supporting points.

For example, the focus of this presentation is actually a comparison—I'm saying that a speech is like a meal. If you can remember that, it shouldn't be too hard to remember my supporting ideas.

At the beginning of the speechwriting process, many speakers aren't sure how to focus their messages. At this stage, it's important to ask, "If your audience remembered only one thing, what would you want it to be?" The answer is often a range of choices.

When I'm searching for the focus for a speech, I look not only for the idea that is the most intellectually compelling, but the one that has the most emotional power for the speaker. That's because we remember ideas when they are presented to us with both clarity and feeling.

I once wrote a commencement address for the head of an education foundation. He'd been asked to speak to the graduating class of an environmental school in Idaho. He wanted to say that the lessons the graduates had learned in school really do apply in the outside world and they would succeed in their

chosen field because they had been so well prepared. This was not a particularly original thought, but one he felt strongly about.

The speaker was also an avid trout fisherman. In fact, he was planning to go
fishing the very next day. So to give his speech added punch, we compared fishing and school. He talked about you have to be patient, choose the right place to
do your work, and so forth. He told the students that by graduating they had
landed a big fish, and that their skill would land them more big fish in the future.
It sounds corny as I recall it, but my point is that he delivered it with real feeling
because he loved both fishing and education so much. They loved it.

Having a focus not only helps tie the speech together, it helps answer what I
consider to be the most important question in speechwriting: "What should I
leave out?" Usually the answer is, "Much—even most—of the material I've
found." If the idea or example doesn't support your main point in some way,
drop it, no matter how fascinating it is. Save it for another speech.

This will help you keep the speech to 20 minutes or so. That's important,
because most audiences begin losing concentration after that amount of time. If
you're asked to speak for longer than that, find ways to break it up, perhaps
with Q&A, slides, a video, or some kind of interactive exercise. Remember: a
speech is like a meal. We can only eat so much at one sitting, and we can only
hear so much at one sitting. Mark Twain said that few sinners are saved after
the first 20 minutes of a sermon. That's true of just about any oral presentation.
So keep it short.

Then you can think of the Q&A as a kind of dessert. Leave room for it, and
time. You don't want your listeners to feel like that grand old lady who died during dinner. She was the sister of an 18th century French writer named Brillat-
Savarin, and she expired at the table one night just before her 100th birthday.
Her last words were, "Bring on the dessert. I think I'm about to die."

I'm going to stop there while you still have room—and we still have time—
for dessert. I'll be happy to answer your questions.

Copyright © 1998–2003 The Executive Speaker® Company.

Comment
Comment: This story exemplifies the use of focus and the combination of clarity and feeling.
Comment: This advice bridges to considering the appropriate length of the speech.
Comment: Repeats the theme.
Comment: Another voice heard.
Comment: Tully completes her comparison, does not review in the conclusion, and ends on a memorable note.
Comment: Ta da boom!
Comment: Invites Q and A, just as she advised.

FINDING STRUCTURE AND SUBSTANCE

1. Outline the body of Tully's speech. The comments in the margins help you by identifying main points and subpoints.
2. List the forms of supporting material in the speech in the order in which they appear.

ACTIVITY 8.1

● COMPARING WRITTEN AND ORAL COMMUNICATION

This section coordinates spoken and written forms for several designated purposes, since some information is best distributed in writing, whereas other
information requires face-to-face communication. Communicators should recognize and differentiate between the characteristics of written and oral communication styles (Table 8.1), moving seamlessly between the two. Good
writing is good thinking, and well-written documents have "voice" and a sense
of "audience," so either style may be spoken or written, At times, an "oral"
style is chosen to close distance with readers, or a "written" style is used to add

TABLE 8.1 • Oral versus Written Communication Style

Oral Style	Written Style
Carefully chosen and highlighted background to topic	Broader literary review and background to topic; extensive parenthetical citation
Use of first and second personal pronouns	Primary use of third person pronouns
Predominantly active voice	Some use of passive voice
Examples chosen for this audience	Generic examples
Energy communicated through voice, facial expression, and movement	Energy represented by form and format, but not directly communicated
Evident interest in audience/participants as well as the topic	Interest in the topic stronger than interest in audience
Responsive to audience facial expressions	Distanced
Interaction with graphs and data for explanation	Lack of time constraints for studying complex graphs and data
Request for feedback before closure	Controlled closure without feedback
Sensitivity to the ephemeral nature of spoken communication coupled with the immediate change of the listeners	Responsible use and awareness of the permanent nature of written communication

formality. Be cautious, since being too "chatty" in writing may come across as too familiar, and being too stilted in speaking may seem distanced and cold. All in all, each form should align with your role in the communication, and your meanings should be clearly accessible to the receivers.

 TYPES OF INFORMATIVE SPEECHES AT WORK

As an employee and a professional, you will be in the informative chain, presenting briefings, technical reports, status reports, professional development training, and client orientations. Your informative purposes will include instructing, reporting, describing, explaining, and teaching. Mark Van Doren (personal communication, February 1966) called these processes "the art of assisting discovery." Let's begin with three fundamental tasks—description, instruction, and demonstration. These tasks may constitute the specific purpose of a speech or may fulfill a subordinate purpose within the presentation. Sometimes, instructors or supervisors request one of these tasks; thus, you should understand their reasonable expectations.

Essential Elements for Descriptions, Instructions, and Demonstrations

Three important types of informative communication are description, instruction, and demonstration. *Descriptions* tell what something is. *Instructions* tell how to do something, and *demonstrations* show how to do something.

Reality @ WORK 8.1

Descriptions

Descriptive speeches introduce inventions, reveal discoveries, and depict products' functions to audiences. Descriptions often appear early in other speeches in which the primary purpose is to instruct or to demonstrate. Important guidelines for descriptions are as follows:

- Open with an overview of the entity and its purpose, importance, or contribution.
- Orient the audience with a preview of main points.
- Use clear transitions and signposts.
- Define essential technical terms.
- Use comparison, contrast, and examples to preclude possible ambiguities and misinterpretations.

Instructions

Explanations and real examples support instructions. Recall times when you received complicated instructions, and consider what did and did not help you. Several techniques are generally helpful:

- Create a view of the desired outcome at the outset of the presentation.
- Sequence instructions in chronological performance steps.
- Signpost each step as it is added.
- Define new, essential, and ambiguous terms.

Additional and alternative approaches should be considered, depending on the technical level of the product or procedure:

- State a procedural step; explain reasons for the step; and state, illustrate, or demonstrate an example. Repeat for each step.
- State the product's purpose(s); demonstrate the product; and review how product features fulfill the stated purpose(s).
- Introduce the product and application procedure; demonstrate a straightforward, typical application; recap the procedural steps; and lead participants in hands-on learning of the application.

- Instruct participants on the basic functions of a product; give time for participants to manipulate the product experimentally; and respond to a question-and-answer session or conduct a discussion with conclusions.

Demonstrations

Demonstration presentations require a sophisticated set of skills. Practice is essential for effective demonstration presentations. Most demonstrations involve visual learning. Chapter 9 is particularly helpful with choices and dynamics to support this type of learning. These presentations lead audiences to construct an understanding of what something is, what is to be done, and how to do it. Use the guidelines for instructions, plus these additional suggestions:

- Keep the goal in mind. (Are listeners supposed to do what you are demonstrating, or are they to understand a process?)
- At all times think from the audience's point of view. (Could *you* follow your speech if you were unfamiliar with the topic?)
- Point out and make visible each feature or step in a procedure being demonstrated.
- Clarify cause-and-effect relationships.
- Solicit audience feedback on critical points. (Speakers can't lead "lost" audiences.)
- Apply contrast and comparison skillfully.
- Examples should be typical, not unusual. Audiences must understand the ordinary before comprehending the extraordinary. Save exceptions for late in the speech or at the ends of main points.
- Use preview, internal summaries, and review to anchor the demonstration with the audience.

Briefings and Briefs

Briefings are oral informative reports; similarly, *briefs* are written informative reports. Their purposes are either (1) to update a listener concerning an event or (2) to provide background information for particular situations. U.S. cabinet members brief presidents on their areas of responsibility, and diplomats expect briefings before going into negotiations (and even before going to dinner) with other nations' leaders. Volunteers and professionals are briefed in preparation for service in emergency situations or for service in another culture. A team of doctors may be briefed on a difficult case before examining the patient.

  Briefings are most helpful when they include objective information, general guidelines, and the emotional tones of interactions.

- Be concise and focus on the topic.
- Enumerate main points as you speak.
- Be precise about cultural, professional, and legal parameters.
- Give relevant examples.

Note the challenges inherent in the communication setting, specific audience, and use of visuals. When are briefings in the field and "on the scene" best used?

- Detail probable events and topics.
- Anchor key ideas, possibly with enumeration.

If a party only receives an official briefing orally, notes or a recording should document the information exchanged. Written briefs, delivered alone or with oral briefings, should do the following:

- Introduce and overview the topic.
- Enumerate or use headings for main points.
- Quote legal guidelines and constraints, citing sources.
- Provide details on qualifying events.
- Give typical examples.
- Exemplify important exceptions.
- Identify taboo and politically sensitive topics.
- List helpful further resources.
- Cite all references.

Reports

Reports are the most routine informative presentations given at work. Reports of workplace subjects are generally concise and matter-of-fact. Reports assume audiences are interested in the subject of the report. They also assume that time is precious and that the audience is not there to be entertained. *Status reports* respond with accountability to describe progress, problems, and compliance. A *walk-through* is a special kind of report in which presenters demonstrate products and orient clients to contractual and custom features.

Some reports are primarily written, others spoken, and many combine the two. Frequently agencies and organizations require standardized forms for documentation. Reports may be used to communicate horizontally among peers, upward to management, or downward to employees. The most common purposes fulfilled by reports in organizations are summarized in Table 8.2.

Although varied by organizational requirements and in formalities, reports keep employees and shareholders updated. Audiences like previews, overviews,

Even reports among peers should be well-organized, concise, and accommodate the ways the listeners learn.

TABLE 8.2 • Communicators' Decisions about Informative Messages

Purpose	Examples	Suggestions
To monitor and control internal operations	Periodic status reports from a work team; monthly budget reports; safety reports	Make budget and safety reports brief. Use standardized procedures. Update time lines and Gantt charts for managers and teams. Discuss project status and unresolved problems in meetings or one-on-one discussions with management.
To announce and explain policies and procedures	Announce hiring policy changes; explain new crisis management procedures; explain procedures for employee travel	Do not assume audiences/employees are as familiar with the issues as policy and procedure developers are. Explain clearly. Support with visuals and handouts. Facilitate a question-and-answer session.
To report progress on implementation of organizational policies and procedures	Reporting status in transforming a bureaucratic to a team-oriented organization; reporting new technology available at the organization	Target appropriate receivers. Don't assume reports are distributed. Support critical changes with presentations and discussions at meetings. Tell audiences what they need or want to know about your background and expertise.

TABLE 8.2 • Communicators' Decisions about Informative Messages (continued)

Purpose	Examples	Suggestions
To report compliance with regulatory requirements	Reports of compliance in response to laws supporting needs of disabled persons	Submit formal status reports of progress and degree of compliance. List compliance measures, present evaluated responses, and provide statistical support.
To provide information for decision making and problem solving[a]	Research report; field report; failed mission analysis; analysis and forecast	Be prepared for Q and A. Prepare written documentation minutes from discussion. Separate facts from inferences and predictions. Cite sources.
To communicate status of clients' projects	Oral and written reports to management team	These are very important reports for everyone involved. Prepare carefully and have necessary and helpful supporting material. Be clear about what management requires. Document status in a written report, possibly in a standardized form, perhaps one provided online.
To convey completion reports to clients	Walk-through with clients at completion of a project; hands-on training with purchased technical equipment	Consider these reports as closure to an individual project, but a bridge to future projects. Give a well-prepared presentation, but be responsive to clients' verbal and nonverbal messages throughout the presentation. Use realistic scenarios for training. Provide guided hands-on experience. Assure clients of technical support as contracted.
To report personal workplace assignments and activities	Written report from off-site regional meeting to management or relevant team; debriefing discussion	For a meeting you attended, send a hard copy or e-mail an agenda, pertinent actions taken, and comments in light of the organization's needs. For discussions, bring notes to remind you of all relevant material as needed. You may leave a list of key points and facts.

---

[a]   Based, in part, on Bovée and Thill (1995), p. 414.

and tables of contents to let them know in what order information will be covered. A compelling organization clearly communicated gives audiences a structure of the report on which to rely. For reports, in general:

- Respect an audience's right and need to know.
- Be accurate.
- Don't overwhelm the audience with more information than they need.
- Avoid unnecessary jargon, technical terms, and unclear or undefined terms.
- Support your words with visuals.
- Back up what you say in writing.
- Connect and explain what you write with speaking.

The following template works for written and oral reports, but you should adapt it for written or oral communication style. Find out ahead of time what your audience prefers—a brief written report with a detailed presentation and full discussion or a detailed report with a presentation that quickly highlights key points. For presentations in which you orally highlight key ideas, include cross-references to written points in an outline or by page number. Be sure that both presentations are in accord conceptually.

I. Introduction
   a. State the problem/project and give a brief background.
   b. State the importance or relevance of the topic to the audience.
   c. Present the original objectives for the project (including problem-solving projects).
   d. In one sentence, overview the progress status for the project.

II. Body
   a. List or explain key aspects of the project or problem. (A simple list or time line is all some reports need, with a statement of where a team stands in regards to completion. Other reports require clear, thorough explanations to audiences unfamiliar with the project or problem.)
   b. Describe changes, unexpected events, new information, and confounding variables that have taken place or come to light since the initiation of the project or the last report. Explain team response in light of those revelations.
   c. Present realignment of the plan in light of progress and changes. (If the audience is a policy body, present the obvious path or logical options for continuation.)
   d. Summarize or preview the next stage of the project and project completion.

III. Conclusion
   a. Briefly review the project status, plan, and project.
   b. Bring closure with a thank you or compliment that connects the project to the audience.

STATUS REPORT ON A FUNDING GRANT

In teams of three to five members, interview a nonprofit agency that is a grant recipient. Review the requirements for the grant, the terms of agreement in the agency's application, and the project status regarding progress toward the agency's stated goals. Using the report outline from this section, prepare a written report (using paragraphs with headings or complete sentence outline), and orally deliver a status report to the class.

**ACTIVITY
8.2**

Alternative Activities

1. *Prepare and present a status report on an organizational change.*
2. *Present a status report on a patient under treatment.*

Technical Communication

Many informative presentations, oral and written, include technical material. From a few examples, we can deduce helpful guidelines. An article on CNN.health.com, "More SARS Cases Investigated in U.S.," provides several examples of making technical information comprehensible to the typical consumer. The story from Atlanta, Georgia, led with the following sentence: "The Centers for Disease Control and Prevention said Friday it is investigating 22 suspected cases in the United States of the mystery pneumonia from Asia that does not seem to respond to common treatments and whose cause is not known."

Lectures

Didactic speeches directly inform listeners, usually without interaction or verbal feedback. A lecture, one of the most common forms of speaking directly, is usually between 20 minutes and two hours in length. Shorter presentations, however, may also be direct and noninteractive. Direct speaking is an efficient way to cover material, primarily because the speaker can plan and control the use of time. Speakers often must anticipate different levels of expertise among their audience members, and to accommodate everyone to some extent, they incorporate a background summary while including new information.

Like classroom informative speeches, direct speaking is *expository* speaking and is the method of choice for most speakers at conventions. Research presentations generally follow scholarly journal formats, and smart presenters take advantage of differences in written and spoken style rather than repeat a paper aloud. Exceptions are when material is highly technical or politically sensitive.

Concept Presentations

Concepts are all in our heads. We only really *know* a concept when we can use it in our thinking. Concepts do not land like a piece of mail in a mailbox; concepts grow in a person's mind. The cycle of learning posited by David Kolb (1984) leads participants in concept development (see the section Kolb's Learning Stages and Styles, later in this chapter). All four styles—assimilators, convergers, divergers, and accommodators—use either *watching* or *doing* to support learning a concept. A concept may be attacked from different directions to give an audience a better chance of catching on.

Even a seemingly simple concept, such as "Welcome our hotel guests as if this were your home" requires considerable training to develop the concept. (Is this welcome indicated with a kiss on each cheek or an invitation to dinner? Should employees invite guests to watch TV with them and put their feet on the sofa?) Notice how commercials and advertisements offer example after example over time to form in viewers' minds vivid concepts of their organizations: "Like a good neighbor," "Have a Coke and a smile," and "Reach out and touch someone."

Verbal examples are adequate when learners can recall similar experiences to those being described. When they do not have a cache of experience, providing an experience is invaluable. "Concept" forms as they work and think within the experience, either real or vicarious. For example, a concept of how to conduct an online conference forms as a person observes or participates in one. Simulations in banking or marketing similarly lead to a concept of how banks or markets work. You will clarify your concepts of presentational speaking as you participate by speaking in class.

FACILITATING INFORMATIVE COMMUNICATION WITH TECHNOLOGY

Technology offers both channels and forms of support for informing—in other words, both form and substance. Let's consider the channels and venues for technologically assisted learning. *Distance learning* formats include individual and independent configurations as well as satellite conferences and broadcasts from multiple sites. Through the Web, participants across the globe receive training on demand at their own pace. About 20% of organizational training takes place online. Other distance learning technologies that supplement face-to-face instruction are CD-ROM (40%), online via internal computer network and via the Internet (50%), diskette (7%), and other computer means (4%) (Eitington, 2002). Satellite conferences and broadcasts combine many of these sources as they serve audiences from multiple sites.

Some formats enable presenters and participants to have limited interaction. A preprogrammed tutorial, for example, may combine instruction with rather constrained trainer–trainee interaction. *Web computer-based training* (WCBT) and *web electronic performance support system* (WEPSS) are terms referring to individual learning formats.

Broadening the interaction possibilities, virtual classrooms in face-to-face, real-time formats typically utilize cameras and monitors at two or more locations. A *virtual classroom* is a computer-generated space in a computer-mediated communication system. Instructors also use formats for interacting with participants by way of teleconferences, videoconferences, and online programs (Longoria, 2003). A web/virtual asynchronous classroom (W/VSC) is one type of virtual classroom support (Eitington, 2002).

More and more, organizations are using training products that are available online. Regardless of the topic, descriptive and relevant training programs reflect good teaching and learning practices (Berkowitz, 1998).

Technology also provides substantial and fitting support for presentations. In such cases, the technology becomes the vehicle for information, often in a format superior to other visual support. Think of the computer-generated visuals

TV journalists use to present the weather, and the three-dimensional and rotated drawings military personnel use to present technology under development. In business, an Excel spreadsheet can be shown on screen, and various values may be substituted for data entries to create "if–then" possibility data. Creating some of these visuals may not be in your immediate future, but many are already created and ready to view, as seen in Activity 8.4. Notice that some sites require fees of some sort, if you plan to use them, whereas others grant permissions for single usage.

We are fortunate as never before to have the technology hardware, software, and resources available to support our informative presentations. Easily available does not equate to easy, however. One step at a time, decide what you need, and then explore how to use it. Technological support helps an audience only to the extent that the presenter artfully and skillfully uses it.

• ANALYZING THE SITUATION: ASSETS

Your goal is to share information in a way that can be understood by listeners. You actually lead listeners to understand, remember, and utilize data and ideas in ways that they couldn't formerly.[1] Admittedly, business reports are straightforward and practical; still, informative presentations are often intense, exciting, sobering, or celebratory. In rebuttal to those who would say that informative speaking lacks passion, consider the passionate descriptions spoken by embedded wartime reporters or by geneticists who worked on mapping the human genome. So, when you are asked to make an informative presentation, think creatively as you seek connections with what people can and will learn. Understand the speaking situation before determining your informative specific purpose. Ask event planners what they have in mind, what the boundaries are, and what you should accomplish.

Indeed, learning about the overall situation in advance of an event is a speaker's responsibility. You also want to assess a situation's inherent advantages and constraints. Figure 8.1 condenses material in an assessment tool for ASSETS, an acronym meaning audience, speaker, setting, event, topic, and story. The "pocket reference" in Quick Start 8.1 prompts you to analyze and incorporate various aspects of the presentation situation.

● QUICK START 8.1   Assets • • • •

Audience

- Who will be there?
- What are the audience's knowledge and skill sets?
- How do they learn?
- What do audience members have in common? Are they culturally similar?
- How many are in the audience?

---

[1] As you recall, to inform is *not* to advocate, argue, convince, or motivate. Nor does to inform mean to repeat what the listeners already know, as in "covering" a subject (Eitington, 2002, p. 209).

FIGURE 8.1 • ASSETS Model: Audience, Speaker, Setting, Event, Topic, and Story

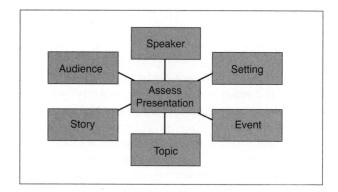

- Who are they in relation to one another and to you? What are the power and interpersonal dimensions present?
- What are their expectations? Do they expect to learn a concept or hear a brief report on a project?
- What is your window of opportunity? How long can you hold their attention? When must they have the information?

Speaker

- As a presenter, are you seen more as a public speaker or as a facilitator?
- What is your expertise?
- What is your rapport and history with the audience?
- What are your communicating strengths?

Setting

- What is the physical setting? Is it conducive to participation and interaction?
- What technology is available for presentations?

Event

- What is the occasion? Why is everyone there? Is this a weekly staff meeting or an annual report to the board of directors?
- Are you the entire agenda, or will there be other speakers and business items?

Topic

- What will you talk about? Is it essential information for the immediate future, or is it a routine report?
- Is the topic complex or straightforward? Is it controversial?
- Are the audience members at the same level of knowledge and understanding regarding the topic? Do they speak the same technical or professional language?

Story

- What is the "story" in this presentation? If your presentation were written up in the news, what would the headline and opening statement be? "What's the scoop?"

• SPEAKING TO PROFESSIONALS AND OTHER MATURE AUDIENCES

The diversity of audiences challenges speakers to be wise in facilitating learning through their choices of approaches and material. Workplace audiences have an attitude of independence and a set of expectations about meeting immediate needs. Certainly, adult audiences don't tolerate disengaged teaching, physical discomfort, or boredom well or for long. The things we learn that make us more effective with workplace audiences, not too surprisingly, have been shown to better engage college audiences as well. Once an audience becomes bored, the presenter faces a tough job in motivating listeners to tune in.

One way to figure out why audiences are bored is to examine the strength of each factor on a diagnostic differential (Figure 8.2). Determine which factors are within your control and which ones are not.

Although you cannot make someone learn something, presenters can stimulate listeners' intrinsic motivations (such as the love of having fun) and remind them of extrinsic ones (such as the desire for professional advancement). Theoretically, if we understand how audience members learn, we can predict which instructional strategies will be most effective. We turn to Malcolm Knowles, David Kolb, and David Sternberg, among others, to (1) describe employees as learners and (2) present principles for informing them. Adult learners exemplify several learner characteristics:

- They require a trusting and open climate and enjoy freely expressing ideas.
- They prefer a problem-solving orientation to content orientation.
- They learn by doing and through experiences.
- They relate new material to an extensive slate of prior experiences.

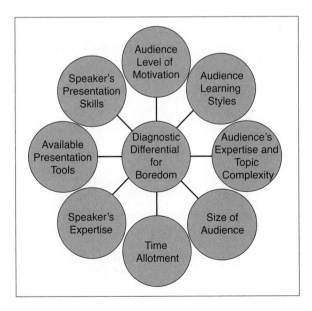

FIGURE 8.2 • Diagnostic Differential for Boredom

- They have well-formed personal goals and objectives, and they take ownership of what they learn and sense their progress toward those goals.

Experience is an excellent teacher, but once people are out of school, being in a traditional educational setting feels exposed and uncomfortable. As Szasz (1973) puts it, "Every act of conscious learning requires the willingness to suffer an injury to one's self-esteem. That is why young children, before they are aware of their own self-importance, learn so easily; and why older persons, especially if vain or important, cannot learn at all."

Several general strategies are especially helpful when talking to adults in college and to career-centered adults:

- Learning should be in the context of tasks they are to perform.
- Build personal ethos (credibility and feelings of good will and acceptance). Encourage cooperation, and avoid overly zealous competition or political maneuvers. Avoid intimidation.
- Move from familiar content, examples, and experiences to new, unfamiliar material. Facilitate discussions of related experiences or refer to shared experiences.
- Coach, rather than lecture, as much as possible. Let learners express what they know.
- Help learners to accumulate experiences, including mistakes and correctives.
- Involve learners as active participants during the presentation. Offer instructional options that engage different learning styles, such as computer simulations, hands-on construction, role play, creative products, puzzles, group problem solving, self-tests, tabulated votes on issues, and independent research.
- Use preview, review, and internal summaries. List objectives that participants can check off as they become satisfied with their learning.

Almost everyone enjoys *knowing,* but not everyone enjoys *learning.* Fortunately, as we mature, we increasingly appreciate the learning process, especially when a speaker-leader is skilled. That's why so many speakers appeal to audiences' interests and use humor.

Reality @ WORK 8.2

USING NARRATIVE TO ENGAGE AN AUDIENCE

One speaker who made learning enjoyable was Robert E. Allen of AT&T, as he spoke to the Economic Club of Detroit on "Telecommunications Reform: When Revolution Is in the Details" on March 10, 1997. He earned his audience's attention with a narrative closely tied to a preview of the topic. Notice how he transitions from event to story to topic:

Customers are of course king *whenever* the competition gets intense. And today, they're demanding, and getting, new capabilities that are allowing them to live as people have never lived before. You may have read newspaper reports a while ago about a Norwegian by the name of Jans Amgust. Jans decided to go ice fishing in an ocean inlet near Oslo. He walked out on the ice, drilled his hole, and settled down. It took him a while before he noticed that the patch of ice he was sitting on had broken away and was drifting off into the North Sea. But don't worry about Jans. He whipped out his cellular phone, called the nearest fire department, and the Norwegian Royal Coast Guard rescued him within 30 minutes—along with his sled.

Advanced communications technologies are often life-savers. But, day to day, consumers are leading such complex lives that they look mainly to communications as a way to simplify. And their communications providers are scrambling to meet their expectations.

Perhaps we generalize about audiences' characteristics because we're concerned that we will be overwhelmed trying to meet too many individual needs. The benefits accrue, however, from choosing techniques reflective of good audience analysis, and most audiences share several characteristics, such as a predominantly female, professional group in health careers. Also, you can acquire a presentational style that combines appeals to the preferences of different segments of the audience.

• DESIGNING PRESENTATIONS FOR VARIOUS LEARNING STYLES

People listen to people they respect, but more important, they listen to those who respect them. When participants perceive disrespect, they are likely to feel resentment, anger, embarrassment, shame, or disdain for a speaker. It is therefore essential, as a presenter, to create mutual respect in a spirit of worthy union with audiences. Presenters should exude confidence without disdain, and authority without condescension. Recognizing diverse talents and intellectual strengths supports respectful attitudes.

An extremely helpful approach, David Kolb's (1984) cycle of learning, is used widely for informative purposes. The four-stage model in Figure 8.3 suggests we best learn concepts and materials that we *feel, watch, think,* and *do.* Worth noting, Kolb adds *feeling* (an emotional connection) and *thinking* (a cognitive connection) to the more common *watching* and *doing.* As often as is practical, presenters should apply all four stages, because by covering all four, they uncover "what makes learners tick" (Selnow, 2003).

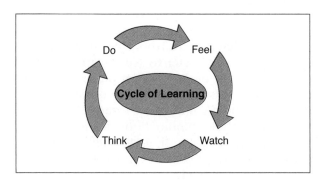

FIGURE 8.3 • Kolb's Cycle of Learning

SELF-TEST: EXAMINING YOUR PREFERENCES IN KOLB'S CYCLE OF LEARNING

Jacob, a Denver client, phones to request you join his executive team for a portion of a working retreat, because the topic of the retreat is integral to the software you are designing. The executive team will be helicoptered in three days earlier. The private lodge is near Telluride, Colorado, and you jump at the chance (maybe you can stay an extra vacation day to ski), but first you need directions to the lodge. Jacob suggests you fly directly to Telluride (the highest commercial airport in the United States) but tells you there is no public transportation to the site, so he'll have a rental car waiting for you. He says he'll e-mail a map but will be out of touch until you see him in Telluride, since the lodge isn't in a cell for phones.

Jacob e-mails a map and, in an area with no roads, pencils in "Wilson Ranch Circle, 10 miles, allow 45 minutes." Concerned about driving to a remote site in winter, you call Jacob for more specific directions. Your flight time will give you only three hours to get to the lodge, and you are determined to locate the site before arriving in Telluride. Assuming you can't "rent a sherpa," choose two strategies, selecting the sources that would be most useful to *you*:

1. Use a computerized map, such as DeLorme's Street Atlas software. (Some private roads are not mapped.)
2. Contact the fire department or city police department. (Remote sites may not be served.)
3. Contact a Telluride realtor. (How? Who would you choose?)
4. Use a GPS program on your laptop. (Which one? What would it cost?)
5. Contact a search-and-rescue volunteer. (How? Who?)
6. Contact a professional mountain guide at a sport shop. (How? Who?)

Select how you would like to receive the information from your sources. (Choose two.)

1. A description of terrain, distances to travel, and compass directions
2. Someone talking through the directions by phone
3. Descriptive details about landmarks to watch for
4. Instructions telling which way to turn and describing marked and unmarked intersections
5. A mark on your GPS program
6. A hand-sketched map promised by your contact person, who will interact with you while talking through the map after your arrival (you need a back-up ahead of time with this one)
7. Feedback when you rehearse how to get there

In Activity 8.8, you explored your preferences for who your sources are and how they give you information. Maybe you prefer to see a map or to hear descriptions. Perhaps you have a good sense of direction or prefer to depend on technology. Did you prefer watching, thinking, feeling, or doing, or some combination? Kolb found that most people combine two stages (watching, thinking, feeling, or doing), and he labels these combinations "learning styles." Find your preferred stages in Table 8.3 (second column) to determine your style in the far left column. In the two right columns, read the associated preferences and strengths of people who share your style.

TABLE 8.3 • Kolb's Learning Styles, Stages, Characteristics, and Strengths

This learning style . . .	combines these stages . . .	and so these learners prefer . . .	because their strengths are . . .
Assimilators (Sideline analysts) Prefer detached work involving abstract ideas	*Thinking and Watching* (Opposite from accommodators)	• Sound logic • Deductive reasoning • Critiquing ideas of others • Systematic analysis	• Interpreting and understanding a wide range of information • Fitting diverse information into a logical form • Creating systematic models • Bringing order to a seeming chaos of ideas
Convergers (Press box coaches) Prefer tasks over social interaction	*Thinking and Doing* (Opposite from divergers)	• Deductive reasoning • Single best solution • Accuracy and clarity	• Technical tasks • Practical application • Problem solving • Decision making
Divergers (Halftime coaches) Use social interaction to stimulate perspectives	*Feeling and Watching* (Opposite from convergers)	• Social interaction • Brainstorming • Many concrete examples	• Imagination • See different perspectives • Drawing generalized conclusions from concrete examples
Accommodators (Sideline coaches) Interact with others to motivate and carry out plans	*Feeling and Doing* (Opposite from assimilators)	• Creative approaches • Involvement in new experiences • Intuitive thinking • Hands-on experiences • Vivid and emotional language, examples, and imagery	• Carrying out plans and tasks • Discovering hidden possibilities • Taking risks • Motivating others

To appreciate the broad spectrum of ways we take in information, spend time exploring the various styles. Follow them logically, but don't try to memorize Table 8.3. Once you are more familiar with learning style concepts, try identifying strategies in Activity 8.4. These experiences lead you toward shaping your informative strategies for particular audiences.

PRESENTING WITH STYLE

First, from the material in Table 8.3, list professions and careers that you think would fall under each style. (Kolb has researched careers and styles.)

Second, match the following statements from actual presentations with the targeted learning style(s).

1. "You know there is an easier way to organize your small business's records, but you don't have the hours it would take to evaluate all the available software. At the end of my presentation, you will be able to choose the best solution for your business."

2. "In my introduction, I showed you the menu page from each of the top five software packages. You may already have spotted the package that seems right to you."

3. "Let's see how each package holds up to your scrutiny."

4. "You have a form in front of you. Mark your preferences as we discuss each package."

5. "You see five stations in the room. Each is set up with one software package and an expert in using that software. We will rotate to all the stations to become familiar with the packages."

6. "Please refer to the color of your handout packet. Join the expert wearing a hat of that color first. When the expert passes the hat to another expert, you stay with that color throughout the session. Go to your color-coded station now."

7. "You will see a bright glare when two of our experts remove their hats. Let me assure you that the glare will cease the moment they again cover their heads (tipping of hats to see shaved heads), but you can find the hat that matches your packet as soon as they don another hat."

8. "Take ten minutes in your teams to brainstorm all the features you may want in a piece of software for managing your businesses. During a break, a team recorder will then provide for each of you a printed copy of your combined results. Circle your highest priorities."

9. "Here are site maps for each software package. Analyze which one most closely fits your and your customers' needs."

10. "I will tell you the stories of five small businesses and how they arrived at their choices of software."

SUMMARY

As informative speakers, we aim to assist discoveries by others. Informative purposes include professional development training, reporting, and instructing. Briefings, technical reports, status reports, professional development training, and client orientations are informative presentations you can expect to give in your work environment.

To effectively inform an audience at work, speakers should (1) understand how audiences learn, (2) assess available material and knowledge, and (3) make good choices for teaching and informing. They also should analyze their audiences, themselves as speakers, and their settings, events, topics, and stories. Find out ahead of time what your audience prefers—a brief written report with a detailed presentation and full discussion, or a detailed report with a presentation that quickly highlights key points. Respect an audience's right and need to know. Speakers' awareness of learning styles, adult learning principles, various intelligences, and immediate needs engages learners in meaningful experiences. As David Kolb's cycle of learning notes, people learn best what they feel, watch, think, and do.

Reports are the most routine informative presentations for the workplace. For technical reports, oral and written, communicators should consider their audience's levels of expertise, moving from the familiar to the unfamiliar and clearly defining terms. For instructions and demonstrations, they should use a straightforward, typical explanation and recap procedures and sequences. Briefings are oral informative reports; in tandem, briefs are informative written reports to (1) update a listener concerning an event or (2) provide background information for particular situations.

Technology offers channels and support for presenting information. Distance learning formats include individual and independent configurations as well as satellite conferences and broadcasts from multiple sites. Some templates enable presenters and participants to interact, emulating face-to-face interaction. •

ACTIVITIES

1. **Technical Support, Team Work, and Presenting to Others:** Assign teams or individuals website topics for class presentations. The website for the PBS series *The Secret Life of the Brain* (www.pbs.org/wnet/brain) exemplifies a well-designed educational website for this activity.

2. **Journaling the Experience:**

   a. Read the following passage and list the statistical data reported by CNN. For the next product, "think backwards": Deduce how the original data may have looked when it was first compiled.

   The World Health Organization is reporting 337 cases of Severe Acute Respiratory Syndrome in 14 countries, including 10 deaths, [CDC Director Julie Gerberding] said. The WHO figures do not include the U.S. cases. No deaths have been reported in the United States, Gerberding said. . . . Among the 22 suspected U.S. cases are two Americans who stayed at a hotel in Hong Kong that has been implicated as the initial source of the spread—"the place where almost all the international cases appear to have been exposed, in February," she said. . . . The Hong Kong Health Department is tracking down others who stayed in the hotel—particularly the ninth floor—at that time, she said. Hong Kong health officials have identified 203 patients with the illness. About a third of them involve family members and other close contacts of infected people, and the others involve health care personnel.

   b. After describing the *effect* of SARS, the report explores what the Centers for Disease Control and Prevention has learned in its search for *cause*. Analyze the following passage. Is cause established? How are paramyxoviruses defined? Compare CNN's definition in this extract with another definition provided at www.tulane.edu/~dmsander/WWW/335/Paramyxoviruses.html on February 16, 1999. CDC is working with other laboratories to find the cause of the disease. Labs in Germany and Hong Kong have found patients harboring particles of what appear to be paramyxoviruses—responsible for such common illnesses as mumps and measles—which they say may turn out to be the cause. It also includes a subfamily of viruses that can be transmitted between animals and people.

3. **Ethically Speaking:** Prepare a brief presentation in response to this statement: "A speaker's first priority is accuracy, even when the subject matter is too technical for the audience to understand."

4. **Presenting to Others and Team Work:** PC Training

A typical workplace informative task is teaching a technical skill. Several principles of learning guide training decisions for teaching the use of personal computers (Knowles, 1984):

- Participants want to know why they're learning specific things (for instance, certain commands, functions, operations, etc.)
- Participants prefer task-oriented instruction instead of rote memory. Activities should focus on familiar tasks they can do on computer.
- Participants have different backgrounds and previous experience with computers.

In teams of four or five, choose a personal computer software product. Each team member should select one function of the product to teach. Possible products include Microsoft Word or DeLorme Street Atlas. As an alternative, choose a research procedure on a library website, such as WilsonWeb. Decide on a team presentation strategy, including specific purpose, introduction, body pattern of organization, and conclusion. List methods the team will use and how you will get feedback on your effectiveness after the presentation, as in the following example:

Specific purpose: After hearing our presentation, the audience will be able to work with folders in Microsoft applications.

Organization: Logical sequence

Member 1 teaches creating folders in Microsoft.
Member 2 teaches saving documents in folders.
Member 3 teaches using Explore to find folders and documents.
Member 4 teaches moving documents in Explore.

Instructional methods: Demonstration, explanation, instructional handouts.

Evaluation of instructional effectiveness: Several participants will perform the function with help from the rest of the audience. All participants will respond to questionnaires about their feelings of efficacy (self-confidence in skills).

Teach the class the skills by your instructional strategy. Alternatively, teach one other team the skills with hands-on learning.

5. **Presenting to Others:** Demonstrate a procedure to an audience. Choose a tightly delineated topic that is unfamiliar to the audience. For example, don't try to teach how to build a bookcase (too broad) or how to assemble a "some assembly required" bookcase (too familiar). Teach, instead, how to miter a corner (*tight*).

6. **Journaling the Experience:** Research what Peter Senge means by a "learning organization" and the discipline he calls "personal mastery." How does learning information fit into "expanding the ability to produce"? Write a half- to one-page reaction paper in your journal to Dr. Senge's statement that "[L]earning organizations are not possible unless they have people at every level who practice it" (see the following extract for the context of this statement).

> Learning is a discipline. . . . "Learning" in this context does not mean acquiring more information, but expanding the ability to produce the results we truly want in life. . . . And learning organizations are not possible unless they have people at every level who practice it. (Senge, 1994, pp. 141–142)

FOR FURTHER READING

A quick introduction to learning styles can be found at www.businessballs.com/kolblearningstyles.htm and www.engr.ncsu.edu/learningstyles/ilsweb.html

Gardner, H. (1993). *Creating minds: An anatomy of creativity seen through the lives of Freud, Einstein, Picasso, Stravinsky, Eliot, Graham, and Gandhi.* New York: Basic Books.

Gardner, H. (1993). *Multiple intelligences: The theory in practice.* New York: Basic Books.

Gardner, H. (2002). The tipping point between success and failure: A psychologist's view. Submitted to *Nexos,* April 2002. Available at http://www.pz.harvard.edu/Pls/HG.htm

Williams, W. M., Blythe, T., White, N., Li, L., Sternberg, R. J., & Gardner, H. (1996). *Practical intelligence for school.* New York: HarperCollins.

A summary of Peter Senge's vision of a learning organization is discussed at http://www.infed.org/thinkers/senge.html#_The_core_disciplines and at http://www.solonline.org/.

Go to Fripp.com under articles for some suggestions on "Selling Your Way to Success: How to Present Your Proposal at an Executive Meeting."

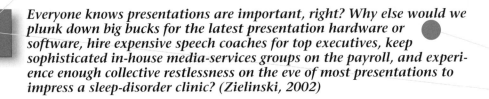

Everyone knows presentations are important, right? Why else would we plunk down big bucks for the latest presentation hardware or software, hire expensive speech coaches for top executives, keep sophisticated in-house media-services groups on the payroll, and experience enough collective restlessness on the eve of most presentations to impress a sleep-disorder clinic? (Zielinski, 2002)

Visual and Other Sensible Support

9

The Function of Media Support

Designing for the Senses

Guiding Principles for "Sensible" Support

Functions and Guidelines for Visual Support

Presenting Sensationally

Speakers and Listeners as Visual Support

Three-Dimensional Supporting Material: Artifacts, Manipulatives, and Objects

Two-Dimensional Supporting Material: Transparencies, Posters, and Handouts

Presentation Software

Mixed Media Support

Distance Presentation: Video Conferences and Distance Instruction

Custom Designs

Whether giving public speeches or presenting services and products to clients one on one, you and your organization will benefit from good choices. This chapter explores media and message designs to complement and support spoken words.

OBJECTIVES

After studying the content of this chapter, you will be able to

- Match experiential support to audiences' needs
- Create visual and other experiential support
- Integrate experiential support to optimize communication

• • • • TIPS   • • • • The "Senses" of Chapter 9 • • • •

Sense carries four meaningful denotations in this chapter.

1. "Making sense" is synonymous to communicating.
2. When someone says, "I sense . . . ," the person usually means, "I interpret what you say or do to mean . . . ."
3. We take in information about our world through the five senses—"sensitively" through touch, sight, sound, taste, and smell.
4. To be sensible is to be reasonable or wise.

Thus, people take in information through the five senses and interpret, or make sense, of what they have gathered. To be sensible—sense-able—requires two sets of skills:

1. The ability to be open and flexible in gathering information through the senses
2. The ability to apply reasoning, value, and experiences for learning

So you see, communication through the senses is the most sensible way to make sense.

• • •

• THE FUNCTION OF MEDIA SUPPORT

Stop right here—really, read no further if you can't keep communication purposes as a primary focus when deciding on support, visual or otherwise. Some people get carried away, and others get overwhelmed, but both tendencies can be tempered by recentering on basic questions:

- To whom am I communicating?
- What am I communicating?
- How can I communicate best?

We learn by seeing, by listening, and by doing. Some topics fit a particular instructional style, but many skills and information can be approached in a variety of ways.

- Most people prefer *visual* experiences. Visual learning includes what the observer sees in visual aids, including studying how the speaker does something.
- About 15% of people prefer to listen. Sometimes they speak just to hear themselves talk, so they can process through hearing.

- Another 25% learn physically, which includes touch, participation, and internalizing a speaker's nonverbal facial and physical cues.

EXPERT ADVICE

Reality
@ WORK
9.1

Randall Englund (2002, p. 88), coauthor of *Creating an Environment for Successful Projects: The Quest to Manage Project Management* and a senior consultant at the Strategic Management Group in Philadelphia, describes his learning style: "I like to see the big picture. Graphics help me get to the point more quickly, especially graphics that link together so I can see how the pieces fit. Complex images or concepts come more easily when they build in sequence. Seeing real people doing real tasks lends credibility." He thinks his engineering training explains his left-brain dominance, but he has come to appreciate his intuitive side, and he has noticed that he learns fastest when both sides are engaged.

Englund refers to work on various intelligences—interpersonal, logical, visual, musical, verbal, intrapersonal, and kinesthetic—noting that each of us is probably strong in a couple of areas and can improve in other areas. Englund advises presenters, "Since people have different styles and ways of processing information, problems can result. An effective presenter needs to respect different learning styles. The best way to do that is to offer variety within a presentation."

Techniques that Englund uses in his presentations to project managers are musical interludes pertaining to an upcoming point, handouts with blanks to fill in, visuals of puzzle pieces showing chapters in his book, assessment tools, discussions, and PowerPoint flowcharts. "Creating an experience that people remember involves activating more of their senses: sight, hearing, touch. If you can engage your audience members according to their preferred learning styles, months later they will remember the stories you told and points you made in your presentation."

A straightforward approach is to determine people's tendencies in acquiring knowledge and recall how they interact with ideas, people, and things. Then you are ready to take advantage of their preferences as you design your presentations.

DESIGNING FOR THE SENSES

Appealing to people's learning preferences usually means utilizing different media. Speakers as artists choose their media (tools) and channels (paths). The examples in Table 9.1 match senses to the media that access them. Good presentational use of media is well informed and strategic, not a random use "just because it's there." Do you agree with the choices made in Table 9.1?

Entertainment, especially television, has changed the way people tune in. Audience members metaphorically "channel flip" through ideas and approaches, and sensitive speakers match the pace and need for change.

FEELING, WATCHING, THINKING, AND DOING

For three presentational tasks in Table 9.1, describe how you would involve an audience through touch, sight, and action. For instance, for presentation task 11, comparing high- and low-quality photographs, a speaker can show emotionally compelling (feeling) photographs as examples (watching) and provide

ACTIVITY
9.1

TABLE 9.1 • Sensible Paths for Media

Presentational Tasks	Sensory Channels	Media
1. Demonstrate how to refinish an antique table to 50 people	Visual	Face-to-face demo with refinishing tools and products Video
2. Introduce a sales force to new frozen entrées (products they will market)	Visual, sight, smell, taste, touch/texture	Food product experience using all five senses
3. Teach a software application	Touch, visual, aural, experience	A hands-on walk-through on a PC Projected active product
4. Promote a new vocalist to three out-of-state recording companies	Aural, visual	Recording Photo portfolio
5. Make statistical comparisons on sales in four regions	Visual	PowerPoint graph or chart Handouts Poster graph or chart
6. Present features of a newly bioengineered fiber to fashion designers	Visual, tactile/touch	A variety of samples of fabrics using new fiber for each participant Handouts for reference Demonstration of drape, weather resistance, etc.
7. Teach Red Cross first aid class CPR	Visual, touch	Charts Resusci Annie demo and practice PowerPoint graphics
8. Balance a ledger—teaching the skill	Visual, experience	PowerPoint interactive Excel sheet Demonstration Handouts Chalkboard, poster, or PowerPoint
9. Teaching critical care patient assessment during clinical rounds	Visual	Patient charts, appearance of patient
	Aural	Equipment beeps, things a patient might utter responsively to requests or pain
	Smell	Signs of infection
	Touch	Response to touch; examination of patient; room temperature, etc.
10. Teach the parts of a digital camera	Visual	Illustration on poster or screen
11. Compare high- and low-resolution photographs	Visual	Enlarged hard copy or projected photos

additional photographs for analysis (thinking). Audience members can sort through a final group of photos to select the most appropriate ones for a given topic and audience (doing).

Two previous chapters on informative speaking scrutinized verbal support; this chapter focuses on selecting, planning, and developing support using the five senses in additional ways.

● GUIDING PRINCIPLES FOR "SENSIBLE" SUPPORT

Speakers don't always look like speakers. For example, a representative of a musical instrument company plays pianos for more than half of a presentation to piano instructors, and a factory tour guide explains what visitors will see before entering but can only shout a few answers to them once they enter the factory. These presentations are somewhat lengthy and not generally the types given in a communication class, but in the workplace, you very well may design similar presentations.

Visual and other "sensible" supporting material strengthen speeches when used correctly. Overall, remember these five principles:

1. *Be purposeful* in everything you show and do.
2. *Motivate* audience members to pay attention. Intrigue them, inspire them, or compel them to listen, but always connect them with what they are doing.
3. *Provide media aids* for all audience members at the same time. If the support is designed for viewing, be sure the audience can actually see it. If it is designed to be touched, let everyone have that experience simultaneously or in a set time frame.
4. *Don't overwhelm the senses.* Audience members may become random in their attention if you do so.
5. *Lead and direct* the audience's attention. Vary pace, yet establish a rhythm; identify a style, but integrate variety.

● FUNCTIONS AND GUIDELINES FOR VISUAL SUPPORT

Visual support strengthens both informative and persuasive speaking purposes because

- Visuals support audience comprehension.
- Visual support increases listener memory and retention.
- Most people are visual learners, and for those who are not, visuals corroborate other "sensible" channels.
- We tend to remember only about 10% of what we hear, but we will probably retain as much as 65% of what we both see and hear (Zayes-Baya, 1977–1978). Retention after three days for speech alone is about 10%; for visual alone, about 20%; and for speech and visual combined, close to 65%. The three methods are closer (70%, 72%, and 85%, respectively) if measured after only three hours.

Discuss several ways the speaker uses the falcon to his audience's benefit.

- Visual support helps persuasive purposes. A study by the 3M Corporation showed that speakers incorporating visual aids into their presentations were 43% more likely to persuade their listeners than those who relied on words alone (Vogel, Dickson, & Lehman, 1986).
- Visual support increases speaker credibility.
- Visuals show a speech's foundation of ideas when a speaker shows main points or key words. A map reveals connections as well.

Now that we are clear about *why* speakers use visual support, we are ready for some important general guidelines for how to use it.

- **Limit each visual** to one main concept.
- **Minimize the number of words** per visual. (Twenty words on one visual will generally tax the viewer, unless words are limited and revealed during the explanation.)
- **Letter clearly and largely**, using letters and numbers easily read by the back row of viewers. (Generally, letters should be $3/_4$ to 1 inch high for every 10 feet the visual is from the viewer.) Sans-serif fonts (that don't have caps or shoes) are better reading from a distance.
- **Label data and structures** clearly and accurately, but with as few words as possible.
- **Use good contrast** in color choices, such as black on white or yellow, or the inverse.
- **Avoid clutter.** Eliminate visual distractions.
- **Match visuals to the topic**, not the topic to the visuals.
- **Design visuals to support audience understanding and retention.** Make them memorable.

• • • • **TIPS**   • • • • **Slides as Presentation Aids** • • • •

Slides can refer to a variety of electronically created visuals, including presentation software visuals (such as PowerPoint), transparencies, and photographs.

• • •

VISUAL DESIGN CAN REFLECT AUDIENCE ANALYSIS

Reality @ WORK 9.2

"Use design to communicate that you know your listeners," says Jennifer Rotondo (2002), a Microsoft Certified Expert and Advanced PowerPoint trainer. "Customizing a presentation to a client or to attendees shows that you care enough to research who they are and what they're about" (p. 1). She assures presenters, "Working your audience research into slide design may take more preparation, but the result is a more polished presentation that adds to the power of your content" (p. 3). Once you have your audience in mind, here are her suggestions:

- Personalize the presentation. "The ultimate goal in your design is to indicate that you understand [the client's] market, product, and mind-set." Use design to reflect that you understand how restrained or upbeat they are.

- Use design to pace the presentation. Anticipate how quickly you need to get to the heart of the presentation or the bottom line. She suggests that if you are allotted 30 minutes, you should keep the main presentation to less than 15 minutes, getting to the point in the first few minutes. This allows question-and-answer time while still ending punctually.

- Design "secret slides," anticipating audience questions. Hidden slides are ready to show when listeners want more specific information. To hide a slide, select it and go to Slideshow, then Hide Slide. The slide will appear with a gray box in the slide sorter, but not on the screen, unless you right-click and select Go. By Title or Slide Navigator will show the labels you gave these slides.

- Keep your text short, so you can elaborate.

- Use parallel construction. Start all bullets with a noun or a verb consistently.

- Use graphics and other visuals when they better represent information.

• PRESENTING SENSATIONALLY

From looking at a speaker to viewing graphs, slides, and handouts, the eyes busily assess and acquire data. *Visual aids* can gain attention in an introduction, review main points in the conclusion, show the structure of the main points, or support a main point. Visuals should not be used to show off; rather, they should support specific communication and aid learners.

Form and substance do not necessarily exclude one another. For instance, graphs combine form and substance when the relationships that they illustrate show substantive content that exceeds verbal description. The words *chart* and *graph* are often used interchangeably, but in this chapter, *chart* refers to mapping or illustrating connections and related ideas, as in organization charts, flowcharts, and the phrase "chart the path."[1] *Graphs* show analyses of statistical data in regard to variables' relationships and occurrences. *Tables* present data and information, so that they are easier to interpret visually. The forms of visual support we will study are grouped as follows:

- Speakers and listeners as visual support

- Three-dimensional visual support

---

[1] PowerPoint uses the command Insert Chart to import visual data from a spreadsheet, such as Excel. These "charts" can be tables or graphs.

- Two-dimensional visual support
- Handouts

After we look at these visible categories, we let presentation software—PowerPoint in particular—lead the way to mixing media for us. Presentation software is most often used for two-dimensional support, but it also can insert audio and videos. The chapter concludes with a final section that peruses specific kinds of designs.

●—●—● SPEAKERS AND LISTENERS AS VISUAL SUPPORT

"Christopher Columbus didn't have a globe to study," Professor Vincent Clark explains to his community college students as he circles his luminous, shaved head with his hands. In case some don't get it, he continues to point to his head anytime he talks about the world being round. Why is his head an effective visual aid for his audience? The class "feels" the logical leap that Columbus had to make from a traditional concept of flat land represented on a flat map to a "vision" of a world pictured on a sphere. Students internalize the analogy—laughing all the way.

Audiences scrutinize speakers to see if they're enthusiastic, sincere, well informed, and confident. With any luck at all, speakers start with audiences looking at them. They can use this attention to become their best visual aids. Speakers actually become visual support for the subject matter, such as when demonstrating a sport or creating a piece of art. When you *are* the visual support, consider these guidelines:

- Look the part. Your clothes and appearance "speak" to the audience. Don't clutter the scenery with overdone jewelry, an extreme hairstyle, or complicated, high-contrast fabric patterns.
- Use your hands purposefully to lead visual attention, to illustrate a shape, to perform a procedure, and to frame your face.
- Avoid hiding behind speaker stands and other equipment.
- If you are demonstrating with your whole body, such as in teaching a dance step, consider what each listener can see during every moment of the presentation.
- Don't visually compete with other visual support.
- Think of your background. Should an audience member take a black-and-white photograph of you while you are speaking, would the photo show good contrast and balance and be visually compelling?

Audiences can participate and be visual aides. Using one or more of the audience members creates a perspective of the speaker as leader. One student speaker used her classmates as support in her speech. Earlier, she had asked two classmates to dress—one appropriately and one inappropriately—for job interviews. Another speaker, a health career major, asked a classmate to be the patient in order to teach a respiratory therapy technique. Involving audience members is also effective when teaching techniques in workshop settings.

Speakers gain knowledge from their speaking experiences, but you can get a head start in selecting visual aids by analytically and critically considering which visuals go with which media. In some jobs, if you are lucky, you will have staff (artists, photographers, and technicians) to assist you in creating visuals. Often, however, you are on your own. Variables to consider when planning presentations are costs versus benefits, time, and the reliability of equipment. Activity 9.2 invites you to consider visual options.

THE WAYS AND MEANS OF MEDIA

As you continue to read about visual support, critically consider which types of visuals best lend themselves to certain media. Return to fill in this activity's matrix.

ACTIVITY 9.2

1. Make notes on limitations to keep in mind when considering each media aid. (These have been started for you.)
2. Use the matrix to match *media* to *visual support*. Rate each pair according to the following instructions.

   Rate (A = high, B = medium, C = low) how well each medium suits each visual support.

   Rate (1 = high, 2 = medium, 3 = low) how useful the matched pair would be for an informative presentation you plan to give *three* times.

   For example, you might give the first pair (photographs + slide projector) a rating of A-2.

MEDIA	Slide Projector (must be shown in darkened room)	PowerPoint with Computer/ Projector or Monitor	Transparency Overhead Projector (limited in color)	Poster Flip Chart (susceptible to damage)	Chalkboard or Dry Board (spontaneous, but time-consuming)	VCR/ Camcorder/ Monitor or Distance Learning Setup	Document Camera (expensive, unavailable at many sites)
VISUAL SUPPORT							
Photographs	A-2 (if 35-mm slides are already available)						
Key Words							
Graphs							
Charts							
Illustrations							
Graphics and Line Art							
Diagrams/ Flowcharts							
Videos							
Details on Small Objects							
Demonstrations (procedures with large equipment)							
Demonstrations (techniques with hand-held instruments)							

THREE-DIMENSIONAL SUPPORTING MATERIAL: ARTIFACTS, MANIPULATIVES, AND OBJECTS

A middle-school audience gained perspective on the size of a prehistoric mammoth when an archeologist showed them a baby mammoth's rib, but when he actually took them to the mammoth dig, they experienced something he couldn't carry around. A graphic representation of how mammoths were positioned at the site helped them imagine the dramatic moment of the animals' deaths, even though the skeletons were mostly buried. The archeologist's arms rounded, flowed, and entwined as he described the female mammoth lifting up her baby to get the youngster to higher ground.

In the preceding example, the archeologist took advantage of the differences between two-dimensional and three-dimensional visuals. The real object (mammoth rib) had more immediate impact than would a photo of it. The artist's rendition of the probable positioning of the mammoths helped the class "see" what they couldn't see in real life. At the mammoth dig site, the class got an experience that used all the senses—clay, dust, and big bones. (Maybe future archeologists will show classes holograms as three-dimensional visuals.)

Three-dimensional support may consist of artifacts, manipulatives, or other objects. Objects are usually brought to audiences, but audiences may be taken to objects. *Artifacts* are items made by human hands, such as art, furniture, and tools. *Manipulatives* are objects the audience handles for participatory learning. Other objects (not made by people), such as plants, mineral crystals, and insects, may also support a presentation.

A particularly useful piece of equipment for showing small objects and techniques is the *document camera*. It projects to the audience in real time items (objects, books, transparencies, etc.) that are displayed on the open, horizontal screen or by means of video, computer, or DVD. If you have access to one, by all means become familiar with it.

Three-dimensional, real objects have several advantages:

- They uphold reality in an explanation and support speaker credibility.
- They draw audience attention and interest.
- They provide real visual perspective and can be turned and seen from different angles.
- Remember to help the audience easily see the objects and understand why and how you are using them.
- Use document cameras to zoom close to small objects, manipulate them, and visually project the images.
- When demonstrating intricate tasks, a graphic enlargement is helpful.
- *Do not* ask listeners to pass around objects during your presentation, and as a point of caution beware of living, active visual aids. Children and puppies steal the show and are sometimes difficult to manage. If anything can go wrong, it likely will, which brings us to safety precautions with equipment. Peeling an apple may not seem difficult until you are doing it

Visual comparisons make clear impression on audiences. Showing these cultures with a document camera would involve an audience in a detailed examination of the two cultures.

in front of an audience. It is your responsibility to make audiences feel safe during your presentations.

• TWO-DIMENSIONAL SUPPORTING MATERIAL: TRANSPARENCIES, POSTERS, AND HANDOUTS

When the "real thing" is too awkward to use or impossible to bring, turn to other forms of visual support. People process two-dimensional support—"flat support"—differently from real objects and three-dimensional support. There is sharper focus, because it is easier for us to think through the relationship of a single cause measured against a single effect than to introduce another variable, or third dimension.

Flat media are used to deliver diverse content, as in the following examples:

Mary projected a photographic digital slide of Michelangelo's *David* when she talked about the large hands and athletic posture Michelangelo sculpted.

Kevin used a poster-sized photograph of a new car model to launch sales.

Dwight pointed to an enlarged schema of an audio system.

Georgette graphed her company's profit curve over the past five years.

Sam used a scatter plot to show his company's distribution of U.S. stores.

Illustrations help audiences understand and are predominantly pictorial, including photographs, art graphics, flowcharts, statistical charts, and graphs. Illustrations have remarkable flexibility for speakers' purposes:

- Illustrations can be shown in hard copy, by projection, in action videos frame by frame, and with handouts, to mention a few possibilities.
- Illustrations can be used in place of actual objects, especially with dangerous items (e.g., microscopic views of the smallpox bacteria) or with unreasonable or unavailable items (e.g., the layers of a glacier).
- Illustrations can clarify ideas, directions, relationships, and information.
- Illustrations can use visual coding, such as colors and shapes.

Although the guidelines for creating visuals certainly apply here, several are worth expanding:

- Make sure people can see without straining. When people squint to see, they frown. The effort may not seem worth it to them after a while, and they might tune out.

- When 35-mm slides provide the best visuals, practice with the projector and the slides. Ask someone to dim and bring up the house lights. Use a slide for a specific purpose; then plan to have the lights brighten again on cue.

- Adjust slide shows to correct time segments. Remember, however, that slide shows do not substitute for speech presentations. Use them sparingly.

Transparencies

Transparencies are images copied to clear acetate or another transparent medium for projection by an overhead projector onto a screen. Projection equipment—an overhead projector—is standard in most presentation rooms, making transparencies one of the most easily used visuals. Words and simple graphics are suitable for transparencies.

Transparencies can be photocopies or printed on clear sheets made for PC printers. Many copy centers create quality color copies as well as black-and-white ones. You can quickly create a transparency with permanent marker pens. As you can see, transparencies for overhead projectors yield several advantages:

- The equipment is simple and dependable.
- The $8\frac{1}{2}$" × 11" transparencies sheets are easily stored or carried in a briefcase.
- Speakers don't have to turn their backs on audiences to use transparencies.
- Transparency visuals are easily seen, even in light-flooded rooms.
- Speakers can write on visuals interactively and can use a pencil as a pointer on the transparency. (Use a felt-tipped, nonpermanent pen on a permanently printed transparency to add immediacy to a presentation.)
- Transparencies can be stacked to layer in features.
- A piece of typing/printing paper can cover parts of visuals until presenters are ready for the audience to see those parts.
- Transparencies can be eliminated or added during the presentation to adapt to time constraints.

Reality @ WORK 9.3

A CONVENTIONAL PRESENTATION

Zack looked forward to presenting his kinesiology research at a national convention. His invitation letter requested one copy of his paper for the print center and 30 copies for the presentation. The letter also said that a limited number of overhead projectors could be reserved through the convention hotel. Zack

immediately e-mailed a request for a projector and requested a confirmation. (He kept the original e-mail and confirmation in his briefcase.) He knew he did not want to pass out papers until after his presentation, and now he needed to decide which parts of his talk needed visual support.

On Microsoft Word he used a large font for keying selective representative statistics, which he reproduced for two of his transparencies. He also simplified a line graph of results, coloring the graph line red and enlarging the label for each axis. Finally, he created transparencies with one hypothesis written on each. Zack planned to use these two transparencies early in his talk, and he would use a marker to write in the results to the hypotheses during his talk. He found a black-and-white illustration of the type of exercise equipment used for the research. He scanned the illustration and printed it on his laser printer from his PC. Satisfied with his six visuals, he sequenced masters that he printed on typing paper and compiled 30 copies—just in case the projector didn't show up. He packed his visuals, handouts, and copies in his briefcase.

In addition to the general guidelines for creating visual aids, pay attention to several items:

- Focus the projector and adjust the screen.
- Put your transparencies and notes in order before you begin a presentation. Write cues on your notes to remind you when to move to a transparency. Rehearse these transitions.
- Practice using notes and transparencies, so that you spend most of your time maintaining eye contact with your audience.
- Look at the overhead projector, not the screen, when pointing to something on a transparency.
- Keep features under wraps until they are relevant. Keep transparencies in order as you remove them.
- Turn off the projector light and move away from the projector when you're not using it. (A fan will continue to run for a few minutes and turn itself off when the $200+ bulb is cool.)
- Verbally signpost visuals. For instance, "Now let's look at a graph of this year's sales."
- Don't depend on transparencies for speaker notes throughout a presentation. Transparencies used solely to project outlines hypnotize people and draw criticism.

Keep the Cardboard: Poster Boards and Flipcharts

Although poster boards and flipcharts are awkward to carry onto airplanes and up elevators, they are sometimes helpful:

- Posters and large charts can be placed close to audiences.
- They provide interactive communication while using visuals.
- Posters stand alone as visual sources, without depending on other people for equipment or relying on working equipment for a successful presentation.
- They can remain displayed to remind listeners of key concepts.

FLIP CHARTS FOR FLEXIBILITY

ShippingPax announced a corporate reorganization. As human resources manager, Maggie planned inquiry sessions at each branch site. She wanted to show details of the new formal organizational chart but keep an informal climate. Maggie decided that a flipchart would serve her presentational purposes and also establish the closeness she wanted. She could stand up to present to larger audiences, and she could sit to encourage participation and questions from more reticent groups.

In addition to following the general guidelines for creating visuals, in designing posters and charts:

- Provide blank sheets in a flipchart between visuals, and turn poster boards not in use to their blank sides.
- Posters and charts should be heavy duty so that they will not roll up or curl off an easel during a presentation.
- Provide an easel at 6 inches to 2 feet above audience eye-level viewing. Pack a couple of clothespins, masking tape, and thumbtacks for emergencies, such as when a fan in the room flips your chart for you.

Handouts

Learners often benefit from the reinforcement of written and graphic directions for practice later. Audiences can take handouts with them, and with handouts, everyone can see the information. Speakers can choose points to discuss in depth or choose to overview a topic. This is especially important for convention speakers discussing complex topics and research. Furthermore, listeners spend more time listening for understanding and less time copying notes.

Especially helpful for convention speakers, handouts can provide comprehensive coverage of a topic, list and credit sources and provide details, such as websites, telephone numbers, and mailing addresses. Handouts are frequently problematic during presentations, because listeners are thumbing through them. There are a couple of ways to deal with this problem. You can mention that handouts with [list their features] are available after the presentation. Another way is to distribute handouts several minutes before the presentation, so recipients can satisfy their initial curiosity. Announce during your introduction, "We will refer to the handouts together at a couple of points in the presentation. For now, you can set the handouts aside." Overall, handouts give a sense of security and ownership, often allowing listeners to follow up with questions, gathering additional material and trying applications.

A FOWL SITUATION

Wildlife specialist Iguana Svetlana (Iggie to her friends) was contacted from the remote site of an oil spill, where wild birds were struggling for their lives. Iggie knew that sundry volunteers already would have gathered to take care of the birds. Her job was to make the volunteer efforts count for the most. This required setting up an organization, with shifts and systems. She also needed to teach triage and techniques for caring for the birds. She was told that a makeshift conference room had been set up, with the only power being a small generator.

Make a master plan showing the kinds of information she should communicate and which presentational aids she should use. Which things should be taught first?

● PRESENTATION SOFTWARE

Kathleen Hall Jamieson, in *Eloquence in an Electronic Age* (1988), suggests that presenters should consider how contemporary audiences learn and engage through presentations. Earlier in our history, politicians declaimed from trains' cabooses, and nomadic vendors hawked their wares. A new face in town commanded attention then, but now audiences are accustomed to an assault of stimuli, much of which is on screen. Jamieson challenges communication texts and professors to "mesh the best of the old and the new" (p. 246), certainly a philosophy inherent to this text. Visual learners and students for whom English is a second language apparently are better at taking notes and understanding how material is organized when instructors use PowerPoint or similar support (Petrie, 2003). When 150 recruiters at a prestigious university were questioned, 75% wanted at least "basic" presentation software skills from their applicants (Davis, 1996, p. 74).

Presentation software opens audio and video support possibilities, even for novices. By definition, presentation software is an application program used

> to create sequences of words and pictures that tell a story or help support a speech or public presentation of information. Presentation software can be divided into business presentation software and more general multimedia authoring tools, with some products having characteristics of both. Business presentation software emphasizes ease- and quickness-of-learning and use. Multimedia authoring software enables you to create a more sophisticated presentation that includes audio and video sequences. (Whatis.com, 2004)

Examples of presentation software used in businesses are Microsoft PowerPoint and Lotus Freelance Graphics, Adobe Persuasion, Corel, and Harvard Graphics. Multimedia authoring tools with added presentation capability are Macromedia Director and Asymetrix's Multimedia Toolbook.

This chapter discusses Microsoft PowerPoint because it is installed on most personal computers, is the one you are most likely to have access to in business and academic locations, and is the software that set the paradigm for digital visual support. PowerPoint's capabilities include video, audio, and interactive features. Also, the quickly achieved sophisticated results are attractive for speakers. Like other visuals in general, PowerPoint should *support* a presentation, not *substitute* for a speaker's responsibility.

You need to experience a software application to understand how easy it is to give in to cluttered design when you get carried away with the technology. Presenters quickly fall in love with the advantages of PowerPoint, so before we explore the package, a few cautions should be kept in mind:

- Speakers may become too tied to technical aspects of presentations and ignore communicating core messages.

- Projection systems vary, and some require low light in the room, making it difficult for audiences to clearly see speakers.

- Speakers are tempted to look at the screen projection rather than at the audience.

- Slides used solely for outlined notes are hypnotizing, automatic, and undermine active listening.

- Eye-popping visuals can steal the show, reducing speakers to technicians.

- Speakers may spend too much preparation time preparing visuals and forget to practice speaking.

● ● ● ● TIPS   ● ● ● ● Using PowerPoint Effectively ● ● ● ●

- Control your PowerPoint presentational support; don't let it control you. Do not use automatic timers on slides.

- Be visually straightforward and uncomplicated. Bells and whistles can divert listeners' attention unnecessarily. Learn to use the features you need to support ideas rather than finding ideas that will use the features you know how to use.

- Ahead of time, find out what version of PowerPoint and what operating system you will be using at the presentation. Save your work in a form that will work on that system. Many new users have created elaborate slide shows with imported pictures, only to find that they could not save them or transport them for presentation. You have several options, one of which is to burn a CD. Second, if the presentation computer is online, you may be able to e-mail the files to that computer. Third, there are several ways to compress, or "zip," data, in order to get more on a disk. You may bring the presentation on a laptop and connect (if you bring cables to connect them) to the monitor or screen. Finally, sometimes you may need to eliminate some of the memory-gulping visuals.

- During the presentation, control the lighting in the room for optimal effect.

- Consciously look at the audience to see whether they are connecting with you and understanding what you are presenting.

- You can point to things on the screen or monitor with your mouse. Sometimes, it is effective to walk up to the screen and use a long pointer, keeping audience attention in one location.

- An egregious error is to write most of your speech on slides, then read from the screen to the audience.

- Display an enthusiasm that lets the audience know the presentation was prepared for *them*.

● ● ●

PowerPoint is rewarding, even after a few minutes, so devote time to learning the basic features of PowerPoint. Although features are added periodically, the format has remained basically the same for several years.

• MIXED MEDIA SUPPORT

Visuals aren't the only "sensible" aids available to speakers. Audible aids are available through recordings on CDs, tapes, and records. Speakers can combine more than one form of sensory support. Be vigilant about holding the presentation together by having consistent structural elements, but variety within the structure. A short film clip with audio and video in itself uses two media. Using a chart with key terms while showing an actual object on a document camera is another logical mix. Murphy's Law, you recall, is "If anything can go wrong, it will." Keep the media support straightforward, and plan what to do if something fails.

MIXING IT UP WITH MEDIA

1. List equipment needed for each of the following speeches.

2. What communication problems are inherent in each of the presentations?

    a. Texas ornithologist (bird expert) Jean Schwetmann taught a community group how to recognize their backyard birds by sight and sound. She played professional recordings of several of the birdcalls, and she imitated the sounds of others. Jean showed an enlarged photograph or lithographic print of each bird as she played its song. Often, she asked what words a bird's song matched. She invited the audience to participate in replicating the birdcalls, which many did with delight.

    b. Burley Sedberry, a commercial music artist, demonstrated a sound mixing board, like the ones used in Nashville for professional eight-track recordings. Half a dozen listeners gathered around Sedberry's seat at the controls as he pointed out audio slides, input sources, and output controls. Then he laid a percussion track, a horn track, a vocal track, and a keyboard track. He selected a volunteer to adjust the input volumes for each track and played the four tracks back simultaneously.

    c. Zach Ginsburg, a history professor, introduced his students to Winston Churchill. He "became" Churchill as he waddled through the halls of the White House, discussing issues with President Franklin Roosevelt. From a history website, he played the recorded voice of Churchill delivering addresses to the British people. In addition to photographs of Churchill, Clark projected American cartoonists' versions of Churchill. He asked the students what Churchill might say about world politics today.

    d. Chef Jean Paul L'Enfant swiftly created Crepes Angelique on an induction cooktop. As the aroma filled the country club hall, the chef assured the audience that they would be served crepes from the kitchen. The audience appreciated the attractive printed recipe card at each of their places and focused on the chef's techniques.

    e. Artist Rosemary West faced the gathered painters to explain which brushes and paints to use before turning to paint her canvas. She gave her students time to paint the same areas, walking among them to give advice, before she proceeded with her demonstration.

ACTIVITY 9.4

    f.   Ken Burns combines historic photographs, music, and expressive commentary for his remarkable television documentaries, such as those on the Civil War, baseball, and jazz.

You can learn to use audio, video, interactive spreadsheets, and web pages in a PowerPoint presentation, but don't do it all at once. Instead, when you really need a feature for a particular purpose, get some help and learn to incorporate that feature. Take it one step at a time.

Reality @ WORK 9.5

THE GEEK SQUAD

Robert Stephens leads the "special agents" of the Geek Squad, a 24-hour, 7-day-a-week on-site emergency response team. "They drive ice cream trucks from 1974, painted black. They wear black suits, white socks, and pant legs three inches too short. They've forgotten more about computers than you'll ever know. They're the Geek Squad, and their advice may be the only line of defense between you and a high-tech presentation nightmare." They rescue crashed programs and often are hired to attend high-profile presentations, standing by in case of a high-tech Code Blue.

Stephens offers five tips to ward off trouble when it's your job to prevent technical difficulties in high-risk conditions (quoted in Matson, 1997, p. 130):

1. Bring two of everything—especially laptops and modems. (Borrow or rent a spare laptop for the day.)

2. Back it up! (Use Zip drives or burn your presentation onto a CD-ROM.)

3. For major presentations have on-site technical support.

4. Beware the Internet. Real-time on the Internet increases your logistics challenges tenfold. Stephens recommends storing a site on your hard drive and using your browser to open that file.

5. Don't let computers replace creativity. "Don't show your technical savvy. Show your creative savvy."

DISTANCE PRESENTATION: VIDEO CONFERENCES AND DISTANCE INSTRUCTION

Video conferences, satellite conferences, distance learning, and *distance instruction* (different names for similar events) connect participants at different sites who communicate by means of computer networks. They are used to address audiences at several locations, live, and with some interaction among sites; to teach off-site classes; and to meet as committees and teams.

The technical format lends itself to using other audio and video technical support. "Attendees" appear live on camera for audio and visual active interaction. For conferences focused on presentation, the audience may or may not be on camera to interact with presenters. Even panel members don't have to be at the same location. They may use monitors to see other presenters. We see something similar on TV when a news interviewer discusses an issue with two people in other locations, and the interviewees are shown simultaneously on a split screen.

In the ultimate distance communication, a teacher participating in a live uplink at NASA Dryden asks the crew of the International Space Station a question.

• • • • **Using Video Conferencing Effectively** • • • •   • • • • **TIPS**

- Learn and follow procedures for reserving a video-equipped conference room. Do not assume that camera, computer, and so forth will be set up and ready to go. Sometimes the computer area is configured uniquely for that room and purpose.

- On a monitor, everything in sight seems important, almost of equal interest. Therefore, remove clutter and "busy-ness" from the background and from your personal appearance.

- Become familiar with the equipment. Schedule some practice sessions. Learn from experts, and practice with the equipment. If possible, have someone who is experienced with the equipment available the day of the conference.

- Think of the camera as your most interested listener. Speak into the camera, and remember there are people at the other end.

- Stay in camera range and take on the role of leader.

- Vary the visual scenery for the audience. This can be done with PowerPoint presentations of points, film clips, document camera views, views of audience members on-site, and switching to audience members off-site for their comments or questions.

- Remember that you may be on camera as a listener as well as a speaker. Your interest and reactions communicate volumes.

                                                                        • • •

● **CUSTOM DESIGNS**

Tables, Graphs, and Charts

Statistical support, when shown as well as told, is often the most convincing supporting material. It also can be the most boring and confusing, when a spreadsheet in all its impenetrable technical glory appears on the screen. In these cases, the audience may not be able to read the table or recognize your point of reference.

• • • • **Terminology** • • • •   • • • • **TIPS**

Tables display visually organized information and data. If the data are statistically analyzed, they can be displayed on a graph.

Graphs have a mathematic or statistical basis. Occurrences are plotted on a matrix to give substance for understanding the abstract analyses. The visual representation should be chosen to illustrate variables' relationships.

Charts usually show connections and paths, such as maps, schemas, and flowcharts. Charts may also list key words or concepts. The word *charts* may be used as an inclusive term.

• • •

- *Pie graphs* are aptly named, because they look like pies, sliced and ready to serve. The pie represents the whole, with each slice showing a percentage of the whole. Clearly explain what the whole is before dividing it into its parts or percentages. Pie charts are useful when showing seven or fewer slices. An example is percentages of an organization's budget, divided by division.
- *Bar graphs* give visual comparisons, such as annual organizational profits over the past five years, enrollment figures by semester for this year as compared with last year, and average annual rainfall by area of the country. *Histograms* are one type of bar graph that groups data to present in block form. Histograms work off averages, which can simplify the picture the statistics bring. Of course, oversimplification can distort the same data.
- *Line graphs* are plotted by data points, which are then connected to show a trend over time. These graphs are sometimes called "fever charts" because they take limited information, such as body temperature taken every hour, and "connect the dots" to determine whether there is a pattern. More than one line can be plotted to show a comparison of two entities over time. Usually the plot points (dots) are eliminated to give a cleaner visual showing only the resulting line.

• • • • **TIPS** • • • • **Clarifying Visual Support** • • • •

- Focus information so that a viewer can understand the basic information in a few seconds.
- Use charts, graphs, and tables to summarize and highlight important points. If you are concerned about an audience getting all the details, provide handouts.
- Keep lettering and numbering big. Use approximately $3/4$ to 1 inch of lettering height on the screen per 10 feet of distance to your farthest viewer from the screen. That is, if the farthest viewer from the screen is 25 feet, you will want to have a 2- to 2.5-inch letter height on the screen.
- Keep lettering and numbering bold, so that it stands out without blurring when viewed at a distance. Sans serif fonts generally are better for reading from a distance. (Sans serif fonts are those that don't have "caps" and "shoes," such as Arial and Britannic.)

- Use contrasting colors. Black on white and black on yellow (or the inverse) are two of the best combinations in well-lighted rooms. Yellow on a dark background is one of the more easily read combinations when projected in darkened rooms. Black on dark red, blue, green, or purple is difficult to see. Colorblind viewers have difficulty discerning between red and green, blue and green, and blue and yellow of equal color values. Try squinting to view your visual to see whether the words pop out at you.

- Limit the amount of material on any one chart, graph, or table. If you are concerned about the audience understanding how the content fits together, show a simplified overview slide, then bring up more detailed ones. Icons with puzzle pieces or chain links remind the viewers where you are in your schema.

- Test each visual with a quick glance. Turn your head from side to side without stopping and see which parts of the visual grab your attention first.

- Considering your audience, assess whether your visuals accurately communicate, do not offend, and bring added value to the presentation.

• • •

Photography

A photograph is one of the most refined forms of visual support. On one hand, black-and-white photographs creatively bring clarity to some ideas. On the other hand, capturing color brings liveliness in a different way. Photographs often support biographical presentations. They also give close-up views of equipment features, the interior of a human heart, cellular structure, details in art, architectural details, and expressions on faces. They shine with expansive pictures of cityscapes, aerial shots of Earth, and seas of people at political conventions.

Photographs can be shown several ways: by document camera, as a poster, by slide or digital imaging, and as photocopies. They are available online for cutting and pasting into PowerPoint, and can be cropped or touched up to eliminate distracting features. One of the most flexible approaches for including a photo is to scan it, crop it to the area you want, and import it into your PowerPoint presentation. Scanners are often available to students in campus libraries or learning centers. Copy centers also scan images and save them on disk or CD for a fee. Almost any noncopyrighted image can be included in a presentation.

As with all forms of support, be purposeful in using photographs. The pictures interest you because you have researched the topic, but the audience may miss important messages in the pictures if you do not take time to show and explain them. Make the image large enough for all viewers. Vary the visual tempo. Do not fall into a hypnotic pattern—picture, explain; picture, explain; picture, explain; and so on. When the photograph makes the point, fill a screen or poster with the image.

All in all, you are now equipped to be artist and technician, creator and analyst, as you orchestrate your presentations. Gain experience step by step, so you are skilled and flexible.

SUMMARY

An effective presenter respects the different ways people prefer to learn. Speakers sometimes combine more than one form of sensory support, such as touch, taste, and smell—certainly important in chef school.

Think from the audience's point of view, and keep in mind the asset that visuals and other types of "sensible" support offer.

General guidelines for creating visual support include limiting the number of words and material on a visual, presenting one concept per visual, eliminating distractions, matching visuals to topics, and supporting audience understanding and retention. Visual aids can gain attention in an introduction, review main points in the conclusion, show the structure of the main points, or support a main point.

Visuals include the speakers and listeners themselves, various types of three-dimensional visual support, several types of two-dimensional effects, and handouts. Variables to consider when planning these visuals are costs versus benefits, time, and the reliability of equipment. Three-dimensional support includes artifacts and manipulatives. Two-dimensional support includes illustrations, transparencies, charts, maps, and graphs, and handouts that provide detailed information not included in a presentation.

Presentation software, such as PowerPoint, enables us to combine a variety of audio and video support. Like other visuals, however, PowerPoint should support a presentation, not substitute for a speaker's responsibility for communicating ideas and information. Video conference presentations are another increasingly popular use of technology, since they reduce travel budgets in organizations. This trend challenges all of us to learn the skills of appearing on camera.

Statistical support, when shown as well as told to an audience, is often the most convincing supporting material and should be designed carefully. Tables display visually organized information and data. Graphs make visual sense of statistical analyses, using familiar forms, such as pie graphs, bar graphs, and line graphs. Charts usually show connections and paths, such as maps, schemas, and flowcharts, or they may list key words or concepts. Use charts, graphs, and tables to summarize and highlight important points. •

ACTIVITIES

1. **Technical Support:** At the online site of the Center for Association Leadership, read "Ten Cool Technologies to Enhance Your Face-to-Face Meetings." The URL is as follows: www.centeronline.org/knowledge/tencool.cfm?ID=2048
   Do further research about one of the technologies suggested, and e-mail a research summary and related hyperlinks to your professor.

2. **Ethically Speaking:** Read about Doar Inc. (www.doar.com) at their website or in the *Small Firm Business* (Fall, 2004) article, by M. K. Flynn, "Still Using Flipcharts?" (www.doar.com/marketing/web/smallfirmbusiness.pdf) or in a *Presentations* magazine (October 2002) article, by S. Regenold, "The Courtroom Becomes a Visual Display."

In small groups, discuss the effects that visuals can have during a courtroom trial. What ethical guidelines would you impose on yourself (if you were a lawyer) during a trial?

3. **Journaling the Experience:** Journal your understanding of integrating presentational aids in a conference with a board of directors, client group, or an organization's staff. DeVito (1996) relates a prime example of "visual aid abuse" in *The Elements of Public Speaking*, 6th edition:

Visual aids should be graphics, pictures of things, not, repeat NOT, word outlines of a speaker's notes. Visuals are to help the audience. . . . I recall one time General Partridge, a four-star Air Force General, was listening to a presentation. The man briefing him put up a slide that had 17 complete sentences on it. He said, "Now I think these sentences very well summarize my main argument in support of the proposition. You can read them."

General Partridge interrupted, "Yes, I can read them, but I don't want to. Please go ahead."

Note: Paul R. Beall, a noted management consultant, communication teacher, lecturer, and college president, provides this example in *Pass the Word: The Art of Oral Communication* (Manhattan, KS: Sunflower University Press, 1993, p. 47).

4. **Team Work:** *Presentations* is an outstanding magazine about the technology available for presentations, and a helpful online version is also available at presentations.com. As a team, create a file that demonstrates that the team can insert and edit clip art (show the file before and after editing), insert a photo as a JPEG file, insert a sound, and add a video.

5. **Presenting to Others and Team Work:** Read "Delivering Your Presentation: Presenting as a Team" at http://presentations.com. Develop a team proposal for a change your team would like to see on campus. Plan an eight- to ten-minute presentation with media support. After all teams make their proposal pitches, decide on one that an administrator at your college should see. Arrange to present your proposal to him or her.

6. **Journaling the Experience:** Explore a variety of kinds of charts through the SkyMark website at www.pathmaker.com/resources/tools.asp. Summarize hints for one familiar type of chart you anticipate using when you are employed and one less familiar type of chart that you want to remember for its potential usefulness in management.

FOR FURTHER READING

Extensive information about equipment and articles regarding presentations are available at http://www/presentations.com

For examples of charts and other visuals, see http://www.smartdraw.com/resources/examples/business/index.htm

Lowe, D. (2003). *PowerPoint 2003 for dummies*. Hoboken, NJ: John Wiley & Sons.

Lucas, R. (1999). *The big book of flip charts*. New York: McGraw-Hill.

Westcott, J., & Landau, J. H. (1996). *A picture's worth 1000 words: A workbook for visual communications*. San Francisco: Jossey-Bass.

People tend to be tenacious about an idea for one of two reasons. Either they're excited by it or they're fearful of what they may lose if the idea fails (Komisar, 2001).

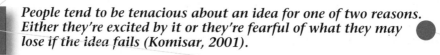

Quick Start to Persuasive Speaking

10

Destination Topic Choice

Advice for Packing: Selecting

Set Your Itinerary

The Guide in Persuasion

Given the complexities of getting another person to agree with you much less do something about it, it is a great challenge to provide a "Quick Start" for persuasive speaking. Like learning to play a musical instrument, mastering a complex set of skills is a lifelong process. But, also like learning to play the instrument, you have to start somewhere—trying out new skills and developing a broad understanding. Suppose in your job you must present product proposals to clients, request an increase in the departmental budget, or prove the cause of a technical problem. It's tempting to say, "Well, I'll just give them the facts, and the facts will speak for themselves," or "They know I'm an expert, and I shouldn't have to prove anything to them." But sometimes the data don't speak for themselves, and sometimes listeners don't draw the conclusions you think are self-evident. So it's up to you to provide the map and be their guide to the destination of your conclusion. That map and destination are the components of persuasion.

With the power to persuade others should come the responsibility of doing it ethically.

Plato insisted that since persuasion could be used for evil ends, training in its tactics should be restricted to people who were ethically righteous by virtue of their privileged education and upbringing. Wrong, argued Aristotle. If you don't teach people how persuasion takes place, they will become unwitting victims of any unscrupulous persons who do have such knowledge. (Quoted in Reardon, 2001, p. 85)

This chapter presumes that you'll design and apply the highest values shared by ethical communicators, as we now move quickly into the brush strokes and machinations of persuasion. This chapter walks you through the persuasive process, explains key components for persuasive presentations, and helps you develop and deliver a persuasive speech. Try your hand at a classroom presentation in order to jump start your skills for workplace situations.

"Persuasion is the act of motivating an audience, through communication, to voluntarily change a particular belief, attitude, or behavior" (Adler & Elmhorst, 1999, p. 418).

OBJECTIVES

After studying the content of this chapter, you should be able to

- Analyze the convergence of audience, speaker, and occasion
- Recognize fact, value, and policy topics
- Research a persuasive topic
- Deliver a persuasive speech to an audience

Everybody prepares differently, but if you don't know where to begin, the task seems overwhelming. This chapter prepares you for a trip in which you decide on your destination (in this case, your stance on an issue), research the area, and organize your route before guiding trusting sojourners to the same destination.

DESTINATION TOPIC CHOICE

In business, the topic usually comes to you rather than you selecting the topic. A classroom or workshop gives more latitude in selecting topics, but the audience *is* real, and you, as a speaker, have the opportunity to influence listeners. Respect the classroom experience for the value it holds.

Situational Analysis

"Presentations are about objectives, benefits, and actions" (Matson, 1997, p. 3). Once a topic has been decided, Michael Fors, a corporate training manager at Intel, asks key questions in deciding a speaking strategy. Notice how his questions frame the blend of speaker, audience, and occasion (quoted in Matson, 1997):

1. What's my core message?
2. How does that message benefit my audience?
3. What barriers are there to people accepting the message?
4. What common ground (values, experience, goals) do I share with the audience?
5. When I finish, what do I want the audience to do?

The audience, the speaker, and the occasion merge as a *situation* for a particular presentation event. The speaker's expertise and communication capability are important factors in choosing a topic, but it's a mistake to ignore audience and occasion—often a mistake with disastrous outcomes, especially in persuasion.

Audience

One of the most common errors communicators make—especially with technical messages—is to ignore the abilities and needs of their listeners. Speakers who are uninformed about their audiences, in effect, speak in foreign languages to strangers. Often presenters give all the necessary facts and draw appropriate conclusions, only to lose listeners in an overly technical and unconvincing presentation. That's why it's important to learn (1) what an audience has in common with one another and with you, (2) how familiar they are with the topic, and (3) how important the topic is to them.

Audience Preconceptions   Shared attitudes, beliefs, and values provide the foundation for persuasion. *Attitudes, beliefs,* and *values* are terms referring to "feelings," or preconceptions, about the speaker, occasion, and topic's worth. *Attitudes* are the tendency to be for or against an idea, person, or object. Coaxing a listener to agree with you does not guarantee that the listener will have a change of heart. For instance, a listener may be convinced that nuclear energy is more efficient and less costly than natural gas, yet maintain an unfavorable attitude about nuclear power plants.

Beliefs state a person's perception of truth. They are central to a person's way of seeing the world and of making decisions. Someone, for instance, may hold a basic belief that the death penalty is wrong or that everyone has the right to a free public school education.

Values speak to the relative importance of an idea, such as how valuable our children are and how important accumulated wealth is. As a speaker, make an early connection with the audience's attitudes, beliefs, and values. Parent–teacher organizations find common ground in the value they place on children. Labor unions negotiate with management on the common ground that reasonably compensated workers make better employees.

Following advice from scholarly research in communication, Kathleen Reardon (2001, pp. 200–201) looks for appropriateness, consistency, and effectiveness (using the acronym ACE) when choosing how to approach particular audiences. Some persons are best persuaded to do what others do in a work situation because it is *appropriate,* following such values as loyalty or dedication. Others answer the strong appeal of *consistency*—"the way we've done it for years" and "if it ain't broke, don't fix it"—where they marry a course of action with other beliefs they hold. *Effectiveness* relies on understanding what the audience wants most. For instance, some clients are willing to invest in a more expensive but more reliable product, whereas others will compromise on reliability to keep a product affordable.

> ● **EXAMPLE 10.1**

STUDENT EXAMPLE

The Granola Foods company wanted employees to stay on campus during lunch to eliminate or cut down on the time it took for a mass exodus to area restaurants. Amar landed on an idea: picnic tables for the tree-lined center courtyard. The employees liked the idea because on nice days they primarily wanted to get out of the building for lunch, but "knew" management wouldn't budget high-end picnic tables when there were already tables in the company cafeteria. Nevertheless, they wanted Amar to try to win their case.

Amar focused on the following *thesis:** "Lost work time will decrease, and morale will increase, if employees have an inviting place on campus to visit and eat lunch." Then he wrote his *specific purpose:* "After hearing my presentation, management will buy tables for the courtyard." Next, Amar summarized employees' discussion into a few points:

1. Traffic is congested, and time is lost driving to lunch.
2. Employees want a break from being in the building all morning.
3. The courtyard has covered areas, and the weather is comfortable most of the year.

Next, Amar imagined possible objections management might have:

1. Commercial-grade tables are expensive.
2. Additional litter and trash increase maintenance.
3. Employees don't currently eat in the cafeteria.

Amar knew that he needed to find common values with the management. He found several: The value of a productive organizational culture with fewer cliques, effective use of resources, and avoiding traffic congestion and lost time. Those became his main points as he addressed management:

1. Granola Foods wants a productive corporate culture, with open communication among various groups and a positive feeling about the environment.
2. Low-maintenance, commercial tables economically utilize existing space. Well-placed receptacles minimize cleanup.
3. The mental model can shift to staying on campus for lunch with this positive, productive, and employee-initiated project.

Amar's careful analysis of attitudes, values, and beliefs paid off. Employees and management joined forces to create "common ground" for lunch.

---

* A central idea statement in a persuasive speech is commonly called a *thesis* or *principal argument.* These terms communicate that the speaker has taken a stance on an issue that has more than one point of view.

── ●

Audience Demographics The audience demography provides generalizations about listeners' characteristics. Age, gender, socioeconomic status (income, education, and occupation), culture or ethnicity, and special interests are your audience's vital signs. David Gunby, a leadership trainer at EDS, says, "You should know as much as you can about whom you're speaking to. What are their expectations? Where are they positioned on the issue? What's their knowledge level? What are their demographics and culture?" (quoted in Matson,

1997, p. 3). He advises colleagues to conduct informal research a few days before a presentation. Analyze the classroom audience before selecting a topic and planning your speech.

Speaker

You, the speaker, are the critical connection between the topic and the audience on a particular occasion. The speaker shapes people's opinions and conclusions. In speech class, you can persuade real people, empowered to act upon your message.

What you can do in a given amount of time—topic feasibility—also depends upon you. How much time do you have to research, design, and practice? How big a persuasive job is reasonable with *this* audience?

Another factor centered on you is the audience's attitude about you. Are you a Republican speaking to a Democratic audience? Maybe you are a nurse speaking to a group of doctors. Do you have high credibility with this audience? Remember to establish your credibility through narratives, expert quotes, and cited sources as needed. Let the audience know that you are one of the "good guys" and that you will fill them with good information and sound reasoning.

Occasion

You are fortunate to be able to get classroom experience, where you pretty much know the physical setting. You already know that this is an assigned speech and that there are others who will speak today. You know your college, and you know the community. You know where you will stand, where your audience will sit, the lighting in the room, and the technical support to expect.

In a professional setting, consider these aspects of occasion analysis:

- Is this a regularly scheduled meeting, or is it a special occasion?
- Are you and the listeners in specialized roles, such as client and developer?
- What is expected of the speaker on this occasion?
- Who will be present, such as honorees or dignitaries?
- What is the meeting's agenda? Will someone be speaking before or after you?

Occasion shapes the message, as in this case: Steven Spielberg makes his remarks in the Pentagon on August 11, after receiving the Department Defense Medal for Distinguished Public Service, 1999 in recognition of the impact his movie "Saving Private Ryan" has had on the American people.

A speaker rallies support for issues of the labor union he represents.

- Are you early or late in the program?
- How will the room be arranged?
- What technical support can you expect?

Types of Topics

In persuasive speaking, analyzing a topic to form an argument and take a stand on an issue is not belligerence. It is *argument*—stating a position on an issue, supporting a thesis, and advocating a perspective. Persuasive speeches may attempt to (1) *convince* or *inspire* the audience to agree with or reject a point of view, (2) further *commit* them to an idea, or (3) *actuate* the audience to do something as a result of the speech.

Which of the following indicate the speaker aims to *convince* an audience that his or her point of view is correct, and which indicate that the speaker's goal is to motivate the listeners to follow up with *action*?

1. After hearing my speech, the audience will volunteer time to the American Red Cross.
2. After hearing my speech, the audience will donate blood at their local American Red Cross chapter.
3. After hearing my speech, the audience will value the work done by the American Red Cross around the world.
4. After hearing my speech, the audience will trust the safeguards to assure uncontaminated blood and plasma from the American Red Cross.

Fact

One type of thesis argues that something is factual and true. For instance, the statement that "global warming changes the plant ecology of South American rain forests" either is or isn't true, and yet people argue for both sides. Topics of fact are usually informative topics, but they can also be persuasive. Arguments of fact usually seek to convince the audience of the accuracy of a point of view.

Value

Issues of what is good or bad, moral or immoral, and worthy or unworthy are value topics. The speaker seeks to convince the audience that the issue is valuable and that they should act on it (actuate). You could argue that one solution is better than another, such as the use of protected lands to correct fuel shortages. Or you could align the audience with the worthiness of fine arts in U.S. culture, to advocate increased funding.

Policy

When you ask "What should be done?" you are concerned with policy. You may advocate

- Keeping the current policy (status quo)
- Eliminating the current policy
- Making a radical change of policy
- Making modifications of current policy (status quo with modifications)

Making or changing policy takes on the burden of proving that doing so solves some problem. Policy may be on a national, state, or local level, or it can support a specific entity, such as public schools in Oregon.

Certainly, the speaker should convince the listeners that the policy is correct. Sometimes, the audience is, also, to do (actuate) something, such as vote for a bill or donate blood. If you think your topic is a policy topic, analyze the proposal and ask:

- What is the current policy?
- Who is responsible for making the policy, and how?
- What should the policy be?
- What do you want the audience to do or think about the policy?

Your Topic

Browse through topical lists for ideas for your persuasive subject. Write a general statement of topic. Useful lists can be found at http://memory.loc.gov/ammem.

After selecting a topic that you find interesting, narrow the focus to the area of the topic that will interest you and the audience most. Interesting support and sound reasons should catch their attention. Be realistic in how much change to expect from the listeners. Usually, changes are gradual. Consider what is feasible in the time limit.

● **EXAMPLE 10.2**

CLASSROOM EXAMPLE

Joel cares about the problem of violence in the public schools, their causes, and some solutions proposed by various experts. His speech assignment is limited to seven minutes. What are possible speech topics in this area of interest?

1. He could establish that violence is a problem, showing the extent of the problem.
2. Another approach would be to convince the audience of one or more causes of violence in public schools.
3. Joel could focus on just one cause, such as bullying, and advocate a solution.
4. He could tell the audience that there are multiple causes, but that bullying is an identifiable cause and that we can initiate specific solutions for a relatively small cost.
5. Joel could identify several causes and lead the audience to conclude with him that his proposal would best answer those causes.

Joel makes a preliminary decision to go with option 3, focusing on the bullying cause and its solution. He remembers a CNN report on violence in which a couple of experts were interviewed. Also, his sister teaches in a local high school. The idea of discussing one cause that he can support with evidence and of showing the connection to a solution seems feasible. He is not sure yet that this is a realistic goal or if he will find adequate information, but this gets him started.

Persuasive Specific Purpose and Thesis

A persuasive specific purpose statement is a planning tool. You may never actually use the statement in your delivered speech, but you need the specific purpose statement as your "true north" to guide your preparation. (Refer back to Amar's specific purpose regarding the outdoor table topic.) The persuasive specific purpose states what you intend to convince the audience to believe or actuate the audience to do. Be clear in your purpose statement as to where you want their thinking to be after your speech. In this regard, think of *how far* you can move *how many* of your listeners on the topic. Use words such as *agree, support, vote for, donate to,* and *volunteer* in your statement. Your initial specific purpose statement is a "best guess" of a direction to follow. You can revise the statement any time during your speech preparation as you get a clearer picture.

You may be ready to write your *thesis,* or you may need to research and develop your reasoning further. *Thesis* is the appropriate term for a statement expressing a position on an issue for persuasion. Following are examples of specific purposes and theses for Joel's speech.

● **EXAMPLE 10.3**

CLASSROOM EXAMPLE CONTINUED

- *Specific purpose statement for his persuasive speech to convince:* "After hearing my speech, the audience will be convinced that bullying is one cause of violence in public schools, and the audience will agree that the Appreciating Diversity Program offered in three grades will be an effective partial solution."
- *Thesis:* "The Appreciating Diversity program for Winstrom Public Schools will be effective in reducing bullying, a common cause of violence."

  However, if Joel discovers that the local public schools are currently deciding whether to use the program and are depending on volunteers or a vote of confidence, he may wish to get the audience members more involved.

- *Persuasive speech to actuate:* "After hearing my speech and recognizing that bullying is one cause of violence in public schools, the listeners will vote for Appreciating Diversity in their local schools."
- *Thesis:* "We should support a referendum for a program, Appreciating Diversity, when it comes for a vote May 3 of this year, in order to reduce bullying, a common cause of school violence."

● ADVICE FOR PACKING: SELECTING

You now have a general idea of your destination: your topic, specific purpose, and thesis, so it's now time to pack the best material available that fits your topic and your audience.

Gather Information about the Topic

The information comes from your prior knowledge and from your topical research material. Because you can't use everything you have and not everything you have is appropriate for your presentation, later you will carefully select material from among your collection that works best with your presentation's specific purpose.

Prior Knowledge

Canvas your own knowledge about the topic. Joel, in our example, had heard a CNN program and had visited with his sister about her public school teaching experience. He recalled times he had bullied and been bullied. He asked some friends about their experiences.

Exploring New Terrain

Look back at Chapter 6 to refresh your knowledge of how to use a college library's electronic databases. Like Joel, you may want to do keyword searches in Newsbank, Infotrac, Wilson Web, and area-specific databases. Use the Allyn & Bacon speech site under "Research Navigator" at www.abacon.com.

Start with three to five credible articles, print them as hard copies, and examine them to see whether your preliminary thoughts were accurate. You may find that you no longer agree with your original stance, that there are other solutions you think are better, or that the cause you wanted to present has weak support. Be open to truth and faithful to an ethical approach. When you converge on truth, you will be more persuasive.

Credible Sources

Credible sources are your best path to an accurate understanding of the topic. They also are the underpinnings of ethical persuasion. Some people think all that is needed are a couple of facts communicated with passion. Unfortunately, that *is* all it takes with a lot of uninformed or lazy listeners, a dangerous assumption to make about a college audience. If you are not an authority in the field, rely on sound information from expert sources. Perhaps cite a source for key information or note the source on a visual, or quote or paraphrase experts. The library's purchased databases are prescreened to give you more reliable sources. (Review Chapter 6 to learn the difference between online information in general and expensive databases of scholarly material available to you through the library.) If you read an article from a newspaper or periodical, see if you can find related articles on the same topic in another periodical, and seek diverse opinions through your reading.

Select Supporting Material

You have gathered material to pack, but it won't all fit into the suitcase. Indeed, you have more information than you can use and probably more information than an audience is willing to hear. Be selective in what you keep. Keep your persuasive specific purpose in mind as you look at various forms of support and consider which types you will select from your research. The forms of support are defined in the following subsections, with examples from persuasive speeches included. The first three forms of support have received increased attention in recent research literature on persuasion.

Narrative

Narratives are stories. Former president George H. W. Bush engaged audiences with the power of the narrative in his "Thousand Points of Light" speech, profiling the "common" citizen as extraordinary. Others soon followed in similar style, recognizing the influence and requirements of television as the medium of the public. Narratives can explain, exemplify, or persuade. Characteristic of a narrative is good story-telling, a dramatic rendering of the tale.

Sarah Brady, along with her husband Jim Brady, spoke on gun control at the 1996 Democratic National Convention. In the speech, she wove personal narrative as a unifying strand amidst factual support. The appendix contains the full text of the speech, in which you can follow the close link of the narrative to the persuasive purpose. Following are two narrative excerpts from the speech:

> Fifteen year ago, Jim was White House press secretary. Our son Scott, who's up here, was just two years old. All our dreams had come true. But then one rainy afternoon in March, our dreams were shattered by an assassination attempt on President Reagan. President Reagan was shot. And so was Jim. We almost lost Jim that day. And we almost lost the president. But thanks to the heroism of the Secret Service and the determination of the physicians and staff at George Washington Hospital, Jim lived. And so did the president. Thank God. But our lives would never be quite the same. . . .
>
> We've traveled from coast to coast during the past 10 years. We've met thousands of gun violence victims and their families. Their stories continue to break our hearts. Especially those involving the children. . . . (Allyn & Bacon, Longman Archives at www.pbs.org/newshour/convention96/floor_speeches/brady.html)

Self-Disclosive Style

Closely aligned with narrative is a self-disclosive element in a speech. Pamela Benoit (1997), in *Telling the Success Story: Acclaiming and Disclaiming Discourse*, discusses how to present personal successes without coming across as arrogant.

Visuals clarify and support a speaker's points. If the audience were larger, how should the speaker adjust his visual support?

The perceived motive of the speaker more than the narrative content is crucial in an audience's assessment of the speaker. "It is the rare communicator who develops the ability to artfully present success stories for self-enhancement, and for the encouragement, hope and transformation of the audience" (Detwiler, 1999, p. 1). Personal narratives are in themselves self-disclosive, since they give information about the speaker.

Visuals

Audiences today expect a visual experience. For one thing, they are looking at the speaker. During presidential election years, the candidates try to "look presidential." The speaker's enthusiasm, passion, or seriousness about an issue may be the most persuasive message to some audiences.

Visuals may support the message or may *be* the message. Jim Brady, severely limited and seated in a wheelchair, sent a strong visual message. Driving education classes use simulations and videos to convince drivers to use safe driving techniques. Statistical graphs are some of the most compelling evidence for many topics. Speakers need to be especially aware of what the audience is seeing, when it is seeing it, and whether they are all seeing the same thing at the same time. Otherwise, the effectiveness is neutralized. For instance, passing around a statistical chart disrupts the audience's attention, but showing it at one time on a chart or projection controls the audience's attention.

Explanation

Explanation is an important tool to help an audience understand something. The relationship between how much they want to know and what they already know is pivotal to persuasion. Hence, motivation and familiarity determine the effectiveness of explanation. Explanation is also used to let the listeners know that an action is going to bring a desired outcome.

Warren Buffet (quoted in Loomis, 1999) spoke to several business groups about the general level of stock prices. In those speeches, explanation supported each point. Here are two explanations he used:

> Let's start by defining "investing." The definition is simple but often forgotten: Investing is laying out money now to get more money back in the future—money in real terms, after taking inflation into account. (p. 2)

To understand why that happened, we need first to look at one of the two important variables that affect investment results: interest rates. These act on financial valuation the way gravity acts on matter: The higher the rate, the greater the downward pull. That's because the rates of return that investors need from any kind of investment are directly tied to the risk-free rate that they can earn from government securities. So if the government rate rises, the prices of all other investments must adjust downward, to a level that brings their expected rates of return into line. Conversely, if government interest rates fall, the move pushes the prices of all other investments upward. The basic proposition is this: What an investor should pay today for a dollar to be received tomorrow can only be determined by first looking at the risk-free interest rate. (p. 3)

Notice in the first explanation that he used definition. In the second explanation, he explained the effect of interest rates. He also used analogy, causation, paraphrasing, and application.

Example

Examples are specific instances. They may be real or hypothetical, brief or extended. Choose examples carefully, keeping in mind the audience's reaction to the example. Bishop Desmond Tutu, South African Nobel Laureate, listed three examples in addressing the World Economic Forum in Davos, Switzerland. Notice the different persuasive images that come to mind as he mentions each example. Keep in mind his audience and the strength of his message.

> No corporate chief will say to you that they are ready to encourage the violation of human rights. Why? Because they are concerned that they should not have the disapproval of people. I think the fact that the world can admire someone like Nelson Mandela, but even more surprisingly, a Mother Theresa who had no world power, if anything she had the opposite. And yet the world admired her. And Princess Di—why was this outpouring of money? In part it was because she had been a caring person, she touched people with AIDS, she went and struggled against landmines—but the world recognizes goodness—hankers after goodness—and excoriate the opposite. You might be the most powerful person, economically, but you are not necessarily the most admired. (Tutu, 2001)

Statistics

Statistics are numbers used to summarize a collection of examples. By pooling examples of a characteristic, the pattern of occurrences can be examined. Too frequently, uninformed or unethical uses of statistics mislead an audience. Familiarize yourself with several basic types of statistics in order to understand statistics in your source material and to present accurate information to your audience.

Measures of correlation show how closely things are related. For instance, students' numbers of hours studying for an exam correlated positively with their exam grades. The results showed a "high, positive correlation." That is, the more hours studied, the higher the grade. (Correlations range from -1 to 0 and from 0 to 1. The closer the correlation is to 1, the higher the positive correlation. The closer the correlation is to -1, the higher the negative correlation.)

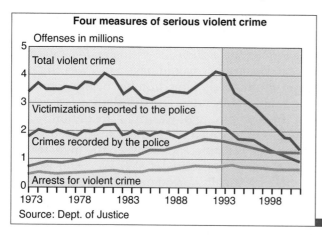

Four measures of serious violent crime

Offenses in millions

Total violent crime

Victimizations reported to the police

Crimes recorded by the police

Arrests for violent crime

1973   1978   1983   1988   1993   1998

Source: Dept. of Justice

What information does this chart statistically summarize? Write at least two accurate statements based on the data.

Correlation is not necessarily causation. Suppose you find that the students who studied the most also had slept less in the 72 hours prior to the exam. Although hours of sleep and study hours had a negative correlation (more sleep, lower grades) and study hours and higher grades had a positive correlation, we could not say that sleep deprivation *caused* higher grades. It could be—but we don't know. Further study would be needed. Suppose then that you find that among the sleep-deprived students, only the students who did not have Thursday-night social events made higher grades. Does that mean that students with no social life made higher grades? Hmmm. Hopefully, you see how important it is for communicators to not only present the statistics but also to interpret them meaningfully for an audience.

Percentages express some portion of 100, with 100 being the entire data set or item. If 7 of the 11 people taking the exam are female, then 64% (rounded) of the class is female. Always let the audience know what the "whole" is. Notice how then First Lady Hillary Rodham Clinton (1995) defined the "whole" for each statistic: "Women comprise more than half the world's population. Women are 70% of the world's poor, and two-thirds of those are not taught to read and write."

Measures of central tendency tell you the pattern of occurrences. *Mean, median,* and *mode* describe events in a set of occurrences. For example, here are the number of traffic tickets issued in 11 consecutive days in Middletown, USA: 40, 53, 75, 75, 75, 80, 82, 85, 95, 98, and 100. Add all the scores and divide by the number of scores to get the *mean,* or average, which, in this case, is 78. The *median,* on the other hand, is the middle of the ordered list—this time, 80. The *mode,* another statistic, is the most frequently appearing grade (in this case, 75).

The White House supplies current demographics for the United States at www.whitehouse.gov/fsbr/demography.html. Here is how the government describes the change in "household income":

> The real median income of households in the United States rose by 2.7 percent between 1998 and 1999, from $39,744 to $40,816. This is the fifth consecutive year that household income increased. Real median household income is now at the highest level recorded since the Census Bureau started

compiling these estimates in 1967. (White House, Social Statistics Briefing Room, 4 June 1997)

Notice in the preceding example that *median* shows the *middle* salary in the United States, not the *average*. The average would have a few wealthy persons' incomes offsetting a disproportionately large number of the country's impoverished population. If we could see the range and distribution, we would have an even clearer picture of the distribution of wealth in the nation.

Measures of difference tell the extent to which scores differ from the average or from one another. In the test scores, the difference between the highest and lowest grades $(100 - 40)$ is 60, so the *range* of the grades is 60. We could assume from so large a range that the grades are really spread out.

Expert Testimony

Attorneys call witnesses to the stand to give evidence in support of their argument on behalf of their clients. Speakers quote other authorities to support their theses, and a carefully articulated quotation inspires an audience. John J. Sweeney, president of the AFL-CIO, cited an article when speaking in Chicago at the Rainbow/PUSH Coalition Breakfast:

> In an article in the *New York Times* two weeks ago, Lou Uchitelle pointed out the cruel irony of our new, free-market global economy: while middle-class Americans are supposedly the most politically powerful block of voters in our country, the middle class is finishing last in the race for economic improvement. (Sweeney, 1998)

Repetition and Restatement

"After seven, after *seven* long years, Congress finally passed the Brady Bill and President Clinton kept his promise: He signed it into law. Thank you, *thank you*, Mr. President." Sarah Brady repeats two phrases to add emphasis. Repeating key phrases helps the audience remember them. Repeating a conclusion makes it more accessible when listeners later use it in their reasoning. This alone makes repetition persuasive. Say something often enough and some people will begin to believe it.

Check Your Support

Pack the most useful items for the finite time of a presentation. You don't want to include irrelevant material just because it's interesting. Remove the unnecessary weight of irrelevant items. Your support should have appropriate situational "fit," potential to persuade, and relevant support for your stance on an issue.

Choose supporting material that is meaningful to your listeners. Anticipate their reactions to what you say in the context of this particular occasion. Effective speakers connect with their audiences through fitting stories and examples.

Choose material that fits the occasion. A kick-off address for government-supported children's insurance is not a good fit with the speech you gave to a group last week on risky stock options.

Allow for the cultural dimensions of the occasion. Some audiences rely heavily on the speaker's credibility to determine the effect the speaker's message has. Students in the United States and other cultures of Greco-Roman tradition are taught to listen logically, critically examining evidence and reasoning. These audiences are more likely to listen for statistical support and scientific approaches. For other audiences, the personal narrative is the most compelling feature.

Two principles are especially helpful in guiding choices of support material. First, the *law of selective exposure* says that generally listeners actively seek out information that supports what they already believe and avoid information that contradicts their opinions and beliefs. However, if listeners aren't sure about their opinions on an issue, they are more likely to listen to various perspectives. That is why you will want to choose supporting material that will inform listeners' reasoning without causing them to become unnecessarily defensive.

Second, the principle of *inoculation* notes that the less a listener has thought about an issue, the greater the speaker's potential influence. Your choice of supporting material, then, depends on how resistant an audience is to your stance. When you get a flu shot, you have been inoculated against that year's prevalent strains of influenza. Exposure to a weakened version of a type of flu prompts your body to build up antibodies to fight the infection. Similarly, when you have had ideas challenged in the past and built up arguments to fight off the attacks, you are more resistant to persuasion.

An argument combines evidence and reasoning, advancing toward a persuasive conclusion. Supporting material is evidence, and each piece should contribute toward the conclusion.

• SET YOUR ITINERARY

The basic decisions made for the informative speech apply also to the persuasive speech. Check your progress via Table 10.1 as you prepare. This section gives special attention to finding patterns for guiding an audience.

One Audience, One Topic, and One Route

With the audience and topic in mind, think in general about (1) how to travel with the audience to your destination and (2) which appeals will motivate them in that direction.

Audience Attitude

Audiences may be favorable, unfavorable (hostile), neutral, or apathetic toward your topic.

Unfavorable or Hostile In general, use inductive reasoning for a hostile audience. It is the safer approach. First, present examples that they agree with; then later in the speech, state the overall stance of your message. After an audience has agreed with you on several less threatening ideas, it is more likely to agree with your more challenging idea, out of a sense of consistency or appropriateness.

TABLE 10.1 • A Speaker's Guided Decisions

Step by Step: A Worksheet for Your Decisions	Text Pages
1. Write a specific purpose statement, recognizing the types of appeal that will affect your audience. Write a thesis statement that is consistent with your specific purpose statement.	269–270, 260–261
2. Research the topic through credible sources.	261–262
3. Examine reasoning and seek a variety of support.	262–266
4. Determine your position on the topic. Adjust your specific purpose and thesis to reflect your stance.	260–261
5. Write out each main point as a claim in a declarative sentence, and arrange the claims logically to persuade the audience.	270–271
6. Examine the support for the main points. (Will your support compel the listeners to agree with you? Have you selected support that helps the listener understand or remember that main point? Have you varied the forms of support?)	262–266
7. Plan the introduction.	271–274
8. Plan the conclusion.	274–275

Favorable   A favorable audience more likely wants to get down to business. A deductive approach has the speaker state the position early in the speech, logically applying it to various specific examples.

Mixed   For an audience with mixed attitudes, you can use both induction and deduction. Start with examples with which everyone finds points of agreement, then present the generalization, and finally apply the generalization to examples that further support your claim.

Neutral   Neutral audiences are like cars idling in neutral. Their motors are running, but they're neither moving toward nor away from the speaker's position. The combined approach for the mixed audience is again appropriate. Recent scholarly work gives us insight into neutral audiences:

- When listeners already hold strong, accessible attitudes on a topic, they are more prone to systematically process and carefully examine information (Fabrigar et al., 1998).
- When listeners feel ambiguous toward a subject, they, too, will analyze it attentively (Maio et al., 1996).
- For some listeners, the enjoyment or need for vigorous thinking keeps them engaged (Cacioppo et al., 1996), especially when the message is presented in clear, not overly complex language (Hafer et al., 1996).

Apathetic   Apathetic audiences simply don't care—at least, not about this topic. Their tendencies have been studied by other scholars. They will more often rely on familiar sayings and put in just enough effort to be satisfied with their own thinking (Eagly & Chaiken, 1993). They also like stances about which they can easily generate arguments or supporting examples (Schwarz, 1998). It is the speaker's job to convince them that the issue is important before proceeding to the speaker's position on the issue. Phrases that signal broader value, such as "family values," may increase their attentiveness (Garst & Bodenhausen, 1996).

Types of Appeal

Appeals speak persuasively to needs and desires in the listeners. Classical rhetoric supplies the terminology: ethos, logos, and pathos.

Ethos   *Ethos* refers to speaker credibility. It includes the competence and goodness of the speaker and the intention of good will. The audience likes to know that the speaker's purpose is not self-serving exploitation. Ethos should permeate the speech, although it is often indirect. A speaker's nonverbal communication carries much of the ethos.

Logos   The appeal to reasoning, or logic, is *logos*. *Logos* means "the word" in Greek, in terms of a representational, connected matrix. It is the attraction and persuasion of structure and support in the speech. It relies neither on emotion nor on whom is giving the speech, since "the words" connecting the parts should stand on their own persuasively.

Pathos   *Pathos* appeals to emotion (you can recognize the root word in *sympathy, empathy,* and *pathetic*). Deeply ingrained psychological appeals reside in every listener. Playing on these heart strings is highly persuasive, when not overdone. Narrative, with its emphasis on the dramatic, makes full use of pathos.

Audience Basic Needs

Abraham Maslow's hierarchy of needs (Figure 10.1) suggests that basic needs are configured in a hierarchy ranging from the most compelling lower-order

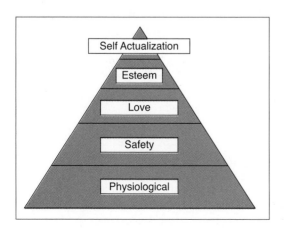

FIGURE 10.1 • Maslow's Hierarchy of Needs

needs to higher-order needs. Persuasive presentations, directly or indirectly, appeal to some of these needs.

Structuring Argument

Organizational patterns guide speakers' development of arguments with audiences. A speaker should examine different options for structuring a persuasive speech. Construct a map, similar to the one you did for the informative speech (see Chapter 7), to get a clear picture of where you are going and where you want to take the audience. Put your thesis in the middle as the destination. Roads lead to each main point and subpoint, or satellite. Supporting materials are in the outermost satellites. If something doesn't fit logically into your map, it probably doesn't belong in the body of your speech.

In making an argument, remember that a rhetorical argument is made up of

1. A claim
2. Evidence to support the claim
3. Reasoning to connect the evidence to the claim

The principal argument becomes your thesis and takes several forms, usually a claim, generalization, or conclusion from evidence, which may or may not be stated at the beginning of the speech.

**ACTIVITY
10.1**

ARGUING FROM CLAIM

In the following example, notice how the evidence is connected to the claim.

Claim: Male students academically benefit more from a community college education than from the first two years of a four-year baccalaureate program.

Evidence: The percentage of two-year colleges transferring male students who complete a baccalaureate degree is higher than that of those completing the first two years at four-year colleges.

Reasoning: Baccalaureate degrees demonstrate academic success and are beneficial.

1. *Logically join two of the statements in the example with "because."*
2. *Should someone ask you to prove the claim, which statement in the example would you use?*
3. *Which statement in the example connects academic benefit with completing a four-year degree?*

• • • • **TIPS**   • • • • **Writing Claims** • • • •

Write each main point as a claim that tells why your thesis is true. Think in terms of "This is true . . . because of these two [three, four, or five] things." The "things" are declarative statements—*claims*—about the thesis, each of which must be supported.

• • •

CONNECTING EVIDENCE TO CLAIM

For the sample speech in Quick Start 10.1 (see pages 277–179), the speaker's thesis (basic claim) is: College students should be protected from hepatitis B through a federal policy of vaccination and professional responsibility of the medical community. Let's suppose that as a health education major, she became aware of how extensive hepatitis B is on college campuses and began to search for possible solutions. She decided that a solution to alleviate the problem fell under (1) federal policy and (2) professional practices that she claimed should be the solution.

The major claim of a speech often is divided into more limited claims, before proceeding with evidence to prove the claim. One way to think about claims is to imagine an adversary who challenges you at every turn:

"*How* can you claim college students are at risk?"

"*Why* should they be protected?"

"*How* can a federal policy solve a portion of the problem?" "*Why* should they?"

"*How* can the professional medical community solve a portion of the problem?" "*Why* should they?"

"*Why* is this combination a good solution?" "Is it the *best* solution?"

"*What* will happen if this solution is or isn't put into place?"

After the speaker establishes that there is an extensive problem with the disease, she knows she must lead the audience to believe that her claim is true and that her solution is the best solution.

1. *Answer three of the "friendly adversary's" challenges, and list the evidence supporting each claim.*
2. *What is the difference in the way speakers address imagined "why" questions and imagined "how" questions? Explain the importance of each type of hypothetical question.*

ACTIVITY 10.2

Arguing from claims gives you a good foundation for other persuasive structures. Several additional ones are discussed in Chapter 11, in the section Designing Persuasion.

Right from the Start with an Introduction

Getting off to a positive start with an audience is critical. Introductions prepare the listeners. You may wish to review key elements of the introduction in Chapter 7. In general, five things should be accomplished in the introduction:

1. "Don't miss a thing." The audience's attention should be focused on you and your speech. (attention technique)
2. "Look at the compass." The audience should know the topic of the speech and have a sense of direction. (statement of topic)
3. "Know why we're going there." The audience should understand the importance of the topic. (importance of topic and motivation to listen)
4. "Trust the tour guide." The audience should have confidence in you and in the quality of your material. (speaker's credibility)

5. "Know the itinerary." The audience should have an idea of how you will sequence the material. (preview)

Gain the Audience's Attention

Not a moment should be wasted in persuasive efforts. Keep your end goal in mind from the opening words. Engage your audience immediately by asking a question, giving a thought-provoking quotation, presenting startling or sobering statistics, using a brief narrative, or sharing humor.

State the Topic

Listeners want to know the topic right away. You wouldn't want to deceive them by saying you were going to speak on improved admissions procedures at a hospital, and then spend three-fourths of your speech belaboring the inadequacies of emergency room staffing. Make a clear statement about the topic you are addressing, which may state your position on the topic if you have a very favorable audience.

Establish the Importance of the Topic and Motivate the Audience to Listen

The audience needs to know why the topic is important to them. Delaying this risks losing listeners. Statistics can represent the extent or severity of the problem, and narratives impress listeners with how people are affected. Quotations from experts can likewise emphasize the importance of the problem.

Build Speaker Credibility

Speakers must maintain credibility throughout a persuasive speech, and this process begins in the introduction. The credibility of the speaker may be the single most important factor in the speech, and it can be quite fragile. Listeners judge what they hear, leaning heavily toward speakers they perceive as (1) trustworthy, (2) competent, and (3) similar to them.

CONTEMPORARY VOICES 10.1: TRUSTWORTHINESS

Goleman (1998, pp. 89–90) discusses requirements for credibility under the concept of *trustworthiness,* which requires

- Maintaining integrity and displaying honesty
- Letting people know your values, intentions, principles, and feelings
- Being steadfast and consistent
- Speaking for tough, principled stands
- Being ethical and above reproach
- Being reliable and authentic

Competence is the sum knowledge and expertise the speaker owns in the subject or area of study. Like trustworthiness, competence is perceptual. Some listeners don't discriminate among different areas of expertise, and generalize that if the speaker is competent in one field, he or she is competent in many fields. This halo effect can also be negative when an audience forms the generalization that the speaker is incompetent.

William O'Connor (1999, p. 561) weaves his personal background into his introduction in a speech given at Sunderland University on May 5, 1999:

> Come back with me to 1967 for a moment while I share some of my personal experiences with you to make a point. When I graduated from Rensselaer Polytechnic Institute, with a Bachelor's Degree in Electrical Engineering, I immediately began working in the General Electric Company, USA, as a flight control engineer. At that time, I never imagined that I'd be spending hundreds and hundreds of hours in my later career, as a president of companies and a CEO of GTECH, on changing the way people work in order to optimize business results.

Mentioning a common ground of interests, background, experiences, or values increases credibility. Hillary Clinton (1995) in her remarks to the plenary session of the United Nations Fourth World Conference on Women, establishes commonality:

> Whether it is while playing with our children in the park, or washing clothes in a river, or taking a break at the office water cooler, we come together and talk about our aspirations and concerns. And time and again, our talk turns to our children and our families. However different we may be, there is far more that unites us than divides us. We share a common future. And we are here to find common ground so that we may help bring new dignity and respect to women and girls all over the world—and in so doing, bring new strength and stability to families as well.

Preview Main Points

After establishing credibility (in the passage you read earlier), O'Connor previews his main points, signposting (underlined text) each one:

> First, let's examine some of the characteristics of the traditional system— what it does and why it has worked well until recently. Then I will address what needs to be transformed to better meet the needs of mid- and large-sized corporations today and into the future. And, finally, I will share with you what we are doing at GTECH to meet the competitive challenges of the next century. (O'Connor, 1999, p. 561)

INTRODUCTIONS IN PERSUASIVE SPEECHES

ACTIVITY 10.3

Analyze student Amy Celeste Forman's introduction in the following extract. How does she open to get the audience's attention? When do you first know what her topic is? At what point do you think this topic might be important to you? Does she indicate the extent and severity of the problem? Does she use an attention-arousing statistic? How does she initiate her speaker credibility? Can you anticipate from her preview what the main points are and how they will be organized?

> One morning in the fall of 1994, Harvard president Neil Rudenstine overslept. While we're all prone to occasionally hitting the snooze too many times, for Rudenstine, who was in the middle of planning a $1 million a day fund-raising campaign, this was a cause for alarm. He had a habit of making notes late into the night, to the football coach, to *Harvard Crimson* editors, to residence hall staff. His sleep habits were scrambled, his daily life was plagued with unfinished tasks. In short, Neil Rudenstine was suffering from the same problem most

Americans are, but fail to recognize. He was facing the problem of working too hard, and taking too little time for himself. The *Annals of Internal Medicine* reports that 24 percent of people surveyed complained of fatigue that lasts longer than two weeks. As a society, we're all feeling the effects of the Information Age, where we're bombarded by work to be done, information to digest, and the fear of falling behind. As a nation, we are exhausted to the breaking point. Because of the nature of this problem, it is one that is seldom addressed. People who put in 60 or 70 hours a week at their jobs are looked at as a real asset. Students who study constantly are viewed as models. It's only when we consider the results that this "all work and no play" attitude have on us emotionally, physically, and in our relationships with friends and family that the problem emerges. Today, we will examine exactly what the problem is, the effects it has on us, and how we can bring balance and control back into our lives.

Source: Amy Celeste Forman (1997), a student from Morehead State University, "What Exactly Are We Working For?" *Winning Orations of the Interstate Oratorical Association,* pp. 50–52, ed. Larry Schnoor. Mankato, MN: Interstate Oratorical Association. Amy Celeste Forman was coached by Tony Glover and Lisa Shemwell.

Journey's End with Conclusion

A conclusion echoes what was started in the introduction. By this point the audience has completed a logical and well-supported journey. Conclusions should never introduce another main point. They *follow* the main points, and that means that the culminating, climactic point should have been presented before the conclusion. This is the journey's closing and these are the speaker's parting words, a fitting time to reminisce about where you've been, to anchor the experience, and to bring closure.

Review of Main Points

Early in your planning, you decided what you wanted the audience to think by the end of your speech. The review anchors the trip route you and your audience have traveled. A review may again list the reasons a problem exists or the reasons the problem needs attention. A review may also encapsulate the logical points, so that listeners can hear the argument one last time, tightly stated.

• • • • TIPS • • • • Nodding in Agreement • • • •

Weld main points in the conclusion with signpost clauses, such as "Since we agree that . . . ," "caused by . . . ," "the obvious and best solution is . . . ." Give the audience time to mentally register each part, soliciting a virtual head nod from them.

• • •

Final Memorable Statement

In the introduction, you attracted the audience's attention with an opening remark. For the conclusion, you are challenged to impart a memorable story, quote, question, or astute remark they will remember. This residual's effect goes into "accessible memory." Quickly recalled memories are likely to continue to influence the listeners in the future.

PERSUASIVE CONCLUSIONS

ACTIVITY
10.4

Compare Amy Forman's introduction in "What Exactly Are We Working For?" (see Activity 10.3) to her conclusion, provided here. Does she review the same main points? How does she change her wording? How does she end her speech? Do you think the end will stick with the audience? What would be other ways to close?

> Today, we have examined the problem of all work and no play. We have seen the effects, physically and mentally, that it can produce. And most importantly, we have examined some solutions to the problem. It is important for our physical and mental health that we each take stock of the effects work is having on us and obtain a balance between work and play. After all what are we working for if we're too busy or exhausted to enjoy the results?

Special Excursions

Two custom-tailored schemas are Monroe's motivated sequence and story-telling, or the narrative.

Monroe's Motivated Sequence

The "motivated sequence," developed by Alan H. Monroe in the 1930s, is widely used for all sorts of persuasive messages, from advertisements to board-room pitches. It is effective for moving an audience to action, such as giving blood at the American Red Cross, joining an organization, and conserving natural resources. The introduction and conclusion are seamlessly sequenced by steps, positioned to be psychologically motivating.

Step 1: Gain Attention   Attention-gaining techniques are effective in this step: Ask a question, use narrative or a dramatic story, tell a joke, refer to the audience or what is happening, use a visual, or give a compelling statement about the importance of the topic.

Step 2: Establish Need   In the second step, show that a need, or problem, exists. This crucial step induces listeners to experience a need so deeply that they are compelled to find a solution. Having lost their equilibrium or security, they need a solution to feel right again. The audience must experience the need before you move to the third step. Support your claim with evidence, and emphasize the seriousness of the problem.

Step 3: Satisfy the Need   Once listeners experience this "needy" uneasiness, they agree that something must be done about the problem. Mentioning your solution earlier in the sequence will weaken the effect.

Step 4: Visualize the Need Satisfied Step 4 coaxes listeners to imagine a future scene. Vivid wording and imagery evoke reality and passion in this step. The speaker may take one of three approaches:

- Visualize the benefits the audience will experience with your proposal.
- Visualize the negative effects they will suffer if they don't adopt your ideas.
- Visualize first the negative consequences, followed by the positive consequences of your proposed action.

Step 5: Call for Action Call the audience to action. State exactly the action you want them to initiate and how to complete it. Distribute United Way Pledge cards, provide addressed envelopes to write a local legislator, tell when the Red Cross chapter will be on campus to collect blood donations, and so forth. If you state your expectations clearly, you are more likely to get the desired response. Because this is the conclusion of the sequence, emotional appeals are often integrated.

The Story as Structure in Narrative

Perhaps weaving a narrative is one of your most effective styles. These stories can be real or hypothetical. Gerry Spence (1996), called the "winningest trial lawyer" (never having lost a criminal case), weaves a story about a supervisor who wants a production engineer to agree with him about the causes of a production problem. To do this, Spence compares two approaches. One way is to have the supervisor cite statistics on decreasing worker production and the loss of profit and then suggest a remedy (solution). Spence prefers the second approach, developing argument in a narrative:

> I went over to Z Area today. The workers looked dead. Their faces were empty. I thought, My God, have I just walked into the morgue? I walked up to a mechanic and said, "How you doin'?" He didn't even look up. He mumbled a reply I couldn't hear. The other people in Z Area were hardly moving. Finally I pulled the mechanic over, stuck a fresh stick of chewing gum in my mouth and offered him one, and said, "What the hell is going on here?" At first he shrugged his shoulders. Finally he said, "Do you really want to know?" That was the first time I saw any life in his eyes. And when I said, "Yeah, I really want to know," he said, "Okay, you asked, so I'll tell you." Here's what he told me. . . . (Spence, 1996, p. 116)

> A speaker can follow up with an outline on the causes of the breakdown, the poor communications with the other areas, the feeling of futility the workers experience with flaws in the machinery, the stymied production, and the resulting worker apathy, the story provided structure for the main points. (pp. 116–117)

Spence (1996, p. 120) advises attorneys to ask four questions in preparing arguments:

- What do we want?
- What is the principal argument that supports us?

- Why should we win what we want? That is, what facts, what reasons, what justice exists to support the thesis?
- What is the *story* that best makes all of the above arguments?

Once you can answer these questions, you can present the thesis (principal argument) and support the argument with the dramatic story.

> The German philosopher Hans Vaihinger, in . . . *The Philosophy of 'As If,'* proposed that in addition to inductive and deductive thought, there exists an original thought form he calls "fictional thinking." Myth, religious allegory, metaphor, aphorisms, indeed, the world of legal fictions and analogy are examples of fictions we use every day in thinking. An ordinary road map is actually fiction, for nothing like the map exists. Yet we can move accurately, assuredly in the real world as a result of our reliance on the fictional representation of the map. An argument that depends upon "fictional thinking," as Vaihinger called it, is the most powerful of all arguments—the parables of Christ, the stories of tribal chieftains, the fairy tales and fables that are the very undergarments of our society. Jorge Luis Borges, who won the Nobel Prize for literature, Gabriel Garcia Marquez, and Joseph Campbell have all made the same argument, that "fictional thinking" is the original form of human thought, that it harkens to our genes. (Spence, 1995, pp. 114–115)

• THE GUIDE IN PERSUASION

Persuasive construction is fascinating, artistic, and skillful. We'll use a model speech to give us an idea of how the pieces fit together. Following the speech is an outline, taken to the level of subpoints. Read in Quick Start 10.1 how Maria Ciach leads others to agree with her point of view.

● QUICK START 10.1   Model Persuasive Speech • • • •

Maria E. Ciach (1994), of West Chester University, Pennsylvania, delivered this speech at the 1994 Interstate Oratorical Association contest.

Hepatitis B: What Every College Student Doesn't Know

Early in November, 24-year-old Wendy Marx visited her doctor with some slight nausea, low-grade fever, and the chills. Her doctor diagnosed her with a case of the flu, and sent her home to drink lots of liquids and get plenty of rest. Three weeks later, Wendy's liver was raging with infection and she lapsed into a coma. It wasn't until then that her doctor diagnosed that Wendy was suffering from Hepatitis B. Without an emergency liver transplant, Wendy would only have 24 hours to live.

As shocking as it sounds, cases like Wendy's are not unique. The *Journal of the American Medical Association* of March 16, 1994, reports that over 300,000 people between the ages of 18–39 will contract life-threatening cases of Hepatitis B each year. Even more frightening, the *American College Health Association* of May 28, 1993, reveals that Hepatitis B has now reached near epidemic proportions in colleges and universities across the country.

Every college student in America is in the highest risk group in the nation, and thousands of us will die each year. These deaths are slow and painful, much like those of AIDS, but different, in that Hepatitis B is completely preventable. Even though a safe and highly effective vaccine has been available for over the past ten years, the Centers for Disease Control reported on February 4, 1994, that cases of acute Hepatitis B have actually increased since the vaccine was first introduced.

In order to learn how the spread of Hepatitis B can be stopped we will, first, expose the extent of the dangers posed by Hepatitis B; second, determine why Hepatitis B continues to spread; and finally, show how the Hepatitis B vaccine provides a very simple solution to a very deadly problem.

When the Hepatitis B vaccine was first introduced in 1982, the medical community assumed that reports of the disease would decrease dramatically. However, the September 24, 1993, *Mortality and Morbidity Weekly Report* states that the number of chronic infectious carriers has already crested at 1.5 million people and continues to grow. Of those infected, approximately 30,000 people will actually develop the acute form of the disease and, without immediate medical attention, they will die. What's worse, the *American Family Physician* of April, 1992, reports that in the past ten years, our chances of contracting Hepatitis B have increased by over 37 percent. And according to *Mortality and Morbidity Weekly Report* of February 4, 1994, every four weeks about 4000 students are infected throughout the country.

However, the statistics don't reveal the pain and suffering experienced by the victims. *Nursing* of March, 1992, states that once a person contracts Hepatitis B, the prognosis is grim. Initial symptoms usually include vomiting, fatigue, muscle ache, bone pain, and some right upper quadrant discomfort. Over one-third of the acutely stricken victims will develop into hepatocellular carcinoma, a form of incurable liver cancer fatal four to six months after its onset, if not sooner.

However, the most dangerous aspect of Hepatitis B is how easily the disease can be spread. The *Wall Street Journal* of February 2, 1993, reports that Hepatitis B is spread through homosexual and heterosexual activity, through the sharing of drug paraphernalia, and from mother to child. But that's not all. The virus can last for up to a week outside of the human body, predominantly on the surfaces of counter tops in doctors' offices, restaurants, and also on the desktops of college classrooms.

Right now, take a look at your hands. You may be examining the hangnail you've been picking at all morning or maybe the paper cut you received from your schematics. That's all the opening you need in order to contract this life-threatening virus. Thus, it is no coincidence that the *FCA Consumer* of May, 1993, reports that over 30 percent of the people who contract Hepatitis B lead low-risk lifestyles and have no idea how they contracted the disease.

Hepatitis B kills more people in their college years than any other sexually transmitted disease; and yet, students everywhere are not getting the vaccine that could potentially save their life. Why? Simply, it is due to the lack of effort by the government, the medical community, as well as patient ignorance.

When we arrived at college, we all made sure that our tuberculosis Tine test and measles vaccinations were up to date, and if they weren't, we received our shots at our college health clinic. That's the law. However, Hepatitis B vaccinations are not mandated by the government, but merely "urged" by the American College Health Association one year ago. It took over ten years of increasing rates of Hepatitis B on college campuses just to get the government to "urge" students to take a responsibility that the government refused to shoulder. Three organizations, the Immunization Practices Advisory Committee, the U.S. Public Health Service, and the American

Academy of Pediatrics, concocted a plan on May 28, 1993, that only recommended certain groups of people, including college students, to get the vaccine. The government left the matter up to the individual.

The medical community has been additionally noncommittal, with squabbles over which fields of doctors should be held responsible for giving out the vaccine. The *New York Times* of March 3, 1993, stated that many pediatricians don't want to give out the vaccine, thinking that it would be best for the children to get the vaccine in their teen years. However, many family doctors feel it is the duty of the pediatrician to give out the vaccine, along with other childhood vaccinations. Because no doctors feel responsible for giving out the vaccine, none of their patients are receiving it.

Moreover, we suffer from ignorance concerning how to protect ourselves. According to Marjorie Haas, the Director of Health Services at the University of Delaware, in a telephone interview on December 3, 1993, most college students don't even know about Hepatitis B. Few colleges and universities have programs designed to educate students about Hepatitis B, leaving many students to suffer needlessly later.

What we must now do is make our college campuses safe against Hepatitis B. Well, our colleges are always doing things to make our surroundings safe, but this undiscriminating killer will not be deterred by a security light, a safety desk, or a self-defense course. And no 911 number can stop it.

First, our federal government must make the Hepatitis B vaccine mandatory at either childhood vaccination or as part of a mandatory prematriculation vaccination. The U.S. Public Health Service must be appointed to regulate the vaccine program to make certain the plan is implemented, just as it regulates and enforces other vaccinations.

Second, health officials must enforce what the government implements, following the lead of the University of Delaware. In a telephone interview on December 3, 1993, the Director of Health Services stated that within five years the Hepatitis B vaccine will become mandatory for all students.

Unfortunately, the national government and medical community are slow to reform. However, there is a step we can all take to protect ourselves.

It's simple: Get the vaccine. Dr. David Estock of St. Francis Hospital stated in a personal interview on August 13, 1993, that the vaccine is 95 percent effective and reported cases of side effects have been minimal. The vaccine is cheap, highly effective, and is available throughout the country at our family physicians, area hospitals, and even some college health clinics. Ask your university health center or family physician about the Hepatitis B vaccine because it can save your life.

After examining the extent of the dangers posed by Hepatitis B, determining why Hepatitis B continues to spread, and showing that the vaccine provides such a simple solution, it's clear that cases like Wendy's are unnecessary.

Wendy required two liver transplants and thousands of dollars before she eventually left the hospital and is now a permanent infectious carrier of Hepatitis B. Stated Wendy in the *Los Angeles Times* of June 2, 1992, "it's a tragedy that anyone should get this. I only wish I had known about the disease." It's time to get smart, be safe, and get vaccinated. Because Hepatitis B is not an incurable illness, just an illness we're failing to cure.

——— ●

Source: From *Winning Orations, 1994* (1995). Mankato, MN: Interstate Oratorical Association, pp. 31–33. Permissions granted from Shnoor (ed), 1995. Winning Orations of the State Oratorical Association. (See References as attached.)

FIGURE 10.2 • **Organizational Chart Template**

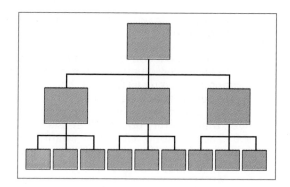

●
ACTIVITY 10.5

MAP A PERSUASIVE SPEECH

Map Maria Ciach's speech, starting with the thesis, connecting the main points to the thesis, and subordinating subpoints under each main point. Use a template such as that shown in Figure 10.2 to map her structure to three levels.

━━━━━━ ●

With a map of the speech body, outlining the speech is a cinch. Ciach's speech outlines to four levels (Quick Start 10.2) to include supporting material, but at three levels, it looks like Figure 10.2. The specific purpose is left blank for you to complete, on the basis of the outline.

● **QUICK START 10.2   Outline of Model Speech** • • • •

Ciach, Maria

1994

Persuasive Presentation Outline

Title: Hepatitis B, What Every College Student Doesn't Know
General Purpose: To persuade
Specific Purpose: After hearing my speech, the audience will _____
_____
_____
_____

Introduction

I. Wendy almost dies with Hepatitis B. (attention getter)

II. Hepatitis B is in epidemic proportions in colleges, making college students the highest risk group of a painful and potentially lethal disease. (importance of the problem and a motivation for the audience to listen)

III. Cite the *Journal of the American Medical Association,* the *American College Association,* and the Centers for Disease Control with recent statistics about the spread of Hepatitis B. (building speaker credibility)

IV. Hepatitis B is preventable with vaccination. (statement of the topic—problem)

V. To learn how the spread of Hepatitis B can be stopped, we will expose the extent of the dangers posed, determine why the disease continues to spread, and show how the vaccine provides a simple solution to the deadly problem. (preview of main points)

Body

I. Dangers posed by Hepatitis B are extensive. (first main point: development of the problem)

    a. Hepatitis B is a danger to us now. (subpoint)

        1. Since the introduction of the vaccine, instead of decreasing numbers, the numbers of those carrying and contracting the disease have grown. (statistical support)

        2. Our chances of contracting the disease have increased by over 37 percent. (statistical support)

    b. Hepatitis B brings suffering and possible death. (subpoint)

        1. Symptoms are debilitating. (explanation as support)

        2. Patients developing hepatocellular carcinoma will die within six months. (factual support)

    c. Hepatitis B is easily spread. (subpoint)

        1. The disease can transfer through homosexual and heterosexual activity, drug paraphernalia, and from mother to child. (factual support)

        2. The disease lasts up to a week outside the body, predominantly on countertops and desks. (explanation)

II. Hepatitis B kills more college students than any other sexually transmitted disease due to the lack of effort by the government and the medical community, and due to patient ignorance. (second main point: development of causes)

    a. After more than ten years, the government merely "urged" students to get the vaccine and left the matter up to the individual. (testimony)

    b. The medical community responds by shifting responsibility to different groups for giving the vaccine. (explanation, testimony)

    c. Most students do not even know about the disease. (testimony)

III. Campuses protect students in other ways and should also protect them against Hepatitis B through a federally mandated, locally implemented program. (third main point: presentation of three-part plan as a solution)

    a. The federal government must make the vaccine mandatory, with an available and regulated program. (subpoint)

    b. Health officials must enforce the government plan. (subpoint)

    c. You can take responsibility for your own protection by requesting the vaccine. (subpoint)

Conclusion

    I. We examined the extent of the dangers of Hepatitis B, determined why it continues to spread, and showed that the vaccine is the solution. (review)

    II. Wendy said, "It's a tragedy that anyone should get this. I only wish I had known about the disease." (closure for introductory narrative)

    III. Be smart, be safe, and get vaccinated. It is not an incurable illness, just an illness we're failing to cure. (final memorable statements)

Practicing initially by talking through the outline, the speaker becomes familiar with what is easy and hard to remember. Speaker notes similar to those shown in Figure 10.3 usually serve best.

FIGURE 10.3 • Speaker's Notes

Intro
    Wendy's story
    Epidemic proportions in colleges
    JAMA, the *American College Association,* and the CDC, statistics on spread
    Hepatitis B is preventable with vaccination. (statement of the topic—problem)
    Preview—dangers, spread, solution
Body
    Dangers
        Current dangers
        Since the introduction of the vaccine, the numbers have grown.
        Our chances of contracting the disease have increased by over 37 percent.
    Symptoms
        Suffering and possible death
        Hepatocellular carcinoma
    Contagious
        Through homosexual and heterosexual activity, drug paraphernalia, and from mother to child.
        Lasts up to a week outside the body, predominantly on countertops and desks. [3 minutes]
    Hepatitis B kills more students than any other STD because of government and medical community, and patient ignorance
        Government—after more than ten years, they "urged"
        Medical community shifts
        Most students do not know about the disease.
        Campuses should protect students against Hepatitis B through a federally mandated, locally implemented program. [4 minutes]
        Feds must make it mandatory
        Health officials must enforce
        You can request the vaccine
Conclusion
    We examined the extent of the dangers, determined why it spreads, and showed the solution.
    Wendy said " It's a tragedy that anyone should get this. I only wish I had known about the disease."
    Smart, safe, and vaccinated. It is not an incurable illness, just an illness we're failing to cure.

The notes in Figure 10.3 show how a speaker can jot down key phrases in the correct sequence as a guide to giving the speech. Practice at least ten times, delivering your speech from your notes. Include cues for ideas you might forget, and omit the ones that come to mind easily. Occasionally check your notes while speaking to see that you are on track. Some speakers practically memorize their notes as they practice.

"A speech is more than ideas. It is sound! It is music! It is rhythm! It is poetry! It is performance!" (Klepper 1995, cited in Flaherty, 1999). The audience perceives everything about you and your delivery as a part of your message. When we remember great speeches, we recall the words, the voice, and the vision of the speakers: "Ask not what your country can do for you"; "I have a dream"; "I consider myself the luckiest man on the face of the earth." When you remember parts of your classmates' speeches, you will remember how they looked and sounded when they said it. Chapter 7, Quick Start to Informative Speaking, gives practical advice on delivering a classroom speech. Chapter 5 explains additional effects of nonverbal delivery. The Tips box in this section shares hints for successful delivery from speech trainers and personal coaches in the business world. Read suggestions from Flaherty (1999), noting things you already do comfortably and finding some effective behaviors to add.

SUMMARY

Persuasion motivates an audience to change a belief, attitude, or behavior. To select a topic, analyze your audience, understand yourself as a communicator, and recognize the dynamics of the occasion. Persuasive speeches may attempt to convince the audience to agree with or reject a point of view, to increase their commitment to an idea, or to actuate them to do something.

Persuasive speakers use a variety of supporting material, including the narrative, self-disclosive information, visuals, explanation, testimony, and statistics. They examine their material according to what will persuade the audience and what will support the thesis. Audiences may be favorable, unfavorable (hostile), neutral, or apathetic toward a topic. In general, use inductive reasoning for a hostile audience, and a deductive approach for an audience that supports the speaker's position.

Appeals speak persuasively to needs and desires in the listeners. Ethos refers to speaker credibility. Pathos evokes psychological and emotional connections. Logos appeals to the reasoned argument, supported with evidence. Persuasive topics directly or indirectly appeal to basic needs.

Several organizational patterns help speakers develop arguments. Problem–cause–solution is a helpful route for organizing the main points. The speech purpose can center on convincing the audience that a problem exists, establishing cause, promoting a solution, or any combination of the three. Speakers should start after cause in the sequence only if the problem is clearly conceded by the listeners. Likewise, the audience must be convinced that the solution will eliminate or respond to the cause. People change their minds and behaviors gradually. Pushing an audience too far, too fast can have a boomerang effect. Monroe's motivated sequence and storytelling, or narrative, are additional "organizing sets" that persuasive speakers use.

The introduction gains the listeners' attention and prepares the listeners with a statement of topic or thesis and the speaker's position or direction on the topic. The audience should know the importance of the topic and have confidence in the speaker and material. Similar to informative speaking, persuasive speaking reviews and gives a final memorable statement in the conclusion. •

ACTIVITIES

1. **Technical Support:** "Be a Virtual Audience Member": Increasingly, the Internet is an interactive medium of communication that invites you to be a virtual audience member for live events. You may also participate in live chat as a venue for discussing your topic ideas.

   Describe a link at which you become a virtual audience member. www.worldlinktelevision.net/streams/chat.php3

2. **Ethically Speaking and Presenting to Others:** In a three-minute presentation, advocate support for a nonprofit organization or social movement. A good source for issues is idealist.com.

3. **Journaling the Experience:** Journal your observations of propaganda devices you hear in spoken communication, as discussed at www.propagandacritic.com/.

4. **Team Work:** In teams of two, map or outline an original persuasive speech on a national policy issue.

5. **Presenting to Others:** Individually, design and deliver a five- to seven-minute speech, using a claim organizational pattern.

6. **Journaling the Experience:**

   a. Imagine you are researching the problem of air pollution from haze in national parks. One of your sources is a May 29, 2001, news release from the U.S. Environmental Protection Agency. How would you use the following statistics to make the problem meaningful to the audience?

      In some parks, like the Great Smokey Mountains, visibility on the haziest days is cut by as much as 80 percent.

      The proposal will affect facilities built between 1962 and 1977 and that emit more than 250 tons of visibility-damaging pollutants every year.

      Without air pollution, people could see about 140 miles in the western United States and 90 miles in the East: but in many parts of the country visibility has been reduced in these regions to 33–90 miles in the West and 14–24 miles in the East.

   b. Martin Scorsese, in his acceptance of the John Huston Award for Artists Rights on February 16, 1996, argued for preserving movie films, documentaries, and newsreels as historical art. "There are a hundred million feet of nitrate film, at a cost of $2.00 per foot. It's $200 million that need to be transferred to safety. By losing them, we lose an important part of our history, our culture."

      Discuss how Scorsese probably compromised exacting accuracy in his statistics in order to communicate with the audience. When do you think rounding numbers for speech communication is justified?

FOR FURTHER READING

Flaherty, T. S. (1999). *Talk your way to the top*. New York: Berkley Publishing Group.

Lundin, H. P., Christensen, J., & Strand, P. (2002). *Fish! tales: Real-life stories to help you transform your workplace and your life*. New York: Hyperion.

Spence, G. (1996). *How to argue and win every time*. New York: St. Martin's Press.

Winning Orations, (Mankato, MN: Interstate Oratorical Association) publishes winning college and university competition speeches annually.

Vital Speeches, as has been brought to your attention previously, is an excellent source of models and resources for supporting material, especially for persuasive speeches. This periodical is available through CIOS at your university library or by subscription at www.votd.com.

Jon W. Dudas

The truth is that presentations, both internal and external, are the most visible extension of a company's vision, goals, and culture. As such, they are an important reflection of a company's identity. Presentations are a double-edged sword, though: They can either enhance the way a company is perceived by its customers and clients, or they can detract from it, causing an unfortunate disconnect between what a company says it is and how it presents itself (Zielinski, 2002).

Designs for Persuasion in Organizations

11

Specific Persuasive Applications in Organizations

Designing Persuasion

A ll communications have persuasive elements, and as we influence others, we also open ourselves to be influenced. Persuasion is inherent in every type of communication—interpersonal, small group, team, and public communication—and ranges from mild influence to impassioned calls to action. When we express our emotions, ideas, desires, and intentions, we legitimize our worth, establish our values, and extol our reasoning. With a straightforward approach about communicators' decisions and choices, this chapter focuses on words and logical patterns used for persuasive effects.

OBJECTIVES

After studying the content of this chapter, you should be able to

- Design and deliver persuasive presentations that fulfill organizational tasks
- Form arguments with logical patterns
- Incorporate persuasive evidence
- Use language powerfully and persuasively

SPECIFIC PERSUASIVE APPLICATIONS IN ORGANIZATIONS

Sometimes you're on your own to deliver a traditional speech at work, but often persuasive presentations are well-planned *interactions* rather than speeches. A typical picture is a client, department, or management audience of 5 to 20 listening to a team of presenters. Participants greet one another and establish a friendly tone. Someone calls the group to order and briefly states the business of the meeting, then turns the meeting over to the presenting team. A team leader formally introduces presenters, introduces the topic, and suggests an organization of the meeting. A preview then assures listeners that their topics will come up in an orderly fashion. The team has a well-prepared presentation of the subject. Different team members address different parts of the report (sometimes divided by topic, other times by expertise). The tone is confident, engaging, professional, communicative, conversational, and informative. The agenda is, at the core, persuasive.

Other teams invite an interactive style from the beginning. They give an oral briefing, pass out hard-copy summaries, and then open the floor for questions and discussion.

Proposing Projects

Project proposals to clients attempt to gain business in response to clients' perceived needs. The process usually is initiated with a *Request for Proposal* (RFP), which is a printed announcement that invites individuals and organizations to submit a proposal for a client's upcoming project. In response, proposals attempt to convince clients of the provider's outstanding capacity, ability, and economy in meeting those needs. A team customarily delivers a project proposal, in writing and speaking, to several key employees of the client organization gathered in a conference room.

Nonprofit organizations rely on grants, loans, philanthropists' monies, and volunteers' services. Foundations' websites post millions of dollars annually. Some RFPs are sent selectively by mail or posted in publications. Proposals for policies seek to influence the direction an organization will take. Applications and guidelines for narrative responses are provided online or by request.

For-profit businesses span organizational boundaries in search of those who will pay for their services For instance, different hotel chains bid to associations' site committees for upcoming conventions. Software developers try to convince clients that they are the best group to create a custom product. Whatever the proposal type, presenters should provide substantial support, showing that they understand the complexity of the job and that they have sufficient resources to meet those needs. Presenters need to convince clients that they can successfully handle the project.

Promoting Ideas (Issue Selling)

Employees compete for the attention of top policy makers in regard to organizational issues. "To do so, they engage in calling the organization's attention to key trends, developments, and events that have implications of organizational performance" (Dutton & Ashford, 1993, p. 398). In such a demanding scene, how will you make your priorities heard? Learning organizations prefer addressing issues as they surface, making their responses at the lowest possible level. With such a philosophy, employees at all levels are cast in advocacy roles, thus bypassing the constraints of hierarchical communication.

Issue selling is a voluntary, specific set of employees' communication behaviors, intended to influence organizational agendas. These grassroots initiatives attempt to achieve focus on such topics as flexible work days, gender equity, and environmental sensitivity in product development. To do this, they must persuade people above the initiators to agree and possibly take action on their issue (Dutton & Ashford, 1993). The decision of whether, how, and when to speak out "may be invisible, but it is by no means rare" (Meyerson & Scully, 1995, p. 586).

CONTEMPORARY VOICES 11.1: PROACTIVE INFLUENCE

What we do is a result of what we *decide,* rather than what we *react* to. To be proactive requires taking responsibility for our own lives and initiating things to happen in our lives (Covey, 1989). Covey categorizes methods of influence under (1) *example*—who you are and how you act; (2) *relationship*—whether you understand and care; and (3) *instruction*—what you tell me (p. 83).

Product championing and *innovation championing* are very similar to issue selling. In these cases, employees promote ideas for new products, solutions for production problems, and marketing opportunities. Perhaps joining a trend toward organic produce, a team suggests developing a hydroponics gardening facility, or maybe an appliance manufacturer's marketing designer thinks parents of toddlers are a market for a safety-designed cook top. In these initiatives, employees upwardly advocate ideas that "informally emerge in an organization" (Archilladis, Jervis, & Robertson, 1971, cited in Ashford, 1998). Done well, issue selling and innovation championing are ways to share visions.

Communicating Vision

"There are three keys to the mint of increased productivity in manufacturing. One is better tools. Another is better processes. And the third is trained, empowered, and motivated people" (Stonecipher, 1996). When a leader communicates a compelling vision, employees rally to the organization's goals. Motivational speeches boost groups' energy, and leaders inspire commitment. High energy, volume, and movement characterize motivational speeches. They typically "look toward the future," "overcome great odds," "make a difference," and "picture success."

FAMOUS ON THE BIG SCREEN

Speakers such as Suze Orman, Kenneth Blanchard, Zig Ziglar, and Tom Peters speak to enormous audiences as they promote basic principles for everyday life. Their presentation strategies include on-stage discussion, distance conferencing on a big screen before a large audience, video, PowerPoint slides, handouts, and audience interaction. Employing a full spectrum of support, they take full advantage of narrative and disclosure and add analogy, metaphor, rhyme, rhythm, repetition, humor, audience participation, narrative, and narration, depending on their listeners' needs and shared values.

Reality @ WORK 11.1

Motivation is not only for the stage and big audiences. Inspiration in conferences carries over to the workplace, and inspiration from classes spreads across individuals to create invigorated campuses. "Narratives, personal disclosure, emotional appeals, and visuals have just as much value in everyday-life presentations as they do in the public arena."

ACTIVITY 11.1

GO FISH!

The "FISH! Philosophy" was inspired by the fishmongers of Seattle's Pike Place Fish Market, who brought creative energy and commitment to their jobs. "The CEO of ChartHouse Learning, John Christensen, encountered the market accidentally one day and instantly noticed that something unusual was going on. A bunch of fishmongers—not MBA professors or leadership gurus—were showing him how to bring more fun, passion, focus, and commitment to work." ChartHouse Learning filmed hours of the fun-filled fish marketplace. ChartHouse Learning's website, https://www.charthouse.com/charthouse/vidTlr_fish.asp? previews a clip of the FISH! Philosophy. The *FISH!* film (1998) has been translated into 14 languages, and the accompanying book has been published in 11 languages, distributed in 27 countries.

Four principles emerged from the film footage. Explore the site to find explanations of the fishy main points:

1. Play.
2. Make their day.
3. Be there.
4. Choose your attitude.

Plan a motivational interaction, discussion, *or* activity for a department or business supporting one of the fishy main points, or plan a motivational speech to follow a viewing of the film. Videotape or audiotape your 5- to 10-minute presentation.

Communicating in Crises

Proactivity precludes many disasters, but some unexpected crises call for organizations to skillfully handle internal and external communication. "A major, unpredictable event that has potentially negative results . . . and its aftermath may significantly damage an organization and its employees, products, services, financial condition, and reputation" (Benoit & Lindsey, 1987, pp. 136–146).

Crisis communication is made up of the cumulative messages given to the public and to an organization's employees in response to a crisis. *Crisis communicators* are specified employees who speak on an organization's behalf. The characters of the Chinese symbol for "crisis" combine "danger" and "opportunity" (Hoffman, 1994), and that is the approach of crisis communicators. When crises implicate organizations, communication is the vehicle of understanding and the substance of correction. This chapter's discussion of crisis communication focuses on communication within organizations, rather than between organizations. Words, their contexts, and channels determine how messages are received. Who delivers these messages? Perhaps you will be the vocal official.

Crises are events of a magnitude to interrupt an organization's ability to conduct business as usual. Crisis communication tries to change negative perceptions of an organization's involvement in an event. Crisis communicators know that a company's profits, image, and employees depend on minimizing possible damage to the organization's credibility (Ulmer & Sellnow, 2000). The problem is that there "are going to be situations in the global marketplace for which there are no solutions" (Howard, 1998).

Management is responsible for two interdependent processes: crisis management and crisis communication. *Crisis management* focuses on taking care of technical and human problems caused by the crisis. *Crisis communication* decides what to say to media, involved parties, the community, stockholders, and other stakeholders (DiSanza & Legge, 2000, p. 297). Professional speechwriters Hampton, Nekvasil, Ricks, and Stark warn, "A badly chosen or poorly prepared spokesperson can severely hamper an organization's response to a crisis," and give advice for communicating with the public:[1]

1. Have templates and generic text for potential crises on file.
2. Create an information management and dissemination system for communicating directly and through media. Maintain a baseline of knowledge outlining the known facts.
3. Involve appropriate leaders about confidential or sensitive information. Remember it is honest and nondisclosive to announce when you will not address certain issues.
4. "Write by committee" of experts to get immediate, pertinent input.
5. Define the various audiences and their respective concerns.
6. Acknowledge the emotional component of the crisis, and say it first.
7. Stay focused on what has to be said, in defense against aggressive interviewers.
8. Have a prepared statement. Be direct, honest, and to the point. Don't argue or blame. Avoid speculation and hyperbole.
9. Address anticipated public questions and concerns directly, or have the information available.
10. Shorter isn't always better. A 12- to 18-minute speech gives time to address issues, diffuse emotion, and make points. Too short and listeners are likely to substitute their own thoughts, fears, and expectations.
11. Avoid using prepared visuals too early in a crisis. They take time and can come across as "canned" or "slick."
12. Pay attention to personal appearances and possible perceptions.

---

[1] The following list is based on an article by Lawrence Ragan Communications, Inc. Crisis conversations in 12 steps. *Lawrence Ragan Communications.* Available: www2.ragan.com

ACTIVITY 11.2

CRISIS COMMUNICATION

William L. Benoit (1995) organizes the most common responses for attempting to reframe an organization's involvement during times of crisis:

- Denial (We didn't do it.)
- Evading responsibility (It's not our fault.)
- Reducing offensiveness (We didn't cause it; they made us do it; this was beyond our control; we were trying to do good things, and this bad thing happened.)
- Corrective measures (We will make this change, so that this bad thing will never happen again.)
- Mortification (We did it, and we're so very sorry.)

1. *Research an organizational crisis, how the public learned about it, and the organization's response. Some earlier crises have been analyzed extensively in view of the effects of the communication following the crisis. You may use one of them (see following list) or a more recent crisis, such as with Enron, Arthur Andersen, the World Trade Center attack, the* Columbia *disaster, a number of interactions nationally and internationally regarding Operation Iraqi Freedom, and the communication concerning Hurricane Katrina's destruction. Which of Benoit's reframing strategies (excuses) did they use in their communications?*

   - *In 1993, the Washington State Health Department learned that an unusual number of children were being treated at Children's Hospital in Seattle for infection by* E. coli, *largely attributed to hamburgers purchased at Jack in the Box restaurants (Ulmer & Timothy, 2000).*
   - *In 1982, seven people died, apparently resulting from cyanide-tainted Tylenol capsules manufactured by Johnson & Johnson.*
   - *In 1989, an Exxon ship, the* Valdez, *hit a reef in Prince William Sound, Alaska, and dumped 240,000 barrels of crude oil into the water.*
   - *The tobacco industry was accused of biased interpretations of research suggesting harmful effects of tobacco products and of increasing the addictive qualities of tobacco products.*
   - *Texaco responded to accusations of racism when audiotapes containing racist and derogatory language about specific minority employees were released.*
   - *ValuJet responded following a crash in the Everglades of Florida that was caused, according to outside sources, by management policies that cut short safety considerations.*

2. *According to sophists, the outcome is all that matters: "The ends justify the means." Plato argued that not only was sophistry unethical, but also that valid information presents a better argument. Which of these approaches is most evident in the crisis you researched?*

3. *In teams, create an ethical code and sequenced procedure for organizational communication in response to crises.*

In short, when a situation implicates one's organization, and the word hits the press, someone must respond. Lines of communication must also be developed *inside* the organization so that employees hear the official response before or within moments of the public announcement. Considerable confusion, fear, and suspicion emerge from uninformed and ignored employees. For these and other reasons, it is important for management to directly and completely communicate with employees. As employees become satisfied with answers, they, too, can answer questions from outside the organization. Important, too, is their acceptance of official reasons for the problem and plans for corrective action.

• DESIGNING PERSUASION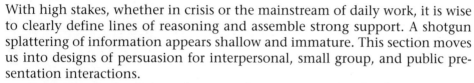

With high stakes, whether in crisis or the mainstream of daily work, it is wise to clearly define lines of reasoning and assemble strong support. A shotgun splattering of information appears shallow and immature. This section moves us into designs of persuasion for interpersonal, small group, and public presentation interactions.

Persuasion isn't what we do to people—persuasion is what happens *inside* them. No matter how much communicators design, research, strategize, and emote, unless someone decides to be persuaded, presenters do not persuade. Perhaps we don't want to admit we are swayed by what others say, and yet persuasion is at the core of human connection.

For ethical communicators, persuasion is an interaction between communicators toward the perceived common good. In the interaction, speakers make requests of listeners, but listeners also ask speakers to do things *for* them, such as reason for them, get evidence for them, and take away the world's ambivalence.

"The chief communication mechanism that promotes compliance must be a give-and-take process in which each party can influence and accommodate the other's understanding of what solicitation and response mean" (Sanders & Fitch, 2001). We find elements of this compliance assembled in ethos, pathos, and logos.

Ethos (Trustworthiness)

Be credible, then communicate your credibility; be trustworthy, then communicate your trustworthiness. With mutual respect among interactants, communication strives for win–win solutions whenever possible. To be effective in the process, you must also be memorable in a positive way.

Trust

"I like doing business with someone I can trust" is a widely repeated sentiment. When audiences see you as sincere, unselfish, and expert, they are prone to trust you. Trust precedes influence, leading thinkers agree. Goleman (1998) says that trustworthiness is an emotional intelligence competence, and Covey and Senge write extensively about the importance of a trusting relationship. Sometimes trustworthiness is displayed in the tough, principled stands (Goleman, 1998).

Appeals of *ethos* include communicating the intent to help others, that is, *"feelings of good will."*

> Ethos joins communicators as worthy participants, who are connected and open. They want to understand people more than they want to impress them. A keynote address at a convention of engineers and technical professionals chided earlier technical writers and speakers: "Often their prose created such obstacles to understanding, through its jargon and density, that it created the *ethos* of the expert: one whose esoteric knowledge makes him . . .

Trust must be built between speaker and listeners. Principal Deputy Assistant Secretary of Defense for Public Affairs Lawrence Di Rita addresses an audience of journalists during a Pentagon press briefing on July 28, 2004. If you were in this speaker's position, how would you build rapport with an audience of journalists?

a member of a priesthood, a wizard whose mysteries aren't supposed to be understood by the uninitiated. (Lukazewski, 1997)

On a larger scale, trust at an organizational level grows out of trust sustained at a personal level. Trust and power are "generated at the interpersonal level and either trust or power dominates the relationship. . . . Power occurs at the level of the structural framework of relationships and is highly conducive to developing trust between individual organizations" (Bachmann, 2001).

Interestingly, at an annual meeting of the Council of Programs in Technical and Scientific Communication, discussion erupted on the phrase "tyranny of audience." There was considerable agreement that too much attention is given to what the audience wants and too little to what the audience needs. *What the audience needs* indicates that speakers should care about their listeners' well-being.

Research confirms that people are more likely to be persuaded by highly *credible* communicators (Allen, 2002), but also, more specifically, that material from someone the listeners see as an expert is more influential if you let them know who said it *ahead* of time. On the other hand, if the source is not well known, hence less credible to the listeners, the material should come first, then the source (Allen, 2002; O'Keefe, 1987). Many naïve listeners, once they accept *you* as credible, don't want to spend time hearing the sources, but critical listeners intend to learn the sources. Most listeners fall somewhere in between, and so presenters learn to incorporate their sources smoothly.

Testimony in communication means quotations from experts, whether they have been gathered in person or through written material. Interesting implications rest in certain types of testimony: reluctant and biased testimony. *Reluctant testimony* comes from sources that provide "evidence in conflict with their own self-interests" (Benoit & Kennedy, 1999, p. 376). *Biased testimony* gives evidence in accord with sources' self-interests and, as would be expected, is trusted less than reluctant or objective testimony. Surprisingly, though, reluctant testimony equals objective testimony in the ratio of favorable to unfavorable thoughts in receivers' minds.

An interesting research design yielded a clear outcome concerning biased and reluctant sources. The researchers (Walster, Aronson, & Abrahams, 1966) constructed two messages (one advocating more power for the courts, the other advocating less) and two persuasive sources (a convicted criminal and a successful prosecutor). The prosecutor was more persuasive when advocating less power for the courts, and the criminal was more persuasive when advocating more power for the courts.

Pathos (Motivation and Emotion)

The artistic appeal of pathos spans motivational and emotional dimensions, the psychology of which is as complex as people themselves. People are uniquely emotional creatures, and their motivations align with their emotions. Understanding these dimensions fuels an endless trek, so we should benefit from what scholars have learned.

"Three central motives have been identified that generate attitude change and resistance" (Wood, 2000, p. 539):

1. Concerns about self
2. Concern about others and the rewards and punishments others can make happen
3. Interest in truly understanding reality

Strong motivators are "So, how does this affect me?" "What can they do for/to me?" and "I want to know the truth."

APPEALING TO THE BOARD

Dr. Harriet B. Harral (personal communication, August 30, 2003), at the time president of Good Will Industries of Ft. Worth, Texas, led the organization through a major building program. In the final stage of planning, discussion centered on what to put in the central courtyard leading off the grand hall of the building. She led them to visualize a beautiful garden: "Picture this—people strolling through a garden. Employees enjoying trees and flowers during breaks. An interesting sculpture." All they could hear was more money being spent. Asphalt would be cheaper.

Her volunteering colleague, Judy Harmon, said, "Perhaps you simply should have said, 'Look. Make it pretty and people will rent it.'" Judy was right. Although Harriet played her last ace to get the board to agree to a garden, it wasn't until several months later, when revenues started showing up in reports, that a surprised and thrilled board proclaimed it the "Harriet B. Harral Garden."

Reality @ WORK 11.2

Truth is a strong motivator. A prime example is in health care, where some people don't want to know if their health is in danger, whereas others prefer knowing. For instance, people are willing to test for heart disease because the disease is more troubling than the test, but people generally aren't as motivated to exercise and diet to avoid heart disease. They are more moved by the ideas of weight loss and added energy (Wood, 2000).

Which of the three central motives do you think would most strongly involve audience in the panel discussion at the Military Family Forum?

"Seek first to understand, then to be understood," counsels Covey. When people think you understand them, they lower their defenses and listen. Active listening responses, sharing stories, and sharing woes, on the whole, produce a feeling of being understood. Working on shared goals with teams brings about similar effects, but in public speaking, presenters must respond to what they already know about the audience and whatever immediate feedback (laughter, head nods) they're getting. Listeners' sad or happy moods (either one and equally strongly) influence the effects they have. "Message strength has a weak effect on people in a happy mood, whereas message strength has a strong effect on those in a sad or neutral mood" (Mitchell, 2000).

Pathos wraps its arms around motivation, psychological appeals, and emotional appeals. Pathos pulls heart strings and builds empathy. It is the human connection. Sarah McGinty, in *Language as a Power Tool* (1999), advises presenters to adjust their style and use of language to an audience. Imposing jargon and professionally specific terms plays one-upmanship and produces resentment. Also, be careful about politically and personally sensitive language.

Logos (Logical Patterns)

The ability to think critically is vital to a world in which personality and image too often substitute for thought and substance" (Lucas, 2002).

Caution! Precaución! Attenzione! Vorsicht! This section could be dangerous to your mental health. It requires clear thinking.

Logos—the dimension that we dissect, analyze, and put back together again—consists of evidence and reasoning. For the presenter, evidence comes from the collected data, testimony, and other material. Reasoning is the process of moving listeners' thinking from point A to point B.

Inductive and *deductive* describe thinking (reasoning) processes as well as certain patterns of organization for presentations. This text leans toward using *inductive* and *deductive* to describe thinking processes and discusses organizational patterns for speeches according to their functions, use of support, and placement of thesis.

Contrast inductive thinking with deductive thinking using the example of Table 11.1. Table 11.2 summarizes basic differences between inductive thinking and deductive thinking.

TABLE 11.1 • An Example to Contrast Inductive and Deductive Logic

Inductive Thinking	Deductive Thinking
1. The house lights went out. 2. The television clicked off by itself. 3. The dishwasher stopped running. 4. The air conditioner has turned off. 5. The street lights are out. 6. I can't turn on my hair dryer. *Generalization:* We are having a power outage.	1. All electrical appliances need power to work. 2. My hair dryer is an electrical appliance. *Conclusion:* Therefore, my hair dryer needs power to work.

If a presenter states a thesis and then supports it with a number of cases (no matter the sequence), the presenter is using inductive reasoning, not deductive, unless each case is individually deduced from the thesis.

TABLE 11.2 • Characteristics of Inductive and Deductive Thinking

Inductive Thinking	Deductive Thinking
An inductive thinker arrives at a conclusion on the basis of observations, experiences, and other evidence.	A deductive thinker begins with an indisputable fact or principle, noting a specific case to which the principle is applied conclusively.
We learn inductively. We learn about gravity long before we know the word, because we drop things and see what happens.	We predict deductively like this: Balls roll. This marble is a ball. Therefore, this marble rolls.
Inductive reasoning collects *specific* incidents and from them forms a *tentative conclusion,* or *generalization.*	Deductive reasoning moves from a *general* and broad principle to one or more *specific cases.* It *concludes* that the principle applies to the specific case.
Inductive Rhetoric	*Deductive Rhetoric*
The thesis is the generalization of the argument.	The thesis is the conclusion, which is not the generalization presented as the accepted principle.
When the presentation design mirrors the thinking, speakers present evidence, building a case until the audience feels compelled to accept the presenter's generalization, which is not stated until late in a speech. This works especially well with an unfavorable audience, because they accumulate points of agreement before a conclusion is drawn.	When the presentation design mirrors the thinking, speakers state something accepted by the audience as obviously true, show how a specific case falls within the boundaries of the first statement, and conclude that what is true for the inclusive category is true for the specific case. This works well with a favorable audience, who already agree with the thesis.
With a favorable audience, an inductive presentation may place the generalization at any point. Examples can build to stating the generalization, and additional evidence can support it afterward.	With an unfavorable audience, a speaker may induce a generalization, support it, and then deduce that it applies to a particular case.
An inductive pattern may organize the entire speech or portions of the speech.	A deductive pattern is more frequently seen *within* a speech than as an organizational pattern.

Inductive Applications

Everyone learns inductively, and we can build arguments that way. In doing so, we develop needs, build backgrounds (including failed attempts), and then conclude that certain projects, proposals, solutions, and studies will or will not work. One example builds upon another, and pieces of evidence accumulate, as the presenter points an audience toward the desired conclusion.

In presentations the generalization may come at any point in the presentation, depending on the audience's receptivity and expertise. Try moving the generalization in the Meyerson example (see Activity 3 at the end of this chapter). Imagine giving two pieces of evidence, then the generalization, and then saying, "In further support . . ." to add more evidence. The sequence is different, but the thinking is the same: basically, that totaling all this evidence leads us inevitably to this one conclusion.

Inductive patterns are especially useful with resistant or hostile audiences. Numerous examples and ample evidence build a conclusion. The strength of the argument depends on the relevance of the examples and the respect afforded the evidence from the audience members' perspectives. Inductive patterns can "quicken the dead" (i.e., apathetic audiences) when examples particularly meaningful to them are used. As their heads bob in agreement and faces light up with empathy, you know you have them paying attention, and probably in the palm of your agreeable hand.

Characteristically, accumulated evidence is accurate, perhaps convincing, but less than conclusive in an inductive argument.

Deductive Applications

Deductive arguments begin by presenting an accepted principle or generalization. Ideally, all listeners accept it as undeniably true from the outset. Then, a presenter shows that a specific case falls within the subject set of the generalization. Finally, the speaker applies the generalization to the case. The *syllogism* is one of the most frequently used forms of deductive reasoning. Perhaps a landscape architect wishes to "prove" that roses will survive multiple growing seasons (see Example 11.1). The architect would start with the known principle as the major premise, connect it to the subject (roses) in the minor premise, and deduce the generalization as a conclusion. Multiple conclusions can be deduced from the same major premise.

● **EXAMPLE 11.1   Formal Syllogism**

All perennials survive a growing season and bloom again. (major premise)

Roses are *perennials.* (minor premise)

∴ Roses *survive a growing season and will bloom again.* (conclusion)

Syllogisms consistently require three terms, with one of the three terms in both premises. The term occurring in both premises must be modified by *all* or *none* at least once.

- The *major premise* is a known fact or principle: All perennials survive a growing season and bloom again.
- The *minor premise* clarifies that the specific subject (roses) falls within the major premise's generalization: perennials.
- The *conclusion* is then logically drawn that the specific item in the category (roses) *must* have the characteristics of the major subject. (Once the conclusion is drawn, the logical path is open to apply it as a generalization for another syllogism, in a sort of chain effect.)

More common than formal syllogisms are enthymemes. *Enthymemes* are not formally structured, unlike syllogisms. They are like syllogisms, but with an assumed or unspoken part. Can you supply the assumed or missing parts in these examples?

- Where there's smoke, there's fire.
- If he went to MIT, he's smart.
- Eat your salad; it's good for you.
- We insulated the attic, so our electric bill will be lower this year.

Enthymemes present tentative conclusions based on probable premises. Unlike syllogisms, neither premises nor conclusions for enthymemes can be proven (Roskell & Jolliffe, 2004). When enthymemes express beliefs that are widely shared by an audience, the audience probably will accept the conclusion even if the reasoning is imperfect or the premises are questionable (Crowley, 1994, p. 159).

COLORFUL ARGUMENTS

In teams of four, conduct a one-hour library search to find examples of inductive and deductive reasoning in speeches (check *Vital Speeches*) and news editorials. You may find the example imbedded in a speech's organization, an individual point, or as a speaker develops support. In the next hour, pore over the examples, using five highlighter pens—green, pink, yellow, blue, and orange.

ACTIVITY
11.3

1. *Inductive arguments*
   Highlight generalizations for inductive arguments in green.
   Highlight key examples or evidence in pink.
2. *Deductive arguments*
   Highlight the major premise or general principle in blue.
   Highlight the minor premise or specific instance in orange.
   Highlight conclusions for deductive arguments in yellow.
3. *Create two posters: one poster of your clearest inductive argument and one poster of your clearest deductive argument. Label whether the deductive argument is a syllogism or enthymeme.*

FIGURE 11.1 • Toulmin's
Requirements for an Argument

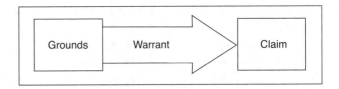

Toulmin's Model of Argument

One way to visualize arguments is to use philosopher Stephen Toulmin's model of argument, displaying three requirements for an argument (Figure 11.1). The idea for which you are arguing (the one you hope to convince your audience about) is the *claim*. The *grounds* are the evidence supporting the claim. The *warrant* is the "logical leap" made between evidence and claim (Keene, 1979).

Three other features may be added to the argument (Brydon & Scott, 2000):

- If the warrant is disputed, there needs to be *backing* to support the warrant.
- There may also be an exception, or *rebuttal,* to the argument, which would deny the claim.
- Unless an argument is 100% certain, it will need to have a *modal qualifier* (sometimes simply called a *qualifier*) to indicate the level of certitude of the claim.

Paraphrased to fit the structure of Toulmin's model, these features would look like Figure 11.2 for deductive reasoning and Figure 11.3 for inductive reasoning.

Problem, Cause, Solution

Inductive conclusions use the following:

1. *Causal* reasoning (establishing the cause-and-effect relationship)
2. *Analogous* reasoning (comparisons between two or more things that seem similar in some respects)
3. *Generalizations* (assertions about all members of a class of objects) to connect supporting evidence

FIGURE 11.2 • Paraphrase of
Toulmin's Model for Deductive
Reasoning

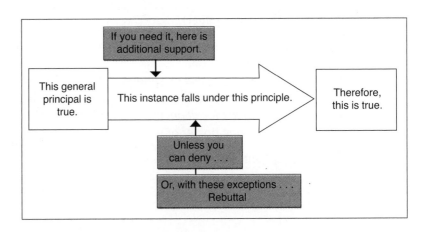

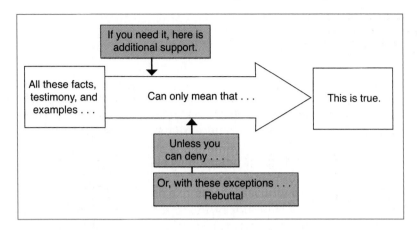

FIGURE 11.3 • **Paraphrase of Toulmin's Model for Inductive Reasoning**

Premises are statements of relevant evidence, including examples that are connected "reasonably" to a generalization. Deductive reasoning is also based on cause—*because* this item falls in this inclusive class, we can prove that it has the characteristics of the category.

Let's see what else falls along the "problem–cause–solution" continuum. You may argue all three: Prove that there is a problem, explain a probable cause or causes, and advocate a solution. Usually, you focus on only one or two aspects of the continuum. The diagram in Figure 11.4 opens a range of organizational possibilities.

Keep in mind two principles of persuasion as you organize your speech:

1. Have a realistic goal.
2. Take one step at a time.

The 180-degree turnaround is more often myth than reality. People change gradually, including changing their minds and their behaviors. "The greater and more important the change you want to produce in your audience, the more difficult your task will be" (DeVito, 2000, p. 389). Pushing an audience too far, too fast produces a boomerang effect. Let's say a developer addresses a city council that wants to keep the community "just the way things are." The speaker may show possible benefits to growth or that the status quo will destroy the community in the long run.

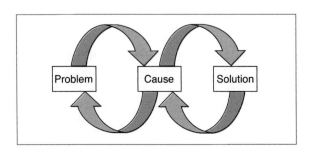

FIGURE 11.4 • **The Problem-Cause-Solution Continuum**

Prove a Problem   An entire speech may try to convince an audience that a problem exists. If that's your choice, give your audience evidence that a problem exists, is extensive, and belongs to them. The problem may be developed inductively or deductively.

Often, the problem is presented with several claims as declarative statements, with each claim supported by evidence. If you choose this approach, your support may include a definition of the problem, testimony from authorities, examples relevant to the listeners, and explanations of how this will affect them.

Some problems are self-evident, but listeners must become sensitive to them to be moved to action. Other problems, even important ones, may have to be pointed out. Before the public was made aware of the problems of diminishing rain forests, people were not prone to support measures to protect them. The public was educated that rain forests provide the sources of many medicines and an environment for unique observations. Occasionally, a speaker even creates a problem. The listeners never dreamed they needed air bags on cars, self-wicking socks, or soy until someone pointed it out.

Prove the Cause(s) or a Portion of the Cause   Causation states that something happens *because* of something else. When an audience already agrees a problem exists, the "open link"—the ambivalence in the problem chain—may center on the cause of the problem. If that's the case, establish clearly that one thing happening makes another thing to happen—which, of course, is the problem.

For example, with an audience sympathetic to protecting rain forests, the speaker can point to a probable cause, such as industrial encroachment. As another example, a researcher may argue the probability of a particular cause of a cancer in order to get funds for research to determine whether that really is the cause. In business, an advertising executive attempts to persuade a client that his or her ad campaign would be the most successful approach for the client's business would be the *best* approach for increasing the client's profit.

As you see in Figure 11.4, causes may be "linked" to problems, solutions, or both. You may either reason from effect to cause or from cause to effect. Furthermore, the causes or the effects may be in the past, present, or future, as shown in the Gandhi example in Contemporary Voices 11.2. In the first two types, the effects are problems; in the last type, the effect is a solution.

1. A problem is an *effect,* or outcome, due to several *causes.*
2. A problem exists *because* of one or more reasons. (Some call this the "reasons why" pattern.)

CONTEMPORARY VOICES 11.2: SEVEN DEADLY SINS

In this example, the effect is the problem, and it is a problem from the past, the present, and the future.

Stephen Covey, in *Principle-Centered Leadership* (1992), teaches corporate leaders to heed the "seven deadly sins" presented by Mahatma Gandhi.

Thesis: Seven things, if practiced, will destroy us.

1. Wealth without work
2. Pleasure without conscience
3. Knowledge without character
4. Commerce (business) without morality (ethics)
5. Science without humanity
6. Religion without sacrifice
7. Politics without principle

1. *In studying the organization of this argument, what is the effect? What are the causes?*

2. *If you present these causes in a speech, the audience may have difficulty remembering all seven unless you grouped them. Which ones could you group for subpoints? What would your main points be?*

CONTEMPORARY VOICES 11.3: WORKPLACE EXAMPLES

Peter Senge, in *The Fifth Discipline* (1994), explains how mental models affect our perceptions and deeds. Notice how he gives the reasons for the problem in his thesis and his central idea.

Thesis: Many of the best ideas in business fail to get put into practice because they conflict with deeply held internal images of how the world works. That is, some of the best ideas conflict with a person's "mental models."

Central idea: Organizations have difficulty converting to "localness," that is, distributing control throughout the organization, because of these reasons.

I.   Senior managers fear that they will become unneeded or less important in the organization if they lessen the amount of their control.

II. Collaborative efforts toward common corporate-wide goals become more complex.

Although causal reasoning can be used to support points, it can also be an organizational pattern for the entire speech. The "reasons why" pattern proves the causes of the event or problem. It may be a single reason or more, although an audience has difficulty retaining more than five reasons.

The combined causes to a problem may overwhelm both speaker and audience, so you may choose to present only one cause, accounting for a portion of the problem. This is a good strategy when an audience sees an easy solution to that cause. The U.S. Environmental Protection Agency (EPA) is concerned about haze in the national parks, including Yellowstone and Grand Canyon. They chose one cause and targeted plants and facilities built between 1962 and 1977 that emit annually more than 250 tons of visibility-obscuring pollutants, such as sulfur dioxide, nitrogen oxide, and particulate matter, or soot.

Beware of false causation. Just because two events coexist does not mean that one causes the other. More people who wear wedding rings get divorces than those who don't. Do wedding rings, then, cause the high divorce rate? One line of reasoning would say that only married people get divorced, so of course they would be more likely to have rings. Others would say dissatisfaction in the relationships, not wedding rings, led to the divorces. Rings don't cause divorce, nor do rings cause unhappiness. False causation often leads to ineffective solutions. For example, let's say you show that tourism on Galveston Island has increased in the last year, and, during the same year, the shrimp population has gone down. Does that mean that the tourists are ordering too many shrimp in local restaurants, or could there be an entirely different reason, like exporting more shrimp to other states? Establishing the right cause has a better chance to lead to the right solution.

Present a Solution   Often a speaker advocates a solution to follow the presentation of the problem or both the problem and cause. The speaker should prove that a particular action *will solve* the problem, show that it is *one way* to solve the problem that has other benefits, demonstrate that it is the *best way* to solve the problem, or show that it has the *flexibility* to solve many problems, including this one. Even if the problem is presented in one introductory sentence, state the problem clearly for the audience. The solution should clearly connect to the stated problem.

Camille Dillard, representing Kitchen Aid, had five minutes to present four new small kitchen appliances at a trade show. She presented each product and demonstrated how it answered various needs. For instance, with several food processors on the market, she showed that her product was easier to clean than the competitors. Her plan was to persuade her audience that her food processor was the *preferred solution* in regard to cleaning. She could then show its multitask capability to prove added benefits.

ACTIVITY 11.4

REASONABLY UNREASONABLE

Read about several marketing successes and errors in Japan at www.culturalsavvy.com/marketing_in_japan.htm

1. *Give examples of deductive reasoning in the article.*
2. *Give an example of critical missing pieces of information from research.*
3. *How could these errors have been avoided?*

Powerful Language

Outstanding communicators are artists with words. They carefully select the words and phrases that prompt their listeners to imagine what they are describing. They use wording that connects to emotion and reasoning. Certainly, if the most effective uses of language filled a persuasive message, there would be no time for words that distract and detract from the desired effects.

Unfortunately, some communicators' habits and poor choices send their listeners on tangents or outright repulse them. Careless choices in language use weaken the appeal of a message. For example, an overuse of qualifiers, those inserted feedforward messages such as "perhaps," "maybe," and "a little," weaken impact. Women use more qualifiers at work than men, but McGinty (1999) says that regardless of gender, "When you're in charge, the words you choose place you in the center of a situation. When you're not in control, you use qualifiers" (quoted in Warshaw, 1998). Here are the ten worst choices of disabling language that will probably undermine persuasive efforts:

1. Offensive word choices, in general or for the listener in particular (derogatory language, crude language, harsh terms for the circumstances, racism, sexism, and other politically incorrect phrases)

2. Profanities and obscenities (religiously and socially unaccepted language)

3. Grammatical errors, especially in subject–verb agreement, choice of verb tense, and use of pronouns ("It don't . . . ," "Her and me went . . . ," "We done took . . . ," "I be thinking . . .")

4. Inaccurate word choice (such as a confusing word, mistaken word, overly weak descriptor, or exaggerated descriptor)

5. Habitual exaggeration, spinning, or glossing (making something sound better than it is)

6. Inadequate vocabulary (ignorant of specific terms, adequate descriptive language, or words the other communicator understands)

7. Fillers (habitual, extensive, and meaningless uses of words such as *you know, like,* and so on) and disfluencies (*er, uh,* and *ah*)

8. Verbosity (too many words for too few ideas)

9. Overuse of regionalisms, colloquialisms, and clichés ("ain't," "ya'll come back now," "youse guys," "plumb wore out")

10. Inappropriate focus on self or other in pronoun choice ("I" overused to brag, or "you" used when making broad accusations meaning "anyone")

IDENTIFYING DISABLING LANGUAGE

ACTIVITY 11.5

Identify the following messages with one or more of the errors from the list of disabling language.

1. Me and him thought that was a good idea.
2. It don't matter to me what mess you're in, I ain't hepping.
3. Er, uh, get the whatchamacallit to fix the drain, uh, you know what I mean.
4. I told you boys to help that customer.
5. This problem is totally inexcusable and will ruin the company and smear your names all over the community.
6. Perhaps we have a small problem that needs a tiny bit of our attention.
7. Like I spoke up and set her, like, straight, before, you know, we, like, could get on with the job.
8. When you make errors on a shipping order, you'd better come clean.
9. The cat was squashed in the middle of the parking lot, I mean, like, with its guts spilling out.

10. The organization is outsourcing management tasks off-shore and embraces the opportunity to recommend former employees, as the result of restructuring for positions in other companies, so long as there is not breach of confidentiality or conflict of interest.

Language should not be a stumbling block, but rather a powerful force in communication. The "power of words" is not a cliché; it is an accurate description. Martin Luther King powerfully repeated, "I have a dream." John F. Kennedy immortalized the phrases, "Ask not what your country can do for you. Ask what you can do for your country." Let's consider four of the most powerful uses of language.

Figurative Language   Few techniques are as appealing, engaging, and compelling as figurative language. Similes, metaphors, and analogies tap into intricate pictures in our heads to allow us to hold another subject up in comparison. Booker T. Washington mesmerized an Atlanta Exposition Address crowd with an analogy: "Cast down your buckets where you are." Furthermore, enumerated points repeated in heightened moments bolster listeners' recall of presentations.

Tandem dialogues   These blend a strand of the message's information with a strand about the information—describing its importance, exploring its usefulness, and celebrating its availability. This second strand is *metacommunication,* or communication about communication.

Disclosing questions   These insist that listeners think, formulating their own answers and perhaps uncovering the inadequacy of their answers. Good questions personalize topics for the listeners, but they do not attack or embarrass them.

Compelling stories   These impose visions in listeners' minds. Careful sequencing, critical details, and vivid language craft memorable stories and examples to become part of persuasive dialogues to be passed on to other listeners. Stories are powerful because we "relate to stories more easily than to most other forms of communication except smell and touch" (Lukaszewski, 1997). They touch our emotions and the everyday truths where we live.

> Successful stories are generally told in plain language; they're fundamentally positive; they're about people; they're relatively brief; and they have a recognizable beginning, middle, and end. . . . It's the opportunity to get the answers to important questions that draws us to a storyteller, to a verbal visionary. Stories clarify the confusion of our life struggles and the chaos of daily life. (Lukaszewski, 1997)

● **EXAMPLE 11.2   Persuasive Speech**

MINING LAW OF 1872

Ben

1   Top of the World Arizona contains a rarity. It is home to a peaceful, lush tree
2 shaded canyon where wild boars still roam free. However in this sensitive area
3 about 70 miles from Phoenix a Canadian company called Cambior, wants to
4 mine for copper. According to the spring 2002 OnEarth, this company, also
5 responsible for a 300 million gallon cyanide spill in Guyana, plans 600 feet deep
6 pits covering a square mile with an additional square mile used to hold the soil
7 removed. Four hundred tons of sulfuric acid would be poured each day to
8 extract microscopic bits of ore and therefore exposed to the surrounding area.
9 Cambior expects to reap over $620 million worth of copper, while paying only
10 $1,700 for the public land and absolutely nothing in taxes depriving us of over
11 $49 million. The mine was approved and there was nothing the courts could do
12 because the development of this mine is protected by a powerful 130-year-
13 force. A federal lawyer defending the government's approval admitted, the proj-
14 ect "is so invasive to the surrounding forest that it would never be considered,
15 much less approved, were it not for the Mining Law of 1872." A mining law fact
16 sheet from the Mineral Policy Center Website last modified September 5, 2002
17 explains that the law "allows private companies to take valuable minerals,
18 including gold, silver and uranium, from public lands without payment of fed-
19 eral taxes,"' the same companies who were responsible for over half of all
20 reported toxic pollution in the U.S. in 2001. The Mining Law essentially requires
21 our government to give away $2–$4 billion in minerals every year and its com-
22 plete lack of environmental provisions has led to 12,000 miles of polluted rivers
23 in addition to 557,000 abandoned mines, the cleanup of which will cost Ameri-
24 can taxpayers $32–$72 billion. Because of this we need to, first, further examine
25 the problems with the Mining Law of 1872, next explore why this flawed legisla-
26 tion still exists, so that, finally, we can take the necessary steps to stop what the
27 *Christian Science Monitor* of May 22, 2002, contends is "one of the greatest tax-
28 payer heists in history."
29   The year was 1872; the Civil War was almost over, Strom Thurman attended
30 his junior prom and President Grant signed the 1872 mining legislation. He
31 intended to help small pick and shovel businesses of the time; however today
32 its outdated design gives miners an unreasonable amount of power which leads
33 to financial, environmental and cultural abuses. The current Mineral Policy web-
34 site explains that thanks to the Mining Law, anyone—including a foreign corpo-
35 ration—can buy American federally owned land containing hard rock minerals,
36 such as gold, copper, or silver, and pay less than $5 an acre and our govern-
37 ment has almost no ability to refuse. The law applies to over 270 million acres
38 of land which is almost one fourth of all land in the U.S. While obtaining the
39 land to mine so inexpensively might not seem that bad—consider this: unlike
40 any other similar industry, no taxes—federal or otherwise—are required on the
41 extracted hard rock minerals. The industry produced an estimated $22 billion
42 worth of valuable metals in the past 8 years alone—all untaxed. Oil and coal
43 miners pay from 8 to 12.5%—or, in this case, roughly $1.4 billion of what they
44 take, but these companies pay nothing. The Environmental News Service Wire
45 on May 21, explains this has resulted in "enormous taxpayer giveaways and lia-
46 bilities. Companies have received billions . . ." and then left us with cleanup bills
47 adding up to billions of our already limited tax dollars resulting in a continued
48 loss of funding for our schools and service industries such as fire-fighters and
49 police officers.

50   And unfortunately, what they leave behind is even worse. The *Bulletin's*
51 *Frontrunner* of May 22, 2002, argues, The Law's "loose construct has been
52 responsible for unchecked environmental damage." Once a company has
53 depleted a mine, many are simply abandoned without concern for damage left
54 behind. The roughly 500,000 abandoned mines, attests the July 23, 2002, *U.S.*
55 *Newswire*, are responsible for "the pollution of 40% of western watersheds; and
56 nearly 30 mine sites are currently on the EPA's superfund National Priority List
57 of the most contaminated sites in the nation." A Redding, California, mine is
58 home to "the world's worst and most acidic water ever found," according to the
59 Spring 2002 OnEarth. Rightfully said so; a steel shovel left in a puddle overnight
60 was found completely dissolved the next morning. The cleanup tab for that
61 mine alone adds up to $85 million. It's not surprising that the *Washington Post*
62 on June 3, 2002, states "according to the EPA, the mining industry is the
63 nation's top toxic polluter." And this pollution is not contained only to the spe-
64 cific mine sites. In 2000, 1.6 million pounds of cyanide, used in the extraction
65 of gold, were released into the environment, and has since found its way to
66 numerous rivers, streams, and even residential tap water. The July 23, 2002,
67 *U.S. Newswire* reports that mines will disturb over 10,000 acres of surrounding
68 areas. Acid drainage leads to toxic and potentially lethal carcinogenic contami-
69 nants such as arsenic leaking into our water sources. The Agency for Toxic Sub-
70 stances and Disease Registry website explains that cyanide can even pass
71 through soil into groundwater. Low exposure leads to breathing problems,
72 heart pains and vomiting, while in larger amounts can cause serious brain con-
73 ditions, comas, and even death.
74   And even land with cultural or religious significance may not be safe. In Cal-
75 ifornia an area containing ancient Indian trails, pictographs and prayer circles
76 sacred to the religion and culture of the Quechan Indian tribe may soon fall
77 victim to a 1,571 acre open pit gold mine explains the July 20, 2002, *San Diego*
78 *Union Tribune.* Senator Barbara Boxer of California has expressed that the mine
79 "would rip the heart out of the tribe's religious center" and compared it to
80 "making a parking lot out of the Notre Dame Cathedral in Paris, or building an
81 oil rig in . . . Westminster Abby." However if the mining law remains in power,
82 this situation may lead to yet another abandoned filthy mine site in addition to
83 another filthy rich mining company.
84   The Mining Law remains in power due to its innocent beginning, current
85 inadequate laws to combat it and the ability of the mining industry to escape
86 reform. In the tradition of the Homestead Act the mining law allowed settlers to
87 stake a claim on any piece of land where precious metals were found intending
88 to promote westward expansion. In 1976—recognizing that we were far beyond
89 the time in which walking onto a piece of land and claiming it as your own was
90 acceptable—the federal government repealed the Homestead Act. And the min-
91 ing Law? Well, this blight on the land is still with us.
92   Current environmental laws are no match for the jurisdiction of the mining
93 Law. The Mineral Policy Center website reports "all state statutes have major
94 gaps in environmental protection." Even the Clean Water Act, one of the tough-
95 est environmental laws in recent history, does not apply to or protect against
96 the pollution of the groundwater that modern mining often pollutes. Miners are
97 exempt from these laws because of the Mining Law. When the strongest of our
98 environmental laws no longer protects us, reform must be eminent. Sadly,
99 reform has been replaced with a series of failed attempts. The May 17, 2002,
100 *Charleston Gazette* notes that over its 130-year history, the Mining Law has
101 endured numerous reform efforts yet none achieved any results because, the
102 law has been "protected by some powerful forces." The *Washington Post* of
103 April 9, 2002, explains, "The industry would like to create the illusion that

104 they're reforming" by hiding behind lawmakers who can't reach a consensus.
105 "Negotiations . . . have always broken down over details," adds the May 17,
106 2002, *Seattle Post Intelligencer.* Disagreements over royalty percentages, aban-
107 doned mine responsibilities, and the government's ability to reject mines have
108 resulted in decades of debate, failed repeals, and absolutely no action. And the
109 mining industry is just fine with that—they continue to benefit most if the status
110 quo remains.
111   But the theft of America's money and resources cannot be allowed to con-
112 tinue. It's time for action to be taken by our government, our local communities,
113 and by us. Fortunately, some in power are starting to realize it. The *Mining*
114 *Journal* of June 21, 2002, states that a bill has been introduced to reform the
115 mining law once and for all. The bill hopes to "remove mining from the top of
116 the land hierarchy" by giving veto power back to the government. Proposals for
117 each new mine will be reviewed and can be revoked by relevant agencies. Fur-
118 thermore, the bill calls for an 8% royalty on extracted minerals; the same
119 required from coal miners, roughly $123 million a year. And finally, according to
120 the May 17, 2002, *Charleston Gazette* the law would "deny permits to mine
121 owners with a history of environmental pollution," "impose environmental
122 standards," and create an Abandoned Hardrock Mine Cleanup fund to help
123 reclaim abandoned mines. However, the bill should go a step further and make
124 the mining industry a significant part of the cleanup effort both financially and
125 manually. The mining industry will only change their ways if we give them a
126 reason to. And it's not asking a lot, says the May 13, 2002, *New York Times.* "It
127 is only asking the industry to follow the same rules that everyone else does."
128   However, until this legislation is passed, the mining industry has no reason
129 to reform. That is where we come in. There are things that our local govern-
130 ments and community organizations can do to offset the powerful mining
131 industry. The *Washington Post* of April 8, 2002, explains that there are, for
132 example, loopholes in the law that a few states have cleverly taken advantage
133 of. In Montana, an initiative to ban cyanide, which is necessary to leach out min-
134 erals from rock, was passed by voters. In Washington state, necessary water
135 permits were denied to a local mine, in effect "trumping the mining law."
136 Admittedly, both cases have been challenged in courts for years and these are
137 not permanent remedies, but they have kept mining grounded in the mean time
138 protecting our environment and billions of our tax dollars. In the long run, how-
139 ever, continued fights with many local governments may leave the industry no
140 choice but to sit down and negotiate.
141   Finally we must become involved ourselves by becoming more aware of
142 our government's actions surrounding our laws. For more information please
143 visit the mineral policy center website at www.purewater.org, home of the
144 Okanogan Highlands Bottling Company. For five dollars they will ship a half liter
145 of their political action bottled water. Cases are also available. Fifty percent of
146 the profits go to protecting watersheds by fighting the Mining Law of 1872.
147 They also propose an interesting way to make sure that a letter to your senator
148 or representative will not go unnoticed. Instead of throwing away that bottle,
149 apply an address label with a 57-cent stamp and send it to your congress-
150 person, with your letter inside. A sample letter is available on the website.
151   Today we have seen how the Mining Law of 1872 allows for the destruction
152 of our environment while making miners rich with our tax money. However, by
153 examining the problems with the Mining Law of 1872, and exploring why it still
154 exists, we were able to develop solutions to this destructive relic. Let's hope
155 that this ancient legislation sees its end before another beautiful and rare place
156 like Top of the World Arizona falls victim.

ACTIVITY 11.6

PROBLEM, CAUSE, SOLUTION

1. The speech in Example 11.2 is rich with support. It is scripted for a specific audience that expects extensive research and documentation. For some audiences, the documentation would overwhelm the message, in which case factual, verifiable material should stand undocumented. If any come into question in a question-and-answer session, the speaker should be able to cite the sources at that point. Another way to handle a rich background of sources is to project slides with key words or statistics with a source and date. Discuss other ways that documentation can be provided with a presentation.

2. Enlarge and copy the "Problem–Cause–Solution" illustration (Figure 11.4). Locate the arguments of Ben's speech and write the inclusive line numbers to indicate where to find each element.

SUMMARY

Persuasive presentations are essential for organizations. Some presentations are designed to persuade clients to accept the organization's proposals, and others promote ideas upward through an organization. Leading executives expound upon their visions and motivate employees. Crisis communication involves internal and external persuasion.

The numerous challenges for persuasion compel us to learn more about designing presentations for specific situations. Most persuasion takes place interpersonally through interactions, and even public speaking benefits from a dialogic perspective. Trust and credibility, dimensions of ethos and basic emotional intelligence, shape all persuasive efforts. Pathos embraces various psychological appeals. The emotional appeal of pathos makes the human connection through memorable, figurative, vibrant, and powerful language.

Logic, or logos, requires a claim or principal argument, evidence supporting the claim, and reasoning that connects claim and evidence. Two logical derivations are inductive and deductive thinking and rhetorical design. Inductive thinking derives a generalization from example and other evidence, or derives a conclusion on the basis of the facts presented. Deductive thinking takes a general principle and applies it to a specific instance, which clearly falls within the generalization. A problem–cause–solution structure gives a straightforward look at the places that a communicator can establish a thesis. It also provides a structure by which to analyze the substantiality and logic of a line of thought.

ACTIVITIES

1. **Presenting to Others:** Read "The Wow Project" by Tom Peters at www.fastcompany.com/online/24/wowproj.html
Find, create, and sell a "Wow Project" to the class or another appropriate community or college audience.

2. **Presenting to Others:** In pairs, select a debatable topic of policy. Share researched material with one another. Take opposite stances on the policy issue. Choose a logical presentation pattern that you decide is appropriate, given the topic and the class audience. Present a five- to seven-minute persuasive speech to the class on each stance.

3. **Journaling the Experience:** Map examples of inductive reasoning from "Everything I Thought I Knew about Leadership Is Wrong" (Meyerson, 1996) in *Fast Company,* issue 2, p. 71, or at www.fastcompany.com/online/02/meyerson.html To map, place the generalization in the center and draw lines to supporting evidence (satellites).

4. **Ethically Speaking:** Find or create examples of inductive and deductive reasoning errors. Point out where the errors take place.

5. **Technical Support:** From the Internet, cut and paste five statistical charts. Analyze each and comment on their persuasive use of statistical support and how responsibly they are used. *Hint:* Notice the scale used along axes to report performance of stocks, depending on the point being made. Or notice how items are grouped and categorized on pie graphs.

6. **Technical Support (advanced):** In Excel, create a spreadsheet with an attached interactive graph. Import the graph into PowerPoint. Demonstrate to the class how a change in data changes the graphic illustration.

7. **Team Work (two hours):** In newspapers and new magazines, find examples of logical fallacies. Collect your favorite examples to explain to the class in a 10-minute brief presentation.

Example: Inductive Presentation Pattern

- More than 20% of public high school students drop out of school.
- Sixty percent of high school graduates go to college, but 37% drop out by their sophomore year.
- Close to 50% of college freshmen must enroll in remedial classes.
- America has not budgeted the estimated $200 billion it would take to repair, refurbish, and expand schools to eliminate overcrowded, outdated schools.

Generalization: America's public high schools do not meet students' educational needs.

Example: Deductive Presentation Pattern

- All urban America's public high schools have a high special needs population.
- Thomas Jefferson High School is an urban public high school.

Conclusion: Therefore, Jefferson High School has a high special needs population.

FOR FURTHER READING

Taking Sides volumes are specific to topics, such as education, social issues, world political issues, and the like. Each subtopic is treated with two articles: one supporting the claim and the other refuting the claim. This is an excellent way to conceptualize the dominant issues on a topic. See, for instance, the volume on environmental issues:

Easton, T. A., & Goldfarb, T. D. (2003). *Taking sides: Clashing views on controversial environmental issues* (Rev. ed.). New York: McGraw-Hill/Dushkin.

For a variety of official material and data for persuasive speeches, try the government website www.firstgov.com.

Building Connections

PART **IV.**

The interpersonal and small group interactions in organizations are the elements composing the individual's experience of work and the organization's culture, successes, and failures. Chapters 12 and 13 prepare the entering employee for the competencies, configurations, and tasks most common for teams. Special emphasis is given to preparing and conducting meetings in Chapter 13. Chapter 14 explores constructive conversations, formal and informal communication, and the impact of words. Attention is given to distanced conversations conducted through technology and to sexual harassment. Chapter 15 is dedicated to managing the consuming effects of conflict. Chapter 16 leads readers through some of their first and most consequential conversations.

The significant problems we face cannot be solved at the same level of thinking we were at when we created them (Albert Schweitzer, in Covey, 1996).

Teams at Work

12

Coming to Terms: Small Groups and Teams

Team Processes in the Workplace

How Teams Span Boundaries

"Houston, we've had a problem." With these words, astronaut Jim Lovell alerted the assembled team at NASA's Houston Space Center to an unprecedented problem that had crippled his Apollo 13 spacecraft. While everyone on the ground worked to interpret the inexplicable words and data coming from the astronauts and on-board computers, the spacecraft's remaining oxygen supply was seeping into the vacuum of space. While the world held its breath on April 13, 1970, NASA, fixated on imminent tragedy, transformed the third moon-landing mission into a daunting race to save three lives.

Because the problem required more expertise and creativity than any one person had, instinct and practice threw NASA's team into action. NASA's group intelligence went on high alert. The location of this team? In space, aboard Apollo 13, *and* on the ground, in Houston. Its members? Everyone involved in the mission, from technicians and engineers to communications and public relations specialists. While small groups brainstormed spontaneously, task forces gathered specific information. A team worked with a collection of items replicating the ones the astronauts carried with them, and another team sweated it out in a simulator, experimenting with combinations in order to conserve enough battery power to return to earth. Astronauts fed ideas and information from space to Houston. Four days later, the damaged spaceship splashed down in the South Pacific; the lives of Jim Lovell, Jack Swigert, and

Fred Haise had been saved by one of the most dramatic examples of successful teamwork in modern history.[1]

On a somber note, 16 years later, on January 28, 1986, NASA exemplified the profound fallibility of teams. This time a group decided to launch the space shuttle *Challenger* despite launch temperatures that were too low for engineering tolerance. A crew of seven men and women lost their lives as the booster rocket's O-ring seals, too cold to seat properly, allowed hot exhaust gases to escape and ignite the primary fuel tank in a fireball whose televised image Americans will never forget. Nor will they forget the loss of lives in the *Columbia* shuttle upon reentry in 2003. This time, an investigative committee cited NASA's organizational culture—evidently flawed in its communication and processes—as a culprit. Pulling off the "impossible" and accomplishing the unthinkable had become a part of their organizational culture.

Teamwork is not usually as dramatic as these examples; nevertheless, teamwork is a "final frontier" in workplace communication. As Apollo 13 demonstrated, a team is more than the sum of its individuals, and at critical points, teams reach zones of creativity and energy that individuals seldom approach. Unfortunately, as in the *Challenger* and *Columbia* experiences, teams can succumb to group pressure and internal censorship, and even seasoned professionals can talk themselves into poor decisions.

Today's information and service economies place a high value on knowledge and critical thinking. Whereas the assembly line subdivided work into the smallest possible tasks, the new economy moves to reconnect the parts—and the new organization is based not on tasks and workers, but on projects and teams.

Whether you consider yourself a "team player" or the type who prefers to work alone, you can improve your ability to work on teams and collaborative projects by learning more about teams and group behavior (Tullar & Kaiser, 2000). Teamwork is a *learned* (and essential) set of skills. Great teams are not born, but made. This chapter provides a foundation by exploring the theory and application of small group communication.

OBJECTIVES

After studying the content of this chapter, you should be able to

- Define small groups, single-leader units, and teams
- Discuss what teams do
- Recognize and apply techniques commonly used by teams (team scripts), especially reflective thinking, problem solving, and brainstorming
- Recognize and function in supportive team roles
- Avoid unproductive and counterproductive team roles
- Discuss the competencies needed by teams
- Recognize several team configurations.

---

[1] This summary of the Apollo 13 mission is based on Andrew Chaikin's account. See Chaikin, A. (1994). *A man on the moon: The voyage of the Apollo astronauts.* New York: Viking.

CONTEMPORARY VOICES 12.1: SENGE

Most of us at one time or another have been part of a great "team," a group of people who functioned together in an extraordinary way—who trusted one another, who complemented each others' strengths and compensated for each others' limitations, who had common goals that were larger than individual goals, and who produced extraordinary results. . . . What they experienced was a learning organization. The team that became great didn't start off great—it learned how to produce extraordinary results. (Senge, 1994, p. 4)

● COMING TO TERMS: SMALL GROUPS AND TEAMS

Several kinds of *groups* are called *teams,* and sometimes the terms are used interchangeably. Research and terminology come from two different primary sources. The first strand comes from communications scholars, who have long studied small groups and teams; their work traditionally uses the term *small group communication.* The principles of small group communication are the basis for studying workplace teams, which leads us to the second strand of research, this time in organizational theory, which looks at *team behaviors,* such as focus and motivation. This section defines the broader category—small groups—and some terms labeling specific types, and then examines what makes highly productive teams special.

What Are the Characteristics of a Small Group?

The term *small group,* once informal and generic, has developed a more specific definition as researchers have elaborated on the nature and function of small groups. Small groups *must* communicate and connect to be considered small groups. People on their way to work don't become a small group just because they happen to share a bus ride. Individuals meld as a small group to the extent several characteristics are present: communication saturation, cohesiveness, purpose, location, member roles, accountability, processes, and endurance.

In a functioning small group, each member is communicating in some way with every other member. A small group is *communication saturated.*

Individuals in small groups interact *cohesively*—sticking together to shape the group. Groups with a strong sense of cohesion are tightly knit and assume roles quickly.

A small group is able to explain the *purpose* of their work—why it exists and what it is to accomplish. Location sometimes indicates purpose—compare, for instance, a formal boardroom and an office cubicle.

In functional groups, *members* assume various *roles,* some with official titles, such as technical lead, project manager, or recording secretary, and others in response to group needs, such as information provider and thought organizer.

Ideally, official work groups are held accountable for their decisions, outcomes, and products. (Accountability = responsibility + measurement + evaluation.) Accountability affects a team's identity. Without accountability, groups tend to become unfocused and dysfunctional.

Process is the "life" of a group, the way it exists and functions. The specific sequencing of events is *procedure,* but the larger picture that includes procedure, people, input, and output is *process.* Several models describe groups' processes. A popular one is Tuckman's (1965) resilient model of small group development, in which a group moves through five main phases:

1. *Forming* (getting together; identifying belonging and purpose)
2. *Storming* (trying out roles and behaviors, interjecting information and ideas, jockeying for position)
3. *Norming* (settling in on expected behaviors by group members and making their interactions "normal" for the group)
4. *Performing* (adjusting to and focusing on the task; producing an outcome)
5. *Adjourning* (bringing closure to a project; deciding upon follow-up actions, if any)[2]

Finally, frequency and longevity, or *endurance,* define a dimension of "group," that is, how often it gathers and how long it has existed as a group entity. In groups where the membership changes over time, the group entity takes precedence. For example, a *standing committee* changes membership ("Who's our representative from accounting for this year?"), but an *ad hoc committee* exists only for the length of the task ("Who's on the 2006 convention site committee?").

What Is Distinctive About Highly Productive Teams?

Not all small groups are teams. Although some people are assigned to a team, they are a "team" in name only. In a perfect world, an authentic, highly productive team is a group that excels qualitatively, functions cohesively, creates critical work processes, and includes its own leadership (Kinlaw, 1991, cited in Wilson, 2002). In the workplace—perfect or not—a team is expected to perform at a professional level and produce significant, measurable outcomes.

CONTEMPORARY VOICES 12.2: BILL RUSSELL ON THE BOSTON CELTICS

Senge uses a wonderful description of what it means to be on a team, as told by Bill Russell of the Boston Celtics:

> By design and by talent, [we] were a team of specialists, and like a team of specialists in any field, our performance depended both on individual excellence and on how well we worked together. . . . Off the court, most of us were oddballs by society's standards—not the kind of people who blend in with others or who tailor their personalities to match what's expected of them. (Russell & Branch, 1979, quoted in Senge, 1994, p. 233)

Critical team communication connects all members with one another and connects teams with other teams and management. It moves teams along designated paths to get results. Teams can be ideally characterized in several ways.

---

[2] The fifth step is the most forgotten step, probably because it doesn't rhyme with the other steps.

An exuberant team of female pilots celebrates setting a precedence of an all-female team.

Teams primarily exist to accomplish a *task,* and achieve an *outcome.* (Lipnack & Stamps, 1997). The team has a compelling purpose that exceeds the sum total of individual goals.

FOCUS ON OUTCOME

As advisory board to the Sawtooth Chamber of Commerce, your team's task is to attract new business without compromising the historic flavor of the turn-of-the-century mining community. The town is in a box canyon, with a road following the river on a flood plain. Some of the old mine is vacated, but potentially dangerous. The main street is lined with historic brick buildings, and there are two campgrounds on the river. Sawtooth has beautiful summers, and snow five months of the year. Several businesses are built around the ski industry, but Sawtooth is 87 miles from a commercial airport. Recently the State School of Mining has brought classes to the mine site and studied the geology of the area. Outline your team's proposal to develop Sawtooth.

ACTIVITY 12.1

Synergy is a creative, productive energy that comes from synchronizing a team toward a common goal. Synergy brings about shared outcomes and visions that exceed the sum of individual goals. *Group flow*—the ultimate in synergy—is when a group catches on fire and literally outdoes itself (Bennis & Biederman, 1997).

In flow, difficult tasks seem easy, even energizing. Others may call it "being in the zone." "Flow poses a neural paradox: We can be engaged in an exceptionally demanding task, and yet our brain is operating with a minimal level of activity or expenditure of energy" (Goleman, commenting on the neurology of flow, 1998, p. 107). Interestingly, people are in flow at work more often than during leisure time.

High *connectivity* produces interdependence. Ellis and Fisher (1994) suggest that in a group experiencing low levels of cohesiveness, productivity may be expected to be fairly low. Increasing levels of cohesiveness will increase productivity in task groups—up to a point (Evans & Dion, 1995; Kelly & Duran, 1985, in Cathcart & Samovar, 1992; Wilson, 2002, p. 243). After all, you don't have to be best friends with all your teammates.

In addition to individual accountability, the *team* is held *accountable* for its products and outcomes. If the team looks good, each member looks good, and the converse is true as well.

What are quantifiable measures of this team's competence? Is emotional intelligence part of what makes the team function?

Productive norms are the accepted "rules" and habits that govern a group and lead to productivity. "When all is said and done, the norms of a group help to determine whether it functions as a high-performing team or becomes simply a loose collection of people working together" (Katzenbach, 1997).

"Whatever the ground rules, people automatically sense them and tend to adjust how they behave accordingly. In other words, norms dictate what 'feels right' in a given situation, and so govern how people act" (Goleman, Boyatzis, & McKee, 2002).

Group norms lead to team identity, which becomes obvious in an increased use of collective pronouns (*we, us,* and *our,* rather than *I, me,* and *mine*); rituals, such as offering coffee; story telling about shared heroes and villains at work, politics, sports, etc. (one story triggers similar and often repeated stories among members); and fantasy themes (jokes and topics that share emotion among members) (Griffin, 1997).

What Is a Team's Life Cycle?

Norms create culture, and culture explains life cycle, as groups and teams evolve in recognizable stages (Thelen & Dickerman, 1949; Tuckman, 1965; Bales & Strodbeck, 1951; Schutz, 1958). Commonly, these phases appear as orientation, conflict, emergence, and reinforcement (Fisher, 1970, 1980; Ellis & Fisher, 1994; Poole & Roth, 1989).

During *orientation,* members meet one another and establish the reason for gathering, what they are to do, and how they are to function. They build trust and tentatively discuss tasks.

By the *conflict phase,* members perceive their status and roles. They are generally more open, assert more opinions, and polarize their stances. Conflict communication is normal in problem-solving groups and shouldn't be dreaded or avoided. This phase is necessary for task communication and process communication. Through conflict, you begin to identify the task issues that confront the group and clarify your own and others' roles. This clarification leads toward greater predictability, less uncertainty, and the establishment of group norms (Beebe & Masterson, 2002).

In the *emergence phase,* group language tends to become ambiguous and ambivalent, as members sense a need to settle differences and move toward consensus. Language choices communicate both agreement and tactful dissent. Members modify their attitudes and make conscious compromises in this stage.

Finally, consensus is recognized, and the *reinforcement phase* comes into being, wherein "members constantly and consistently express opinions favorable to the proposals and positively reinforce one another's favorable opinions with expressions of agreement and additional social support" (Ellis & Fisher, 1994, p. 160).

PHASE TALK FOR TEAM DEVELOPMENT

ACTIVITY
12.2

The Chamber of Commerce Tourism Committee of Wannabee, Wisconsin, sees a decline in dollars spent on tourism in their area. A dozen statements made during their meeting follow. Label the statements made during this problem-solving conference according to the phase in which they are most likely to occur.

_____ 1. "Does everyone know one another? Good. I've been thinking about this issue; perhaps this is just an off year for tourism."

_____ 2. "I think that other cities are doing a better job of showcasing their beautiful settings."

_____ 3. "I'm prone to agree with the earlier comment about tourism being off. Here are the numbers some of the hotel chains ran."

_____ 4. "Tourism is up in the rest of the state. So I don't think a general decline in tourism is our problem."

_____ 5. "You know, people of all ages like to hike and bike through the countryside."

_____ 6. "I don't think we should ruin our land with trails full of people."

_____ 7. "Yeah, I agree, and the wildlife may suffer."

_____ 8. "Could we designate protected areas for wildlife?"

_____ 9. "I'd rather limit trails to certain areas and not allow motors or engines of any sort."

_____ 10. "So, we agree that visitors would appreciate our natural setting, but we want to keep it beautiful. We need a consultant in parks and wildlife."

_____ 11. "Charging an access fee would offset the cost of park attendants."

_____ 12. "Then we agree to pursue hiring a consultant to develop a plan for trails and advise us in regard to a fee structure."

Is There "One Right Way" When Designing Groups?

Some work is done better when team members are assigned individual tasks, and other business works better in team collaboration. *The Wisdom of Teams* and *The Discipline of Teams* discuss the difference between "single-leader units" and "real teams," as labeled by Jon Katzenbach, who also insists that effective group work requires both single-leader unit and real-team performance.

Single-Leader Units

When a problem is divided into tasks and a group has one leader to coordinate the tasks, the group is a *single-leader unit.* In single-leader units, individual goals are combined into a group purpose, members assume specific tasks, and each person is held accountable for his or her task.

"Real Teams"

"Real teams," in Katzenbach's definition, "require close collaboration among two or more people working together in real time with access to multiple leaders" (Katzenbach & Smith, 2001). They share goals and take on tasks collectively.

Self-Directing and Leaderless Teams

Some organizations use single-leader units, and other organizations empower teams to direct themselves to get a task done (Wellins, Byham, & Wilson, 1991, cited in Adler & Elmhorst, 2002). These "leaderless" teams, a type of Katzenbach's "real teams," and are configured for a given project. The basic dynamics are that members share a vision, respect one another's abilities, and collaborate toward desired outcomes.

As more and more organizations eliminate layers of middle management, self-managing teams become necessary (Sims & Dean, 1985). Self-directing teams dissolve formal team hierarchy to manage themselves. For example, a team that includes an information technology architect, entity programmers, a client liaison, and a business analyst may function entirely on its own expertise, disregarding the diverse hierarchical positions of its members. If, by chance, a group does have a designated leader who isn't highly competent, a high amount of overall distributed group leadership can carry the essentially leaderless group to its goals (Barge & Hirokawa, 1989). Chang and Curtin (1999) researched managed teams that transformed themselves into self-directed ones and found they benefit from communication skills training.

The rest of the team world functions somewhere between "single leader" and "self-directing." In a start-up company, principals (the ones who started it up) usually function as a team-of-the-whole, but a small, proprietary business more often has a single-leader approach. In large organizations, teams even manage other teams.

TEAM PROCESSES IN THE WORKPLACE

A workplace team evolves over time. Its history is more like a soap opera than a 30-minute, got-it-all-solved sit-com. It even has expected roles, or scripts, and themes to play out. This section studies the functions and competencies of teams, the antagonists to their successes, and their productive genres.

What Do Teams Accomplish?

Reality @ WORK 12.1

TEAM SUCCESS AT WHOLE FOODS

Just walk into a Whole Foods supermarket, and you know it's not your mother's grocery store—gleaming stacks of produce, each apple stem and celery stalk facing in the same direction, youthful employees eagerly answering questions and offering samples, fact sheets about wheatgrass juice and residue-free beef, and posters celebrating sustainable agriculture are visible. Whole Foods Market, Inc., a radical experiment in democratic capitalism, is the largest natural-foods grocer in the United States. This countercultural food store has for about two decades used teams, with autonomy and their own slogans, in a highly profitable business model. Cofounder John Mackey says,

> We don't fit the stereotypes . . . "The team," not the hierarchy, is the defining unit of activity. Each of the 43 stores is an autonomous profit center composed of an average of 10 self-managed teams—produce, grocery, prepared foods, and so on—with designated leaders and clear performance targets. The team leaders in each store are a team; store leaders in each region are a team; the company's six regional presidents are a team. . . . Whole Foods is a social system. It's not a hierarchy. We don't have lots of rules handed down from headquarters in Austin. . . . Peer pressure substitutes for bureaucracy . . . [and] enlists loyalty in ways that bureaucracy doesn't.

> And catch this—only teams have the power to hire someone to a full-time position. Bonuses are directly tied to team performance (sales per labor hour), and teammates are really tough on new hires. Teams are expected to set ambitious goals, achieve them, and account for them in a bottom-line retail world. Not lacking in motivation, the teams have actually been asked to tone down their competitiveness. People were working too many hours.

Learning

Teams spend time learning about market demands, technological developments, demographic shifts, and the like. Examples of teams in action include teams performing triage at the World Trade Center site, researching anthrax, and piecing together an exploded space shuttle. Learning, then, involves such skills as statistical analysis, independent research, focus groups, and active research to advance the team's database (Pelosi & Sandifer, 2001).

CONTEMPORARY VOICES 12.3: TEAM LEARNING

Teams are the fundamental learning units in modern organization, so if they can't learn, the organization can't learn (Senge, 1994, p. 10). Although team learning involves individual abilities, team learning is a collective discipline. "Thus, it is meaningless to say that 'I,' as an individual, am mastering the discipline of team learning, just as it would be meaningless to say that 'I am mastering the practice of being a great jazz ensemble'" (Senge, 1994, p. 237).

Learning, however, comes at a price. "Everybody wants to build a learning organization, but nobody actually wants anyone to learn. Learning requires tolerating people who make mistakes. Learning requires tolerating inefficiency.

Learning requires tolerating failure. Learning requires letting people try things that they've never done before, things that they probably won't be very good at the first time around (Professor Jeffrey Pfeiffer of Stanford Graduate School of Business, quoted in Webber, 2000).

CEO Mackey of Whole Foods offers a more positive path: "In most companies management controls information and therefore controls people. By sharing information, we stay aligned to the vision of shared fate."

Learning accumulates intellectual capital, and teams decide to take on endeavors, to define courses of action, and to configure groups and processes.

Making Decisions

Decision making involves choosing among alternatives (Beebe & Masterson, 2000), and decisions set paths of action. Group decision making is slower than one person deciding, but on complex issues, groups produce higher-quality decisions. This may be because face-to-face interaction provides perspectives and prompts a more thorough exploration of the problem.

> There is a world of difference between making a decision alone and making a group decision. The unique chemistry of social interaction can distill the best that each member has to offer, creating a resonance of ideas and a synthesis of viewpoints. A different chemistry can stop the reaction and contaminate the product with erratic reasoning or low commitment. (Hirokawa & Poole, 1986, p. 15)

Many decisions are made during the process of problem solving, including decisions on solutions and their implementations.

Problem Solving

Teams are designed for solving problems. So what's a problem? A *problem* is an unsatisfactory situation that gets in the way of achieving one's goal. Problem solving eliminates, or at least manages, the obstacles that keep a group from achieving its goal. Most teams in business and industry are put together to solve problems (Beebe & Masterson, 2002). Don't think that "problem" automatically means distraught and upset people. Rather, a problem is a hurdle that must be logically overcome, and solving problems energizes and focuses real teams.

Developing Projects

Corporations such as IBM and EDS do most of their work through business units and teams. *Business units* are like internal companies networked to the rest of the organization, and *teams* are the functioning units within a business unit. Their projects grow out of the need to attract clients who want their problems solved.

Looking at a Whole Foods project, let's see how it produces its image. Whole Foods's "Declaration of Interdependence" proclaims a commitment to "diversity, community, and saving the planet." The company is an "upscale retailer with a hip twist—a marketing formula that's worked miracles for 'lifestyle' companies such as Ben & Jerry's, Starbucks, and The Body Shop" (Fishman, 1996). The company dedicates itself to the image by choosing products to match—no artificial colors, flavors, or preservatives; organic produce; and meat and seafood that are free of chemicals and hormones.

A project team or project manager must designate team tasks and individual tasks for teammates. The team tracks each task's progress on an identified timeline. Gantt charts of timelines give a description of each task, who will be responsible, the interim target dates, and the actual dates of completion. Project accountability grows out of such management constructs, measurable by progress on the chart.

Managing Change

As traditional organizations transform into team organizations, change agents come into play. A *change agent* manages change, much as a travel agent manages travel, and a real estate agent manages property sales. Very often teams themselves are the agents of change (Chang, 1999, 2002). Team projects during change include setting an organization's mission, planning for the long range, re-engineering through innovation, assessing change, and implementing new directions.

Presenting to Audiences

Professionals also speak as teams at conventions, present to schools and communities, and launch work programs. Sometimes a team is responsible for keeping other teams informed. Team presentations pool expertise in front of their audiences, a format that is more comfortable and secure for many presenters than individual public speaking.

ROUNDTABLE PRESENTATION

Panels often present information in a "roundtable" format, displaying equality in expertise and contributions. List the strengths and weaknesses in one such presentation, presented in *Discover,* Vol. 24, No. 9 (September 2003), available at www.discover.com/web_pick/index.html

ACTIVITY 12.3

What Strategies Do Teams Use?

Now that we've discussed what teams are and what they do, let's turn to techniques of how they go about accomplishing these feats. Become familiar with the formats—scripts, if you will—that teams commonly use. Prepare to step into these processes, whether in classrooms, boardrooms, or cubicles, because, in the future, you will.

Systematic Problem Solving

Whereas some researchers (Scott M. Poole, in particular) study and theorize how groups *really* solve problems, other researchers identify functions that members *should* perform (Hirokawa & Rost, 1992). Dr. Hirokawa says groups producing high-quality solutions must have five basic functions. *Vigilant thinkers* are essential to the process.[3] They are adept in analyzing, assessing,

---

[3] *Vigilant thinkers* maintain group performance over the five functions. They are mindful (as opposed to mindless) and monitor what the group is doing and how they are doing it.

and evaluating ideas, constantly monitoring the moment and the process. Hirokawa's five functions are as follows:

1. Develop an accurate understanding of the problem.
2. Develop requirements for an acceptable choice.
3. Develop many alternatives to solve the problem.
4. Assess the positive features of the alternatives or options to solving the problem.
5. Assess the negative features of the alternatives or options to solving the problem.[4]

• • • • TIPS   • • • • Special Forces in Open Systems • • • •

Dr. Kevin Barge (1994) identified functions to maximize team contributions in open systems (learning organizations):

1. Network with others.
2. Analyze information accurately.
3. Generate and evaluate solutions.
4. Manage relationships effectively by listening, using feedback, and applying negotiation skills.

• • •

Unstructured teams don't produce as well as structured ones (Gouran, Brown, & Henry, 1978; Putnam, 1979). John Dewey (1910) is credited with defining the steps of *reflective thinking.* Based on the scientific method, this agenda has become a standard format for small group problem solving (Bayless, 1967; Gouran, Hirokawa, Julian, & Leatham, 1993). Variations of the reflective thinking sequence depend on (1) the complexity of the problem, (2) the nature of the group, and (3) the amount of structure needed. Reflective thinking isn't for the faint of heart; it challenges our best thinking skills. Every employee should know how to apply the problem-solving steps.

Step One: Identify and Define the Problem   State the problem clearly. Say it aloud, and write it down. Make sure all team members agree on the definition of the problem and who is affected by it. Explicate the scope, extent, and constraints of the situation. Agree on what key terms mean.

Step Two: Establish Criteria for a Solution   Picture what a solution should and should not look like. That picture helps form and state standards and measurements by which to evaluate possible solutions. Groups who discuss criteria avert many conflicts and political battles. Hold on to the criteria to use later in the process. Do not propose solutions in this step.

---

[4]   All five functions are important, but numbers 1, 2, and 5 are the best predictors of quality group performance (Mullin, Salas, & Driskell, 1994).

Step Three: Analyze the Problem   Problem analysis can take a number of paths. Here are some very useful reasoning processes:

- Break a problem into its parts.
- Establish cause–effect associations.
- Describe symptoms or indicators of the problem.
- Research and learn about the topic.
- Determine how severe and how extensive the problem is.
- Discuss what is already being done and whether it is working.
- Discuss and list the obstacles to reaching the goal.

Step Four: Generate Solutions   Generate possible solutions and propose them to the team. Offer proposals tentatively and objectively, not argumentatively or defensively. Generating solutions often reveals inadequacies in the criteria, and the team can modify criteria as necessary (Brilhart, 1966, cited in Beebe & Masterson, 2002).

Step Five: Select the Best Solution or Best Combination of Solutions   Use previously established criteria to measure proposed solutions and narrow the number of options. Perhaps the problem being solved needs a combination of solutions, or perhaps this problem's solution will answer other business needs at the same time. Not all criteria have the same weight, and so the team may need to prioritize the criteria, preferably in the second step, but possibly here. If several proposals satisfy the criteria, the team may move to other ways to make a choice, such as listing advantages and disadvantages of each proposal, voting, or discussing each in more depth until the team comes to a consensus.

When academic classes work on problem-solving skills, class teams usually end their discussions at this point, since testing and implementation may not be practical. They can get feedback, a substitute for implementation, by asking experts to evaluate the group's solutions, by administering questionnaires, or by conducting a limited (pilot) experiment.

Step Six: Test and Implement the Solution   Carpenters say, "Measure twice, cut once." Testing and measuring is done to minimize or eliminate costly mistakes—mistakes such as public disdain, lives lost, and money and time wasted. The solution chosen is the one the team thinks has the best chance of working. That's their *hypothesis,* but it needs to be put to the test for validation or rejection. Teams test through computer simulations, limited marketing, questionnaires, focus groups, experiments, and pilot studies (Dendinger, 2000). Let the test fit the solution. (Lab rat testing, for instance, informs researchers about pharmaceutical drugs, but rats would be a poor proxy when testing a management style.)

The team decides when it's time to either implement the solution or go back to the drawing board to seek other possibilities. Problem-solving teams do not always have the responsibility of implementation. That can fall on another team.

ACTIVITY 12.4

TEAMS USING REFLECTIVE THINKING

Use reflective thinking steps for your team to design a college's core curriculum.

Form a team of 10 members, who are responsible for developing a college core curriculum. All students will be required to complete the core curriculum to graduate. The core curriculum should be exactly 45 semester hours. Assign 5 team members a major discipline or program to represent. The other 5 should represent professions and businesses in the community. Prepare by reading degree plans and interviewing people like the ones you will represent.

1. Journal the experience, including how closely the group followed the reflective thinking steps and which functions you observed.

2. In a panel discussion, present your core curriculum to the class. Explain the choices made by the team, and follow with an open forum.

Brainstorming

• • • • TIPS   • • • • The Brainstorming Equation • • • •

Creative ideation + Deferred judgment = Brainstorming   • • •

Teams are terrific at generating ideas for things like marketing campaigns. We know the concept of *group creative ideation* most commonly as *brainstorming,* a frequently used script for teams. Alex Osborne (1953) reported in *Applied Imagination* that separating idea generation from idea evaluation yields more and higher-quality ideas. Sometimes the same group will both generate and evaluate, but often another team does the evaluation. Training is necessary to develop fluid brainstormers, but once people know how, trained brainstormers produce more ideas and more outstanding ideas (in the top 5%) than the same number of people working independently. Guidelines for brainstorming are as follows:

• Think of as many ideas as possible. Push for quantity, not quality.

• Avoid criticism, verbally and nonverbally. Don't groan, roll your eyes, or use put-downs in response to others' ideas.

• "Freewheeling" is welcomed. The wilder the idea, the better. Off-the-wall ideas prompt others' creativity and freedom of expression.

• Combine and change. Combine two or more ideas or parts of ideas. Add, reduce, alter, and in other ways change contributed ideas.

If you are invited to a brainstorming meeting, pay attention to how uncritical and freewheeling the established participants are, before joining them. If you lead a brainstorming session, discourage critical comments, push for quantity, and enjoy the rush of wild ideas. Expect occasional low-productivity plateaus, but push through the tendency to give up, reminding the participants that the most original ideas are yet to come. A preordained time limit is motivating. If the team is not fluid, try some starter lines to get ideas moving:

- "What could we do if we had all the funding we wanted?"
- "What could we do if we could hire all the experts we want?"
- "What is your wildest solution?"
- "Let's play with that idea."

"Stoppers" discourage creativity, and "naysayers" block some of the best and most realistic solutions. Because, in brainstorming research, the last 20% of the ideas offered are judged to be the most profitable, it seems quantity *does* breed quality.

BRAINSTORMING

ACTIVITY
12.5

1. You are a photographer in the Northwest Territory who has accidentally been shipped 100,000 unboxed DVDs. The company suggests you get rid of them or use them in some way, rather than shipping them back. For five minutes, members *individually* should brainstorm ideas for using DVDs other than for playing movies at home. Assemble a team of five, post individuals' results for the team to study for five minutes, and group brainstorm ideas to add new ideas for five additional minutes.

   Evaluate your three best ideas, based on (1) creativity, (2) usefulness, and (3) cost.

2. Your team has been asked to present ideas for products made of Polartec fleece. Conduct background research on the product and the company before brainstorming new products.

3. Reconfigure teams. Your new team is a marketing team. Rank the top idea from another team, and brainstorm ideas for marketing it.

Quality Circles

Organizations that use *quality circles* (QC) train employees in their techniques, processes, and values. Total Quality Management and similar movements have been extensively developed and presented in books, websites, workshops, and classes.[5] We can only briefly introduce quality circle scripts, but you should become familiar with their terms and processes. In Total Quality Management organizations, teams continually review their processes and adjust to improve. In their discussions, they apply reflective thinking and can propose larger changes for supervisors to accept or reject.

> The quality circle is perhaps the clearest example of a participative management group. Quality circles evolved in Japanese firms through the efforts of an American consultant, Joseph Juran, who advocated participative decision making as a method of achieving quality control. In 1961 the editors of the Japanese magazine *Quality Control* took up this idea. They believed that

---

[5] See, for instance, Mary Walton's *The Demming Management Method* (New York: Dodd-Mead, 1986) and J. M. Juran's *Juran on Quality by Design* (New York: Simon & Schuster, 1992).

involving first-line supervisors in quality control would increase productivity. . . . Participative management groups became popular in Japan and, consequently, came to the attention of American business and industry (Hirokawa, 1982). Firms such as Lockheed Corporation, J. C. Penney, Uniroyal, General Motors, Firestone, Chrysler, Ampex, R. J. Reynolds, and Bendix instituted quality circles. (Wilson, 2002, pp. 85–86)

Quality circle members must have good communication skills, contribute to a supportive climate, be adequately assertive, and show a willingness to lead. Members should be stakeholders and shareholders in their organization's products. As evidence, organizational profits may be reflected in salaries and bonuses. Circles *must* have top-management support and experience management's overall openness to ideas, criticism, and change. A fundamental and observable axiom maintains that decisions should be made at the lowest possible level, the rationale being that solutions should come from those who are closest to the problem. Nurses, for instance, are on the front line of patient care and can see, firsthand, what's not working and imagine what might work. Decisions are made in the field.

Symposiums and Panel Discussions

Symposiums and panel discussions are good formats for section meetings at professionals' conventions. They distribute responsibility and are relatively easy to coordinate. At a *symposium,* each speaker has a set time to speak, and speakers divide topics into main points and sequence their remarks. A moderator introduces the speakers, previews the topic, and provides transitions. Facing the audience, panels sit in a horseshoe. Occasionally, when the room doesn't configure to a traditional symposium layout, speakers take turns speaking from a lectern. Classroom skills translate readily into business and professional practices. Teams presenting to clients often use a symposium format, and panel discussions allow practitioners to collaborate on problems and issues in an open meeting, where others can benefit.

Symposiums work well when issues are controversial, specialized, or need different areas of expertise or points of view. For instance, a group of students brought together a lawyer, a human resources manager, and an abuse counselor to present a symposium on sexual harassment. One student introduced the topic and told how her class had come to realize its importance. She also introduced speakers and made transitions after each 14-minute presentation. Another student moderated the lively question-and-answer session at the end, and a third student brought the symposium to a close, briefly thanking the speakers for specific contributions they had made that day.

A *panel discussion* is probably the better choice when a topic benefits from lively conversation among the presenters. A panel discussion typically engages three to five presenters in a focused conversation for the benefit of an audience. It is not a debate, where teams are expected to take sides on issues, although discussion can get lively. Instead, the group is eager for information and insights. Instead of dividing and conquering a topic, as is possible with a symposium, panel presenters cooperatively discuss each aspect of the topic.

A presentation typically lasts from 20 to 40 minutes before opening to the audience for questions and comments.

Always analyze audience, occasion, and purpose. You want to know whether the listeners expect overview or in-depth presentations. For some topics a question-and-answer period is where the real action lies. The context defines the participants' role.

• • • • Guidelines for Group Presentations and Panel Discussions • • • •   • • • • TIPS

Preparation

1. Decide on a team leader, select a topic, list two to five possible main points, and, in preliminary research, determine whether adequate material is available.

2. On their own, members gather information and keep a record of sources.

3. In the second meeting, summarize findings and rethink the main points. Finalize the choice of main points, but avoid scripting the presentation.

4. Each member should make a reference notebook, with dividers for each main point. Collect material on *every* main point. You can make notes from sources, photocopy pages, and include entire articles. Highlight key ideas, statistics, and quotes you want to remember to use. If one article covers more than one main point, cut and paste portions under different points. Make sure you keep documentation with each portion. Jot down your questions for the panel as they occur to you on a point.

5. The leader should prepare an introduction and conclusion and anticipate moderating questions following the presentation. The leader should introduce the members by name, interest the audience in the topic, and preview the main points. The conclusion should review the main points, make a closing statement, and open the floor for questions and comments from the audience.

Panel Discussion Presentation

1. Set up a table or desks in a semicircle, opened out to the audience. Name plates are helpful.

2. Following the introduction, the leader states the first main point and opens the floor to the panel for discussion. (Some have a member primed to contribute immediately. Beyond that, there should be no scripting of who says what when.) Members discuss research, add ideas to others' contributions, and ask follow-up questions. Individual contributions usually take one or two minutes. Leaders also contribute and participate during each main point, but focus on all members participating.

3. Suggestions for successful participation:

   a. Research each main point. Explanations, examples, statistics, and quotations support main points better than personal opinions. Use a well-organized notebook.

   b. Listen attentively and stay engaged.

   c. Use affirmation and transition: "I read that article and found this interesting fact to add," "I'd like to add another author's view," and "Did anyone find information on . . . ?"

   d. Credit authors and sources. Remember you are combining material to learn the truth.

e. Be assertive *and* considerate. Listen for times to add material. If you and another participant both begin speaking at the same time, take turns. If the leader starts to close a point too soon, you may interject, "Another thing before we move to the next point . . . ," but support the leader to use time well.

f. Balance your participation with that of other members. Be ready to speak, and discourage domination by any one person. Help members who are hesitant, make false starts, or get interrupted to get to speak.

g. Remember the audience. Speak loudly enough for everyone to hear. Remember that the audience has not studied this topic. Look out at the audience occasionally, but pay closest attention to other participants as they speak, since your behavior models audience attentiveness.

4. Respect the leader's responsibilities when, between points, he or she summarizes and transitions to the next point. The leader concludes the presentation.

5. As the leader fields audience questions, be ready to respond.

● ● ●

What Are the Ingredients for Team Competence?

Essential team competencies include knowledge, reasoning, creativity, application, and emotional intelligence (EI). A team benefits from varying views and expertise in ratio to the complexity of the problem and must collectively possess the skills to get a job done. Team competencies mustn't stop there, however. The personal intelligences (intrapersonal and interpersonal) are not icing on the cake—they are essential. A classic study of group IQ by Wendy Williams and Robert Sternberg at Yale University underscored the critical parts that interpersonal skills and group compatibility play in group performance. They discovered several other interesting facts: A team needed at least one high-IQ member to get good performance, and one contributor was insufficient unless the group had certain other qualities. Teammates who couldn't understand other people's feelings dragged a group under, and "eager beavers" overcontrolled, disallowing their teammates full participation (Goleman, 1998, p. 205).

So we find that not only individuals, but also groups, need all four sets of emotional intelligence: (1) self-awareness, (2) self-management, (3) social awareness, and (4) relationship management. Using Goleman's EI competency areas, this section first looks at what the individual brings to the group (self) and then at how the group interacts (with one another).

First, we need to be *aware* of our behaviors and *manage* them. We're usually better at seeing other people's problems than we are at recognizing our own. Well-conditioned teammates avoid using disruptive behaviors and solicit feedback to make sure they aren't doing so.

Self-centered roles fulfill personal desires at the expense of group needs (called "individual roles" by Benne and Sheats [1948, pp. 41–49]). We want to manage ourselves so that we don't slip into these roles, but we should recognize these behaviors in others, as well, because when a group yields to a dysfunctional member, it reinforces and escalates that member's behavior.

SELF-CENTERED ROLES

Reality
@ WORK
12.2

Abrams' tank	(Put-downs, theft, and greed.) Destroys status of other group members; takes credit for others' contributions. Blocks others' successes.
Attention hog	("Notice how wonderful I am. I assume everybody is here to hear what I think.") Egocentric. Seeks the spotlight by boasting. Exploits team time to tell personal feelings, thoughts, and observations.
Grumpy bear	(Negative and grumpy). Generally negative, stubborn, and disagreeable without apparent reason.
Pity partier	("Poor me.") Tries to evoke a sympathetic response from others and often expresses insecurity or feelings of low self-worth.
Goof-off	("This whole thing is a waste of my time.") Lacks involvement in the group's process, possibly becoming cynical, nonchalant, or lacking in enthusiasm.
Magician	("They'll never know what hit them.") Makes an effort to assert authority by manipulating members or dominating the group; may use flattery or assertive behavior to win attention.
Lobbyist	("Here's the deal.") Speaks for a special group or organization that best fits his or her biases.

Second, team awareness is a type of social awareness, one of the major components of emotional intelligence. Competent teams exist by design. By now, we understand that EI is not optional fluff to keep everyone happy. In fact, sometimes EI doesn't sound nice at all and confronts problems, but EI translates directly into team productivity and profitability.

Richard Chang (2002) tells us what a good team does:

- Clearly states its mission and goals
- Operates creatively
- Focuses on results
- Clarifies roles and responsibilities
- Is well organized
- Builds upon individual strengths
- Supports leadership and each other
- Develops team climate
- Resolves disagreements
- Communicates openly
- Makes objective decisions
- Evaluates its own effectiveness

These qualities make a good diagnostic list to keep teams functioning. As you read about outstanding teams in Reality @ Work 12.3, you will recognize emerging themes of emotional intelligence.

Reality @ WORK 12.3

FOOTBALL, HEART SURGERY, AND WINNING TEAMS

In a three-year study, Larson and LaFusto (1989) interviewed a wide range of teams. Championship football teams, a cardiac surgery team, the team that developed the IBM personal computer, and the presidential commission that studied the space shuttle *Challenger* disaster were among 75 outstanding teams studied. What they had in common were results-driven structures, standards of excellence, competent team members, collaborative climates, external support and recognition, and principled leadership. Quite distinctly, they had a strong team identity.

Self-awareness, self-regulation, motivation, and empathy are the founding members' skills that build team skills. With true teamwork all roles become *supporting* roles. Adaptive participants fill roles as needed, so a person may play a couple of roles on one team and very different roles on another.

Social awareness, a third part of Goleman's emotional intelligence, requires supportive roles, traditionally divided into task roles and maintenance roles. *Task roles* help teams do their jobs, and *maintenance roles* sustain group climates. We'll use the present progressive tense ("tasking" and "maintaining") for categories to emphasize that they are fluently acting (doing) team scripts. This textbook has updated and combined task names to make them more memorable, but it nods to the long-standing traditional categories delineated by Benne and Sheats (1948, pp. 41–49).

Tasking Roles

Architect	("Here's an idea.") Proposes new ideas or approaches to group problem solving, such as a different procedure for organizing the task.
Interviewer	("What do you think?" "Do we have data on that?") Asks for a clarification of the values and opinions expressed by other group members. Asks for clarification of suggestions; also asks for facts or other information that may help the group deal with the issues at hand.
Educator	("Research shows several facts.") Provides facts, examples, statistics, and other evidence that pertains to the problem the group is attempting to solve.
Tour Director	("Thus far, this is what we have done, here is where we are now, and that is where we are going.") Summarizes what has happened and keeps the group focused on the task at hand. Clarifies and notes relationships among the ideas and suggestions that have been provided by others.
Judge	("We seem to have adequate information to warrant that conclusion." "That's a good suggestion.") Makes an effort to evaluate the evidence and conclusions that the group suggests. Offers affirmation of values.
Stock broker	("This is exciting work—just the beginning—what more can we do?") Attempts to motivate and stimulate the group to greater productivity.

| Technician | ("I'll get those handouts to everybody.") Helps the group achieve its goal by performing necessary tasks such as distributing papers, setting up the room, or duplicating copies. |
| Historian | ("I've written down the solutions we have so far.") Writes down suggestions and ideas of others; makes a record of the group's progress. |

Maintaining Roles

Cheerleader	("Cool idea!") Offers praise, understanding, and acceptance of others' ideas and suggestions.
Diplomat	("Let's get along with one another." "What if we do it this way?") Mediates disagreements among group members. Attempts to resolve conflicts by trying to find an acceptable solution.
Emcee	("Let's hear what everyone thinks before we move on.") Encourages quieter members to participate and curbs lengthy contributors.
Pace setter	("This is good progress." "Let's see if we can complete this part today." "We are discussing actions before exploring the problem.") Helps to set standards and goals for the group; keeps records of the group's process and evaluates the group's procedures.
Choir member	("Fine with me.") Goes along with the suggestions and ideas of other group members; listens to discussions and decision making.

Ultimately, teams must interact with other teams intelligently. This last characteristic completes the fourth quadrant for an emotionally intelligent team. In an impressive study,[6] ten "star teams" of 150 self-managed teams yielded distinguishing qualities that included those documented by Chang (2002) as well as the qualities of open communication (even confronting underperforming teammates), self-awareness and self-confidence as a team, proactivity and a drive to improve, team flexibility, organizational awareness, and the ability to build bonds to other teams (Goleman, 1998, p. 220).

What Are Seven Contributors to Team Incompetence?

At least seven deadly sins interfere with teams' effectiveness, especially in EI's fourth quadrant, interaction with others. They include (1) too much conformity (Asch, 1952), (2) counterproductive cohesiveness (Mullin & Cooper, 1994), (3) social loafing (Comer, 1995; Karau & Williams, 1993), (4) self-serving political manipulation, (5) mismatched groups, (6) groupthink (Janis, 1982), and (7) risky shift (Myers, Murdoch, & Smith, 1970; Cartwright & Zander, 1968).

---

[6] GE, Abbott Laboratories, and Hoechst-Celanese (a German chemical company) requested identification of the competencies that characterize outstanding teams. In response, Vanessa Druket analyzed 150 self-managed teams at a plant run by Hoechst-Celanese.

With thought and imagination, you can readily realize how overconformity, overcohesiveness, and social loafing undermine a team, so we'll move to some multifaceted conformity and cohesiveness problems—groupthink and risky shift, along with political manipulation and inner team mismatches.

Political Manipulation

Egocentrism, greed, and power addiction expose the seamier side of office politics. Teams trying to make a good impression often take on more than they can handle and finish with a poorly developed product. An obsession with image undermines productive work, because employees spend far too much energy avoiding blame. The ladder of success tempts some teams to become stingy with their knowledge.

People make better decisions in groups than even the brightest can make individually, unless a few things happen. Research at Cambridge University showed that bickering, interpersonal rivalry, or plays for power compromised otherwise brilliant teams, which ultimately made bad decisions (Belbin, 1996, cited in Goleman, Boyatzis, & McKee, 2002, p. 173).

Mismatches and Personality Clashes

With the right blend, teams can crank out work in short order and much more smoothly than a team with one or more team members mismatched to the task or to the team.[7] Most of the time, increasing communication increases understanding and appreciation, but sometimes better understanding only escalates the conflict. That's when you find out for sure you don't like what's going on.

Another area where mismatching occurs is "basic personality attitude." Basic personality attitude is a fairly stable personality trait. Each person falls somewhere along a range from positive to negative in his or her attitude about life in general. People have temporary joy or sorrow outside their usual realm, but they return to their basic attitude time and time again. Misery does occasionally love company, and some people seem to thrive with fellow gripers, but in researching a variety of positive and negative combinations, only one pairing shows clear preferences. In short, positive people far prefer working with other positive people.

Groupthink: Cohesiveness Gone Awry

The same qualities that bring harmony, such as group cohesiveness and interdependence, can also distort a group's willingness to listen and to think critically. Irving Janis (1982) studied highly motivated teams that had historically significant failures, such as America's escalation of the Vietnam War and the American invasion of Cuba (the Bay of Pigs). Presidential cabinets and advisors during those tough times were bright and outspoken. It was puzzling that such

---

[7] By *mismatched,* we mean that members' personalities, skills, or abilities do not match the style and needs of the team.

disastrous decisions came from such competent teams. Even NASA's highly knowledgeable teams, trained to make quality decisions and celebrated for their triumphs, were devastated by disasters when they succumbed to the self-protective thinking of what Janis labeled *groupthink*.

> This situation [the explosion of the space shuttle *Challenger*] was the product of flawed decisions as much as it was a failure of technology. The pressures on the National Aeronautics and Space Administration (NASA) to launch a space shuttle at the earliest opportunity were intense, despite evidence that this course of action was inadvisable. A decision to delay the launch was undesirable from NASA's perspective because of the impact it would have on political and public support for the program. In contrast, a successful launch would have appeased the public and politicians alike, and would have amounted to another major achievement. NASA engineers claimed that pressure to launch was so intense that authorities routinely dismissed potentially lethal hazards as acceptable risks. (Whyte, 1989, cited in Tubbs, 2001, p. 237)

Groupthink (for simplicity, modified into three categories) causes teams to think and behave in several predictable ways.

Good Guys Win

- Illusion that the group is invulnerable: *We are invincible.* "We are Enron, mighty and powerful. Nothing can bring us down."
- Unquestioned belief in the moral goodness of the group, ignoring moral consequences of the decision: *We are the good guys.* "If we show good results on these lending institutions, the stock will go up, and everybody wins."
- Stereotyped views of other, "evil" groups: *They are the bad guys.* "Management is too busy winning and dining powerful clients to care about our needs." "Well, that idea came out of accounting; just ignore it."

United We Stand

- Group pressure to conform: *You're either with us or against us.* "You sound like one of them." "Aren't you going to vote like the rest of us?" "Come on. Join in."
- Illusion of unanimity: *We are of one mind, one voice.* "We move forward together and give a united front." "Don't mess with any of us." "We stick together."
- Self-censorship to avoid saying things the group doesn't agree with: *I hate to stick out like a sore thumb.* "I don't totally agree, but I'll keep this idea to myself."

Don't Want to Hear It

- Tendency to rationalize or discount negative information: *No big deal in the grand scheme of things.* "One pilot study showed dangerous side effects with our new drug, but it was conducted in a small clinic."
- "Mindguards" against threatening information: *Our minds are made up; don't confuse us with more facts.* "Our engineers told us that the O-rings

haven't been tested at these temperatures, but they are notoriously conservative."

Risky Shift

Risky shift, for better or worse, means that people are more likely to shift toward a more extreme decision when they function together than when they decide on their own. People get bolder as they discuss things with others. For example, no *one* person would have chosen the bolder marketing scheme, cutting-edge solution, or untested approach that the group chose *after* discussing it. Although risky shift implies a riskier choice, interestingly, a conservative group may shift to an even more conservative posture (Gammage, Carron, & Estabrooks, 2001). Instead of "Let's cut him back on the medication," it becomes, "Let's take him off any treatment." The shifts are more likely to occur when groups skip or take shortcuts in the reflective thinking steps.

HOW TEAMS SPAN BOUNDARIES

Many teams function across boundaries in time, space, and culture. If you're assigned to several teams, you'll soon notice that each team has its own culture. Teammates have a unique style of interaction, rhythm of work, patterns of dialogue, and logical strategies. Teams across oceans, moreover, complicate the group tenor with different nationalities, ways of doing business, and assumed roles. Outsourcing a project may mean "off-shoring" it for another national entity to do the work abroad.

Communicating across borders and oceans amplifies the diversity of teams. Lipnack and Stamps (1997, 2000) see the challenges of unconventional and diverse teams:

> By implication, traditional work means that people speak the same language and take their nonverbal cues from the same broader culture. Virtual teams break this traditional cultural boundary mold. When people occupy different places and come from different organizations, they can be certain that they will have to communicate across culture and custom with different languages. . . . Two people from different professional upbringings can have almost as much problem communicating as two people who grow up speaking English and Japanese. When teams go global, their language and culture issues clearly loom larger. . . . Not only is the workforce becoming more diverse, but the task requirements of complex work demand that a more diverse group of people work together, whether in traditional settings or in virtual teams. When people know they are at a distance—culturally and linguistically as well as spatially—they are more conscious of the need to be explicit and intentional about communication. (Lipnack & Stamps, 2000, pp. 18–19, 170)

Virtual Teams

"A virtual team is a group of people who work interdependently with a shared purpose across space, time, and organization boundaries using technology" (Lipnack

& Stamps, 2000). Virtual teams do not "go to the office." Each person works from his or her own location, perhaps at home, on the road, or in his or her private office. So you could say that virtual teams work in virtual offices, that is, offices that have no walls and in fact lack a physical location. Cyberspace offices buzz as documents shuttle by e-mail, phones ring for brainstorm sessions, and the CEO's weekly speech streams to monitors.

A team is virtual if it is located in different places *or* if it functions at different times. The usual picture sees virtual teams communicating by phone conferencing and teleconferencing and with voluminous e-mail on a quick-return basis. Like other project teams, virtual ones share documents, compare schedules, and conduct threaded discussions (Imperato, brief article, 2000). The most difficult experience to reproduce online is the face-to-face interaction that builds understanding and trust and takes place so naturally when everyone is located at the same place (Lipnack & Stamps, 2000). To accommodate, Pfizer, a pharmaceutical company, convenes teams face to face to build trust and connection before sending them to home locations to do their work virtually.

A VIRTUAL TEAM

Susan, Jessica, Anna, and Sarah are employed by a consulting group that applies information technology to business applications. The surprise is that the group has almost 200 employees, but no office. These employees function on virtual teams in a virtual office that claims cyberspace as its residence.*

So where do Susan, Sarah, Anna, and Jessica work? From Friday through Sunday they work from home, and most Mondays through Thursdays they are on site with clients, depending on requirements of their current projects. They meet with one another by e-mail and other virtual means to prepare bids for potential clients, to do research, and to solve problems. Anna recalls that at the beginning of one project, she was literally staring at a blank notebook and a computer screen. She e-mailed team members to find out their expertise on the project, then contacted human resources to do a search for other employees who had worked on similar projects. She followed the leads she was given, and continued with Internet research. Her attitude is, "The information is out there somewhere. I just have to find it and learn it." With a background in statistics and operations research, she is well educated to do just that.

"Pull out your teams' résumés, and learn other projects your team members have been on," Jessica adds. Until a project is assigned, these consultants do not know with whom they will work, nor where, nor the duration of that project. "You set out the goals for a five-week project. If your skills do not fit the project, no matter how much I want to work with you, you are not right for that project." But there is another benefit that is especially meaningful: "You have to switch teams to get to know the people in the organization." When asked about preferences in teammates, she replied, "Switching teams makes transparent how good you are. You have to prove yourself every time. Of course, in switching teams, you get to start over, but if someone is not functioning well on teams, they won't last."

Reality @ WORK 12.4

---

* At the time of this interview (personal communication, March 11, 2002), Susan, Jessica, and Sarah composed one team, and Anna was on a separate project at the same location. Anna met Jessica and Sarah face to face for the first time at this interview.

They agreed with the characteristics of outstanding teams we've discussed in this chapter and added a few others, along with advice:

- Be generous: Have an attitude of sharing.
- Be creative, spontaneous, and capable of brainstorming.
- Be approachable.
- Be accountable and responsible.
- Be flexible.
- Be supportive.

Mediated Teams

Mediated teams take advantage of different media for their communication. Global corporations such as DaimlerChrysler use Internet meetings as a way to reduce travel costs and "to produce the synergy that global mergers and acquisition promise" (Tullar & Kaiser, 2000; Ball, 1999). Even teams on location are probably "co-located"[8] part of the time and mediated when they cannot get together. In studies of the effects of audio conferencing, video conferencing, and other less tangible variables on 45 mediated decision-making teams, Yoo and Alavi (2001) concluded that the most important variable is how cohesive the group is. Productive mediated conferences, predictably, benefit from members' prior experience together, trust, and focus on a worthy task.

Group Support Systems (GSS) is an electronically mediated process to help groups exchange information and make decisions. It helps teams work over the Internet asynchronously (with one another but at different times, just like occurs with using e-mail). Groups trained in GSS, as compared with untrained groups, exhibit higher team participation, waste less time and energy, work together better, and make significantly more accurate judgments than untrained groups (Tullar & Kaiser, 2000; Benbasat & Lim, 1993).

In virtual offices, work is either synchronous or asynchronous, and sometimes both. *Synchronous* meetings occur as telephone and video conferencing, as audio-enabled Web meetings in virtual team rooms, or as interactive video. For audio conferences, participants at each location gather around a speakerphone. Video conferences require video cameras and monitors to utilize the channels of communication, whereby a signal is sent by satellite to monitors at the various locations (O'Hair, Freidrich, & Dixon, 2002). Document cameras make close-ups of pictures, documents, and three-dimensional objects visible. With them a person can manipulate an item, zoom in to point out details, and show other evidence on the spot. The organizations where you will work are very likely to have virtual conference rooms.

---

[8] Located in two or more places simultaneously.

Most often, mediated team communication uses *asynchronous* meetings. Conversation threads pick up and leave off at individuals' convenience. Likewise, discussion boards allow employees to post messages and leave responses at their convenience.

Cross-Functional and Cross-Organizational Teams

Cross-functional teams include participants from different departments or areas of expertise. A long-range planning team, in which all areas should provide input, and a project team consisting of an architect, a marketer, a product developer, and an engineer are a couple of examples of cross-functional teams.

Some teams function across organizational boundaries, for instance, a United Way task force composed of members from member agencies. To function, this type of team must come to understand its members' organizational cultural differences, their preconceived expectations, and their communication styles. No wonder a great deal of time is spent developing a process for a cross-organizational team to function before it can get to the business at hand. As you work in these environments, you'll recognize when organizations negotiate a shared process and when, instead, one becomes the "alpha" leader. An organization can either provide the operative process model or can show the broad capability to adjust to other models. "You really do need to do your homework if you're going to bring your teams online. Your job is to diffuse complexity" (Lipnack & Stamps, 1997, p. 163).

SUMMARY

Never before have teams been so essential to organizations. Small group characteristics are communication saturation, cohesiveness, purpose, location, member roles, accountability, processes, and endurance. Single-leader units operate under the direction of a leader who coordinates members' individual tasks to accomplish the team goal. Real teams share responsibility and accountability for accomplishing their goal. In the workplace, teams must perform at a professional level, with significant outcomes. They are task focused, synergistic, have productive norms, and develop through phases. Teams learn, solve problems, make decisions, develop projects, and facilitate organizational change. Teams use productive techniques such as systematic problem solving (reflective thinking), brainstorming, and quality circles, and teams present to clients, in the community, and at conventions.

Emotionally intelligent teams engage participants who are aware of the team as a whole and can interact appropriately with it. They can take on necessary task and maintenance roles for a team. These teams can function with teams outside their organization.

Good characteristics do not exclusively produce good results. When competent teams arrive at inane conclusions, often groupthink, office politics, and members who are mismatched to a team or a task are to blame.

Virtual, mediated, cross-functional, cross-organizational, and leaderless teams indicate how flexible today's workplace really is. Technology has prompted a boom in virtual teams, although communicating across borders and oceans amplifies diversity. ●

ACTIVITIES

1. **Journaling the Experience:** Journal the group activities you experience in this unit of study. Pay attention to the roles and behaviors of other group members.

2. **Team Work:** Briefly describe three groups you belong to, such as your extended family, a church or synagogue group, a friendship group, a sports team, and your shift at work. Each group should be fewer than 20 people. You may have a hundred family members get together for a reunion, but the cousins within three years of one another in age—about ten of them—may be "your group." As another example, you may feel very much a part of your church group, but the study class members are the ones you keep up with regularly.

3. **Presenting to Others:** In an informative panel discussion, present an environmental issue to the class.

4. **Team Work:** Your ship sank offshore of a remote, deserted island. You and your seven teammates are the survivors: John, a dentist; Herbert, a taxi driver; Joy, a civil engineer and mother; Phillip, Joy's two-month old son; Truitt, a marine biologist; Raul, a professional basketball player; and Cheri, an artist. Each team lists items saved from the ship and brought to the island with them on the life raft, not to exceed 100 pounds. Each team receives an items list by chance (could be their own). The survivors afloat come across the final living survivor, Blake, a college student, who weighs 150 pounds. The survivors must decide how to save Blake (assuming they want to) *and* live on the island for an undetermined amount of time.

5. **Technical Support:** As a team project, create a "driving safely" videotape to explain how to align the rear view and side mirrors for optimal visibility on most automobiles. Play the tapes for a panel to comment on their relative effectiveness.

6. **Technical Support:** Go beyond the chapter's limits, researching and summarizing, in two paragraphs, GSS and Delphi Techniques for group work.

7. **Technical Support:** Form a class team to explore teamwork-oriented sites, such as eRoom.net (www.eroom.net) and HotOffice (www.hotoffice.com). Report several features and available training.

8. **Ethically Speaking:** Read the article cited at the end of this paragraph, write a position paragraph agreeing that families should be present during pediatric resuscitation, gather in small groups, and read your paragraphs to one another. Discuss ethical dimensions of the article. What are the different perspectives of what is helpful? List the values upheld with each position. McGahey, P. R. (August 2002). Family presence during pediatric resuscitation: A focus on staff. *Critical Care Nurse,* pp. 29–34.

FOR FURTHER READING

Buckinghom, M., & Coffman, C. (1999). *First, break all the rules: What the world's greatest managers do differently.* New York: Simon & Schuster.

Katzenbach, J. R. (1997). *Teams at the top.* Boston: Harvard Business School Press.

Katzenbach, J. R., & Smith, D. K. (2003). *The wisdom of teams: Creating the high-performance organization.* New York: HarperBusiness.

Lipnack, J., & Stamps, J. (1997). *Virtual teams: Reaching across space, time, and organizations with technology.* New York: John Wiley & Sons.

McDermott, L. C., Brawley, N., & Waite, W. W. (1999). *World class teams: Working across borders.* New York: John Wiley & Sons. (The authors draw from their experience with Pfizer, Colgate, AT&T, Coopers & Lybrand, and Motorola to give a hands-on guide for developing, launching, leading, and evaluating world-class teams.)

An excellent tutorial site is http://www.vta.spcomm.uiuc.edu/.

Despite the evidence to the contrary—including the fact that Michelangelo worked with a group of 16 to paint the ceiling of the Sistine Chapel—we still tend to think of achievement in terms of the Great Man or the Great Woman, instead of the Great Group. (Bennis, 1997)

Communication in Leadership

13

Practical Leadership for Workplace Teams

Leading Meetings

Problem-Solving Skills Applications

Power in Organizations

Standpoints on Leadership

I t's hard to think of teams as leaders, but perhaps the vision is changing. In Washington, D.C., the Korean War veterans' memorial honors Korean War veterans with life-size, bronze figures advancing in the field, and the Vietnam Memorial Wall displays a list instead of solo statues. Leadership ebbs and flows not only with a designated leader, but also among members of a team.

With more than 40% of U.S. employees working in self-managing teams (Ramsay, 1999), no one is exempt from leadership roles in the workplace. The questions are "When will your leadership be needed?" and "How competently and ethically will you lead?" Recently hired college graduates are astonished to find themselves leading teams within weeks of starting a job. It only makes sense to study those skills and concepts that will equip you to fill roles alongside or within a team. Furthermore, no matter whom you lead or how you do it, you are also being led and should wisely interact with different types of leaders.

This chapter follows in a logical sequence from the previous chapter and begins with leadership practices and how to lead meetings. With such practical matters in hand, it turns to principles and types of power and concludes with an overview of major theories. The motivations for learning this material are forthright—we want to get along with our bosses, we want to competently lead others; and we want to maintain ethical standards throughout.

OBJECTIVES
After studying the content of this chapter, you should be able to

- Recognize the types of teams and ways to lead within them
- Differentiate between defensive and supportive climates
- Conduct productive meetings
- Analyze a working relationship in terms of power
- Recognize perspectives on leadership
- Lead ethically

 PRACTICAL LEADERSHIP FOR WORKPLACE TEAMS

Inexperienced professionals are left to sink or swim in some of their first leadership roles, especially in leading teams and conducting meetings. In new roles, some people manage projects and meetings, but fail to *lead* people. The act of *managing* is tied to a position of authority (manager). Managers operate in a management system in which they, too, are managed. Managers manage tasks, human resources, and units. Some managers are good leaders, and some are not.

Conversely, some leaders are good managers, and some are not. *Leading,* in comparison to managing, is "a social phenomenon that emerges as a result of interaction" among all group members (Hirokawa & Poole, 1986, p. 212). True leaders encourage people to interact and progress toward a shared goal. People follow their lead largely because of how they feel about the leader.

A manager is in a position to direct personnel and may also be a leader, but leadership means more than management. Bennis and Nanus (1985) say, "Managers do things right, leaders do things the right way" (p. 3). Through charisma and communication skills, leaders mediate between their groups and an overall environment. For instance, Winston Churchill had legitimate power as the prime minister to meet with foreign leaders, but by his personality and unique combination of abilities, he became an international leader of his time. Even in classrooms, leaders emerge among peers and influence classes' climates and interactions.

Cross-Functional Teams

Typically, *cross-functional teams* bring together talent from different areas to prepare client proposals, design new products, create organizational infrastructure, and otherwise address broader, more generalized issues. Leaders of such teams need skills in negotiation and eliciting team cooperation. Team members remain answerable to their primary areas while working under the leadership of the cross-functional project manager. Even when communicating in English, teammates speak different "languages" due to nationalities, disciplines, vested interests, or businesses. For instance, an accountant, an engineer, a systems architect, and members from marketing and human resources on one team will speak from different backgrounds and employment.

When the core business depends on teams, managers assign employees to multiple projects on a planning matrix to coordinate human resources. Some employees are assigned to a proposal project for the duration, and other employees—functioning as boundary spanners—are assigned percentages of their work time on more than one project across departments, projects, or organizations.

Proposal Teams

New employees may soon find themselves designated as proposal managers. As novices, they have not developed networks (within the organization or with other organizations), they hold limited authority, and they haven't established their expertise. They pull up everything they can remember from college courses, request advice from their own managers, pay close attention to messages from all directions, and communicate very carefully, while pressured by deadlines. Reality @ Work 13.1 captures this type of experience.

JOURNALING INITIAL EXPERIENCES

Reality @ WORK 13.1

Justin signed a contract with E-Technical Corporation (ETC) one month after receiving his B.S. in Management Information Systems. With only a vague notion of what his job would be like, he felt like a freshman all over again. As was his habit, he kept a journal, having found the process helpful in keeping a realistic perspective and working through the emotions of events. Read journal excerpts from his first weeks.

Week 1: Introduced to my human resource manager, Janice. She will keep up with me and my paperwork, it seems (wish I had someone to do that in college!). Signed insurance, security, and other official forms. My mentor is Debbie—seemed nice, knew almost everyone. I'm on a proposal team (manager: Ken, six months out of college). I asked how I could help, and Ken told me to just watch, and I'd catch on. So, I observed, listened as others made decisions, and, by the end of the week, dug in and wrote 20 hours of code. (Why had they manipulated an old program, instead of updating systemwide? Oh, well, I'm just the freshman here.)

Week 2: Assigned to work on hot new project in Miami (always wanted to go to Miami). Can't believe my luck! Great learning opportunity. Left my "old" team after one week. Teamwork makes so much sense at ETC. I'm loving work—totally happening! Everyone gets along great—even with a dork named Maraul. What planet beamed him in? Still haven't seen much of Miami—probably just a bunch of sand and bikinis.

Argh! Made a major error and slowed up the team. Feel terrible, heard a couple of groans and, thankfully, a few laughs, but no one griped. Flew home Thurs. evening. Cleared e-mail at office Friday. Played basketball after work with some of the guys. Studied a new programming language some, over the weekend.

Week 3: Back in the office and spending 20% of my time writing code for another team, while finishing up the proposal for the Miami client. I feel as if I've been at ETC half my life. I must say, it's really interesting to interact with a creative, diverse team. My proposal team has systems analysts, programmers, an accountant, a design engineer, and personnel from marketing.

Week 4: We present our proposal to a potential client Thursday. Sure glad I gave presentations in speech communication class. I really want to do a good job Thursday.

Good grief! Now I'm assigned to another start-up proposal for 50% of my time. Talk about fragmented—I'm having an identity crisis! I can't let the proposal presentation get pushed to the back. There's no place to hide in front of your team, other managers, and potential clients.

Successful proposal presentation—PowerPoint, flowcharts, and all. By the way, Maraul saved the day more than once. I underestimated how sharp he is. Maybe I'm the one from another planet. I'm still amazed that a major corporation like ETC trusts us to meet directly with clients and develop proposals. Celebrated completing the proposal after work on Friday.

Week 5: Had lunch with Debbie, my mentor. She told me my manager said good things about me. Seems project managers do a lot of talking about who works well with a team and cranks out the work. I liked hearing Debbie say she heard I had "caught on quickly" and "handled the presentation like a pro." Do a good job, and they are competing to get you on their teams. The better the project, the better the bonus pay.

Week 6: Debbie must have mentioned that I am studying a program language on weekends—now I'm assigned to a team using it. This team has more experience with proposals than most—pretty impressive, actually. Seems they are working up a proposal for a porcelain plant in Dresden, Germany, for managing worldwide orders and billing. We sent three of our team to Dresden, and we conference online much of the time. I can't believe they are paying me to have so much fun.

Weeks 7–9: Haven't had much time to write in my journal. We've reached three benchmarks and been checked off by the "red team" within a day of schedule. (Of course, we worked all one weekend to reach one of those goals.)

Week 10: The project manager told us to go home Monday afternoon, because of all the weekend work, but I had another meeting and stayed anyway.

It's Tuesday, and they have lost their minds! I've been assigned to manage a proposal team. First, I need to check with Janice in HR to see how much of my time is still assigned to the Dresden project.

Successful team leaders challenge the group with fresh facts and use positive feedback, recognition, and rewards extensively (Katzenbach & Smith, 1993). A 10-year case study of teams (in this case, for writing aerospace proposals) revealed other effective practices to adopt when proposals and projects are your job (Kent-Drury, 2000):

1. *Multilevel tracking to produce a consistently successful product.* Become very familiar with the organization's system for planning, tracking, and allotting time and resources. Establish benchmarks, checkpoints, and feedback loops to yield higher quality than would a single end goal.[1]

2. *Effective negotiation of accountability and responsibility.* Successful managers cooperate, negotiate, and compromise with their teammates. Status reports are more effective when individuals are apparent (not transparent) to upper management. Managers make "rounds" to check each person's progress and respond to problems. Reward prompt completion, and keep people informed of incomplete tasks to boost efforts—nobody likes to be the one blocking completion.

3. *Neutral work space dedicated by the organization to the proposal team's use.* With so much done in cubicles, teams make good use of controlled-access bullpens. These designated and centralized spaces allow a degree of security for clients' products, and the high-profile activity of the bullpen creates a positive work climate.

WHEN LEADERS MAKE TEAMS SICK

"If teams are the cure, what's the disease?" quips Mark Fischetti (1998, p. 170), who describes five insidious maladies, hoping leaders won't succumb.

1. *Collective amnesia* is the fault of senior executives who appoint a team without asking whether the project needed a team in the first place.

2. *Group myopia* comes from a deficiency of clear, inspiring goals.

3. *Leadership phobia* occurs when a leader doesn't want to lead. Clinical symptoms include poor decision-making skills and a perception that the price of failing is too great.

4. *Chronic cantankerousness* is when every item becomes a quarrel. By the time members have argued about where to hold the meeting and who will write it up, their moods are ripe for all-out infighting.

5. *Losing life support* kills teams who lose funding, equipment, information, and space to operate.

Reality @ WORK 13.2

---

[1] *Benchmarks* are interim points of accomplishment at a given level of quality. Each benchmark is an identifiable goal along the project time line. *Checkpoints* provide item-by-item reviews of completed tasks on the time line. *Feedback loops* are open channels of communication to management and teammates. They avoid delays in getting messages to those who need to provide supplies, incorporate changes, and solve related problems.

Climate Control

Generated in bullpens, spread among cubicles, and leaking from executive offices, *group climate* is palpable when you walk in the door. Studies of group attitudes and climate show the following:

- Positive people have a way of finding one another when thrust into a group, perhaps because emotions and attitudes "leak" even when participants try to hide them (Ekman, 1982, 1992).
- A morose pessimist on teams, even if very knowledgeable, endangers team energy and momentum.
- People with an upbeat attitude are more likely to be satisfied with the team, and with their own influence, when the team also has a positive outlook. Managers are more likely to also positively label the team.
- Researchers suggest that teams with similar positive attitudes are prone to act as a team, instead of a group of individuals, and exhibit better performance than bitter or skeptical teams.
- Healthy, confident teams characteristically seek out positive directions to move (Barsade, Ward, Turner, & Sonnenfeld, 2000).

Supportive climates are typically positive, productive, and desirable, as opposed to defensive climates, which are generally negative, counterproductive, and undesirable, with a few exceptions. Defensive behavior seems appropriate during interviews, legal proceedings, and arbitrations. Long-term productivity must have supportive climates and must offset defensive ones. Dr. Jack Gibb (1961) observed behaviors characteristic of each type of climate, considering defensive climates generally counterproductive. Helpfully, Gibb categorizes contrasting defensive and supportive factors, as shown in Table 13.1.

One of the best ways to develop sensitivity to defensive behaviors and substitute supportive behaviors is to practice in hypothetical scenarios, as in the next activity.

●
**ACTIVITY
13.1**

COMMUNICATION CLIMATES

Mark received a memo from Don (vice president in charge of acquisitions of Concept VII) to attend a meeting to "decide whether to submit a bid to do an outsource project for Mountain Starre." As manager of human resources responsible for staffing, Mark knew that they were tightly staffed for the next six months, due to three unexpected projects. He also recalled that the CEOs of Concept VII and Mountain Starre had golfed recently.

In preparation, Mark called together several project managers and technical leads to collect thoughts on the potential project. They wanted Mountain Starre as a client but couldn't spare anyone. Another manager asked what resources Mountain Starre could contribute. Two technical leads warned Mark that the project might be a no-win situation because, from what they had heard through the grapevine, Mountain Starre's RFP was to interface three businesses with incompatible data formats. They would need to configure the other businesses or design three separate products for each. Mark felt better prepared for Don's meeting, but knew these weren't all welcomed messages.

TABLE 13.1 • Defensive and Supportive Behavior

Defensive	Supportive
Evaluative: Judging persons or their ideas or behaviors. "You did what? You know that's against policy."	*Descriptive:* Reports sense data and factual information; seeks information. "A customer complained about an item, and a new clerk refunded her purchase."
Control: Seeks to take away others' perceptions of choices. "That's irrelevant." "Hire three people before next week."	*Problem orientation:* Focuses on aspects of problems and approaches for solutions. "How many people short are you in this department?"
Strategy: Manipulative plotting or political moves to "win." "Why don't you attend the department meeting, and I'll go to the trade show?"	*Spontaneity:* Unfiltered responses true to the thoughts and feelings of the moment. "I would love to go to the trade show. Wouldn't you?"
Neutrality: Noncommittal or apathetic, failing to state one's position. "Thanks for putting thought into this. I need to get others' input."	*Empathy:* Feeling with others and responding sensitively and helpfully. "You must be frustrated by all the delays."
Superiority: Perceived imbalanced worthiness and abilities, snobbishness. "I'll take care of that issue, so it will be done right."	*Equality:* Valuing all members for their unique perspectives, knowledge, and ideas. "We have three interesting ideas given so far. Anyone want to add to this?"
Certainty: Dogmatism, refusal to entertain other points of view, the final authority of self. "My mind's made up; don't confuse me with the facts."	*Provisionalism:* Secure in understanding other perspectives; accept new information for evaluation; uses expressions such as "in my opinion" and "as far as I know."

Don opened the meeting, "We have an exciting opportunity to outsource for Mountain Starre with a product that could open a new service line for us. So let's discuss it. We'll just go around the table here and give everyone a chance to make comments." Marketing saw this as a great opportunity, and accounting didn't anticipate any complications with the new account, but then some skepticism arose:

CTO (Chief Technical Officer):   This would be quite a challenge. [lengthy technical explanation] I think it is more involved than Mountain Starre realizes.

Don: If anybody has the expertise to do this job, we do. I'm sure nobody wants to see this account go to a competitor.

CTO: But what if we can't do it in their time frame? What if we fail to deliver?

Don: Write it up in the bid for the job, but be reasonable.

CTO: It will be a steep learning curve, and that takes time they won't want to pay for.

Don: Are you saying your people can't do it?

CTO (warily):   I'm just saying it's complicated, time consuming, and expensive.

Don: Let's go to you, Mark. What do you have to say?

Meaningful, well-planned meetings are more likely to produce high participation and ownership and low resentment levels.

1. *What has shaped the communication climate to this point in the meeting?*
2. *What seems to be Don's agenda? Is he likely to take "no" for an answer?*
3. *If you were Mark, what would you say?*

Work teams have meetings that range from those called on-the-spot to brainstorm a problem to those that carry a level of formality and require planning. The next section examines the skills involved in leading these meetings.

LEADING MEETINGS

Efficient, effective meetings are rooted in discipline and effort on the part of meeting initiators, managers, and participants alike. Most business people play all three of these roles over the course of a year—and sometimes within a day. (Carlozzi, 1999)

Employees are in meetings nearly half the work day, and they don't want their time wasted. Employees at 15 corporations listed on a pocket recorder what they were doing at work at 20-minute intervals. "An analysis of almost 90,000 working days showed that an impressive 46 percent of the time was spent in meetings of one sort or another" (Coleman, 1983, quoted in Adler & Elmhorst, 2002, p. 276). The way you run a meeting displays an apparent level of professional competency. "If you master meeting management, you will gain a reputation as someone who is organized and knows how to get things done. Fail to run a good meeting, and people won't want to attend your meetings or trust your project management skills" (Bredin, 2000). This section provides an organized approach to preparing for meetings, leading a meeting, and following up afterward. (You may want to bookmark these pages for future employment use.)

Clarify

Be sure you know what the meeting is about before you commit others' time to it. When matters are clear to you, you are ready to inform others about the meeting.

- *Why are you meeting?*
- *Who will be attending, and why?*
- *Where are you meeting?*
- *When are you meeting?*

• • • • **Deciding Who Attends** • • • •   • • • • **TIPS**

- If you anticipate issue conflicts and are at liberty to select participants, consider including participants who are willing to articulate different perspectives.
- Overlapping areas of expertise and interests may help trim the size of a group.
- Intense decision making and problem solving may bog down with more than 8 to 10 participants (Grensing-Pophal, 1999).

• • •

Notify

Make someone responsible for notifying participants and arrangement staff or notify them yourself, in writing (mailed or e-mailed), and request confirmation. For a pressing, last-minute issue, phone them: "Our client called with several issues this morning [purpose] and asked for a 24-hour turnaround [justifying short notice]. The team [participants] is meeting at ten o'clock [time] this morning [date] in Conference Area B [place]. Can you attend? [request confirmation]. See you in 30 minutes [affirm confirmation and restate the time]. Bring your interface design ideas and sketches [materials to bring]."

Arrangements vary, depending on the site, the size and resources of your organization, those attending, the distances participants must travel, and how extensively organizations are involved.

1. Contact appropriate location staff to ascertain that the facility is available for the time you plan.
2. Contact participants, giving as much notice as possible. Use the checklist in Figure 13.1.
3. List and follow up on contacts for equipment, refreshments, and other physical arrangements. For lengthy meetings, locate smoking areas and restrooms. Know whom to contact for equipment and emergencies. Assign people to tasks. Prepare nametags or place cards, if helpful. On the meeting day, contact the local arrangements staff and check the meeting room.

Become Familiar with *Robert's Rules of Order*

Leaders largely depend on meeting protocol to guide them through treacherous moments. The definitive script for parliamentary procedure is *Robert's Rules of Order,* used extensively in large and small meetings, including the U.S. Senate, college boards of trustees' meetings, student governments, and, of course, the English Parliament (should you happen to be there). Almost everyone is familiar with it, but leaders especially appreciate the orderliness and civility built into the system. Review the steps of conducting meetings by

√ Meeting objectives (results-oriented, specific, clearly stated, and realistic)

√ Team or group to convene (include individuals' titles and affiliations if participants will not know one another—for example, "George Wilson, Chair of Emergency Response Committee; Capt. Russell Analusa, City Police Department; Glen Macik, Executive Vice President, Charity Hospital")

√ Day and date ("Tuesday, February 7, 2006")

√ Time ("10:00 A.M.–2:00 P.M.") and special provisions ("Lunch provided at noon" or "List of nearby restaurants for lunch break from noon until 1:00 P.M.")

√ Place (map to building, if needed; parking, floor and room number or name; equipment available at site or by request, with form for request included)

√ Travel information, if applicable (flight, shuttle, accommodations)

√ Agenda (jot reminders on individuals' agendas, if they have meeting responsibilities)

Robert's Rules. You can find a number of helpful resources online, including the following:

National Association of Parliamentarians, www.parliamentarians.org/parlipro.htm (provides a sample meeting agenda and how to present various motions)

Survival Tips for Parliamentary Procedure, www.calweb.com/~laredo/cuesta5.htm

Robert's Rules of Order Revised, www.constitution.org/rror/rror—00.htm

ACTIVITY 13.2

PARLIAMENTARY PROCEDURE

In teams of three or four, review parliamentary procedure to answer the following questions.

1. *What should you do if you notice an error in the minutes from the previous meeting? What if someone presents an error, but suggests something else erroneous?*

2. *Is unfinished business the same thing as old business? Which term is correct?*

3. *When do standing committees give their reports?*

4. *How do you address the group?*

5. *How do you introduce a new topic?*

6. *Which is correct to say: "I make a motion" or "I move"?*

7. *What if someone amends your motion, and you don't like it? What should the chair do? What can you do?*

8. *Why are motions seconded? How many times can a motion be seconded?*

9. *When should a leader elect to use parliamentary procedure?*

Prepare an Agenda for a Meaningful Business Meeting

The agenda should be available to everyone attending, both by being sent earlier and being provided again at the meeting. A meeting agenda by parliamentary procedures lists standard items: (1) opening the meeting and introductions, (2) reading of the minutes, (3) reports, (4) unfinished business, (5) new business, and (6) adjournment.

Conduct Meaningful Business Meetings

People attend meetings for different reasons—some for the topic, some to affect outcomes, some to network, some as a job requirement, and some with political aspirations. Leaders must prepare to use time well and to remain socially sensitive to conflicting needs.

Open the Meeting

Set the tone immediately. Call the meeting to order, introduce visitors, and welcome all participants. Reiterate meeting goals and create a constructive, productive climate. Provide background information to instill group unity, momentum, and focus.

Encourage Participation

[E]ach institution is autonomous and has to do its own work the way each instrument in an orchestra plays only its own part. But there is also the score, the community. And only if each individual instrument contributes to the score is there music. Otherwise there is only noise.

—Peter F. Drucker

- Know the participants and their areas of interest or expertise. Recognize them by name, as far as possible.

- Study attendees' nonverbal communication to see who will engage readily in discussion early in the meeting. Establish eye contact after announcing a topic to prompt these extraverts.

- Look for participants who seem ready to say something, but are hesitant to interrupt. Create an opportunity for them to speak.

- Pay attention if someone mentions an item of concern or raises a question during a break time. That person is either planting a seed for someone else to speak up or is testing the waters to see how the message is received before introducing it into a meeting.

- Use questions skillfully to encourage meaningful discussion.

The following types of questions are useful for generating and directing discussion.

- *Assembly* questions are directed to the entire group for anyone to answer. "You have just seen two marketing presentations. What are your reactions to them?"
- *Individual* questions single out an individual for an answer. "Jan, you have worked in this area. What resistance should we anticipate?"
- *Volley* questions deflect a question back to the one who originally asked it. "That's a good question, Lewis. What would you do in that situation?"
- *Transfer* questions pass the question on for someone else to answer. "Susan has brought up a valid concern. Who has an answer for the problem in her area?"

Stay on Track

Minutes from the previous meeting are read immediately following the opening and introductions. They are approved (by vote) as read or amended and approved as amended. A leader may further summarize an earlier meeting to update the group. In meetings held according to *Robert's Rules of Order,* standing committee reports are next, followed by ad hoc committee reports. Then "old business" items are discussed, and appropriate action is taken on each. New business is saved until after old business has been brought to closure or tabled for another meeting. Some leaders require that they know any new business items early enough to include on the agenda.

Balance task and relationship issues. Direct the group toward its objectives and, at the same time, be sensitive to relational and emotional dimensions. Members usually are satisfied if their ideas are written down and they're assured the group will return to them.

• • • • TIPS   • • • • **Voice Choice in Minutes** • • • •

An accurate report of an action in a meeting could read, "Joe Daniels proposed a cut in salary for professional personnel." That reporting style could dampen honest participation, however. When a committee decides that the minutes should accurately reflect meeting content while protecting members' anonymity, the recording secretary has choices:

1. Passive voice: "A proposal to cut salaries for professional personnel was approved."
2. Active voice that speaks for the committee as a whole: "The committee approved a proposal to cut personnel salaries."

• • •

Close the Meeting

The leader closes the meeting, announces future meetings, and states actions for follow-up. A skillful closing anchors the effectiveness of the meeting in the minds of those attending. In parliamentary procedure, the chair says, "Is there any other business to discuss? [pause] If not, the meeting is adjourned."

Once again Brother Hank has opportunity to demonstrate his decision-making skills.

We reveal ourselves through our decisions.

Follow Up

Follow-up brings closure by delivering what the meeting promised. Sometimes, leaders request additional feedback after an action is completed. The entire group should receive updated, written results.

● PROBLEM-SOLVING SKILLS APPLICATIONS

Meetings, like other team purposes, are built around problems. Problem-solving and leadership dexterity come with practice. Return to Chapter 12 to review the steps of reflective thinking before applying them to solve problems.

PROBLEM SOLVING FOR WILD HORSES

Working as a team, research the situation with wild horses in Nevada. Role-play a congressional environmental standing committee. Operate with a designated leader, and make all members responsible for collecting and presenting information at the first meeting. The issue before you is what to do about wild horses in the state. Use the following questions and comments as prompts to help you thoroughly consider the problem. Make a decision as a team. Inform the other class teams of your team's decision.

1. **Identify and define the problem:** "How can we most clearly state the problem?" "What do we mean by 'wild' horses?" (Research this topic online.)
2. **Establish criteria for a solution:** "How much time do we need?" "We have to stay within the conservation budget." "We want this historical lineage to be saved in as natural an environment as possible." "What are our limits in funding and resources?" "Does everyone agree on the kind of solution we want to create?"
3. **Analyze the problem:** "Where in Nevada are they?" "Why do we need to do something? Are they a danger to people or property? Are they endangered or in danger?" "How many horses like this exist?"
4. **Generate several possible solutions:** "We need to study their behavior." "Let's keep a veterinarian on call to care for horses in harm's way." "Let's round the horses up." "Save their DNA." "We need a very long fence around an area

ACTIVITY
13.3

Herds of wild horses on rangeland
present challenges to various groups.

away from housing." "We should test them for diseases." "Provide access to
water at all times." "What about helicoptering them into the Red Rock Canyon
National Conservation Area?" "Can we control their natural enemies?" "Other
western states could help." "I propose a research team of veterinarians and
historians of the Old West." "What else could we propose?"

5. **Select a solution or combination of solutions, evaluating proposed solutions against the established criteria:** "The research team sounds feasible
   with our budget, but we may not have a year to save them." "We can get
   immediate feedback from them about water, diseases, and natural enemies." "Contacting other states allows more freedom for the animals and
   possibly more support in this cause." "Do we agree that this is what we
   want to propose?"

6. **Test the solution:** Obviously, your team is not going to fly to Nevada and
   force the state to test your solution(s). You can, however, decide how a congressional committee could go about checking out the validity of your
   approach. "Who can field test the solution?" "Can we work with one team
   of wild horses and get the results before moving ahead?" "What sort of
   model or simulation is available for testing?"

7. **Plan follow-up:** "Shall we prioritize actions we support, depending on available funds?" "How shall we follow up on today's meeting?" "Let's each present one part of the proposal during class time." "I think they need a written
   copy as well." "Would someone please state our follow-up plan for the
   records." "Let's include how we will communicate it to others."

Whether leading meetings or participating on problem-solving teams, you
have experienced the effects of power. This next section introduces the principles and types of power as they function in organizations.

POWER IN ORGANIZATIONS

Leadership entails an exercise of power. Power is inherent to any interaction,
and by definition, leadership influences other people.

Principles of Power

All communications have a power dimension, obvious in some but opaque in others. Power principles explain a great deal of what happens in the workplace.

Communications in Organizational Cultures Assume Dimensions of Power

Motivational messages in one organization are disgusting ones for another. Culture—national, professional, racial, dominant gender, community, and organizational—frames interpretations of organizational messages in terms of power.

CONTEMPORARY VOICES 13.1: LEADERSHIP TRAINING, CULTURE, AND POWER

Goleman (1998) studied cultural effects of leadership-development initiatives when organizations were experiencing major change processes, finding that these initiatives must respond to cultural context to be effective. Organizational change processes must start at the top and be an organizational priority (pp. 232–233).

Power is an aspect of relationship communication. When a spouse tells a partner, "I'll take care of the checkbook," more than information is exchanged: This is a message of who has power over the checkbook. In business these dynamics play out in terms of who is included in a meeting, who has access to the business's confidential information, where someone parks, and who gets the new wireless laptop. The political messages in these acts are usually more powerful than the information and rationales offered.

Power Is a Function of Perception

Leaders hold power only to the extent that others perceive them as powerful. When the perception is openly acknowledged, the power increases. Medical doctors hold power regarding our decisions about our health, because we perceive they know more about that subject, but if we conclude that a doctor knows everything about everything, we may erroneously empower the doctor to influence how we vote, where we buy a house, and whether we are doing our own jobs right. Because power ebbs and flows in relationships, a changed perception has an immediate effect. Also, power must be used to remain potent. Imagine what would happen to a governor, coach, or manager who stopped exercising the prerogative to make decisions and apportion resources.

Power Comes through Many Sources and Is Unequally Distributed

People do not have equal amounts of power, no matter how unfair it seems. Power originates and renews itself from a number of sources. An NFL quarterback, a popular recording artist, an astronaut, a box office–attracting actor, and a brilliant geneticist hold power, and others are born or marry into power.

The Person Who Has the Most to Lose Has the Least Power

The principle of least interest (or lesser interest) means that whoever has the least interest has the most power. We watch this at work on the dating scene, with the dilemma of letting someone know you are interested, but not *too* interested—available, but not too available. You can see the principle at work when project managers select members for their teams. When an employee has a choice of projects, the courting intensifies.

People Gain Power by Empowering Others

> If you're uncomfortable with the idea of vesting people with the power to fire their boss, then you're not ready for the task of leadership in the next century.
>
> —Jim Collins

Leaders extend their influence by equipping others to act on their own. "The most important and effective way to build personal power is to empower others. Good project managers mentor employees, empower them to make decisions, provide training, and get them what they need, including information. The more they empower others, the more their power grows" (K. Kostohryz, personal communication, 2003). It's a natural progression as empowered, motivated employees build their own circles, which, in turn, add to their leaders' collective power.

Types of Power

People earn power through education, through honorable actions, because of their jobs, and because of attractive personalities (French & Raven, 1959). There's some truth to the saying that with power, you use it or lose it. However, that's when self-awareness, understanding others, and communication skills come into play. Abusing power depletes reserves. As you learn the basic forms of power, consider how misused power can backfire.

Legitimate: Power by Virtue of Position of Authority

The president of the United States holds official and legitimate powers, regardless of how people in the country voted. Legitimate power comes with a person's position in the hierarchy at work and may exist independent of respect or expertise.

Expert: Knowledge as a Primary Source of Power

One good example of expert power is seen in the value placed on computer skills today. Also, people usually choose and pay their doctors, lawyers, real estate

Legitimate power has its privileges.

"Wait until you see the
president's office."

What evidence of expert power and legitimate power do you see in this communicator?

agents, and accountants for their specific areas of expertise. Your professors are in the business of giving power away when they teach you their subject disciplines.

Coercive: Power to Punish

Supervisors have varying degrees of coercive power, ranging from the power to assign undesirable shifts to the power to fire employees. In order to have coercive power, a person must determine what others want, control what they want, and use their desire as leverage against them. Coercive power resides in the use of salary, promotion/demotion, recognition, inclusion, and reputation.

Reward: Power to Reward

In relationship to coercive power, the power to reward grants another person's needs or wishes. "If you do a good job on this data analysis, you will be invited to present in Hawaii in March." Usually the same person holds both coercive and reward power—for instance, the power to give a raise (reward) versus freezing a salary (coercive).

Referent ("Charisma")

Charisma, or *referent power,* belongs to the person others want to follow or emulate. The group respects, likes, or in some other way is attracted to the referent power holder. Referent power is partially a function of personality and presence. Talkativeness and an energetic presence are qualities that surface with many, but not all, holders of referent power. Earned respect falls under the category of referent power.

CONTEMPORARY VOICES 13.2: PRIMARY GREATNESS

Covey (1992) says "primary greatness" goes beyond technique and positive personality traits to include "[a] character rich in integrity, maturity, and the abundance mentality" (p. 58). "If we use human influence strategies and tactics to get other people to do what we want, we may succeed in the short-term; but over time our duplicity and insincerity will breed distrust. Everything we do will be perceived as manipulative" (pp. 57–58).

Information Power: Insider Information

Information power is a more recent addition to the list of powers (Raven & Kruglanski, 1975). People can be powerful because they know what others want to know. A person can get "inside" information along the grapevine, perhaps from playing tennis with a boss or mingling during breaks at conferences.

Connection Power

Closely related to information power is the power of the "right connections" (Hersey & Blanchard, 1982). Knowing the right people gives access to inside information and carries a certain amount of clout.

Persuasion Power: Compelling Presentation of Logic

Persuasion power melds expert power, referent power, and strong communication skills. A different brand of power seems to be wielded by people with the ability to make information clear, communicate vision, and persuasively reason to conclusions and actions.

●
**ACTIVITY
13.4**

THE BOSS'S EAR

Five years out of college, Jim is one of twenty architects at Drew, Dietz, & Dillard, Inc. (DD&D, Inc.). About two months ago, a client—Protocol, Inc.—turned down Senior Architect Martha Dabney's design for an office building. Procrastinating and pressed for time, at the last minute she asked Jim to redesign the exterior for better flow. She had another deadline on an important project and hoped Jim's minor changes would satisfy Protocol. As Martha left Friday, she said, "Thanks, Jim, for getting this done before Monday. I know I can depend on you. You know, this could be high profile for your work. By the way, I know I haven't done your performance review this year, but we'll schedule it next week."

Fritz Dietz (the Dietz in DD&D) was also working late Saturday and stopped by Jim's desk. Jim asked his advice on a couple of points, and soon they were working side by side on more extensive changes. They discussed what Protocol wanted, analyzed the problems, brainstormed for solutions, and churned out a design in the wee hours. They were both exhilarated, and Fritz uncharacteristically declared, "It's been a long time since I've had so much fun collaborating with a creative, upcoming architect. Why has Martha been hiding you?"

Jim presented the design to Martha on Monday but didn't get the enthusiastic response he expected. "Thank you, Jim, for working this weekend. I didn't know you were going to take Fritz's time. I'll look this over, probably make a few changes, and try to convince the client this will work. We'll talk about your performance review later." Jim wondered why she tacked that last comment onto this conversation. He knew he needed Martha's stamp of approval to get a salary step increase. Two days later, Martha told Jim, "The design was certainly not what Protocol expected, but I convinced them to accept the design. Good job. By the way, I've turned in your performance review. No need for us to talk."

Jim got a different picture when Fritz called him to his office. He said Protocol was thrilled—so thrilled the chief executive wanted Fritz and Jim to design three other office complexes. "Jim, these are big projects, just what DD&D needed to stay competitive. I'll work with you closely, and I've arranged with Martha to move you over to my area. You'll be putting in some long hours, but it will be worth it, I promise." Jim was stunned. He knew this was a chance for a promotion, but what if he were moved back with Martha at the end of the projects?

Martha was relieved, but knew she blew it in not realizing the future Protocol could offer. Everyone liked Fritz, and Martha knew to be careful about what she said, but she emphasized to Fritz and others that she had done most of the work on the initial design, and they had used 90% of her design. Meanwhile, Jim was enjoying himself thoroughly, including conversations with "the other Ds," and he was working longer hours than ever.

1. *What forms of power do Fritz, Martha, Jim, and Protocol each hold?*
2. *What are their sources of power?*
3. *Explain how one person can hold more than one form of power.*
4. *What were turning points in the power dynamics?*
5. *What evidence do you notice of power used directly? Indirectly?*

When Leaders Follow and Followers Lead

Without followers there would be no leader. According to Peter Drucker, "To lead, one must follow because it is only from the viewpoint of the follower that we can reflect on the basis of followership, which when turned around becomes the essence of leadership" (Drucker, 1981, p. 14). Stephen Covey advises adopting a stewardship mentality, and others similarly look to "servant leaders."

Responding to Manipulative Messages

Power does not rest entirely with legitimate power, and to avoid being unduly manipulated, one should think ahead about responses to supervisors (see Table 13.2). Manipulators rely on scripts and games. Your safeguards and responses stabilize the moment and deter future abuse.

• STANDPOINTS ON LEADERSHIP

Leading means someone is following; thus, leadership is an interactive, social process (Fisher, 1982; Shaw, 1981; Cartwright & Zander, 1968; cited in Hirokawa & Poole, 1986). Leadership is not always positive and ethical influence, but it *is* influence. Contrast the leadership of Hitler and Stalin with that of Martin Luther King, Winston Churchill, Mother Teresa, Albert Schweitzer, Michael Dell, and Jack Welch. Whereas *leadership* refers to a process (example: "We attribute the team's success to good leadership"), *leader* refers to a person, a role, or a position (example: "The leader should set the tone for the meeting").

"Leadership is an influence process which is directed toward goal achievement" (Shaw, 1981, p. 317); more specifically, a communication perspective states, "Leadership is human (symbolic) communication which modifies the attitudes and behaviors of others in order to meet group goals and needs" (Hackman & Johnson, 1991, p. 11). For another authoritative definition of leadership, we turn to *Bass & Stogdill's Handbook of Leadership* (Bass, 1990): "Leaders are agents of change—persons whose acts affect other people more than other people's acts affect them. Leadership occurs when one group member modifies the motivation or competencies of others in a group" (pp. 19–20).

TABLE 13.2 • Possible Responses to Manipulative Messages

If the boss says . . .	You can respond . . .
"You need to be a team player." (*Variations:* "You're not being a team player." "He's not being a team player." "This is a team." "When we leave this room we will stick together.")	"I value each person on the team and I will continue to contribute to the team." Reaffirm the value you place on the team and your position on the team without succumbing to pressure.
"Yes, . . . but . . ." (*Variations:* "That's a good idea, but. . . ." "Maybe. . . ." "Do you really think that would work?" "We don't have the resources.") Leaders using this style limit productive meetings in the future.	"We've all given ideas, and you seem to have something in mind. How do you think we can solve this problem?" This game is set up to make the boss look good when the boss has "the best" solution. Turn the tables before being cut down.
"We are here to decide whether to adopt this course of action. Put your concerns on the table today, so we can take care of them. We are excited about this opportunity." Leaders pensively nod their heads, "We can fix that, etc.," followed by "Will that work?" The assumption is that you will agree, since your "only objection" has been solved.	"I had prepared for a decision-making session. I am sensing that the decision is apparent or has been made." The decision *has* already been made. Superiors are willing to do whatever it takes to follow through on a preordained commitment.
A "by invitation only" meeting is announced to everyone on e-mail, and key people—even you—aren't included.	Approach the leader setting up the meeting and say, "I understand a master design team is meeting, and you are leading it. Congratulations." Give the person a chance to respond. "Will the team include someone from engineering? Engineering brings critical expertise."
"You're really a harsh project manager." "You don't realize the pressure you put on us." "I can't do my job and your job, too." An employee is immediately and aggressively offensive when criticized.	"Could you be more specific?" Wait for the answer. "What would you prefer me to do?" Wait. "Thank you for that feedback. I learn from your comments, and I know you also benefit from feedback. We all have development needs." You have modeled how to receive feedback nondefensively.
"I have special circumstances," or the knee-jerk response, "Everyone has special circumstances." These two opposite messages plead for or deny individual attention.	"How do you think the team can work with these circumstances? Can you trade off with someone?" "That is what is so terrific about this group. We pitch in for one another. Here's a possible solution."
"Of course, I wouldn't have done it that way," or other vague allusions to inadequate work performance.	"I'm glad you have been thinking about this project." This response surprises the critic. "After looking at a number of options, we decided this was the way to go." With other innuendoes about poor work, ask for a meeting to discuss specifics. Usually, you get a neutralizing response, such as, "Oh, I wasn't saying you did anything wrong" and even, "Don't get defensive," to which you should answer, "I'm always open to learning."

In *Transforming Leadership,* Terry Anderson (1995) explains that simple theoretical models are inadequate to explain the complexities of leadership, and yet if a model becomes too complex, it is cumbersome and impractical. "The challenge is to state [theoretical models] clearly enough so they become tools that can be tested and used. Research on leadership effectiveness reveals that at this point, we are still groping for the 'magic formula'" (Anderson, 1995, p. 276). That would explain why some applications seem more faddish than practical.

"The trick involved in discovering, predicting, and training for effective leadership is to resist the common-sense mythology of leadership and take advantage of the complexity" (Fisher, quoted in Hirokawa & Poole, 1986, p. 215). Academicians and researchers have spent considerable time studying leadership and separating myth from wisdom.

Trait Theory of Leadership

The oldest documented perspective on leadership, *trait theory,* leans toward the view that leaders are born, not made. For centuries, leaders were seen as predestined to lead. Consider the description of the anointing of King David of the Old Testament. He was presumably tall and handsome, skillful, and godly. Social scientists have searched for traits that identify "born leaders," and there isn't a set recipe for leadership, but leaders do seem more likely to show "self-confidence, dominance, enthusiasm, assertiveness, responsibility, creativity, originality, dependability, critical-thinking ability, intelligence, and ability to communicate effectively (Bass, 1995, p. 413)." Yet in a review of research, Bernard Bass (1995) draws an important conclusion:

> Although leaders differ from followers with respect to . . . personality, ability, and social skills. . . . Traits do not act singularly but in combination. . . . The leader who acquires leadership status in one group tends to emerge as leader when placed in other groups. Thus, perhaps the best prediction of future leadership is prior success in this role. (p. 413)

Still, the question looms: Does success breed success, or is it merely an indication?

Peter Drucker debated the prototypical view of the charismatic leader with "inexhaustible energy, imposing physique, superior intelligence, magnetic personality, and extraordinary technical skills" (Flaherty, 1999, p. 272). "Eisenhower, George Marshall, and Harry Truman were singularly effective leaders, yet none possessed any more charisma than a dead mackerel" (Drucker, 1981). Then perhaps leadership is more than genetics—more than having a magical, charismatic DNA. Maybe the magic is in a leader's style.

Leadership Style

Theorists (Lewin, Lippitt, & White, 1939) analyzed whether any one leadership style leads to superior outcomes. The styles they used, by design, reflected how governments around the world did business: autocratic, democratic, and laissez-faire.[2]

---

[2]   *Laissez-faire* is French for "let them do," pronounced *lay-say-fare.*

- *Autocratic leaders* are authoritarian and controlling. They assign employees to tasks; direct communication; and organize use of time, tasks, and materials. Examples are dictators (benevolent or otherwise), strong-willed head coaches, and CEOs who require their stamp of approval for all decisions.

- *Laissez-faire leaders* pretty much let people do what they want to. These leaders abdicate leadership power, allowing groups to function without formal structure. They respond to what the group requests, but they don't take ownership in outcomes. Some start-up businesses that depend on creativity and spontaneity function with leaders who, in effect, say, "Do your thing, and let me know what you need."

- *Democratic leaders* encourage the participation of all group members for all aspects of the group process. Democratic leaders pay attention to task and group processes. These leaders maintain a productive climate, with no one dominating. Head coaches who respect the input of their coaching staff and support collective decisions, and presidents who rely on their cabinets and advisors exemplify democratic leadership.

ACTIVITY 13.5

RECOGNIZING LEADERSHIP STYLE

- Sherman, after 10 years in the military, accepted a position as manager of Kaufee Associates' accounting department. He understands the chain of command and communication according to rank. Sherman assigns each employee the job to do now and waits for each task to be completed before telling them what to do next. Sherman is hands off, and he expects the job to be completed correctly and on time. Employees follow orders and march to Sherman's tune, and Sherman, in turn, is in tune with his boss. Sherman hands out praise and criticism to individuals, not groups, and sets an example as the ideal employee—punctual, hardworking and focused, obedient, and loyal.

- Henri, a commercial artist by education, was recently promoted to be Kaufee Associates' director of marketing design. He trusts the employees' competence and thinks they need room to think and create. He does not impose his ideas and is generally hands off. Henri responds quickly to supply materials and information when asked. He neither imposes formal structure nor determines policy. To upper management, he explains what the department is producing and gives rough estimates of completion, but he tries not to tie down his employees. Henri sometimes does menial or tedious tasks to free employees for creative missions. Occasionally, Henri comments spontaneously about a project or product. He avoids evaluative or advisory remarks.

- Thomas is Kaufee Associates' manager of product development. He values his employees' ideas and logical abilities. He encourages departmental and unit discussion and prefers consensus for reaching decisions. At the outset of meetings, Thomas sketches the steps to get to the group goal and assists with the process. He eagerly participates in meetings and discussions, and as a "regular member," he offers, but does not impose, his own ideas and suggestions. He may advocate and justify a solution, but seldom will he override a group decision. Members fluidly work among themselves and gather information from outside the department without going through channels. Thomas represents the department's views to upper management, and he gives the department immediate feedback from management.

1. *Match each leader with either an autocratic, democratic, or laissez-faire leadership style. Justify your decisions.*
2. *Which one would you prefer working for? Why?*
3. *Do an Internet search to review basic beliefs of Theory X and Theory Y managers, according to McGregor's theory. Which style would a Theory X manager use? Theory Y?*

Participants are more satisfied with democratic leadership (Foels, Driskell, Mullen, & Salas, 2000; Jurma, 1978) and are more productive in nonstressful situations (Rosenbaum & Rosenbaum, 1971), but no one leadership style is most effective in *all* situations. Military troops in a hostile wilderness respond quickly to authority (Korten, 1962); in contrast, some free-spirited teams lose their productive rhythm when a manager decides to formally structure the work. More recent literature uses "traits" as a way to point to observable behaviors, such as creativity, self-confidence, self-monitoring ability, enthusiasm, and verbal ability. That standpoint is a forerunner of a *functions* approach, which we look at next.

Functional Leadership Perspective

You may have noticed that in identifying traits and styles, scholars research communication behaviors. The *functional perspective* takes a forthright approach to communications, saying that anyone in the group can perform any number of functions. We all have leadership responsibility in work groups, and we should assertively and generously engage in those functions as needed (Fiedler, 1967). You studied some functions in Chapter 12 under the categories of tasking and maintaining roles. From a leadership perspective, *task leadership* includes the following:

- Initiating the generation of ideas
- Coordinating members' ideas in the direction of the goal
- Summarizing the essence of the discussion on the topic
- Elaborating and clarifying productive ideas

Process leadership makes a point of building and *maintaining* a satisfying group climate (Beebe & Masterson, 2002, p. 315).[3] To achieve this goal, Bennis (1997) notes that leaders of "Great Groups" must do the following:

- *Provide direction and meaning.* People want to know that their work makes a difference.
- *Generate and sustain trust.* The group must possess adequate trust in itself and its leadership to weather internal conflict, external challenges, and general discouragement.

---

[3] "Building" and "maintaining" pick up on an industrial metaphor. Building assembles the parts in a way that they will function, and the assemblage must be maintained or it will stop performing.

- *Display a bias toward action, risk taking, and curiosity.* A sense of urgency energizes groups.
- *Purvey hope.* Leaders give a vision of "what can be" and how to attain it.

What can you do to accomplish these inspiring, but abstract, process goals? In one study, 18 leaderless discussion groups worked for over four months without assigned structures, so that leadership had to emerge informally to the point where there was an undisputed leader in each group (Drecksel, 1984). After thoroughly analyzing her data results from an elaborate research design, "Drecksel was unable to find any evidence to suggest why or how leaders are different" (Fisher, 1985, cited in Hirokawa & Poole, 1986, p. 210). Drecksel could only conclude that the sole difference between leaders and nonleaders is that leaders show more variety in their communication behaviors.

Searching still for functions, Fisher (1985) suggests that leaders are interpreters and organizers of available information for the group—"leaders as mediators." He notices that these leaders are flexible and adaptive as they

- Interact with a large repertoire of communicative functions
- Avoid simplifying information too quickly
- Adapt when sources of information differ, when communicating with different people, and with varying issues
- Exhibit greater overall complexity over time on a variety of topics and with different participants

Although Goleman objects to any suggestion that people are interchangeable, he searches for a "list of ingredients for highly effective leaders" with considerable success (Goleman, Boyatzis, & McKee, 2002, p. 250). After analyzing data from close to 500 competence models of global companies, Goleman and his researchers support the assumption that higher cognitive capabilities, such as IQ and technical skills, are found in star leadership. Big-picture thinking and long-term vision are especially important. The higher that leaders rise on the organizational ladder, the more emotional intelligence (EI) competencies show up as dominating capabilities (Spencer, 2001, cited in Goleman, 1998).[4]

Emotional competence and broad-spectrum communication skills, including adaptive skills, mandate a more complex explanatory theory. Barge and Hirokawa's communication competency model of group leadership (1989) marries functional and situational approaches of leadership studies. In their model, the constantly shifting situation requires a repertoire of skills. The "shifting sands" of context set up a situational, or contingency, approach to leadership.

Situational or Contingency Leadership

Situational, or *contingency,* approaches claim that leadership requirements depend on the situation. There is no one "best" style or set of functions. The kind of leader needed is contingent upon variables of the situation, which include the following:

---

[4] Perhaps Goleman's list of emotional capabilities reframes functionalism.

- The goal, purpose, and task of the group
- The abilities, experience, values, and ethics of the participants
- The motivation and expectations of the participants
- The amount of respect, trust, and compatibility among the participants
- The skills, commitment, values, and experience of the leader
- Time constraints
- The culture

Organizational contexts add these dimensions:

- The type of organization
- Organizational culture
- The distribution of power
- Organizational politics
- The temporal context (time in the organization's life and in history)
- Organizational values
- The physical setting of the interactions

Thinking that a more easily applied model was needed, Hersey and Blanchard (1996) offered their *Situational Model,* one well known in business circles. The authors work from assumptions of adaptive behavior from earlier models. Their model (Figure 13.2) combines one axis of task (from high to low) and another axis of relationship (from high to low). Examine it to understand each of Hersey and Blanchard's categories.

- *Telling* is highly directive (high task, low relationship).
- *Selling* is also directive, but seeks to influence the group to buy into the idea (high task, high relationship).

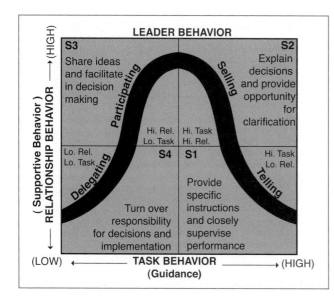

FIGURE 13.2 • **Hersey and Blanchard's Situational Leadership Model**

- *Participating* concentrates on relationships and input by all members (high relationship, low task).
- *Delegating* encourages the group to direct itself, as the leader adopts a hands-off position (low relationship, low task).

As a group matures to own the ability and motivations to assume a task, leadership moves from *directive leadership* toward *facilitative leadership*. This process occurs in stages:

- Telling works well for beginning groups who need direction.
- Selling coaches groups on how to move in a productive direction.
- Participative support turns more responsibility over to a maturing group.
- As groups mature, leadership shifts to delegating, allowing more autonomy.

Emergent Leadership

If you want to lead, avoid appearing withdrawn, obnoxious, rigid, bossy, or clueless. In groups where no one is appointed leader, who emerges as leader? Professor Ernest Bormann, in the Minnesota Studies, found that it's more a matter of who *submerges*. Most leaderless groups do not select leaders; instead, they eliminate nonleaders (Beebe & Masterson, 2002, p. 325). By this process of residuals, like the game "musical chairs," members are eliminated one at a time, leaving the last one to sit in the leadership chair. Of course, the first people to be voted off the island, so to speak, are the ones who do not participate early in the discussion. (How can you lead, if you're not even participating?) And it's also a problem if you don't know anything to contribute. Next, overaggressive and dogmatic members are seen as too inflexible to lead the group (Geier, 1967). Overly authoritarian members and those who are mismatched (process-oriented in a task-oriented group or vice versa) are also sent packing (Baker, 1990). On the other hand, emergent leaders typically display effective listening skills (Johnson & Bechler, 1998), task ability, and commitment to the group's goal (De Souza & Klein, 1995).

Transforming (Transformational) Leadership

"Resonant leaders shatter the mold that was cast in the image of the captains of industry." Increasingly, champions lead not by authority alone, but by the indispensable art of relating well to others. "Leadership excellence is being redefined as companies strip out layers of managers, as corporations merge across national boundaries, and as customers and suppliers redefine the web of connection" (Goleman, Boyatzis, & McKee, 2002, p. 248).

Transforming leadership reshapes organizations that have significantly new missions. Imagine being the leader responsible for an organization transforming from a nonprofit, academic research team to a team in a for-profit pharmaceutical company or from a military battalion to military peace keepers. The goal of transformational leadership is to "transform" people and organizations in a literal sense—to change them in mind and heart; to enlarge vision and understanding; to align behavior with beliefs, principles, and values; and to bring about self-perpetuating changes (Covey, 1992, p. 287).

Transforming leaders are *change agents* facilitating drastic reformations. Change can be (1) gradual, incremental, and fairly comfortable or (2) abrupt and discontinuous.

CONTEMPORARY VOICES 13.3: LONG-TERM CHANGE FOR STABLE RESULTS

"You would save big bucks by increasing span of control and tapping the energies and talents of people" (Covey, 1992, p. 279). To look to the long haul, beyond quarterly reports:

1. Build a sense of internal security so that the organization can adapt to the marketplace. People need security before they can be flexible.

2. Make a cultural change to principle-centered decisions, working toward improvement from the inside out—not waiting to be made to do something or merely copying the competition. "Today, nothing fails like past success" (p. 280).

3. Create a common vision and a set of principles. Management focuses on increasing financial and human capabilities, but such improvements are temporary unless continuous quality improvement anticipates the market and works on both product and process (p. 281).

SUMMARY

Leadership skills and concepts equip us to assume roles as a group needs them. A team composed of members from different departments, disciplines, or organizations is called a cross-functional team. Successful team leaders challenge the group with fresh facts and possibilities and use positive feedback, recognition, and reward.

Certain behaviors characterize supportive as opposed to defensive groups, suggesting that defensive climates are counterproductive to group activity. Evaluative messages frequently create defensive climates. In supportive climates, participants present facts and seek helpful information. Likewise, perceived unequal power or ability to contribute fosters a defensive climate.

Leaders' skills become transparent in meetings. Leaders largely depend on meeting protocol to guide them through treacherous moments. Special formats for making decisions and solving problems include the scientific method of problem solving, brainstorming, nominal group technique, buzz groups, and focus groups.

Power is inherent to any interaction, and by definition, leadership influences others. Culture frames power, and leaders have power to the extent that others perceive them as powerful. People do not have equal amounts of power, no matter how much we protest. People gain power by empowering others. People earn power through such things as education, honorable actions, jobs, and attractive personalities. Power can be categorized as legitimate, expert, coercive, reward, information connective, and persuasive.

Perspectives on leadership include trait theory, leadership style, functional leadership perspective, situational or contingency leadership, and emergent leadership. Transforming leadership leads individuals and organizations to reshape themselves into different missions and ways of doing work, and into whole new entities. •

ACTIVITIES

1. **Presenting to Others:** Draw a cartoon or write a dialogue of a team with group members displaying the characteristics of people who will not be chosen as leader of the team. Present your dialogue to the class.

2. **Technical Support:** Read an episode of "The On-going Saga of the Project From Hell" in *PMTalk Newsletter* (online at www.4pm.com). Find suggestions in this chapter you can adopt to avoid making the same errors. List three additional suggestions you learn from the article.

3. **Journaling the Experience:** The terrorist attacks on the World Trade Center and Pentagon caused extreme, devastating, and abrupt shifts. Unprecedented in American history, they tested the ablest of leaders and the wisest of organizational theorists to respond.

   On Peter Drucker's web page, Leader to Leader (www.pfdf.org), read ideas from other leadership professionals about responding to change, written *before* September 11, 2001. Write one page evaluating the wisdom of the expert's opinions in retrospect.

4. **Ethically Speaking:** Give a three-minute oral report on an article quoting a successful leader on leadership practices. Preferred sources include *Fortune, Business Weekly,* and *Fast Company* (online at www.fastcompany.com). Comment on the ethics of the leader's approach.

5. **Presenting to Others:** Present your vision for a nonprofit organization. Local interviews and national websites provide good overviews of organizations such as local chapters of the American Red Cross, American Cancer Society, and chambers of commerce.

6. **Presenting to Others:** As you interact with others with the intention of influencing them, do you exercise Covey's characteristics of principle-centered leaders? In a reflective essay, describe areas in which you recognize your strengths. Discuss how you can strengthen the other areas. Conclude your essay with three things you can do each day in response to Covey's description.

7. **Technical Support:** Report on how you played the game at the following site: www.bricksorclicks.com/

8. **Journaling the Experience:** As this year's chair of the Service to Community committee, you ask for ideas. Boyd comes to you one day, very excited, and suggests that town citizens give up driving vehicles for one week and donate the saved gasoline money to the local hospital. Assuming you think Boyd's idea out of the question, what can you say to Boyd? Role-play a conversation with him.

FOR FURTHER READING

Covey, S. R. (1992). *Principle-centered leadership* (1st Fireside ed.). New York: Simon & Schuster.

Goleman, D., Boyatzis, R., & McKee, A. (2002). *Primal leadership: Realizing the power of emotional intelligence.* Boston: Harvard Business School Press.

For lists of books on leadership and interesting websites to explore, see www.articles911.com/Leadership/Suggested_Books/ and www.work911.com

A helpful list of resources for leaders is collected at www.netpresenter.com

Exemplary leaders create a climate of candor throughout their organizations. They remove the organizational barriers—and the fear—that cause people to keep bad news from the boss (Bennis, 1999).

Consequential Conversations in Interpersonal Communication

14

- The Interpersonal Communication of Conversation

- Words in Conversations

- Communication along the Organizational Chart

- Patterns of Pointed Conversations

- Closing Distances with Conversations, Both Wired and Wireless

Join a spider on the web. Sit quietly with him in the center, alert to vibrations. "What's that?" he says. "Is that an enemy, lunch, or maybe both?" Imitate the spider—Be still. Touch the web. How strong and clear are the signals? Who's there? What is the content? How strong is the emotional signal? There is much to learn from the web, "but perhaps the most important thing is the knowledge that the web exists—that we will pick up whatever vibrations are sent out, because we are connected" (Levinson, 1981, quoted in Eitington, 2002, p. 217).

Conversations spin webs of networks and create climates in organizations. If we study them, they reveal whether an organization is liberal or conservative, for profit or for service, present- or future-oriented, and dynamic or static. It's not unusual to attend a meeting only to learn that most of the issues were decided in prior conversations. At some time in your career you will experience the consequences of the conversations discussed in this chapter.

OBJECTIVES

After studying the content of this chapter, you should be able to

- Direct messages through formal and informal organizational communication channels

- Build and use communication networks
- Use words mindfully
- Respect cultural differences in business conversations
- Recognize interpersonal strategies, including deception
- Use caution with sensitive subjects, especially issues of discrimination
- Facilitate conversations through technology

THE INTERPERSONAL COMMUNICATION OF CONVERSATION

Interpersonal communication is one-to-one and usually face-to-face communication. To have interpersonal communication, at least two people must have a practical and meaningful relationship. Impersonal communication follows social norms, but interpersonal communication uses unique, personal, and psychological information (Miller & Steinbert, 1975; Miller & Sunnafrank, 1982).

Interpersonal communications keep us connected at work and "are crucial to the survival of individuals, teams, and organizations today" (Eisenberg & Goodall, 1997, p. 233). We certainly can't pay attention to all aspects of a conversation as it is happening, but we *can* mindfully monitor, focus, and select items to sustain for discussion (Burgoon, 2000).

Constructive Conversations

Business is fundamentally a conversation. If we focus on business gone wrong to crowd out any discussion of what might go right, if we allow the number crunchers to overwhelm the idea people, we make it harder to change the negative trends that we all find so, well, negative. Business conversation is the source of new ideas, new energy, and new directions. It shapes what we work on and how we work on it, day in and day out. What we talk about—with employees, with customers, and with colleagues—is a powerful force in determining what actually happens inside companies. (The Founding Editors, 2003)

Alex Broer, vice chancellor of Cambridge University and a former director of research at IBM, says that innovations are built like jigsaw puzzles: "The ideas of an individual must fit into a matrix of innovation that spreads across a group of researchers around the world. . . . You have to *talk* to everybody" (quoted in Goleman, 1998, p. 101).

CONTEMPORARY VOICES 14.1: FAIR, OPEN, AND ETHICAL

Goleman (1998, p. 174) lists communication as a major component of emotional intelligence (EI) and says emotionally intelligent people

- Are effective in give-and-take, registering emotional cues in attuning their message
- Deal with difficult issues straightforwardly

Every conversation is potentially highly consequential. Goleman says emotionally intelligent individuals search for accurate information, listen well and seek mutual understanding. Here two men examine data in their deliberations toward solving a problem.

- Listen well, seek mutual understanding, and welcome sharing of information fully
- Foster open communication and stay receptive to bad news as well as good

Goleman (1998, pp. 89–90) also presents "trustworthiness and conscientiousness" as an EI competence and lists additional characteristics. Emotionally intelligent people

- Act ethically and are above reproach
- Build trust through their reliability and authenticity
- Admit their own mistakes and confront unethical actions in others
- Take tough, principled stands even if they are unpopular

Interpersonal Skills of Conversation

Experts report that interpersonal skills can be taught. Those trained with direct instruction, case studies, and role-play performed better in interviews and other business conversations than those who relied on spontaneity (Waldron, Lavitt, & McConnaughy, 1998). With a similar approach, this textbook now studies specific skills for effective, ethical, and expressive communication—especially in consequential conversations. From a review of communication and organizational literature, Table 14.1 lists the top six skills.

● WORDS IN CONVERSATIONS

"Consequential conversations" are dialogues with significant outcome. The words that we use in conversation are chosen on the basis of (1) our motivations and intentions, (2) predictions of how the other person will interpret the words and why, (3) organizational and personal contexts, (4) cultural appropriateness, and (5) our predictions about long-term and short-term consequences. Only after listeners assess messages do they feel confident in their responses (Berger, 1997). This section examines words that mislead us. Burgoon (2000) reminds us that in some cases, in spite of good intentions, miscommunications grow out of mindless messages. The following three examples are fun.

- A computer software corporation perplexed its employees: "As of tomorrow, employees will only be able to access the building using individual

TABLE 14.1 • Interpersonal Skills of Effective Communicators

Trustworthiness	Trust, essential for relationship building and conversation, can be visualized as spiraling trust and self-disclosure. Other skills crumble without trust. Anything from an untrustworthy source causes doubt. With experience, most professionals find trust the most essential quality in those with whom they deal.
Openness	Through openness, communicators learn to trust one another. Open mindedness—one dimension of openness—implies that a communicator is nondefensive and ready to listen.
Empathy	Empathic persons can imagine themselves in others' situations and emotional states. Out of empathy, they are better able to respond appropriately to the other person.
Descriptiveness	Descriptiveness objectively, nonjudgmentally reports a situation. Descriptive communicators avoid words and statements that betray their preferences or judge others.
Positivity (attitude, approach, message, perspective)	Positive qualities generate interpersonal energy. Positive people are more attractive. Repeatedly frowning, making negative statements, and forecasting gloom and doom assumes rejection prematurely. "I guess you wouldn't want to do this, would you?" is better asked as a straightforward message: "Would you do this?" or more positively, "Would you enjoy this opportunity?"
Expressiveness	Expressive communication is the opposite of monotonous or disinterested communication. Expressive messages are sent by words, tone of voice, and facial expression. Expressive words have vitality, levels of emotion, and shades of meaning.

security cards. Pictures will be taken next Wednesday, and employees will receive their cards in two weeks."

- "What I need is a list of specific unknown problems we will encounter." (from a shipping company)

- "We know that communication is a problem, but the company is not going to discuss it with the employees." (from a major provider of communications services)

As we can see, mindless messages characteristically don't make perfect sense. Tragically, misleading messages can lead to more serious outcomes, as in communication mishaps between air traffic controllers and pilots. The message here is to pay attention to what we say and how someone may interpret it. Be clear. Furthermore, every word has some emotional attachment for each of us, and emotive language can come across as encouraging, discouraging, comforting, or alarming, depending on the communicators and the circumstances.

Verbal Blunders

Conversational blunders, whether verbal or nonverbal, generally come from mindlessness, maliciousness, or ignorance.

- Communicators may err from lack of information (*ignorance*). The cures for ignorance are education, experience, investigation, and research.

- *Maliciousness*, however, is an ethical problem. Mean-spirited individuals intentionally pit one person against another, manipulate conversations to benefit them, and make ruthless statements. Malicious blunders include manipulative word choices, put-downs disguised as humor, hurtful double entendres, and deception.

- *Mindless* communication blunders are habitual social patterns of thoughtless communication. Mindlessness causes people to stumble, appear ignorant, or speak inappropriately. One should not be *overly* mindful—one should relax, be one's self, and trust the relationship—but seldom is total mindlessness safe and productive, even in the most intimate relationships.

Mindful communication selects words that encourage and foster productivity. Jack Griffin (1998) suggests, "Use *we, us,* and *our* to emphasize what we have in common. Other words that foster cooperation and alliance are *team, thanks, together, offer, idea, helpful, open mind, thanks, collaborate,* and *analysis.* Avoid words that communicate loss and limitations, such as *impossible, disaster, crisis, non-negotiable, one-time offer, stupid, cheated, afraid, blame, unreasonable,* and *wasted*" (pp. 11–17).

Perhaps you can decide if the following types of verbal blunders are primarily due to ignorance, maliciousness, or mindfulness.

Fraudulent Facts

Inferences and assumptions presented as if they were facts spell trouble. Sending fraudulent facts victimizes receivers and makes liars of senders. Receivers lose trust in those senders or become cynical about communicators in general.

FACTS AND INFERENCES

Assuming that the following story is factually accurate, respond to the numbered items with T (the statement is true), F (the statement is false), or ? (the statement could be true or false; you don't know). In a small group, discuss your answers.

ACTIVITY 14.1

> Working four hours overtime on a Friday, a systems analyst completed encrypting data code that required high security. Company protocol mandated a single data copy to be locked in the vault, located on the first floor. The project manager burned a CD, packed a briefcase, and punched the elevator down button. As the door opened, a muscular, darkly clothed, armed individual demanded the CD. Contents were removed from the briefcase, and the individual quickly disappeared. Immediately security was called.

1. A systems analyst encrypted code requiring high security.
2. The robbery happened after normal working hours.
3. The thief was muscular.

4. The systems analyst thought he was alone in the building.
5. Someone assisted the analyst by copying the data.
6. The analyst took the elevator down to the first floor, where the vault was located.
7. Someone demanded a CD.
8. A CD was taken from the briefcase.
9. A man in dark clothes was in the elevator.
10. An armed individual appeared at closing time.
11. Although security people were called, they did not arrive in time to be effective.
12. At least two people were on the first floor.
13. The CD was taken before the employee could lock it in the vault.
14. No one worked overtime on Friday.
15. Three people are involved in the story: the systems analyst, a security guard, and the thief.

Key

1. T 2. ? 3. ? 4. ? 5. ? 6. ? 7. T 8. ? 9. ? 10. ? 11. ? 12. ?
13. ? 14. F 15. ?

Fuzzy Language

To avoid misleading others, we should be cautious about using unclear and confusing words, or *fuzzy language.* Five of the fuzziest types of language are as follows.

• *Imprecise:* "I'll get to that report as soon as I can." (Is that today or next week? Is this your way of saying you don't plan to do it?) "They won't let me register." (Do "they" have a legitimate reason to keep you from registering, such as nonpayment or failing your classes?)

• *Ambiguous:* "His salary is not even close to yours." (Does that mean his salary is higher or lower?) "Journal your headaches for a month." (Is the patient to write about thoughts at the time of the headaches or record the frequency, duration, and severity?)

• *Overly abstract* (as opposed to concrete): "It is better to stick with the tried and true, than to try something new." (In what situations? Eating escargot? Experimental chemotherapy? Space flight?)

• *Indecisive:* "We may have to go with the first suggestion." (Do we or don't we? What is the decision tied to?)

• *Evasive:* "It can't be helped." (Does the speaker mean "I don't know how to change this situation" or "I will not give the time required to solve this problem"?)

ACTIVITY 14.2

FUZZY LANGUAGE

Label the verbal problems, and explain problems each message can cause.

1. Take two pills, once in the morning and once in the evening.
2. We only interview college graduates.

3. I'll fly in and see you at 8:00 tomorrow.
4. I will ship it second-day air sometime today.
5. The building's design must be subdued and modern.
6. We have a zero-tolerance policy on sexual harassment.

—————— ●

Jargon

Every business and profession has its own terminology, familiar to those in the field but confusing to the general public. Jargon ranges from "technospeak" (abbreviated technical terminology) to acronyms. Employee benefit presentations, for example, leave heads spinning. With messages such as these, no wonder:

> The deductibility of employee death benefits raises other concerns as well. In one case the court permitted a buyer to deduct payments resulting from a postacquisition death (*M. Buten & Sons, Inc.,* TCM 1972-44). But in another case where the death occurred before the acquisition, the buyer had to capitalize rather than deduct the payments. (*David R. Webb Co.,* 77 TC 1134, 1981). ("Taxation of Pending Claims," 2003)

Technology especially has its own language and recycles common terms. For instance, as people access computers wirelessly, we hear more about "pull" (information access) and "push" (proactive delivery) of information through "application processes" (Rosenberg & Zimmer, 2001, para. 4). Even the techies don't agree on what "convergence" and "seamless" specifically mean.[1] But perhaps more detrimental than such obvious jargon are ordinary words with specific, extraordinary meanings. For instance, to "burn a disk" certainly does not mean to throw it into the fireplace embers, and "protective relaying" in the electric utility business has nothing to do with passing a baton in a track race.

Dogmatic Language

Dogmatic persons have opinions on almost everything and state them unequivocally. Avowing "My mind's made up; don't confuse me with the facts," they reek of insecurity. A closed-minded stance alienates people, since dogmatic messages are probably exaggerated, understated, or overly confident. "You *totally ruined* our chance to win over that client." "This is the *only* method that works." These communicators attempt to belittle a situation or person, appear humble, or divert attention from issues.

Words That Denigrate, Marginalize, and Harass

The use of words to discriminate against gender or gender orientation, ethnicity, religion, age, or disability is illegal at work. The courts are clear about some issues, although others remain open to interpretation. Damage begins

---

[1] Go to www.commweb.com/article/COM20011112S0005 to see a discussion of these terms.

subtly, perhaps with assumptions about roles, grammatical usage, or overgeneralizations, and builds to open and sweeping denigration. To *discriminate*, in this sense, means discriminating *against* persons and includes denigrating, marginalizing, and harassing messages. Language to *denigrate* promotes messages intending to belittle or put down someone, as in racism, sexism, and heterosexism.

Marginalizing, a subversive type of denigration, pushes persons to the fringes of organizational information and action. They only receive the least consequential messages and are excluded from more meaningful conversations.

Gender-biased subtleties weave into messages: "An applicant should send a résumé with *his* application form." "*Firemen* are the heroes of New York." "We've planned a tour *for the wives,* while meetings are in session." "What a sissy!"

Word choices also reveal prejudices: "Southerners are mostly 'good ole boys.'" "Yankees are rude." "They're just a bunch of flag-waving hippies." "We have three minority applicants, so we should interview one of them." "This job needs someone young and up-to-date." "'Jew' him down on the price." The slippery slope leads to name-calling and slurs, exposing the bleak face of intolerance.

Verbal harassment is aggressive, damaging language and is illegal in the workplace. Verbal harassment includes berating a person in front of other people, telling racist or sexist jokes, using racial or gender slurs, threatening bodily harm, making sexual overtures, and soliciting sexual favors. Verbal expression is protected by the right to freedom of speech, but threatening and demeaning remarks are not protected because they potentially cause employees psychological and physiological harm and affect their job performance.

Because employees are in the inferior bargaining position in employment, they are entitled to protection from workplace harassment. The law protects all people from verbal abuse, even highly sensitive and fragile "eggshell victims." Even if an employer isn't aware of sensitive matters for a hypersensitive individual, he or she is liable for "offending" such a person. For instance, an employer may not know that religious profanity repulses some employees and that another employee, who was once assaulted and raped, is traumatized by sexist language. Organizations can't afford to tolerate foul language, profanity, obscenities, and insults. Even when it is not directed at someone but is simply overheard, an employer is liable.

Sexual Harassment

Workplace harassment targeting race, ethnicity, age, or disability, to name several topics, is illegal and is perpetrated through verbal messages. In recent years, widely publicized scandals such as the Bill Clinton–Paula Jones case, the Clarence Thomas–Anita Hill hearings, the Navy Tailhook trial, and the controversy surrounding the resignation of Senator Bob Packwood have increased the national attention given to sexual and gender harassment. These scandals have raised awareness concerning the difficulty women face in reporting and discussing sexually oppressive behaviors.

Sexual harassment is defined as "unwanted sexual attention that would be offensive to a reasonable person and that negatively affects the work or school environment." It manifests—often verbally—"deeply held beliefs, attitudes, feelings, and cultural norms" and "reflects the abuse of power" (Brandenburg 1997, pp. 1, 39). Although sensitivity to sexual harassment is nothing new, some developments are fairly recent, such as encouragement for resolution through communication within organizations rather than in the courts.

"Although it has been outlawed under Title VII of the Civil Rights Act of 1964 and prohibited under Title IX of the Education Amendments of 1972, many companies . . . have yet to develop adequate policies and procedures for addressing sexual harassment." Two Supreme Court rulings encourage resolution within organizations by "requiring harassed employees to work within their companies to resolve grievances before turning to the EEOC [Equal Employment Opportunity Commission]," thereby placing "responsibility on the employer to set guidelines for preventing sexual harassment and on the employee to follow them" (Barrier, 1998). In light of these court rulings and in response to victims' needs, "Internal grievance procedures may save time, minimize emotional and financial expense, and be more sensitive to all persons" (Brandenburg, 1997, p. 53).

Thus, in addition to communication strategies such as intervention and mediation, employers should write a policy and provide oral explanations and feedback. A suggested procedure is as follows (Kimble-Ellis, 1998; "Protecting Employees," 1998).

1. Develop a strong company policy that specifies in writing outlawed behaviors and penalties for their demonstration.
2. Establish grievance procedures for reporting, processing, and resolving complaints.
3. Provide sexual harassment training for all employees, explaining what sexual harassment means and how it can be recognized, confronted, and averted.

Whether employer or coworker, each employee should learn how to intervene when an employee is harassed. Berkowitz (1998) identifies the following steps to train employees to intervene helpfully (pp. 3–4).

Air Force General Counsel Mary L. Walker (left) holds a copy of the report on the U.S. Air Force Academy sexual misconduct study during a press briefing. She is joined by Brig. Gen. Ron Rand, director of Air Force public affairs.

1. Help learners to *recognize* sexual harassment incidents by providing them with appropriate and relevant definitions and examples of sexual harassment.

2. Help learners to *interpret* which behaviors signify harassment.

3. Encourage participants to *share* their experiences and their intolerance for certain behaviors as a means of illustrating their common ground.

4. Encourage participants to feel *responsible* for dealing with the problem.

5. Teach *intervention* skills and provide opportunities to practice them. Use role-play scenarios to help participants find comfortable and appropriate ways to express their discomfort with another's behavior.

6. Help participants be *free of retaliation.* Explore participants' fears about retaliation and provide examples of how interventions will be supported.

• • • • TIPS • • • • **The Law Speaks on Sexual Harassment** • • • •

- A grievance officer or committee must adhere to certain guidelines: The complaint must be specified, usually in writing; complainants, witnesses, and the accused must be interviewed; a determination will be made as to whether sexual harassment has occurred; the findings will be presented to both parties, along with the consequences of the action; and employees are required to accept mandatory arbitration.

- *Quid pro quo harassment* occurs "when submission to or rejection of such [unwelcome sexual] conduct by an individual is used as the basis for employment decisions affecting such individual" ("Protecting Employees," 1998, p. 3).

- *Hostile environment harassment* occurs "when unwelcome sexual conduct causes the environment to become hostile, intimidating, or offensive, and unreasonably interferes with an employee's or student's work" ("Protecting Employees," 1998, p. 3).

• • •

The Reality of Image and Reputation

People generally want the acceptance and trust that come from a positive image, as seen by others. Our reputations are others' reality, and we shape our reputations through what we disclose, how we excuse our errors, and how we seek compliance from others. *Self-revelations* intended to shape others' images of self include tying decisions and behavior to worthy organizational values, revealing personal values, allying with good or powerful people, and stating credentials. Here are some examples:

- "To protect our client and for the good of the company, we want to create a cost-effective product." (organizational values)

- "My children come first." "I don't take advantage of people." "I saw him at church last Sunday." (personal values)

- "I played tennis with your CEO just last week." "I do all of Oprah's parties, when she's in town." (allying)

- "As an architect, I find flaws in the design." "Dr. Hill was my mentor at Johns Hopkins." "So you're familiar with Goleman's work on EI." (stating credentials)

Conversely, when we damage our own reputations, we become both per-petrators and victims. The fragility of reputation is startling, and "mere words" can mar or ruin a reputation. Following a damaging revelation or a faux pas, persons decide how important it is to restore their reputations. "Human beings frequently must attempt to restore their reputations after alleged or suspected wrong-doing" (Benoit, 1995). Two common excuses you'll recognize are cate-gorized as "It's not my fault" and "It's not as bad as it sounds." Variations include "It could have been worse" and "You don't understand."

Compliance-gaining strategies are short-order verbal means to convince some-one to do something our way. The pressure on the person to maintain image is obvious in these strategies:

- *Compliments:* "You did a great job on that presentation. The statistics blew them away."

- *Altercasting:* "I know you are the type to meet a deadline, so I'll count on seeing you in the office Saturday" (positive altercasting); "Only a deadbeat would ask others to finish his project" (negative altercasting).

- *Value identification:* "As a parent of five, you certainly want better schools. We will rely on your vote for the new school bond."

- *Trading favors and imposing obligation:* "I'll give you a break on this bid, but remember me in the future."

From image maintenance to harassment avoidance, we recognize the power of words. As words create conversation, and conversations create relationships, they lead to verbal activity that creates organizational culture.

Organizational Words, Culture, and Lore

Organizational culture is constructed of image, policy, and conversation. Ordi-nary conversations exert "extraordinary influence on the rhythms of the work and the environment of the workplace" (Trice & Beyer, 1993, p. 123). William Ouchi's (1981) study of the Japanese work culture and Peters and Waterman's (1982) presentation of leading American corporations put a spotlight on orga-nizational culture. Narratives convey history, alleviate stress and anxiety, and build organizational and personal images. Leaders craft stories in order to share a vision, whereas other lore travels informally along grapevines and through networks, predominantly as horizontal communication. To study organiza-tional lore, researchers analyzed extensive and detailed stories of firefighters (McCarl, 1985) and ambulance workers (Tangherlini, 1998). They found that the telling and retelling of events as stories, complete with plot, heroes, and villains, were crucial in stressful job cultures.

• COMMUNICATION ALONG THE ORGANIZATIONAL CHART

My Big Fat Greek Wedding is a movie about the joining not only of two people, but also of two families. The new groom is swept into a new family culture. Similarly, when you accept a position, you marry into an organizational culture.

One characteristic of the culture is how information flows through it. The *organizational chart* is an open, straightforward map of organizational structure that prescribes the formal communication among employees. The equally important informal map is not so obvious, on which communication flows downward, upward, and horizontally (laterally), and not always according to the organizational chart.

Vertical Communication

Organizational charts illustrate official communication and prescribe paths for employees to follow, as in Figures 14.1 and 14.2. Some organizations are much taller than others, but basically, organizations function in a hierarchy with stacked levels. Generally the hierarchy looks like a triangle or pyramid, which sometimes is inverted. As hierarchies become flatter, horizontal communication increases, and as they become taller, vertical communication increases. Organizational charts prescribe communication paths for their organizations and map the span of control of each executive, management, and supervisory level. When someone advises you to "communicate through channels," this is what they are talking about.

Policy communication and official announcements primarily travel from the top downward to employees—and they usually move rapidly. The higher a message is initiated, the greater the number of employees who officially receive it down the line. At the very top, when a CEO issues a directive, it moves downward through all organizational layers. Any time a message travels in a series of transactions, the message is in jeopardy of losing parts, having elements added, and getting distorted. Executives often counteract these tendencies by sending carefully worded, written messages simultaneously throughout the company or to the next level of management. Other suggestions for receiving messages from employees higher in the organization include detecting remnants of reduced messages and asking about portions you suspect are missing. Be careful of criticizing the message sender. Your supervisor may reflect the CEO's management style, for instance.

Although top-down communication flows quickly, upward communication (e.g., from a line worker to the CEO) struggles against the current. Employees' spoken and upward feedback arrives at the top abbreviated and censored, if at all. Written feedback may move unenthusiastically from desk to desk through channels, or e-mailed responses may skip levels, be inhospitably received, and anger mid-management. When a message *is* welcomed, there is the danger of it having disproportionate effect because others from the trenches haven't been heard.

As you can see, both downward and upward communications face challenges characteristic of vertical communication. Table 14.2 summarizes these characteristics.

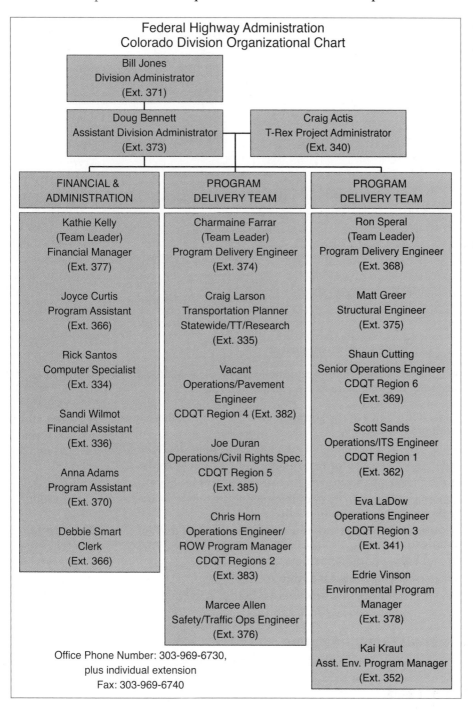

Federal Highway Administration
Colorado Division Organizational Chart

Bill Jones
Division Administrator
(Ext. 371)

Doug Bennett
Assistant Division Administrator
(Ext. 373)

Craig Actis
T-Rex Project Administrator
(Ext. 340)

FINANCIAL & ADMINISTRATION	PROGRAM DELIVERY TEAM	PROGRAM DELIVERY TEAM
Kathie Kelly (Team Leader) Financial Manager (Ext. 377)	Charmaine Farrar (Team Leader) Program Delivery Engineer (Ext. 374)	Ron Speral (Team Leader) Program Delivery Engineer (Ext. 368)
Joyce Curtis Program Assistant (Ext. 366)	Craig Larson Transportation Planner Statewide/TT/Research (Ext. 335)	Matt Greer Structural Engineer (Ext. 375)
Rick Santos Computer Specialist (Ext. 334)	Vacant Operations/Pavement Engineer CDQT Region 4 (Ext. 382)	Shaun Cutting Senior Operations Engineer CDQT Region 6 (Ext. 369)
Sandi Wilmot Financial Assistant (Ext. 336)	Joe Duran Operations/Civil Rights Spec. CDQT Region 5 (Ext. 385)	Scott Sands Operations/ITS Engineer CDQT Region 1 (Ext. 362)
Anna Adams Program Assistant (Ext. 370)	Chris Horn Operations Engineer/ ROW Program Manager CDQT Regions 2 (Ext. 383)	Eva LaDow Operations Engineer CDQT Region 3 (Ext. 341)
Debbie Smart Clerk (Ext. 366)	Marcee Allen Safety/Traffic Ops Engineer (Ext. 376)	Edrie Vinson Environmental Program Manager (Ext. 378)
		Kai Kraut Asst. Env. Program Manager (Ext. 352)

Office Phone Number: 303-969-6730,
plus individual extension
Fax: 303-969-6740

FIGURE 14.1 ●
Organizational Chart of the Federal Highway Administration, Colorado Division

FIGURE 14.2 ●
**Organizational
Chart of the
Federal Aviation
Administration,
Eastern Region**

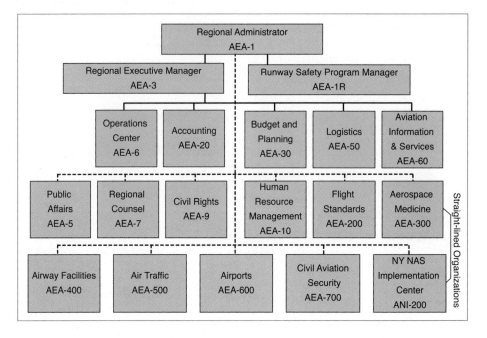

Regional Administrator
AEA-1

Regional Executive Manager
AEA-3

Runway Safety Program Manager
AEA-1R

Operations Center AEA-6 | Accounting AEA-20 | Budget and Planning AEA-30 | Logistics AEA-50 | Aviation Information & Services AEA-60

Public Affairs AEA-5 | Regional Counsel AEA-7 | Civil Rights AEA-9 | Human Resource Management AEA-10 | Flight Standards AEA-200 | Aerospace Medicine AEA-300

Airway Facilities AEA-400 | Air Traffic AEA-500 | Airports AEA-600 | Civil Aviation Security AEA-700 | NY NAS Implementation Center ANI-200

Straight-lined Organizations

● ● ● ● **TIPS** ● ● ● ● **Upward Communication** ● ● ● ●

Messages communicated sequentially by levels are susceptible to distortions, omissions, and additions to their original information and intent.

- Check "up" the organizational ladder for preferred types of information and feedback.
- Match message to channel and consider supervisors' preferences.
- Keep supervisors informed on team and project progress.
- Distill messages accurately, to avoid unnecessarily long ones.
- Maximize facts; minimize opinions. Report objectively, and reserve opinions to those specifically requested.
- Allow your superiors to be human, and respond to their needs for informality at times.
- Do not soften or hide bad news.
- For personnel issues, be problem oriented.
- Realize that coworkers are aware whether you have the boss's ear.

● ● ●

Horizontal Communication

Horizontal (lateral) exchanges occur among peers. They may be among staff, team members, or individuals representing different branches of an organization. For instance, a planning department needs to work with a transportation department to develop a mass transit system. An Army five-star general and a Navy admiral may communicate laterally at the Pentagon while solving tactical problems before reporting back to the Joint Chiefs of Staff. In almost all organizations of significant size, officially endorsed horizontal and vertical

TABLE 14.2 • **Characteristics and Strategies of Vertical Communication**

Characteristics of Vertical Communication	Strategies for Skillful Vertical Communication
Communication flows downward from the top of the organization.	Choose carefully among available communication codes (written or spoken) and channels (group discussion, presentation, written memo, etc.).
The organizational climate's tone is set at the top and trickles down level by level.	Your supervisor may reflect, imitate, or adapt to the CEO's communication and management style. To criticize one may be to criticize both.
The higher a person is in an organization, the more distanced that person is from information and attitudes at other levels.	Value employees who will give you honest feedback. Create feedback opportunities, and don't shoot the messenger.
Feedback from lower organizational levels is probably *leveled*—compressed and weakened—as it moves up through channels. Leveling alleviates long or complicated messages, due to information overload, inept listening, personal motives, or the sensitivity of subjects.	Detect "remnants" of leveled messages—those fractions that indicate there is more to a story. Your messenger may have gotten a report third or fourth hand. Ask specific questions about sensitive issues.
Parts of messages become *highlighted*—given emphasis or importance in the way the messages are told. Highlighting is often a result of personal experiences and motives, because the items that interest people are easiest for them to remember.	Departmental and personal agendas shape messages, preserving key information to move upward. Ask about the portions you suspect are missing. Get feedback from other sources.
Employees at the level immediately below a supervisor (all the way up to the CEO) feel exposed and vulnerable.	Shared communication training sessions create a common ground for value clarification and improvement.
Downward communication has a strong power dimension.	Although a supervisor may communicate as an equal, those supervised are cautious.
Messages moving downward take on increased importance, because they were sent from "on high."	Send clear and adequate messages downward, anticipating their interpretations. Realize motives can be distorted through interpretations.

communications coexist. We call employees who communicate business across organizational parameters, as in the preceding examples, *boundary spanners.* Boundary spanning may be a part of the formal organization or it may form to generate ideas or solve problems.

As organizations flattened in the 1980s and 1990s, horizontal communication became more dominant. Brown and Gray (1995) explain the communication implications of flattening workplaces:

> The real genius of organizations is the informal, impromptu, often inspired ways that real people solve real problems in ways that formal processes can't anticipate. Learning is about work, work is about learning, and both are social. There are different kinds of knowledge for work: explicit knowledge with individual mastery and tacit knowledge. Tacit knowledge is the capacity to do

something without necessarily being able to explain it. In many technical developments, the practice and knowledge are "embedded in the community that created it. The only way to learn the practice is to become a member. The best way to access the knowledge is to interact with the community". (p. 79)

Cultivated Grapevines

Less official, informal communications flow along the grapevine, like the old game of gossip, from person to person to person to person, in a series of communications. Disregarding who *should* talk to whom, grapevines thrive in most workplaces. Hardy tendrils cross hierarchical boundaries, strengthen old connections, and create new ones.

Reality @ WORK 14.1

CO-PRODUCING

Searching for ways to increase productivity with their field staff, Xerox commissioned an anthropologist from the Xerox Palo Alto Research Center to travel with a group of Xerox tech reps to study their work patterns. The anthropologist noticed that tech reps made it a point to spend time together, perhaps gathered at a local parts warehouse or hanging around the coffee pot to swap stories from the field. "The tech reps weren't slacking off; they were doing some of their most valuable work." The tech reps weren't just repairing machines; they were also figuring out ways to repair machines better. In these conversations, technicians functioned as "knowledge workers" through unmapped channels (Brown & Gray, 1995, pp. 78–79).

The Xerox tech reps discussed in Reality @ Work 14.2 cultivated solutions "on the grapevine." Others agree that grapevines can be productive. "Employees gathered around the water cooler aren't necessarily fueling the rumor mill" (Allerton, 2000). What *are* they talking about? A thousand large companies responded to a nationwide poll, and 40% of executives said that business-related topics were the topics of these informal discussions. Another 12% said sports, politics, and personal issues were discussed, and 9% thought gossip kept their attention (Allerton, 2000).

Executives have no choice about the grapevines in their yards. When you prune grapevines, you lose control of them, and they return with increased vigor. Decision makers can easily locate grapevines, since vines seek out people in power. Smart executives feed grapevines a lot of accurate information *before* the hottest news spreads along the vine. Grapevines are notorious for using persuasive narratives and stories to engage listeners.

Reality @ WORK 14.2

GENDER, GOSSIP, AND MOBILE PHONES

We gossip a lot. Most of the much-vaunted human capacity for complex language is dedicated to gossip. Perhaps the most striking findings of recent research on human conversation is that about two-thirds of our conversation time is entirely devoted to social topics and the minutiae of everyday social life—in a word, gossip (Fox, 2001, 6–7).

Men are more likely to gossip with work colleagues, partners, and female friends. Women, on the other hand, gossip more with same-sex friends and family. Women sound more animated and high-pitched, give more details, and request more feedback than men. Men sound more serious and talk more about themselves while gossiping. Men and women gossip about the same general subjects, and although only about five percent of gossip for men and women is critical and negative about others, even this "negative gossip" teaches rules and creates social bonding.

Men gossip more than women, especially on their mobile phones (33% compared to 26%). We are using space-age technology to return to stone-age gossip (25).

Confidential Communication

Passing along secrets is a secret bearer's way to brag about being "connected" and valuable. "People in the know" attract others, and inner circles are powerful, energizing, and addictive. Like individuals, organizations have comfort levels of organizational disclosure, but the temptation to tell is almost irresistible. Employees who will respect confidentiality are valuable. They can either stop the announcer or stop the broadcast. Remember, nothing is off the record, and if you say it is off the record, it is even more enticing for employees to put it on the grapevine. Unfortunately, people suspect that most, if not all, of what they are hearing is true.

It's a different matter when secrets are organizational knowledge. An employer may ask you to sign a confidentiality agreement to be hired or to keep a job. The question is which part of that knowledge capital belongs to you, and which part belongs to the organization.[2] *Confidentiality agreements,* similar to *nondisclosure agreements,* are written legal contracts between you and your employer regarding inside knowledge of the organization. These agreements limit discussion about topics such as new projects or development to being between certain parties. The types of information deemed confidential are sometimes designated specifically, but more often with broad terminology. For instance, upon resignation, you might relinquish your rights to make decisions based on prior knowledge in your next job. You may even be asked to agree to not work for competitors for a certain period of time. Be sure you are well informed *in writing* of the constraints of the agreement you sign. Interestingly, the agreement—mostly in writing—binds you from giving information—mostly in conversation. Some topics are discussed outside the workplace because conversations are difficult to initiate with people in power.

CONTEMPORARY VOICES 14.2: WHEN IS SPEAKING UP THE RIGHT THING TO DO?

I met her on a plane, my seatmate for a few hours on a flight out West. We'd been chatting for a while when she found out I was writing about emotions at work. Then her story spilled out: "We do safety testing for the chemical industry, assessing their materials and how they handle them for risks like combustibility. We verify that their procedures for handling these substances meet federal

---

[2]   *Knowledge capital* is the organizational worth of what you know and can do. Intellectual capital includes knowledge but extends to your aptitude and background for learning, reasoning, and using other cognitive skills. "What can you do for me now?" expresses a value for knowledge; "What is your potential for a learning organization?" expresses a value for intellect.

safety standards. But my boss doesn't care if the report is accurate; he just wants it done on time. His motto is, Get the job done quick as you can and get the money.

"I recently found that the calculations for one job were wrong, so I redid them. But the boss gave me grief about it because it took more time than he wanted. I have to do what this guy tells me, even though I know he's incompetent. So I'm always redoing calculations at home, on my own time. Everyone's unhappy that the boss pushes us this way."

Why does she put up with it?

She tells me about a messy divorce, having to take care of her two children on her own, being stretched. "I'd leave if I could, but I need the work. Jobs are tight just now. . . .'

After a long, reflective silence, she continues. "He signs all the work, even what we do. At first it bothered me that he was taking all the credit, but now I'm relieved—I don't want my name on those reports. It doesn't feel right to me. There haven't been any accidents, like fires or explosions, but there might be someday."

Shouldn't she speak up, report what's going on?

"I've thought about saying something to someone, but I can't say anything because I signed a secrecy agreement when I was hired. I'd have to leave the company and then be able to prove in court what I said—that would be a nightmare." (Goleman, 1992, pp. 91–92)

What you learn as a part of your job adds to an organization's intellectual capital, and most companies are paranoid about losing it. Conversation is at the core of *organizational intelligence,* a specialty of learning organizations. "Most information never gets written down—it's just floating in people's heads. That's why the most valuable network is the human network." (Jan P. Herring, after 20 years with the CIA, then at Motorola, established the first business-intelligence system based on national security principles) (Imperato, 1998, 269).

Technology ventures are especially guarded in allocating intellectual property rights, including technologies brought to new jobs from previous employment. Employers may require written assignment of copyrights, patents, trademarks, and trade secrets that may develop as a part of the employment relationship. Because of the possibility that a recruit from another organization might be encumbered by previous agreements, companies are cautious in hiring to minimize the risk of unqualified hires or being encumbered with excessive recruiting fees. How confidentiality is discussed will differ depending on whether the agreement favors the employee or employer.

Culture and Conversation

Strong cultural components in business transactions are possibly the most worrisome obstructions to successful outcomes (Adler, 2001, and Hall & Hall, 1990, cited in Chen & Chen, 2002). The communication challenges of multinational corporations include language proficiency and transaction protocols. In blended corporations, communication errors and frustration exist among native speakers as well as non-native speakers (Charles & Marschan-Piekkari, 2002). Each culture has a unique way of solving problems (Kluckhohn & Stodbeck, 1969, cited in Chen & Chen, 2002).

GUANXI AND SAVING FACE IN THE PEOPLE'S REPUBLIC OF CHINA

Foreign investors continue to be reticent and intimidated by the cultural expectations of Chinese business conversation. Confucianism, Buddhism, Taoism, and other pervasive influences overshadow dramatic sociopolitical change in recent years. The top ten factors (ranked by Hong Kong business negotiators) that affect Chinese business negotiations are relation, face, harmony, reciprocity, credibility, authority, patience, status, gift giving, and seniority (Chen & Chen, 2002, p. 403). One Hong Kong business person in the study said, "If you are considered their own people in the PRC, they will take special care of you; that makes business move much more smoothly. . . . After you have built up a good *guanxi* and become an in-group member, you will gain a lot of advantages." (*Guanxi* is an expression of relationship.) "Face"—upholding a respectable image—is also critical, because "[t]heir attitude would change sharply if you lose their face in negotiation. They may even become uncooperative" (p. 402).

Reality
@ WORK
14.3

BUSINESS CONVERSATIONS IN OTHER CULTURES

Business protocol includes gift giving, negotiating tactics, appointments, business entertaining, and cross-cultural communication. Complete the following exercise using the information provided at www.executiveplanet.com/community/items. Provide quotations from a country's site in support of each answer.

ACTIVITY
14.3

1. *Name at least one culture in which*

    a. *Business conversations work best with older and more reserved businesspeople and an indirect sense of humor.*

    b. *You will be welcomed several times at your first meeting, and "yes" may actually mean "possibly."*

    c. *You should expect to wait for appointments and should schedule your own appointments 2 or 3 hours apart.*

    d. *You should avoid giving compliments.*

    e. *It would be a mistake to introduce a business plan that does not treat everyone as equals or that will have detrimental side effects for the environment.*

    f. *You should expect to provide business cards, on which you include your academic degrees and awarded titles and the date of the organization's founding, to build personal and organizational credibility.*

Networks

Networks appear on organizational charts and thrive on grapevines. How we deal with them depends on our character—our ethics—especially since networks connect people we live with day in and day out, such as coworkers, supervisors, recruiters, clients, and friends of friends. Networking at its best is more than knowing whom to call—it is a mutually beneficial connection among people. We work inside our circles of influence, so it is a matter of knowing how to engage in them. For every hour a star puts into seeking answers through a network, an average person may spend three to five hours collecting data (Goleman, 1998).

Rozakis and Rozakis (1998) define networking as "finding the right strings and pulling them" and offer some suggestions for doing that (pp. 283–284):

- Attend conferences, seminars, and professional training
- Stay linked professionally to your trade organizations
- Continue work-related travel
- Socialize with colleagues after work
- Use online service and World Wide Web sites, such as CareerBuilder
- Join a community or civic group
- Contact your alumni associations

They add that office politics are strategies people use to gain and maintain competitive advantages in their careers. To survive in today's cutthroat economy, you must be politically savvy (Rozakis & Rozakis, 1998, p. 98):

- Every business is competitive. The leaders of the pack get the goodies.
- Like death and taxes, office politics are inescapable.
- Play fair; it pays off big.

• • •

As we mature physically, psychologically, and professionally, we move from dependence (on others) to independence (from others) to interdependence (with others). Only in maturity do we stand on interdependence to marry others' complementary abilities in order to accomplish loftier goals. Our circles of influence include people who trust us, interact with us, and understand our personal power. Our circles of influence can be expanded or diminished, but only inside these circles can we make a difference in the world (Covey, 1992).

Mentors

Ultimately, mentors fall within the circles of influence. *Mentorships* are mutually beneficial connections between two employees, where one person is in a nurturing leadership role with the other. Often, an expert may mentor in a skill set, advance your career, align you with key people, teach management skills, and lead in separating personal points of view from facts and reality (Argyris, 1976, 1993). The best way to learn in an organization is through observing and interacting with worthy mentors and practicing their behaviors (Deegan, 1979; Rossett, 1990).

Organizations assign mentors in various ways, such as matching mentors to new employees by rotation or by volunteers, encouraging employees to ask an experienced employee, or allowing the relationships to develop informally. Since different mentors can help you grow in different ways, it's a good idea to cultivate more than one mentor.[3] (When a single bright star falls, the star's protégés may, too.) However, don't overcommit, because mentoring requires

---

[3]   *Grow* is synonymous in some organizations with *develop*. This leads to strange syntax, such as, "The organization is growing Harold for a technical lead position" and "What is your growth plan?" (No, it is not a tumor.)

energy and time from those involved. Finally, remember to be collegial toward your mentors' other mentees, who will be part of your career network.

"The great thing about mentoring is that it shifts easily to meet training needs, whether you're expanding your business or you're not hiring. When you're growing, it's great to help integrate your people. When you're not, it can help people make the next leap in their careers," says Lory Lanes of Intel, New Mexico (Warner, 2002, p. 116).

Peer mentors help new employees acclimate to office routines and protocols. By interacting with them, you can also model communication practices in that organization, discuss decision making and make the internal process transparent, and steer them away from wasted efforts. Of course, you will listen and, as they accumulate experience, celebrate their accomplishments and show them how to deal with errors. Discussing professional development opportunities and including them in team-building activities builds their maturing professionalism.

• PATTERNS OF POINTED CONVERSATIONS

Careers that once seemed like individual pursuits, such as those involving scientific invention, today rely on collaboration. Conversations have patterns affected by the cultures and organizations in which they take place. Typical business conversations can be described as having five stages:

1. Greetings
2. Topic orientation
3. Topic discussion
4. Closure of topic
5. Farewells

First, greetings establish rapport, which may be as simple as waiting at an office door ("Hi. Excuse me. I have a quick question. Got a minute to talk?") or be more official, as in the example in Activity 14.4. Greetings and feedforward on upcoming business are positively worded in introductions. In the dialogue in Activity 14.4, Rawlin takes the role of host, since they are on his territory, but each person establishes rapport, gives appropriate compliments, and builds credibility (with a hint of one-upmanship) at the outset.

Second, topic orientation transitions from the greetings and trust-building part to the business topic (as Frank does in the dialogue) and sets a discussion agenda.

DIALOGUE

Frank: Hello. I am Frank Spielberg, systems design consultant with ABC Consulting Group. I am here to discuss the ABC's Downsworth project in more detail.

Rawlin: Thanks for coming. Congratulations on getting the project. I'm Rawlin Stone, project manager for Downsworth. We'll be working together. Let's sit at the table by the window. We have wireless capabilities for your laptop if you need them.

ACTIVITY 14.4

F: Thank you. I'll get set up. What a wonderful view this is!

R: Copley Square is prime real estate here in Boston, and you can see why. Frank, would you like a cup of coffee or Sprite? I already have a cup going.

F: Sprite sounds good. May I get it?

R: It's right here.

F: Thanks.

R: This project is one of Netline's highest priorities. It's getting a lot of attention. I understand you just moved here. How do you like Boston?

F: I feel like I'm coming home—I graduated from MIT.

R: No wonder you like the view! You can see your alma mater from here. How long have you been with ABC?

F: About four years. I helped open branches in Helsinki and London.

R: Helsinki and London! Do you enjoy the traveling?

F: Actually, I lived at each location for a couple of years. ABC believes in technological support for all their projects, internal and external. After your project is completed, I will still be available for support. Why don't we start by going over the contract specs?

R: The specs specify our needs. I'd like to point out features we have in other projects that we don't want in Downsworth. Then we can iterate the contract specs. As we emphasized earlier, we want this site custom designed, not reworked from other applications. This afternoon the rest of the team will join us to explain some constraints and some external requests. Does that sound OK to you?

1. *How do Rawlin and Frank establish personal credibility? Do they maintain equilibrium without bragging?*

2. *How do compliments affirm another person's credibility?*

3. *Describe the American business conversation. Contrast it with a different cultural pattern, by referencing Executive Planet at www.executiveplanet.com/community/items*

4. *How is a conversation analogous to a tennis match?*

5. *What examples of subtly competitive one-upmanship do you see?*

In the *conversation body*, Frank and Rawlin will discuss the issues at hand. Pertinent facts, individuals' opinions and interpretations, reports of consequences, and intentions are elements of business conversations, as are questions and answers. Business conversations do best with organized agendas, although they may be offered informally. Just as in presentations, they may follow chronological, logical, spatial, geographical, or topical patterns of organization. Another arrangement is by familiarity, difficulty, or emotional loading in topic. Initial exchanges discuss less complex and less sensitive issues in order to build a discussion base for more difficult subjects.

Conversations must come to *closure*, and culture guides appropriateness. First is an exchange of *feedforward* messages, indicating it is time to wrap up the conversation, usually including some type of *summary*. Next comes *agreement, additions,* or *corrections.* Finally, business is *completed, follow-up meetings* are scheduled, and *farewells* are exchanged. Frank and Rawlin conclude this way:

R: Frank, I'm impressed by how clearly you understand what we need with this product at Netline. Have I answered all your questions?

F: You've helped me get a picture of your specifications, Rawlin, and I'd like to take this to my team to get their ideas. Perhaps our team can get together with the Downsworth team before we submit our proposal. When would be a good time for your team? We'll get together whenever you say. . . .

    . . . Good. So we'll see you next Thursday. The proposals are due the 19th of the month. I'm certainly happy to meet you and look forward to our meeting Thursday.

R: Me, too. I'll reserve a conference room for us all day. See you Thursday at 9:00 in the morning.

Conversations with Clients

Organizational lore is full of stories about conversations with clients, told repeatedly to make a point. These are critical, consequential conversations that ring true to clients' values, expose organizational authenticity, and intuitively, rather than logically, present evidence on your values and "the company you keep."

For communicating with clients, become familiar with cultural patterns of conversation and observe your organization's preferred interaction patterns.

- Know what you're talking about.
- Model respectful conversation.
- Be appropriate.
- Focus on the client's needs.
- Be organized, and think clearly.
- Speak the client's language, and communicate clearly.

Detecting Deception

Most people wish they could detect lies, even if they don't like what they may learn. Paul Ekman explains the results of extensive research in *Telling Lies* (1992). Contrary to what we think, we do little better than 50/50 in detecting when another person is deceiving us, even with close friends and family. Carefully observing the same person or types of people over time increases our chances of detecting lies, but even then, we often miss their "important" lies. Fortunately, we detect truthfulness better than we can tell about lying. Lies are mixed messages in which the liar either (1) deceives with a verbal message supported with nonverbal signals, or (2) tells the truth verbally while nonverbally signaling that it's not the truth.[4] Researchers continue to seek definitive behaviors of

---

[4] Incongruous messages occur when the verbal and nonverbal dimensions of a message contradict one another, for instance, snarling "I'm thrilled you're here." Verbal messages are quotable and seem more concrete, but nonverbal messages overpower verbal messages, if contradiction is detected. When a colleague hesitates in stating a positive response to a request you make, you may wonder whether the person really wants to do it.

liars, but skilled liars are excellent actors, and they learn to act as if they are telling the truth. Muscle twitches and insufficient detail give some people away, but nervousness or excitement can also be the cause of these behaviors. Perhaps exposing truth is more a matter of seeing from the other's perspective than it is adding up specific behaviors.

The CIA, FBI, ATF, and several metropolitan police departments do just that to provide current, intensive training for their interviewers, perhaps explaining why they score higher than the norm in lie detection. As presented in the *FBI Law Enforcement Bulletin* (Sandoval & Adams, 2001), approaches such as active listening and neuro-linguistic programming (NLP) are especially effective in law enforcement interviews.

ACTIVITY 14.5

CAN FACTS LIE?

1. *Is deception always intentional?*
2. *Can consumers be deceived by giving them too much information?*
3. *In light of the following material on aspirin and acetaminophen, write a reaction paper (two or three paragraphs) to this statement: "Organizations should tell consumers the whole truth."*

* If a heart attack occurs, aspirin can reduce damage to the heart, especially if taken within 30 minutes of an attack. Aspirin may also increase the risk of another type of stroke (*hemorrhagic*) caused by bleeding into and around the brain, especially in women, and yet the misuse of aspirin and other over-the-counter pain-relieving medication is a growing problem, with more than 100,000 people hospitalized every year (Lewis, David, & Archibald, 1983).

* Middle-age women can cut their risk of strokes but not heart attacks by regularly taking low doses of aspirin, and the pills help prevent both problems in women 65 and older, a major study found. The results are opposite what is known about aspirin in men, where its benefit for stroke is limited and its ability to prevent heart problems is legendary ("Study: Aspirin," 2005).

* Acetaminophen products are advertised as a safe alternative pain reliever, without aspirin's side effects (stomach irritation, Reye's syndrome), but even small overdoses of acetaminophen have caused liver failure. At least 33 people in the United States under the age of 13 have died of acetaminophen poisoning between 1970 and 1991. There have been 152 serious illnesses ranging from hospitalization to serious disability (Hu, n.d.).

CLOSING DISTANCES WITH CONVERSATIONS, BOTH WIRED AND WIRELESS

When it comes to subtle negotiations, complex issues, or time-sensitive decision making, talking to someone is usually more effective and efficient than sending typed messages back and forth. E-mail, video conferencing, and electronic bulletin boards and chat rooms provide venues for one-on-one conversations, and are all about convenience, speed, and documentation. "Velocity is vital as we pursue e-business, e-learning, and e-relationships. These emerging forms are organic and tribal" (Boyatzis, 2001, p. 2). E-mail is the most familiar tool, and yet who would argue that voice-to-voice and face-to-face meetings build business relationships more efficaciously?

E-mail

"E-mail is a bit like a conversation at the water cooler that can be instantly forwarded to 500 people" (Gwynne & Dickerson, 1997). E-mail generally imitates conversation, and it's helpful to imagine the other party as if you were there in person. That's why first person (*I, me*), second person (*you*) and contractions (*don't, didn't, can't*) are used, and emoticons ("smileys") are sometimes inserted. In addition to being cost-effective and instantaneous, e-mail provides networking in a familiar, retrievable format globally. E-mail serves three basic purposes: (1) informing, (2) requesting, and (3) responding (Guffey, 2002), as senders post schedules for departments, inform managers of completion dates, explain decisions, and provide data or ask questions.

A more legalistic informative use is communicating policy or offering contractual agreement. Messages can be filed and retrieved electronically and, therefore, documented and tracked. In contrast to chatty exchanges, these informative business communications use a detached, formal writing style and should be treated as official policy and contractual documents.

Request memos may be individually or group distributed, depending on the request. They should be straightforward in making the request and clear about how to respond by a particular date.

REQUEST MEMOS

Reality @ WORK 14.4

In sending request memos, consider the audience. Especially when sending a request up the ladder, be careful about marking high-priority too readily. Karen Kostohryz (personal communication, September 10, 2003) says to always consider the organizational rank of the recipient: "The higher the audience the more abridged a version needs to be. For every level I go up, I cut my e-mail by half." She finds that bulleted and numbered lists highlight points succinctly. Limited use of bold or underline focuses attention to key ideas. She has learned from e-mails she receives that long, rambling messages usually mean that senders didn't think through their messages or edit them adequately.

If you request "read receipts," you will know whether someone opened your message at the other end. "Your job is to make them happy, learn their communication style, and tailor to them. If they don't read e-mail, then contact them another way, by phone, for instance."

When receiving e-mail, notice whether it was "CC'd" (a copy sent) to you for the purpose of keeping you informed and in the loop or sent directly to you, with the expectation of a reply. Always reply to direct messages. Responses to these memos should answer with the information requested and be written in the tone of the original memo. If you notice an ambiguous remark, write a response that clarifies it.

• • • • **Is Paper Pointless?** • • • •   • • • • **TIPS**

Learn the behaviors of your zoo's inhabitants. Some supervisors prefer hard copies for filing request responses; others prefer e-mail. If you think a message should be private, send your response by hard copy only through "snail mail," marked confidential and in a sealed envelope.

• • •

A *Time* magazine article warns, "As informal as it may be, e-mail is writing and constitutes a permanent record, to the eternal delight of any number of plaintiff lawyers and special prosecutors (Yes, your company reads your e-mail.)" (Gwynne & Dickerson, 1997). Other warnings to heed about e-mail make this "top ten" list.

1. Never, ever discuss personnel issues via e-mail.
2. Don't spam, use obscenities, or send offensive humor.
3. Don't reprimand by e-mail.
4. Don't forget what you agreed to do. Flag e-mail invitations to remind you of obligations, or set action items.
5. Don't lose track of important correspondence. File e-mail records in electronic folders, labeled appropriately.
6. Don't hide behind e-mail when interaction with immediate feedback is needed.
7. Don't forward correspondence meant only for you, even when it is in response to a group mailing. Respond directly and only to the sender in most cases. Avoid "Reply to all" except when it is information that should be shared with all.
8. Don't clutter people's in-boxes. Some companies prohibit sending systemwide messages (to "everyone" or "everybody") and forwarding jokes, cartoons, and similar messages at work.
9. Don't be evasive, cute, or threatening with subject lines. Use the subject line to overview a message's contents and provide a topic for filing and quick reference.
10. Don't neglect the basics. Writing in "all caps" is shouting, and "no caps" is lazy. Check grammar and spelling.

Technology-Assisted Conversations

We have a growing number of tools for electronic collaboration. Audio conferencing and video conferencing are both *teleconferencing* (*tele-* means distance), as is conferencing by telephone. Video conferencing allows communicators to give and interpret visual feedback. The term *video conferencing* generally assumes that audio is included, because both audio and video bounce off satellites and stream to communicators. Technology helps reduce travel budgets, and some conversations are actually more productive when done virtually.

Video Protocol

In recent years, the combined effects of homeland security concerns and belt-tightening in a tough economy have made video conferencing an attractive alternative to travel. The Web conferencing market is expected to grow at a projected cumulative average growth rate of 35% and reach $2 billion by 2008.

Webcams have moved beyond classrooms and into mainstream business. And it's no wonder, with falling equipment prices and an ever-increasing number of third-party service providers.

Conversations on camera use most of the same skills as other conversations, with a few adjustments:

- Know where the cameras are and treat them like people, both when you are talking and when the other person speaks.
- Don't exaggerate facial expressions.
- Coordinate supporting visuals with video equipment.
- Consider what others see at all times.
- Be responsive to messages. This is a conversation, not television.
- Create immediacy by using the other person's name, shared experiences, and the other person's opinions.
- Maintain business decorum. Look sharp, don't eat or chew gum, and above all, be respectful.

VIRTUOSOS

Dr. Laura Esserman, a Stanford-trained surgeon and MBA, pilots a project with 24 breast cancer patients following their diagnoses. Esserman facilitates virtual collaboration with doctors nation-wide. The patient is given a printout with her diagnosis, specific information about her cancer, and possible treatments with correlated data. Patient and doctor use the material in discussing treatment options. Esserman says that she can bring many doctors' opinions together with real time research data and specialists' counsel, no matter where in the world the patient is located. "With tools like these, we have . . . the opportunity to get a second—and even a third and a fourth—opinion while their primary doctor stands by." (Overholt, 2002, p. 108)

Protocol for Voice Channels

Web-based applications can integrate streaming audio with traditional telephone communication, so that someone can join a conference conversation with a mobile cell phone while others are seeing each other face to face, but remotely.

Distance communications between offices, conference rooms, and site locations alter some of the communication protocol. Chapter 12 discusses media-assisted small group conferencing, and protocol is less stringent for two persons interacting, but a technical design imposes structure nonetheless. Some systems automatically announce who is joining and who is leaving the conversation, to increase awareness and accountability.

- Agree on call protocol before the scheduled conversation. Affirm the agenda of the conversation. Have notes and pen handy. Use silent keyboards, if using computers.
- Find out who will be participating and who will be listening in. Before you agree to confidentiality, learn your organization's policy. No matter how friendly a conversation seems, business is business.

- Your voice is your "face." Communicate interest, sincerity, and other emotions with inflection and tone.
- Give the call your full attention—no multitasking and no interruptions. Make technical arrangements to block or divert other incoming calls.
- Control for outside noises. Don't add any of your own—papers rattling, pen tapping, gum smacking, nose blowing.
- Don't interrupt a speaker unless absolutely necessary.
- Introduce yourself when you join a conversation in progress.
- Be sensitive to remaining time and proportional use of time.
- Let other persons know when you are about to leave a conversation.

SUMMARY

Business is fundamentally a conversation that reveals the character of an organization. Interpersonal communication is one-to-one communication, so to have interpersonal communication, at least two people must have a practical and meaningful relationship. High-quality interpersonal communication emphasizes trust, openness, and descriptive skills in positive and expressive messages.

An organizational chart illustrates downward and upward communication paths. The higher a message is initiated, the greater the number of employees who officially receive it. Horizontal communication occurs among and between teams and departments. Less official, informal communications flow along the grapevine. Confidentiality agreements are written legal contracts between an employer and employee that protect inside knowledge of the organization.

Networks and mentors support efforts at work. Networking provides camaraderie, emotional support, creative collaboration, and combined resources, and it requires building and nurturing relationships. Mentorships are mutually beneficial connections between two employees.

Mindless communication explains many conversational blunders. Mindlessness in substantial conversations causes people to stumble and appear ignorant, mostly because they weren't thinking. ●

ACTIVITIES

1. **Team Work:** Read "Simulated Outbreak Shows Limitations of Emergency Plans," available at www.medicalpost.com/mpcontent/article.jsp?content=/content/EXTRACT/RAWART/3738/22B.html and "Communication Breakdown Hampers Acute Care," available at www.medicalpost.com/mpcontent/article.jsp?content=/content/EXTRACT/RAWART/3624/04A.html

   In teams of three to five members, discuss the communication problems inherent to a system in these medical communities. Create a chart of problems and correctives to show to the class.

2. **Technical Support and Ethically Speaking:** Read "Why Aren't There More Women at the Top?" by Trisha Krauss at www.fastcompany.com/online/37/

bookreport.html and discuss the biases at work regarding what Peggy Orenstein points out as the most basic difference between men and women: Women have babies. Find other online articles discussing how women's goals may differ from men. Write a one-page reaction paper to this statement: Women's conversations reflect different goals and values from men.

3. **Ethically Speaking:** At www.pbs.org, research the work and lives of a white surgeon and a black medical genius in "American Experience: Partners of the Heart." In small groups arrive at team consensus as you ask and answer questions central to the article.

4. **Technical Support and Ethically Speaking:** Go to media.whatcounts.com/ insider_secrets.pdf to read insider's tips on e-business. Discuss the ethical use of e-mail for business purposes.

5. **Journaling the Experience:** Search for websites using the keywords "confidentiality agreements" and "intellectual property." One such site is mytechnologylawyer.com. Identify the differences between agreements written from an employee's perspective and from an employer's. List four items you plan to look for in confidentiality agreements, especially as a contingency for employment.

6. **Presenting to Others:** Find an opportunity to listen to a group tell you their tales of work. In a 3-minute presentation, describe their culture through the lens of their stories. What was the oldest story in the organizational culture? What story characteristics indicate to you that the narrative has moved from a person's story to an organization's story?

FOR FURTHER READING

Elgin, S. H. (2000). *The gentle art of verbal self-defense at work.* Englewood Cliffs: Prentice Hall.

Rozakis, L., & Rozakis, B. (1998). *The complete idiot's guide to office politics.* New York: Alpha Books.

Scott, S. (2002). *Fierce conversations: Achieving success at work and in life, one conversation at a time.* New York: Viking Penguin.

Tannen, D. (1990). *You just don't understand: Women and men in conversation.* New York: William Morrow.

Tannen, D. (1994). *The argument culture.* New York: Random House.

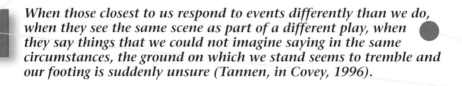

*When those closest to us respond to events differently than we do,
when they see the same scene as part of a different play, when
they say things that we could not imagine saying in the same
circumstances, the ground on which we stand seems to tremble and
our footing is suddenly unsure (Tannen, in Covey, 1996).*

Conflict at Work

15

Conflict Chemistry

Managing Self

Communicating in Conflict

A Variety of Perspectives: Conflict Theories

onflict is a normal occurrence among people in organizations, with individuals trying to meet needs, reach goals, compete for resources, and form affiliations. On one hand, escalated conflict can destroy relationships, careers, and organizations. On the other hand, conflict can be a rich, largely untapped resource for increasing "organizational and individual performance, as well as preventing harmful effects of unchecked authority or solidarity" (Morrill, 2000). Conflict is inevitable, and conflict has the potential to infuse relationships with interest, intrigue, creativity, and originality. Surprising to some, the absence of conflict often indicates a relationship void of genuine connection. We don't have to fear conflict. In fact, experts advise us to *not* suppress conflict within the organization: "The use of powerful people to prevent conflict from surfacing stifles the free expression of ideas, a fundamental condition for effective decision-making" (Maier & Solem, 1952).

Responding productively to conflict is quite different from stirring up conflict. Some people apparently don't know their hearts are beating unless they are fighting with someone somewhere. They mistakenly think aggressively presenting ideas and "standing up for themselves" makes them more worthy human beings. Linguist Deborah Tannen (1998), in *The Argument Culture: Moving from Debate to Dialogue,* exposes a cultural obsession with contentious conflict. She talks of Victor Klemperer, a German Jewish professor who recorded language distortions introduced by Hitler and other Nazi communicators, and of Kathryn Ruud, who studied Klemperer and the language usage of Nazis in the years before the Holocaust. Ruud was alarmed to find very similar verbal manipulations in radio talk shows in the United States. "It is commonplace to hear ordinary citizens, including many who would never listen to right-wing talk radio, talk in disparaging, contemptuous ways about the president and other politicians and leaders. . . . People pick up phrases, ideas, and attitudes from what they hear and repeat them as if they were their own—repeat them because they have *become* their own" (Rund, quoted in Tannen, 1998, pp. 83–84). Conflict should be treated with respect, recognizing when sincere people clash over ideas and organizations pursue goals at cross-purposes. Adversarial stances are important and necessary when good-faith efforts fail, but we fail if conflict *becomes* the culture.

In the United States, we are a people held together by our own communication. It is extremely important that we understand conflict and use it ethically and productively. The ethics of conflict rests on the truth, a quality that we can control for ourselves but not from others. Commitment to the truth means "a relentless willingness to root out the ways we limit or deceive ourselves from seeing what is. . . . It means continually broadening our awareness, just as the great athlete with extraordinary peripheral vision keeps trying to 'see more of the playing field'" (Senge, 1994, p. 159). This chapter examines the chemistry, attitudes, styles, and emotions of conflicts. It describes some categories of "difficult people" and examines skills for dealing with such people ethically, expressively, and effectively. Finally, you can compare your perspective on conflict with some leading theories in the field.

OBJECTIVES
After studying the content of this chapter, you should be able to

- Define conflict
- Recognize five types of conflict
- Analyze an individual's style of engagement
- Recognize the effects of culture in conflict
- Explain the motivations for some difficult people's behaviors
- Apply skills for ethical and helpful communication in conflicts
- Analyze conflict from several theoretical perspectives

CONFLICT CHEMISTRY

Conflict is the interaction of interdependent people who perceive incompatible goals and interference from each other in achieving those goals (Hocker & Wilmot, 1985).

> Two persons + Communication + Interdependence + Goals + Perceived interference = Conflict
> Two persons + Communication + Interdependence + Goals + Perceived cooperation = Solution

Points of agreement may require lengthy discussions, problem solving, and negotiation. Here you see an international meeting on security policy held in Munich, Germany.

According to the first equation, communication is the catalyst for conflict; according to the second equation, communication is part of the solution. Communication, then, is measured according to the other person's perceived intention. Therefore, communication can lead to competition, cooperation, or both (Folger, Poole, & Stutman, 1997). Conflict involves goals (Tracy, 1991; Pavitt & Kemp, 1999) and therefore contains strategy (Haslett, 1987; Kellermann, 1992; Pavitt, 1999). Conflict also requires some sort of confrontation, and so combatants perceive that in order for one to win, the other must lose (mutual exclusion). The outcomes range from acquiring goals to achieving domination, and sometimes to destruction. Conflict varies in intensity, from routine and low-key spats to wars demanding physical, financial, and emotional resources. A particular conflict's chemistry depends on the subject of the conflict, people's attitudes about conflict, and cultural teachings.

Subjects of Conflict

Probably the largest leap of understanding comes when attempting to discern where the conflict lies. It may be about topics, personalities, values, or procedures.

Substantive Conflict

Substantive conflict, also called *simple conflict,* centers on issues or topics. These conflicts are provoked by limited time, human resources, money, or other resources. One party wants *A* and another party insists on *B,* and to satisfy one seemingly precludes satisfying the other.

General strategies for dealing with substantive conflict seek out and rely heavily on facts and expert knowledge. We know that when groups are actively gathering information, they propose twice as many solutions as those not involved, and the solution is likely to be higher in quality than any ideas prior to the conflict (Guetzkow & Gyr, 1954).

Let's look at an example that illustrates a genuine clash, in which employees make independent and opposing choices of consultants bidding for a job.

Ann takes the lead: "OK, we agree to eliminate Bumpkin Corporation from the bid list. That gets us down to two, and Kringe has the better product." Stan replies, "Yes, but, clearly, Dwindle and Dawdle meet our specifications more closely." Ann and Stan aren't attacking one another, nor are they disagreeing that the criteria for selection are wrong. They are disagreeing on substance—which consultant to hire.

Value Conflicts

Some conflicts surround values at polar opposites, and others don't disagree on core values so much as on how to prioritize them. Conflicts arise from commitments to such values as public service, honesty, community spirit, responsible employment, and maximum profits. Value conflicts are the most entrenched and most difficult to resolve. For this reason, build on shared values and minimize clashing values. Use phrases such as "Since we all value. . . ."

ACTIVITY 15.1

CONFLICTING VALUES

1. Your manager values prompt arrival and active participation by everyone in all team meetings. You also value being a part of the team, being prompt to meetings, pleasing the manager, and putting clients first. As one meeting time approaches, you are on the phone with a client who is having a problem with one of your teammates, and he asks you to keep the call confidential. You are late for the meetings.

   How can you prioritize these valuable activities? How do you make a decision?

   Do you communicate your decision with anyone? What do you say?

   What if your action becomes the norm for other teammates?

2. "The hospital budgeted for ten billboards within the city limits. That should reach a larger segment of the market."

   "I disagree. We are a service institution. I'm not sure what purpose billboards serve."

   What are the clashing values in this dialogue?

   What values do the interactants share?

3. Yuri, a department head, believes in open communication among all levels for problem solving. Rebecca, a manager under Yuri, insists on communication through formal channels. A conflict occurs when one of Rebecca's team members discusses an idea directly with Yuri, without involving her.

   What values clash?

   How reasonable is each stance?

4. You expect John to stay at the office late to finish a project, but his daughter expects him to be at her school theater production.

   Do you encourage John to finish or to go see his daughter?

   Would John's work history affect your decision?

Ego Conflict: Personal Clashes

If value conflicts are the most seldom resolved, ego conflicts are the most difficult to manage. They also are the most damaging to interpersonal relationships. With ego conflicts, the interactants feel personally attacked and become defensive. Fights become nasty and destructive or simmering and subversive, and often the combatants have long forgotten what started the fight. The three primary sources of ego conflict at work are (1) personal and personality clashes, (2) self-serving goals, and (3) emotional reactions (Falk, 1982). The ones most frequently observed at work are as follows:

1. Passing the buck
2. Spreading false rumors
3. Going over a person's head or behind a person's back
4. Avoiding issues or ignoring pointed messages
5. Wasting time
6. Insulting a person's competence or doubting a person's motivation
7. Reneging on promises
8. Dwindling resources and higher demands
9. Power plays and playing favorites
10. Discrimination against people

Consider the example in "Substantive Conflict" about Ann and Stan deciding which consultant to hire. The conflict could escalate as an ego conflict if Ann retorted to Stan, "You are so wrapped up in rules that you are going to eliminate the group that can give us a superior product." Stan might reply, "Rules make business fair, and *I* am fair. You just think the Kringe sales rep is good looking."

Belligerent workplace warriors want others to fear them. Contrary to what they think, catapulting insults and slinging personal attacks can return to destroy the attackers and their own businesses. You can hear one-upmanship played in pre-meeting small talk, but disdain ignites fury. "As soon as we communicate verbally or nonverbally that [the opposition has] little or no value or worth, it is likely that the confrontation will fail to produce positive results in the short or long term" (Anderson, 1992, p. 117). Because meetings can mediate conflict on issues and facilitate healthy discussions about values, obvious ego conflicts show up at meetings as petty, self-serving, and inappropriate.

Procedural Conflict

Ego conflicts are often disguised as procedural conflicts, hoping the gavel will fall in their favor. A *procedural conflict* is a disagreement about how to conduct business. Tension arises among (1) those who feel the need to adhere to an agenda and procedural rules, (2) those who prefer a free-flowing discussion, and (3) those who mix official business and their own socially satisfying discussions. Although groups may use procedural protocol as a way to avoid, delay, or withdraw from an issue, genuine conflict can erupt over procedural issues alone (Putnam, 1979, 1983).

Do not let procedural conflicts become the heavy hand that overwhelms reasonable people making decisions. Create a climate of "reasonableness." Use tools presented in other chapters, such as parliamentary procedure as set forth in *Robert's Rules of Order,* decision rules such as consensus and majority rule, and orderly steps of problem solving. Also, check out the productive team membership roles discussed in Chapter 12.

When an agenda has several items requiring tough decisions, resolving each issue one at a time is ideal and orderly, but sometimes any single solution spills into other parts of the problem and into other issues. In Activity 15.2, imagine leading a team of athletic directors from small northwestern colleges. How would you bring order and introduce sequence to the meeting?

ACTIVITY 15.2

INTERDEPENDENT PROBLEMS

Label the comments from the first participant in each dialogue, as excerpted from the meeting, as (a) genuine conflict over procedure, (b) a withdrawal tactic, or (c) an avoidance or delay tactic.

1. Paul: Let's set up the rotation schedule before we get into the issue of gate earnings.

   Gene: Yeah, we're pretty much in agreement on scheduling and can crank that out in a hurry.

2. Butch: Don't ask my opinion about gate receipts. That doesn't concern me.

   Paul (laughing): You wish.

3. Alena: Every college should have an equal vote on this committee, no matter its size.

   Butch: Hold on. Some colleges are eight times the size of others. Let's straighten this out before moving to other business.

4. Jake: Recruiting is new business. Let's not discuss recruiting at the same time we discuss colleges currently on probation—clearly old business.

   Paul: But part of the probation issue is related to past practices of recruiting. I know this is a concern at *your* college, Jake, but we must discuss recruiting *and* probation at some point in these preseason meetings.

5. Alena: Women's golf is on probation because it hasn't been a part of our programs before. That's different from being on probation for violation of rules.

   Jake: Probation is probation. It means an unproven program, for whatever reason. I say we put all probation issues on the agenda together.

6. Gene: I'd prefer to talk about gate receipts after lunch.

   Butch: Will you be able to get that information from your box office manager by then?

Write a paragraph quoting what you would say at this point to bring logical order and productivity to the meeting.

Pseudo-Conflict

The imposter among the types of conflict is the *pseudo-conflict.* Judging from outward appearances, ideas are clashing, but beneath the surface, it's a sham. You may think you're in a fight, only to find that you don't really disagree at all. False conflicts occur when there is inadequate or inaccurate communication, such as the following.

- *Misunderstood actions, words, or phrases.* "When I said to cut the budget for human resources, I didn't expect you to totally eliminate their funding."

- *Misperceptions of desired outcomes.* "I am not opposed to *expanding* the business. I want to increase sales through specialty sports stores."
- *Inaccurately assigned motives.* "You misunderstand my intentions. I am increasing your travel budget to compensate you, not to require that you travel more."

As you can see from the preceding examples, most pseudo-conflicts can be resolved with added information and communication.

Personal Styles of Engagement

SELF-TEST: CONFLICT STYLE

Take the following test twice, first thinking of conflict with family or friends, and the second time thinking of conflict at work or school. Score each time separately, using "yes = 1."

1. I avoid being "put on the spot." I keep conflicts to myself.
2. I use my influence to get my ideas accepted.
3. I usually try to "split the difference" in order to resolve an issue.
4. I generally try to satisfy the other's needs.
5. I try to investigate an issue to find a solution acceptable to us.
6. I usually avoid open discussion of my differences with the other.
7. I use my authority to make a decision in my favor.
8. I try to find a middle course to resolve an impasse.
9. I usually accommodate the other's wishes.
10. I try to integrate my ideas with the other's to come up with a decision jointly.
11. I try to stay away from disagreement with the other.
12. I use my expertise to make a decision that favors me.
13. I propose a middle ground for breaking deadlocks.
14. I give in to the other's wishes.
15. I try to work with the other to find solutions that satisfy both our expectations.
16. I try to keep my disagreement to myself in order to avoid hard feelings.
17. I generally pursue my side of an issue.
18. I negotiate with the other to reach a compromise.
19. I often go with the other's suggestions.
20. I exchange accurate information with the other so we can solve a problem together.
21. I try to avoid unpleasant exchanges with the other.
22. I sometimes use my power to win.
23. I use "give and take" so that a compromise can be made.
24. I try to satisfy the other's expectations.
25. I try to bring all our concerns out in the open so that the issues can be resolved.

ACTIVITY 15.3

Scoring: Add up your scores on the following questions:

1.	2.	3.	4.	5.
6.	7.	8.	9.	10.
11.	12.	13.	14.	15.
16.	17.	18.	19.	20.
21._____	22._____	23._____	24._____	25._____
_____	_____	_____	_____	_____
Avoidance Totals	Competition Totals	Compromise Totals	Accommodation Totals	Collaboration Totals

Assertiveness index = (Competing + Collaborating) − (Avoiding + Accommodation)
Your score: _____

Cooperativeness index = (Collaboration + Accommodation) − (Competing + Avoiding)
Your score: _____

Source: Adapted from M. A. Rahim and N. R. Mager. (1995). "Confirmatory Factor Analysis of the Styles of Handling Interpersonal Conflict: First-Order Factor Model and Its Invariance across Groups," *Journal of Applied Psychology 80*(1):122–131. (Self-test adaptation as in Wilmot & Hocker, 2001, pp. 132–133.)

Based on the conceptualizations of Follett (1940), Blake and Mouton (1964), and Thomas (1976), Rahim and Bonoma (1979) differentiated the styles of handling interpersonal conflict on two basic dimensions: concern for self and for others (Figure 15.1). The first dimension explains the degree (high or low) to which a person attempts to satisfy his or her own concern. The second dimension explains the degree (high or low) to which a person attempts to satisfy the concern of others. Combining the two dimensions results in five specific styles of handling conflict. Descriptions of these styles are presented in the following list (Rahim, 1983).

1. *Integrating* style (high concern for self and others) involves openness, exchange of information, and examination of differences to reach an effective solution acceptable to both parties. It is associated with problem solving, which may lead to creative solutions.

2. *Obliging* style (low concern for self and high concern for others) is associated with attempting to play down differences and emphasizing commonalities to satisfy the concerns of the other party.

3. *Dominating* style (high concern for self and low concern for others) has been identified with win–lose orientation or with forcing behavior to win one's position.

4. *Avoiding* style (low concern for self and others) has been associated with withdrawal, buck passing, or sidestepping situations.

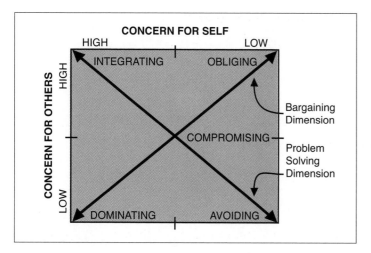

FIGURE 15.1 • Conflict Styles

Source: Rahim, M. A., Antonioni, D., & Psenicka, C. (2001). A structural equations model of leader power, subordinates' styles of handling conflict, and job performance. *International Journal of Conflict Management,* 12(3), 191–211.

5. *Compromising* style (intermediate in concern for self and others) involves give-and-take whereby both parties give up something to make a mutually acceptable decision.

Beyond these styles, the "hero" is the *collaborative style.* "Collaboration is an 'invitational rhetoric' that invites the other's perspective so the two of you can reach a resolution that honors you both" (Foss & Griffin, 1995, cited in Wilmot and Hocker, 2001, p. 161). Table 15.1 summarizes characteristics of six styles, gives typical messages, and presents typical outcomes for you to compare.

Cultural Expectations in Conflict

Culture and gender factor into persons' attitudes. We've all observed conflict in our families, schools, workplaces, and communities.

CULTURAL TEACHINGS ON CONFLICT

What have you been taught about conflict? Checkmark the items you have heard and find mostly true. Put an X by the items you have heard but find mostly false.

ACTIVITY
15.4

_____ 1. You have to stand up for yourself.

_____ 2. The one who shows anger first is the one who loses.

_____ 3. Sticks and stones may break my bones, but words will never hurt me.

_____ 4. A good person makes peace, not war.

_____ 5. Turn the other cheek.

_____ 6. Deep inside, I know what I am worth, no matter what others say.

_____ 7. Insults tell more about the speaker than the listener.

_____ 8. The best defense is a good offense.

_____ 9. Weak people don't defend themselves.

_____ 10. Fight fire with fire.

TABLE 15.1 • Five Conflict Styles

Style	Characteristics	Typical Messages	Characteristic Outcomes
Avoidance	Refuses to talk about it or walks away Changes topics Criticizes to divert the focus from a decision Passive	"We don't need to talk about that." "It'll work out." "Arguing won't help." "I wouldn't know." "Let's just try to get along with one another." Silence and irrelevant responses	Frustrates and aggravates others Can rob others of their effective power Can show a lack of caring Effective for conserving energy or avoiding costly conflict
Competition	Involved, strategic Confrontational Pushy, adversarial Goal-centered One-upmanship Put-downs, hostility Threats Stonewalling Highly active	"You are either for us or against us. Which is it?!" "That's stupid." "Don't give an inch!" "Here is what I can do." "This *is* what is going to happen." "I don't see your business doing anything we can't do." Use of language to attack, find weakness, and establish dominance	Win–lose positioning Can create enemies or alienate others; fear Initiates attack and counterattack with other competitors Can energize interaction or be destructive Knows when the goal is reached Effective in competitive contexts or in response to hostile confrontation Inappropriate in some relationships and hurts the relationship
Compromise	Win–lose approach Fairness May be active negotiation May be a passive division of resources Moderately active	"You take half of the profit, and I'll take the other half." "Let's just split the difference." "Would you be happy with that much of it?" Language of concession and negotiation	Everybody gets part, but not all, of what they want May feel treated fairly or may feel deflated by an "empty victory" Effective when there is no possibility of a solution that suits everyone or there is a limited "prize"
Accommodation	Agrees for the sake of agreeing Hides true preferences; denies needs Tries to smooth and make peace Passive	"Whatever you want." "Your idea sounds good." "I really don't have an opinion." "I'll work it out somehow." Conciliatory language	Others make the choices Resentment by either or both parties Feeling of appreciation or support by other Disrespect for the accommodator
Collaboration	Integrative Likes problem-solving and team work Consensus building Assertive—high concern for self and for other Goal-oriented and recognizes other's goal Active	"I'm sure we can work together on this." "Let's pool our information and come up with a solution." Uses descriptive and problem-centered language Avoids personal attacks Takes responsibility Open to criticism	Win–win approach to problem solving Satisfied with interaction Creates allies and collaborative networks Flow of ideas Time consuming Development of productive process

_____ 11. I'll make them think twice before they cross me a second time.

_____ 12. Some groups don't like us. Watch out for them.

Numbers 1, 8, 9, 10, 11, and 12 show a tendency toward angry expressiveness.

Numbers 2, 3, 4, 5, 6, and 7 show a preference for not expressing anger.

━━━━━━ ●

Cross-Cultural Conflict

An Israeli professor visiting the United States . . . met an American scholar prominent in her field, and she almost immediately launched into a run-down of the points on which she disagreed. She hoped thereby to show the American how carefully she had read her work—and begin a fruitful exchange of ideas. But the American professor was offended by the assault: She did not consider it appropriate to begin an acquaintance by criticizing. Not eager to let herself in for more of the same, the American professor assid-uously avoided the Israeli visitor for the remainder of her stay, exactly the opposite of what the visitor had hoped to accomplish (Tannen, 1998, p. 211).

Every culture experiences conflict, but cultural expressions differ in style and degree. Conflict can even be offered positively, when arguing *within* an established group indicates intimacy.

ETHNIC CONFLICT

Reality @ WORK 15.1

Ambassador John W. McDonald asserts, "There is no such thing as intractable, insolvable conflict" (quoted in Wagner & Minerd, 1999, p. 56). His organization by invitation trains community leaders for the long haul to "develop the skills to resolve conflicts after the peace treaties are signed" (p. 56). McDonald says that the collapse of the Soviet Union, one of the last global empires, is one reason there is so much conflict today: "Empires ruled by force and fear and kept the lid on ethnic conflict." But he points to some 5,000 ethnic groups living in 185 nations as evidence that ethnic conflicts can be resolved (Wagner & Minerd, 1999).

Apparently, cultures and the organizations in them need orderly proce-dures, rules, or rituals to set parameters for disagreements. Some generalities are helpful: Harmony is valued highly in such countries as Japan, China, Thai-land, and Vietnam, where persons publicly appear agreeable in order to help the other party "save face," even when they clearly do not agree. People from these cultures have low tolerance for open conflict. A Greek or Italian, on the other hand, is more likely to be openly and directly confrontational. Germans tend to display intellectual prowess through arguments and flagrantly dis-pute others' positions. Without boundaries, fights are more likely to become uncontrollable, violent, and physical, so good advice is to err on the side of politeness.

Because we are from different "gender and ethnic cultures," we need to work diligently at understanding one another's meanings.

Conflicts arise from attitudes.

"These feminist types don't last too long."

Gender in Conflict

Cultural conflict rules are different for men and women, and of all dynamics that separate genders, the practices in conflict are the most significant.[1] According to primitive roles, males confronted the enemy to protect their tribe and family, while women built relationships and alliances to insulate themselves and their offspring from danger. Even now, males and females learn to deal with and use conflict so differently that it is as if they were from distant countries. Males and females are acculturated within gender to experience and respond differently.

Men and women are equally willing to deal with confrontation in important matters, but women are less likely to enjoy fighting just for the sake of fighting. Men are more likely than women to banter or argue on less essential issues, engaging in the "game" at a business level. Men may find a good fight

---

[1]   The range of normal behavior among men and among women is very wide—in fact, it is more varied than the difference between the sexes. "The forces of gender are far more complex than a simple male–female dichotomy suggests. Many variations exist, shaped by culture, geography, class, sexual orientation, and individual personality" (Tannen, 2002, p. 1671).

entertaining and energizing. Fighting creates a bond, whether fighting with other males or against them, because of the allies, adversaries, and conversational scripts it creates. Women, on the other hand, prefer harmony in their work environment and will withdraw, ignore, or accommodate on small issues, even at personal expense. Because women are more likely to be the peacemakers behind the scenes, they are often astonished at how men heartily disagree on issues and walk away as if nothing troubling had happened.

Regardless of gender, participants are more likely to report using an accommodating style if the other person is female (Berryman-Fink & Brunner, 1987). Typically, both genders compete more at work and accommodate more at home. It follows that active, collaborating strategies of negotiation at work should improve the trust level, satisfaction, and sense of fairness among work associates (Wilmot & Hocker, 2001).

Madeleine Kunin, who served as the first woman governor of Vermont, and later as assistant secretary of education and ambassador to Switzerland, writes that speaking in public and dealing with conflict were her most important challenges. "No matter how politically skilled one became, controversy could not be avoided. . . . Speaking out always carried a price." She had to communicate outside her native culture—she was a female in male-land. "The fearful idea that by speaking out I would no longer be a good girl, that my words might antagonize those who heard me, was deeply rooted. If I said the wrong thing at the wrong time I risked punishment: I might not be liked. Worse yet, I would not be loved" (Kunin, 1994, quoted in Tannen, 1998, p. 202).

Even though it is probably impossible for an individual to disregard all cultural teachings, individuals still sculpt personal conflict styles (Bazerman, 2000). We can manage our personal styles, if we choose to.

• MANAGING SELF

No matter the driving force of a conflict, conflict management requires self-management and self-discipline. If we can't manage ourselves, what right do we have to manage others? Especially when others confront us, we must manage our own needs, self-messages, and emotions before responding. As important as emotions are to us, no emotional experience is perfectly communicated to others.

Perhaps life was going well until the clashing moment. "In such a situation you may not have been aware of making a specific choice about whether to engage or not, yet that choice defined all future interactions" (Wilmot & Hocker, 2001, p. 135). At that moment, it seemed as if the other person or the event made you angry or caused you to act a certain way. To understand the emotional dimensions of conflict, this chapter first discusses attitudes about conflicts and their possible outcomes, and then discusses the emotional experience during conflict. *Attitudes* are collections of past experiences that shape present emotional experiences. Earlier this chapter studied personal style preferences in conflict, and now it examines (1) approaches to conflict, (2) expectations about outcomes, and (3) skills for communicating emotions.

Passive, Aggressive, Assertive, or Argumentative Approaches to Conflict

The self-test in Activity 15.5 leads to concepts about aggression, assertiveness, argumentativeness, and passivity.

WHICH ARE YOU? PASSIVE, AGGRESSIVE, ASSERTIVE, OR ARGUMENTATIVE

Think of situations in which you have experienced conflict and respond to the following statements with one of the following choices:

1 = usually false
2 = occasionally true
3 = usually true

1. I have a short fuse and am angered easily. I like to "vent," and I feel better after a heated fight.
2. I am blunt by nature and don't mind taking charge of any situation.
3. The end result justifies whatever means you use to get there.
4. I take credit wherever I can, because I don't want to be seen as a loser.
5. I make a mental note of others' offenses and errors, so that if they criticize me, I have ammunition.
6. Most people bend the truth to get their point across.
7. I believe "the best defense is a good offense," so I am quick to attack verbally.
8. Compromise is a "dirty word," because the other person wins some ground.
9. A boss has the right to say anything. With power, you use it or lose it.
10. I am quick to recognize put-downs, criticism, and snide remarks, and I can put others in their place.
11. Although others take credit for my ideas and work, I will be quiet and wait until others realize my value to the organization.
12. It is wrong to argue. When others hurt my feelings, I must keep it to myself.
13. Frequently, my feelings are hurt because of others' rude remarks.
14. Others describe me as reliable, patient, and agreeable.
15. I don't really care what others do, and I do not feel responsible for them or their work.
16. I am tired of being blamed for others' errors.
17. I am often unsure of my point of view, so I generally agree with the ones present.
18. Other people cannot hurt me. "Sticks and stones may break my bones, but words will never hurt me."
19. I am scared to confront others, because of what they may say about me.
20. I avoid argumentative people. I feel like the loser in most conflicts.
21. I recognize my responsibilities to the organization and to the people who work there.
22. Multiple solutions exist for most problems. I enjoy seeking the ones that meet many individuals' needs.
23. I tell the truth out of respect for others and for myself.
24. I enjoy listening to others' ideas and knowing about their successes.

25. I am comfortable making decisions and communicating them to the people affected.
26. I enjoy interacting with people of different points of view.
27. I choose my words carefully and avoid personal attacks.
28. Often discussions bring out better solutions than any one person brought into the discussion.
29. I treat others the way I want to be treated.
30. I share responsibility for the outcome of my team, for better or for worse.
31. A good argument is like playing a sophisticated intellectual game.
32. Sometimes I take the opposite side for the sake of the argument.
33. I feel energized after a lively argument.
34. I prefer arguing with someone who is knowledgeable.
35. When discussions get boring, I introduce a controversial topic.
36. I am at my best when logically advocating a position at work.
37. I expect people to tell me openly when they disagree.
38. I am skilled at listening for faulty reasoning.
39. I take heated discussions with opposing views personally.
40. Arguing brings issues to the surface and facilitates problem solving.

Scoring: The first ten items describe an *aggressive* individual, items 11 to 20 describe a *passive* individual, items 21 to 30 indicate *argumentativeness*, and the final ten items describe an *assertive* individual.
   Use the following scale as an informal indicator of your preferred type.

   11–13 points = Weak tendency toward type
   13–20 points = Moderate tendency toward type
   21–30 points = Strong tendency toward type

Aggressive communicators (competitive style) use their abilities to get their ways at all costs. They often have difficulty with self-control, are more likely to be self-centered, and more often have shallow relationships. Convinced that their views are correct, they don't consider the ideas of others. They are likely to feel entitled to other people's time and energy and come across as dominating and hot-headed.

Passive communicators (avoidance, accommodating, and sometime compromise styles) are just the opposite. Passivity assumes, "I'm not involved, and nothing affects me" or "There's nothing I can do about it, so why try?" In still another common form, passive communicators try to inordinately control themselves and their resources. They manipulate others (and sometimes distort their own thinking) in order to take care of their own discomfort before attending to the needs of others (passive aggressive behavior). They feel "forced" to lie and deceive, because they are so uncomfortable confronting others. Trying to please everyone, they may appear two-faced.

Assertive communicators (collaborative style) know where to draw the line between their rights and others' rights. They accept responsibility and expect others to do the same. Honest and open, they tactfully speak up to tell the facts as they see them. They have good self-awareness and predict and interpret others' emotions well.

Argumentative communicators (most often found in competitive, compromise, and collaborative styles) eagerly and logically debate issues. They enjoy intellectual competition and respect others who can hold their own with knowledge and skillful reasoning. Argumentative people even argue with themselves in order to think through all sides of an issue. In fact, if you agree with an argumentative person, that person may switch sides for the sake of a lively argument.

Win–Lose, Lose–Lose, and Win–Win Expectations for Outcomes

"Leaders who manage conflicts best are able to draw out all parties, understand the differing perspectives, and then find a common ideal that everyone can endorse. They bring the conflict to the surface, acknowledge the feelings and views from all sides, and then direct the energy toward a shared ideal" (Goleman, Boyatzis, and McKee, 2002, p. 256). For *win-lose* expectations people who see themselves as winners may feel entitled to whatever others have. People who see themselves as losers are likely to become dependent and depressed, withholding their ideas and expending a minimum of their (feeble) effort.

Lose–lose (nobody wins) thinks every proposal is a loser and looks no further. This predisposition lives in pessimists, cynics, and severely depressed individuals. "If we cultivate more clients, we will have more work, have to hire more people, and risk more investments" and "Why should I try to solve this problem? I would probably make a bad situation even worse."

Win–win requires creatively approaching a problem, welcoming challenges, and expecting multiple solutions. Win–win enters the dialogue expecting to satisfy the needs of all parties involved. Contrary to what some people think, win–win is not seeing the world through rose-colored glasses. Instead, it looks for answers, while others eliminate possibilities with their negative thinking or competitive approaches.[2] Groups who avoid win–lose and majority rule show superior quality in decision outcomes, as compared to those engaging in other tactics (Barnlund, 1959). Furthermore, consensus groups are more creative than majority-rule groups (Hall & Watson, 1970).

Managing and Communicating Emotions

Granted, sometimes emotion is hard to manage, but managing the self is the foundation of maturity. Sometimes our common sense betrays us, and such is the case with emotions.

Managing Emotions

Events do not cause emotional reactions, as we might think. In fact, we do not experience any particular emotion until we *interpret* what the event means and evaluate its importance to us. Have you ever wanted to laugh at something naughty a child did to "make" you mad? Or perhaps you felt satisfied that

---

[2] A side note for a different perspective: Many Asian cultures value the coexistence of both winners and losers for balance and harmony.

Honest discussions include communicating attitudes responsibly and giving feedback openly.

someone was trying to "make" you jealous. In the first few seconds, we make decisions about how to use that first pure shot of emotion. Allowing the first notion that comes to mind to became the behavioral choice makes us victims of our own habits.

Throughout the text, we have discussed perception, cultural context, meanings, language, and empathy. We are therefore equipped to entertain numerous interpretations, not just the first ideas that cross our minds. We are in control of our own thinking and can explore possible intentions by the sender.

Anger and depression are probably the first emotions that come to mind when we think of conflict. Long-lasting bitterness is the most physically harmful emotion to the angry person. Anger is also the most destructive emotion to interpersonal relationships. People who are quick to anger do not have short fuses so much as they take things personally. Anger signals that something is important, but managing that anger is essential for managing difficulties.

CONTEMPORARY VOICES 15.1: GOLEMAN ON EMOTIONAL RESPONSES

Daniel Goleman warns us not to succumb to an emotional hijack, becoming hostages to emotion's physiology. Sense data coming in for processing prompts a knee-jerk (habitual) interpretation, quickly bypasses the reasoning part of the brain, and heads for the primitive brain, which only knows "fight or flight." In that old brain mode, the body prepares for an emergency, heightening blood pressure and releasing hormones. Following a physiological, chemical release, the body takes hours to return to normal. Emotional intelligence requires assessing what is truly dangerous and looking openly for possible interpretations, intentions, and responses.

Communicating Emotions

Sometimes we need to communicate a feeling directly to the other person; other times low-keyed, logical dialogue is the best option. Whatever the choice, we still communicate emotion by what we say and quite often by what we *don't* say, by how we act and how we avoid acting. When parents block toddlers from getting what they want, they are in conflict, and toddlers try screaming, crying, throwing something, or refusing to talk (basically, whatever works). Some adults immaturely, like the toddler, act out their emotions.

TAGGING EMOTIONS

Giovanni:	Geez! This sucks! Who does she think she is, telling me how to do my job?
Helena:	You're talking about the new supervisor, Cassie?
Giovanni:	Yeah. What the hell! I'm *not* doing the inventory *her* way. Takes too long. Unreasonable witch.
Helena:	I'm afraid you'll get in trouble if you don't do it her way.
Giovanni:	Now *you're* on my case. I don't have to defend myself to you. You act just like management—egotistical.
Helena:	I worry that you may lose your job, and I like having you here, but I resent your attacks on me.
Giovanni:	Mortgage is due and my kid is sick today. I bought that Harley this year, too.
Helena:	You are worried about your financial responsibilities.
Giovanni:	Damn right. Uh, forget what I said. You didn't deserve that.

Discuss in dyads (two people):

1.   *Who is experiencing strong emotion in this scenario?*
2.   *What is Helena's role in the communication?*
3.   *What emotions do Giovanni and Helena express? How do they express them?*
4.   *Do you find evidence that either or both of them made conscious choices regarding whether to communicate emotion?*

Imagine how you would respond to a class teammate who neglected her responsibilities in a group assignment. Next, imagine your supervisor asking you to work over the weekend because he didn't finish a report. Would the tone of your response be the same? Observing and making choices about one's own behavior is called *self-monitoring,* a very emotionally intelligent thing to do. Before communicating emotions, weigh the advantages and disadvantages according to the situation and persons in conflict, as in Table 15.2.

• • • • **TIPS**   • • • • **Engage Brain before Opening Mouth** • • • •

Before expressing your feelings, quickly think through a few questions:

- Are your motivations ethical?
- Is your emotional state pertinent to the situation?
- Do you want the other person to know your emotions?
- Do you think the other person will listen to you without becoming defensive?
- Is this an appropriate time, place, and setting for this communication?

• • •

Determine whether an emotion is relevant to the discussion and to the outcome. Understand the feeling and, if you choose to express it, decide *how*

TABLE 15.2 • Advantages and Disadvantages of Communicating Emotions

Advantages	Disadvantages
It is a part of building positive relationships.	You may become more vulnerable.
Personal emotions are effects that are not easily debated by the other person.	Some see it as showing weakness or become uncomfortable acknowledging it.
The other person does not misinterpret your feelings.	The other person may "smell blood" and pursue the issue relentlessly.
The overall communication becomes more accurate.	Accuracy does not guarantee progress toward conflict resolution.
You avoid blaming others and take responsibility for your own feelings and behavior.	Responsible behavior is new and insecure for some people who prefer to think others "make them feel" the way they do.
You take away the perception that the other person can control how you feel.	The other person may resort to a pseudological approach.
If the other person wants to cooperate, he or she will function with better understanding.	If the other person wants to escalate conflict, he or she will have more ways to hit where it hurts.

to express it. If you are satisfied that this is appropriate, use these guidelines to formulate your message:

- Show responsibility for your own feelings. Usually this is done with an "I" message.
- Label your emotions clearly and accurately with words, usually with adjectives (*happy, concerned, confused*) or verbs (*worry, resent, look forward to*).
- Anchor the message in the present, not the past or the future. Use the present tense when reporting a current emotion.
- Tell what your emotions relate to or what you are reacting to.
- Be aware of your tone of voice and facial expression to indicate your trustworthiness in word choice.
- Tell whether you expect something from the other person.

The following is a helpful, although oversimplified, formula for key elements:

am	because	I expect you to . . .
I + feel + adjective + when . . . + and so		I would like . . .

Can you find all the elements in these model messages?

"I feel discouraged when I don't get feedback on my work, and I want you to tell me whether I am doing good work or not."

"I am very happy to be on your team. You acquire such interesting projects. You can count on me to be productive."

"I experience frustration every time I try to learn something from that dad-blamed instruction manual. Please talk the steps through with me."

●—●—● COMMUNICATING IN CONFLICT

Conflict may be born of clashing personal styles (personalities) or clashing positions on issues. Because all messages have both emotional and content dimensions, communicators should be quick to determine how to address these dimensions.

● ● ● ● **TIPS**   ● ● ● ● "If" ● ● ● ●

- If people's emotional needs are met, they move on to issues more readily.
- If you can influence the communication context, focus on one thing at a time.
- If you listen and give nondefensive responses, others are more likely to be open.

● ● ●

Ego Conflicts Surround Difficult People

The bully is your boss. A pleasant colleague doesn't deliver the goods. A coworker loudmouth snipes during meetings. You despise the "bull of the woods" who doesn't bother with accuracy while climbing the organizational ladder. These are the truly difficult people.

A Zoo of Difficult People

When ordinarily well-intended individuals find their goals thwarted, they intensify their usual approaches. In *Dealing with People You Can't Stand,* Brinkman and Kirschner (1994, pp. 4–33) introduce their "most unwanted" difficult people. The first three types of difficult people feel a strong need to be in control.

1. The *Tank* is pushy, confrontational, pointed, angry, and aggressive. Tanks damage indiscriminately.
2. The *Sniper* is full of snide remarks, sarcasm, rudeness, or derogatory nonverbal behaviors such as rolled eyes.
3. The *Know-It-All* really does know a lot, but can't take criticism, contradiction, or correction. This person overwhelms with long arguments, discredits others, and dominates time. "Know-It-All" is also quick to blame others.

The next three types are pessimists and perfectionists who come unglued when "things aren't right."

4. The *Nothing Person* gives minimal feedback, even when the other person desperately needs it. "Nothing" is usually uncomfortable and uncertain, so with nothing positive to say, he or she says nothing. "Nothing" often throws back a problem, refusing to have anything more to do with the problem or the people.

5. The *No Person* feels hopeless and can kill ideas and hope with a single word. Disguised as a mild-mannered person, "No Person" declares, "Forget it; it will never work," and enlists others into negative thinking.

6. The *Whiner* feels at the mercy of a merciless world. The whiner is a perfectionist who wants equally miserable colleagues. "It's all wrong," Whiner whines.

And then there are those who desperately want to get along with others.

7. The *Yes Person* wants to avoid confrontation and tries to please everyone. "Yes" overcommits, has no time for himself or herself, becomes forgetful of earlier commitments, and eventually becomes resentful.

8. The *Maybe Person* procrastinates regarding decisions, hoping for a better solution, until the decision makes itself.

Some people, when they feel they are not getting enough attention, make poor communication choices to get the attention they think they deserve.

9. The *Grenade* has a brief period of calm before erupting explosively, ranting and raving about items that have little to do with the present situation. The Grenade is likely to be even more volatile for subsequent events.

10. The *Friendly Sniper* (a variation of the Sniper) is playful and actually likes you. Many relationships include playful sniping, but those who repeatedly play the game are hurting beneath the surface.

11. The *Think-They-Know-It-All* bluffs his or her way to the spotlight by fooling enough people into believing the ruse and being swayed by the appearance of irritation.

Difficult people are pitied for their weaknesses, feared for their assaults, and shunned because of their annoying ways, but they do what they have learned to do and what gets them what they want.

Responding to Difficult People

Let's see what Brinkman and Kirshner (1994, p. 73) say about dealing with the more aggressive difficult people: Tanks, Snipers, and Grenades.

Tanks (aggressive, competitive)   Attacking, defending, and withdrawing backfire on you. Instead, hold your ground and gain respect. Aggressive people require assertive responses. Avoid turning into a Tank. Take a deep breath of self-control, while maintaining eye contact. The Tank will open a round of fire, but let him finish and ask if he wants to say anything else. "Is that everything? All right, then, I'll get back to work." If you have something you must say, interrupt by saying Tank's name as you normally would in conversation until the person gives you full attention. Immediately repeat Tank's main point to show you've been listening. Get to the bottom line with a concise message. Allow Tank to roll away with dignity.

Snipers (aggressive, competitive)   Because Snipers feel compelled to get things done, if they think someone is blocking them, they will sneakily attack through rude remarks. Don't become an easy target by letting Sniper know your feelings are hurt. (He or she will dish out more.) To get sniping to stop, you're going to have to learn how to live with it, because if the Sniper can't get you to react, the behavior loses its value (Brinkman & Kirschner, 1994, p. 86).

What you can do is *expose* the Sniper, who thrives on covert activity. There are several possibilities to consider.

- Question the relevance of the snippy remark: "What does your remark have to do with our team-building effort here?"

- Question the intention of the Sniper: "When you said . . ., what were you really trying to say?"

- With a Sniper holding a grudge, bring the grudge to the surface in a private conversation: "Several times you have made remarks about women managers. For instance, . . . and . . . . What message are you trying to send with these remarks?" Follow with, "In the future, if you have a problem with something I do, come talk to me directly, so we can work it out."

Grenades   Grenades get their pins pulled when they don't feel adequately appreciated, and they then demand attention. They lose control and explode. Blowing up at a Grenade in return or disliking the Grenade from a distance only feeds the dynamics that set up the explosion in the first place. If the Grenade starts to "lose it," then take control of the situation.

Grenade: Nobody cares how hard I've worked. This whole organization is heartless. They don't care about the customer, the environment, ethics . . .

You: Dale, Dale, we do care how hard you've worked. You are very appreciated. Please don't assume we don't care. And the solution was right on target, just like you predicted.

As you talk, reduce the intensity of the message and tone. Give everyone a break, and promise to reconvene later to work things out. Messages that may help are

- "I want to have less conflict with you. What made you so angry today?"

- "How can I be most helpful at the times you lose your temper?"

- "What response would you have preferred from me?"

Disallowing Victimization

"For there to be prey, the prey must agree to play the role of the prey" (Spence, 1996, p. 195). How do we engage in conflict without being a wimp or a jerk? Preparation equips us with general strategies that inform the heart as well as the mind (based on Spence, 1995):

- Be generous in assessing motivations and attributions. Identify others' threatened goals and intentions.

- Find shared values and emphasize them. Affirm the person, and focus on issues. Agree with what you can. Show appreciation.

- Use sound reasoning and a reasonable tone of voice.

- Listen and paraphrase. Ask key questions. Identify your needs and others' needs.
- Use narrative to engage others' empathy and understanding.
- Be credible and ethical, and radiate good will. Connect with others positively, so that they experience your expectations of all that is good and reasonable in them.

When we follow these suggestions, we do not frame and reduce people to "opponents," while we stand tall and refuse victimization. It takes high principles and skills to use language constructively and responsibly.

> When little children do harm with their language, we make allowances for their lack of experience. When adults who are physically or mentally impaired do harm with their language, we make allowances for their lack of competence. We make similar allowances for adults who are simply ignorant. In all such cases we do everything we can, consistent with the individual's capacities, to discourage the offensive language behavior, but we try to be tolerant. We assume that if the person's circumstances were different, the language would be different as well. This is rational—even admirable.
>
> But when verbal violence is committed by educated and competent adults in positions of responsibility, allowances should *not* be made. The grammar of verbal violence is part of their internal grammar. They are skilled in its use, just as they are skilled in any other aspect of their language. And when the adult is an executive or professional, such language behavior constitutes Malpractice of the Mouth. (Elgin, 2000, p. 101)

"If someone says X, what can I say back?" When others are at their worst, how can we be at our best? The key to dealing with a variety of situations is developing flexibility. The following subsections examine two attack patterns that difficult people use and how to deal with them, based on Elgin's *The Gentle Art of Verbal Self-Defense at Work* (2000).

The Bait + Sheltered Attack   The bait is an "if you really" type of phrase followed with an insult. That is, a presupposition precedes an attack.[3]

• • • • **Response to a Bait + Sheltered Attack** • • • •   • • • • **TIPS**

1. Ignore the bait, no matter how tempting or outrageous.
2. Respond directly to a presupposition.

                                                                  • • •

Attack 1: "If our organization *really* mattered to you, *you* wouldn't have accepted that other time-consuming community project."

Response: "What makes you think I don't care about this organization?" (Immediately focus on the presupposition.)

---

[3] A *presupposition* is anything that a person understands to be part of the meaning, even if it is not outwardly stated.

Attack 2: "*Even* an old-timer like you could operate *this* computer."

Response: "I am surprised you would draw such a conclusion about people older than we are. I know many retirees who are very competent on computers. In fact, my neighbor designs software, now that she is retired from teaching. You know, John is in his office. Let's ask him whether this is a common assumption."

The Intonation Attack   A second common attack pattern uses intonation. Verbal attacks have strong stresses in the tone of voice, which produce an "abnormal melody."

• • • • **Response to the Intonation Attack** • • • •

1. Behave as if the attacks are serious questions or claims.
2. Talk in full and at length without defensiveness.

• • •

Attack 1: "WHY did you write about such a STUpid TOpic?" (Uppercase indicates exaggerated intonation.)

Response: "I believe the subject first occurred to me while I was reading the *Journal of the American Medical Association.* Yes, that was it. It was the January, 2003, issue. I wouldn't have noticed it, except my sister's husband is an otorhinolaryngologist—an ear-nose-throat doctor, you know—and we were waiting for him at his office. I looked for something to read and saw an article about the emotional effects of losing a sense of smell. In communication we call the study of the communication of smell olfactics. I was curious about the physiology and thought others would find that interesting." (You get the idea. Continue until you are sure the other person never wants this to happen again. Each time the person makes a snide remark, try the same "Boring Baroque Response.")

Difficult people and those from whom we must defend ourselves engage primarily in ego or relational conflict. Another type of conflict we recognize and to which we must respond in some way is substantive conflict.

Substantive Conflict

Substantive conflict deals with disagreements about specific issues or proposed solutions. The different attitudes (assertive, aggressive, passive, and argumentative) and expectations of outcomes (win–lose, lose–lose, lose–win, and win–win) are the groundwork for skillful communication in substantive conflict.

Strategies for Substantive Conflict

Conflicts do not take place in a vacuum, and topics are brought up, responded to, reiterated, and developed as a unique event between the interactants.

1. *Be ready.* Expect the unexpected. We don't always pick our battles—some pick us and surface without warning. *Sound* sure-footed: "I'm glad you brought this to my attention." "Do you have time in an hour? Let's get the team together."

2. *Know when to introduce a topic.* Pay attention to the topics that are being avoided or hidden, sometimes by diverting to a different issue. If an issue that affects your choices is omitted, introduce the issue with an appropriate statement or question: "We haven't discussed how this project will be budgeted."

3. *Actively pursue an understanding of the other person's position.*

   "I'm not sure how to interpret what you just said."

   "I wonder whether we are thinking the same thing."

4. *Know when to let a topic go.* Recognize when an issue is dead or has been discussed to death (Reardon, 2000). Also, don't argue a point that the other party already agrees with and lose what you have already won.

5. *Follow the leader, and lead the follower.* Pay attention to the other person's reaction for your next cue. Think carefully about how much you can expect to affect other interactants. We all can be effective with some people and in some areas.

6. *Persistence pays when you are low in formal power.* Lower-power people in a conflict can increase their power by persisting in their requests.

7. *Consider the possibility of a bigger pie.* Do not initially assume limited resources.

8. *Swiss cheese or fractionation strategy (Fisher, 1969).* If you take enough bites out of the slice of cheese, it becomes full of holes until it's totally consumed. Break a problem into its parts or issues to make it more manageable for debate, compromise, or negotiation.

9. *Two-column method.* Analytical listeners identify emerging themes, competing interests, and perceived costs and rewards. The two parties' interests can be organized in two columns to clarify the conflict. A similar approach is to identify the "pros" and "cons" of each proposition.

Comparing Styles

In a groundbreaking study (Lawrence & Lorsch, 1967), six different types of organizations preferred "problem-solving" as the method for conflict resolution, with "competing" as the back-up. Several studies later tested which styles worked best in a variety of situations. Table 15.3 summarizes the research analyzed by Folger, Poole, and Stutman (1997) in their discussion of styles, strategies, and tactics used in conflicts. Read across the table this way: "This (style) when (context) caused these (results)."

Following are six criteria for deciding whether to engage in a specific conflict:

1. How do you want to present yourself or your organization publicly?

2. How important are the issues to you or your organization?

3. How important are the issues to the other person or organization?

TABLE 15.3 • **Comparative Studies of Conflict Resolution Methods and Their Results**

Method	Style Pairing Comparisons	Results
Negotiating; bargaining[a]	Competitive matched with competitive	Stalemates
	compared to	
	Competitive matched with collaborative	Higher mutual agreement, but competitors won more than half the time
Negotiating and needing bargaining toughness[b]	Assertive toughness by one party only	More favorable final agreement[d]
	compared to	
	Equally tough, but fair[c]	Optimal solution
	compared to	
	Uncompromising toughness	Counterattacks and stubbornness
Managing	Forcing (competitiveness)	50% "bad" results (measuring managers' effectiveness[e])
	compared to	
	Problem solving (collaboration)	100% "good" results
Approaching a task	Problem solving	Effective (measuring task accomplishment[f])
	compared to	
	Accommodating behaviors	Less effective
Managing conflict in engineering firms[g]	Problem solving	Most effective
	compared to	
	Smoothing behaviors	Less effective, but effective
Intense or active problem solving	Group problem-solving path to solutions[h]	Comparatively lower-quality solutions
	compared to	
	Exposing conflict by competing, compromising, and problem solving	Higher-quality solutions
Matching interactions	Matching (each party matches the move made by the other party, reciprocally)	Contagion of matching behaviors; induces competitive parties to cooperate, even in the larger group
Negotiating; bargaining	Threats	More compliance[i]
	compared to	
	Promises	Less compliance

Source: Folger, J. P., Pode, M. S., & Stutman, R. K. (1997). *Working through conflict: Strategies for relationships, groups, and organizations.* New York: Longman.

[a] Filley (1975)
[b] Bartos (1974)
[c] Bartos (1974)
[d] Chertkoff & Esser (1976)
[e] Phillips & Cheston (1979)
[f] Jones & White (1985)
[g] Burke (1970)
[h] Putnam & Poole (1987)
[i] Rubin & Brown (1975); Pruitt & Rubin (1986)

4. How important is the relationship?

5. What are the time constraints?

6. What is the level of trust between the parties?

CONFLICT WITH THE BOSS

Two hundred people who took on their bosses in conflict say these are some things they learned (Hornstein, 1997):

- Brutal bosses don't just survive—they thrive. Some of these bosses are protected from *their* bosses because they are delivering exactly what upper management wants, and they are protected at the top.
- Don't talk like a victim. Humility with brutal bosses invites assaults. Don't apologize, and don't confess.
- In order to survive the trauma, "don't suffer in silence." Confide in a trusted coworker. Pretending to be tough only causes you to suffer more.

Negotiation

As you have already noticed, one way to deal with apparent conflict is negotiation. Negotiations actively engage all parties and may be competitive or collaborative. In *Getting to Yes: Negotiating Agreement without Giving In,* Fisher, Ury, and Patton (1991) advise separating relationship conflicts from substance conflicts (p. 21). Deal with people problems directly in three areas: perception, emotion, and communication. Having covered perception and emotion elsewhere, we can narrow the focus to negotiation and communication.

We negotiate in many contexts, but negotiation[4] is often seen in the context of labor union–management communication. These negotiations demonstrate three common phases, which have much in common with problem-solving models (based on Morley & Stephenson, 1997, cited in Folger, Poole, & Putnam, 1997):

Distributive Bargaining Phase

- Preparing cases
- Taking on roles to represent "sides"
- Testing the feasibility of possible demands
- Establishing criteria for appropriate settlements
- Assessing the power of each side
- Evaluating the strength of the cases being made

Problem-Solving Phase

- Exploring solutions according to criteria
- Some tactical maneuvering

---

[4] *Negotiation* and *bargaining* are usually used synonymously.

- Establishing a working relationship and exploring possible solutions to problems

Decision-Making Phase

- Agreeing between parties
- Exploring implications of the solution(s)
- Testing feasibility and implementation

CONTEMPORARY VOICES 15.2: GOLEMAN ON NEGOTIATION

A negotiation can be viewed as joint problem solving, since the conflict belongs to both parties. The reason for the negotiation is that each side has its own competing interests and perspective and wants to convince the other to capitulate to its wishes. Agreeing to negotiate acknowledges that the problem is shared and that there may be mutually satisfying solutions available. Herbert Kelman, a Harvard psychologist who specializes in negotiations, points out that the process of negotiation restores cooperation between conflicting parties. (Goleman, 1998, p. 180)

In two paragraphs, report a time you negotiated for a better grade or increased privileges with a teacher or employer. How did the resolution change your relationship?

Negotiating parties develop their own rules and norms, and for most conflicts, negotiation is preferred over litigation. For some conflicts, everyone involved would benefit from the assistance of a third party, as in the following three forms of intervention.

- *Adjudication:* A legally binding intervention in which an authority calls parties together to resolve the conflict. Primarily used when negotiation breaks down, it forces a negotiation between parties.
- *Arbitration:* Also a legally binding intervention, in which parties come together voluntarily.
- *Mediation:* Brings in a third party to lead and facilitate a negotiated agreement.

 A VARIETY OF PERSPECTIVES: CONFLICT THEORIES

By now, you probably have some of your own thoughts about conflict. You may find a colleague of like mind among leading theorists and theories. First, firm up your own theoretical views of conflict in Activity 15.6.

ACTIVITY 15.6

TEST YOURSELF: POINTS OF VIEW ON CONFLICT

Answer True or False to each statement after considering your experiences in conflicts.

1. Sometimes a person imagines being in conflict with me, and I am unaware a problem exists.
2. I can avoid conflict by communicating clearly.

3. I have to discuss terms and examples with others to see whether we are in agreement.
4. I have to mentally imagine a conflict in order to engage in it.
5. I think communication makes a conflict into a fight.
6. In retrospect, I have difficulty determining when a conflict actually began.
7. The best defense is a good offense.
8. Conflict is destructive, and I avoid it as much as possible.
9. I only get angry when I'm around arrogant and unkind people.
10. Others procrastinate and cause delays in a job. Sometimes I am forced into an impossible situation, but I delay a job as little as possible.

After reading an overview of various theories, match a theory to each of the statements. How can you benefit from a variety of theoretical approaches?

Theories are perspectives that help us better conceptualize and analyze a process. Let's meet a few relevant to the study of conflict.

- *Reciprocity theory* retraces interactions. "He hit me first" challenges many parents to find out who started the conflict. It sees each interaction as reciprocating to an earlier act or message. Reciprocity theory holds that individuals adapt their communication in response to the immediate, prior communication by the other party.

- *Verbal aggressiveness theory* holds personality traits responsible for the aggressive "nature" of individuals (Infante & Wigley, 1986; Infante, Rance, & Womack, 1997). People low in argumentation skills (a positive trait) and motivation are more likely to become aggressive (a negative trait). Low-argumentative persons are uncomfortable in conflict, associate arguing with suffering and unpleasantness, and, when pushed to the limit, have a tendency to launch personal attacks on the opposing party.

- *Attribution theory,* studied in Chapter 2 applies to conflict as well. Individuals commonly attribute others' behavior to dispositional factors and their own behavior to situational factors. To maintain and enhance self-esteem, individuals often defensively attribute actions resulting in negative consequences to external forces and attribute positive consequences of the action to themselves (Folger, Poole, & Stutman, 1997).[5]

- *Cognitive theory* says that the true location of communication is in the mind; therefore, conflict does not exist until you perceive it exists. Cognitive theorists emphasize perception; encoding and decoding functions; predicting and planning for messages; and message strategies.

- *Interactional theory* ties meaning to context. Meanings emerge as a part of the interactants' communication and are negotiated between the interactants.

---

[5] For a discussion of conflict theories, see "Contemporary Theories of Conflict" in Folger, Poole, and Stutman (1997).

●
**ACTIVITY
15.7**

PERSPECTIVES ON CONFLICT

Cognitive and interactional theories give us two perspectives for the dialogue of Danylle and Frank.

> Frank (Chief Projects Coordinator): The problem is sheer, absolute ignorance!
>
> Danylle (a team manager): I resent you calling this team stupid. Another team did the proposal, and we don't know what management agreed to.
>
> Frank: That's what I meant. Your people can't be expected to work in ignorance. You all should have been included in the initial meeting with the client. Since it's too late for that, we need to set up a meeting. Why are you so defensive?
>
> Danylle: I thought you were blaming us. OK, the meeting should start us in the right direction.
>
> Frank: Sure. We cure ignorance by involving smart people at the outset.

1. *When does the actual conflict begin, according to our definition of conflict?*
2. *Did the speakers change their initial perceptions? How?*

SUMMARY

By definition, conflict is the interaction of interdependent people who perceive incompatible goals and interference from each other in achieving those goals. Conflict can be over issues (substantive—or simple—conflict), values, or procedures. Egos can clash, or sometimes a conflict only seems like a conflict, and the parties actually do not disagree.

One way to determine one's style in conflict is to find one's intersection between "concern for self" and "concern for other." Scales of aggressiveness and involvement refine the placement of individuals' styles, which can be classified as avoidance, competition, compromise, accommodation, and collaboration.

Cultures and genders view conflict differently. Women and men are equally willing to deal with confrontation in important matters, but women are less likely to enjoy fighting just for the sake of the sport. Attitudes and approaches also shape outcomes of conflict. Some people passively avoid or withdraw from conflict, and others charge in without regard to anyone's needs but their own. Those with assertive attitudes (usually a win–win approach to problem solving) stand up for their needs but do not feel entitled to others' resources.

Anger is a common emotion in conflict. Ethical argument involves taking responsibility for one's own emotions and expressing them without blaming others. Difficult people range from irritating "Yes" people, who readily agree to take on tasks but don't follow through, to "Tanks," who destroy everything in their path. Skillful communicators keep their wits about them when confronted by a verbally abusive person.

Overall, problem solving is the preferred style for dealing with conflict in organizations, although competing and compromising have also succeeded, contingent on the situation. For low-importance and costly (in terms of resources or time) issues, many prefer less aggressive styles, such as avoiding and smoothing. ●

1. **Technical Support and Journaling the Experience:** Read "Open Mouth, Close Career?" at pf.fastcompany.com/online/20/openmouth.html Summarize in your journal what you can learn from Carol Roberts' experience and Dan Oestreich's advice.

2. **Team Work:** Divide the class into three teams. One-third of the teams will represent college administration, and another third will represent students. The final third will represent faculty. Through research and discussion, form a position on the length of a semester and the number of "break" days. Negotiate a final solution.

   Burke (1998) and Anderson (1988) say that not all styles of dealing with conflict are equally effective. Which of their styles matches most closely with competition? Which ones match with collaboration, with withdrawal, and with smoothing? (Styles are listed in order from least effective to most effective.)

   - *Forcing* coerces the other person to accept the forcer's stance and, thereby, to "lose." Forcing may be physical force or psychological manipulation. Forcers coerce because they can.

   - *Withdrawal* means retreating, walking out, or tuning out.

   - *Smoothing* soothes the communicators, makes peace, envisions positive aspects, and creates a respite from sensitive issues. Everyone feels better, but progress halts.

   - *Compromise* brings parties together to "meet somewhere in the middle." Each person wins some and loses some.

   - *Confrontation with problem solving* invites opponents to the table. The debate focuses on the *problem,* and *persons* are not attacked. The persons collaborate to move toward an agree-able solution.

3. **Presenting to Others:** Research a strategy for dealing with conflict. With a partner, role-play for the class how that technique works.

4. **Team Work:** Divide the class into four teams. The "Creative Problems" team will configure three or more jigsaw puzzles (under 150 pieces per puzzle) into two packages of mixed pieces. You do not have to include all the puzzle pieces in either package. You may mix them any way you like. You may put in some odd pieces from other puzzles. Present the problem to the two conflicting teams ("The Dynamics" and "The Champions"): "You have a package of puzzle pieces. If either team completes a puzzle, that team gets 50 points plus one point for every puzzle piece linked into place. If you do not complete a puzzle, you earn 2 points for every linked piece. You have two class periods to finish your product." The fourth team, "The Superiors," may ask five questions that the Creative Problems team will answer with "yes" or "no." The Superiors, now having limited insider knowledge, will observe the processes of the Dynamics and the Champions, making notes of the strategies each uses. The Dynamics and the Champions may request the help of the Superiors to mediate their interactions for solutions, at the cost of 75 points per team.

5. **Journaling the Experience:** Explore at least four websites on conflict, negotiation, or mediation. Since sites regularly revise and update, you may need to do a

general search for the organizations' names. For each website you explore, write a brief description of the purpose of the site.

For whose use is the site designed?

Which ones are individuals more likely to use? Which ones are organizations more likely to use?

What are two major features of each site?

6. **Presenting to Others and Ethically Speaking:** The United States Supreme Court records the court's majority opinion (a ruling), as well as the court's minority opinion. Prepare a three-minute position presentation agreeing or disagreeing with one of the following statements:

a. "Minority opinions do not reflect the decision of the court and should not become a part of public record."

b. "Leaders who require consensus coerce dissenting parties into agreeing with the majority position."

FOR FURTHER READING

Numerous articles on conflict are available online at http://workhelp.org/content/blogcategory/72/60

Eidelson, R. J., & Eidelson, J. I. (2002). Dangerous ideas: Five beliefs that propel groups toward conflict. *American Psychologist, 58*(3), 182–192. (This article reporting research through the Solomon Asch Center provides a good summary of five belief domains that may cause large-scale conflicts in the workplace due to engaging groups defined by ethnicity, nationality, religion, or social identities.)

The following sites serve as resources for mediation and arbitration:

Academy of Family Mediators http://www.igc.apc.org/afm

Victim Offender Mediation Association http://www.spidr.org

American Arbitration Association http://www.adr.org

Institute for Global Communications and Peace Net http://www.igc.apc.org/igc/issues/cr

National Conference on Peacemaking and Conflict Resolution http://www.web.gmu.edu/departments/NCPCR

Women in Distress http://womenindistress.org/signs.htm

International Association of Facilitators http://neo-humanista.org/IAFWEB

Nova Southeast University http://www.nova.edu/ssss/DR/univ.html

Higher education is the only business that has a ceremony for firing its customers. Colleges spend thousands of dollars on recruiting students, and then, after four years, those colleges make students dress up in a gown, march them across a platform, and then fire them . . . . Educational institutions that survive will move . . . to a model that turns students into members of a network . . . that keeps them engaged over the course of their life (Masie, in McCauley, 2000).

Interviews and Appraisals

16

Clear the Way

Interviewing for Employment

Interviewing Applicants for Employment

Performance Appraisals and Correctives

A graduate from a top MBA program sought the advice of a director of the career center at Harvard Business School:

"Right out of school, she decided that she wanted to start a chain of pizzerias that were of better quality than California Pizza Kitchen," James Waldroop recounts. "So she spent six months on the idea, raising capital and talking to some consultants. She finally determined—and I agreed—that her idea wouldn't work. So she pulled the plug. She had an interview coming up for a marketing job that she wanted to land more than anything in the world. But she felt this great embarrassment over the pizzeria experience. I walked her through the questions that the interviewer was probably going to ask, and she realized that pulling out of the venture was actually a very mature decision—which was a great point to make in the interview. The weight was lifted from her shoulders, and she got the job. The point is that even just discussing things that you feel embarrassed about can be enormously relieving." (Rosenfeld, 2001)

Interviews and appraisals are complex, consequential tasks. Whether conducting or responding in these structured interactions, you need to anticipate what will happen, how you will respond, and how you will feel during the process. This chapter discusses skills for getting a job, skills for hiring others, and skills for using critical feedback productively.

OBJECTIVES

After studying the content of this chapter, you should be able to

- Interview well for employment
- Interview others for employment
- Interact in an assessment interview
- Give and receive criticism in a corrective interview

    This chapter forms the bridge between what you have learned in college and your opportunity to use it. There's a certain kind of tension and excitement as you prepare to enter a career. You want your skills in order and your knowledge packed, but you don't want to take extra luggage that will only slow you down. So, clear the way.

 CLEAR THE WAY

Certain character traits damage self-concept and hold others at a distance, creating problems at several levels in the workplace. Waldroop and Butler (2000) categorized problematic tendencies as follows:

- Individuals with the *imposter syndrome* feel they don't belong where they are or don't deserve the opportunities.
- *Meritocrats* fight the good fight until everyone is out of patience and worn out.
- *Heroes* constantly try to do too much and push too hard. Heroes will "expend whatever resources are necessary and make whichever sacrifices have to be made. They storm the castle, take out the bridge, and blast through the wall—when 100 yards away there's a door that could have been taken instead" (Waldroop & Butler, 2000).
- *Peacekeepers* see themselves as diplomats but are really afraid of conflict. They try to keep peace at all costs.
- *Procrastinators* feel ashamed, rationally or not, of their perceived inabilities.

    Once people can reasonably identify with successes, let go of lost causes, ease up on others, and face fears of conflict and failure, they are ready to function more fully as professionals. With the pathway clear, we are ready to practice the skills of employment interviews and assessments.

INTERVIEWING FOR EMPLOYMENT

Employment interviews epitomize consequential conversations. In them we recognize the potential of a single statement to redirect our lives—where we work, with whom we work, and for whom we work. The Speech Communication Association (1997) analyzed responses from questionnaires sent to personnel interviewers at 500 businesses. Over 90% of the respondents said communication skills are essential for success, but only 60% found applicants to be prepared with those skills by the time of their interviews. Furthermore, approximately 90% agreed an employee's ability to communicate is a determining factor for promotions. So it is not surprising to see corporations specifically seek communication skills and initiative in their applicants.

According to the Bureau of National Affairs, the employment interview is the single most important factor in getting a job offer (Peterson, 1997). Unfortunately, employers who are untrained in employment interviewing often fail to find the best candidate from their pool of applicants (Moulton, n.d.). In those cases, the burden rests squarely on applicants to communicate how well they fit the job and how much the organization will benefit from hiring them.

Getting slated to interview is a job in itself. Colleges and universities conduct job fairs and provide placement offices to assist their graduates in getting jobs. Other organizations advertise recruiting visits. As a newer twist, a few companies have screened applicants with an unexpected phone quiz, in which they ask technical questions in the applicant's field of study.

Inside Information

Learn about an organization before interviewing with it, and find how your values and credentials fit its needs. Determine the core business (what the organization makes or does), the size and scope of its operations, and the challenges, competition, and constraints with which it deals. Study job descriptions, websites, online sources (America Online, Prodigy, Csi-Compuserve, Monster.com), and published articles about the organization.

One headhunter (Corcodilos, 1997) suggests that the real matchmaking of job and applicant takes place before the interview. Investigate a prospective employer to find out whether you and the company are a good fit or not.

Kenton Green of Ann Arbor, Michigan, while completing a doctorate in electrical engineering and optics at the University of Rochester, researched potential employers to learn about their culture, goals, and competitors. "I would find an article published by someone in my field who worked at a company I was interested in. Then I'd call that person and ask to talk, mention my employability and discuss the company's needs. One of two things happened: I'd either get an interview or learn we weren't a good match after all" (quoted in Corcodilos, 1997).

Perhaps you don't feel as qualified as Kenton Green may have been, but an employer *wants* to hire you. If you fill the bill, the employer can stop interviewing and get back to work.

Presenting Yourself in Résumés and Cover Letters

Résumés alone won't get you a job, but they can get you in the door. A résumé introduces you on paper. It presents your work history, academic achievements, and contributions within organizations.

A résumé can be ready at a day's notice, if you keep it up to date. A *job-specific résumé* matches a job to your experiences and descriptions. For a job-specific résumé, let descriptions emphasize skills for the job, for instance, "Led 20 employees in a technical team to develop an international project involving three airlines" or "Technical designer for an international airline product," depending on whether you want to emphasize your leadership or technical experience. Also, edit the general résumé to include relevant entries:

June, 2003–current   Global Software, Inc.

Systems Analyst   Austin, TX

Led a design team of 20 employees in developing Web-based support for three regional airlines in five contiguous European countries.

Quick Guide for Résumés

There is no one right way to write a résumé, but there are many wrong ways. Here are some guidelines for preparing successful résumés. Examples 16.1 and 16.2 present typical résumés.

- Begin with a brief description of what you have to offer and the kind of job you seek. Reflect the job you want in your description, but don't narrow it to that position alone. An introductory summary statement is generally preferred over objectives.

- Most organizations prefer a chronological organization under major headings, such as education and training, work experience, and community service.

- Arrange the sections of a résumé so that the top half of the first page presents your strengths. If your education is recent and stellar, let them see that first, followed by distinctions. Include a list of skills, such as "skilled in Java script, Microsoft Excel, and web page design." If you have been out of school for a while and have gained expertise in a related area, put your experience, expertise, or technical training and certification up front.

- Avoid using italics or other fonts that are difficult to read. Electronic scanners won't read all fonts, especially uncommon ones..

- Electronic scanners identify key descriptors, such as *manager, engineer,* and *physical therapist,* and action verbs, such as *supervised, organized,* and *developed.*

- Traditional organizations respond well to white or cream-colored, high-quality paper and a matching legal-size envelope. Use adequate postage.

- Check for sample résumés, other tips, and lists of action verbs at helpful college and university websites, including the University of Wisconsin's: www.bus.wisc.edu/career/pubs/sampleresumes/Tips.htm

- Match the organization's style. If it is conservative, show restraint and dignity. If the organization is known to be highly creative and upbeat, let measured creativity surface, but present yourself professionally, not as "cute."

- For artistic and product-oriented jobs, mail your résumé, cover letter, and portfolio work, if requested, personal websites are another way (generally expected in business and technical fields) to showcase your work.

- Carefully follow directions for submitting résumés, as included in the application. Find out how the organization prefers to receive your résumé—by mail, by e-mail, or both.

- You can apply to companies that have not posted job openings. Personnel managers, human resources managers, and other key managers may have contact information on the organization's website. You usually can submit a cover letter and résumé by e-mail.

EXAMPLE 16.1

SAMPLE RÉSUMÉ

Madison Travinsky

7801 Progression Drive
Talkome, Florida, 30890
Business: 802-555-6278
Email: mat@hof.rr.com

SUMMARY
Motivated and talented project manager with broad experience in marketing and advertising. Versatile learner, self-motivating, productive, and creative. An ethical and effective communicator interpersonally, with a team, and in presentations. Extensive knowledge of children's products globally. Enjoy managing teams with diverse experience and challenging projects.

EDUCATION
B.S. Degree in Business, Marketing and Finance (1995) **graduated cum laude** (3.82 GPA)
University of Southern Florida, Tallahassee, Florida

Continuing Education Short Course, "Marketing Abroad, England, France, and Italy"   2004
Webster University, Talkome, Florida

Graduate Course, Research Design and Statistics (Business MBA program)
Baylor University, Waco, Texas   Spring, 2005

CAREER HISTORY & ACCOMPLISHMENTS
Executive Assistant to the Mayor, Talkome, Florida   2003 to present
Responsible for the budget for the Office of the Mayor. Coordinated public appearances and press releases for the mayor. Worked directly with heads of local and state media, attorneys, and executive directors of major philanthropies. Conducted research and made recommendations for platforms and programs for the mayor. Prepared a successful $8.2 million federal grant proposal to provide affordable housing locally.

Director of Marketing, Southern Division, Baby and Company   2000–2003
Responsible for overseeing marketing developments in southern market segment for Baby and Company. Managed department of 57 employees on 8 teams in five states. Developed the 2003 marketing strategy, which yielded 22% growth in profit.

Project Manager, Innovative Plastics, Inc.   1995–1999
Coordinated three teams for the development of toys for seven clients. Key liaison with clients in multimillion dollar corporations. Built a reputation of returning clients to Innovative Plastics. Responsible for reports to clients' executive boards and Innovative's CEO and Board of Directors.

MEMBERSHIPS & AFFILIATIONS
Mayor's Councils of America Affiliate Member, Florida Chamber of Commerce Member, Historic Florida Foundation, Rotary Club President.

SAMPLE RÉSUMÉ
Justin Thyme

1214 Ambition Way
Snowyton, Minnesota 55810
Home: 972-789-6321   Business: 972-123-456   fax: 972-123-4568
Email: thyme@earth.com

Objective

To contribute experience, training, and skills as a project manager.
Highly motivating, outcome-driven, and people-oriented, experienced in:

Business and Market Analysis
Computer Software Systems Integration
Global Business Development

Experience

2004–2006   TinyTunes, Inc.   Nashville, Tennessee
Business Analyst
- Expanded territorial sales by 400% in response to initial analysis.
- Designed and developed sales tracking analysis by area.
- Initiated development of multilingual products.

2001–2004   Hill & Hagan, Attorneys at Law   Crockton, Minnesota
Intern
- Researched global business relations of clients.
- Prepared and presented businesses' briefs to counsel.
- Awarded the firm's sole undergraduate scholarship for 2003 and 2004.
- Developed a computerized filing system for Hill & Hagan's clients in Germany, Austria, and Poland.
- Integrated databases from client with filing system.
- Coordinated philanthropic activities of firm.

1999–2000   ABC Mart   Dresden, Minnesota
Associate
- Customer Services. Productively dealt with customers who returned or exchanged merchandise. Won and implemented proposal to improve customer satisfaction.
- Stock Manager, Electronics. Managed six weekly shifts of four employees. Named outstanding manager two years.
- Improved method for tracking inventory that eliminated redundant orders and saved 11% from previous year's cost.

Education

2000–2004   Central State University   Crockton, Minnesota
- Bachelor of Science, *cum laude.* Business Administration and Computer Science.

2004–2006   South-central University   Mythplace, Tennessee
- Master or Business Administration, Marketing

2005   Microsoft Training   Orlando, Florida

Interests

American Red Cross, Cross-country Skiing, Choir, and Racquetball

Cover Letters

Include a cover letter with a résumé. In the opening line, it should connect the readers to you as someone they want to work with. Address the letter to specific individual(s) rather than "To whom it may concern." Explain (1) how you became interested in the job or organization, (2) how your values and abilities align with theirs, and (3) the unique benefits that will come from hiring you. Be positive, sincere, and straightforward. A sample letter is provided in Example 16.3.

● **EXAMPLE 16.3**

SAMPLE COVER LETTER

Ursula Heisler

822 Vintage Way
Greeley, CO 80631
Home: 970-345-8900
Cell: 970-344-5358
fax: 970-345-8900
e-mail: uheisler@hoc.rr.com

October 20, 2004

Mr. Elin R. Aught, Manager of Human Resources
Destiny Utilities
Fort Collins, CO 80521

Dear Mr. Aught:

Problem-solving skills, team membership and leadership excellence, a high aptitude for learning, a penchant for details, and knowledge capital from employment in two states are qualities I want to bring to a position in the utility industry. Ever since I read the June, 2000, IEEE journal, I have followed the assertive projects at Destiny Utilities. The Assistant Accountant position currently posted on Destiny Utilities' website describes an excellent match for my interests, experience, education, and aptitudes.

Destiny Utilities' job description emphasizes the challenges of cross-departmental tasks. As an undergraduate in accounting at University of Colorado, Boulder, I chose to intern with Essential Energy, Inc., a Texas engineering consulting firm. As a research assistant during the initial phases of legislated deregulation, I worked with engineers preparing to meet with the Energy Regulation Council of Texas (ERCOT). I was responsible for explaining how engineering practices would impact accounting procedures and policies. For this work and upon the recommendations of my supervisors, I received the Outstanding Intern Award for 2002, University of Colorado's School of Business.

After completion of an accounting degree and within my first month of full-time employment at Greeley Utilities, I was appointed to a team responsible for recommending billing policies and online applications to the Greeley Utilities' Board of Directors. I shouldered a major research assignment for the project and was credited with four of the recommendations to significantly simplify the billing process.

I have the background to confidently choose a career in an organization and would like very much to discuss the Assistant Accountant position with you. I will be in Fort Collins next week and will contact your office to schedule a time to meet. If you wish to schedule an earlier time, please contact me at the numbers or addresses provided.

Thank you for your time and consideration.

Sincerely,

Ursula Heisler

Study appropriate attire to wear to an interview at organizations where you would like to work.

What to Wear

"Corporate attire" is safest for interviews. Dress conservatively. *The Complete Idiot's Guide to Office Politics* suggests you call ahead and speak to a secretary or administrative assistant and ask about the dress code (Rozakis & Rozakis, 1998). *Corporate wear* means long-sleeved white shirts, dark suits, and ties for men. A nice watch is the only jewelry. Likewise, corporate wear for women means suits, one-inch heeled and closed-toe shoes, and conservative jewelry. *Business* or *corporate casual* usually means khaki slacks, a striped or subtle plaid woven cotton shirt, and a neutral, contrasting blazer. Women adapt with tailored slacks or skirts, blouses, and blazers.

Women should wear conservative jewelry and subtle cosmetics. If you are shopping for that one good "interview suit," keep in mind that for men and women, dark gray, black, and navy solid or pinstripe suits get the highest marks for competence and credibility (Sundaram & Webster, 2000).

Of the many factors affecting whether someone gets a job, attractiveness is often the tie breaker. Attractiveness is not limited to physical traits, as seen in one study (Osborn, 1996) that showed posture being as important as body build in influencing how attractive others think we are. Physical attractiveness becomes less important as the perceiver learns more about the person. For *first* impressions, however, new acquaintances judge that attractive people are more likely to be friendly, credible, and competent (Reis, Nezlek, & Wheeler, 1980).

Who Will Be There?

Standard interviews are traditional interviews in which an applicant sits down with management, professionals, and personnel directors. The most common interview format remains a one-on-one interview, but you may be interviewed by several people at the same time or with several applicants together. A typical *interview board* includes a recruiter, a human resources manager, and a department or team manager. For technical and highly specialized jobs, experts join the board.

Organizations are as eager to find the right employees as you are to find the right job. "Now, with shareholder scrutiny, hiring slowdowns, and diminishing budgets, no manager can afford to hire the wrong person. Companies ranging from J. P. Morgan Chase to General Electric Co.—and hundreds more—are

TABLE 16.1 • **Getting What You Pay For in Hiring**

Interview Style	Accuracy in Predicting Performance (%)
Standard interview	7
Résumé analysis	37
Work sample test	44
Assessment center	44
Situational interview	54

Data are from *Handbook of Industrial and Organizational Psychology,* as summarized in Merritt, 2003, p. 63.

switching to the new methods" (Merritt, 2003, p. 63). In the 1980s, companies experimented with innovative formats to get strengths and weaknesses to surface in their finalists. Such interviews involved a cast of interviewers and assessors. A comparison of the relative accuracy of hiring strategies illustrates the reasoning behind the shift from traditional to novel approaches. As you see in Table 16.1, the best predictor for job success is the situational interview, with 54% predictive ability. Today, hiring practices usually combine interview styles.

What Will Interviewers Ask?

What interviewers ask depends on what they are looking for. Some organizations start with work sample tests and skills tests. Other organizations use off-site consulting groups to assess emotional intelligence, interpersonal skills, personality, nonverbal communication, oral response abilities, critical thinking, and style preferences.

If the situational interview has the highest predictive ability, how do organizations design these interviews? "Ever since Microsoft made headlines for its unconventional approach to interviewing, more and more companies are looking for that certain approach that will uncover just the right quality of mind" (Kane, 1995). *Experiential, situational,* and *behavioral interviews* are similar in that they test applicants with novel situations that require thinking in the moment. Interviewers challenge applicants by describing technical problems, irate customers, or difficult clients, and ask how the applicant would handle the situation. Answers are followed up with probing questions to determine the applicant's depth of understanding and experience (Kelly, W., 2004, personal communication). Interviewers could, for instance, set up situations requiring marketing ideas responding to a given demography, employees competing for resources, and medical patients with difficult families.

Interviewers pay attention to the applicant's behaviors: facial expressions, tone of voice, awareness of others, emotional control and appropriateness, and creativity. They also have antennae attuned to ethics, values, openness, and priorities. Of course, onterviewers must work within guidelines about discrimination and invasion of privacy issues.

Interview boards may be seated formally behind a table or in informal arrangements of comfortable chairs.

Dialogic, Interactive Model

Anticipate what will go on during an interview, and prepare for commonly asked questions. Think in terms of introduction, body, and conclusion—just like a speech presentation.

"Failure to ask questions tells the employer that you don't care much about the job or that you aren't very bright and are accustomed to accepting whatever anybody hands you" (Griffin, 1998, p. 63). Asking questions will help you determine whether this is a job you want. The questions also tell some things about you. Usually, interviewers are open to questions during an interview and at the end of an interview. Just don't attempt to control the interview and frustrate your interviewers. The Tips featured on page 452 give questions that may be appropriate for you to ask. Table 16.2 models an interviewee's responses and allows you to complete the interview dialogue.

TABLE 16.2 • An Interview Dialogue

The Interview Dialogue	The Silent Agenda
Interview Team (TEAM): Hello, I'm Joseph Grice, Director of Human Resources. Did you have a good flight?	Grice thinks: I'll introduce myself, have a little small talk, and be ready to introduce the interview team. The team for each interview decides ahead of time who asks which questions, but we make it seem conversational.
Interviewee (YOU): Hello, Mr. Grice. I'm happy to meet you. Thank you for making all the arrangements. It was a beautiful day for seeing the city from the air.	Grice thinks: This is an upbeat and positive applicant.
or	
My drive was very pleasant, but I do appreciate your offer to fly me in.	Grice thinks: You are appreciative and do not exploit the organization. You recognize, you do not take for granted, and you appreciate acts of thoughtfulness and support.

TABLE 16.2 • (continued)

The Interview Dialogue	The Silent Agenda
TEAM: We're glad you're here. Let me introduce Barb Milam, Manager of Engineering, and Glen Watson, Design Engineer for Transmission.	Team thinks: You seem composed and confident, since you look at each person as he or she is introduced.
YOU: I recognize your names from the Zenon Project. I am so pleased to meet you. I looked up your article after seeing Zenon cited in my management text. I would like to hear more about that project sometime.	Team thinks: You are familiar with the organization's work and have done your research. You made a meaningful connection. You go beyond what is assigned in a class; you probably will do the same at work.
TEAM: We can talk all day about that one. Is that what interested you in this organization?	Your compliment is acknowledged, and the topic is switched to this job and perhaps your career goals.
YOU: ~~Honestly~~, I became aware of ABC, Inc., a couple of years ago, when George Peterson became CEO and applied some of Peter Senge's ideas. I was interested in how his five disciplines would work here.	(You started to use an "honest" qualifier. "To be perfectly honest with you," "actually," and "to tell the truth," indicate you had considered not being honest and truthful.)
	Team thinks: You know who the CEO is, and you know some of his philosophy and history with the organization. You are familiar with a top name in organizational literature.
	(You are careful to not judge this organization's application of Senge's disciplines.)
TEAM: Of course, some things sound good in a book but don't work here. What was it about Senge's work that you liked?	Team thinks: Let's test your knowledge and also see how you handle disagreement.
YOU: Mental models make sense to me, although that was not a new idea at VMI, and his discussion of mental models lets me know that some paradigms may inhibit problem solving. I agree with the need to stay open to learning new things. I am interested, though, in your perspectives, because there's nothing like real life to test the theories.	Team thinks: Smart. You choose a discipline from Senge that is not controversial, and no, you are not bluffing. You understand the basic tenets.
	(You are flexible and not dogmatic. You do not assume you know all the answers.)
TEAM: That's good insight. Yes, *The Fifth Discipline* is on every employee's bookcase. We find that some people are so competitive that they don't share information in-house, and others are so open outside the organization they don't respect confidentiality. I guess you can say we are still learning. Just last week we got an e-mail on confidentiality.	You just got a compliment. With that connection they disclose to you their reservations with some of the application of Senge's principles.
	They introduce a new topic to see what you do with it.
YOU: What is your policy on confidentiality?	Team thinks: You know to ask pertinent questions.

(continues)

TABLE 16.2 • (continued)

The Interview Dialogue	The Silent Agenda
TEAM: Pretty much it says to keep information and ideas in-house, especially if it is a new development, but keep your ear to the ground about what other companies are doing. Anything you create as a part of ABC belongs to ABC. I can get you a copy of the confidentiality agreement, if you like.	Team thinks: Good question from an interviewee. This is not a popular issue, so we will offer information but not continue with specifics of the agreement.
YOU: I would like to see a copy. What you have said sounds consistent with what I would expect.	Team thinks: You evaluate new information with background knowledge.
TEAM: I don't recall learning about that in college. Where did you pick up on confidentiality agreements?	Team thinks: Let's see if you care about the credibility of sources.
YOU: It was in my first business management course, and I discussed it with my brother, who works at NASA.	Team thinks: You know where you learned it. You checked it out with someone whose opinion you trust.
TEAM: Speaking of college, what have you found most valuable about your college experience?	Team thinks: Are you mindful about education and experience?
(Additional questions with your responses to why you chose your major, how college has prepared you for a career, and which subjects you like best and least.)	Team thinks: You are mindful and prepared. You expose your values.
TEAM: I see that you worked on campus in the math department and two summers for the Learning Technology Center. Describe an experience you had in one of these jobs and what you learned from it.	Team thinks: We have read your résumé. Let's see how you process job experiences.
YOU: Those were good jobs to learn from. As a math department tutor, I worked with professors who were far ahead of me in math and who rattled off formulas and applications I hadn't yet studied. They seemed to expect me to understand, and so I studied and asked questions until I did. That's when I discovered that I am a very self-motivated learner, and I can learn from a lot of sources. As a tutor, however, I couldn't assume that about others, and I began to realize how threatening and emotional learning math is for some people.	Team thinks: You acknowledge the question and set the tone. You work well with others, both those who know more and those who know less than you. Team thinks: You do not take an inferior or superior stance. You accept responsibility. You are a self-starter. You have emotional intelligence in empathizing with others.
Those experiences helped me on the job at the Learning Technology Center. I led a team supporting learning technology for evening classes. It was a sink-or-swim learning experience. For instance, there was one history professor who loved using online teaching tools. He would surf into the distance during a class, or the	You use key words: *team, lead,* and *support.* You are responsible and adaptable.

TABLE 16.2 • (continued)

The Interview Dialogue	The Silent Agenda
university system would shut down, and he'd call us to "come fix this old equipment." We knew that he would chew out whoever showed up. It was definitely an emotional event for him. The first thing I would ask him was when he could take a break, so we wouldn't interrupt his class. That was so he could save face with the class.	You are culturally sensitive to the power structure in a university and help the professor save face.
I initially was the one to go, but I made a point to take a new student employee with me, in order to mentor the employee in dealing with similar situations. I suggested we commiserate with him about the problem, compliment him on what he was doing for his class, and ask for some time to "try to fix the problem." After a while, employees competed to go to see who he would like best!	You value mentoring. You have interpersonal communication skills. You enjoy the accomplishments of others.
TEAM: Good, so you've had experience working with teams. Would you describe the tech center job as stressful?	Team thinks: We want to know your attitude about stress.
YOU: Stressful? No, at times challenging, but not stressful. I enjoy being in a position to make decisions, solve problems, and make a difference.	Team thinks: You frame tasks and responsibilities positively. You are not intimidated by problem solving.
TEAM: You don't sound like someone who gets stressed easily. Can you think of a time you were, and what you did about it?	Team thinks: We approve of your answer. Here's a question about how you deal with stress.
YOU: [Tell about a stressful situation that you handled with finesse.]	
TEAM: Tell us what interested you in this job.	Team thinks: I don't think this applicant is as naïve as the last applicant, who said, "The money." Let's see.
YOU: [Answer with specifics, and tell how the organization can benefit from your competency.]	
TEAM: What do you see yourself doing in five years?	Team thinks: How motivated are you? Do you plan for your future? What career path do you want?
YOU:	
TEAM: If a team member makes a significant error, what would you do?	Team thinks: What supervisory skills do you have?
YOU:	
TEAM: If you made a mistake as a part of a team, what would you do?	Team thinks: Are you open and honest? Who will you tell? Will you be part of the solution?

(continues)

TABLE 16.2 • **(continued)**

The Interview Dialogue	The Silent Agenda
YOU:	
TEAM: What are your three best qualities?	Team thinks: Can you identify overarching values and connect them to our organization?
YOU:	
TEAM: We've been asking you a lot of questions. Do you have any questions for us?	Team thinks: Can you take charge and lead this part of the interview?
YOU:	

• • • • TIPS   • • • • Questions Interviewees Might Ask • • • •

Early in an Interview

- *Qualifications:* "May I highlight some of my qualifications for this job?" or "Is there something on my résumé that you would like to know more about?" (Use this one if the interviewer is at a loss for words and questions.)
- *Nature of job:* "What creative challenges do you see in this job?" "What problem-solving opportunities does the job offer?"
- *Job fit:* "How would you describe the person who is an ideal fit for this job?" "What, in your opinion, are the most important qualifications for this position?" "How would you describe the organizational climate? Energetic? Open? Dynamic? Frantic? Stormy?"

If the Interviewer Is Very Knowledgeable about the Position

- *Specifics:* "What results would you like me to produce?"
- *Organizational priorities:* "What organizational priorities affect this department?"
- *Problems:* "What are the problems for the department currently?"

Later in an Interview

- *Organization's concept:* "Is this a newly created position? When was the need recognized?"
- *Salary:* "What is the salary structure for this position?" "What health insurance and retirement options do you offer?"
- *Abdicator:* "Was the person who formerly held this position promoted?" (A positive way to ask, "What happened to the last guy?" If the person continues in a positive role or relationship with the organization, ask to meet with him or her.)

Follow Interviewers' Cues for Closure

- *Visualization:* "Do you see how I can be a part of this team and produce for this company?"
- *Procedure:* "What is my next step in this process?"
- *Omissions:* "Is there additional information you would like me to provide?"
- *Response:* "When can I expect to hear from you?"

• • •

If Interviewers Ask Illegal Questions

Employers are forbidden by law to ask questions about your marital status, age, ethnic or national origins, religion, and sexual orientation (Wilson, 1991, cited in Bovee and Thill, 1995, p. 394). Decide ahead of time how to deal with awkward requests. If interviewers ask illegal questions deliberately, you may want to rethink whether you want the position.

Remember, a business may ask questions if the questions relate directly to a safety concern inherent to the job. As a rule of thumb, be brief and stick to facts. If you think that a company has intentionally discriminated against you in the hiring process, you have legal recourse, but it is a costly and time-consuming process.

For this section, assume that you want the job and that the infraction came from naivete. One choice you always have is to answer openly, but, when necessary, there are other ways to step around the question. For instance, you can say without elaboration, "Yes," "No," "I don't see how this is relevant," or "I don't think this is an appropriate topic for our interview." The following Tips box offers other answers to bungling questions.

• • • • **Handling Illegal Questions** • • • •   • • • • **TIPS**

- *Are you married?* (The interviewer wants to know whether your home life will interfere with your job or whether you will share confidential information.) "My spouse and I are professionals, and we keep our work and personal lives separate."

- *Do you have children? What arrangements have you made for child care? Do you have custody?* "I have two children who are cared for."

- *Do you plan to have [any, more] children?* (This is more frequently asked of women than men for pregnancy and child-rearing decisions.) "Yes, eventually, and I plan to establish a career as a part of that plan." "We have no immediate plans." "We are focused on developing our careers. I have handled a demanding job and a pregnancy, and I took three months' maternity leave. I continued working online at home and on site two days a week. The results were so effective that the company added it to policy."

- *How old are you [for applicants older than 40]?* (This question libels employers to civil and criminal suits.) "I continue to develop professionally, and, furthermore, I am now at a confident point for developing, even with complex challenges." "Younger than my résumé indicates, since I moved up rapidly on my last employer's career track." "I don't know of any constraints or limitations this job poses for me."

- *What is your religious background? Which church do you attend? Are you a member of a lodge?* "My values align with the mission of this organization." "Although I worship regularly, I do not impose my beliefs on others." "My religious beliefs are in accord with my professional behavior and this company's ethical code." "Are there specific religious requirements for this position?"

- *What is your sexual orientation? Do you have a spouse or partner? Are you gay?* (Usually, if this subject is raised, the topic is brought up casually. In any form, it is inappropriate.) "I'm assuming from that question you want to know whether I keep my personal life private, and you can see, based on this interview, that I do." "I would like to spend this time discussing my credentials for this job."

- *Were you born in the United States? Where are you from? What is the origin of your name?* (This is an illegal question during an employment interview.) "Yes, I am." "I proudly became a citizen in 2001." "I am in the process of becoming a naturalized citizen." "Although I retain my birth citizenship, the United States is my home, and I will soon be a U.S. citizen."
- *Have you had cancer? Do you have a chronic illness or disability?* "I am fully capable of doing this job." "As you see, I use a cane. I'll try not to injure anyone with it."

● ● ●

Follow-up

At the end of the day, you still have obligations to the host organization. Review business cards you collected and write down names of people whom you met. Write thank you letters to those who interviewed you or made arrangements for you. Use a formal business letter style, be specific about something that was especially helpful, and thank the interviewers for the opportunity. If you are not informed of their hiring decision in a reasonable time, call to ask where they stand in their decision.

● ● ● ● TIPS   ● ● ● ● **Don't Shoot Yourself in the Foot** ● ● ● ●

- Use your home or cell phone and your home mailing address for contacts from potential employers. Keep your cell phone fully charged, "silent" in meetings and interviews, and with you.
- Do not spend scheduled work time or office resources on your search for a new job.
- Be clear with potential employers and recruiters about keeping contact confidential until you want to inform your employer.

● ● ●

INTERVIEWING APPLICANTS FOR EMPLOYMENT

It's time to change hats. Think of yourself not as the one being interviewed, but as the one doing the interviewing. "You can't build a great company without great people. The problem: How do you know the great people when you see them?" (Carbonara, 1996).

Wearing the interviewer's hat, you want to hire the right people, and you want to do it the right way.

Preparation

Interviewers plan their interviews. They set in place a procedure for contacting applicants and scheduling interviews. Contact persons should be skilled in making the contact, knowing what to say, handling questions, and arranging travel. Likely, the contact person, often a recruiter, secretary, or executive assistant, will be the first person the interviewee meets. Someone must take responsibility for coordinating all participants' visits.

Shape the interview context by considering the room, furniture arrangement, and general comfort. Interviews usually take place on location in an office or conference room at an organization. The location makes a strong impression and sets the tone. American cultural distance for business conversations is 4 to 12 feet, and the near phase (4 to 8 feet) seems most comfortable for interviews. Placing chairs about 5 feet apart in an open conversational arrangement or sitting around a conference table that allows the same distance are two ways to invite interaction without intimidating the interviewee. The interviewee should be able to easily turn to face each interviewer. Check room temperature, lighting, and chairs (they should be of similar height), and the availability of water plus hot and cold drinks. If your organization records interviews, opens conference lines, or has other special arrangements, let the interviewee know to expect that and explain why it is done. Otherwise, arrange conversational privacy and avoid interruptions.

Discuss the goals of upcoming interviews with involved colleagues. Find out if the organization is seeking specific skill sets and which characteristics team members need. When you know what you are looking for, you are more likely to find it.

Assemble the right people to conduct an interview. Company policy may mandate that certain people be present, and common sense says to include management, human resources, and an expert in the job-opening area. Discuss interview strategy ahead of time—what the tone of the interview should be, who asks what and in what order, the time frame, and how the interview will be closed.

Conduct the Interview

Structure the interview. A reasonable plan would be 2 to 3 minutes for opening, a minute to set boundaries of how the interview will progress, 30 to 40 minutes for open-ended questions, 10 to 16 minutes to allow the candidate to ask questions, 5 minutes to sell the company, and 2 to 3 minutes to inform the candidate what will happen from here and close.

Ask questions skillfully and with genuine interest. Follow the interview strategy, and sequence questions so that one leads logically to another. Eliminate questions that were coincidentally answered in earlier responses. Prepare follow-up questions and follow-up to follow-up questions—often the most revealing. Consider several types of questions to elicit the type of information you seek:

- *Closed questions* can be answered with a simple "yes," "no," or a brief answer. ("Were you responsible for a budget in your last job?" "Are you fluent in a second language?")

- *Open-ended questions* prompt the responder to create an answer from his or her experiences and knowledge. ("How would you deal with a client who expects a number of changes in a contractual project?")

- *Probing questions* usually follow a response to probe a layer deeper. ("What do you mean when you say you'll negotiate with the client? What risks are you taking?")

- *Leading questions* "lead" a responder to answer a certain way. ("Don't you agree that no one has the right to expect changes without putting in extra time?")

- *Hypothetical behavioral questions* create hypothetical situations and challenge the responder to describe productive behavior he or she would display in the situation. ("If you were given two equally good solutions by two employees who were constantly at odds with one another, how would you choose the solution to implement, and how would you deal with the employees?")
- *Experience behavioral questions* ask the responder to recall a time he or she was in a situation and describe how he or she handled it. ("Describe a mistake you made, and tell what you learned from it.")
- (Refer to the website www.businessballs.com/ under "Job Interviews" for additional sample questions and answers.)

 ## PERFORMANCE APPRAISALS AND CORRECTIVES

> The most important thing in life is not to capitalize on your successes—any fool can do that. The really important thing is to profit from your mistakes.
>
> —William Bolitho, *Twelve against the Gods*

"Performance appraisal appears to be a simple management tool; yet experience demonstrates just the opposite. That members of an organization should know how they are performing is obvious. And that superiors should tell subordinates about their performance is equally obvious. Yet some superiors avoid this crucial task, while others experience anxiety and discomfort doing it" (Kikoski & Litterer, 1983). The Civil Service Reform Act of 1978 left little choice but to conduct periodic appraisals of employees' individual job performances. Essentially, appraisers need basic nonverbal attending skills, skills in questioning, and the ability to use paraphrasing, reflection of feeling, and feedback (Kikoski, 1998).

Appraisal Interviews

As an employee, at the minimum expect annual evaluations and discussions concerning your workplace performance. A maxim holds that "whatever is measured is what is done." Organizations have sophisticated systems for reviewing their employees' competence, at all levels of employment. The most common term for periodic appraisals is *performance evaluation.* Progressive companies incorporate upward, downward, and lateral evaluations. A popular and more recent format is the *360-degree assessment,* which gathers feedback from anyone who has worked with a particular employee.

Consistent Messages from Supervisors

All employees must be informed of performance expectations before performing the tasks and certainly before being evaluated. The goal for evaluating the performance of individuals is to give fair and honest feedback in order to help employees grow with an organization. Honest praise should be part of the feedback, and negative marks should be springboards for employee development through training. When performances fall short of expectations, consistent consequences should still apply, even when that means reassignment so that both organization and individual can find a better match.

When responding to appraisal, be positive, open, and honest. Keep nonverbal communication consistent with verbal messages.

Performance evaluations can be positive experiences for both employer and employee if they are used consistently. Half of the appraisal equation is the employee's response to the evaluation instrument, and the other half is the supervisor's response. Discussion—genuine dialogue, not lecturing or complaining—should follow. A supervisor should not dominate an evaluation, and neither should the employee responding to the evaluation.

Responding Appropriately

Upcoming appraisal interviews generate considerable energy and anxiety in most organizations. "Receiving a performance evaluation need not be a stressful event. There are ways to minimize stress and ensure that the performance evaluation is a positive experience for both the company and the evaluate" (Koziel, 2000). A preparation period precedes the face-to-face evaluation. During this time the employee reflects on expectations and goals and the extent to which he or she has met them. This is an opportunity to examine unmet goals and determine a path of correction. Perhaps the employee will ask for training or company resources to support the correction.

If you are the one being evaluated, communicate with a positive attitude and show potential for growth in the organization. Openness and honesty, rather than excuses and deception, are essential for productive appraisals. Be ready to set goals for the next year or evaluation period. Present a plan for meeting those goals and show how they are appropriate for the organization. Integrate personal goals with organizational goals and communicate them clearly to the superior. Perform in the present, but look to the future.

Corrective Interviews

All levels of employment are vulnerable to dismissal, even high-ranking executives. A landmark study (Leslie & Velsor, 1996) with Fortune 500 companies, multinational corporations in North America, and similar ones in 10 European countries looked for reasons that top executives were fired, forced to leave, or placed in jobs where they couldn't advance. The top two reasons were rigidity and poor relationships, especially "being too harshly critical, insensitive, or demanding, so that they alienated those they worked with" (Goleman, 1998, p. 40).

Never do we feel more singled out than when we are criticized. Asked to recall uncomfortable situations, most people easily recall critical messages, whether they were on the giving or receiving end. Emotionally intelligent professionals see that criticism can be productive, even when uncomfortable. Criticism can guide employees to improve their skills and judgment. Of course, we need to be able to sort out good coaching from pompous put-downs and grandstanding. This section examines the dynamics of criticism—giving it, taking it, and responding to it.

Giving Criticism

Giving criticism is different from "being critical." *Critics,* by definition, identify themselves to those receiving criticism, target a topic, and direct their criticism to a person or organization positioned to make a change. Criticism can be directed toward an employee whom you supervise, your supervisor, a peer, or an organization.

Whether giving or receiving criticism, be clear about your motives and your relationship with the other person. Realize it is often very difficult for some people to speak up at work "because they're afraid, but that fear—of being labeled as a whiner, or as someone who isn't a team player—prevents people from sharing criticisms and ideas that might ultimately benefit their companies" (Ryan & Oestreich, 1998). You also mustn't criticize solely to make yourself feel better or to make someone else feel worse.

Criticism should come with a warning label: "Confrontation is the most risky of all communication skills, and is actually least likely to succeed" (Anderson, 1992, p. 115). When criticizing employees whom you supervise, recognize the anxiety that the receiver will likely experience. Keep an even tone of voice, one that balances support of the employee and confidence in the worth of the criticism.

Assess   First, assess your responsibility, knowledge, expertise, and familiarity with the situation. Usually the problem deals with basic expectations, such as punctuality, cooperation with cohorts, appropriate communication with clients, and confidentiality issues. At the same time, assess how clearly organizational procedures have been communicated to employees.

Determine the level of this corrective discussion. Most organizations use this sequence:

1. Present the problem, explain what must change, make a development plan, and schedule future feedback.
2. Meet again to assess progress in the development plan, and repeat, clarify, and possibly modify the employee's development, whether it is treatment or training.
3. Present a deadline for measurable and acceptable change, underscoring the consequences of low performance.
4. Summarize the problem, the plan, the amount of progress, and the consequences or next step in placing the employee appropriately. (This could mean moving the employee to another position or firing the employee.)

Make Your Commitments and Motives Clear   Start by telling the person your motives in what you are about to say and why. As an employee, you assume commitments to the organization and to your department or team. As a supervisor, you add a commitment to the development of the employee whom you supervise. As Anderson (1998) says, "You have to earn the right to confront by proving ahead of time to others that you care about their development as persons, that you are seeking to develop a relationship with them, that you are attempting to build rather than tear down" (p. 113). An employee should realize your support and be confident in your interest in his or her progress.

Make the Core Issue Clear   Present the problem and focus on the core issue. It is generally better to deal with only one issue. Remember, the problem is the person's behavior, not the person. Address issues, not personalities. Give the facts about unacceptable behavior, including consequences from the employee's behavior and development and other correctives that must be put into place. When behavior is counterproductive to the mission of the organization, is unacceptable to you, and is in your field of influence, the appropriate skill is confrontation. An employee should be told clearly what the problem is and what to correct.

Keep a perspective of the strength of the effect on the recipient. On the other hand, don't hem and haw, clear your throat, and make small talk. Use concise, clear wording. Make your point and stop. Avoid blanket criticism; be specific. Give the person time to absorb the message and react. Follow through on what is settled in the discussion.

Generally, criticize in private   When others are present, the critic is in danger of embarrassing a boss, forcing a decision on an issue, complicating an issue, or humiliating an employee. Public criticism reflects more strongly on the giver than the receiver, so consider the possible effect and what could backfire.

Use good timing with "critical conversations"   Starting a workday with criticism clouds an employee's thoughts with defensiveness, self-doubts, and intense internal dialogue that may interfere with productivity for the day. Concluding the day with criticism leaves residuals of isolation and depression and usually a lack of resolution.

Receiving Criticism

Even when we ask for it, criticism isn't easy to receive, and frankly, some critics are inept in giving it. Show your true mettle when you're in harm's way. You very well may lay groundwork for progress, if you handle the situation well.

"DEVELOP" PRODUCTIVE RESPONSES

Benjamin says, "John, this report will never fly with the board. Were you thinking at all? You gave absolutely no statistical data to support your claims." John uses the DEVELOP method to respond.

- **D**etermine the core message.

  John analyzes silently, "Benjamin thinks the board won't approve the project because the report doesn't have enough supporting data. He wants me to add statistics to the report."

- **E**valuate intentions, motives, and expertise.

  John considers, "Benjamin needs the board to approve a project critical to the success of the department. He's frustrated with the lack of statistics in the report. Benjamin generally supports my work. There is no need to respond to the personal attack, unless it is repeated. Benjamin is probably right. He works with the board more often than I do."

- **V**erify the message.

  John says, "You are right. I did not include statistical and technical data." (John agrees with the one fact that was presented. He does not agree that he is an unthinking, incompetent employee, who needs to apologize for being on the planet.)

- **E**nlighten the critic about you and your goals.

  John continues, "I definitely want the board to approve the project."

- **L**earn from the critic.

  "This board likes seeing the numbers, you say. How can I best present them so that they will be meaningful?"

- **O**pen the interaction to positive change. Be proactive, not reactive.

  "Thank you for the suggestions to get the project approved. Do you have other ideas to discuss?"

- **P**roduce results and articulate the product.

  "This came together quickly, with the analyses I ran on Excel. Here is the amended report."

Receiving criticism well and using it for improvement communicates collegiality and openness. Your most lucid critics can be your best friends. After all, they may be the ones who are close enough to help you. A study of workplace communication styles revealed that friendly workers were more productive than the people who kept an emotional distance (Sanchez-Burks et al., 2003).

SUMMARY

Interviews are most frequently used for hiring, assessing, and correcting employees in organizations. The employment interview is the single most important factor in getting a job. Research an organization and follow its application process, probably an application form, résumé, and cover letter. Résumés present work history, academic achievements, and contributions within organizations. In job-specific résumés, applicants match education and prior experiences to desired job descriptions. Cover letters highlight applicants' characteristics and attitudes.

The most common interview format is a one-on-one interview, but an applicant may be interviewed by several people at the same time or with several applicants interviewed together. A typical interview board includes a recruiter, a human resources manager, and a department or team manager. Today, organizations' hiring practices combine interview styles. The best predictor for job success is the situational interview, in which interviewers challenge applicants with situations and problems.

Applicants should prepare for commonly asked questions and anticipate other challenges. Applicants can also ask questions to help them determine whether they have found good job fits. Although interviewers should use legal and ethical guidelines, especially with discrimination and privacy issues, applicants should know what legally cannot be asked and should be ready with responses to inappropriate questions.

Organizations with job openings should initiate procedures for contacting applicants, scheduling appointments, establishing a location, discussing hiring and interviewing goals with colleagues, and planning questions.

Assessment interviews give on-the-job feedback and work evaluation. These discussions usually occur annually, but may be at shorter intervals. Organizations generally have forms and procedures to facilitate assessments. Upward, downward, and peer feedback provide input for 360-degree evaluations, used by many companies. Assessment interviews should incorporate development plans for employees, written in a collaboration of supervisor and employee.

Skillful criticism guides employees to improve job performance and judgment. Critics should identify themselves to those receiving criticism, target a topic, and direct their criticism to a person or organization in a position to change a situation. Criticism can be directed toward an employee whom you supervise, your supervisor, a peer, or an organization. Receiving criticism with equanimity opens a dialogue to initiate—even negotiate—appropriate correctives. •

ACTIVITIES

1. **Presenting to Others and Team Work:** Divide the class into interview panels of three to five members each, numbering the panels (panel 1, panel 2, etc.). Each panel will post a job description of a professional position immediately after college. The individuals of the numerical panel that follows each panel (e.g., panel 4 follows panel 3) will interview for the job; that is, each person on panel 4 will be interviewed by panel 3. Panel 1 will be interviewed by the last panel. Panels should work together to plan the interview according to suggestions in this chapter. The panels should write up feedback critiques for everyone that they interviewed. A final hiring decision should be made.

2. **Journaling the Experience:** As you prepare to "hire" others and to be interviewed, monitor and journal your emotional feelings. How can participating in both roles increase your emotional intelligence?

3. **Technical Support:** Explore www.fastcompany.com/online/16/webjobs.html
Read "35 Ways to Land a Job Online" by Gina Imperato (1998). Explore the resources Imperato suggests. List five tips and three helpful websites you plan to use.

4. **Ethically Speaking:** Write a position paper regarding the following statement: "Performance evaluations are an effective way to get rid of an employee while protecting oneself and the organization from legal action."

5. **Technical Support:** Microsoft Word includes Résumé Wizard, which can be accessed by choosing File, New, General Templates. Choose from Elegant, Contemporary, and Professional formats or use the Wizard to walk you through. Check the categories you wish to include. Click Finish. Fill in your credentials by overtyping in each category.

    1. First, create a detailed résumé for your records only, and save it as "resume detail.doc." The detailed résumé includes all your accomplishments, education, experiences, affiliations, and skills relevant to professional work and working in a community.

    2. Second, narrow your detailed résumé to a powerful professional résumé that is one to two pages long. Save this version as "resume professional.doc." This one is ready when a résumé is requested by someone introducing you to speak, in response to professional honors, and the like.

    3. Generic résumés seldom harvest jobs. Customize your general résumé for one of these pre-graduation jobs:

        a. Weekend Supervisor, Guest Reception, University Recreation Center (responsible for overseeing employees in various activity areas, enrolling new members, keeping usage statistics, opening and closing a $1,000,000 facility)

        b. Merchandizing Designer, Hometown Hardware (responsible for changing store window designs weekly)

        c. Director of Activities, Camp of the Wild (responsible for recruiting activity leaders, creating camp activity schedule, and resolving problems in this area)

FOR FURTHER READING

Try a simulated interview through www.merlot.org/artifact/ArtifactDetail.po?oid= 3000000000000165508

For more information on interviewing, try www.collegegrad.com/intv

Psychometrics is a Jungian personality approach. You can preview it at www.psychometrics.com/scales/values.htm

References

Adler, M. (1983). *How to speak, how to listen.* New York: Macmillan.

Adler, R. B., & Elmhorst, J. M. (1999). *Communicating at work* (6th ed.). New York: McGraw-Hill.

Adler, R. B., & Elmhorst, J. M. (2002). *Communicating at work* (7th ed.). Boston: McGraw-Hill.

Aguinis, H., Simonsen, M. M., & Pierce, C. A. (1998). Effects of nonverbal behavior on perceptions of power bases. *Journal of Social Psychology, 138,* 4.

Allen, M. (2002). Effect of timing of communicator identification and level of source credibility on attitude. *Communication Research Reports, 19* (1), 46–55.

Allerton, H. E. (2000, March). Myth buster (brief article). *Training & Development.* Retrieved April 1, 2005, from http://www.findarticles.com/p/articles/mi_m4467/is_3_54/ai_61649783

American Psychological Association. (2001). *Publication manual of the American Psychological Association* (5th ed.). Washington, DC: Author.

Anderson, T. D. (1992). *Transforming leadership: New skills for an extraordinary future.* Amherst, MA: Human Resources Development Press.

Anderson, T. D., Ford, R., & Hamilton, M. (1998). *Transforming leadership: Equipping yourself and coaching others to build the leadership organization* (2nd ed). Boca Raton, FL: CRC Press.

Andrews, P. H., & Baird, J. E., Jr. (2000). *Communication for business and the professions.* Boston: McGraw-Hill.

Applegate, J. Don't fear public speaking. *Succeeding in Small Business.* Retrieved August 17, 1999, from CNNfn.com

Arbelle, S., Benjamin, J., Golin, M., Kremer, I., Belmaker, R. H., & Ebstein, R. P. (2003). Relation of shyness in grade school children to the genotype for the long form of the serotonin transporter promoter region polymorphism. *American Journal of Psychiatry, 160,* 671–676.

Archer, D., & Akert, R. (1977). Words and everything else: Verbal and nonverbal cues in social interpretation. *Journal of Personality and Social Psychology, 35,* 443–449.

Argyle, M. (1972). *The psychology of interpersonal behavior.* London: Penguin.

Argyle, M., Alkema, F., & Gilmour, R. (1971). The communication of friendly and hostile attitudes by verbal and nonverbal signals. *European Journal of Social Psychology, 1,* 385–402.

Argyris, C. (1964). *Integrating the individual and the organization.* New York: John Wiley & Sons.

Argyris, C. (1976). *Increasing leadership effectiveness.* New York: John Wiley & Sons.

Argyris, C. (1982). *Reasoning, learning and action: Individual and organizational.* San Francisco: Jossey-Bass.

Argyris, C. (1993). *Knowledge for action.* San Francisco: Jossey-Bass.

Argyris, C. (1993). *On organizational learning.* Cambridge, MA: Blackwell.

Aries, E. (1996). *Men and women in interaction: Reconsidering the differences.* New York: Oxford University Press.

Aries, E. (1998). Gender differences in interaction. In D. Canary & K. Dindia (Eds.), *Sex differences and similarities in interaction: Critical essays and empirical investigations*. Mahwah, NU: Erlbaum.

Asch, S. (1952). *Social psychology*. Englewood Cliffs, NJ: Prentice Hall.

Ashford, S. J. (1998). Out on a limb: The role of context impression management selling gender-equity issues. *Administrative Science Quarterly, 43*(1), 23–57.

Atwater, L. E., Carey, J. A., & Waldman, D. A. (2001, September). Gender and discipline in the workplace: Wait until your father gets home. *Journal of Management, 27*, 537–561.

Auden, W. H. (1966). Prologue: The birth of architecture. In *About the House*. New York: Random House.

Bachmann, R. (2001). Trust, power and control in trans-organizational relations. *Organizations Studies* (electronic version).

Baker, D. C. (1990). A qualitative and quantitative analysis of verbal style and the elimination of potential leaders in small groups. *Communication Quarterly, 38*, 13–26.

Bales, R. F., & Strodbeck, F. (1951). Phases in group solving. *Journal of Abnormal and Social Psychology, 46*, 485–495.

Ball, J. (1999, August). Your career matters: DaimlerChrysler's transfer woes—workers resist moves abroad—and here. *The Wall Street Journal*, p. B1.

Balu, R. (2000, January). Starting your startup. *Fast Company, 31*, 81.

Barge, J. K. (1994). *Leadership: Communication skills for organizations and groups*. New York: St. Martin's Press.

Barge, J. K., & Hirokawa, R. Y. (1989). Toward a communication competency model of group leadership. *Small Group Behavior, 20*, 167–189.

Barker, J. A. (1992). *Paradigms: The business of discovering the future*. New York: HarperBusiness.

Barnlund, D. C. (1959). A comparative study of individual, majority, and group judgment. *Journal of Abnormal and Social Psychology, 58*, 55–60.

Barrier, M. (1998, December). Sexual Harassment. *Nation's Business, 86*(12), 14–19.

Barsade, S. (1998). The ripple effect: emotional contagion in groups. Working paper, Yale School of Management.

Barsade, S., & Gibson, D. E. (1998). Group emotion: A view from the top and bottom. In D. Gruenfeld et al. (Eds.), *Research on managing groups and teams*. Greenwich, CT: JAI Press.

Barsade, S. G., Ward, A. J., Turner, J. D. F., & Sonnenfeld, J. A. (2000). To your heart's content: A model of affective diversity in top management teams. *Administrative Science Quarterly, 45*(4), 802–836.

Bartos, O. J. (1974). *Process and outcome of negotiations*. New York: Columbia University Press.

Bass, B. M. (1990). *Bass & Stogdill's handbook of leadership*. New York: The Free Press.

Bass, B. M. (1995). Concepts of leadership: The beginnings. In J. Thomas Wren (Ed.), *The leader's companion* (pp. 49–52). New York: Free Press.

Bayless, O. L. (1967). An alternative model for problem-solving discussion. *Journal of Communication, 17*, 188–197.

Bazerman, M. H. (2000). Negotiation. *Annual Review of Psychology, 51*, 279–314.

Beatty, J. (1999). Good listening. *Educational Theory, 49*(3), 281–299.

Beebe, S. A. and Masterson, J. T. (2002) *Communicating in small groups: Principles and practices* (6th ed.). Boston: Allyn & Bacon.

Belbin, R. M. (1996). Brilliant teams with bad decisions. In *Team roles at work*. Boston: Butterworth-Heinemann.

Benbasat, I., & Lim, L. (1993). The effects of group, task context, and technology variables on the usefulness of group support systems: A meta-analysis of experimental studies. *Small Group Research, 24*, 430–462.

Benne, K. D., & Sheats, P. (1948). Functional roles of group members. *Journal of Social Issues, 4*, 41–49.

Bennis, W. (1997, Winter). The secrets of great groups. *Leader to Leader, 3*, 29–33. Retrieved from http://www.pfdf.org/leaderbooks/l2l/winter97/bennis.html

Bennis, W. (1999, Spring). The leadership advantage. *Leader to Leader, 12*, 18–23.

Bennis, W., & Biederman, P. W. (1997). *Organizing genius: The secrets of creative collaboration*. Reading, MA: Addison-Wesley.

Bennis, W., & Nanus, B. (1985). *Leaders: Strategies for taking charge*. New York: Harper & Row.

Benoit, P. (1997). *Telling the success story: Acclaiming and disclaiming discourse*. Albany: State University of New York Press.

Benoit, W. L. (1995). *Accounts, excuses, and apologies: A theory of image restoration strategies*. Albany: State University of New York Press.

Benoit, W. L., & Kennedy, K. A. (1999). On reluctant testimony. *Communication Quarterly, 47*(4), 376–387.

Benoit, W. L., & Lindsey, J. J. (1987). Argument strategies: Antidote to Tylenol's poisoned image. *Journal of the American Forensic Association, 23,* 136–146.

Berger, C. R. (1997). *Planning strategic interaction: Attaining goals through communicative action.* Mahwah, NJ: Lawrence Erlbaum Associates.

Berkowitz, A. D. (1998, October). How we can prevent sexual harassment and sexual assault. *Educator's guide to controlling sexual harassment, 6*(1), 1–4.

Berryman-Fink, C., & Brunner, C. C. (1987). The effects of sex of source and target on interpersonal conflict management styles. *Southern Speech Communication Journal, 53,* 38–48.

Better Hearing Institute and American Academy of Otolaryngology. (1987, June). How noise can harm your hearing. *Good Housekeeping,* 215.

Bibeault, D. (1981). *Corporate turnaround: How managers turn losers into winners.* New York: McGraw-Hill.

Bippus, A. M., & Daly, J. A. (1999). What do people think causes stage fright? Naïve attributions about the reasons for public speaking anxiety. *Communication Education, 48*(1), 63–72.

Blake, G. (1998, June 6). Savoir-faire in the systems department: IS managers talk about interpersonal skills. *Corporate University Review.* Retrieved November 8, 1998, from http://www.elibrary.com/s/edumark

Blake, R. R., & Mouton, J. A. (1964). *The managerial grid.* Houston: Gulf.

Blakeman, M., et al. (1971). *Job-seeking skills reference manual* (3rd ed.). Minneapolis: Minnesota Rehabilitation Center.

Blum, D. (1998, September–October). Face it! *Psychology Today,* 32–70.

Bond, J. F. (1999). Hands out and heads up. *Incentive, 173*(4), 85.

Bostrom, R. N. (1996). Memory, cognitive processing, and the process of "listening": A reply to Thomas and Levine. *Human Communication Research, 23*(2), 298–306.

Bovée, C. L., & Thill, J. V. (1995). *Business communication today* (4th ed.). New York: McGraw-Hill.

Boyatzis, R. (1994). Stimulating self-directed learning through the managerial assessment and development course. *Journal of Management Education, 18*(3), 304–323.

Boyatzis, R. E. (1999). Developing emotional intelligence. In Cherniss, C., & Goleman, D. (Eds.), *Developments in Emotional Intelligence.*

Boyatzis, R. E. (2001, May 28). Unleashing the power of self-directed learning. Retrieved January 17, 2002, from the Consortium for Research on Emotional Intelligence in Organizations Web site: http://www.eiconsortium.org/research/self-directed_learning.htm

Boyatzis, R. E., Leonard, K., Rhee, K., & Wheeler, J. V. (1998). Competencies can be developed, but not in the way we thought. *Capability, 2*(2), 21–41.

Boyatzis, R., Cowen, S., & Kold, D. (Eds.). (1995). *Innovating in professional education: Steps on a journey from teaching to learning.* San Francisco: Jossey-Bass.

Brady, S. (1996). Guns and gun control. Speech presented at National Democratic General Convention. Boston: Allyn & Bacon. Available: Allyn & Bacon, Longman Archives at http://www.pbs.org/newshour/convention96/floor_speeches/brady.html

Brandenburg, J. B. (1997). *Confronting sexual harassment:* What schools and colleges can do. Williston, VT: Teachers College Press.

Bredin, A. (2000, April 24). Practice, preparation help make meetings productive. *Los Angeles Business.* Retrieved June 14, 2002, from http://www.findarticles.com

Brinkman, R., & Kirschner, R. (1994). *Dealing with people you can't stand.* New York: McGraw-Hill.

Brody, M. (1998). *Speaking your way to the top.* Boston: Allyn & Bacon.

Brown, J. S., & Gray, E. S. (1995). The people are the company. *Fast Company, 1*(1), 78–81.

Bruton, J. K. (1994, April). The subjective side of cross-cultural communication. *Special Warfare, 7,* 28–31.

Bryant, B. (1987). *Quality circles: New management strategies for schools.* Ann Arbor, MI: Prakken.

Brydon, S. R., & Scott, M. D. (2000). *Between one and many: The art and science of public speaking* (3rd ed.). Mountain View, CA: Mayfield Publishing Co.

Buller, D. B. (1987). Communication apprehension and reactions to proxemic violations. *Journal of Nonverbal Behavior, 11,* 13–25.

Burgoon, J. K. (1991). Relational message interpretations of touch, conversational distance, and posture. *Journal of Nonverbal Behavior, 15,* 233–259.

Burgoon, J. K. (2000). Mindfulness and interpersonal communication. *Journal of Social Issues, 56*(1), 129.

Burgoon, J. K., Birk, T., & Pfau, M. (1990). Nonverbal behaviors, persuasion, and credibility. *Journal of Nonverbal Behavior, 15,* 233–259.

Burgoon, J. K., Coker, D. A., & Coker, R. A. (1987). Communicative effects of gaze behavior: A test of two contrasting explanations. *Human Communication Research, 12,* 495–524.

Burgoon, J. K., & Le, B. A. (1999). Nonverbal cues and interpersonal judgments: Participant and observer perceptions of intimacy, dominance, composure, and formality. *Communication Monographs, 66*(2), 105–124.

Burke, K. (1998). Responding to participants' learning styles: Hear, see, touch, and move them. In R. Dunn & K. Dunn (Eds.), *Practical approaches to individualizing staff development for adults* (pp. 49–55). Westport, CT: Praeger.

Burley, A. M. (1982). *Listening: The forgotten skill.* New York: John Wiley & Sons.

Butler, D., & Geis, F. L. (1990). Nonverbal affect responses to male and female leaders: Implications for leadership evaluations. *Journal of Personality and Social Psychology, 58,* 48–59.

Cadogan, M. P., Franzi, C., Osterweil, D., Hill, T. (1999, January). Barriers to effective communication in skilled nursing facilities: Differences in perception between nurses and physicians. *Journal of the American Geriatrics Society, 47*(1), 71–75.

Calgary Herald. (1994, November 12), p. J1.

Carbonara, P. (1996, August–September). Hire for attitude, train for skill. *Fast Company, 4,* 73.

Carducci, B. (2000, January). Shyness: The new solution. *Psychology Today, 33,* 38–78.

Carducci, B. J., & Zimbardo, P. G. (1995, November/December). Are you shy? *Psychology Today, 28,* 34–82.

Carli, L. L. (1999, Spring). Gender, interpersonal power, and social influence. (Social influence and social power: Using theory for understanding social issues). *Journal of Social Issues, 55*(1), 81.

Carlozzi, C. L. (1999, February). Make your meetings count. *Journal of Accountancy,187,* 53–55.

Carnahan, J. (1999, June 14). Born to make barrels. *Vital Speeches of the Day, 65*(17), 529–531.

Carnevale, A. P., Gainer, L. J., & Meltzer, A. S. (1989). *Workplace basics: The skills employers want.* Alexandria, VA: American Society for Training and Development.

Carton, J. S., Kessler, E. A., & Pape, C. L. (1999). Nonverbal decoding skills and relationship well-being in adults. *Journal of Nonverbal Behavior, 23,* 91–100.

Cartwright, D., & Zander, A. (1968). Leadership and performance of group functions: Introduction. In *Group dynamics: Research and theory* (3rd ed.). New York: Harper & Row.

Cashman, K. (2000, November). Value-creating communication. *Executive Excellence, 17*(11). Retrieved November 8, 2002, at EBSCO host.

Cathcart, R. S., & Samovar, L. A. (Eds.) (1992). *Small group communication: A reader* (6th ed.). Dubuque, IA: Wm. C. Brown.

Chaikin, A. (1994). *A man on the moon: The voyage of the Apollo astronauts.* New York: Viking.

Chang, R., & Curtin, M. J. (1999). *Succeeding as a self-managed team: A practical guide to operating as a self-managed work team.* San Francisco: Jossey-Bass/Pfeiffer.

Chaplin, W. F., Phillips, J. B., Brown, J. D., Clanton, N. R., & Stein, J. L. (2000). Handshaking, gender, personality, and first impressions. *Journal of Personality and Social Psychology, 19*(4), 110–117.

Charles, C., Gafni, A., & Whelan, T. (1997). Shared decisionmaking in the medical encounter: What does it mean? (or it takes at least two to tango). *Social Science of Medicine, 44,* 681–692.

Charles C., Gafni A., & Whelan T. (1999). Decisionmaking in the physician-patient encounter: Revisiting the shared treatment decisionmaking model. *Social Science of Medicine, 49,* 651–661.

Charles, M., & Marschan-Pierkkari, R. (2002, June). Language training for enhanced horizontal communication: A challenge for MNCs. *Business Communication Quarterly, 65*(2), 9–29.

Chaudron, D. Elements of quality. Retrieved January 3, 2002, from Organized Change Consultancy Web site: http://www.tqm.organized change.com/tqmelem.htm

Chen, G., & Chen, H. (2002). An examination of People's Republic of China business negotiating behaviors. *Communication Research Reports, 19*(4), 399–208.

Chertkoff, J. M. & Esser, J. K. (1976). A review of experiments in explicit bargaining. *Journal of Experiential Social Psychology, 12,* 464–485.

Clinton, H. R. (1995, September 5). *Women's rights are human rights.* Remarks to the United

Nations Fourth World Conference on Women Plenary Session in Beijing, China. Retrieved May 30, 2001, from http://douglass.speech.nwu.edu/clin_a64.htm

Coleman, D. (1983, February). The electronic Rorschach. *Psychology Today, 17,* 35–53.

Comer, D. R. (1995). A model of social loafing in real work groups. *Human Relations, 48,* 647–667.

Corcodilos, N. (1997). *Ask the headhunter.* New York: Plume.

Covey, S. R. (1990) *The seven habits of highly effective people: Powerful lessons in personal change* (1st Fireside ed.). New York: Simon & Schuster.

Covey, S. R. (1992). *Principle-centered leadership* (1st Fireside ed.). New York: Simon & Schuster.

Covey, S. R. (1996). *Quotes & quips: Insights on living the seven habits.* New York: Simon & Schuster.

Crowley, S. (1994). *Ancient rhetorics for contemporary students.* New York: Macmillan.

Cuban, M. (1999, June 21). Looking to hire the very best? Ask the right questions. Lots of them. *Fortune, 139*(12), 68.

Dahle, C. (1998, June). Your first seven seconds. *Fast Company, 15,* 184.

Davis, M. (1996). Plugging into the office of the future. *Public Management, 78,* 37.

Deegan, A. (1979). *Coaching.* Reading, MA: Addison-Wesley.

Del Valle, C. (1998, March 10). Degree of touch. *Newsday,* p. B13.

Demetrius, J.-E., & Mazzarell, M. (1998). *Reading people.* New York: Random House.

Dendinger, M. J. (2000, June). How to organize a focus group. *Meetings & Conventions,35*(9), 32.

De Souza, G., & Klein, H. J. (1995). Emergent leadership in the group goal-setting process. *Small Group Research, 26,* 475–496.

Detwiler, T. J. (1999, Spring). Telling the success story: Acclaiming and disclaiming discourse. *Southern Communication Journal, 64*(3), 269–270.

Deur, J. (1999, September 15). Trends in telecommunications. *Vital Speeches of the Day, 15*(23), 728–731.

DeVito, J. A. (1999). *Messages: Building interpersonal communication skills.* New York: Addison-Wesley Longman.

DeVito, J. A. (2000). *The elements of public speaking* (7th ed.). New York: Longman.

Dewey, J. (1944) *Democracy and education.* New York: Macmillan.

Dipbooye, R. L., Arvey, R. D., & Terpstra, D. E. (1977). Sex and physical attractiveness of raters and applicants as determinants of résumé evaluation. *Journal of Applied Psychology, 62,* 288–294.

Dipboye, R. L., Fromkin, H. L., & Wiback, I. (1975). Relative importance of applicant sex, attractiveness, and scholastic standing in evaluation of job applicant résumé. *Journal of Applied Psychology, 60,* 39–43.

DiSanza, J. R., & Legge, N. J. (2000). *Business and professional communication.* Boston: Allyn & Bacon.

Dodd, C. (1995). *Dynamics of intercultural communication* (4th ed.). Madison, WI: Brown & Benchmark.

Douglas, J. M., O'Flaherty, C. A., Snow, P. C. (2000, March). Measuring perception of communicative ability: The development and evaluation of the La Trobe communication questionnaire. *Aphasiology, 14*(3), 251–268.

Drecksel, G. L. (1984). *Interaction characteristics of emergent leadership.* Unpublished doctoral dissertation, University of Utah.

Drucker, P. (1973). *Management: Tasks, responsibilities, practices.* New York: HarperCollins.

Drucker, P. (1977). *An introductory view of management.* New York: HarperCollins.

Drucker, P. (1981, January 6). Leadership: More doing than dash. *Wall Street Journal,* p. 14.

Drucker, P. (2000). Managing knowledge means managing oneself. *Leader to Leader, 16,* 8–10.

Duncan, A. (2002). *Speaking beyond the podium* (5th ed.). Dubuque, Iowa: Kendall/Hunt.

Dutton, J. E., & Ashford, S. J. (1993). Selling issues to top management. *Academy of Management Review, 18,* 397–428.

Dzurinko, M. D. (1999, April). Giving presentations with pizazz. *Information Outlook, 3*(4), 34–35.

Eagly, A. H., & Johnson, B. T. (1990). Gender and leadership style: A meta-analysis. *Psychological Bulletin, 108,* 233–256.

Eagly, A. H., Makhijani, M. G., & Klonsky, B. G. (1992). Gender and the evaluation of leaders: A meta-analysis. *Psychological Bulletin, 111,* 3–22.

Eagly, A. H., & Chaiken, S. (1993). *The psychology of attitudes.* Fort Worth, TX: Harcourt Brace Jovanovich.

Edelman, G. (1987). *Neural Darwinism: The theory of neuronal group selection.* New York: Basic Books.

Ehninger, D., Gronbeck, B., McKerrow, R., & Monroe, A. (1986). *Principles and types of speech communication* (10th ed.). Glenville, IL: Scott Foresman, and Co.

Eisenberg, E. M., Goodall, H. L. (1997). *Organizational communication: Balancing creativity and constraint* (4th ed.). New York: St. Martin's Press.

Eitington, J. E. (2002). *The winning trainer* (4th ed.). Boston: Butterworth-Heinemann.

Ekman, E., & Friesen, W. (1975). *Unmasking the face: A guide to recognizing emotions from facial expression.* Englewood Cliffs, NJ: Prentice Hall.

Ekman, P. (Ed.). (1982). *Emotion in the human face* (2nd ed.). New York: Cambridge University Press.

Ekman, P. (1992). *Telling lies: Clues to deceit in the marketplace, politics, and marriage.* New York: Norton.

Ekman, P., Sorenson, E. R., & Friesen, W. V. (1969). Pan-cultural elements in facial displays of emotion. *Science, 164,* 86–88.

Elgin, S. H. (2000). *The gentle art of verbal self-defense at work.* Englewood Cliffs, NJ: Prentice Hall.

Ellis, D. G., & Fisher, B. A. (1994). *Small group decision making: Communication and the group process* (4th ed.). New York: McGraw-Hill.

Englund, R. (2001, February). Cater to the learning styles and senses of your audience. *Presentations,* 88.

Erickson, B., Lind, E. A., Johnson, B. C., & OBarr, W. M. (1978). Speech style and impression formation in a court setting: the effects of "powerful" and "powerless" speech. *Journal of Experimental Social Psychology, 14,* 166–179.

Eslinger, P. (1998). Neurological and neuropsychological bases of empathy. *European Neurology, 39,* 193–199.

Evans, C. R., & Dion, K. L. (1995, November). Group cohesion and performance. *Small Group Behavior, 22,* 175–186.

Fabrigar, L. R., Priester, J. R., Petty, R. E., & Wegener, D. T. (1998). The impact of attitude accessibility on elaboration of persuasive messages. *Personality and Social Psychology Bulletin, 24,* 339–352.

Falk, G. (1982). An empirical study measuring conflict in problem-solving groups which are assigned different decision rules. *Human Relations, 35,* 1123–1138.

Fears, D. (2003, June 21). Some tout racial identity, some say it is demonizing. *Washington Post.*

Fiedler, F. (1967). *A theory of leadership effectiveness.* New York: McGraw-Hill.

Filley, A. C. (1975). *Interpersonal conflict resolution.* Glenview, IL: Scott Foresman.

Fischetti, M. (1998). Team doctors, report to ER. *Fast Company, 13,* 170.

Fisher, B. A. (1970). Decision emergence: Phases in group decision-making. *Speech Monographs, 37,* 53–66.

Fisher, B. A. (1980). *Small group decision making: communication and the group process* (2nd ed.). New York: McGraw-Hill.

Fisher, B. A. (1985). Leadership as medium: Treating complexity in group communication research. *Small Group Behavior, 16,* 167–196.

Fisher, R., & Ury, W., with Patton, B. (1991). *Getting to yes: Negotiating agreement without giving in.* New York: Penguin Books.

Fishman, C. (1996, April). Whole foods is all teams. *Fast Company, 2,* 103.

Flaherty, T. S. (1999). *Talk your way to the top.* New York: Berkley Publishing Group.

Flynn, M. K. (2004, Fall). Still using flipcharts? *Small Firm Business, 17.* Retrieved from www.doar.com/marketing/web/smallfirmbusiness.pdf

Foels, R., Driskell, J. E., Mullen, B., & Salas, E. (2000). The effects of democratic leadership on group member satisfaction. *Small Group Research, 20,* 676–701.

Folger, J. P., Poole, M. S., & Stutman, R. K. (1997). *Working through conflict: Strategies for relationships, groups, and organizations.* New York: Longman.

The Founding Editors. (2003, January). It's a new year. Can we change the conversation? *Fast Company, 66,* 20.

French, J. R. P., & Raven, B. (1959). The bases of social power. In D. Cartwright (Ed.), *Studies in social power.* Ann Arbor, MI: University of Michigan, Institute for Social Research.

Gammage, K. L., Carron, A. V., & Estabrooks, P. A. (2001). Team cohesion and individual productivity. *Small Group Research, 32,* 3–18.

Gardner, H. (1983). *Frames of mind.* New York: Basic Books.

Garst, J., & Bodenhausen, G. V. (1996). "Family values" and political persuasion: Impact of kin-related rhetoric on reactions to political campaigns. *Journal of Applied Social Psychology, 26,* 1119–1137.

Garvey, M. (1949). *Duration factors in speech intelligibility.* Unpublished master's thesis, University of Virginia.

Gaut, D. R. L., & Perrigo, E. M. (1998). *Business and professional communication for the 21st century.* Needham Heights, MA: Allyn & Bacon.

Geier, J. (1967). A trait approach to the study of leadership. *Journal of Communication, 17,* 316–323.

Geus, A. (1997). *The living company.* Boston: Harvard Business School Press.

Gibb, J. R. (1961, September). Defensive communication. *Journal of Communication, 11,* 141.

Gibson, M. K., & Papa, M. J. (2000, February). Blue-collar workers develop strong cultures, show generational differences. *Journal of Applied Communication Research.* Retrieved November 30, 2001, from http://www.natcom.org/Publications/JOURNALS/JACR/jacr0200.htm

Gilmore, D. C., Beehr, T. A., & Love, K. G. (1986). Effects of applicant sex, applicant physical attractiveness, type of rater and type of job on interview decisions. *Journal of Occupational Psychology, 59,* 103–109.

Gladwell, M. (2000, May 29). The new-boy network. *The New Yorker, 76*(13), 68–86.

Goldstein, H. (1940). *Reading and listening comprehension at various controlled rates* (Contributions to Education, No. 821). New York: Teachers College, Columbia University.

Goleman, D. (1992). *Emotional intelligence: Why it can matter more than IQ.* New York: Bantam.

Goleman, D. (1995). *Emotional intelligence: Why it can matter more than IQ* (Paperback edition). New York: Bantam.

Goleman, D. (1998). *Working with emotional intelligence.* New York: Bantam Books.

Goleman, D., Boyatzis, R., & McKee, A. (2002). *Primal leadership: Realizing the power of emotional intelligence.* Boston: Harvard Business School Press.

Goode, E., Schrof, J., & Burke, S. (1991, June 24). Where emotions come from. *U.S. News and World Report,* pp. 54–62.

Gouran, D. S., Brown, C., & Henry, D. R. (1979). Behavioral correlates of perceptions of quality in decision-making discussion. *Communication Monographs, 45,* 193–218.

Gouran, D., Hirokawa, R., Julian, K., & Leatham, G. (1993). The evolution and current status of the functional perspective on communication decision-making and problem-solving groups. In S. Deetz (Ed.), *Communication yearbook, 16.* Newbury Park, CA: Sage.

Grahe, J. E., & Bernieri, F. J. (1999). The importance of nonverbal cues in judging rapport. *Journal of Nonverbal Behavior, 23*(4), 254–269.

Gregory, H. (1993). *Public speaking for college and career* (3rd ed.). New York: McGraw-Hill.

Gregory, R. (1998, December 19). Snapshots from the decade of the brain: Brainy mind. *British Medical Journal, 317,* 1693–1695.

Grensing-Pophal, L. (1999, October). How to become an effective leader. *Nursing Library.* Retrieved June 14, 2002, from http://www.findarticles.com

Griffin, E. (1997). *A first look at communication theory* (3rd ed.). New York: McGraw-Hill.

Griffin, J. (1998). *How to say it at work: Putting yourself across with power words, phrases, body language, and communication secrets.* Englewood Cliffs, NJ: Prentice Hall.

Guetzkow, H., & Gyr, J. (1954). An analysis of conflict in decision-making groups. *Human Relations, 7,* 367–381.

Guffey, M. E. (2002). *Business Communication Today* (4th ed.). Mason, OH: South-Western.

Gwynne, S. C., & Dickerson, J. F. (1997, April 21). Lost in the e-mail. *Time this week.* Retrieved November 29, 2000, from http://europe.cnn.com/ALLPOLITICS/1997/04/14/time/Gwynne.html

Hackett, G., & Betz, N. I. (1981). A self-efficacy approach to the career development of women. *Journal of Vocational Behavior, 18,* 326–339.

Hackman, M. Z., & Johnson, C. E. (1991). *Leadership: A communication perspective.* Prospect Heights, IL: Waveland Press.

Hagedorn, J. J. (2001, July 12). Understanding various communication barriers. *New Stratis Times-Management Time.* Retrieved November 8, 2001, from EBSCO 2W82001200107123540

Hall, E. T. (1966). *The hidden dimension* (2nd ed.). Garden City, NY: Doubleday/Anchor Books.

Hall, J., & Watson, W. H. (1970). The effects of a normative intervention on group decision-making performance. *Human Relations, 23,* 299–317.

Hall, J. A., & Veccia, E. M. (1990). More "touching" observations: New insights on men, women, and interpersonal touch. *Journal of Personality and Social Psychology, 59,* 1155–1162.

Hamilton, C. (2001). *Communicating for results* (6th ed.). Belmont, CA: Wadsworth.

Hamilton, D. L. (1979). A cognitive-attributional analysis of stereotyping. In L. Berkowitz (Ed.), *Advances in Experimental Psychology, 12*, 53–84.

Hammer, M., & Champy, J. (2001). *Reengineering the corporation: A manifesto for business revolution.* New York: HarperBusiness.

Harvey, S. (1999, December 11). "Hey! What team does she play for?" *Los Angeles Times.* Retrieved from latimes.com

Haslett, B. J. (1987). *Communication: Strategic action in context.* Hillsdale, NJ: Erlbaum.

Hersey, P., & Blanchard, K. (1982). *Management of organizational behavior* (4th ed.). Englewood Cliffs, NJ: Prentice Hall.

Hesselbein, F. (2001, Winter). Speaking a common language. *Leader to Leader, 19*, 4–5.

Hirokawa, R., & Poole, M. S. (1986). *Communication and group decision-making.* London: Sage.

Hirokawa, R. Y., & Rost, K. M. (1992). Effective group decision making in organizations: Field test of vigilant interaction theory. *Management Communication, 5*, 267–288.

Hocker, J. L., & Wilmot, W. W. (1985). *Interpersonal conflict.* Dubuque, IA: Wm. C. Brown.

Hodgetts, R. M. (1995, Summer). Evolve! Succeeding in the digital culture of tomorrow. A conversation with Rosabeth Moss Kanter. *Learning Organization Online.* Retrieved December 31, 2001, from http://home.nycap.rr.com/klarsen/learnorg/kanter.html

Hoffman, J. C. (1994). Just what is a crisis? *Prometheon.* (brief article). Available: http://www.speaking.com/speakers/judyhoffman.html

Holahan, C. K., & Sears, R. R. (1995). *The gifted group in later maturity.* Stanford: Stanford University Press.

Hornik, J. (1987). The effect of touch and gaze upon compliance and interest of interviewees. *The Journal of Social Psychology, 127*, 681–683.

Hornik, J., & Ellis, S. (1988). Strategies to secure compliance for a mall intercept interview. *Public Opinion Quarterly, 52*, 539–551.

Hornstein, H. A. (1997). *Brutal bosses and their prey: How to overcome abuse in the workplace.* New York: Riverhead Books.

Hoult, J. (2000, October). Negotiation 101. *Fast Company.* Retrieved July 14, 2001, from http://www.fastcompany.com/feature/00/act_podziba.html

Hu, A. (n.d.). Asian health: The dirty secret is that Asians really are healthier. *Index of Diversity: Health.* Retrieved April 3, 2005, from http://www.arthurhu.com/index/ahealth.htm#acet

Hutchinson, K. L., & Neuliep, J. W. (1993, Winter). The influence of parent and peer modeling on the development of communication apprehension in elementary school children. *Communication Quarterly, 41*(1), 16–25.

IEEE-USA. (2000, November 3). Study notes change in perceptions toward older Americans in workplace. *PR Newswire.* Retrieved from http://www.findarticles.com

Imperato, G. (1996, December). Flight of the nerd. *Fast Company.* Retrieved July 3, 2000, from http://www.fastcompany.com

Imperato, G. (1998, August). 35 ways to land a job online. *Fast Company, 16*, 192.

Imperato, G. (2000, July). Real tools for virtual teams (brief article). *Fast Company, 36*, 378.

Infante, D. A. & Wigley, C. J. III, (1986). Verbal aggressiveness: An interpersonal model and measure. *Communication Monographs, 53*, 61–67.

Infante, D. A., Rance, A. S., & Womack, D. F. (1997). *Building communication theory* (3rd ed.). Prospect Heights, IL: Waveland.

Iwata, E. (1995, March 27). Getting accustomed. *Orange County Register.* Santa Ana, CA, d06.

Izard, C. (1979). *The face of emotion.* New York: Appleton-Century-Crofts.

Jaffe, C. (1995). *Public speaking: concepts and skills for a diverse society* (2nd ed.). New York: Wadsworth.

Jaffe, C. I. (2002, Winter). Balancing the old and the new. *American Communication Journal, 5*(2).

Janis, I. L. (1982). *Groupthink: Psychological studies of policy decisions and fiascoes.* Boston: Houghton Mifflin.

Jamieson, K. H. (1988). *Eloquence in an electronic age.* New York: Oxford University Press.

Jim Moran Institute for Global Entrepreneurship, Florida State University. (n.d.). Improving communication in the workplace. Retrieved June 21, 2004, from http://www.cob.fsu.edu/jmi/newsletter_articles/communication.asp

Johnson, S. D., & Bechler, C. (1998). Examining the relationship between listening effectiveness and leadership emergence. *Small Group Research, 29*, 452–471.

Jones, S. (1994). *The right touch.* Cresshill, NJ: Hampton Press.

Juran, J. M. (1992). *Juran on quality by design: The new steps for planning quality into goods and services*. New York: Simon & Schuster.

Jurma, W. E. (1978). Leadership structuring style, task ambiguity and group members' satisfaction. *Small Group Behavior, 9*, 124–134.

Kane, K. (1995, November). The riddle of job interviews. *Fast Company, 1*, 50.

Karau, S. J., & Williams, K. D. (1993). Social loafing: A meta-analytic review and theoretical integration. *Journal of Personality and Social Psychology, 65*, 681–706.

Kare, A. (1998, October). The face of feeling. *Broadcast Engineering, 40*(11), 102.

Katz, D., & Kahn, R. L. (1966). *The social psychology of organizations*. New York: John Wiley & Sons.

Katzenbach, J. R. (1997). *Teams at the top*. Boston: Harvard Business School Press.

Katzenbach, J. R., & Smith, D. K. (1993, March–April). The discipline of teams. *Harvard Business Review, 71*(2), 111–119.

Katzenbach, J. R., & Smith, D. K. (2001, Fall). The discipline of virtual teams. *Leader to Leader, 22*, 16–25. Retrieved January 9, 2001, from http://www.pfdf.org/leaderbooks/121/fall2001/katzenbach.html

Keene, M. L. (1979, Spring). Teaching Toulmin logic. *Teaching English in the two-year college, 3*, 193–198.

Kelly, M. S. (1966). *Brainstorming*. Unpublished master thesis, Baylor University of Waco, Texas.

Kellermann, K. (1992). Communication: Inherently strategic and primarily automatic. *Communication Monographs, 59*, 288–300.

Kent-Drury, R. (2000, March). Bridging boundaries, negotiating differences: The nature of leadership in cross-functional proposal-writing groups. *Technical Communication, 47*(1), 90–99.

Kikoski, J. F. (1998, December). Effective communication in the performance appraisal interview: Face-to-face communication for public managers in the culturally diverse workplace. *Public Personnel Management*. Retrieved November 4, 2000, from *Electric Library*.

Kikoski, J. F., & Litterer, J. A. (1983, Spring). Effective communication in the performance appraisal interview. *Public Personnel Management, 28*, 33–42.

King, P. E., Young, M. J., & Behnke, R. R. (2000). Public speaking performance improvement as a function of information processing in immediate and delayed feedback interventions. *Communication Education, 49*, 365–374.

Kinlaw, D. C. (1991). *Developing supervised work teams: Building quality and the competitive edge*. Lexington MA: Lexington Books.

Kirtley, M. D., & Weaver, J. B., III. (1999). Exploring the impact of gender role self-perception on communication style. *Women's Studies in Communication, 22*(2), 190–209.

Knapp, M. L., & Hall, J. (2002). *Nonverbal behavior in human interaction* (3d ed.) New York: Holt, Rinehart & Winston.

Kolb, D. A. (1984). *Experiential learning*. Englewood Cliffs, NJ: Prentice Hall.

Komisar, R. (2001, Winter). The business case for passion. *Leader to Leader, 19*, 22–28.

Korten, D. C. (1962). Situational determinants of leadership structure. *Journal of Conflict Resolution, 6*, 222–235.

Kotter, J. P. (1982). What effective general managers really do. *Harvard Business Review, 60*, 156–167.

Koziel, M. J. (2000, December). Giving and receiving performance evaluations. *CPA Journal, 70*(12), 22.

Kramarae, C. (1989). Redefining gender, race, and class. In C. Lont & W. Friedley (Eds.), *Beyond boundaries: Sex and gender diversity in communication* (pp. 317–412). Fairfax, VA: George Mason University Press.

Kruger, J., & Dunning, D. (1999). Unskilled and unaware of it: How difficulties in recognizing one's own incompetence lead to inflated self-assessments. *Journal of Personality and Social Psychology, 77*, 1121–1134.

Kunin, M. (1994). *Living a political life*. New York: Knopf.

Lapakko, D. (1997) Three cheers for language: A closer examination of a widely cited study of nonverbal communication. *Communication Education, 46*(1), 63–67.

Larson, C. E., & LaFusto, F. M. J. (1989). *Teamwork: What must go right, what can go wrong*. Newbury Park, CA: Sage.

Lawrence, P., & Lorsch, J. (1967). Differentiation and integration in complex organizations. *Administrative Science Quarterly, 12*, 1–47.

Lawrence Ragan Communications. PR Spotlight: Crisis communication: Inside the spin zone. *PR Reporter*. Retrieved June 15, 2004, from http://www.employeecomm.com

Lehman, C. M., & Lehman, M. W. (1989). Techniques: Essential element in the promotional strategies of professional service firms. *Journal of Professional Services Marketing, 5*(1), 17–28.

Leslie, J. B., & Velsor, E. V. (1996). *A look at derailment today: North America and Europe.* Greensboro, NC: Center for Creative Leadership.

Levine, R., & Bartlett, K. (1984). Pace of life, punctuality, and coronary heart disease in six countries. *Journal of Cross-Cultural Psychology, 15,* 233–255.

Lewin, K., Lippitt, R., & White, R. K. (1939). Patterns of aggressive behavior in experimentally created social climates. *Journal of Social Psychology, 10,* 271–299.

Lewis, H. D., David, J. W., & Archibald, D. G. (1983). Protective effects of aspirin against acute myocardial infarction and death in men with unstable angina: Results of a Veterans Administration cooperative study. *NEJM* (309), 396–403.

Lewis, L. K. (2000, February). "Blindsided by that one" and "I saw that one coming": The relative anticipation and occurrence of communication problems and other problems in implementers' hindsight. *Journal of Applied Communication Research, 28,* 44–67.

Likert, R. (1967). *The human organization.* New York: McGraw-Hill.

Lipnack, J., & Stamps, J. (1997). *Virtual teams: Reaching across space, time, and organizations with technology.* New York: John Wiley & Sons.

List, K., & Renzulli, J. S. (1991). Creative women's developmental patterns through age thirty-five. *Gifted Education International, 7,* 114–122.

Littlejohn, S. W. (1992). *Theories of human communication.* Belmont, CA: Wadsworth.

Longoria, J. (1998, 2003). The virtual classroom. Retrieved June 28, 2004, from http://www.fiu.edu/~longoria/self-p/concept.htm

Loomis, C. (1999, November). Mr. Buffett on the stock market. *Fortune, 140*(10). Retrieved November 21, 1999, from http://www.pathfinder.com/fortune/1999/11/22/buf.html

Lucas, S. E. (1995). *The art of public speaking.* New York: McGraw-Hill.

Lucas, S. E. (2002, Winter). Speechmaking, pedagogy, and civic responsibility. *American Communication Journal, 5*(2). Available: *American Communication Journal online.*

Lukaszewski, J. E. (1997, August–September). Becoming a verbal visionary: How to have a happy, successful, and important life. *Executive Speeches, 12,* 23–30.

Lukazewski, J. E. (1997). How to develop the mind of a strategist. *Communication World, 18*(5), pp. 3, 9.

Mack, D., & Rainey, D. (1990). Physical attractiveness and selection decision making. *Journal of Management, 16,* 723–736.

Maier, N. R., & Solem, A. R. (1952). The contribution of a discussion leader to the quality of group thinking: The effective use of minority opinions. *Human Relations, 5,* 277–288.

Mallory, M. W. (2002, September 8). Women taking over at work. *Waco Tribune-Herald,* pp. A1–A2.

Matson, E. (1997, February). Now that we have your complete attention. *Fast Company.* Retrieved February 4, 2000, from http://www.fastcompany.com/online/07/124present.html

Matsumoto, D. (1989). Cultural influences of the perception of emotion. *Journal of Cross-Cultural Psychology, 20,* 92–105.

Mayer, B. (1987). The dynamics of power in mediation and negotiation. In Umbreit, M. S., *Mediating interpersonal conflicts: A pathway to peace.* West Concord, MN: CPI Publishing.

McCann, M. (n.d.) The generation gap in bosses. Retrieved February 21, 2002, from http://www.globalbusinesscafe.com

McCarl, R. S. (1980). Occupational folklife: An examination of the expressive aspects of the work culture with particular reference to firefighters. Doctoral thesis. Memorial University of Newfoundland.

McCarl, R. (1985). *The District of Columbia's fire fighters' project:* A case study in occupational folklife. Washington, D.C.: Smithsonian Institute Press.

McCaslin, J. (2000, April 24). Inside the beltway. *The Washington Times.* p. A6.

McCauley, L. (2000, October). Learning 101. *Fast Company, 39,* 101–106.

McCroskey, J. C. (1984). The communication apprehension perspective. In J. A. Daly & J. C. McCroskey (Eds.), *Avoiding communication: Shyness, reticence, and communication apprehension* (pp. 13–38). Beverly Hills, CA: Sage.

McCroskey, J. C. (1997). *Why we communicate the ways we do: A communibiological perspective.* A Carroll C. Arnold Distinguished Lecture presented at the annual convention of the

National Communication Association, Chicago, IL, November 20, 1997.

McCroskey, J. C., Andersen, J. F., Richmond, V. P., & Wheeless, L. R. (1981). Communication apprehension of elementary and secondary student and teachers. *Communication Education, 30,* 122–132.

McGinty, S. (2001). *Power talk: Using language to build authority and influence.* New York: Warner Books.

McGregor, D. (1960). *The human side of enterprise.* New York: McGraw-Hill.

McGregor, D. (1966). *Leadership and motivation.* Cambridge, MA: MIT Press.

Mehrabian, A., & Ferris, S. (1967). Inference of attitudes from nonverbal communication in two channels. *Journal of Consulting Psychology, 31,* 248–252.

Mehrabian, A., & Wiener, M. (1967). Decoding of inconsistent communications. *Journal of Personality and Social Psychology, 6,* 109–114.

Merritt, J. (2003, February). Improv at the interview: New techniques show bosses how applicants react to stress. *Business Week Online.* Retrieved April 5, 2005, from http://www.businessweek.com/magazine/content/03_05/b3818082.htm

Messick, S. (1976). *Individuality in learning.* San Francisco: Jossey-Bass.

Meyerson, D. E., & Scully, M. A. (1995). Tempered radicalism and the politics of ambivalence and change. *Organization Science, 6,* 585–600.

Meyerson, M. (1996, April–May). Everything I thought I knew about leadership is wrong. *Fast Company 2,* 71.

Miller, G. (1956). The magical number seven, plus or minus two: some limits on our capacity for processing information. *Psychology Review, 63,* 81–97.

Miller, G., & Steinberg, M. (1975). *Between People: A New Analysis of Interpersonal Communication.* Palo Alto, CA: Science Research Associates.

Miller, G., & Sunnafrank, M. (1982). All is for one but one is not for all: A conceptual perspective of interpersonal communication. In F. Dance (Ed.), *Human communication theory: Comparative essays* (pp. 220–242). New York: Harper & Row.

Miller, G. A., & Licklider, J. C. R. T. (1950, March). The intelligibility of interrupted speech. *Journal of the Acoustical Society of America, 22,* 167–173.

Millet, J. (2004). Communicating across cultures: Using global English. Retrieved June 26, 2004 from http://www.culturalsavvy.com/communicating_across_cultures_using_English.htm

Mintzberg, H. (1975, July–August). The manager's job: folklore and fact. *Harvard Business Review, 53,* 49–61.

Mitchell, R. (1999, June). How to manage geeks. *Fast Company, 25,* 174.

Mladenka, J. D., Sawyer, C. R., & Behnke, R. R. (1998, Fall). Anxiety sensitivity and speech trait anxiety as predictors of state anxiety during public speaking. *Communication Quarterly, 46* (4), 417–429.

Mongan, J., & Suojanen, N. (2000). *Programming interviews exposed: Secrets to landing your next job.* New York: John Wiley & Sons.

Moody, F. (1996, June/July). Wonder women in the rude boys' paradise. *Fast Company, 3,* 85.

Morrill, C. (2000, September). Using conflict in organizations [Review]. *Administrative Science Quarterly.*

Morris, A. H. (2000). Developing and implementing computerized protocols for standardization of clinical decisions. *Annals of Internal Medicine, 132,* 373–383.

Morrow, P. C., McElroy, J. C., Stamper, B. G., & Wilson, M. A. (1990). The effects of physical attractiveness and other demographic characteristics on promotion decisions. *Journal of Management, 16,* 723–736.

Moulton, S. (n.d.) Ideas for finding exceptional talent—interviewing. *Action Insight.* Retrieved April 4, 2005, from http://actioninsight.com/Article16.htm

Mullin, B., Anthony, T., Salas, E., & Driskell, J. E. (1994). Group cohesiveness and quality of decision-making: An integration of tests of the groupthink hypothesis. *Small Group Research, 25,* 189–204.

Mullin, B., & Cooper, C. (1994). The relationship between group cohesiveness and performance: An integration. *Psychological Bulletin, 115,* 210–227.

Murray, T. (2001, April 24). *Listen Up, Doc— Patients want a physician—not a prescription. Medical Post.* Retrieved September 10, 2001, from http://www.elibrary.com/s/edumark.2000 bigchalk.com

Myers, D., Murdoch, P., & Smith, G. (1970). Responsibility diffusion and drive enhancement effects on risky-shift. *Journal of Personality, 38,* 418–425.

Newstrom, J. W., & Davis, K. (1997). *Organizational behavior: Human behavior at work* (10th ed.). New York: McGraw-Hill.

O'Connor, W. Y. (1999). The workplace of the new millennium: Let's be prepared. *Vital Speeches of the Day.*

O'Hair, D., Friedrich, G. W., & Dixon, L. D. (2002). *Strategic communication in business and the professions.* Boston: Houghton Mifflin.

O'Keefe, D. J. (1987). The persuasive effects of delaying identification of high- and low-credibility communicators: A meta-analytic review. *Central States Speech Journal, 38,* 63–72.

O'Keefe, D. J. (1994). From strategy-based to feature-based analyses of compliance gaining message classification and production. *Communication Theory, 4,* 61–69.

O'Leary, V. E., & Ickovics, J. R. (1991). Cracking the glass ceiling. Overcoming isolation and alienation. In U. Sederan & F. Long (Eds.), *Pathways to excellence: New patterns for human utilization.* Beverly Hills: Sage.

Osborn, A. (1953). *Applied imagination: Principles and procedures of creative thinking.* New York: Scribners.

Osborn, D. (1996). Beauty is as beauty does? Makeup and posture effects on physical attractiveness judgments. *Journal of Applied Social Psychology, 26,* 31–51.

Ouchi, W. (1981). *Theory Z: How American business can meet the Japanese challenge.* Reading, MA: Addison-Wesley.

Overholt, A. (2002, March). Virtually there. *Fast Company, 56,* 108.

Pascale, R. T., Millemann, M., & Gioja, L. (2001, April). *Surfing the edge of chaos: The laws of nature and the new laws of business.* New York: Crown Business.

Pavitt, C. (1999). Theorizing about the group communication-leadership relationship: Input-process-output and functional models. In L. Frey, D. Gouran, & M. Poole (Eds.), *The handbook of group communication theory and research* (pp. 313–334). Thousand Oaks, CA: Sage.

Pavitt, C., & Kemp, B. (1999, Spring). Contextual and relational factors in interpersonal negotiation strategy choice. *Communication Quarterly, 47*(2), 133–150.

Pelosi, M. K., & Sandifer, T. M. (2001). *Doing statistics for business with Excel: Data, inference, and decision making* (2nd ed.). New York: John Wiley & Sons.

Peters, T. (1999, May). The wow project. *Fast Company, 24,* 116.

Peters, T. J., & Waterman, R. H. (1982). *In search of excellence: Lessons from America's best-run companies.* New York: Harper & Row.

Peterson, C. D. (1997). *On your own discovering your new life and career beyond the corporation.* New York: John Wiley & Sons.

Petrie, G. M. (2003, November). ESL teachers' view on visual language: A grounded theory. *The Reading Matrix, 3*(3), 137–168.

Phillips, E. & Cheston, R. (1979, Summer). Conflict resolution: What works? *Management Review, 21*(4), 76–84.

Poole, M., & Roth, J. (1989). Decision development in small groups IV: A typology of group decision paths. *Human Communication Research, 15,* 323–356.

Prince, R. A., & File, K. M. (1999). Listen first, talk later. Retrieved September 9, 2001, from http://www.elibrary.com/s/edumark/getdoc.cgi?id

Prose, N. S. (2000). Paying attention. *Journal of the American Medical Association, 283*(21), 27–63.

Protecting employees—and your business. (1998, December): *Nation's Business, 86*(12), 18–19.

Putnam, L. L. (1979). Preference for procedural order in task-oriented small groups. *Communication Monographs, 46,* 193–218.

Putnam, L. L. (1983). Small group work climates: A lag-sequential analysis of group interaction. *Small Group Behavior, 14,* 465–494.

Rahim, M. A. (1983). A measure of styles of handling interpersonal conflict. *Academy of Management Journal, 26,* 368–376.

Rahim, M. A., & Bonoma, T. V. (1979). Managing organizational conflict: A model for diagnosis and intervention. *Psychological Reports, 16,* 143–155.

Ramsay, M. (1999). *Leadership in teams* (CSWT Papers). Denton, TX: Center for the Study of Work Teams, University of North Texas.

Rankin, P. T. (1928, October). The importance of listening ability, *English Journal* (College Edition), *17,* 623–630.

Rapaport, R. (2000). Import jeans, export values. Retrieved June 15, 2000, from http://www.fast company.com/online/00/levi.tyml

Raven, B., & Kruglanski, W. (1975). Conflict and power. In P. G. Swingle (Ed.), *The structure of conflict*. New York: Academic Press.

Reardon, K. K. (2000). *The secret handshake: Mastering the politics of the business inner circle*. New York: Doubleday/Currency.

Reis, H. T., Nezlek, J., & Wheeler, L. (1980). Physical attractiveness in social interaction. *Journal of Personality and Social Psychology, 38*(4), 604–617.

Reiss, S. (1997). Trait anxiety: It's not what you think it is. *Journal of Anxiety Disorders, 11*, 201–214.

Rekha, B. (2000, May). Listen up! *Fast Company, 34*, 304.

Remland, M. S., Jones, T. S., & Brinkman, H. (1995, June). Interpersonal distance, body orientation, and touch: Effects of culture, gender, and age. *Journal of Social Psychology, 135*, 281–297.

Richmond, V. P., & McCroskey, J. C. (1995). *Communication apprehension, avoidance and effectiveness* (4th ed.). Boston: Allyn & Bacon.

Richmond, V. P., & McCroskey, J. C. (1998). *Communication apprehension, avoidance, and effectiveness* (5th ed.). Boston: Allyn & Bacon.

Robinson, J. D. (1998). Getting down to business: Talk, gaze, and body orientation during openings of doctor-patient consultations. *Human Communication Research, 25*(1), 97.

Rogers, C. (1961/1995). *On becoming a person*. New York: Houghton Mifflin.

Rogers, C. (1980/1995) A *way of being*. New York/Boston: Houghton Mifflin.

Rohlander, D. G. (2000, February). The well-rounded IE. *IIE Solutions, 32*(2), 22.

Rosenbaum, L. L., & Rosenbaum, W. B. (1971). Morale and productivity consequences of group leadership style, stress, and type of task. *Journal of Applied Psychology, 55*, 343–358.

Rosenberg, A., & Zimmer, D. A. (2001, November 12). Seamless cross-modal communication. *TechWeb*. Retrieved from http://www.techweb.com/article/COM20011112S0005

Rosenfeld, J. (2001, January). Blam! Maximum success. *Fast Company, 42*, 127.

Roskell, H., & Jolliffe, D. (2004). *Everyday use: Rhetoric at work in reading and writing*. New York: Longman.

Rossett, A. (1990). *Coaching*. Englewood Cliffs, NJ: Educational Technology Publications.

Rotondo, J. (2002, January) Use design to communicate that you know your listeners. *Presentations*. VNU Business Media. Retrieved January 7, 2003, from http://presentations.com/presentations/search/search_display.jsp?vnu_content_id=1350482speaker

Rozakis, L., & Rozakis, B. (1998). *The complete idiot's guide to office politics*. New York: Alpha Books.

Ruquet, M. E. (November 6, 2000). Listening to employees seen as key to agency success. *National Underwriter/Property & Casualty Risk & Benefits, 104*(45), 52.

Russell, C. G. (2000, Spring). Culture, language and behavior: Perception. *Etc., 57*(1), 4–27. Retrieved August 15, 2000, from http://www.texshare.edu/ovidweb/ovid

Russell, W., & Branch, T. (1979). *Second wind: Memoirs of an opinionated man*. New York: Random House.

Ryan, E. S. (1999). Comparing 21st century job-skills acquisition with self-fulfillment for college students. *Education, 3*, 119. Retrieved September 10, 2001, from http://www.elibrary.com

Ryan, K. D. & Oestreich, D. K. (1998). *Driving fear out of the workplace: Creating the high-trust, high-performance organization*. San Francisco: Jossey-Bass.

Sachs, A., Rutherford, M., & Marchant, V. (1999, June 28). What bosses really want. *Time*, p. 74J. Retrieved September 10, 2001, from http://www.elibrary.com/s/edumark

Salovey, P., & Mayer, J. (1990). Emotional intelligence. *Imagination, Cognition, and Personality, 9*(3), 185–211.

Sanchez-Burks, J., Lee, F., Choi, I., Nisbett, R., Zhao, S., & Koo, J. (2003, August). Conversing across cultures: East-West communication styles in work and nonwork contexts. *Journal of Personality and Social Psychology, 85*(2), 363–372.

Sanders, R. E., & Fitch, K. L. (2001). The actual practice of compliance seeking. *Communication Theory, 11*, 263–289.

Sandoval, V. A., & Adams, S. H. (2001, August). Subtle skills for building rapport: Using neuro-linguistic programming in the interview room. *Law Enforcement Bulletin, 70*(8). Retrieved April 1, 2005, from http://www.fbi.gov/publications/leb/2001/august2001/aug01p1.htm

Schafer, E. (1996, June 20). Keynote address, Telemedicine 2000 conference/exhibition, Chicago, IL. Retrieved July 15, 2002, from http://www.ehs.health.state.nd.us/gov/speeches/tele2000.htm

Scherer, K. R. (1982). Methods of research on vocal communication: Paradigms and parameters. In Scherer, K. R. and Edman, P. (Eds.), *Handbook of methods in nonverbal behavior research* (pp. 136–198). Cambridge: Cambridge University Press.

Schneider, B., & Bowen, D. (1995). *Winning the service game*. Boston: Harvard Business School Press.

Schulz, Y. (2001). Attentive. *Computing Canada.* Retrieved November 2, 2001, from http://www.findarticles.com/cf_0/m0cgc/18)27/77755399

Scott, S. (2001). *Fierce conversations: Achieving success at work and in life, one conversation at a time.* New York: Viking.

Segall, M. H., Dasen, P. R., Berry, J. W., & Poortinga, Y. H. (1990) *Human behavior in global perspective: An introduction to cross-cultural psychology,* New York: Pergamon.

Selnow, D. D. (2003). *Public speaking: A process approach.* Belmont, CA: Wadsworth.

Senge, P. (1994). *The fifth discipline.* New York: Doubleday/Currency.

Senge, P. M. (1996). Leading learning organizations. In F. Hesselbein, M. Goldsmith, & R. Beckhard (Eds.), *The leader of the future.* San Francisco: Jossey-Bass.

Shaw, M. E. (1981). *Group dynamics: The psychology of small group behavior* (3rd ed.). New York: McGraw-Hill.

Schnoor, L. G. (Ed.). (1995). *Winning orations, 1994.* Mankato, MN: Interstate Oratorical Association, 31–33.

Schutz, W. C. (1958). *FIRO: A three-dimensional theory of interpersonal behavior.* New York: Holt, Rinehart & Winston.

Shuter, R. (1977). A field study of nonverbal communication in Germany, Italy, and the United States. *Communication Monographs, 44,* 298–305.

Sims, H. P., & Dean, J. W., Jr. (1985). Beyond quality circles: Self-managing teams. *Personnel, 62,* 25–32.

SkyMark Corporation. (2002). Affinity diagram. Retrieved March 25, 2002, from http://www.pathmaker.com/resources/tools/affinity_diagram.asp

Smith, D. E., Gier, J. A., & Willis, F. N. (1982). Interpersonal touch and compliance with a marketing request. *Basic and applied social psychology, 3,* 35–38.

Smith, P. B., & Bond, M. H. (1994). *Social psychology across cultures: Analysis and perspectives.* Boston: Allyn & Bacon.

Society for Organizational Learning. (n.d.). Senge, P. M. Retrieved February 2, 2002, from http://www.solonline.org/com/peo/psenge.html

Spence, G. (1996). *How to argue and win every time.* New York: St. Martin's Press.

Spencer, L. M., Jr., & Spencer, S. (1993). *Competence at work: Models for superior performance.* New York: John Wiley & Sons.

Spencer, L. M., Jr., McClelland, D. C., & Kelner, S. (1997). *Competency assessment methods: History and state of the art.* Boston: Hay/McBer.

Sternberg, R. J. (1995). *In search of the human mind.* Fort Worth, TX: Harcourt Brace.

Stettner, M. (1997, October). Body of evidence. *Successful Meetings, 46*(11), 128.

Stonecipher, H. C. (1996). *Reducing cost: The enemy is us.* Remarks to Defense Manufacturing Conference. Miami, Florida, December 3, 1996. Available: The Executive Speaker at http://www.executive-speaker.com

Study: Aspirin helps women prevent strokes. (2005, March 7). CNN. Retrieved April 4, 2005, from http://www.cnn.com

Sundaram, D. S., & Webster, C. (2000). The role of nonverbal communication in service encounters. *Journal of Services Marketing, 14*(5), 378–391.

Suplee, C. (1999, June 9). Get outta my face! The science and secrets of personal space. *The Washington Post,* p. H1.

Suzuki, S. (1998, April). In-group and out-group communication patterns in international organizations: Implications for social identity theory. *Communication Research, 25*(2), 154–182.

Sweeney, J. J. (1998, August 13). Remarks at Rainbow/PUSH breakfast. Chicago, Illinois. Available: http://www.rainbowpush.org/speeches/1998/index.html

Swenson, J., & Casmir, F. L. (1998). The impact of culture-sameness, gender, foreign travel, and academic background on the ability to interpret facial expression of emotion in others. *Communication Quarterly, 46*(2), 214.

Tangerlini, T. R. (1998). *Talking trauma: Paramedics and their stories*. Jackson, MS: University Press of Mississippi.

Tannen, D. (1986). *That's not what I meant: Conversational style makes or breaks relationships*. New York: William Morrow.

Tannen, D. (1990). *You just don't understand: Women and men in conversation*. New York: William Morrow.

Tannen, D. (1995). The power of talk: Who gets heard and why. *Harvard Business Review, 73,* 5.

Tannen, D. (1998). *The argument culture*. New York: Random House.

Tannen, D. (2002). Agonism in academic discourse. *Journal of Pragmatics, 34,* 1651–1669.

Taxation of pending claims: how to handle liabilities when selling or restructuring a business. (2003, May 1). *Tax Articles.com*. Retrieved April 1, 2005, from http://www.tax-articles.com/tax/taxarticles/irs/irs-article-11467.html

Taylor, B., & Lippitt, G. (1983). *Management development and training handbook*. London: McGraw-Hill.

Taylor, F. W. (1911). *Scientific management*. New York: Harper & Row.

Taylor, S. (1995). Stimulus estimation and the overprediction of fear: A comment on two studies. *Behaviour Research and Therapy, 33,* 699–700.

Thelen, H., & Dickerman, W. (1949). Stereotypes and the growth of groups. *Educational Leadership, 6,* 309–316.

Tracy, K. (Ed.). (1991). *Understanding face-to-face interaction: Issues linking goals and discourse*. Hillsdale, NJ: Lawrence Erlbaum.

Trentham, S. (1998, January). Gender discrimination and the workplace: An examination of rational bias theory. *Sex Roles: A Journal of Research, 38,* 1–28.

Trice, H. M. & Beyer, J. M. (1993). *The Cultures of work organizations*. Englewood Cliffs, NJ: Prentice Hall.

Tubbs, S. (2001). *A systems approach to small group interaction* (7th ed.). Boston: McGraw-Hill.

Tuckman, B. (1965). Developmental sequence in small groups. *Psychological Bulletin, 63,* 384–399.

Tullar, W. L., & Kaiser, P. R. (2000). The effect of process training on process and outcomes in virtual groups. *Journal of Business Communication, 35*(4), 408–427.

Tully, J. (2002). Public speaking. *Tully Communications, The Executive Speaker Company.*

Tutu, D. (2001). Interview by D. Schechter at the World Economic Forum in Davos, Switzerland. Retrieved January 4, 2001, from PBS Online: http://www.pbs.org/globalization/tutu.html

U.S. Department of Defense. (2000, June 14). *Contract pricing reference guides: Volume 5. Federal contract negotiation techniques*. (Chapter 5. Nonverbal Communication). Retrieved May 18, 2001, from http://www.defenselink.mil

Ulmer, R. R., & Sellnow, T. L. (2000, May). Consistent questions of ambiguity in organizational crisis communication: Jack in the box as a case study. *Journal of Business Ethics, 25*(2): 143–155.

Unruh, J. (1996, September 11). Technology: A global vision for the 21st century. *Executive Speaker*. Retrieved May 25, 2004 at http://www.executive-speaker.com

Vogel, D. R., Dickson, G. W., & Lehman, J. A. (1986). Persuasion and the role of visual presentation support: The UM/3M study. *3m Corporation,* 1–20.

Wagner, C. G., & Minerd, J. (1999, November). On the frontiers of wisdom. *The Futurist, 33*(9), 51–56.

Waldron, V. R., Lavitt, M., & McConnaughy, M. (1998, November). Understanding the role of interpersonal communication in a job training program serving an urban poverty area: A longtitudinal case study. Paper presented at the Annual Conference of the National Communication Association, New York.

Waldroop, J., & Butler, T. (2000). *Maximum success: Changing the 12 behavior patterns that keep you from getting ahead*. New York: Doubleday.

Walster, E., Aronson., V., Abrahams, D., & Rottman, L. (1966). Importance of physical attractiveness in dating behavior. *Journal of Personality and Social Psychology, 5,* 508–516.

Walton, M. (1986). *The Demming management method*. New York: Dodd-Mead.

Warner, F. (2002). Inside Intel's mentoring movement. *Mentorship Online.com*. Retrieved April 1, 2005, from http://www.mentorshiponline.com/article.asp?section=articles&id=1001&cat=art-maincat

Warshaw, M. (December 1998). Open mouth, close career? *Fast Company, 20,* 240.

Weaver, J. B., III, Fitch-Hauser, M., Villaume, W., & Thomas, T. (1993, November). *Exploring the impact of gender-role schematicity on communication anxiety.* Presented before the Speech Communication Association, Miami, FL.

Webber, A. M. (June, 2000). Why can't we get anything done? *Fast Company, 35,*168.

Weil, E. (1997, August/September). Power camp. *Fast Company, 10,* 145–153.

Wellins, R. S., Byham, W. C., & Wilson, J. M. (1991). *Empowered teams: Creating self-directed work groups that improve quality, productivity, and participation.* San Francisco: Jossey-Bass.

Westminster firm spurring change in Japan: Traditional face-to-face meetings giving way to teleconferencing. (1997, August 3). *Denver Post,* p. G-01.

Whatis.com. (2004). Presentation software. Retrieved July 8, 2004, from http://whatis.techtarget.com/whome/0,289825,sid9,00.html

What's your company's culture? (2000, December). *Harvard Management Communication Letter. 12*(3), 10.

The White House. (1997, June 4). Social statistics briefing room. Retrieved from http://222.whitehouse.gov/fsbr/demography.html

Whitworth, R. H., & Cochran, C. (1996). Evaluation of integrated versus unitary treatments for reducing public speaking anxiety. *Communication Education, 45,* 306–314.

Whyte, G. (1989). Groupthink reconsidered. *Academy of Management Review, 14*(1), 40–56.

Wilmot, W. W., & Hocker, J. (2001). *Interpersonal conflict* (6th ed). Boston: McGraw-Hill.

Wilson, A. (2000, March/April). Women's ways work. *Psychology Today, 33*(2), 17.

Wilson, G. L. (2002). *Groups in context: Leadership and participation in small groups* (6th ed.). Boston: McGraw-Hill Irwin.

Winning orations, 1994. (1995). Mankato, MN: Interstate Oratorical Association.

Wolff, F., & Marsnik, N. C. (1992). *Perceptive listening* (2nd ed.). Fort Worth: Harcourt Brace Jovanovich.

Wood, J., & Lenze, L. (1989). Gender and the development of self: Inclusive pedagogy in interpersonal communication. *Women's Studies in Communication, 14,* 1–23.

Wood, W. (2000). Attitude change: Persuasion and social influence. *Annual Review of Psychology, 51,* 539–570.

Yoo, Y., & Alavi, M. (2001, September). Media and group cohesion: Relative influences on social presence, task participation, and group consensus, *MIS Quarterly, 25*(3), 371–390.

Young, A. T. (1992, September). Ethics in business: Business of ethics. *Vital Speeches, 15,* 725–730.

Zayas-Baya, E. P. (1977–1978). Instructional media in the total language picture. *International Journal of Instructional Media, 5,* 145–150.

Zielinski, D. (2002). Organizing your message: Strategic presentations. *Presentations.com, VNU eMedia Inc.,* Retrieved January 7, 2003, from http://presentations.com/presentations/search/search_display.jsp?vnu_content_id=1105094

Zull, J. E. (2002). *The art of changing a brain: Helping people learn by understanding how the brain works.* Sterling, VA: Stylus Publishers.

Index

Credits

Page v © Greg Knobloch/Center for Disease Control; vi © U.S. Department of Defense; vii © Scott Bauer/U.S. Department of Agriculture; viii © U.S. Department of Public Health, Center for Disease Control; 3 © Greg Knobloch/Center for Disease Control; 3 © Bob Nichols/U.S. Department of Agriculture; 4 © Bob Nichols/U.S. Department of Agriculture; 8 © John Coletti/Prentice Hall, Inc.; 17 © Charles Kay Ogden, Ivor Armstrong Richards; 18 © Laima Druskis/Prentice Hall, Inc.; 21 © Bob Nichols/U.S. Department of Agriculture; 34 © Greg Knobloch/Center for Disease Control; 41 © Greg Knobloch/Center for Disease Control; 42 © Shawn Moore/Occupational Safety and Health Administration; 44 © Paul Cretien; 57 © U.S. Department of Defense; 57 © Susan Oristaglio/Prentice Hall, Inc.; 58 © U.S. Department of Defense; 71 © U.S. Air Force; 71 © U.S. Department of Defense; 75 © Paul Cretien; 82 © U.S. Department of Energy; 93 © Scott Bauer; U.S. Agricultural Research Service; 100 © U.S. Department of Energy; 102 © Shirley Zeiberg/Prentice Hall, Inc.; 112 © Susan Oristaglio/Prentice Hall, Inc.; 115 © Amber Whittington/U.S. Air Force; 122 © Susan Oristaglio/Prentice Hall, Inc.; 124 © Steve Gorton/Dorling Kindersley; 135 © Angelica Delgado/U.S. Air Force; 138 © Eddie Edge/U.S. Air Force; 146 © Mark Diamond/U.S. Air Force; 151 © Eddie Edge/U.S. Air Force; 163 © Scott Bauer/U.S. Department of Agriculture; 163 © U.S. Department of Defense; 164 © Dorling Kindersley Media Library/Dorling Kindersley; 180 © U.S. Department of Energy; 188 © Christine Whiteman; 195 © Dorling Kindersley Media Library/Dorling Kindersley; 200 © U.S. Department of Energy; 211 © U.S. Department of Energy; 212 © Frank La Bua/Prentice Hall, Inc.; 221 © David Kolb; 228 © U.S. Department of Energy; 234 © U.S. Air Force; 239 © U.S. Department of Energy; 247 © Tom Tschida/NASA Dryden Flight Research Center Photo Collection; 252 © U.S. Air Force; 257 © Helene Stikkel/U.S. Department of Defense; 258 © Laimute E. Druskis/Prentice Hall, Inc.; 263 © Scott Bauer/U.S. Department of Agriculture; 265 © U.S. Department of Justice; 270 © Abraham Maslow; 286 © U.S. Air Force; 294 © R.D. Ward/U.S. Department of Defense; 296 © U.S. Department of Defense; 300 © Stephen Toulmin; 300 © Stephen Toulmin; 301 © Stephen Toulmin; 313 © U.S. Department of Public Health, Center for Disease Control; 313 © Greg Knobloch/Center for Disease Control; 314 © U.S. Air Force; 319 © U.S. Department of Defense; 320 © U.S. Air Force; 344 © John Coletti/Prentice Hall, Inc.; 352 © John Coletti/Prentice Hall, Inc.; 357 © Travis Looper; 358 © Ken Hammond/U.S. Department of Agriculture; 360 © Travis Looper; 361 © U.S. Department of Defense; 369 © Paul Hersey, Ken Blanchard; 374 © U.S. Department of Public Health, Center for Disease Control; 377 © U.S. Department of Public Health, Center for Disease Control; 383 © Jim Varhegyi/U.S. Department of Defense; 387 © Federal Highway Administration, Colorado Division; 388 © Federal Aviation Administration, Eastern Region; 404 © Greg Knobloch/Center for Disease Control; 407 © U.S. Department of Defense; 413 © M. Afzalur Rahim, David Antonioni, Clement Psenicka; 416 © U.S. Air Force; 416 © ; Travis Looper; 421 © Greg Knobloch/Center for Disease Control; Keith Weller/U.S. Department of Agriculture; 446 © Dorling Kindersley; 448 © ; 448 © U.S. Department of Energy; 457 © Keith Weller/U.S. Department of Agriculture.